LOG ON TO IT

FOR CSEC®

THIRD EDITION

Roland Birbal
Michele Taylor

HODDER
EDUCATION
AN HACHETTE UK COMPANY

Orders: please contact Hachette UK Distribution, Hely Hutchinson Centre, Milton Road, Didcot, Oxfordshire, OX11 7HH. Telephone: +44 (0)1235 827827. Email education@hachette.co.uk Lines are open from 9 a.m. to 5 p.m., Monday to Friday. You can also order through our website: www.hoddereducation.com

© Roland Birbal and Michele Taylor 2019

This edition published in 2019

Published from 2015 by
Hodder Education,
An Hachette UK Company
Carmelite House
50 Victoria Embankment
London EC4Y 0DZ

www.hoddereducation.co.uk

Impression number   10 9 8 7 6 5
Year   2023

Cover photo © Sergey Tarasov/Adobe Stock
Illustrations by Stephan Theron, Val Myburgh and Wimpie Botma
Typeset in Bliss Light 11/13 pt
Printed and bound by CPI Group (UK) Ltd, Croydon, CR0 4YY

A catalogue record for this title is available from the British Library.

ISBN: 978 1 5104 5998 4

Contents

Types of computers and their parts

What is a computer?

A computer is a programmable electronic device. It follows a set of instructions to process data. The action of processing data produces information that can be output or stored for future use. Electronic devices use tiny electric currents, flowing through circuits, to perform their operations. Electrons form these currents, hence the term 'electron-ic'.

An example of a fairly simple computer is a calculator; it can process data and output the information from the processing. For example, adding '2 + 6' (the processing) produces '8' (the information). Other computers are much more sophisticated – as you will see later in the chapter.

A computer system refers to the complete computer, which includes all the hardware and software required for the computer to work. A computer system allows users to input, process, output and store data.

What is the difference between data and information?

Data is all the raw facts and figures that a computer processes by following a set of instructions called a program. Data by itself has no meaning; it can be in the form of letters (a, b, c, d ... x, y, z, and so on), numbers (1, 2, 3, 15, 456, and so on), pictures, sounds or symbols. It is only when we attach meaning to data that we get information.

For example, if you collect the temperature of your classroom each day for a month, you have collected data. When you instruct a computer to arrange (sort) this data, you could get information such as:

■ the highest temperature over the period
■ the lowest temperature over the period
■ the mean (average) temperature over the period.

This information may then be useful, for example, to determine whether a classroom is too hot or too cold for comfortable working. If the information were just raw data, it would not be easy to interpret. Hence, the computer has helped you to look at a real-life situation or problem and make some sense of it.

▲ Figure 1.1 Data displayed on a laptop and on a cell phone screen

1

What is the difference between ICT, IT and computer science?

We often confuse the terms 'information and communications technology' (ICT), 'information technology' (IT) and 'computer science', and use them interchangeably. However, these are all very different fields.

Information and communications technology (ICT) involves the use of computer hardware, software and telecommunications devices to store, manipulate, convert, protect, send and receive data. ICT has become an integral part of our daily lives and has a major impact on the way we live, work and play. The banking and finance industry relies heavily on ICT for things like customer service, fraud protection, investment, and more. Using artificial intelligence (AI) in our homes and in products such as smartphones, smart cars and video games makes our lives more comfortable. For example, many of the smart home devices such as lights, thermostats, and air-conditioning units use artificial intelligence to learn our behaviour so that they can adjust the settings themselves to make the experience match our behaviour.

Information technology (IT) deals with the study of data and data processing, and may also apply to the management of computer systems, particularly in a business setting. When used in a business, IT facilitates the business by providing four sets of core services. These core services provide information, tools to improve productivity, business process automation and a means to connect with customers.

Computer science is the study of computer hardware and software design. It includes both the study of theoretical algorithms and the practical problems involved in implementing them through computer hardware and software. The study of computer science has many branches, including AI, software engineering, programming and computer graphics.

Why do we use computers?

The following features of modern computers assist us in our daily lives.

- **Data-processing speed:** Computers are quick; they can perform tens of millions of operations per second. With this speed comes the power to undertake many different tasks, such as predicting weather forecasts, modelling, data crunching and producing thousands of bills for utility companies. Data crunching refers to the analysis of large amounts of data so that it becomes useful in making decisions.
- **Data-processing accuracy:** Computers are very accurate. Errors occur only if there is an error in the way the hardware and software have been set up, or if there are errors in the data that has been input. When errors occur, it is usually because of some human error. Computers can only do what they are set up and programmed to do.
- **Ability to store large amounts of information in a small space:** There are many types of computer storage media that can be used to store large volumes of data and information. For example, a single CD-ROM disc or flash drive can hold the equivalent of a shelf of library books in electronic form.
- **Ability to work continuously:** Computers can work continuously for very long periods, only stopping for upgrading or maintenance checks. In fact, most modern computers can be left switched on all the time if desired, 24 hours per day and 7 days a week.

Note

Can you think of other types of data that you can collect in your class, the computer can process to give information?

▲ Figure 1.2 Robotic vacuum cleaners use AI technology to map their environment, by using navigational sensors.

▲ Figure 1.3 Smart cars have a self-driving mode that combines sensors and software, to control, navigate and drive vehicles.

Hardware and software

To process data to produce information, a computer needs both hardware and software. Hardware is all the physical parts of the computer system you can see and touch. It is all the devices that make up the computer system. These include the internal components and the external components. The internal components are necessary for the computer to function. These include the motherboard, central processing unit (CPU), Random Access Memory (RAM) and Read Only Memory (ROM) chips, and others. The motherboard is the main printed circuit board of a computer; it allows all the parts of a computer to receive power and communicate with one another. The central processing unit (CPU) and the RAM and ROM chips are all on the motherboard. Other components or devices that run the computer or enhance its performance are either part of the motherboard or plug into it via an expansion slot or port.

▲ Figure 1.4 Components on the motherboard of a personal computer

The external components, which are called peripherals, are those hardware devices that are not essential to a computer's function and are usually connected to the computer by a cable, or wirelessly. These devices include keyboards, printers, speakers, mice and hard drives. Software is a set of instructions (called a program) that a computer needs to carry out its tasks. For example, if you want to use the computer to type a letter, or draw a picture, or do some accounting work, you would need different types of software to accomplish these tasks. Some typical examples of software are word processors, spreadsheets, graphics packages and database packages. Both hardware and software are needed to process data.

Did you know?

Did you know that an app you download to your smartphone is software? What are some apps that you or a friend use or are familiar with?

▲ Figure 1.5 The parts of a personal computer

Stages of processing

To accomplish its tasks, a computer has to process data. Processing data to get information involves three stages: input, processing and output.

Input devices such as keyboards, joysticks, mice, touchscreens and scanners are used to get the data and instructions into the computer for processing. The processing takes place in that part of the computer called the central processing unit (CPU). The CPU, also known as the processor, is the 'brain' of the computer. It takes raw data and follows a set of instructions (programs) to convert it into information. The CPU is made up of three components, the control unit (CU), the arithmetic logic unit (ALU) and registers. A register is a temporary storage location that holds a single instruction or data item.

Traditionally, a CPU was made up of a processor with a single core. A core contains an ALU, CU and registers. Most modern processors contain multiple cores; a processor with two cores is called a dual-core processor and a quad-core processor has four cores. They are effectively several CPUs on a single chip. The more cores a processor has, the more sets of instructions the processor can receive and process at the same time, which makes the computer faster.

The speed at which a CPU processes data to convert it to information is measured in megahertz (MHz – millions of machine cycles per second) or for newer machines, in gigahertz (GHz – billions of machine cycles per second). A machine cycle is the sequence of instructions performed to execute one program instruction. Computers that are used for gaming, video editing, compiling code and running intensive virtual reality require very fast processors. One of the fastest processors for personal computers at present is the Intel Core i9-7980XE. This processor is very fast because it is the first consumer desktop processor to contain 18 cores.

Control unit

The control unit (CU) is the main part of the CPU. It directs and coordinates all the activities within the CPU. The CU determines the sequence in which instructions are executed. It does not execute the instructions itself; instead, it sends the data and instructions to the ALU for processing. The CU is primarily responsible for the movement of data and instructions from itself to the main memory and ALU and back. The CU executes an instruction by performing the following steps:

1   The CU fetches the instruction from memory.
2   It decodes the instruction.
3   It fetches the data required by the instruction from memory.
4   The CU sends the data and instruction to the ALU for processing.
5   It sends the data to the memory unit after processing.

The control unit also contains a number of registers. Registers are used to store data and instructions that are needed immediately and frequently. Two examples of registers found in the control unit are the program counter and the instruction register. The program counter holds the address of the current instruction (the instruction being processed) and the instruction register holds the instruction itself.

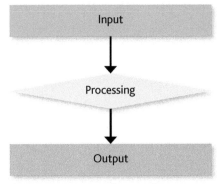

Input
↓
Processing
↓
Output

▲ Figure 1.6 Stages of processing

▲ Figure 1.7 A CPU

Did you know?

The scientific unit of measure 'Hertz' (Hz) is named in honour of the German physicist Heinrich Rudolf Hertz (1857–1894). Hertz did the groundwork for the development of the vacuum tube. He also discovered electromagnetic waves.

Arithmetic logic unit

The arithmetic logic unit (ALU) performs all the arithmetic and logic functions in a computer. For example, if an instruction involves an arithmetic operation such as addition, subtraction, multiplication, division or the comparison of data, the control unit sends the data to the ALU for processing.

Some of the logic functions are comparisons, such as:

equal to =   not equal to ≠
less than <   greater than >
less than or equal to <=   greater than or equal to >=

For example, using the 'equal to' logic function, the ALU compares two values to determine if they are equal. Other logical operations performed by the ALU are AND, OR and NOT.

Primary memory

Primary memory, also referred to as main memory or immediate access memory, is directly accessible to the CPU and holds data and instructions that the computer is processing at the time. Therefore, the data collected in the example of the temperature of the classroom would be placed in main memory while it is being processed. Output devices then translate information processed by the computer into a form that the user can understand. After processing, the data and information can be either stored in a secondary storage device, such as a hard disk, or sent to an output device such as a printer or a computer screen.

Primary memory consists of two types of memory chips: Random Access Memory (RAM) and Read Only Memory (ROM).

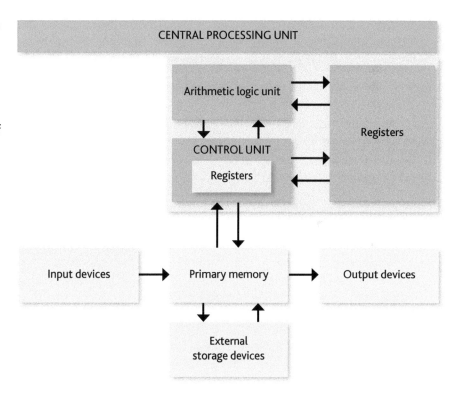

▲ Figure 1.8 The components of a basic computer system

A computer uses RAM to hold data and instructions (programs) temporarily while processing is taking place. RAM also holds the data that results from processing data, which is waiting to be output or stored in a secondary storage medium. RAM is therefore also called working memory.

ROM chips hold the data and instructions necessary for starting up the computer when it is switched on. These instructions are fixed at the time of manufacture and are sometimes described as being 'hard-wired'. This ensures that the instructions stored in ROM are always there, whether the power is on or not. RAM and ROM will be discussed further in Chapter 3.

Exercise 1

1 Computers are often used because they are able to hold lots of _____ in a very small space. They can work _____ and are much better at completing many tasks because of their _____ and _____.
2 The action of _____ data produces information that can be _____ or stored for future use.
3 Two internal components that are necessary for the computer to function are _____ and _____.
4 The external components of a computer are known as _____.
5 Use the words in the list below to identify the devices that are components and those that are peripherals.

> CPU   Keyboard   RAM   Mouse   Printers   Motherboard   Speakers

6 A _____ contains an ALU, control unit and registers.
7 A processor with two cores is called a _____ processor and four cores is called a _____ processor.
8 The _____ unit determines the sequence in which instructions are executed.
9 The control unit is primarily responsible for movement of data and instructions from itself to the _____ and _____ and back.
10 The _____ holds the address of the instruction being processed at the time and the instruction register holds the instruction itself.

Types of computers

Computer systems are classified on the basis of system performance, which in turn affects physical size and cost. Given the rapid pace at which computer technology is changing, classifying computers on this basis is often very difficult, since many of the newer, smaller systems can outperform the larger models of a few years ago. Nevertheless, some broad categories can be defined, as follows.

Desktop systems

A desktop computer system is designed to stay in a single location and must remain connected to a wall outlet. Although desktop systems lack portability, they offer similar or even better functionality to laptops, smartphones and other devices. Two examples of desktop systems are personal computers and gaming consoles.

Personal computers (PCs)

Personal computers (PCs), also called microcomputers, are the most common type of computer. They come in many different shapes, sizes and colours, depending on the manufacturer. PCs are used by one person at a time and fit on an office desk, hence the name 'desktop computers'. A PC consists of a system unit, a keyboard, a mouse and a display screen, and has all the functional elements found in any larger system. It performs the input, control, arithmetic and logic, output and storage functions mentioned earlier in the chapter. It can execute software program instructions to perform a very wide variety of tasks. Individuals, businesses and organisations use personal computers. The processing speed, internal memory capacity and external storage vary with the different models available. Usually, individuals or organisations will purchase a personal computer based on the purpose for which the computer will be used. The processor speed for a typical personal computer ranges from 2.4 GHz to 3.7 GHz. These computers usually have between 4 gigabyte (GB) and 32 GB of RAM and a storage capacity that varies from 40 GB to 1 terabyte (TB).

▲ Figure 1.9 A desktop system (personal computer)

Gaming consoles

A video game console is a highly specialised desktop computer used to play video games. Gaming consoles have many of the same hardware components as computers, but are usually less advanced. This is why they cost much less than a high-end gaming computer. The player interacts with the game through a controller, which is a hand-held device with buttons and joysticks or pads. Gaming consoles are usually connected to a television, which outputs the video and sound. Examples of consoles include the Microsoft Xbox, Sony PlayStation, Nintendo GameCube, and Nintendo Wii. The processor speed for a typical gaming console ranges from 2.4 GHz to 4.1 GHz. These devices usually have between 4 GB and 32 GB of RAM and a storage capacity that varies from 512 GB to 1 TB.

▲ Figure 1.10 A gaming console with game controllers

Mobile devices

A mobile device is a general term used to refer to devices such as laptops, tablets, smartphones and personal digital assistants (PDAs). These devices have similar characteristics such as:

- the ability to access the internet
- a battery that powers the device and can last for several hours
- a physical or onscreen keyboard for entering information
- a small size and light weight, which allows it to be carried in one hand and manipulated with the other hand
- a touchscreen interface in almost all cases
- wireless operation.

> **Did you know?**
>
> Present-day personal computers can perform tasks thousands of times faster than the personal computers of the 1980s.

Laptops

A laptop computer is a portable version of a PC, equipped with a flat liquid crystal display (LCD) screen and weighing about one to four kilograms. The two main types of laptop computers are notebooks and subnotebooks.

Notebooks

A notebook computer is a portable computer that weighs two to four kilograms and is roughly the size of a large thick notebook, around 35 × 25 × 4 centimetres. They have a fairly large LCD colour screen (about 30 cm across) and a fairly large keyboard, usually with a small touch-sensitive pad, which serves as a mouse. Notebook PCs can easily be packed into a briefcase or backpack, or simply held under your arm. They can use power from an electrical outlet or rechargeable batteries. Notebooks are usually just as powerful as a desktop PC, but cost more than their equivalent desktop PC. The processing speed and storage capacity can vary widely depending on the needs of the user. The processor speed for a typical notebook computer ranges from 2.2 GHz to 3.1 GHz. These devices usually have between 4 GB and 32 GB of RAM and a storage capacity that varies from 512 GB to 1 TB. A notebook computer is a very portable device given its relatively light weight and a battery life that varies between 9 hours and 17 hours depending on the brand.

▲ Figure 1.11 A notebook computer

Subnotebooks

A subnotebook computer is a very portable device. It usually weighs between 1 kg and 1.5 kg, can fit in a large jacket pocket and has a battery life of more than 10 hours. It has a small screen and a small keyboard without the mouse function. It can perform many of the same functions as notebooks, but not to the same degree of complexity (difficulty). Similar to a notebook, its processing speed and storage capacity can vary widely depending on the needs of the user. The processor speed for a typical subnotebook computer ranges from 1.6 GHz to 1.8 GHz. These devices usually have between 4GB and 32 GB of RAM and a storage capacity that varies from 256 GB to 1 TB.

Netbooks

A netbook is a small, low-power notebook computer that weighs less than 1.5 kg and has a battery, which can provide between 6 to 12 hours of service before needing to be recharged. It has a smaller screen size (less than 30 cm), smaller keyboard size and less processing power than a full-sized laptop. It is designed to be simple and can be used to perform easy tasks like word processing, email, internet browsing, light entertainment and light productivity. They typically have less RAM and hard disk capacity than laptops. The processor speed for a typical netbook computer ranges from 1.5 GHz to 1.7 GHz. These devices usually have between 2 GB and 4 GB of RAM and a storage capacity that varies from 64 GB to 256 GB.

▲ Figure 1.12 A netbook and wireless mouse

Tablet PCs

A tablet PC is a thin, lightweight mobile computer that typically weighs less than 1 kg and has a battery that can provide between 15 and 18 hours of battery life. It is smaller than a laptop but larger than a smartphone. All tablets use a touchscreen as their primary input device. Users can interact with the device by using their finger or a stylus. They also have the option to connect external devices such as a keyboard or mouse wirelessly.

A tablet can be used for gaming, retrieving information, keeping connected with others, shopping, entertainment or taking notes in meetings and lectures where a laptop may not be practical. A typical tablet has a processing speed of between 1.5 GHz and 2.5 GHz, 2 GB to 16 GB RAM and a storage capacity of between 256 GB and 1 TB.

▲ Figure 1.13 A tablet PC

Smartphones

A smartphone is a mobile phone that performs many of the functions of a computer. It usually has a touchscreen interface, internet access, and an operating system capable of running downloaded apps. Smartphones can be used to make phone calls, surf the web, send and receive email messages, use a variety of apps (WhatsApp, Waze, Facebook and Uber) and play online games. The processing speed and storage capacity of smartphones varies with price. The greater the RAM, ROM and processing speed, the more expensive the smartphone. An average smartphone may have a processing speed of 2.3 GHz, 2 GB to 16 GB of RAM and a storage capacity of between 16 GB and 64 GB.

Wearable computers

The latest trend in computing is wearable computers. Essentially, common computer applications (email, database, multimedia, calendar/scheduler, health monitoring system) are integrated into watches, cell phones, visors and even clothing. For example, the Apple Watch® is a wristwatch that interfaces with the Apple iPhone® and the user can also download apps such as a calculator app, camera app, weather app and many more to the watch.

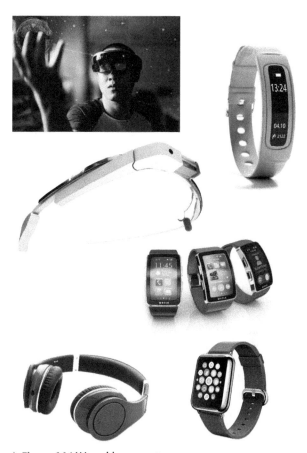

▲ Figure 1.14 **Wearable computers**

Embedded computers

An embedded computer is a special-purpose computer used inside a device and is usually dedicated to specific functions. It is housed on a single printed circuit board that provides all of the circuitry necessary for a microprocessor, RAM, ROM and any necessary components. It is connected to sensors, which are devices that detect changes in the environment such as light, temperature or pressure, and actuators, which are hardware output devices that convert an electrical control signal into physical action. They are commonly used in items such as answering machines, smart televisions, washing machines, cameras, cars, motors, sewing machines, clocks and microwaves. For example, in a microwave oven, the embedded system is designed to take directions from the keypad and turn them into commands. If you program a microwave oven to operate on high for two minutes, the embedded system instructs the high-voltage transformer to operate on full discharge for two minutes. When the two minutes expire, the embedded system commands the transformer to turn off.

The processing speeds, memory and storage capacities of embedded computers are usually much lower than a typical PC computer due to the limited range of commands they are required to perform. For example, the amount of RAM required for a typical application may vary between 64 KB and 1 MB.

▲ Figure 1.15 **The button panel on a microwave**

Exercise 2

True or False?

1 A desktop computer system is designed to stay in a single location.
2 Personal computers (PCs) are also sometimes called microcomputers.
3 A video game console is a highly specialised desktop computer used to play video games.
4 Notebook PCs are too large to be tucked into a briefcase or backpack.
5 A netbook computer is another name for a subnotebook computer.
6 A tablet can be used for gaming, retrieving information, keeping connected with others, shopping and entertainment.
7 The Apple Watch® is an example of a wearable computer.
8 The functions in a microwave oven are controlled by an embedded computer.
9 A modern smartphone has the same processing capacity as a modern desktop computer.
10 The processor speed for a typical netbook computer ranges from 3.5 GHz to 4.1 GHz.

Multiple-choice questions

1 Which of the following is an example of an embedded computer system?
  a Notebook
  b Netbook
  c Tablet
  d Smart television
2 The processing speeds of modern laptop computers can be measured in:
  a gigahertz.
  b kilohertz.
  c gigabytes.
  d kilobytes.
3 Information can best be described as:
  a raw facts.
  b raw data.
  c processed data.
  d none of the above.
4 Which of the following is best suited for taking notes in meetings and lectures?
  a Desktop computer
  b Notebook computer
  c Netbook computer
  d Tablet computer
5 Which of the following is not a feature of a mobile device?
  a Ability to access the internet
  b A battery that powers the device and can last for several hours
  c A physical or onscreen keyboard for entering information
  d Can only operate when plugged into a power outlet

Minicomputers

Minicomputers have become outdated and are rarely used today. They were very popular in the 1960s. Their cost and processing capabilities were somewhere between those of a PC and a mainframe computer. They were used mainly in small manufacturing plants, research labs and businesses. Mini-systems were usually designed to simultaneously (at the same time), support up to about 200 users. They allowed many users to share access to central hardware through work stations called terminals. A typical terminal has a keyboard, a display screen and a cable that connects the terminal to the computer system. Lower-capacity models have as low as 64 to 192 MB of memory, whereas higher-capacity models have as high as 1,024 to 32,768 MB of memory. Direct access storage disks are attached directly to the server or computer and allow a typical minicomputer to manage anywhere from 4 GB to over 18,000 GB of data.

▲ Figure 1.16 Minicomputer

Mainframes

Mainframes are very powerful computers that are very expensive. They offer more processor capacity and greater storage capacity than a typical minicomputer. A mainframe can handle thousands of users simultaneously. They are found in large organisations such as banks, government agencies, insurance companies and corporations, where they perform tasks that require a lot of computational power: typically, bulk data processing such as censuses, industry/consumer statistics and bank transaction processing. The IBM zSeries z14 Model M05 is currently one of the most powerful mainframe computers available. The IBM z14 class mainframe computer can have up to 170 processors operating at 5.2 GHz, up to 32 TB of Redundant Array of Independent Memory (RAIM) and significant amounts of storage as required.

▲ Figure 1.17 The IBM System z14 mainframe computer

Supercomputers ('monsters')

Supercomputers such as the IBM-built Summit, and Sierra, are the world's fastest and most powerful computers in the year 2019. Supercomputers are designed to process complex scientific applications. They are typically used for 'number crunching' in scientific simulations, scientific research and developments in areas such as energy, space exploration, medicine and industry. Number crunching is the ability to perform large amounts of numerical computations quickly. Similarly, the United States Department of Energy's Oak Ridge National Laboratory (ORNL) new Summit supercomputer is providing scientists with incredible computing power to solve challenges in energy, artificial intelligence (AI), human health and other research areas that were simply out of reach until now. The Summit has 9216 processors operating at 4.0 GHz and more than 10 petabytes (PB) of total memory available, and has already set new records in AI and traditional application performance. These systems are very expensive, often costing millions of US dollars.

Did you know?

The processing power and storage capacity of the modern PC is far greater than that of a mainframe computer of the 1960s.

▲ Figure 1.18 A supercomputer

Generations of computers

Computers can be broadly classified into five generations. These generations are based mainly on the basic electronic component that was used to build the computer.

First generation (1945–1956)

The vacuum tube or valve was the main electronic component of first-generation computers. This made the computers very large; they contained many kilometres of electrical wire, used a lot of electrical power and generated a lot of heat. As vacuum tubes were blown so easily, processing was unreliable. Also, each computer had a different binary-coded program called a 'machine language' that told it how to operate, and had to be programmed directly in this machine language. This made the computer difficult to program and limited its versatility and speed.

The Harvard Mark I (electromechanical) was the first computer in this generation. The ENIAC (Electronic Numerical Integrator and Calculator), produced in 1946, was the first computer to use electrical signals for calculating and storing results with no mechanical operations involved. Other first-generation computers include UNIVAC, Burroughs 220 and the IBM 700 series.

▲ Figure 1.19 The ENIAC computer

Second generation (1956–1963)

Transistors were invented in 1947 and these formed the basis for second-generation computers. A transistor is a device used to open and close a circuit in computer processors and digital memory. Computers became smaller, faster, more reliable and more energy-efficient than their predecessors. The machine languages of the first-generation computers were replaced by assembly language, allowing abbreviated programming codes to replace long, difficult binary codes. Some popular second-generation computers include the IBM 1400 and 1600 series, UNIVAC III, NCR 300 series and the Burroughs B500 series.

Did you know?

The transistor is considered to be one of the greatest inventions of modern times. Without transistors, modern computers would not have been possible. The transistor was invented at Bell Laboratories in December 1947 by John Bardeen, Walter Brattain and William Shockley. They were awarded the 1956 Nobel Prize in physics for their outstanding achievement.

Third generation (1964–1970)

With the invention of the integrated circuit (IC), or chip, computers became even smaller, faster, more reliable, more energy-efficient and cheaper than their predecessors. Another third-generation development was the invention and use of 'high-level' languages, which used English words and the base-10 number system to program the computer. Some third generation computers include the IBM System 3 and System 7, UNIVAC 9000 series, NCR Century series and the Burroughs 6700.

▲ Figure 1.20 A third-generation computer

Fourth generation (1971–present)

Fouth-generation computers are still based on the chip, but with many more components packed inside. First, there was large-scale integration (LSI), where hundreds of components were placed on the chip. By the 1980s, very large-scale integration squeezed thousands of components onto a chip. Ultra-large-scale integration (ULSI) increased that number to millions of components. Computers became even smaller, cheaper and much more reliable; their processing capabilities increased accordingly. Some early examples of fourth-generation computers include the IBM System 3090 and RISC 6000, the HP 9000 and the Cray 2 XMP.

As the years have gone by, the size of a chip has decreased to the 14 nanometre (nm) size that is used in the IBM z14 today. Performance gains (improvements) now depend not only the speed of the chip, but also on the system innovation (new technological advances) adding to the complexity on the chip. The requirements that drive the complexity have also changed along the way. An example is the requirement for security in today's digital world. The IBM z14 is capable of processing over 12.5 billion fully-encrypted transactions in a day, the equivalent of 400 Cyber Mondays on a single system.

▲ Figure 1.21 A robot is a fifth-generation computer.

Did you know?

Cyber Monday is name for the Monday after the US Thanksgiving holiday, where shops provide huge discounts to shoppers when shopping online.

Fifth generation (present–future)

Fifth-generation computers will be able to mimic many of the things that so far have only been within the capacity of human beings to achieve, namely that they will demonstrate a certain level of artificial intelligence (AI). For example, fifth-generation computers, including standard PCs, are starting to accept spoken word instructions (voice recognition) and can now assist doctors in making very specific diagnoses (expert systems).

Computers of this generation make use of parallel processing: they are capable of performing multiple, simultaneous operations using more than one microprocessing chip. This makes them especially powerful. The eventual goal of fifth-generation computers is to develop devices that respond to natural language input and are capable of 'learning'. An AI program would eliminate the need for users to write programs, since they could communicate their orders to the computer in ordinary English.

Emerging technologies: Quantum computers

Quantum computers are designed to exploit certain properties of quantum mechanics (a physical science dealing with the behaviour of matter and energy on the scale of atoms and subatomic particles/waves) to solve problems that would be impractical or impossible for a classical (digital) computer to solve. Quantum computers work by using qubits. These qubits are not limited to values of either 1 or 0 like classical bits, but can represent both a 1 and a 0 at the same time through superposition. Qubits, when in a superposition, can be entangled; that is, a state of one qubit (either 1 or 0) can depend on the state of another. Through the use of these qubits, sophisticated switches can be made to compute certain problems that are difficult for classical computers to do.

▲ Figure 1.22 D-Wave 2000Q™ quantum computer

Chapter 1: Summary

- Storage refers to the media and devices used to keep data and instructions for immediate or later use.
- A computer is an electronic device that processes data following a set of instructions.
- A computer system is a complete computer, which includes both hardware and software.
- Data is all the raw facts and figures that a computer processes by following a set of instructions (called a program) to produce information.
- Information and communications technology (ICT) is the use of computer hardware, software and telecommunications devices to store, manipulate, convert, protect, send and receive data.
- Information technology (IT) deals with the study of data and data processing, and may also apply to the management of computer systems, particularly in a business setting.
- Computer science is the study of computer technology (both computer hardware and software).
- We use computers for their great speed, accuracy, large storage capacity and ability to work continuously in solving a variety of problems.
- Hardware is all the parts of the computer system that you can see and touch. It consists of both the internal and external components of the computer.
- Peripherals are external hardware devices that are not essential to a computer's function and are usually connected to the computer by a cable or wirelessly. These devices include keyboards, printers, speakers, mice and hard drives.
- Software is a set of instructions (a program) that a computer needs to carry out its tasks.
- Input, processing and output are the three stages of processing.
- We use input devices to enter data and instructions into the computer for processing.
- The central processing unit (CPU) is the 'brain' of the computer. It comprises the control unit (CU), the arithmetic logic unit (ALU) and registers.
- The control unit is the main part of the CPU. It directs and coordinates all the CPU activities.
- A register is a temporary storage location that holds a single instruction or data item.
- The program counter holds the address of the current instruction (the instruction being processed) and the instruction register holds the instruction itself.
- The arithmetic logic unit (ALU) performs all the arithmetic and logic functions in a computer.
- The primary memory holds data and instructions that the computer is processing at the time.
- Primary memory consists of: Random Access Memory (RAM) and Read Only Memory (ROM) chips.
- The motherboard is the main printed circuit board of a computer that contains the CPU, and the RAM and ROM chips. It allows all the parts of a computer to receive power and communicate with one another.
- Output devices translate information that is processed by the computer into a form that the user can understand.
- We classify computer systems as personal computers, minicomputers, mainframe computers, supercomputers, quantum computers and embedded computers.
- Personal computers (PCs), also called desktop or microcomputers, are the most common computers. We design PCs to be used by one person at a time. A PC can usually fit on an office desk and consists of a system unit, a keyboard, a mouse and a display screen.
- Minicomputers have become outdated and are rarely used today. They were very popular in the 1960s. Their cost, storage and processing capabilities were between those of a PC and a mainframe computer.
- Mainframes are very powerful computers and are very expensive. They offer faster processing speeds and greater storage capacity than a typical mini.
- Supercomputers are the largest, fastest and most powerful computers at present. They are typically used for 'number crunching' in scientific simulations, scientific research and development.
- A mobile device refers to devices such as laptops, tablets, smartphones and PDAs.
- Laptops, notebooks, subnotebooks and netbooks are all portable computers with flat LCD screens.
- A tablet PC is a computer that looks like a notebook computer except that data is entered with a digitising tablet or touchscreen.
- A smartphone is a cell phone that has many of the capabilities of a computer.
- A video game console is a highly specialised desktop computer used to play video games.
- A wearable computer is an electronic device, capable of storing and processing data that is incorporated into a person's clothing or personal accessories.
- An embedded computer is used inside a device and is usually dedicated to specific functions.

Chapter 1: Questions

Fill in the blanks

1   A set of instructions that a computer needs to carry out its tasks is known as a _____.

2   _____ is a set of raw facts and figures.

3   _____ are used to get the data and instructions into the computer for processing.

4   Processing takes place in that part of the computer known as the _____.

5   _____ computers will be able to mimic many of the things that so far can only be done by human beings.

6   The _____ directs and coordinates all the activities within the CPU.

7   A(n) _____ computer is a special purpose computer that is used inside a device and is usually dedicated to specific functions.

8   A _____ is a temporary storage location that holds a single instruction or data item.

9   The _____ holds the address of the current instruction in the control unit.

10 The _____ performs all the arithmetic and logic functions in a computer.

11 The _____ holds data and instructions that the computer is processing at the time.

12 _____ translate information processed by the computer into a form that the user can understand.

True or False?

1   Data and information are the same.

2   The CPU is the main part of the computer.

3   All the data is processed in the memory unit.

4   The control unit sends data from the memory to the ALU for processing.

5   Output devices translate information processed by the computer into a form that the user can understand.

6   A modern mainframe has the same processing power as a very powerful PC.

7   An embedded computer is housed on a single microprocessor board.

8   The most popular computers today are mainframe computers.

9   A register can hold data permanently.

10 The program counter is found in the control unit.

Multiple-choice questions

1   Which of the following devices is not found in the CPU of a computer?
   a   Arithmetic logic unit   b   Secondary storage
   c   Control unit   d   Register

2   Where in the computer would the instructions to add two numbers be carried out?
   a   Screen   b   External storage
   c   CPU   d   Keyboard

3   Which of these is a function of the control unit?
   a   Fetch and decode instructions from memory
   b   Store data for processing
   c   Perform logical operations
   d   Perform arithmetic operations

4   Which of the following types of computers has the fastest processing speed?
   a   Laptops   b   Mainframes
   c   Embedded computers   d   Supercomputers

5   Which of the following is not an example of a peripheral device?
   a   Keyboard   b   Mouse
   c   RAM   d   Speakers

6   A program is a:
   a   hardware device.   b   memory device.
   c   set of instructions.   d   register.

7   Which device is not found in the CPU?
   a   ALU   b   Control unit
   c   Instruction register   d   Printer

8   The ALU processes data and stores it in:
   a   the main memory.   b   the instruction register.
   c   the control unit.   d   the program counter.

9   Which one of the following is not a function of the control unit?
   a   Fetch instructions from memory
   b   Decode instructions
   c   Process instructions
   d   Fetch data for required instructions

10 Complex scientific research is usually done using:
   a personal computers.   b supercomputers.
   c minicomputers.   d mainframe computers.

Short-answer questions

1 Define the terms 'hardware' and 'software'.

2 Using examples, explain the difference between data and information.

3 Draw a diagram showing the three stages of processing.

4 a Draw a block diagram to illustrate the main components of a computer system.
  b Describe the functions of the two main units found in the central processing unit.

5 Explain the purpose of the following devices:
   a input device.   b output device.
   c main memory.

6 State FOUR reasons why we use computers.

7 Describe the features of a personal computer (PC).

8 a Explain the difference between a mainframe computer and a supercomputer.
  b State TWO reasons why a bank may want to purchase a mainframe computer.
  c Differentiate between a notebook computer and a subnotebook computer.
  d What is an embedded computer?

9 Discuss with your classmates how a portable computer could assist these professionals:
   a a teacher.   b a police officer.
   c a newspaper reporter.   d a sales representative.

Research questions

1 Your school principal wants to purchase a very fast desktop computer for the school and a laptop computer for himself. He asks you to prepare a list of the five fastest desktop computers and a list of the five fastest laptop computers. Present the information in a table with the following headings: name of computer, processing speed, manufacturer and approximate cost.

2 Using the internet to conduct your research, make a list of the top five most powerful supercomputers in the world. You are required to create a table with the name of the computer, processing speed, the purpose for which the computer is used, manufacturer and approximate cost.

3 A friend would like to buy a computer to play computer games. She would like you to provide her with a list of suggestions of the specifications for this computer, as well as three computers on the market that she can buy, which would allow her to play most of the modern computer games.

4 Use the internet to research these tasks:
   a Create a timeline to show the evolution of processors.
   b Explain how computers are used in predicting weather forecasts, modelling, data crunching and automation.

Crossword

Across

1 A device in the control unit that is used to store data and instructions that are needed immediately and frequently (8)

3 A set of instructions that the computer needs to carry out a task (7)

5 It represents billions of machine cycles per second (9)

6 Also known as the brain of the computer (9)

7 Performs the logic functions in the computer (3)

Down

2 A special-purpose computer used inside a device (8)

4 A type of intelligence that will be used in fifth-generation computers (10)

Input devices

Objectives

At the end of this chapter, you will be able to:

→ define the term 'input device'
→ explain the term 'data capture' and the different means by which data is captured
→ explain the difference between data verification and validation
→ list typical input devices
→ state some of the characteristics and uses of different input devices
→ select appropriate input devices to meet the needs of specific applications.

A computer needs input, output and storage devices so that it can accept data, process that data and produce useful output. This is sometimes referred to as the Input Processing Output Storage (IPOS) cycle.

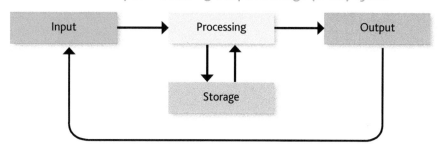

▲ Figure 2.1 Input Processing Output Storage (IPOS) cycle

All the input, output and storage devices connected to and dependent on a computer for operation are called peripherals. Input devices are pieces of equipment that are used to put data into the computer.

Data-processing cycle

When data is collected, it is processed to convert it into useful information. Processing usually involves a set of actions or operations called a data-processing sequence or a data-processing cycle. Figure 2.2 and Table 2.1 show the main stages in a typical cycle, which may include:

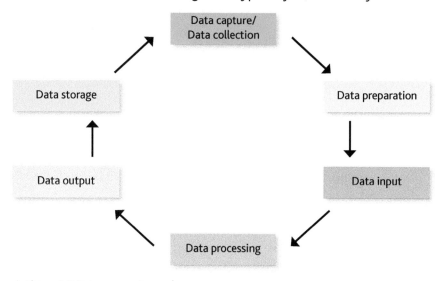

▲ Figure 2.2 Data-processing cycle

Stages	Explanation
Data capture	Data is gathered or collected, manually or automatically, in order to be entered into the computer.
Data preparation	Data is checked for accuracy and manipulated into a format that is acceptable for data input (verified and validated).
Data input	This is where the prepared data is converted to a machine-readable format so that it can be processed.
Data processing	The data is manipulated or changed, based on the instructions given by the computer program.
Data output	At this stage, the processed data or information is transmitted to the user.
Data storage	At this stage, the data, information and instructions are saved for later use.

▲ Table 2.1 Explanation of the stages in the data-processing cycle

Data output is discussed in detail in Chapter 4 and data storage is discussed in Chapter 3.

Data capture

Data capture means collecting data for input. It is the first stage of the data-processing cycle. It is at this point that various input devices are used to input data that the computer will process and/or store.
There are two main ways of inputting data, as listed below:

■ **Manual data input:** Data is entered directly into the computer, one transaction at a time, by hand. This data is usually stored on data capture forms. These forms are usually designed so that the instructions are very clear and concise, leaving no room for misinterpretation. The data from the form is entered manually by data entry personnel. Keyboard, mouse, touchscreen, light pen, graphics tablet and voice input devices are some of the devices used.

■ **Automatic data input/data capture:** Data is entered directly into the computer from source documents. Source documents are documents on which data is first recorded before it is entered into the computer. Data entered from these documents is transferred directly from the document into the computer's memory. Data is captured at the source, for example, directly from barcodes on supermarket items into the computer, or directly from national lottery slips into the computer. In some applications, such as utility bill processing, the bill produced at the output stage of the data-processing cycle has more information added to it and is then input for further processing. This type of document is called a turnaround document. For example, when a customer pays an electricity bill, the amount and date paid are added to the bill. This new information on the bill is then re-input into the system along with additional meter readings to produce the new bill for the customer. Other examples of turnaround documents are a boarding pass or a laser-encoded cheque, such as a bank manager's cheque.

▲ Figure 2.3 A barcode being scanned

Data preparation and data input

Data must be in an appropriate format and checked for accuracy before being entered into the computer. If you put incorrect data into a computer system, the output will be incorrect. Inaccurate data can result in embarrassment and economic loss to individuals and organisations. Therefore, it is very important to ensure that data entering a system has integrity, which means that it is accurate and that it is input into the computer without mistakes.

The causes of inaccuracies in input data are listed here.

- **Mistakes or inaccuracies when collecting the data:** For example, in a greenhouse, the sensors used to collect data such as temperature and humidity may not be working properly, so the wrong data will be fed into the computer that is controlling the greenhouse environment.
- **Software and hardware errors:** Software errors may occur due to a virus erasing or corrupting previously entered data. Hardware errors include:
  - transmission errors – data that has been sent from one device to another within the computer or from one computer to another, is changed due to a hardware failure.
  - read errors – this occurs when an input device is unable to read the input medium correctly.
- **Errors in preparing the data.** This may be due to:
  - typing errors, such as transposition errors – typing digits or letters in the wrong order. For example, if you had to enter the digits 50673 but entered 50763, you would have made a transposition error.
  - misreading characters in a coding sheet, such as replacing a zero (0) with the letter O or vice versa.

People who develop computer systems use two main techniques to ensure that the data entered into a system has integrity. These techniques are verification and validation.

Verification

Verification is a check to ensure that data from the medium it was originally stored on is accurately transcribed or copied into a computer. This may be achieved by visual checks and dual inputs.

- **Visual checks (proofreading):** This involves carefully checking what has been typed, against the original document. Another method is the use of screen prompts. In this case, the user enters data into the computer. After a predetermined amount is entered, it is redisplayed on the monitor screen. The user is prompted to read the data and confirm that it has been entered correctly. If the user has entered any data incorrectly, he or she simply retypes the incorrect parts. The accuracy of this method depends on the thoroughness of the individual checking the document.
- **Dual inputs (double entry):** This method is used when a keyboard is used to enter data. The data to be entered is typed in twice by two different operators and saved. The two copies of the data are then compared. Any differences are detected by the computer. The operators will be prompted to retype the sections that differ until both copies agree.

When the two copies agree, it is assumed by the computer that the data has been entered correctly. This method is much more accurate but is more time-consuming and expensive, as two individuals have to be employed to do the same task.

Validation

Validation is the checking of data for errors before the actual processing takes place. It is used to determine if the data entered is incomplete, inaccurate or unreasonable. The following are some of the validation checks that may be carried out by some or all validation programs.

- **Presence checks:** Presence checks are used to check that data has been entered into a field and that it has not been left blank. For example, a database storing the names of students would require the surname field for each student to contain data. However, this check would not ensure that the correct surname was entered for the student.
- **Data-type checks:** Data-type checks are used to check that an entered value is of a particular type. When a table in a database is created, each field is given a data type. Data may be of typed text, memo, number, date/time, and so on. When data is entered into a specific field, the database will check to ensure that the data is of the correct type. If not, an error message will be displayed and the data will have to be re-entered.
- **Length checks:** Length checks are used to check that the number of characters entered in a field does not exceed the number allocated for the field or is not fewer than specified. For example, each field in a Microsoft Access database has a preset length. This length can be adjusted to reduce storage space and to try to ensure the accuracy of the data entered. For example, a field that is used to store a bank account number would have a fixed number, typically 8 digits, so if 7 are entered, the field will recognise that it is wrong. Another example may be a password, which has to be 6 or more characters, so A123BC would validate, but AB123 would not.
- **Range checks:** Range checks are used to check whether data is within a range of possible values. For example, when entering the months of a date of birth, the range of acceptable numbers lies in the range 1 to 12. Also, the range of acceptable numbers for the number of normal hours worked for a week may be in the range 0 to 40.
- **Format checks:** Format checks are used to check that the data is entered in the format specified by the software. For example, a car registration number should consist of one to three letters followed or preceded by one to four numbers.
- **Check digit checks:** A check digit is an extra digit attached to the end of a string of digits to ensure that if any of the digits are changed by mistake, the error will be detected. Barcode and ISBN numbers in books both contain check digits. When a barcode number is printed on a product or label of a product, the computer calculates and adds a check digit to the end of the number.

Did you know?

When you enter a new password that has to be more than six characters long and contain a number and capital letter, it has to undergo a length validation and a data-type validation. It also has to be validated for consistency – which is why you are asked to enter the password twice.

When the number is input into the computer, a calculation is performed to check whether the check digit at the end of the number is valid. If it is not, then the number has been misread and must be re-inputted. See the following example to check the ISBN: 1-4058-2043.

Starting from the left and moving to the right, multiply the first number by 10, the second by 9, the third by 8, and so on.
We will therefore get:
$1\times10+4\times9+0\times8+5\times7+8\times6+2\times5+0\times4+4\times3+3\times2=157$

1 Divide 157 by 11 = 14 remainder 3
2 The remainder is then subtracted from 11 to give the check digit: 11 − 3 = 8. The check digit is therefore 8. Note that if the remainder works out to be 10, then the check digit of the ISBN will be represented by an X.
3 The number printed on the book will be 1-4058-2043-8.

■ **Parity check:** A parity check is used in data communications to ensure that data is not corrupted during transmission. When data is transmitted, each character is encoded as a 7-bit binary number. An eighth bit is added to make a byte. This bit is called a parity bit and is used to ensure that the data received is not corrupted in any way. A system can use either even or odd parity. In an even parity system, the receiver, for example, the computer getting data from a barcode reader, checks that each received byte contains an even number of 1s. In an odd parity system, the receiver checks that each received byte contains an odd number of 1s. If this is not the case, then an error must have occurred. A request will be sent to the transmitter to ask it to send the byte again.
For example, if a system is using even parity and the letter C has to be sent, the letter must first be encoded. The ASCII code for the letter C is 1000011. Since this code contains an odd number of 1s, a 1 is added to the left-hand side (for example: 11000011) so that the total number of 1s in the byte are even. If the computer is using odd parity, then a 0 is added so that the total number of 1s are odd (for example: 01000011).

▲ Figure 2.4 The 10-digit ISBN is shown above the bar code.

> ### Did you know?
> International books now have ISBNs that are 13 digits long. The 13th digit is still a control digit, which is used to check the correctness of the other digits.

Typical input devices

Typical input devices include these peripherals: keyboards, pointing devices, gaming input devices, scanning devices, smart cards, audio and video input devices and other input devices. We will look at each of these in turn.

Keyboards

The most common input device is the keyboard. A digital code is sent to the computer when each key is pressed. For example, the code 01100001 is produced when the 'A' key is pressed. Keyboards play a pivotal role in the input of data into the computer. Their design is of critical importance for comfort and usability, since users may spend long periods of time entering data. Many keyboards are therefore designed with ergonomics in mind.

▲ Figure 2.5 An ergonomic keyboard

There are two types of keyboards: the alphanumeric keyboard and the special-function keyboard, which can be either wired or wireless. The alphanumeric keyboard contains letters, numbers and symbols in particular layouts. This keyboard is modelled on the typewriter keyboard and is also known as a QWERTY keyboard. Keyboards may be attached to the computer by wires or they may be wireless.

Special-function keyboards are invented for a particular purpose. Some examples are listed here.

- **Braille keyboard:** This keyboard has its keys marked with raised dots to aid the blind.
- **Concept keyboard:** This keyboard contains a flatbed of contact switches covered by a flexible membrane. Whole words, pictures or symbols are superimposed over each contact switch. The computer is then programmed to respond appropriately to these. Concept keyboards are used in education as an early-learning aid, in restaurants so the operator can visually add up the cost of standard menu items, and in messy places where a normal keyboard would be at risk.
- **Left-handed keyboard:** This keyboard is designed for the left-handed individual.
- **Virtual/projection keyboard:** This keyboard is projected onto any surface and touched. The keyboard can register your finger movement and then translate that movement into a keystroke. An example is the touchscreen keyboard of the automatic teller machines (ATM) found in front of banks.

Pointing devices

Pointing devices are used by graphical operating systems such as Windows to show the motion of a pointer or cursor, and to enable the control and selection of objects on the display.

The mouse

The movement of the mouse over a flat surface is mirrored by a pointer on the monitor screen. Buttons on the mouse allow you to make selections from menus, move objects around the screen, and paint or draw.

There are various types of mice: some are designed for comfort and others as a matter of preference. A mice can come with or without a wire attachment, hence we have the wireless mouse.

- The **optical mouse** can slide over most surfaces. It emits a small beam of red light that bounces off the surface into a sensor. The sensor sends coordinates to the computer, which in turn moves the cursor or pointer on the monitor screen according to these coordinates. The advantage of this type of mouse is that you do not need to worry about dirt and cleaning, and it is very easy to manipulate. Since there are no moving parts, the mouse is less likely to fail because there is less wear and tear.
- The **trackball mouse** has a large ball on top rather than underneath. You can roll the ball with the palm of your hand or your fingers. These are found mainly on laptop computers. Buttons placed close by allow you to select features on the screen.

> **Did you know?**
> The measurement for the speed and movement direction of a computer mouse is called a mickey. One mickey is approximately 1/200 of an inch or 0.1 mm.

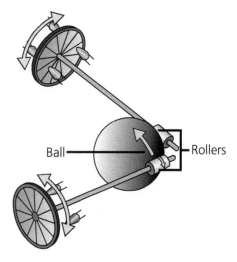

Ball — Rollers

▲ Figure 2.6 The mechanics inside a traditional (mechanical) or trackball mouse

- The **pointing stick mouse** found on laptop computers, looks like a pencil eraser. It protrudes from the keyboard between the B, G and H keys. Pushing on the pointing stick with your finger will move the pointer around the screen. Once again, buttons placed close by allow for selection of features on the screen.
- The **touchpad mouse** contains a touch-sensitive pad and is usually found on laptops. It is a pressure- and motion-sensitive flat surface of about 5 cm × 5 cm, over which you move your fingers to control the cursor/pointer on the screen. Buttons placed close to this surface allow for selection of features on the screen.
- The **gStick**, **pen mice** or **stick mice** (named after Gordon Stewart) are a pen or pencil-type mouse with a wheel and buttons located strategically in relation to a wheel. These mice were designed for user comfort.

▲ Figure 2.7 A pointing stick mouse on a laptop keyboard

Digitising tablets (graphics tablets)

To digitise data means to convert it from an analogue form (like a picture) to a digital form (binary numbers – see Chapter 5). A digitising tablet is a board that can detect the position of a pointing device such as a stylus or a puck on its surface. A stylus is a pen-like pointing device for a graphics/digitising tablet. A puck is a mouse-like device, which is moved over the surface of the tablet. It has cross-hairs to position it accurately and a number of buttons for different actions. Drawings and sketches can be entered easily onto the computer using the digitising tablet.

▲ Figure 2.8 A digitising tablet with a stylus

Touch-sensitive screens

This pointing device lets you interact with the computer by touching the screen. The pointer is the human finger. There are three forms of touchscreens: pressure-sensitive, capacitive surface and light beam. These screens are used in bank ATM machines, for example. They allow you to perform actions on your bank account by following instructions and options on-screen, using your finger to choose the option you wish.

Gaming input devices

In gaming, the input devices are trying to do fewer things than the input devices you use for other types of computing. Often you want them to look like the thing a player is using in the game, for example, in a driving game, the steering wheel and pedals of a car. We are going to look at joysticks, gaming pads, gaming wheels, dance pads, hybrid controllers and motion-sensing game controllers.

▲ Figure 2.9 A graphics stylus

Joysticks

A joystick is a pointing device that enables the user to control the movement of an object on the screen by operating a small lever. It is used mainly for computer games such as flight simulators.

▲ Figure 2.10 A gamer using a joystick

> ### Did you know?
> The light pen was used on cathode ray tube (CRT) monitors. You used a pen with the screen in a similar way to how you would work with a modern touchscreen with your finger. However, today their use has become obsolete with the invention of LCD monitors and touchscreens.

Gaming pads

A gaming pad enables a user to
move an object on the screen by
pressing buttons or moving sticks.
It is held with both hands.

▲ Figure 2.11 A gamer using a gaming pad

▲ Figure 2.12 A gaming wheel

Gaming wheels

This device is a steering wheel that simulates driving by turning the wheel.
Pedals are also used with this device to simulate the acceleration and
braking system of a car.

Dance pads

A dance pad, which is also known as a 'dance mat' or 'dance platform',
contains a matrix of square panel sensors that a player steps on while
following directions from a game.

Did you know?

Input devices are being developed
to use brainwave patterns. These
brainwave detection input devices
include brain activation headsets,
helmets and headbands.

▲ Figure 2.13 A dance pad

Hybrid controllers

A hybrid controller combines aspects of a keyboard, gaming pad, mouse and joystick. It is designed so that a gamer can use it with only one hand.

Motion-sensing game controllers

This device uses motion sensing to detect position and track motion, allowing a game player to imitate a player's actual movement, such as swinging a tennis racket. The Wii Remote and Xbox Kinect (discontinued in 2017) are examples of motion-sensing game controllers.

▲ Figure 2.14 A hybrid controller

Exercise 1

1 What is the most common input device?
  a Mouse   b Printer   c Monitor   d Keyboard
2 Which of the following is not a pointing device?
  a Joystick   b Printer   c Keyboard   d Mouse
3 A device that enables the user to control the movement of objects on the screen by operating a small lever is a:
  a touch-sensitive screen.   b joystick.   c puck.   d light pen.
4 Which of these has a ball positioned at the top?
  a Optical mouse   b Pointing stick mouse   c Touchpad mouse   d Trackball mouse
5 Which type of keyboard would most likely be used by a person with a physical disability?
  a Concept keyboard   b Alphanumeric keyboard
  c Virtual keyboard   d Left-handed keyboard

Scanning devices

Scanners

Scanners were originally designed to scan pictures (image scanners) but now their use is extended, for example, to scan text into a word processing program. There are various types of scanners, as listed.

- **Flat-bed scanner:** The picture is placed on a flat scanning surface and the image is captured, similarly to how a photocopying machine works. Household versions are inexpensive, costing less than 100 US dollars.
- **Hand-held scanner:** The scanner reads the picture as the user drags the scanner over it. The quality of the image provided by this scanner is poor, but it is useful for quick data capture.
- **Drum scanner:** This is usually used in the publishing industry (magazines, books) to capture images with high detail. These scanners tend to be expensive, often costing thousands of US dollars.
- **Sheet-fed scanner:** The sheet that contains the image is fed through rollers and the picture is scanned as the paper passes through.
- **Photo scanner:** This scanner is used to scan photographs because it supports high resolution and the colour depth required to capture a good image.

Did you know?

Your cell phone can now be used to scan documents. A good camera combined with apps that can adjust the camera and image for the best results have made it exceptionally easy for you to scan documents with your cell phone.

▲ Figure 2.15 Flatbed scanner

Magnetic ink character recognition (MICR) reader

Magnetic ink character recognition (MICR) readers are mainly used in the banking industry to read cheques. Bank cheques have the following information printed on them with magnetic ink:

- the cheque number
- the bank branch number
- the customer's account number.

After the customer has written a cheque, the bank encodes the amount of money using a special magnetic ink that contains iron oxide.

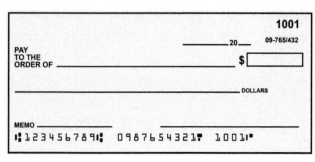

▲ Figure 2.16 A bank cheque

The cheques can then be read by an MICR reader. As the document passes into the MICR reader, the shapes of the characters can be recognised electronically. The characters have to be printed in a special font since the reader can only recognise a specific font and a limited number of characters. Some readers can only recognise 14 characters.

Advantages of MICR readers

- Documents are difficult to forge.
- Documents can still be read after being written on, folded, marked, and so on.

Disadvantages of MICR readers

- MICR readers and printers are expensive.
- The system can accept only a few characters.

Optical mark reader (OMR)

An optical mark reader (OMR) detects the position of black marks on white paper. The documents to be read have empty boxes pre-printed on them. The user makes pencil or ink marks to fill the appropriate boxes, as shown in Figure 2.17. The intensity of the reflected light from these marks on the form is detected by the OMR. This is sometimes called 'mark sensing'. The computer records the position of the marks and analyses it to determine the meaning of the data. OMRs are used mainly for assessing multiple-choice examinations or questionnaires given out by market researchers.

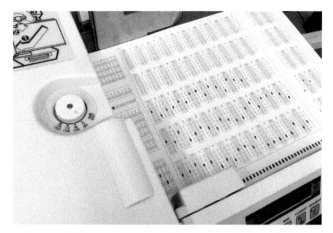

▲ Figure 2.17 Optical mark recognition on a multiple-choice paper

Optical character recognition (OCR)

Optical character recognition (OCR) is used for reading characters from paper, using special OCR readers. The shapes of different characters are detected by shining light on them from a photo-electric device and sensing the patterns of reflected light. The reader looks at each pattern (say, a letter, like 'R') individually. Sophisticated software allows each pattern to be compared with a set of stored patterns until the closest match is found. This match is translated into electronic text in the computer, so it can be manipulated by the user.

Advantages of OCR

- OCR is great for converting large volumes of printed data into a form that can then be manipulated on the computer, for example, in a word-processing program. It can, therefore, be used to create computer archives of old printed books and documents, thereby preserving these in a searchable electronic form for the future.

Disadvantages of OCR

- OCR has difficulty translating handwritten text to electronic text if the letters in that text are not formed properly. OCR also has difficulty recognising certain unusual fonts.

Barcode readers

A barcode is a set of vertical lines of differing thickness with a string of numbers printed at the bottom. The barcode is read by a scanner in which a laser beam scans the barcode and the light is reflected back into the scanner. The information received by the scanner is sent to a computer for processing. The system gives fast and error-free data entry into the computer. Barcodes provide a quick method of recording the sale of items. You can see barcodes on items in supermarkets, books in libraries, and so on.

QR code

A QR code is short for Quick Response code and is similar to a barcode. Much like a barcode, it holds information about the item to which it is attached and requires a scanner to read it. These days the most common scanning device would be a camera on a phone. Unlike barcodes that hold information in one direction horizontally, QR codes hold information in two directions – vertically and horizontally. This allows it to store more information than the regular barcode.

QR codes can be customised to include graphics such as a small logo. It also has an error margin of 7–30%, which will allow the code to be read despite it having some damage or being dirty.

Point of sale (POS) system

Barcodes form part of the POS system usually found at retail outlets. A terminal is connected to a central computer that records details after the barcode of an item has been scanned. The price of the product is displayed on a monitor at the point of sale. Meanwhile, the central computer calculates the amount due, including VAT, and prints an itemised receipt. The information recorded can also be used for stock control and sales analysis.

▲ Figure 2.18 A scanner being used to 'read' a barcode

▲ Figure 2.19 QR code

Did you know?

Anyone can now create their own QR code and link them to their product or website. Due to their increasing popularity, they are now being used in games and augmented reality applications (Augmented reality applications add additional digital elements, such as a 3D moving model appearing when a smartphone is held over a 2D picture.)

Advantages of point of sale (POS) systems

- Customers get a quicker and more accurate service, which improves efficiency.
- Supermarkets can get instant or continuous stock checks.
- Saves on paperwork.

Disadvantages of point of sale (POS) systems

- Barcodes cannot be read by people.
- Barcodes hold less information than QR codes.

Radio frequency identification (RFID)

Radio frequency identification (RFID) uses radio waves as a means of identifying animals, persons and objects. A chip connected to a small antenna makes up the RFID tag. Information such as a serial number is transmitted to an RFID receiver, which converts the radio waves to digital information so that it can be processed by the computer.

RFID tags are used for tracking animals, for example, as they can be embedded in the skin of the animal and the tag can be read once the animal is within range of the reader. Some stores are now tagging their merchandise with RFID tags to record POS information, and also as a means of security to reduce theft. Alarms can be raised when someone tries to exit a store without paying for an item. The disadvantage of RFID is that it is a lot more expensive than barcoding. See Table 2.2, which compares barcodes to RFID.

▲ Figure 2.20 An RFID tag

Barcodes	RFID
Barcodes must be passed over a reader to be read.	RFID tags can be read once the items are within range of a reader.
Barcode labels can be ripped, soiled or removed, making it difficult or impossible to read them.	RFID can be tagged on the surface (for example, as part of a label on something in a shop) or embedded in the object (for example, as a plastic pill that can be injected under the skin of an animal. Since radio waves can travel through non-metallic material, the RFID chip can be covered in plastic for further durability.
Barcodes do not identify single unique examples of a single product-type. For example, they distinguish between milk made by two different manufacturers, but cannot distinguish between two identical cartons with two different expiry dates from the same manufacturer.	RFID can distinguish between two identical cartons from one manufacturer with different expiry dates.
Barcodes are much cheaper than RFID and effective for certain tasks.	RFID tags are more expensive than barcodes, but more effective for certain tasks.
We cannot reuse barcode tags.	RFID tags can be reused again and again.

▲ Table 2.2 Comparing barcodes to RFID

Magnetic stripe codes

A magnetic stripe is a short length of magnetic-coated tape printed on the surface of, or sealed into a ticket or card. It contains information to identify the ticket or card and its user.

The card is read by swiping it – moving the magnetic stripe through a reader so that the stripe can be read. The reader detects the patterns of magnetism in the magnetic stripe and converts these to data. Such stripes are found on bank cards that identify the cardholder's bank account, so that the cardholder can perform banking transactions.

Cards with these magnetic stripe codes can provide quick identification of people entering buildings, allowing access to the cardholder. These cards are therefore also used for security purposes. Examples of other uses are in phone cards and debit cards for cell phones. The magnetic stripe in this instance contains information about the amount of money left 'on' the card.

▲ Figure 2.21 A magnetic stripe card being read by a reader

Advantages of cards with magnetic stripe codes

- They are easy and cheap to produce.
- The stripe can store enough information for simple transactions.
- They reduce the amount of paperwork that would otherwise be involved in a transaction.

Disadvantages of cards with magnetic stripe codes

- The data can be changed, altered, forged or erased by magnetic fields.
- The stripe can be damaged by scratching.
- The stripe can store only a limited amount of information.

Exercise 2

Crossword

Across
1 Has difficulty translating handwritten text to electronic text (3)
3 This type of stripe is found on a ticket or card and holds information (8)
4 A scanner used in the banking industry to read cheques (4)

Down
2 A type of scanner found in the publishing industry, to capture images of high detail (4)
5 This chip uses radio waves as a means of identifying people, animals or objects. (4)
6 A set of vertical lines of various thickness (7)
7 Similar to a barcode, but holds information horizontally and vertically (2)(4)

Audio and video input devices

Audio and video input are rapidly growing fields In computing. We are going to look at voice data entry and voice response units; sound capture; MIDI instruments; digital still cameras and digital video cameras.

Voice data entry, voice recognition and voice response units

Voice recognition systems require the use of a microphone. This system accepts the spoken word as input data or commands. Human speech is very complex because it carries tones, inflections and emphasis of various parts of words and phrases. The computer is programmed to recognise certain patterns of speech. Using a microphone, human speech is coded into a sequence of electronic signals. These signals are compared to a set of stored patterns. If they match, the command or data being entered is accepted by the computer and is processed. We are seeing more systems like this, from simple voice response systems to the voice assistant systems, such as Siri and the Google Assistant™ virtual personal assistant built into modern smartphones.

▲ Figure 2.22 Some smart appliances now respond to voice recognition, such as this refrigerator

Simple commands can be used to control machines or even 'type' letters into a word processor. Voice recognition has become important in many areas of our lives. It has made life easier for people with movement difficulties, who, with suitable equipment can now operate a wheelchair, switch lighting on and off, and even open doors using voice commands.

Advantages of voice data entry, recognition and response units

- No typing is required.
- The system can be used remotely, for example, by telephone.

Disadvantages of voice data entry, recognition and response units

- The system's recognition of words, although quite good, is not 100% accurate.
- The system is not suitable for use in noisy places.
- Some training of the system is needed to understand your particular voice patterns.

Sound capture

All modern computers contain a built-in microphone for sound capture. This means that you can record your voice, for example, to make comments that are embedded in a word-processing document. A sound card on your computer is required for recording voice or music. The sound card digitises the information into a form that the computer can understand.

MIDI instruments

Electronic musical instruments can have a MIDI port (musical instrument digital interface) for input into the computer. The instrument produces the sounds but sends the computer a record of all of the keys pressed and settings selected. The sounds are digitised and stored as a file. The file can be displayed on screen, edited and played back using appropriate software.

▲ Figure 2.23 A MIDI port

Digital cameras

Digital cameras capture an image and store it in memory within the camera. These cameras have a sensor that converts the light into electrical charges. The processor in the camera converts this information into digital data and stores it on flash memory or a flash RAM card. The digital images can then be uploaded from the camera to a computer where they can be displayed, manipulated or printed. The memory can be erased so that more images can be captured. Unlike normal RAM memory (sometimes called temporary memory or volatile memory) where the information is lost when the computer is switched off, flash RAM is non-volatile. This means that the images are not lost when the camera is switched off. The resolution of the camera is measured in pixels. The larger the number of pixels the camera has, the clearer the image and the greater the detail captured.

▲ Figure 2.24 A digital camera showing the viewfinder screen

Advantages of digital cameras

- Photos can be shown on a small screen on the camera, and resized and erased as you go along so that you only store the images that you really want on the camera.

Disadvantages of digital cameras

- It is relatively easy to lose or erase a digital camera's memory cards. Always transfer the photos to the computer or CD.

▲ Figure 2.25 A compact digital camera

Digital video cameras

The digital video camera (also called a digital video camcorder or DVD camcorder) works in much the same way as a movie camera, where light is focused onto a film treated with chemicals. The chemical reaction of the film to the light intensity forms the image on the film. Similarly, in a digital camera, light is focused onto an image sensor called a charge-coupled device, which contains thousands of light-sensitive diodes called photosites. These detect the light intensity and record an image. The digital video camera or camcorder detects not only light intensity but also levels of colour to reproduce a coloured image. The camera takes many pictures per second to give the impression of movement.

Other input devices

Other devices include biometric systems; remote controls; sensors and interactive whiteboards.

Biometric systems

Biometrics refers to the science of identifying an individual through their body characteristics such as face geometry and hand geometry (for example, fingerprints), iris or retinal scans and vein and voice patterns. All these forms of identifying an individual can be input into a computer system set up for security purposes. Fingerprint and face recognition are already becoming common in smartphones, but in the near future, they may become even more common, for allowing access to buildings and bank accounts, for example.

Retinal scans use a ray of light directed into the eye to identify the distinct network of blood vessels at the back of the eye. Fingerprint readers scan the imprint made by the pattern of ridges on the finger and compare it to a set of patterns stored in memory. Fingerprints are considered unique, as no two individuals have the same fingerprint.

Remote controls

A remote control emits a beam of infra-red light that carries data signals. Commonly used for input to televisions, stereo systems, VCRs and DVD players, they are now being used by computers as a wireless means of communication.

▲ Figure 2.26 A biometric access machine

▲ Figure 2.27 A retinal scanner

▲ Figure 2.28 Remote control with a beam of infra-red light

Sensors

Chemical or physical changes in humans and their environment can be converted to electrical signals using sensors that pass information to a computer, where it is analysed, stored and manipulated by specialist software. These sensors are useful in the fields of medicine, environmental planning and preservation, weather reporting, and so on. A variety of sensors can be used to measure such things as heat, light, sound, pressure, strain, acidity (pH), oxygen concentration, humidity, pulse, water level, water flow, speed, tilt or even something like a door or a valve opening or closing.

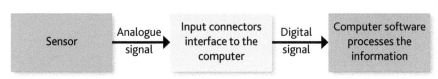

▲ Figure 2.29 How a sensor system works

Did you know?

Self-driving cars, also called autonomous or driverless cars, use a wide array of sensors to allow the car's computer to build a picture of what is around the car, how fast they are moving and in what direction they are moving. These cars use cameras, proximity sensors and laser sensors to do this.

Interactive whiteboards

An interactive whiteboard is a touch-sensitive whiteboard that connects to a projector and a computer. The projector projects the image of the computer's desktop into the whiteboard. The user can interact with the computer by using their finger or a pen on the whiteboard. This device is now being used in some schools in the Caribbean.

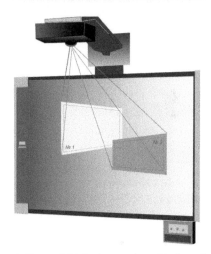

▲ Figure 2.30 An interactive whiteboard

Emerging technology

Technology is always changing and evolving. There are new input devices being developed in order to make data entry easier, faster and more efficient, even for people with physical disabilities. Here are a few of those technologies:

Wearable input devices:

Smart Glasses are designed like a pair of eyeglasses, which allows you to interact with a computer anywhere and anytime, much like a hands-free smartphone. You can communicate with the glasses using voice commands, as there is no mouse or keyboard. Examples are: the Google Glass™ wearable computing device and Oculus.

Gesture recognition or motion tracking input devices allow the user to control the function of the mouse pointer or keyboard function through motion control. Keyglove is an example of a wearable glove that virtually controls both the mouse and keyboard. Another example is Massless pen, which is a pen that can be used to create 3D designs in a virtual environment by movements in the air.

Surface Electromyography (EMG) are sensors that measure muscle movement or activity and are used in bionics. For example: Mouth-based interfaces (designed for people with disabilities) have sensors that are applied to the face or throat to attempt to recognise the patterns of muscle movement required for speech.

Other emerging input devices:

Electronic paper and electronic ink (e-paper and e-ink) are digital paper-like technologies that have the look and feel of paper and are part of green technology.

Chapter 2: Summary

- Input devices are pieces of equipment that are used to put data into a computer.
- The data-processing cycle consists of five stages: data capture, data input, data processing, data storage and data output.
- Data capture is the first stage of getting the data into the computer. The two main data input means are manual and automatic.
- A source document is a document on which data is first recorded before it is entered into the computer.
- A turnaround document is one that has the look and feel of paper, is produced as output at one stage of the data-processing cycle, has more data added to it and is re-input for further processing.
- Verification is the checking for accurate transcription or copying.
- Validation is the checking of data before it is processed to see that it obeys the rules that have the look and feel of paper and are applied to it.
- Presence checks – checks that data has been entered into a field.
- Data type checks – checks that an entered value is of a particular type.
- Length checks – checks that the number of characters entered in a field does not exceed the amount allocated for the field or is not less than specified.
- Range checks – checks of whether data is within a range of possible values.
- Format checks – checks that the data is entered in the format specified by the software.
- Check digits checks– an extra digit attached to the end of a string of digits to ensure that if any of the digits are changed by mistake, the error will be detected.
- Parity checks – used in data communication to ensure that data is not corrupted during transmission.
- The most common input device is the keyboard of which there are two types: alphanumeric and special-function keyboards.
- Pointing devices are used to move a pointer or cursor on the computer screen, and enable the control and selection of objects on the display. These devices include the mouse, digitising tablet, touch-sensitive screen, light pen and others.
- Gaming input devices include joysticks, gaming pads, gaming wheels, dance pads and motion sensing devices. Joysticks are pointing devices.
- Other devices include biometric systems, remote controls, sensors and Interactive whiteboards.
- Scanning devices use laser beams and reflected light to interpret and convert images, pictures and text into digital form.
- Magnetic ink character recognition (MICR) is used mainly to read cheques whose data is encoded with magnetic ink.
- Optical mark readers (OMR) detect the position of black marks on white paper. They are used mainly in multiple-choice exam marking and assessing market research questionnaires.
- Optical character recognition (OCR) senses the patterns of reflected light off scanned text via a photo-electric device and compares it to the patterns in memory. The text is converted and stored in the computer and can be manipulated by the user, for example, in a word-processing program.
- A barcode is a set of vertical lines of differing thickness with a string of numbers printed at the bottom; it holds information about a product or item.
- A QR code is a two-dimensional graphic that functions in a similar way to a barcode but holds more information about a product or item or can link to a URL.
- Radio frequency identification (RFID) is the use of embedded chips and radio waves to identify individual unique examples of animals, people and objects.
- Voice recognition systems recognise certain patterns of speech and accepts them for processing by the computer.
- Video input devices capture images and audio and store them in memory.
- Biometrics refers to the science of identifying an individual through their body characteristics such as face geometry, fingerprint, hand geometry, iris, retina, vein and voice patterns.
- Sensors can be used to measure heat, light, sound, pressure, strain, acidity (pH) and other changes in the environment.

Chapter 2: Questions

Matching descriptions

Match each item in Column A with its description in Column B. Write the number and the correct letter.

Column A	Column B
(1) MICR	(a) Found on items in the supermarket
(2) Braille keyboard	(b) For playing games
(3) Joystick	(c) A card containing a tiny memory chip
(4) Barcode reader	(d) Used to assess multiple choice exams
(5) OMR	(e) Used by visually impaired persons
(6) OCR	(f) Used to read bank cheques
(7) Smart card	(g) Translates text on paper into electronic text on the computer

True or False?

1 Source documents are documents on which data is first recorded.

2 Source documents and turnaround documents are the same.

3 RFID must be passed over a scanner.

4 A smart card contains a microchip embedded in the card.

5 Digital cameras do not require film.

6 Biometric devices are less accurate than passwords.

7 Remote controls are now used by computers as a wireless input communications device.

8 OMR is used to read cheques.

Multiple-choice questions

1 Which of the following is not a validation method?
   a Range check
   b Check digit
   c Dual input
   d Format check

2 Checking for accurate copying of data is known as:
   a validation.
   b verification.
   c source document.
   d data capture.

3 Which one of the following is not an advantage of magnetic stripe codes?
   a Easy and cheap to produce
   b Strip can store enough information for simple transactions
   c Data can be changed, altered, forged or erased by magnetic fields

d Cut down on paperwork that would otherwise be involved in a transaction

4 Which of the following is not true about barcodes?
   a Cheaper than RFID
   b Can be reused again and again
   c Can become difficult to read if they are ripped, soiled or removed
   d Must be passed over a reader

5 OCR:
   a detects marks on paper.
   b detects the unique ridges in a fingerprint.
   c understands and easily converts handwritten text.
   d detects the shape of characters.

6 Which of the following is a scanning device?
   a Optical mark reader
   b Touch pad
   c Light pen
   d Remote control

Short-answer questions

1 Give definitions for (a) a verification check and (b) a validation check.

2 If some data passes a validation check, does this mean that the data is correct?

3 Suggest the name of a field in a student database on which a range check can be used.

4 Using the method illustrated in this book, calculate the check digit to complete the ISBN number 167053442.

5 You have been asked to select input devices that would be used by physically-challenged persons in an organisation. List FOUR devices and explain the kind of person who would be able to use the device and why.

6 State TWO advantages and TWO disadvantages of the smart card over the magnetic stripe card.

7 A pharmaceutical research company has decided to introduce biometric systems for security reasons. Consider TWO alternatives and discuss the advantages of using biometric systems over those systems.

8 State TWO disadvantages of a digital camera or a digital video camera.

9 Explain how sensors work and list FOUR types of sensors.

10 What is RFID and how does it work?

11 Explain the differences between a barcode and a QR code.

Challenge questions

1 Five different types of customers have asked you to assist them in selecting input devices for their use. Recommend suitable devices for each of them.

a A stay-at-home mother with two small children – a 3-year-old and an 8-year-old. She has a small budget but uses the internet often. Her children also use the computer.

b Ms Patrick has a small home office and works mainly from home but communicates with the head office frequently. She is a real-estate agent for a local real-estate company. She often needs to send documents to the head office.

c Mr Jay is a pharmaceutical sales representative who is always commuting to and from his various clients. While he is on the road he is frequently in contact with his clients and also head office. He also sends and receives sensitive information between his clients and the head office.

d Mr Tom is a freelance animator and graphics designer with a well-established clientele of big and small companies and individuals. He designs and produces advertisements for his clients.

e The manager, Mr MacFarlan, is from a large business college that conducts video conferencing of many of its classes. He wants to suitably equip the staff of more than 100 employees.

f Mr Joseph is interested in becoming a DJ (disk jockey). He has been disk jockeying for family and close friends but is now being offered more jobs in his community. He needs the right input devices for his career path.

g Darcy is an aspiring author who has written a few books. She is accustomed to writing on paper and has recently upgraded to a computer. She is told that there are input devices that can make her job easier.

2 A large supermarket in your area is considering implementing a self-checkout system as a means of reducing their costs. A number of the top managers agree; however, many feel that it will encourage shoplifting. What input devices are needed for such a system? What input devices could be put in place or used to monitor such a system?
(A self-checkout system is one in which the customer scans the barcode, weighs the produce, bags the items and pays for the items without the assistance of an attendant or checkout person.)

Research questions

1 A non-profit organisation in your community that cares for children with physical and mental disabilities has asked you to recommend some input devices that would assist the children in their daily lives. Select at least THREE devices and explain how these devices would help to improve the lives of the children, making reference to the disability on which each device will have an impact.

2 Select one emerging input device and describe its use and function and justify its possible future potential.

Crossword

Across

3 Has difficulty translating handwritten text to electronic text (3)

4 Type of scanner found in the publishing industry, to capture images of high detail (4)

6 Type of scanner where the image must be fed through a device containing rollers (two words) (8)

7 Type of scanner where the image is placed on a level surface (two words) (7)

Down

1 A set of vertical lines of various thickness (7)

2 User drags scanner over image (two words) (8)

5 Used to read cheques (4)

3

Primary and secondary storage

Objectives

At the end of this chapter, you will be able to:

→ define what primary and secondary storage are
→ explain the difference between primary and secondary storage
→ explain the functions of RAM and ROM
→ explain the differences between ROM, PROM, EPROM and EEPROM
→ name the units of storage: bits, bytes, kilobytes, megabytes, gigabytes and terabytes
→ list some characteristics of secondary storage media, such as magnetic tapes, magnetic disks, optical discs, flash memory, memory cards, USB drives and solid state storage
→ explain the advantages and disadvantages of cloud storage and local storage
→ explain the uses of magnetic stripe cards, smart cards and RFID tags.

▲ Figure 3.1 A motherboard showing RAM slots

Storage

Storage refers to the media used by a computer and mobile devices to keep data, information and software for immediate or later use. It is the physical material on which the data is stored, such as magnetic tapes, magnetic disks and optical discs. The device that reads or writes the items to the media is known as a storage device. These devices include magnetic tape drives, magnetic disk drives and optical disc drives. Sometimes the storage medium is a fixed (permanent) part of the storage device, for example, the magnetic-coated disks built into a hard drive. The storage medium can also be removable from the device, for example, a CD-ROM can be taken out of a CD drive. **Reading** refers to the process of moving the data or information stored in a storage medium into memory. **Writing** is the process of moving data or information from memory to a storage medium.

Storing data, information and software is an essential part of everyday computing. For example, a student may need a storage device and medium to store digital photos, contacts, email messages and school assignments. A bank will need storage for customer information, bank investments, loans, employee information, and so on. Storage can be grouped into two categories: primary storage and secondary storage.

Primary storage

Primary storage, also called main memory or immediate access store (IMAS), is a group of chips that resides in the motherboard (main circuit board) of the computer. The distance that the electrical signals have to travel from the CPU to primary storage or vice versa is much shorter than the distance between the CPU and secondary storage devices, which are connected to the motherboard via cables. This shorter distance, along with the design of the chips, allows for a faster exchange of data and instructions between the CPU and primary storage. This speedy access is necessary since the CPU can only act on data and instructions held in primary storage. So for the computer to work fast, the primary storage must be accessible as quickly as possible.

Primary storage consists of two types of memory chips: Random Access Memory (RAM) and Read Only Memory (ROM) chips. A memory chip is an integrated circuit (IC) made up of millions of transistors and capacitors.

Random Access Memory (RAM)

A computer uses RAM to hold data and instructions (programs) temporarily, while processing is taking place using that data and program. It also holds the data that results from processing – data that is waiting to be output or stored in a secondary storage device. RAM is therefore also called working memory.

Programs and data stored in secondary storage must therefore first be loaded into RAM before they can be processed. For example, before a letter can be typed, or data for a spreadsheet entered, the CPU must first load the application programs – such as a word-processing or spreadsheet program – into memory. These application programs, and whatever the user inputs using them, are held in RAM until the application is closed or the power is turned off.

If programs and data are not stored on a secondary storage medium, they will be lost when the power is turned off or the computer is rebooted (started up again). This is because the information in RAM is volatile; it is temporary and changeable. The information in RAM can also be accessed directly and easily by the CPU, hence the term 'random access'. RAM chips are limited in storage capacity. Most personal computers sold today come with 4 GB (gigabytes) to 32 GB RAM as standard; extra RAM can easily be added, expanding the computer's capacity. RAM needs to be installed in pairs. If your motherboard supports 16 GB of RAM and has four slots, you can install four 4 GB sticks or two 8 GB sticks to reach your maximum. RAM chips are also expensive and are a major determinant of the final price of a computer. RAM chips are very costly for several reasons. Firstly, extremely complex equipment is required to fabricate the chips and, because impurities in or on the silicon can cause defects, the environment must be extremely clean. Secondly, programming the machines to fabricate the chips requires significant engineering expertise, which can be quite expensive.

▲ Figure 3.2 RAM chips

Did you know?

Having more RAM may not make your PC run faster; it just allows you to do more things at once. Having a lot of memory allows you to quickly switch back and forth between the different applications without your computer freezing or slowing down.

Cache memory

Currently, processors can operate at speeds much greater than memory can supply the necessary data. In an effort to speed up processing, most microcomputers have cache memory (pronounced 'cash'). Cache memory is very fast memory that the processor can access much more quickly than main memory or RAM. Cache is made of high-speed static RAM (SRAM) instead of the slower and cheaper dynamic RAM (DRAM) chip that is used for main memory.

Generally, most programs access the same data or instruction over and over. By keeping as much of this information as possible in SRAM, the processor avoids accessing the slower DRAM. Cache memory works by attempting to predict which data/instruction the processor is going to need next, loading that in memory before the processor needs it, and saving the results after the processor is done with it. This speeds up processing. Table 3.1 shows some of the differences between DRAM and SRAM.

	Dynamic RAM (DRAM)	Static RAM (SRAM)
Size	Smaller in size	Larger in size
USE	Used in main memory	Used in cache memory
Expensive	Is cheaper	Is more expensive
Power	Consumes less power	Consumes more power
Time	Requires more time to access stored data	Requires less time to access stored data
Storage capacity	Has higher storage capacity	Has less storage capacity
Refresh rate	Needs to be refreshed thousands of times per second	Does not need to be refreshed

▲ Table 3.1 Some differences between DRAM and SRAM

Read Only Memory (ROM)

Read Only Memory (ROM) chips hold the data and instructions that are necessary for starting up the computer. When you switch on your computer and the microprocessor tries to execute its first instruction, it has to get that instruction from somewhere. It cannot get it from the operating system because the operating system is located on a hard disk, and the microprocessor cannot get to it without instructions that tell it how to do this. Those instructions are stored in a ROM chip, which stores the BIOS (Basic input/output system). The BIOS is a program that tells the computer how to load the operating system. It also performs a power-on-self-test (POST) for all of the different hardware components in the system to make sure everything is working properly.

The instructions stored in ROM are fixed at the time of manufacture and are sometimes described as being 'hard-wired'. This ensures that the instructions stored in ROM are always there, whether the power is on or not. ROM is therefore non-volatile: it cannot be easily changed, because it is 'read only'. ROM is also sometimes found in some input and output devices, such as scanners and printers.

ROM cannot easily be modified and therefore provides a measure of security against accidental or malicious changes to its contents. Users of a system cannot infect ROM chips with a virus. Variations of ROM chips, namely PROM and EPROM, which allow some flexibility in storing data and instructions, are also available.

▲ Figure 3.3 A ROM chip

- **Programmable ROM (PROM):** This is a type of ROM that can be programmed using special equipment; it can be written to, but only once. This is useful for companies that want to make their own ROMs from software that they write themselves: when they change their code, they can create new PROMs without requiring a whole ROM manufacturing plant.
- **Erasable programmable ROM (EPROM):** An EPROM is a ROM that can be erased and reprogrammed, which can make it more useful than an ordinary PROM, although EPROM chips do not last as long. Erasing is done by exposing the chip to ultraviolet light of a specific frequency for a specified period of time. Reprogramming may become necessary if there are updates to the current data, or instructions that are held in EPROM.
- **Electrically erasable PROM (EEPROM):** This is a special type of ROM chip that can be erased and reprogrammed repeatedly by a user. A chip is erased by exposing it to an electrical charge, which erases the entire chip. Unlike EPROM chips, EEPROM chips do not have to be removed from the computer to be reprogrammed. EEPROM is non-volatile and can be used to hold data and instructions that need to be updated regularly. Flash memory is a type of EEPROM and is also used in many electronic devices such as CompactFlash cards known as 'electronic film' for digital cameras, memory cards and video game systems.

▲ Figure 3.4 AN EEPROM chip

Units of storage

A computer consists of many two-state (or bistable) devices that process and store data. A bistable device is one that can be set to one of two states at any one point in time. An example of a bistable device could be a light bulb that can be either in the 'on' or 'off' state. On a magnetic disk or magnetic tape, the two states can be represented by a magnetised spot or an unmagnetised spot. In a microchip, the transistor is similar to an electronic switch that can turn current on and off.

The binary number system, which consists of two digits 0 and 1, is used by computers to represent the two states. These two binary digits are also known as bits (short for binary digits). A single bit is the smallest unit of storage and can represent one of two values, 0 and 1.

The amount of data and instructions that can be stored in the memory of a computer or secondary storage device is measured in bytes. A byte is made up of a combination of eight bits and has the storage power to represent one character. A character can be a letter, a number, a symbol, a punctuation mark or a blank space. A word is the number of bits the CPU can process in one operation. With modern general-purpose computers, word size can be 32 bits or 64 bits, depending on their architecture and when they were manufactured. Table 3.2 below shows larger units of storage.

Name	Symbol	Binary measurement	Number of bytes	Equal to
kilobyte	KB	2^{10}	1 024	1024 bytes
megabyte	MB	2^{20}	1 048 576	1024 KB
gigabyte	GB	2^{30}	1 073 741 824	1024 MB
terabyte	TB	2^{40}	1 099 511 627 776	1024 GB
petabyte	PB	2^{50}	1 125 899 906 842 624	1024 TB
exabyte	EB	2^{60}	1 152 921 504 606 846 976	1024 PB
zettabyte	ZB	2^{70}	1 180 591 620 717 411 303 424	1024 EB
yottabyte	YB	2^{80}	1 208 925 819 614 629 174 706 176	1024 ZB

▲ Table 3.2 Larger units of storage

Exercise 1

1 The media used by a computer and mobile devices to keep data, information and software for immediate or later use is known as _____.
2 A storage device is used to _____ or _____ data and information to and from media.
3 The process of moving data or information stored in a storage medium into memory is known as _____, while _____ is the process of moving data or information from memory to a storage media.
4 Primary storage consists of _____ and _____ memory chips.
5 A memory chip is an integrated circuit (IC) made up of millions of _____ and _____.
6 Programs and data stored in secondary storage must first be _____ into RAM before they can be processed.
7 RAM memory is said to be _____ because it is temporary and changeable.
8 _____ is very fast memory that the processor can access much more quickly than RAM.
9 _____ chips hold the data and instructions necessary for starting up the computer when it is switched on. It is commonly used to store system-level programs such as the _____.
10 Instructions that are fixed at the time of manufacture are sometimes described as being _____.

Secondary storage media and devices

Secondary storage, also called auxiliary or backup storage, is used to store data and instructions when they are not being processed. Secondary storage is more permanent than the main memory since data and instructions are retained when the power is turned off. Secondary storage is also much cheaper than primary storage and is unlimited – you can have as much of it as you can afford.

A computer for home use will not need as much secondary storage as a computer used in a large organisation such as a bank, a hospital or an insurance company. As a result of this diverse range of storage needs, a number of secondary storage devices are available. Devices are chosen for a particular use based on their:

- storage capacity (how much data the device can store)
- access speed (the time needed to locate the data and transmit it to the CPU)
- size (necessary for storage on shelves or portability)
- portability (ability to be easily removed and used on another system)
- cost.

The most commonly-used secondary storage devices are magnetic storage (magnetic tapes and magnetic disks), optical storage (CD-ROM, CD-R, CD-RW, Blu-ray, DVD-ROM, DVD-R and DVD-RW), and flash memory (solid state drives, USB drives and memory cards).

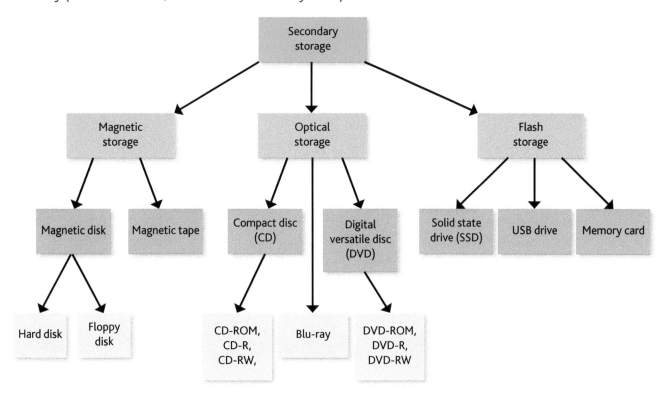

▲ Figure 3.5 Types of secondary storage

Magnetic storage

There are two types of magnetic storage: magnetic tapes and magnetic disks.

Magnetic tapes

Many companies still rely on massive magnetic tape libraries for backups and archives. Magnetic tape is a ribbon of plastic material coated with a metal oxide film on which data is recorded as magnetised or unmagnetised spots. The magnetised spot is created by a magnetic field surrounding a current-carrying conductor (write head of the tape drive) in the area of the magnetic tape. The magnetic field causes the magnetic material on the tape to switch between two states of polarity, which results in magnetised and unmagnetised spots. Data is stored as these magnetised and unmagnetised spots, which are represented by the binary digits 0 and 1.

On mainframe computers, the tape is stored on reels or cartridges and read with a magnetic tape drive. Magnetic tape is not suitable for data files that are revised or updated often because it stores data sequentially. This means that data is retrieved in the order in which it was stored. Accessing data is also very slow, as you cannot go directly to an item of data on the tape. It is necessary to start at the beginning of the tape and search for the data as the tape goes past the heads.

Advances in the technology have resulted in newer tape drives that deliver high-performance streaming with very large capacity, and a high level of reliability and availability for long-term storage. For example, the new IBM TS2280 Tape Drive uses next-generation LTO Ultrium 8 cartridges to store up to 30 TB of compressed data per cartridge – twice the capacity of previous generations. These magnetic tapes are also erasable, reusable and less expensive than hard disks. The following text summarises the characteristics of magnetic tapes.

Summary of the characteristics of magnetic tapes:

- provide sequential access to data stored
- easy to transport and store
- cheaper than hard disks
- mostly used for backups or archives (tertiary storage)
- shelf-life of over 30 years for the new LTO Ultrium 8 cartridges
- must be stored in a suitable environment (smoke, dust, temperature and humidity must be carefully controlled)
- difficult to update files (cannot make changes to a record without writing over the entire tape).

▲ Figure 3.6 A tape drive and magnetic tape cartridge

Magnetic disks

Magnetic disks are one of the most widely-used secondary storage media for computers. All magnetic disks provide direct access to stored data. This means that you can go directly to a piece of data without having to access any other data either before or after the data you want. Like tape, it is magnetically recorded and can be re-recorded over and over. The two main types of magnetic disks are floppy disks and hard disks.

Floppy disks

A 3.5-inch (90 mm) diskette or floppy disk is a removable, flexible plastic disk, coated with a magnetisable material. The disk is contained in a hard plastic case to protect it from dust and grease. [The term 'floppy' refers back to the 5.25-inch (134 mm) diskettes that were used in the 1980s and were actually soft and flexible. These are no longer used.]

Data is stored as magnetised spots on concentric rings known as tracks. They were relatively slow to access because of their rotation speeds. Floppy disks held 1.44 MB of information.

By 2006, computers were rarely manufactured with installed floppy disk drives. Floppy disks have been replaced by data storage methods with much greater capacity, such as USB flash drives, flash storage cards, portable external hard disk, optical discs, and storage available through computer networks.

▲ Figure 3.7 Floppy disk

Hard disk drives (HDDs)

Every computer has at least one internal hard disk drive to store software and data. If you are using a Windows operating system, this drive is typically called the C: drive. The combination of the hard disk, read/write head and the circuitry is called the hard disk drive (HDD). A hard disk drive may contain one or more hard disks, which are also called platters.

Hard disks are one of the most widely-used secondary storage media for computers. They are thin but rigid, inflexible disks made of highly polished metal. All hard disks provide direct access to data stored.

The surface of each side of a hard disk is covered with a substance that can be magnetised, which allows data to be stored on both sides as magnetised or unmagnetised spots. The hard disk constantly rotates at a high speed and may have one read/write head per hard disk (moveable head) or, on more expensive hard disks, every track in each hard disk may have its own read/write head (fixed head).

The access time (time to get data) from a spinning hard disk with one read/write head is a combination of:

- seek time – how long it takes the head to get to the right track
- rotational delay or latency time – how long it takes for the data to rotate under the head
- transmission time – the time taken to read the data and transmit it to the CPU.

▲ Figure 3.8 The inside of a hard disk drive

For fixed-head hard disk drives, where each track on the hard disk has a read/write head, the time taken to access data and instructions is reduced, as the seek time is eliminated.

Hard disks are much slower than internal memory. To increase the speed at which data is written to and read from a hard disk, a cache, also often called a buffer, is included in most modern hard drives. The purpose of this cache is similar to other caches used in the PC. For hard disks, the cache is used to hold the results of recent reads from the disk, and also to 'predict' and hold data that is likely to be requested in the near future, for example, the data immediately after the one just requested. The use of cache improves the performance of any hard disk, by reducing the number of physical accesses to the disk on repeated reads.

Before any data can be stored on a hard disk it must be formatted. Formatting sets up the tracks and sectors. In the case of a hard disk drive that has more than one hard disk, formatting sets up the tracks, sectors and cylinders. A cylinder is made up of all the tracks of the same number from all the hard disks that make up the hard disk drive, which can be read or written to at the same time. For example, if you start from the bottom of a stack of hard disks, track 5 of the second hard disk will be directly above track 5 of the first hard disk. Track 5 of the third hard disk will be directly above track 5 of the first and second hard disks, and so on. These are all put on top of one another to resemble a tin can with no top or bottom – a cylinder.

The computer keeps track of what it has put where on a hard disk by recording the addresses of all the sectors used – a combination of the cylinder, track and sector numbers. Data is written down the hard disks on the same cylinder. This works quickly because each hard disk has a read/write head for each side, and they all move together. So, for one position of the read/write heads, the computer can put some data on all the platters (individual hard disks).

Almost all PCs come with a hard drive that is housed inside the system unit and attached to the motherboard by a special cable. These hard drives are not removable and vary in storage capacity from about 500 GB to 8 TB or more. The hard disk, which is housed in the hard drive, usually stores application software (word processor, database, spreadsheet, and so on) and the operating system. Two additional types of hard drives that can be used with a PC are external hard drives and removable disk drives.

- **External hard drive:** An external hard drive can be used if there is no space in the system unit to house another hard drive. It may come with its own power source and is connected to the system unit via a special cable. External hard drives can be easily removed and connected to another computer, which allows some portability and flexibility of use. External hard drives come in a variety of capacities, ranging from 1 TB to 8 TB, with a typical example being the Seagate 8TB Innov8.

For larger computer systems, hard disk drives consist mainly of removable hard disk packs, fixed disk drives and RAID storage systems.

- **Removable hard disk pack:** This may contain between 6 and 20 hard disks aligned one above the other in a sealed unit. The storage capacity is usually very large, ranging from 1 TB to 10 TB or more.
- **Fixed disk drives:** These are similar to those found in PCs. They have high-storage capacity and are more reliable than removable hard disk packs. A mainframe computer may have between 20 and 100 fixed hard disks housed in a single cabinet.
- **RAID (Redundant Array of Independent Disk) storage system:** A RAID storage system consists of a cabinet that may contain a large number of disk drives (up to 100). Besides holding more data than a fixed disk drive, it stores multiple copies of data on different drives. If one drive fails, others can take over, thereby allowing the data to be recovered. Data is transmitted to the CPU using multiple data paths.

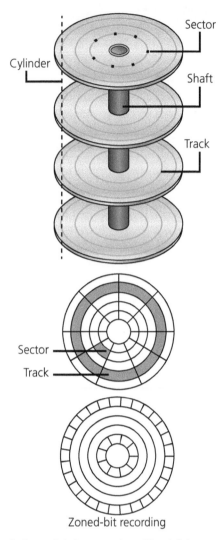

▲ Figure 3.9 Cross-section of hard disks in a hard disk drive to show how it is arranged and divided into tracks, sectors and cylinders

▲ Figure 3.10 External 2 TB hard disk

The following is a summary of some key characteristics of hard disks.

Summary of some key characteristics of hard disks:

- direct access
- fast data transfer speeds
- vast storage capacity.

The largest hard disk drives today exceed (are more than) 10 TB, for example, Toshiba's helium-filled MG07ACA Series disk can store 14 TB on a single 3.5-inch (90 mm) drive. Overall, hard disk drives are about five to eight times cheaper per TB than flash disks, which at present is the only advantage they have over flash memory storage.

▲ Figure 3.11 A RAID cabinet

Optical storage

Optical storage is any type of storage in which data is written and read with a laser.

Optical discs

Optical discs are discs that are read by laser lights. The disk is made mainly of a type of plastic (polycarbonate). The data is stored on a layer inside the plastic. A metal coating (usually aluminium) reflects the laser light back to a sensor. The main types of optical discs are compact discs (CDs), DVDs and Blu-ray.

CD-ROM

CD-ROM stands for Compact Disc-Read Only Memory. This means that you can only read (access) what is on the disk, but you cannot add or change anything. The data is encoded and read optically with a low-intensity laser light. The data is represented as a series of pits and lands. A pit is a little depression formed by the laser burning into the data layer when the CD is created. The land is the part between the pits or the smooth surface. Reading a CD is done by shining a laser light at the disk and detecting changing reflecting patterns. When the laser beam reflects off the smooth surface (land), it is interpreted as a 1 bit. When the laser enters a pit there is no reflection, which is interpreted as a 0 bit.

The speed at which the data is accessed depends on how fast the disk spins. The faster the disk spins, the faster the data can be transferred to the computer's memory. The speed of a CD-ROM drive is indicated by a number followed by an 'X'. Typical CD-ROM drive speeds are 48X, 50X, and so on. The higher the number, the faster the disk spins, resulting in faster data access.

Because of their large storage capacity (up to 750 MB), CD-ROMs are used to store software packages for sale or distribution. They are particularly useful for storing multimedia (text, graphics, sound and videos) and application software packages such as encyclopaedias, word processors, training programs, games and graphics packages.

CD-R

CD-R stands for Compact Disc-Recordable. This disk allows you to write data onto the disk, once only, using a CD recorder (burner). The disk then becomes CD-ROM, as the contents cannot be changed. It is ideal for storing data that does not need to change. A typical use is to create music CDs. The storage capacity of CD-R, like all CDs, is a maximum of 750 to 800 MB.

▲ Figure 3.12 CD-R discs

CD-RW

CD-RW (Compact Disc-Rewritable) was a very common choice for backup storage. The data layer of these disks uses a phase-changing metal alloy film. By using a higher-intensity laser light, the film can be melted to level out the marks made by the laser burner when the data was stored, effectively erasing previously stored data. New data can then be recorded, using a lower-intensity laser light to burn the new data. In theory, you can erase and write on these discs as many as 1,000 times. Therefore, it is an ideal backup storage device for storing data that changes frequently.

DVD discs

Types of DVDs (Digital Versatile Discs) include DVD-ROM (Read-only), DVD-R (Recordable) and DVD-RW (Rewritable). They look similar to a CD-R disc but can hold much more information for these reasons:

- The tracks on a DVD are placed closer together than those on a CD, thereby allowing more tracks.
- The pits in which data is stored are much smaller on a DVD than on a CD. As there are more pits, more information can be stored.
- Some DVDs are double-sided. This allows data to be stored on both sides, which dramatically increases the disc's capacity.

▲ Figure 3.13 A DVD player ejecting a disc

A typical DVD disc can hold between 4.7 GB and 17 GB of information. They are used mainly for storing movies.

Blu-ray

As well as storing even larger amounts of data (up to 25 GB on a single-layer disk and 50 GB on a dual-layer disc), Blu-ray is suitable for recording, rewriting and playback of high-definition (HD) video. Whereas CDs and DVDs rely on a red laser to read and write, this format uses a blue-violet laser, hence the name Blu-ray. The following is a summary of some characteristics of optical discs.

Summary of some characteristics of optical discs:

- much sturdier and more durable than tapes or floppy disks
- not usually sensitive to being casually touched, though they too can get dirty or scratched
- unaffected by magnetic fields
- provide direct access to data stored.

Care of optical discs

Optical discs are not indestructible. It is important that they are handled with care, or data may be lost. Data loss results from:

- physical damage (breaking, melting, scratching, and so on)
- blocking of the laser light due to dirt, paint, ink and glue
- corrosion of the reflective layer.

Some guidelines for handling optical discs correctly include the following:

1 Store CDs and DVDs in their cases when not in use to prevent them from being scratched or getting dirty.
2 Avoid soiling the surface of a CD – hold it by the edge or centre hole.
3 Keep your CDs clean by gently wiping both sides with a clean damp cloth from the centre to the outer edge, and not around the disc. Wiping in a circle can create a curved scratch, which can confuse the laser. For stubborn dirt, use a CD/DVD cleaning detergent.
4 Do not write on the top side of the CD with a ballpoint pen or other hard object, as this can damage the data layer on the other side. Use a CD marker instead.
5 Do not write on the top side with a fine-point marker or with any solvent-based marker. (Solvent may dissolve the protective layer.)
6 Do not expose a CD to high temperatures or humidity for an extended period of time, as the CD may warp.

Flash memory storage

The modern computing industry is continually developing new products to assist the computer user. One of the latest storage media is flash memory storage. Flash memory technology is based on EEPROM (Electrically Erasable Programmable Read Only Memory) technology and has no moving parts. As with EEPROM, flash memory is non-volatile. However, reading from and writing to flash memory is much faster than with EEPROM. This is because data in flash memory can be erased a block at a time, instead of only a single byte at a time, as with EEPROM. The compact nature of flash memory enables it to be incorporated into very small solid state devices that are available in all shapes and forms. These devices are rapidly becoming an integral part of modern living. Types of flash storage include solid state drives, USB flash drives and memory cards.

Solid state drive (SSD)

Solid state drives (SSD) are flash memory storage devices that are designed to store data without reading or writing on rotating disks, as hard disk drives (HDD) do. SSD is non-volatile, contains no moving parts, and stores data electronically rather than magnetically, which results in faster data transfer and swift input/output (I/O). SSDs offer better data integrity, consume much less energy and are extremely robust; tolerating extreme temperatures, shock and vibration from natural disasters, and even being dropped. Most SSDs at present have a capacity ranging from 500 GB to 4 TB and more. The recent introduction of massive SSDs has resulted in much larger capacities, such as Nimbus Data's 100 TB ExaDrive. These massive SSDs are quickly replacing HDDs as high-capacity storage devices in desktop and laptop computers to speed up processing, and in data centres for cloud storage. SSDs are used in PCs, cell phones, cable TV set-top boxes and video game consoles. One disadvantage of SSDs is that they are more expensive than HDDs.

> **Did you know?**
> Many manufacturers no longer include CD-R, CD-RW, DVD-R and DVD-RW drives in personal and laptop computers. This is mainly because optical storage is still limited to storing in gigabytes, whereas most hard drives and flash storage devices are storing more and more terabytes.

> **Did you know?**
> Flash memory got its name because a block of memory cells is erased in a single action, or 'flash'.

▲ Figure 3.14 A hard disk (left) versus the SSD (right), which has no mechanical parts

USB flash drive

USB flash drives are used to store or move data and applications from one personal computer to another, almost instantly. Connecting to computers by way of USB ports, flash drives are plug and play devices, so there is no need to download any software or drivers before using them. These devices, which are referred to by different names such as flash drive, flash pen, thumb drive, key drive and mini-USB drive, are small (about the size of your thumb or a large car key) and plug into a USB port on the computer. Such small flash drives can have storage capacities ranging from 16 GB, 32 GB and 64 GB to 128 GB, 256 GB and more. Newer versions, such as the Samsung T3 SSD, have a capacity of 1 TB. Some flash drives include password protection and the ability to run software right off the USB drive.

▲ Figure 3.15 A USB flash drive

The following is a summary of some characteristics of USB flash drives.

Summary of some characteristics of USB flash drives:
- easy to use
- convenient (small size – can be placed in a pocket or on a key chain)
- highly compatible – 'plug and play' (no software needed)
- fast access
- password protection
- disk write protection switch (prevents data from being accidentally written over).

Flash memory cards

Flash memory is particularly well known today because of the popular flash memory cards used in digital cameras. These include CompactFlash (CF), SmartMedia (SM), MultiMediaCard (MMC), Secure Digital (SD) and Memory Sticks (MS). For example, the Sony Memory Stick is an extremely versatile storage card for digital images and more. This type of flash memory comes in the form of a card shaped like a stick of chewing gum, with dimensions of 21.5 × 50 × 2.8 mm and a storage capacity ranging from 64 GB to 256 GB. The Memory Stick weighs just four grams and has a data-protection tag feature on the reverse that enables users to protect data written on the flash memory.

Flash memory is also used in many electronic devices including PCs, cell phones, tablets, cable TV set-top boxes and video game consoles.

▲ Figure 3.16 Different types of flash memory cards

The following is a summary of some characteristics of flash memory cards.

Summary of some characteristics of flash memory cards:
- physically very small
- highly portable
- high data capacity, ranging from 32 GB, 64 GB, 128 GB, 256 GB, and even more
- high data transfer speed to the device they are part of or attached to (camera, PC, and so on).

Table 3.3 on the following page, shows the advantages and disadvantages of secondary storage devices.

Storage device	Storage capacity	Advantages	Disadvantages
Magnetic tapes	Up to 1.6 TB per tape cartridge	• Easy to transport and store • Cheap • Mostly used for backups or archives	• Provides sequential access to data stored • Must be stored in a suitable environment (smoke, dust, temperature and humidity controlled) • Difficult to update files (cannot make changes to a record without writing over the entire tape)
Fixed hard disks	Up to 15 TB	• Direct access • Fast data transfer speeds • Vast storage capacity	• Not portable
Removable hard disks	Up to 16 TB	• Direct access • Fast data transfer speeds • Vast storage capacity • Portable	
Optical discs	CD – up to 800 MB DVD – up to 17 GB Blu-ray – up to 50 GB	• Direct access • Fast data transfer speeds • Portable • Easy to clean with a soft cloth • Unaffected by magnetic fields	• Data on CD-ROMs cannot be changed • Access times are slower than hard drives
Solid state drives	Varies with devices usually 500 GB to 4 TB. For massive SSDs, it can reach up to 100 TB	• Highly portable • Faster data transfer speeds • Higher storage capacity • Faster access times than HDD • More durable • Lighter weight	• Cost is higher than HDD • Data recovery in the event of data failure is more difficult than HDD
Flash memory cards	Varies with devices; usually 32 GB to about 256 GB	• Physically very small • Highly portable • High data transfer speed to PCs • Large storage capacity compared to CDs • Direct access	• May need special software to be used with PCs • Can break easily • Relative high cost
USB flash drives	Up to 1 TB	• Easy to use • Convenient (small size – can be placed in a pocket or on a key chain) • Large storage capacity compared to diskettes • Highly compatible – 'plug and play' (no software needed) • Fast access, direct access • Password protection • Disk write protection switch (prevents data from being accidentally written over)	• Can be easily lost because of its small size • Can become corrupted over time • USB plug can become damaged with constant use

▲ Table 3.3 Advantages and disadvantages of secondary storage devices

Cloud storage

Cloud computing is the use of a network of remote servers hosted on the internet to store, manage and process data, rather than using a local server or a personal computer. Cloud storage, also referred to as 'The Cloud', is a service where data is remotely maintained, managed and operated by a cloud storage service provider. The service allows the users to store data online so that they can access it from any location via the internet. The rapid growth of cloud storage has resulted in hundreds of companies offering a variety of cloud storage services. Services, like Google Drive™, Amazon S3, OneDrive, Box and Sky Drive, allow users to save their files in one of many massive online data centres. These companies offer different packages based on the amount of storage a company may require. Some companies offer monthly and yearly plans. For example, companies charge between $1.04 to $1.15 US dollars for a one-year plan for the first 50 TB. The next 500 TB can cost between $10.00 to $11.00 and for the next 500 TB, the cost is even cheaper.

As the cloud's popularity continues to grow, more and more businesses are using the application as a backup program for their software and documents. By utilising these applications, anyone can access their documents anywhere, worldwide. Individuals are no longer tied down to just one electronic device in one set area, but can instead revise a version of a document on their laptop at home and then access it for a presentation the next day from their computer at work. In addition, multiple users can collaborate on projects by having access to the same file.

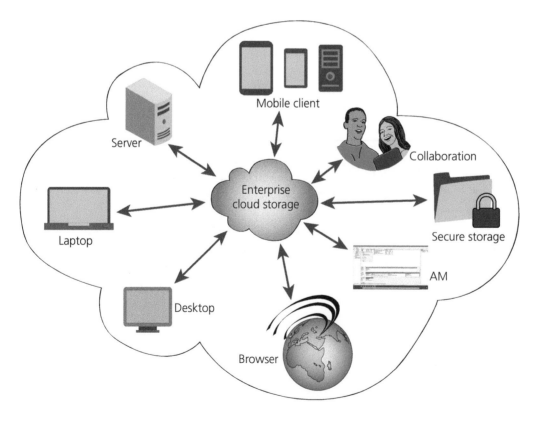

▲ Figure 3.17 Cloud storage

Advantages of cloud storage

Some advantages of cloud storage include the following points.

1 **Ease of use:** All cloud storage services have desktop folders for Mac® and PC users. This allows users to drag and drop files between the cloud storage and their local storage.
2 **Accessibility:** Stored files can be accessed and shared from anywhere via an internet connection. Cloud data storage allows the data to be shared in numerous remote locations, whether from an office across the country or overseas, or employees working from home.
3 **Disaster recovery:** Cloud data storage can be used as an off-site backup, as it is not affected by events and disasters such as theft, floods, fire, and so on.
4 **Cost savings:** The relatively low cost of cloud storage often allows businesses and organisations to reduce annual operating costs. Companies can pay for as much storage as they require at a relatively inexpensive cost per TB.

Disadvantages of cloud storage

Although cloud storage has many advantages, it also has disadvantages.

1 **Usability:** It is much slower than local backups.
2 **Accessibility:** It requires an internet connection to access your data.
3 **Data security:** There are concerns about the safety and privacy of data stored remotely.
4 **Software:** In order to manipulate your files locally through multiple devices, you need to download the service on all devices.

Local storage

Local storage refers to storage devices that are used on-site to store or backup data within a company or organisation. These devices, which are directly attached to the computer or network, include hard drives, solid state drives, flash drives and tape drives. Some advantages and disadvantages of using local storage include the following points.

Advantages of local storage (storage on your server)

1 **Control:** You have complete and total control over the data. As the data is stored locally on a server, you have control over the hardware.
2 **Accessibility:** Your data is easily accessible. Having your data right at your fingertips is a huge convenience. There is no worry about upload or download speeds for retrieving your data. Additionally, there is no need for an internet connection to access your data.
3 **Speed:** As local storage devices are often connected directly to your computer, accessing information can be quicker.

Whereas there are advantages to storing data locally, but there are also some disadvantages.

Disadvantages of local storage (storage on your server)

1 **Disaster recovery:** Data that is stored locally is much more susceptible (vulnerable) to events such as fires and floods. Local storage and local backups could be lost.
2 **Cost:** Local storage of data requires the use of hardware, such as file servers and network cabling, which can be expensive.
3 **Data safety and security:** An on-site data storage can crash at any time, resulting in damaged or no data. However, this potential hazard can be avoided by putting the data online.

Exercise 2

1 A _____ can be a letter, a number, a symbol, a punctuation mark or a blank space.
2 A _____ is the number of bits the computer can process in one operation.
3 Magnetic tape is not suitable for data files that are revised or updated often because it stores data _____.
4 _____ access means that you can go directly to a specific piece of data without having to access any other data, either before or after the data you want.
5 The _____ time is the time taken to get data from a spinning disk with one read/write head.
6 A _____ is made up of all the tracks of the same number from all the metal disks that make up the hard disk, which can be read or written to at the same time.
7 _____ disks are disks that are read by laser lights.
8 Flash memory technology is based on _____ technology and has no _____ parts.
9 Flash memory can be erased a _____ at a time instead of only a single byte at a time, as is the case with EEPROM.
10 Cloud computing is the use of a network of remote servers hosted on the internet to store, _____ and _____ data.
11 _____ stripe cards have a magnetic layer or a stripe that contains minimal information for the user.
12 _____ cards or chip cards contain an _____ chip that stores and transacts data.
13 _____ uses electromagnetic fields to automatically identify and track tags with an implanted chip attached to objects.

Other storage media

Magnetic stripe cards, smart cards and RFID tags, which were discussed in Chapter 2 Input devices, also provide storage for specific uses and applications.

Magnetic stripe cards

Magnetic stripe cards have a magnetic layer or a stripe that contains minimal information for the user. Typically, the user access number is the most identifiable information. In the case of a bank, the card may contain information such as the user's name, account number and the card's expiration date. When used in a hotel, personnel at the hotel desk will imprint the user information at check-in and usually set a time limit for its use until checkout. The door lock is triggered once the magnetic stripe is read and verified by the hotel door card reader.

▲ Figure 3.18 A magnetic stripe card is used to open an electronic door lock at a hotel.

Smart cards

Smart cards, also referred to as chip cards, contain an embedded chip that stores and transacts data. The chip can include plenty of additional information when compared to a magnetic stripe card. Smart cards can be used in e-commerce (electronic commerce) to make it easy for consumers to securely store information and cash for purchasing. For example, when used in a hotel, the holder can use it to access his or her room, and can also use other services in the hotel, such as restaurant, utility or laundry, to get a joint record of all bills at one place. Smart cards can also be used by students in a university to make purchases from money prepaid to the card. In health institutions, the card can be used to store patient medical records and vaccination data.

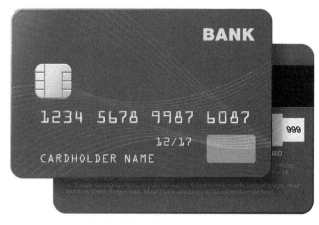

▲ Figure 3.19 A smart card

Radio frequency identification (RFID) tags

RFID is an ID-identification-system. RFID uses electromagnetic fields to identify and track tags attached to objects automatically. It relies on a small chip that is implanted in a tag. When used in a supermarket or warehouse, the chip can record and store data, such as a serial number, price or purchase record of an item. The tag can be attached to all sorts of items: merchandise, shipping containers, vehicles, and even pet or animal collars. An electronic scanner then uses radio signals to read or track the ID tag.

▲ Figure 3.20 An RFID protection sleeve to secure a credit card

Emerging technologies

Phase Change Memory is a technology that competes with classic flash technology. This optical technology offers faster writes than typical flash, and also does not degrade as fast as flash with usage over time. IBM and Intel are currently working on this technology.

DNA storage

DNA can be used to store not only genetic information for many thousands of years, but also data. As DNA is much denser than modern storage mediums, it would be possible to store all the data we have on DNA that would take up the space of only a few trucks. Currently it is not cost-effective to use this technology, but the cost may decrease enough to make it viable in the future.

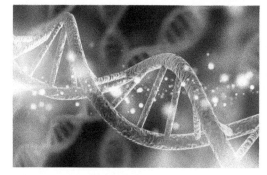

▲ Figure 3.21 A DNA strand

Helium drives

Hard drives are usually filled with air. However, helium-filled hard drives have been pushing the capacity boundaries of hard drives. The Western Digital 10 TB hard drive has surpassed Seagate's 8 TB air-filled hard drive (the largest hard drive at the time). By using helium instead of air, helium-filled drives use less power to spin the disks (helium offers less resistance compared to air), they run cooler, and they can pack in more disks. These high performance drives are likely to get cheaper and be more widely used in the near future.

Chapter 3: Summary

- Storage refers to the media and devices used to keep data and instructions for immediate or later use.
- Primary memory, which resides on the main circuit board, consists of RAM and ROM chips.
- Random Access Memory (RAM) is immediately available to the processor and holds data and instructions temporarily, while processing takes place. It also holds processed data that is waiting to be output or stored in a secondary storage device. Data can be read from and written to RAM. RAM is volatile, limited and expensive.
- Read Only Memory (ROM) chips hold data and instructions necessary for starting up the computer when it is switched on. Data can only be read from ROM chips. ROM is non-volatile.
- PROM and EPROM are variations of the ROM chip that allow data to be added, once in the case of PROM and many times for EPROM.
- A bit is the smallest unit of storage.
- A byte is made up of a combination of eight bits and represents one written character.
- A word is the number of bits a computer can process in one operation. The word length is the number of bits in a word.
- One kilobyte (KB) is approximately 1,000 bytes, one megabyte (MB) is approximately one million bytes and one gigabyte (GB) is approximately one billion bytes.
- Secondary storage devices store data and instructions permanently, to be used when required.
- Storage is chosen for a particular use, based on its storage capacity, access speed, size, portability and cost.
- Magnetic tapes, magnetic disks (hard disk), optical discs (CD-ROM, CD-R, CD-RW and DVD), USB drives, flash memory and solid-state storage are secondary storage devices.
- Magnetic tapes are erasable, reusable and inexpensive. They have large storage capacities but only allow sequential access. They are mostly used for emergency backup purposes.
- Sequential access refers to the accessing of data in the order in which it was stored.
- Magnetic disks provide direct access to stored data.
- Direct access means that you can go directly to a specific piece of data without having to access any other data.
- External hard drives can be easily removed and connected to another computer.

- Hard disks are thin but rigid, inflexible disks made of highly polished metal with a storage capacity from around 500 GB to 8 TB and more. The hard drive usually stores application software (word processor, database, spreadsheet, and so on) and the operating system.
- RAID stands for redundant array of independent disks. A RAID storage system consists of a cabinet that may contain a large number of disk drives (up to 100).
- Formatting a disk means writing electronic information on the disk so that the computer can recognise the disk as a valid storage device and data can be stored.
- Optical discs (CD-ROMs, CD-Rs, CD-RWs, DVDs and Blu-rays) provide direct access to stored data.
- USB flash drives are a new type of flash memory device with storage capacities from 16 GB to 256 GB or more. They are small and plug into a USB port on the computer. No additional software is needed for Windows 7, 8 or 10.
- Flash memory is non-volatile, solid-state memory that can range from 32 GB to 400 GB. These devices can be incorporated into small devices such as digital cameras, cell phones, tablets, cable TV set-top boxes and video game consoles.
- Solid state storage (SSS) is a type of non-volatile flash memory storage that stores and retrieves data electronically without any moving parts. Storage capacities range from 500 GB to 4 TB. Massive SSDs can store up to 100 TB.
- Cloud storage is a cloud computing model in which data is stored, maintained, managed and backed up on remote servers accessed from the internet, or 'cloud'. Advantages of cloud storage include ease of use, accessibility, disaster recovery and cost savings. Some disadvantages include slower access, the need for an internet connection, concerns with data security and the need for software in all machines.
- Local storage involves storing data and information on a server on site. Advantages of local storage include greater control and accessibility of data. Disadvantages include greater susceptibility to disasters, the cost of equipment to store data and less protection from loss of data in a computer crash.
- Magnetic stripe cards, smart cards and RFID tags can store information and can be used in a number of ways.

Chapter 3: Questions

Fill in the blanks

1 A _____ can hold the code for one character.

2 A _____ is the smallest unit of storage.

3 _____ is the data access method used by magnetic disks.

4 A _____ is about 1 billion bytes.

5 Magnetic tapes are mainly used _____.

6 Optical discs are read by _____.

7 The concentric circles in a disk are known as _____.

8 The tracks with the same number in each disk in a disk pack are known as _____.

9 _____ memory has no moving parts.

10 _____ is the use of a network of remote servers hosted on the internet to store, manage and process data.

True or False?

1 Primary storage consists of RAM and ROM chips.

2 A magnetic disk has a number of concentric circles called tracks.

3 RAM chips hold data permanently.

4 The user inputs data and instructions into a ROM chip.

5 A byte has the capacity to represent one character.

6 EPROM chips cannot be erased.

7 Magnetic tapes allow direct access to data stored.

8 Magnetic tape is difficult to update.

9 A USB drive cannot be easily removed from a system.

10 Blu-ray is the most suitable type of optical disc for storing high-definition video.

Multiple-choice questions

1 What does the acronym ROM stand for?
a Random Only Memory
b Read Only Memory
c Read Optical Module
d Random Organising Memory

2 Which device holds data and instructions when it is not in use?
a Primary storage   b System unit
c Monitor   d Secondary storage

3 The smallest unit of storage is a:
a byte.   b bit.
c megabyte.   d terabyte.

4 Another name for primary storage is:
a secondary storage.
b immediate access storage.
c magnetic tape.
d hard disk.

5 Where are data and instructions held so that they are available to the CPU for processing?
a ROM   b DVD
c CD-ROM   d RAM

6 When a disk is formatted, which of the following happens?
a All data on disk is erased
b Becomes damaged
c Data files are copied onto disk
d Contains files to boot up the computer

7 Magnetic tape is used to:
a hold data necessary for starting up the computer.
b back up large amounts of data.
c hold data that the computer is processing at the time.
d do none of the above.

8 Which of the following is a disadvantage of cloud storage?
a Usability (much slower than local backups)
b Cost savings
c Disaster recovery (can be used as an off-site backup)
d Ease of use

9 Which of the following storage media use laser technology to read and store data?
a USB drive   b Hard disk
c Magnetic tape   d CD-ROM

10 Which of the following would be the BEST option to expand your laptop's secondary storage capacity?
a Use magnetic tape
b Store data on DVDs
c Store data on CD-ROM
d Use solid state memory devices

Short-answer questions

1 Explain the functions of RAM and ROM.

2 Explain with the use of examples the difference between the terms 'storage device' and 'storage medium'.

3 What is the function of secondary storage?

4 List the criteria used in selecting a secondary storage device for a particular use.

5 What kinds of secondary storage devices do large computer systems use?

6 State whether EACH of these storage media is a primary or a secondary storage medium.
   a RAM   b Magnetic tape
   c Solid state memory   d PROM

7 Explain, using examples, the terms 'serial access' and 'direct access'.

8 Define the following terms: 'bit', 'byte', 'word' and 'word length'.

9 Define the terms 'track', 'sector' and 'cylinder'.

10 Explain what happens to a disk when it is formatted.

11 List THREE precautions for the care of optical discs.

12 Give the similarities and differences between each of the following pairs:
   a RAM and ROM
   b Hard disk and magnetic tape
   c Primary storage and secondary storage

13 Define the term 'SSD'. List devices that use SSDs.

Research questions

1 The manager of your community sports club wants to purchase a personal computer to perform some of the clerical and accounting work of the club, such as to store information about club members, create and maintain club accounts, create word-processed documents and flyers for advertising club events. The manager would also like to buy a personal computer that can be used for playing some of the latest computer games. You are required to:
   a create two lists of three computers each that the manager can choose from to satisfy both requirements. Each list must state the type and speed of the processor and the primary and secondary storage capacity of the computer.
   b give reasons for each choice.

2 Solid state storage devices are becoming very popular as secondary storage devices. Using the internet to conduct your research, create a table of three types of solid-state storage devices. The table should indicate the following:
   a The range of the storage capacities of each device
   b The advantages of each device
   c The disadvantages of each device
   d Where each device is used.

3 Use the internet to conduct research to complete the following tasks:
   a Create a timeline to show the development of storage options over the last 10 years.
   b Explain the term 'holographic storage'.

Crossword

Across
1 Memory device used in digital cameras and cell phones (5)

4 Holds data and instructions necessary for starting up the computer (3)

5 Stores movies with high-quality sound and video (3)

6 This medium only provides serial access (4)

7 A type of storage that holds data on a permanent basis for later use (9)

Down
1 Performing this operation on a disk erases all the information (10)

2 The number of bits the computer can process in one operation (4)

3 It contains millions of transistors and capacitors (4)

4

Output devices

Output devices are pieces of equipment that are used to get information or any other response *out* of a computer. If the output can be read by human beings, it is said to be human readable. If the output cannot be understood by humans, it is said to be machine readable.

There are two types of output. Softcopy output or temporary output refers to information displayed on a screen or in audio or voice form through speakers. This kind of output disappears when the computer is switched off. When the computer is off, neither the screen nor the speakers work because they are always linked to and driven by the computer. Hardcopy output or permanent output is output printed onto paper.

The main output devices that you are likely to come across are shown in Figure 4.1.

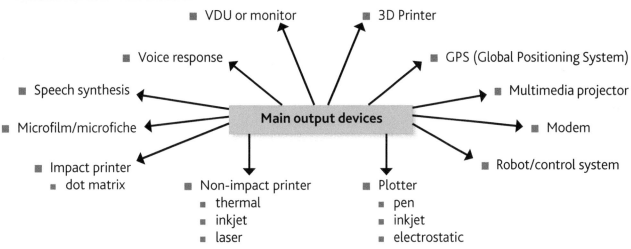

- VDU or monitor
- 3D Printer
- Voice response
- GPS (Global Positioning System)
- Speech synthesis
- Multimedia projector
- Microfilm/microfiche
- **Main output devices**
- Modem
- Impact printer
  - dot matrix
- Robot/control system
- Non-impact printer
  - thermal
  - inkjet
  - laser
- Plotter
  - pen
  - inkjet
  - electrostatic

▲ Figure 4.1 Main output devices

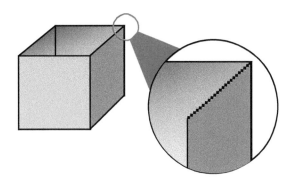

▲ Figure 4.2 Example of the pixels on a close-up view of an image

Softcopy output devices

Softcopy devices produce a temporary output, something that cannot be saved. We are going to look at three groups of softcopy output devices:

- visual output devices
- sound output devices
- modems.

Visual output devices

Monitors

The monitor (also called 'the screen') or visual display unit (VDU) can output still or moving pictures. The screen is similar in appearance to that of a television and helps the user to interface visually with the computer. Images and text are formed by many tiny dots of

▲ Figure 4.3 A flat panel monitor (on the left) and a cathode ray tube monitor (CRT)

coloured light called pixels (short for picture element). A pixel is the smallest unit on the screen. Screens have pixels in three colours (blue, green and red) that can be turned on or off to make different colours. The pixels are so numerous that when placed together in certain patterns, they appear to form a smooth image on the screen.

CRT monitors

Cathode ray tube (CRT) monitors have become almost obsolete because flat panel displays are lighter, brighter, cheaper, thinner and easier to make with larger numbers of pixels (higher resolution).

Flat panel display monitors

There are three types of flat panel display monitors.

- **LCD (liquid crystal display):** This display uses liquid crystals, which is a substance that can change states from liquid to solid and so change its appearance when an electric current is passed through it. An LCD display is small, light and flat with no moving parts and therefore uses much less power than the CRT display. It is, therefore, used extensively on laptop computers.
- **Plasma display:** In this display, light is created by a plasma discharge from phosphors placed between two flat panels of glass. This works a bit like each pixel being a fluorescent light that can be switched on or off. Plasma displays were popular for televisions, but improvements in LCD and LED technologies have made these less popular.
- **LED display:** This display uses an array of light-emitting diodes (LEDs). These electronic components can be manufactured in different colours and act as tiny lamps or pixels to create the image. OLED (organic light-emitting diodes) and flexible OLED displays use a giant complex molecule/organic material whose properties can make the display flexible, bendable and foldable. It also uses less power than traditional LCDs. OLEDs are used in televisions and smartphone screens.

> **Did you know?**
>
> The CRT was invented in 1897 by the German scientist Karl Braun. It was first used in the cathode-ray oscilloscope, a scientific instrument used to display data about electric currents. Later, it became the basis of television. The first successful transmission of moving television images took place in 1925, by the Scottish inventor, John Logie Baird.

> **Did you know?**
>
> QLEDs (quantum light-emitting diodes) or dots that range in size from 2 to 10 nanometers (about 50 times smaller than in a typical computer monitor) and produce different colours depending on their size. Samsung's new QLED TV can blend into its environment by matching the background around it.

Characteristics of monitors

A monitor's full capabilities depend on several factors:

1. The graphics/video card or adaptor being used
2. The monitor's size
3. Its resolution
4. Its 'image aspect ratio'
5. Its 'refresh rate'.

Let us look at these characteristics in more detail.

- **Graphics/video card or adaptor:** This is an electronic link between the computer's processor and the monitor – it is a circuit board that connects the processor to the monitor. It determines the display resolution, the number of colours available and the refresh rate of the monitor. Both the type of monitor and the graphics card determine the resolution. The adaptor contains VRAM (video RAM) that supports a certain resolution. You cannot set a resolution higher than the adaptor can support. The more powerful the card is, the more capable the monitor will be in all these aspects.

▲ Figure 4.4 Different resolutions shown on a monitor

- **Size:** This is the diagonal dimension of the screen. Common sizes range from 17 to 24 inches (43 to 61 cm).
- **Resolution:** Resolution determines the clarity and sharpness of an image when displayed on the screen. The more pixels there are on a screen, the higher the resolution, and the greater the level of detail that can be shown in an image. Some common resolutions are:
  - VGA (video graphics array) = 640 × 480 pixels
  - SVGA (super video graphics array) = 800 × 600 pixels
  - XGA/XVGA (extended graphics array/extended video graphics array) = 1024 × 768 pixels
  - SXGA (super extended graphics array) = 1280 × 1024 pixels
  - UXGA (ultra extended graphics array) = 1600 × 1200 pixels
  - QXGA (quad extended graphics array) = 2048 × 1536 pixels
  - WUXGA (widescreen ultra extended graphics array) = 1920 × 1200 pixels
  - HD (high definition) = 1920 × 1080 pixels
  - 4K or UHD (ultra high definition) = 3840 × 2160 pixels or 8K UHD = 7680 × 4320 pixels.
- **Image aspect ratio:** This refers to the width to height ratio of an image on the screen. Most monitors have a 4:3 width to height ratio. Note that some of the pixel dimensions listed above can be reduced to this ratio mathematically. Work them out and see for yourself.
- **Refresh rate:** This is the number of times the image is repainted or refreshed on the screen per second. We think that the content displayed on our screen is still, but in fact, the image is being repainted continuously. If this process is slow, the screen may appear to flicker.
  - The refresh rate is measured in Hertz (cycles per second). For example, 150 Hertz (Hz) means the screen is refreshed 150 times a second.
  - As the refresh rate becomes faster, the flickering on the screen becomes less noticeable.
  - As the resolution becomes higher, more lines need to be scanned across the screen, or repainted, per second.

> **Did you know?**
> 4K and UHD are not technically the same thing. However, because the resolution is close, most people tend to refer to UHD as 4K. 4K refers to a horizontal resolution of 4096 pixels.

Different users will have different requirements. For example:

- Gaming users need a high refresh rate because of the amount of movement in games. They also need high resolution to get the best out of the game, though games often do not use as high a resolution as films, and may use an aspect ratio that is more similar to a computer screen.
- Web browsing does not generally put too high a demand on the graphics card, compared to gaming use. Websites will usually adapt their layout to suit the aspect ratio of the monitor you are using.
- Graphic design and desktop publishing screens need to have high resolution and be able to produce colours very accurately, so that designers can be confident that what they see on a screen will look like the printed result. They may also use wider aspect ratios, as this allows more space on the screen for the software tools and graphics.
- Video editing requires a similar type of screen to that of gaming users, but often needs to support the kinds of resolutions that the finished videos will use, which could be as high as 4K resolution.

▲ Figure 4.5 Video editing requires a high-resolution graphics monitor.

Multimedia projectors

A multimedia projector is used to create and deliver dynamic multimedia presentations (in which sound, photos, video, text and other moving graphics may be combined to interesting effect). The projector connects directly to a computer, television, video/DVD player or video camcorder such as a monitor. Images from these devices are projected through the projector onto a screen or wall. Versions of this projector now have an arm extension with a digital video camera attached. This video camera allows real-time videos and pictures to be projected instantly through the projector onto a screen. For example, the camera can be directed at a page in a book or at someone performing a demonstration; the video camera image is projected through the projector onto a screen or wall. The three types of multimedia projectors are LCD (liquid crystal display), DLP (digital light processing), and LED (light-emitting diode) projectors, and these differ in the way they make the images:

- An **LCD projector** uses a small LCD screen in front of a powerful lamp. This image is then focused onto a screen by the lenses.
- A **DLP projector** uses a chip made with thousands of micro-mirrors to project images onto a screen/wall, as done by most cinema projectors.
- An **LED projector** has arrays of red, blue and green diodes.

See Table 4.1, which compares LCD, DLP and LED projectors.

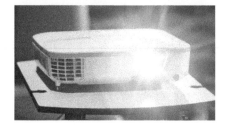

▲ Figure 4.6 An LCD projector and a Pico projector

LCD projector	DLP projector	LED projector
Sharper and higher image quality	Image quality better for moving images	Best quality image
Heavier projector	Lighter and more portable projector	Lightest and most portable
Less reliable	More reliable	Generates the least heat
Quieter projector	Less quiet, more moving parts	Uses the least amount of energy
Uses less power and produces less heat	Generates more heat	Has limited brightness and therefore does not show well when there is a lot of ambient light

▲ Table 4.1 A comparison of LCD, DLP and LED projectors

Sound output devices

Sound output is also a form of 'softcopy' output, as it not permanent, as printing would be. Examples of devices include the following:

Speakers

A simple speaker makes a range of sounds available, such as computer-generated sound, music output, computer-synthesised voice and a normal speaking voice. Microcomputers need sound cards installed to have good-quality sound. In environments where speakers are impractical, headphones, earphones (inserted into the ear canal) or earbuds (they rest outside the ear canal) may be used. Both headphones and earphones now include noise-cancelling technology, which reduces the amount of noise interference from the surrounding environment.

▲ **Figure 4.7** Headphones are larger and are worn over the ears.

Voice response systems

The voice response system selects from a set of digitised prerecorded words, phrases, music, alarms or other sounds stored on disk. The system combines these prerecorded words into responses based on selections made by the user. For example, many phone banking systems use voice response systems. Based on the information given to them when a caller selects options on their telephone keypad, the bank computer outputs voice information to the caller. The sounds must be converted from digital format back to analogue before being output to the speaker.

▲ **Figure 4.8** Earphones are inserted into the ear canal.

Speech synthesis

Speech synthesis called speech-generating devices (SGDs) convert written text into computer-generated speech ('text to speech'). They are used for computer-aided conversations by hearing- and speech-impaired persons, or for converting conversations/text from one language into another.

Modems

A modem (short for **mo**dulator/**demo**dulator), or communications device, sends and receives data, for example, to and from the internet. So it is both an input and an output device. It converts digital data from the computer into analogue data and transmits it over a landline. The modem on the other end converts the analogue data back into digital data for the computer to process. Modems are often built into computers.

> **Did you know?**
>
> You can use a modern smartphone and fast wireless internet with an app such as the Google Translate™ translation service for speech synthesis. Connect to the internet and see what other speech synthesis websites you can find.

Exercise 1

1 Fill in the blanks using A to E below.

    a _____ = resolution   b _____ = pixel   c _____ = refresh rate

    d _____ = speech synthesis   e _____ = voice response systems

    A The smallest unit on the screen   B The clarity or sharpness of an image

    C Selects and plays back prerecorded sounds   D Measured in Hertz

    E Converts written text into computer-generated speech

2 Fill in the blanks.

    Temporary output is also known as _____ output. Monitors are temporary output devices; _____ and _____ are the two types of monitors. The most common is the _____. The electronic link between the processor and the monitor is _____. Three characteristics that affect the capabilities of monitors are _____, _____ and _____.

Hardcopy output devices

You can print information that is in the computer onto paper or film. By printing you create what is known as a 'hardcopy' – something you can hold in your hands.

Printers

Printers are used to present and store all kinds of information on paper, such as letters, legal documents, scientific data and graphs, photographs and advertising material. There are no limits to the amount and type of information that can be printed on paper – just take a look at the paper-based materials around you, in your classroom or in your home.

There are therefore many different kinds of printers, which vary in their speed and print quality, depending on the desired print output. One way of classifying printers is according to the following categories.

- **Character printers:** These print one character at a time, much like a typewriter. They are slow.
- **Line printers:** These are much faster; they print a line at a time, or so it appears as multiple hammer-like keys forming a line of text hit the page at one time. They are used with mainframe computers where high speed is vital for the large volume of printed output required. Line printers print a limited number of characters and do not print graphics.
- **Page printers:** These print a whole page at a time. They are therefore even faster and deal with very large volumes of printed output. Page printers are used for printing books.

The print quality will vary depending on the type of printer, and also the instructions sent to the printer for the quality required. For example, in a standard household or office printer, there is letter quality, near letter quality (NLQ), draft quality printing and photo quality.

Another more common way of classifying printers is as impact printers and non-impact printers. We will now look at these printers in detail.

Impact printers

The print head of an impact printer contains a number of metal hammers that strike an inked ribbon placed between the print head and the paper. These hammers may contain complete characters; alternatively, they may contain 'dots' that are used to build up a character. The dot matrix printer, although almost obsolete, is still used in some industries.

Dot matrix printers (character printers)

Characteristics of these printers include the following:

- Characters are formed from a matrix of dots.
- The speed is usually 30–550 characters per second (cps).
- This is the noisiest of the printer family.
- These printers are relatively fast.
- The print obtained is usually poor. They are useful for low-quality carbon copy printing of text, or printing text on continuous sheets of paper.
- They are not good for printing shaded graphics or photographs.

> **Did you know?**
> There were many other impact printers that have become obsolete. These printers include the Daisy wheel, drum, and chain or band printer.

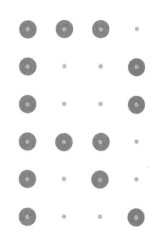

▲ Figure 4.9 An example of how a matrix printer constructs a character

Non-impact printers

The print head of a non-impact printer does not strike the paper, so they are much quieter than impact printers. Most non-impact printers produce dot matrix patterns, as this is how a computer builds up an image. These printers can produce much smaller dots and therefore much higher resolutions than a dot matrix printer. Several technologies are now available and have been used to produce a variety of printers. The main types of non-impact printers are:

- thermal printers
- laser printers
- inkjet printers.

Thermal printers (character printers)

The two types of thermal printers are described in the following text.

- **Direct thermal printers:** These printers use heated elements or pins to form the characters. These elements or pins come into contact with special heat-sensitive paper to form darkened dots where the elements have reached a critical temperature, thus shaping the characters. The pins actually burn the dots into the specially coated paper. Exposure to sunlight and heat tends to darken the thermal printer paper, which also tends to darken over time even at room temperature; the print quality produced by thermal printers is therefore poor.
- **Thermal wax transfer printers:** The print head of these printers melt a wax-based ink from a transfer ribbon onto the paper. These printers do not require special paper.

Thermal printers are widely used in battery-powered equipment such as portable calculators, fax machines and some automated teller machines (ATMs).

> **Did you know?**
>
> The fastest black-and-white laser printers can produce around 40 printed pages per minute. The fastest colour laser printers are only slightly slower, producing around 30 pages per minute.

Laser printers (page printers)

Laser printers are very common in the modern office. They use an electrostatic process. A laser beam and dry powdered ink (called toner) produce a very fine dot matrix pattern. This pattern is transferred to the page over a charged drum and then fused onto it by heat and pressure. These printers can generate a large number of pages per minute depending on the specifications and quality of the printer.

Colour laser printers use four different colour toners and work by printing four times – once with cyan toner, then with magenta toner, then yellow and then with black. The mix of these colours can produce all other colours, and the output quality is very good.

Compared to black-and-white laser printers, colour laser printers are much more expensive – sometimes thousands of dollars more than the black-and-white laser printers.

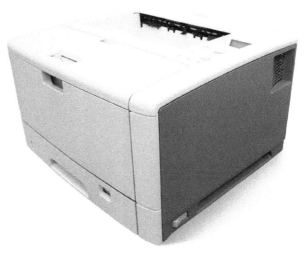

▲ Figure 4.10 A laser printer

Inkjet printers (line printers)

Inkjet printers produce an image by spraying ink onto the paper in a dot matrix pattern. Colour graphics can be produced by spraying cyan, magenta, yellow and black ink onto the page. Inkjet printers can print in both colour and black-and-white. They are very common for home use and the print quality is good, even very good, but not as good as that of laser printers. A typical printer of this type may cost around US$100, though the cost of continuously replacing ink should also be considered.

Characteristics of impact and non-impact printers

Table 4.2 shows the different characteristics of impact and non-impact printers.

▲ Figure 4.11 An inkjet printer

Characteristics of impact printers	Characteristics of non-impact printers
Noisy	Much quieter – useful in hospitals, busy offices, and so on.
Can produce multiple copies by printing on duplicating paper	Much faster printing speeds
Used in a few businesses or industries	Sometimes require special paper
	Do not have multiple-copy facilities, that is, they cannot produce multiple copies by printing on duplicating paper

▲ Table 4.2 Characteristics of impact and non-impact printers

Other types of printers

Mobile printers

A mobile printer is a lightweight, battery-powered printer that can also work with a power source. These are usually thermal or inkjet printers. Many come with the option of being able to connect to a laptop via Bluetooth, IrDA (a way of connecting devices using infrared light), or USB.

Multifunctional printers

Multifunctional printers are sometimes called all-in-one, three-in-one or four-in-one printers. These printers may contain a laser or an inkjet printer, a scanner, a copier, and sometimes fax facilities.

▲ Figure 4.12 A mobile printer

Braille printers

A Braille printer, also called a Braille embosser, is an impact printer that converts text into the Braille code by producing patterns of raised dots on paper, for use by the blind or people with low vision.

Braille readers or Braille display devices

Braille readers, also called Braille display devices, contain a set of round pins that become raised through the flat surface of the device as the computer text output is converted to Braille.

Plotters

A plotter is a peripheral device used to draw high-quality, high-resolution images, graphics, charts, graphs, maps and vectors or coordinate graphics on large sheets of paper. They are useful for producing architectural drawings, building plans, maps and computer-aided design (CAD) drawings, where precision is required. The paper is sometimes laid on a flatbed (flatbed plotter) or on a rotating drum (drum plotter).

There are three main types of plotters.

- **Pen plotters** use a mechanical arm or rail that holds a pen, which can be moved across the page. They are slow and not often used.
- **Inkjet plotters** work in the same way as inkjet printers by spraying ink onto the paper. These are fast and can produce high-quality and high-resolution images. They are often used for creating posters and large photographic images.
- **Electrostatic plotters** work in the same way as laser printers and have similar uses and advantages as inkjets printers.

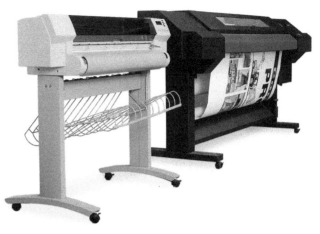
▲ Figure 4.13 Plotters

3D printers

A 3D printer creates a physical object (3D model) by building or layering specific materials such as a polymer, plastic, metal alloy or even food ingredients.

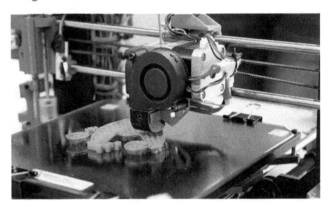
▲ Figure 4.14 A 3D printer

Microfilm/microfiche (COM)

Computer output on microfilm/microfiche (COM) is used to store computer documents by reducing their size so that they fit onto very small photographic prints. They are a physical output, like printing. These prints can be read using a special magnifying machine. Microfilm is a roll of film and microfiche is a rectangular sheet of film on which many frames/pages of information can be stored.

Robotics devices and control systems

Computer processors can send signals (output) to a robotic hardware device to produce a physical action. Robotics devices are very common in the manufacture of high-tech goods, such as cars, television sets, and so on, in a complex factory production line process.

Control systems use sensors to measure physical quantities. Sensors send input to the processor of the controlling computer, which responds by sending an output signal to activate an item of hardware. A smoke detector is an example of such a sensor; once smoke is detected, it sends a signal to the sprinklers in a building or a signal to a fire station.

GPS (Global Positioning System)

A GPS (Global Positioning System) uses a network of satellites to define a position or location on the Earth and displays it on the GPS screen.

▲ Figure 4.15 Microfilm (top) and microfilm reader

Emerging technology

Wearable output devices

Smart glasses, such as the Google Glass™ wearable computing device experiment, are also considered to be an output device. These glasses allow you to see both the real world and virtual content or augmented reality. They superimpose the computer screen on the lenses of the glasses.

▲ Figure 4.16 Smart glasses

Bionic technology, in the form of contact lenses, helps people who are visually impaired to interact with or see the outside world by using technology in the lens to correct whatever visual impairment the user has.

▲ Figure 4.18 A jacket has a screen showing an advertisement

Clothing-based displays are clothing with screens sewn into them to show a message or advertise a product.

▲ Figure 4.17 A bionic lens

Chapter 4: Summary

- Output devices are pieces of equipment that are used to get information or any other response out of a computer.
- Output can be human readable or machine readable.
- Softcopy or temporary output disappears when the computer is switched off.
- Hardcopy or permanent output refers to output printed onto paper, microfiche or microfilm.
- Monitors or VDUs are softcopy output devices that include CRT, LCD and plasma.
- A pixel is the smallest unit on the screen, made up of coloured dots that can be turned on or off to create different shades.
- A monitor's performance depends on the graphics/video card or adaptor, its size, resolution, image aspect ratio and refresh rate.
- Sound is softcopy output. Computer-synthesised voice, computer-generated sound, music output and the speaking voice are output using a speaker.
- Modems are both input and output devices. They communicate information over a telephone line.

- Printers are hardcopy output devices and can be classified as character, line and page printers.
- Printers can be divided into two broad categories: impact printers and non-impact printers.
- Impact printers include dot matrix, daisy wheel, and drum/chain/band printers.
- Non-impact printers include thermal, laser and inkjet printers.
- A plotter is used, for example, in CAD, to draw high-quality graphics, images, charts, graphs, maps and vectors, or coordinate graphics on large sheets of paper.
- Computer output on microfilm/microfiche (COM) is hardcopy output used to store computer documents by vastly reducing their size so that they fit onto photographic prints.
- A 3D printer creates a physical three-dimensional model of an object using specific materials.
- GPSs (Global Positioning Systems) use a network of satellites to define a location on the Earth.

Chapter 4: Questions

True or False?

1 The image aspect ratio is the number of times the image is repainted or refreshed on the screen.

2 Plotters are useful for producing architectural drawings, building plans, maps and CAD drawings.

3 Sensors send output to the processor of the controlling computer.

4 Impact printers have much faster printing speeds.

5 Laser printers produce an image by spraying ink onto the paper in a dot matrix pattern.

6 An LED (light-emitting diode) projector has arrays of red, blue and yellow diodes.

7 Microfiche is a rectangular sheet of film on which many frames/pages of information can be stored.

8 An inkjet printer is an example of a non-impact printer.

9 Headphones are a type of speaker that are placed in the ear.

10 A GPS (Global Positioning System) uses a network of computers to determine position or location on the Earth and displays it on the GPS screen.

Multiple-choice questions

1 A monitor's capabilities depend on all except:
   a resolution.
   b size.
   c refresh rate.
   d print quality.

2 NQL refers to:
   a refresh rate.
   b the number of characters per second.
   c print quality.
   d type of monitor.

3 All the following are non-impact printers except for:
   a the dot matrix printer.
   b the thermal printer.
   c the inkjet printer.
   d the laser printer.

4 Which is not a characteristic of laser printers?
   a Are quiet
   b Have high print speeds
   c Use toner similar to that of photocopiers
   d Can produce multiple copies by printing on duplicating paper

5 Microfilm output is stored on:
   a rectangular sheets of film.
   b photographic paper.
   c magnetic paper.
   d a roll of film.

Short-answer questions

1 Give TWO advantages and TWO disadvantages of a non-impact printer over an impact printer.

2 Explain the difference between a line printer and a character printer.

3 Explain the difference between microfilm and microfiche.

4 A number of output devices can be used to help physically-challenged people. Select TWO and explain how these devices work towards making things easier for the physically challenged.

5 Give ONE advantage of output on microfilm over that on printed paper.

6 A number of output devices produce human readable, as well as machine-readable output. Explain the difference and list ONE of each type of device.

7 Describe how a robotic arm can be used in an assembly line.

8 You are a consultant to a small business that types documents and creates presentations for individuals. Select a suitable printer and explain to your client why you have chosen that printer for their business.

9 List TWO attributes of a monitor that affect its display and explain how the monitor is affected.

10 Explain the difference between LCD and plasma flat-screen monitors.

11 State whether you would use a printer or a plotter to print the following documents:
   a A résumé
   b A prenuptial agreement contract
   c A design for a new gown
   d A recipe
   e The redesign of a bathroom
   f A map to get from the centre of the town to your home.

Crossword

Across
3 Sound output (7)

5 The print head of this printer strikes the paper (6)

7 Clarity of an image (10)

Down
1 Sprays ink onto paper in a dot matrix pattern (6)

2 Permanent output (two words) (8)

4 Specialised output device used to produce architectural drawings (7)

6 Smallest unit on the screen (5)

Challenge questions
1 Five different types of customers have asked you to assist them in selecting output devices. Recommend appropriate devices to them:

   a A stay-at-home mother with a teenager has a small budget but uses the internet often. Her child also uses the computer for schoolwork and entertainment.

   b Ms Patrick has a small home office and works mainly from home but communicates with the head office frequently. She is a real-estate agent for a local real-estate company. She often needs to send documents to the head office.

   c Mr Jay is a pharmaceutical sales representative who is always commuting to and from his various clients. While he is on the road, he is frequently in contact with his clients and also with head office. He also sends and receives sensitive information between his clients and the head office.

   d Mr Tom is a freelance animator and graphics designer who designs and produces advertisements. He has a well-established clientele of big and small companies, and individuals.

   e Mr MacFarlan is a manager for a large business college that conducts video conferencing of many of its classes. He has a staff of over 100 employees who need suitable equipment.

   f Mr Joseph is interested in becoming a DJ (disk jockey). He has been disk jockeying for family and close friends but is now being offered more jobs in his community. Can you recommend some output devices for his career path?

   g Darcy is an aspiring author who has written a few books. She usually writes on paper, but has recently upgraded to a computer. She is told that there are output devices that can make her job easier.

2 There are many types of printers on the market. List a number of questions that you would ask yourself or that a salesperson would ask you when you are purchasing a printer.

Project
■ Your teacher wants to purchase a 3D printer for the class, but is being discouraged by colleagues because of the negative stories they have heard about 3D printing. Your teacher has asked you to assist him in justifying the need for this device by indicating the pros and cons of making use of a 3D printer in the class. A company in the community has agreed to fund the purchase of the printer if a convincing argument can be made.

■ Select one emerging output device. Describe its use and function, and justify its possible future potential.

5

Data storage and representation

Objectives

At the end of this chapter, you will be able to:

→ explain the difference between discrete and continuous data and give examples of each
→ explain what a bistable device is
→ convert a decimal number to binary, and vice versa
→ add and subtract binary numbers
→ represent integers using 'sign and magnitude, one's complement, two's complement and binary coded decimal methods
→ perform subtraction using two's complement
→ explain the term 'character set'.

▲ Figure 5.1 A light bulb is a bistable device, as it only has two states: 'on' and 'off'.

Discrete data and continuous data

Data is all the raw facts and figures that a computer processes. The way in which data is stored and represented depends on the medium storing it and the type of data. Generally, there are two types of data – discrete and continuous.

Discrete data

Discrete data is data that can be counted; for example, the number of cars in a car park or the number of people that responded 'yes' or 'no' to a question. It has no value in between; for example, you cannot say two and a half students are present. Computers work with data represented by the binary numbers '1' or '0', which are discrete quantities.

Continuous data

On the other hand, continuous data (also known as analogue data) is data that can be measured and can be recorded at many different points. For example, the temperature of a liquid can be recorded as 32 degrees Celsius (°C), or as 32.5 °C or 32.53 °C or 32.534 °C, and so on. Other examples of continuous data are length, weight and volume. For a digital computer to process continuous data, it needs to be converted to a digital form. For something like temperature, this is done by measuring at regular, short time intervals (sampling) and converting the measurement to digital data, in a process called analogue to digital conversion.

A bistable device

A computer consists of a number of two-state (or bistable) devices that process and store data as numbers. A bistable device is one that can be set to one of two states at any one point in time. An example of a bistable device could be a light bulb, as a circuit can either pass a current through it or not. In the case of the light bulb, 1 can represent the bulb being 'on' and 0 can represent it being 'off'. Similarly, a bistable device's outputs can be represented by the digits 0 and 1. The binary number system, which consists of two digits 0 and 1, is used by computers to represent the two states, referred to in mathematics as base 2. These two binary digits are also known as bits (short for binary digits).

A single bit can represent 0 or 1. A group of two bits can represent one of four (2^2) values:

00   01   10   11

These four values can represent four different symbols or characters. For example, the numbers 0, 1, 2, 3 could be represented by these four 2-bit patterns:

00   0   10   2
01   1   11   3

With three bits, we can have eight (2^3) 3-bit patterns. This means we can now represent eight different characters (0 to 7):

000   0   100   4
001   1   101   5
010   2   110   6
011   3   111   7

With four bits, we can represent sixteen (2^4) characters, with eight bits we can represent 256 (2^8) characters, and so on. Therefore, with 'n' bits, we will be able to represent 2^n characters.

Number systems

The number system that we use every day is the decimal (base 10) number system. Since computers can only perform binary operations, you need to know how to perform calculations using the binary number system. The next section deals with converting numbers from binary (base 2) to decimal (base 10) and vice versa.

Converting a binary number (base 2) to decimal (base 10)

The decimal number system consists of ten digits (0, 1, 2, 3, 4, 5, 6, 7, 8, 9) and is also referred to as the base 10 number system. The base of any number may be indicated as a subscript on the extreme right of the number (for example, 455_{10} means '455 in base 10'). These digits and their combinations are used to represent numbers in the decimal number system.

Each digit in the decimal number system has a value that depends on its position or place in the number. The place values start at ones (10^0) for the digit of smallest value on the right. $10^0 = 1$, since any number raised to the power of 0 is 1. So 10^0 is the 'ones place' or 'ones column'. Similarly, 10^1 is the 'tens place'. The value of each place increases by a factor of 10, so $10^2 = 10 \times 10 = 100$, for each consecutive digit *moving right to left* until the digit of greatest value is reached: the digit on the far left. You will recall this from your mathematics lessons.

Let us look at the number 325. This number is made up of the sum (addition) of each digit multiplied by its place value. Table 5.1 shows the value of each digit in the number.

> **Did you know?**
>
> The Voyager space probe has binary messages for any intelligent life form it may encounter on its journey through space. Launched in 1977, Voyager 1 and its twin, Voyager 2, were the first space probes to explore the outer planets of our solar system. Voyager 1's primary mission ended in 1980 when it completed its observations of Saturn. Since then, it has been heading into deep space. Voyager 1 and Voyager 2 both carry a so-called 'The Golden Record' — a 12-inch gold-plated copper disk. The record includes samples of music, greetings in multiple language and nature sounds. Binary code printed on the record shows the proper speed at which the record should be played.

Hundreds (H)	Tens (T)	Ones (O)
3 represents 3 hundreds	2 represents 2 tens	5 represents 5 ones
3 × 100 = 300	2 × 10 = 20	5 × 1 = 5
Adding the totals gives 325		

▲ Table 5.1 Value of each digit in the number 325

Another way of setting out the information in Table 5.1 is shown in Table 5.2.

H (10^2)	T (10^1)	O (10^0)	
100	10	1	This row shows the value of each digit in that position: the 'place value'.
3	2	5	Each digit in this row is multiplied by its place value, above.
300	20	5	Sum the totals:
			The result is 325

▲ Table 5.2 Decimal number and place value

Converting a binary number to decimal is very similar, since each digit in a binary number also has a place value that depends on its position in the number. However, in this case, the place value starts at 2^0 for the least significant bit (LSB) and increases by a factor of 2 for each bit that follows, again moving right to left, as in the decimal example just given.

To convert a binary number to decimal, multiply each bit by its place value, starting from the least significant bit (LSB) on the right to the most significant bit (MSB) on the left, and then sum the totals. Examples 1 and 2 illustrate how to do this.

Example 1

Convert 1001_2 to decimal.

Solution

2^3	2^2	2^1	2^0	
8	4	2	1	This row shows the value of each digit in that position: the 'place value'.
1	0	0	1	Each digit in this row is multiplied by its place value, above.
8	0	0	1	Sum the totals.
				The result is 9

Therefore $1001_2 = 9_{10}$

Example 2

Convert 111001_2 to decimal.

Solution

2^5	2^4	2^3	2^2	2^1	2^0	
32	16	8	4	2	1	This row shows the value of each digit in that position: the 'place value'.
1	1	1	0	0	1	Each digit in this row is multiplied by its place value, above.
32	16	8	0	0	1	Sum the totals:
						The result is 57

Therefore $111001_2 = 57_{10}$

Converting a decimal number (base 10) to binary (base 2)

Converting a decimal number (base 10) to binary (base 2) is a simple process. You need to divide the decimal number by 2 and record the remainder until the result is zero, then write out the remainders starting from the last remainder to the first. See the following examples.

Example 3

Convert the number 9_{10} to binary.

Solution

2	9	a 9 divided by 2 gives 4 remainder 1
2	4 R 1	b 4 divided by 2 gives 2 remainder 0
2	2 R 0	c 2 divided by 2 gives 1 remainder 0
2	1 R 0	d 1 divided by 2 gives 0 remainder 1
	0 R 1	Write the remainders starting from the last remainder moving up to the first.
		This gives 1001_2

Therefore $9_{10} = 1001_2$

The process is the same for larger numbers, as shown in Example 4.

Example 4

What is the binary equivalent of 225_{10}?

Solution

÷ 2	225	Remainder
÷ 2	112	1
÷ 2	56	0
÷ 2	28	0
÷ 2	14	0
÷ 2	7	0
÷ 2	3	1
÷ 2	1	1
	0	1
		Write the remainders starting from the last remainder moving up to the first.
		This gives 11100001_2

Therefore $225_{10} = 11100001_2$

Adding binary numbers

Memorise these five sums and remember the points that follow, as this basic information shows you how to add in binary.

1 0_2	2 0_2	3 1_2	4 1_2	5 1_2
$+ 0_2$	$+ 1_2$	$+ 0_2$	$+ 1_2$	$+ 1_2$
				$+ 1_2$
0_2	1_2	1_2	10_2	11_2

Did you know?

A Polynesian culture, the Mangarevans, used a special counting system (partially based on binary) for important tribute goods such as turtles, fish, coconuts, octopuses and breadfruit.

To understand how the above calculations work, you can think of them as follows:

1 $0_2 + 0_2 = 0_2$. This is the same as:

$(2^0 \times 0) + (2^0 \times 0) = (1 \times 0) + (1 \times 0) = 0 \times 0 = 0$.

0_{10} in base 2 is $\mathbf{0_2}$, hence the answer shown.

Similarly:

5 $1_2 + 1_2 + 1_2$ is the same as:

$(2^0 \times 1) + (2^0 \times 1) + (2^0 \times 1) = 1 + 1 + 1 = 3$.

3_{10} in binary is the same as:

$(2^1 \times 1) + (2^0 \times 1) = 11_2$

You also need to remember always, that when adding binary numbers, $1 + 1 \neq 2$, because the digit 2 is not used in binary; similarly $1 + 1 + 1 \neq 3$.

Now let us look at adding in binary with a few examples.

Example 5

Add the binary numbers 01 and 10.

Solution

First, place the binary numbers one above the other, ensuring that the bits with the same weighting are in the same columns. This gives:

```
MSB   LSB
  0    1
+ 1    0
```

Step 1: Starting from the column on the right (LSB), add the digits: $1 + 0 = 1$. Write the 1 in the same column.

```
  01
+ 10
   1
```

Step 2: Add the digits in the second column: $0 + 1 = 1$. Write the 1 in the same column.

```
  01
+ 10
  11
```

Therefore $01_2 + 10_2 = 11_2$

Example 6

Add 011 and 010.

Solution

First, place the binary numbers one above the other, ensuring that the bits with the same weighting are in the same columns. This gives:

```
(MSB)(LSB)
  0 1 1
+ 0 1 0
```

Step 1: Starting from the rightmost column (LSB), add the digits: $1 + 0 = 1$. Write the 1 in the same column.

```
  0 1 1
+ 0 1 0
_____
      1
```

Step 2: Add the digits in the second column: $1 + 1 = 10$. Write the 0 in the same column and carry the 1 to the next column.

```
(carry) 1
      0 1 1
    + 0 1 0
    _____
        0 1
```

Step 3: Add the digits in the third column: 1 (the carried bit) $+ 0 + 0 = 1$

We now have:

```
  0 1 1
+ 0 1 0
_____
  1 0 1
```

Therefore $011_2 + 010_2 = 101_2$

Example 7

Add 1011 and 0011.

Solution

First, place the binary numbers one above the other, ensuring that the bits with the same weighting are in the same columns.

```
(MSB) (LSB)
  1 0 1 1
+ 0 0 1 1
```

Step 1: Add the digits in the rightmost (LSB) column: $1 + 1 = 10$. Write the 0 in the column and carry the 1 to the next column:

```
        1
  1 0 1 1
+ 0 0 1 1
_____
        0
```

Step 2: Add the digits in the second column, including the carry bit: $1 + 1 + 1 = 11$. Write the 1 in the column and carry 1 to the next column.

```
    1 1
  1 0 1 1
+ 0 0 1 1
_____
      1 0
```

Step 3: Add the digits in the third column, including the carry bit: $1 + 0 + 0 = 1$. Write the 1 in the column.

```
    1 1
  1 0 1 1
+ 0 0 1 1
_____
    1 1 0
```

Step 4: Add the digits in the fourth column: $1 + 0 = 1$. Write the 1 in the column.

```
    1 1
  1 0 1 1
+ 0 0 1 1
_____
  1 1 1 0
```

Therefore $1011_2 + 0011_2 = 1110_2$

Exercise 1

1 Give one example of each of the following:
   a continuous data   b discrete data.
2 Give an example of a bistable device other than a light bulb.
3 Why is the binary number system used to represent information in digital computers?
4 Convert the following binary numbers to decimal:
   a 11000   b 01010   c 11101
5 Convert the following decimal numbers to binary:
   a 31   b 26   c 17
6 Add the following binary numbers:
   a $01_2 + 11_2$ b $011_2 + 101_2$ c $1101_2 + 1011_2$

Representing signed integers

An integer is any whole number (positive or negative) that does not have a fractional part. So far, our discussion has focused on unsigned integers – integers we always assume to be positive. However, in practice, we need both positive and negative integers, collectively called signed integers. In the decimal system, the minus sign (–) is used to indicate that a value is negative and an optional plus sign (+) is used to indicate that a value is positive. In binary, there are many different ways of representing signed integers. In this chapter, we will look at four of the more common methods: sign and magnitude, one's complement, two's complement and binary coded decimal (BCD).

Sign and magnitude representation

In the decimal number system, we can represent a negative number by placing the minus (–) sign in front of the number, for example, –3, –245. However, this is not possible in binary as we can only have binary numbers. In sign and magnitude representation, the leftmost bit is used to represent the sign (positive or negative) and the remaining bits represent the magnitude. Usually, a 0 sign bit indicates that the number is positive and a 1 sign bit indicates that the number is negative.

The four-bit binary representation '0001' in sign and magnitude representation is equivalent to the decimal number 'positive one' (+1), whereas '1001' is equivalent to the decimal number 'negative one' (–1). Table 5.3 below shows the sign bit and the bits that make up the magnitude.

Sign bit	Magnitude	Decimal value
0	0 0 1	+1
1	0 0 1	–1

▲ Table 5.3 Sign and magnitude representation

Using four bits we can have 16 different combinations. Using the convention 0 sign bit for positive and 1 sign bit for negative, Table 5.4 shows the range of numbers that can be represented.

0000	0	1000	0
0001	+1	1001	–1
0010	+2	1010	–2
0011	+3	1011	–3
0100	+4	1100	–4
0101	+5	1101	–5
0110	+6	1110	–6
0111	+7	1111	–7

▲ Table 5.4 Range of numbers that can be represented

The range of numbers that can be represented using four bits is –7 to +7. From the table, we can see that when the 0 sign bit of any number is replaced by a 1 sign bit (except for the numbers representing 0), we get the negative of the number. Example 8 describes how a signed integer may be represented using a sign and magnitude representation.

Notice the answer consists of only six bits. To make it an eight-bit number, we need to add two zeroes to the left, which gives 00100011_2. Note that adding the two zeroes to the left does not change the value of the binary string.

$+35 = \mathbf{00}100011_2$

Sign bit magnitude

To get –35 we change the leftmost bit to 1.

$-35 = \mathbf{1}0100011_2$

Sign bit magnitude

From Table 5.4 on page 75, we can see that the two ways to represent the number 0 are 0000_2 and 1000_2. Because of this drawback and a few others, computer scientists have developed other methods, such as one's and two's complement, of representing numbers in the computer.

One's complement

In one's complement notation, positive numbers are represented as usual in unsigned binary. However, negative numbers are represented by simply flipping all the digits. This means replacing all the zeroes with ones and all the ones with zeroes. For example, positive three (+3) in this system is written as 0011_2. To get negative three (–3), we replace the zeroes with ones and the ones with zeroes so that it becomes 1100_2.

When converting a number to its one's complement, the number of bits must be stated. It is, therefore, wrong to say, for example, 'find the one's complement of 100_2'. You need to say, 'find the four-bit one's complement of 100_2'. Look at examples 9 and 10.

This numeric representation system is not used very much today. It was common in older mainframe computers; the PDP-1 and UNIVAC 1100/2200 among many others.

Example 8

Give the eight-bit representation of –35 using sign and magnitude representation.

Solution
First, find the binary representation of 35.

÷ 2	35	Remainder
÷ 2	17	1
÷ 2	8	1
÷ 2	4	0
÷ 2	2	0
÷ 2	1	0
÷ 2	0	1

This gives 100011_2.

Example 9

What is the seven-bit one's complement of 0110?

Solution
1 Add three zeroes in front of the leftmost bit (MSB). This gives 0000110.

2 Flip the bits. This gives 1111001.

The seven-bit one's complement of 0110 is therefore **1111001**.

Example 10

Using four bits, give the one's complement representation of –6.

Solution
1 Find the binary representation of 6, following the process in Example 3 on page 72. This gives 110_2, i.e. $(2^2 \times 1) + (2^1 \times 1) + (2^0 \times 0)$

2 Add zero in front of the leftmost bit (MSB) to make it a four-bit number. This gives 0110_2.

3 Flip the bits. This gives 1001_2.

The four-bit one's complement of –6 is therefore **1001_2**.

Two's complement

This is one of the most commonly used methods of representing signed (positive and negative) integers. The majority of modern computer systems use two's complement form to represent signed binary numbers. This is because there is only one representation of zero and addition and subtraction is made very simple. Using the two's complement system, the circuitry for addition and subtraction can be unified, otherwise they would have to be treated as separate operations.

To represent a number in two's complement notation, first find the one's complement of the number, then add 1 to the result. See Example 11.

Table 5.5 shows the two's complement representation of a four-bit binary number.

Notice, there is only one representation for zero: 0000. This is an improvement over one's complement because when performing arithmetic, you do not need to deal with the two representations of zero.

7	0111
6	0110
5	0101
4	0100
3	0011
2	0010
1	0001
0	0000
−1	1111
−2	1110
−3	1101
−4	1100
−5	1011
−6	1010
−7	1001
−8	1000

▲ Table 5.5 Four-bit two's complement representation

Note that we now have nine bits. Since we are working with eight bits, we discard the leftmost bit. This discarding action (performed by the computer) is a convention used in two's complement notation to maintain the original number of bits specified, in this case, eight. The answer is therefore 00000000, which is the same as what we started with. See Example 12. Then work through Example 13.

Example 11

Find the two's complement of the seven-bit binary number 0011011.

Solution
1 Find the one's complement.

Binary number: 0011011

One's complement: 1100100

2 Add one to the one's complement.

```
  1100100
+       1
  1100101
```

The two's complement of 0011011 is therefore **1100101**.

Example 12

Find the two's complement of the eight-bit binary number 00000000.

Solution
1 Find the one's complement.

Binary number: 00000000

One's complement: 11111111

2 Add one to the one's complement.

```
    11111111
+          1
   100000000
```

(Discard the extra bit)

The two's complement of 00000000 is therefore 00000000.

Example 13

Using six bits, find the two's complement representation of -27_{10}.

Solution
1 Find the binary equivalent of 27. This gives 11011_2.

2 Add a zero in front of the MSB to make it a six-bit number. This gives 011011_2.

3 Find the one's complement of 011011_2. This gives 100100_2.

4 Add 1_2 to 100100_2. This gives 100101_2.

−27 as a six-bit two's complement representation is therefore **100101_2**.

From Example 13, $-27 = 100101_2$. This is possible because in two's complement coding, the place value of all the bits is the same except the MSB, which represents a negative number. Table 5.6 shows the two's complement binary representation of -27.

$-(25)$	2^4	2^3	2^2	2^1	2^0	
-32	16	8	4	2	1	This row shows the value of each digit in that position: the 'place value'
1	0	0	1	0	1	Each digit in this row is multiplied by its place value, above.
-32	0	0	4	0	1	Summing the totals gives -27.

▲ Table 5.6 The two's complement representation of -27

Subtraction of binary numbers

Two's complement can also help us with the subtraction of binary numbers. Consider the following problem:

$1001_2 - 0110_2$

This could be written as $1001_2 + (-0110_2)$.

Instead of performing binary subtraction, it is actually easier to find the two's complement of 0110_2 (*not* -0110_2), and add it to 1001_2. First, we need to find the two's complement of 0110_2:

1 Find the one's complement. This gives 1001_2.
2 Add 1 to the one's complement. This gives 1010_2.
3 Now add 1001_2 and 1010_2:

```
   1001
 + 1010
  10011
```

(Discard the extra bit)

Since we are using only four bits, we discard the extra (leftmost) bit. The answer is **0011**. Now work through Example 14.
   Table 5.7 contains some examples of different binary representations of different decimal numbers:

Binary representation of the number			
Decimal number	One's complement representation	Two's complement representation	Sign and magnitude representation
1	00000001	00000001	00000001
-1	11111110	11111111	10000001
100	01100100	01100100	01100100
-100	10011011	10011100	11100100

▲ Table 5.7 Examples of different binary representations of different decimal numbers

Example 14

Find the value of $9_{10} - 6_{10}$ using four-bit two's complement binary.

Solution
This could be written as $9_{10} + (-6_{10})$.

1 Convert 9 to its binary equivalent. This gives 1001_2.

2 To find -6, we need to find the two's complement of 6. Convert 6 to its binary equivalent. This gives 0110_2.

3 Find the one's complement of 0110. This gives 1001_2.

4 Add 1 to get the two's complement. This gives 1010_2 which is equal to -6.

5 Add 1001_2 and 1010_2.

```
   1001
 + 1010
  10011₂
```

We discard the extra bit because we are using four-bit. The answer is therefore 0011_2.

Binary coded decimal (BCD) representation

BCD representation is very common in electronic devices such as pocket calculators and microwave ovens where a numeric value is to be displayed. In BCD representation, each digit of a number is represented as its four-bit binary code. For example, to store the decimal number 256 using BCD means finding the four-bit binary equivalent of 2, 5 and 6:

256 = 0010 0101 0110   So $256_{10} = 001001010110_2$
       2   5   6

This method can also be used to represent signed integers (+ and −). This system uses four bits to represent a number. We can, therefore, represent 16 different numbers (see page 70, where we saw how three bits can represent eight different numbers; logically, four bits allows 16). However, since we only need ten different codes to represent the digits 0 to 9, we can use any of the remaining six codes to represent positive (+) and negative (−). (+) is often shown as 1010 and negative (−) as 1011.

Therefore the BCD representation of −256 would be:

1011 0010 0101 0110
 −   2   5   6

Example 15

What is the BCD representation of −325?

Solution

1 Find the four-bit representation of each digit.

2 0011 0010 0101
    3   2   5

3 Place the BCD code for negative (1011) to the left of all the other bits.

1011 0011 0010 0101
 −   3   2   5

The BCD representation is therefore **1011 0011 0010 0101**.

Data representation

Various codes have been developed to represent data in the computer and to enable it to be easily transmitted between systems. Data that is represented in computers is made up of characters. Characters include:

- number characters (0 to 9)
- alphabetic characters (lowercase letters and uppercase letters)
- special characters (punctuation marks, $, /, and so on)
- control characters (backspace, delete, insert, and so on).

All the characters that a computer can store and process are called the character set of that computer. Different types of computers may have slightly different character sets, depending on the operating system. Each character is represented by a code consisting of either seven or eight bits, called the character code.

Two of the most common codes used are Extended Binary Coded Decimal Interchange Code (EBCDIC pronounced 'Eb-see-dic') and the American Standard Code for Information Interchange (ASCII pronounced 'As-key'). EBCDIC uses eight bits to represent each character and is able to represent 256 different characters. ASCII uses seven bits to represent each character plus an extra bit called a parity bit, which is added to help to ensure data integrity. We saw how the parity bit worked in Chapter 2.

The standard ASCII code defines 128 character codes (from 0 to 127) of which the first 32 are deliberately defined as control codes. A control code is a non-printable code that is used to tell the computer to carry out a command such as 'start a new line' (the LNFEED character in Table 5.8). This is done by assigning one of the control codes to a command.

Whenever the computer encounters the code, it carries out the command. Control codes give programmers the opportunity to assign commands to actions that they may want to personalise in a particular computer. In many cases, there are many unused control codes.

The remaining 96 character codes are representable (printable) characters (Table 5.8). ASCII code is mostly used in mini and PC computers, whereas EBCDIC is mainly used on large IBM computing systems.

From Table 5.8, we can see that the codes increase by adding 1_2 bit to the previous code. For example, the code for the letter A is 1000001_2. To get the code for the letter B we add 1 to 1000001_2, which gives 1000010_2. This pattern is repeated for the entire character set. From this pattern, we can determine the codes of other characters if we are given the code of any character in the set. Work through Example 16.

Char	7-bit ASCII	Char	7-bit ASCII	Char	7-bit ASCII
A	1000001	a	1100001	0	0110000
B	1000010	b	1100010	1	0110001
C	1000011	c	1100011	2	0110010
D	1000100	d	1100100	3	0110011
E	1000101	e	1100101	4	0110100
F	1000110	f	1100110	5	0110101
G	1000111	g	1100111	6	0110110
H	1001000	h	1101000	7	0110111
I	1001001	i	1101001	8	0111000
J	1001010	j	1101010	9	0111001
K	1001011	k	1101011	blank	0100000
L	1001100	l	1101100	.	0101110
M	1001101	m	1101101	(	0101000
N	1001110	n	1101110	+	0101011
O	1001111	o	1101111	$	0100100
P	1010000	p	1110000	*	0101010
Q	1010001	q	1110001	)	0101001
R	1010010	r	1110010	–	0101101
S	1010011	s	1110011	/	0101111
T	1010100	t	1110100	,	0101100
U	1010101	u	1110101	=	0111101
V	1010110	v	1110110	RETURN	0001101
W	1010111	w	1110111	LNFEED	0001010
X	1011000	x	1111000	0	0110000
Y	1011001	y	1111001	0	0110000
Z	1011010	z	1111010	0	0110000

▲ Table 5.8 Characters and their ASCII codes

Example 16

The ASCII code for the letter A is 1000001. Determine the seven-bit ASCII code for the letter G.

Solution

Let us look at two methods to solve this problem.

Method 1

Since G is near the start of the alphabet, we can add 1 to the codes of the consecutive letters until we reach G.

The code for A is 100001; to get B we add 1 to the code of A, this gives 1000010; to get C we add 1 to the code for B, this gives 1000011: and so on. If we continue adding, we will find that G is therefore **1000111**.

A 1000001   D 1000100   G 1000111

B 1000010   E 1000101

C 1000011   F 1000110

Method 2

Here is another method that may be more efficient.

1 Convert the binary code for A (1000001) to its decimal equivalent.

   1000001 = 65

2 Find the decimal equivalent of the letter G. We know that A is represented by 65, B will be 66, C will be 67 and G will, therefore, be 71. Convert 71 to its binary equivalent.

   71 = 1000111

3 The ASCII code for G is therefore **1000111**.

Chapter 5: Summary

- Data can be classified into two types: discrete and continuous. Discrete data is data that can be counted, whereas continuous data is data that can be measured and recorded at many different points.
- A decimal (base 10) number can be converted to binary by dividing the decimal number by 2 and recording the remainder until the quotient is zero and then writing out the remainders starting from the last remainder to the first.
- A binary number can be converted to decimal by multiplying each digit by its place value starting from the least significant bit (LSB) on the right to the most significant bit (MSB) and summing the results. The place value is a factor of 2 starting from 2^0 for the LSB and increasing by a factor of 2 for each consecutive bit.
- Binary addition follows these rules: $0_2+0_2 = 0_2$, $0_2+1_2 = 1_2$, $1_2+0_2 = 1_2$, $1_2+1_2 = 10_2$ and $1_2+1_2+1_2 = 11_2$
- There are four main ways of representing negation inside the computer: sign and magnitude, one's complement, two's complement and binary coded decimal (BCD). In sign and magnitude, one's complement and two's complement, positive integers (whole numbers) are represented in the same way as unsigned binary numbers.

- In a sign and magnitude representation, the leftmost bit (MSB) is used to indicate the sign (+ or −) of a binary number. Usually '1' represents negative (−) and '0' represents positive (+). The remaining bits give the magnitude of the number.
- Finding the one's complement of a number involves flipping the bits. This means changing the 1s to 0s and the 0s to 1s.
- Two's complement is found by adding 1 to the one's complement of the number.
- The BCD system converts each digit of a decimal number into its four-bit binary code. Negative (−) is represented by 1011 and positive (+) is represented by 1010.
- The character set of a computer consists of all the characters that a computer can store and process.
- Characters (numbers, alphabetic characters, special characters and control characters) are represented by a code called the character code.
- Two of the most common codes used to represent characters are the seven-bit American Standard Code for Information Interchange (ASCII) and the eight-bit Extended Binary Coded Decimal Interchange Code (EBCDIC).

Chapter 5: Questions

Fill in the blanks

1 _____ is data that can be counted.

2 _____ is data that can be measured and recorded at many different points.

3 A bit is short for _____.

4 A single bit can represent one of _____ values.

5 All the characters that a computer can store and process are called the _____ of that computer.

6 ASCII uses seven bits to represent each character plus an extra bit called a _____ bit.

7 The standard ASCII code defines _____ character codes.

8 A _____ code is a non-printable code that is used to tell the computer to carry out a command.

9 Characters are represented by a code called the _____ code.

10 Two of the most common codes used to represent characters are the seven-bit ASCII code and the eight-bit _____.

True or False?

1 A bistable device is one that can be set to two or more states.

2 Each digit in the decimal number system has a value that depends on its position or place in the number.

3 In sign and magnitude representation, 4 bits can represent the range −7 to + 7 numbers.

4 In one's complement, negative numbers are represented by simply flipping all the digits.

5 A parity bit is an extra bit that is added to a byte to help to ensure data integrity.

Multiple-choice questions

1 A bistable device can be set to:
   a 1 state.   b 2 states.
   c 3 states.   d an infinite number of states.

2 A parity bit is added to a byte to:
  a make up 8 bits.
  b ensure data integrity.
  c assist with calculations.
  d represent none of the above.

3 In a sign and magnitude representation, 4 bits can represent:
  a the range –4 to +4.   b the range –3 to +3.
  c the range –7 to +7.   d none of the above.

4 Two's complement is one of the most commonly used methods of representing:
  a signed (positive and negative) integers.
  b unsigned integers.
  c positive numbers only.
  d negative numbers only.

5 Which letter is represented by the ASCII code 100 0101?
  a A   b B   c F   d E

Short-answer questions
1 a Explain the difference between the two types of data. Give examples of each type.

2 Convert the following decimal numbers to binary:
  a 7_{10} b 15_{10} c 25_{10}
  d 71_{10} e 205_{10}

3 Convert the following binary numbers to decimal:
  a 0011_2 b 00110001_2
  c 10111001_2 d 10110111_2
  e 11111111_2

4 Add the following binary numbers. Give the answer in binary form.
  a $101_2 + 110_2$ b $011_2 + 100_2$
  c $01011_2 + 110_2$ d $011011_2 + 01011_2$
  e $110101_2 + 01101_2$

5 a Convert the decimal number 45_{10} to binary.
   b What is the one's complement representation of -45_{10}?
   c What is the two's complement representation of -45_{10}?
   d What is the BDC representation of $_c -45_{10}$?
   e What is the sign and magnitude representation of -45_{10}?

6 The following 8-bit pattern represents the two's complement of an integer:111001101. What is the decimal equivalent?

7 Subtract the binary number 0011011 from 11110010.

8 Explain the term 'parity bit'.

9 Which range of integers can be represented using two's complement with:
  a 4 bits?   b 6 bits?   c 8 bits?

10 What is the decimal equivalent of the following BCD representations? The first four bits represent the sign (1011 for negative and 1010 for positive).
  a 1011 1001 1000 0111
  b 1010 0010 0101 0111
  c 1010 0101 0111 0011 1001

11 Give the ASCII representation of the following statement: 'Meet me at 6'.

12 The ASCII code for the letter 'F' is 01000110. What is the ASCII code for the letter 'K'?

13 Using an example, explain a 'bistable device'.

14 Determine the BCD representation of 65_{10}.

Research question
Conduct research on the internet to explain how fractions and decimals are represented in a computer.

Crossword

Across
4 Data that can be measured and can be recorded at many different points (10)

5 A binary representation that is very common in electronic devices such as pocket calculators and microwave ovens where a numeric value is to be displayed (3)

6 Data that can be counted (8)

Down
1 A number system which consists of two digits 0 and 1 (6)

2 A device that can be set to one or two states at any point in time (8)

3 Can represent one or two values, 0 and 1 (3)

Software: The power behind the machine

Application software

Application software is the term for programs developed to carry out specific tasks or solve particular problems. For example, if you want to type a letter, you would need to use a word processor. To create a highly decorated birthday card would require some type of graphics package. Word processors and graphics packages are examples of application software.

There are many different types of application software available for sale. Each is designed for a particular type of activity. Selecting the right application software to perform a task makes it easier to accomplish the task and will greatly improve the final outcome. When you purchase a new computer, it is usually sold with systems software and some application software. However, depending on your needs, you may have to purchase additional application software. Application software includes entertainment software such as games, home or personal software such as encyclopaedias, productivity software such as word-processing and spreadsheet packages, and specialist software such as desktop publishing and graphics packages. Application software can also be categorised as follows: general-purpose software, integrated software, specialised software, customised software and custom-written (tailor-made) software packages.

General-purpose software

General-purpose software is not written for any specific business or organisation, but can be used or adapted to suit their specific needs. For example, a teacher can use a spreadsheet package to prepare students' end-of-term grades reports, and a word-processing package to write letters to the parents. These same packages could also be used in a business to perform different tasks, such as accounting or memo-writing. General-purpose software packages, also called off-the-shelf software, are usually well tested and relatively cheap.

Integrated software

An integrated software package is a set of related programs combined in a single package that allows data to be transferred easily between the programs and has a similar look across the programs. Examples include Microsoft Office, Adobe® Creative Suite® and the iWork® package used by Apple® Macintosh®.

A basic integrated package may contain word processor, spreadsheet, database, communications and graphics presentation programs. A major advantage of these packages is the ease with which data can be transferred from one component to another.

For example, if you are working on a word-processing document you can quickly incorporate a graph created in the package's spreadsheet component via a simple cut/copy-and-paste operation or by using the object linking and embedding (OLE) option.

OLE allows the transfer and sharing of information between applications. With embedded or linked objects, a document can contain information that was created in different applications. For example, a Microsoft Word document may contain a chart or table from Excel. This information can be edited from inside the Word document that contains the object.

If an object (chart, table, and so on) is linked, the object in the Word file is updated every time the Excel file is updated. However, when you embed an Excel object, information in the Word file doesn't change if you modify the source Excel file. Embedded objects become part of the Word file and, after they are inserted, they are no longer part of the source file.

Some additional advantages of integrated software include the following:

- It takes up less disk space than individual applications.
- You can move much faster from one application to the next.
- It is usually easier to learn, as the user interface for choosing commands is the same.
- It tends to be more powerful and versatile than individual applications.
- It is less likely to crash and contains fewer errors, since it has been widely tried and tested.
- The producers' after-sales service is often good (for example, online help facilities); users can also get support from user groups and magazines.
- It is usually cheaper than purchasing the packages individually.

Some disadvantages of integrated software include the following:

- Not all the features of single applications are included.
- Some integrated packages do not contain all the applications that may be required to complete a task.

Specialised software

Specialised software is software that is written for a specific task rather than for a broad application area. These programs provide facilities specifically for the purpose for which they were designed. For example, a payroll program will usually only be able to deal with all aspects of a company's payroll, that is, for one very specific purpose. Other examples of specialised software are expert systems (software that operates like an expert in a particular field, for example, medical expert systems), accounting programs such as Sage 300 and QuickBooks, and theatre or airline booking systems.

▲ Figure 6.1 Various types of software

Customised software

Software can be customised to better meet the needs of an individual or organisation. For example, macros or plugins can be added to general-purpose software to add increased functionality to the software. Macros are short programs written to automate several steps in software such as databases, spreadsheets and word processors. Plugins are blocks of code that add features to the overall package. The core code of the program allows for these macros or plugins to be added. Macros and plugins can be written by experienced end-users of the program or programmers.

Another method of customising software is to integrate several pieces of proprietary and/or open source software to fit the requirements of the user or organisation. For example, many universities and learning institutions use the CANVAS learning management system to provide digital tools and learning resources for teachers to use in one location. To better suit the needs of the university, an experienced user or in-house programmer can use an application program interface (API) to integrate software such as Office 365, Google Drive™, student information system (SIS) and other features into the base program.

Custom-written (tailor-made) software

This is software that is written to meet the specific needs of a company. Every company is unique and may have unique needs, which is why a solution tailored to achieve a company's goals, based on their specialised requirements, offers many advantages when compared with general-purpose pre-packaged applications. Custom-written software may be written by programmers within the company, or it may be contracted out to a software house (a company that specialises in writing software). This may be necessary because there are no commercial applications or 'off-the-shelf' packages available.

The main advantage of custom-written software is that the solutions it offers give the greatest depth, breadth and flexibility possible in meeting the needs of the organisation, since the software product is tailored to the organisation's specifications. Also, the software developer delivers and installs the software and trains the end-users in the use of the new product.

Some additional advantages of custom-written software include the following points.

- It performs tasks that general-purpose software cannot perform.
- The software can be quickly changed when the needs of the business change, since the source code belongs to the company.

Some disadvantages include the following points.

- **Cost**: The costs of developing the software, on-site installation, support and training are often high.
- **Lengthy development time**: It takes time to acquire the information that is needed and then write the code for the new software.
- **Increased probability of undetected errors**: The probability of undetected errors decreases not only with the length of time a product is in service but also with the number and variety of users. Hence there are likely to be fewer errors in a long-established general-purpose package (possibly used all over the world) than in a custom-written package.

Exercise 1

1. a Define the term 'software'.
   b Define the term 'application software'. Give THREE examples of application software.
   c Explain the terms 'general-purpose software', 'integrated software', 'specialised software' and 'customised software'.
2. a Explain the term 'custom-written software'.
   b List the advantages and disadvantages of custom-written software.
3. Explain the difference between application software and system software.

System software

System software acts as a buffer between the application software and hardware. It manages and supports the resources and operations of a computer system by, for example, providing a common way for application software to store things on a disk. It enables the running of application software, provides user interfaces and the management of the system resources. Five major categories of system software are the operating system, utility programs, device drivers, firmware and language translators. Figure 6.2 shows a conceptual arrangement of hardware, system software, application software and the user.

Operating system

An operating system (OS) is a set of programs that governs the operation of a computer. The OS manages all software and peripheral hardware and accesses the central processing unit (CPU) for memory or storage purposes. It also makes it possible for a system to simultaneously run applications. Without operating system software, the computer cannot function. All PCs, laptops, tablets, smartphones, and servers require an OS. Software developers may use specific operating systems that are better suited to programming and application development, like Linux, as it is highly customisable. The average user will likely use a system like Microsoft Windows for more common everyday usage. The most common operating systems are Microsoft's Windows, Apple's®macOS®, Linux distributions such as Ubuntu or Red Hat, and mobile operating systems for smartphones such as Android and iOS. In some hand-held computers such as smartphones and tablets, the operating system is embedded in a ROM chip that can be rewritten when the system is updated. However, for most PCs and larger computers, the operating system is switched on as soon as you turn on, or 'boot', the computer.

The term booting refers to the process of loading operating system software into a computer's main memory from disk. The instructions to load the operating system are held in the BIOS, also known as the Basic Input Output System. The BIOS is a firmware or set of instructions that resides in a ROM chip on the motherboard. It contains the bootstrap – the program that takes the computer through steps that lead up to the loading of the operating system (OS). The operating system remains in main memory until you turn off the computer.

Types of operating systems

Some older operating systems that were used in PC computers include Windows 98, Windows ME (Millennium Edition), Windows 2000, Windows XP, Windows NT, Apple® operating systems (for example, OS9 and OS X®), OS/2, Linux and Unix. There are Unix operating systems for PCs and mainframe computers.

> **Did you know?**
>
> The Linux operating system was initially developed by a young University of Helsinki student by the name of Linus Torvalds. Linux was released with a General Public Licence and is an example of 'open source' software. This means that anyone can copy, distribute and modify the software's code, thereby building on the source code written by Mr Torvalds. This source code is often used by other individuals to develop new, free programs. These individuals often share the same philosophy of cooperation and openness as the code's original inventor.

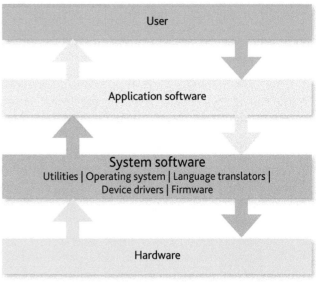

▲ Figure 6.2 Conceptual arrangement of hardware, system software, application software and the user

Functions of the operating system

The functions of an operating system depend on the size and complexity of the computer system. It may also depend on whether the system is a single-user system such as a PC or a multi-access system such as a mainframe or network. A multi-access (multi-user) system is one that allows a number of users with online terminals/PCs to interact with the same computer at the same time. An online system is one where the terminals/PCs and the computer are linked interactively. Although the operating systems of mainframes and networks are much more complex and perform a wider range of functions than those of PCs, the functions of most operating systems can be grouped under the headings discussed below.

Managing computer resources

Managing all the resources of the computer system is a large part of the operating system's function. The operating system allows the user's application software such as word-processing, spreadsheet and database packages to communicate with the computer's hardware. For example, if you are working in a document in Excel and you want to print the document, you simply access the 'Print' command or press the 'Print' button on the standard toolbar. Excel directs the operating system to select a printer (if there is more than one) to print the document. The operating system then notifies the computer to begin sending data and instructions to the appropriate program to get the document printed. Figure 6.3 shows how the operating system acts as an interface between application programs and the hardware.

The operating system also manages the use of input and output devices. This is accomplished by the use of buffers. A buffer is an area of memory that temporarily holds data being transferred to be processed or output. Input buffers take data from a device (for example, a keyboard) and hold the data, releasing it to the CPU at a rate the CPU can cope with. This function is especially important when a number of processes are running and taking up processor time. The operating system will instruct a buffer to continue taking input from the device, but to stop sending data to the CPU while the process using the input is suspended. Then, when the process that needs input is made active once again, the operating system will command the buffer to send data.

The operating system functions in much the same way with output buffers. An output buffer is used to store data waiting to be printed. For example, a program that has to use the printer will transfer whatever needs to be printed to the print buffer and continue processing. In this way, the CPU does not have to be idle while the printer, which operates at a much slower speed, prints the document. The operating system also provides error messages to indicate devices that may not be working properly or not functioning at all.

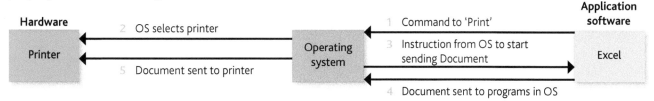

▲ Figure 6.3 The operating system is at the centre of operations, interfacing between software and hardware.

Managing files and memory

The operating system manages all the files on a computer. It keeps track of the locations where programs and data are stored in the computer's memory. For example, when you open a file that has been saved to your hard drive, you are first instructing the computer to find that file, and then open it. The operating system also allows you to easily find files stored in other secondary storage devices. Other file management functions include copying, erasing, renaming and backing-up files. In the case of mainframe computers, the operating system has to share storage between the many programs that may be running at the same time.

Maintaining security

In networks and larger computers, each user is given a username or ID and password to gain access to the computer system. The operating system keeps a register of all these names so that only persons with valid usernames or IDs and passwords can access the system. This prevents access by hackers and unauthorised persons. The operating system also keeps a log of which users logged in, the length of time each user stayed on the system and what they did. Administrators can check the log for breaches and abuse of resources.

Managing tasks

Early computers ran one process at a time. However, because of the fast speed of the CPU and the much slower speeds of input/output devices, the CPU remained idle much of the time. This problem was further compounded with the development of multi-core processors. To reduce the idle time of the CPU and to ensure that each job is executed the following methods are used: multitasking, multiprogramming and multiprocessing.

- **Multitasking** is the ability of the computer to appear to run more than one program at the same time, although at a specific instant in time the CPU is dealing with only one instruction for one of the active programs. The operating system manages which instruction to send to the CPU. For example, many students like to listen to music on their computer while at the same time typing a document or playing a computer game. These tasks appear to be happening simultaneously. As computers are so fast, the operating system can switch the program executed in the CPU so quickly that the user cannot tell that, in reality, the music-playing and typing functions are performed at individual moments in time. In actuality, the CPU processes one instruction at a time but can execute instructions from any active process.
- **Multiprogramming** refers to the computer's ability to run two or more programs at the same time using a single processor.
- **Multiprocessing** refers to a computer system's ability to support more than one process (program) at the same time using multiple processors. This generally increases processing times.

Processing modes

Processing modes describe the ways in which the operating system handles data during data processing. These modes include the following.

- **Real-time processing:** Operating systems that perform real-time processing are designed to respond to an event within a predetermined time. As soon as the data is input, it is processed and output immediately. In some applications, the output is used to influence the input. Completing the operation within a predetermined time is a critical element of any real-time processing system. These types of operating systems are found in environments where computers are responsible for controlling systems continuously; for example, robotics, manufacturing, interactive games, and airline and theatre booking systems. In all these applications, the computer is often a dedicated computer and runs the same program all the time.
- **Batch processing:** In batch processing systems, all data is collected together before being processed in a single operation. Typically, the processing of payrolls, electricity bills, invoices and daily transactions are dealt with in this way. This method of operation lends itself to jobs with similar inputs, processing and outputs where no human intervention is needed. Jobs are stored in a queue until the computer is ready to deal with them. Batch-processed jobs are often done overnight.
- **Multi-user (time-sharing) processing:** Multi-user systems allow several users to have access to computing resources at the same time. Computer game servers use multi-user systems for online gaming. The CPU deals with each user in turn. The CPU allocates a period of time to each user, called time sharing. The processor is so fast that the response time at the most is a fraction of a second and the users feel they are being dealt with immediately.
- **Online processing:** Online processing, also known as transaction processing or pseudo-real-time processing, processes data as soon as it is available. The processing is interactive, which means that processing takes place as a 'conversation' between the user and the computer: the computer responds to the user's input by outputting some data before the user can input any more data.

In all applications, the master file needs to be kept up to date at all times. For example, whenever a travel agent books a seat on a flight, the number of seats that remain available on the flight must be reduced by one immediately. If this update is not done immediately (as might happen in a batch-processing system), then the flight could become overbooked with the same seat being booked more than once. The updating of records must be done quickly (in not more than two minutes). Online systems can also be found in a number of industries, including electronic banking, mail-order processing, stock control in supermarkets and manufacturing.

Providing a user interface

Many operating system functions are never apparent on the computer's display screen. What you do see, however, is the user interface. The user interface is the user-controllable part of the operating system that allows you to communicate, or interact, with it. User interfaces are discussed in more detail later in this chapter.

Utility programs

Utility programs are system software programs that provide useful services, such as performing common tasks and 'housekeeping' routines. Some are included with the operating system (for example, disk repairing programs) whereas others are purchased separately by the user (for example, Glary Utilities Pro 5). Some of the functions performed by utility programs include those listed under the following four headings.

Backup

The 'Backup' utility allows you to make a duplicate copy of every file on your hard disk, which can be stored on an external hard drive or on cloud storage (storage accessible on the internet, for example, Google Drive™, Dropbox, and so on). Figure 6.5 shows the 'Backup' utility option in Windows 10.

▲ Figure 6.4 Backup tapes

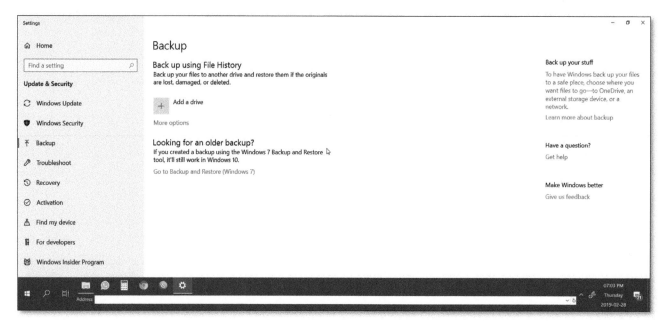

▲ Figure 6.5 Windows 10 Backup window

Disk repair

A disk repair utility scans a hard disk for bad sectors (defective areas) and either makes repairs to these sectors or marks the defective area so that the operating system will not store any data in that location. Figure 6.6 shows the Windows 10 disk repair utility option.

Virus protection

Antivirus software programs are also utility programs. These are covered in Chapter 10.

▲ Figure 6.6 Windows disk repair utility option

File defragmentation

When files are stored in a new computer or hard disk, they are stored next to one another (contiguously). After using your computer for a while, you will probably have deleted old files and added new ones. The computer fills free gaps with new files, including parts of files. After a while, the constituent parts of a typical file are scattered all over your hard disk – they are fragmented. This can really slow down your computer, as the operating system must first find all the parts of a file before they can be put back together and loaded. A defragmenter utility finds these fragmented files and organises them back in a continuous manner – called file defragmentation. Figure 6.7 shows the Windows 10 Defragmenter utility option.

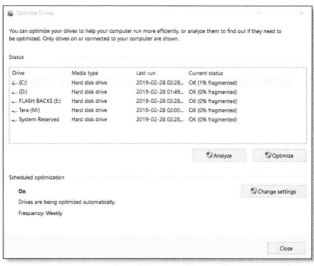

▲ Figure 6.7 Windows 10 Defragmenter utility option

Device drivers

A device driver is a software application that enables a computer to interact with the hardware devices attached to it. A device driver acts as a translator between the hardware device and the programs or operating systems that use it. There are device drivers for printers, displays, cameras, CD-ROM readers, and so on. When you buy an operating system, many device drivers are built into the product. Without the required device driver, the corresponding hardware device will not work. The most updated device drivers can be accessed online from the manufacturer's website. Specialised devices, such as Braille readers or barcode readers, often come supplied with a device driver.

Firmware

Firmware is programming that is added to a computer's non-volatile memory (ROM) at the time of manufacturing, such as the BIOS stored in ROM, as mentioned on pages 39 and 86. It is used to run user programs on the device and can be thought of as the software that allows hardware to run. Hardware makers use embedded firmware to control the functions of various hardware devices and systems, much like a computer's operating system (OS) controls the function of software applications. Firmware may be written into Read Only Memory (ROM), Erasable Programmable Read Only Memory (EPROM), or flash memory. Firmware can be thought of as 'semi-permanent' since it remains the same unless it is updated by a firmware updater. Firmware that is embedded in flash memory chips can be updated more easily than firmware written to ROM or EPROM, which makes it more adaptable.

Language translators

Language translators (assemblers, compilers and interpreters) are programs that translate programs written in a particular programming language into another programming language without losing the functional or logical structure of the original code. In most cases, the program is translated into machine language (the language the computer can understand).

User interfaces

There are four types of user interfaces, both for operating systems and application software: command-driven, menu-driven, graphical and touch.

Command-driven interface

The command-driven interface was an earlier interface used in computing, where you had to type in the command at the prompt on the display screen. For many years, PCs only used the MS-DOS operating system or Linux and Unix with a command line interface. Modern PCs using Windows, macOS® or Linux also have a command line or terminal interface to allow you to type in commands. This interface has been kept in operating systems as, for an experienced user particularly, it can be a fast and efficient way to do some things. However, for a beginner, this interface is complicated, as you have to learn the commands and the options that go with them. An example in the Windows command prompt would be at the C:\> prompt, where C:\ generally refers to the hard disk, you can type the following command:

C:\>delete *.*

This command tells the operating system to erase all the files on the hard disk. Figure 6.8 shows an example of a command-driven interface.

▲ Figure 6.8 A computer screen in MS-DOS mode

Menu-driven interface

A menu-driven interface differs greatly from a command-line interface. It lists menu choices that a user can select to navigate from one place to another within a website or software program. A menu-driven interface does not require a user to memorise commands, which makes navigation easier for the user. As such, users require little training when using menu-driven interfaces. A disadvantage of a menu-driven interface is that it can be difficult for a user to find a command if he or she does not know where the command is located in the menu. This is particularly true for more complex systems that include multiple menus. Additionally, menu-driven interfaces are less flexible and the users can only execute actions that are listed. Cashpoint machines (ATMs) contain a menu-driven interface. Other applications that use a menu-driven interface are gaming consoles, websites, apps, word processors and other office software. Figure 6.9 shows the Windows 10 Disk Management menu-driven interface.

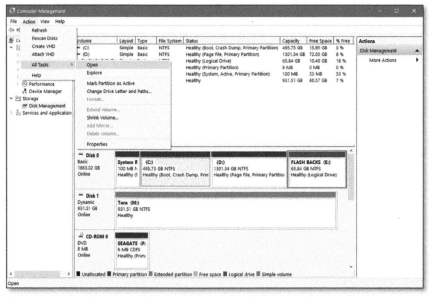

▲ Figure 6.9 Windows 10 Disk Management menu-driven interface

Graphical user interface

The graphical user interface (GUI) (pronounced as 'goo-ee'), also called WIMP (windows, icons, menus and pointing devices), is the easiest interface to use when interacting with the computer. It allows you to use graphics (images), menus and keystrokes, to choose commands, start programs, see lists of files and other options. Some of these images take the form of icons. Icons are small pictorial figures that represent programs, folders, files, tasks, procedures, and so on.

Another feature of the GUI is the use of windows. A window is a rectangular-boxed area on a computer screen. (This is not to be confused with Windows, for example, Windows 7 or Windows 10 with a capital W, which is the Microsoft operating system.) The screen can show different windows at the same time, within which individual application programs may be running. Each window may show a different program, such as a word-processing document in one window and a spreadsheet in another window, or two windows may show two different documents being run by the same program. A window can also show other things, such as a directory of files on your hard drive. The windows appears over a common visual background known as the desktop. Figure 6.10 shows a Windows 10 graphical user interface desktop, without any windows open.

We will look at the Windows desktop as an example of a GUI later in this chapter.

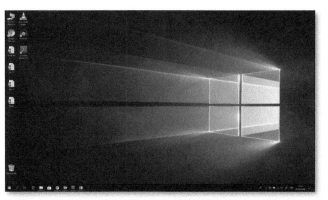

▲ Figure 6.10 A Windows 10 graphical user interface desktop

Touch user interface

Touchscreen devices are found just about everywhere you look, from smartphones, retail stores and restaurants to cars, residential homes and commercial workplaces. They allow users to control a device or machine through a touch-based user interface. A touch user interface (TUI) is a computer-pointing technology based on the sense of touch. It is a graphical user interface using a touchpad or touchscreen display as a combined input and output device (Figure 6.11). A TUI provides a reduction in time to get where the user wants to go in the digital world. Often it takes the form of a simplified version of a GUI, perhaps with larger finger-sized buttons.

Actions may also be simplified to reduce the amount of text you need to enter, so, for example, a user can touch a printed advertisement and connect directly to the online experience provided by the advertiser. This can include initiating a voice-over internet protocol (VoIP), instant messaging (IM), or electronic mail (email) by simply touching the page. Furthermore, electronic commerce (e-commerce) transactions can be initiated and completed with the TUI.

The advantage of a TUI is that it does not need a keyboard, you simply touch the screen. This means that it is ideal for smaller devices such as smartphones and tablets. It also means that for applications like a point of sale terminal, you reduce the number of steps that a user has to choose from (because you only give them buttons to do what you want them to), which makes it simpler to use. In addition, for users with visual impairments, these simplified interfaces can be adapted to work with tactile or Braille input.

▲ Figure 6.11 Touch user interface (TUI)

The Windows desktop

The Windows desktop is one of the most common ways for people to interact with a computer. It is almost certain to be the starting place for your use of computers. In this section, we will look at how you use it, and examine some of the advantages and disadvantages. Some of the tasks and functions that you will perform using the Windows desktop include the following:

- interacting with the CPU and the hard drive
- opening software programs
- managing files, folders and directories
- creating documents
- printing photos
- listening to music.

The Windows 10 Desktop

After booting up a modern PC running Windows 10, the desktop appears as shown in Figure 6.12. You can think of the Windows desktop as being like the traditional office desk. Just as you can move things around on a real desk, putting away items in drawers, and adding and removing objects, you can do the same on your Windows desktop. The Windows desktop contains a number of shortcuts that allows you to access various processes available in the Windows operating system. Some of the default icons contained on the Windows 10 desktop are described below.

- The **Start Menu** lets you launch applications, shut down your computer, access system settings, and much more.
- The **Search Box** allows you to search your computer and the internet at a point, right from the taskbar.
- The **Task View/Timeline** allows you to manage your virtual desktops and move application windows between them.
- **Pinned apps** show the applications that you use commonly and that can be pinned to your taskbar. By default, Windows pins a few for you.
- The **Task Tray** shows any application that is open and that has not been pinned to the taskbar.
- The **Notification Tray** shows icons of applications that are running in the background and provides access to the internet and sound settings.
- The **Clock** displays the current time and date.
- The **Action Centre** is Windows' main notification system. Any slide-out notification that you receive will be stored in this panel until you clear them. The Action Centre also provides quick access to system features such as Wi-Fi, Bluetooth, and so on.
- The **Desktop icons** are the application icons that the desktop holds. You can add your own icons.
- The **Desktop** holds your desktop icons and has a customisable background image.

File Explorer

File Explorer is the utility used for file management functions in the Windows 10 operating systems. It can be used to move, copy, rename, duplicate and delete files, and to browse through the directory.

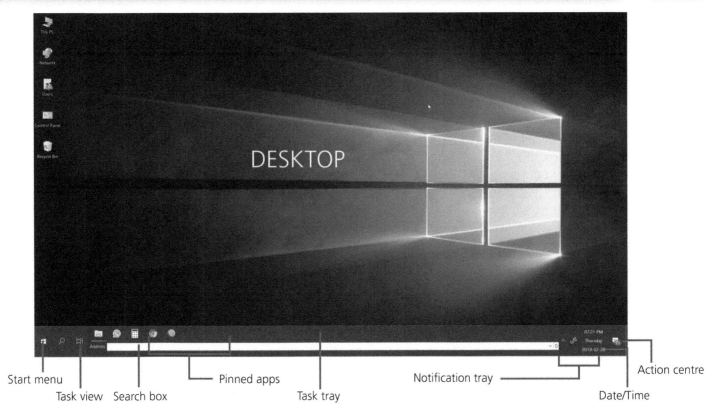

Start menu

Task view   Search box   Pinned apps   Task tray   Notification tray   Date/Time   Action centre

▲ Figure 6.12 Components of Windows 10 desktop

Quick Access toolbar

Here you can save (pin) your most frequently-accessed commands. Quick Access also automatically pins your most frequently accessed folders.

Directories or folders

At first, a new disk will not have any folders on it: there is just the disk itself with a single base position called the root drive of the disk. The root drive will be C:\ for the hard disk, D:\ for CD-ROM, CD-RW, E:\ for an external hard drive and F:\ for a flash

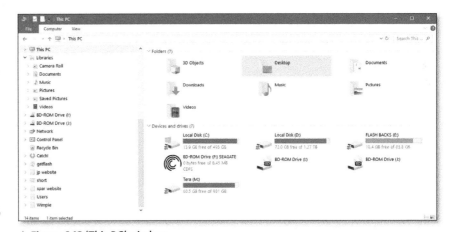

▲ Figure 6.13 'This PC' window

drive, and so on. It is possible to store your documents, programs, music files, and so on, directly on one of these devices, with no arrangement into sections for the different types of files you are adding. However, after a period of time continuously adding files, it will become very difficult to find specific files stored on the disk. You would need to look through all the individual files, in a long list, to find the one you want. A logical system for storing documents would enable you to quickly locate and retrieve the documents when you need them.

One way of keeping all files of a certain type together, so they can be easily viewed and accessed, is to store them in a directory or folder.

Directories or folders are used to hold documents, programs, files and even further sub-directories and folders. There is no limit to the sub-levels you could add. Directories allow you to group files that are in some way related, placing them in one location. For example, on your computer, you may have assignment documents for the different subjects you are doing in school. These might be stored in drive C (referred to as 'This PC' in Windows 10), in the 'Documents' folder. You may have English documents, Social Studies documents, and so on. Each type of

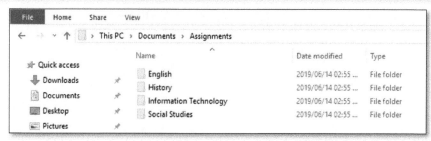

▲ Figure 6.14 Several folders stored in one folder

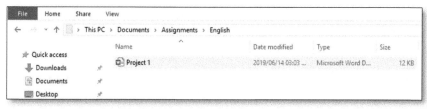

▲ Figure 6.15 Hierarchical structure for storing files

document can be stored in an individual folder corresponding to a particular subject (Figure 6.14). For even easier reference, all the folders for the different subjects could be placed in the one folder called 'Assignments'. The name chosen by the user – 'Assignments' – is an 'umbrella' term for all the subfolders in that folder.

An English assignment document (such as 'Project 1') will, therefore, be stored in drive C (This PC) in the 'Documents' folder, in the 'Assignments' folder and in the 'English' folder. This can be written as 'This PC:\Documents\Assignments \English\Project1.doc' (Figure 6.15). This hierarchical structure for storing files makes retrieval of files very easy – you simply click through the hierarchy of folders to find the file you want.

Creating a folder

To create a folder on the desktop in Windows 10:

1 Right-click on any clear area on the desktop.
2 When the pop-up menu appears, select **New**.
3 Select **Folder** from the menu (Figure 6.16).
4 A folder icon appears on the desktop and you can give it a name.

Folders can be created in a hard drive or flash drive by selecting it, opening it and following the procedure outlined above, or by clicking the **File** menu and selecting **New** and **Folder**. Folders can also be created and stored within other folders.

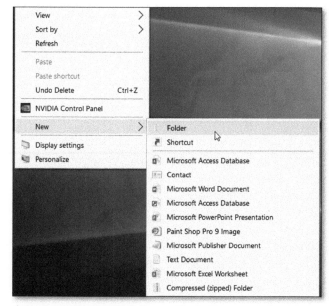

▲ Figure 6.16 Creating a folder on the desktop

Copying a folder

To copy a file or folder:

1 Highlight the file or folder that is to be copied.
2 Right click and select **Copy**.
3 Navigate to the desired location, such as a flash drive, and click the icon.
4 Then click **Paste**.

Deleting a folder

To delete a file or folder:

1 Highlight the file or folder that is to be deleted.
2 Then click **Delete**.
3 The 'Delete Folder' dialog box confirms the Delete request. Click **Yes**.

Note

Deleting a file removes it from its current location and sends it to the Recycle Bin; the file remains there until the Bin has been emptied.

Windows file management

Naming a file

Files or folders are named to identify them. The names given should be logical and should reflect the content of the folder or file. The names of files are usually keyed with initial capital letters. Filenames can be up to 255 characters long (but in practice you will not use filenames that long). In addition, the following symbols cannot be used in a filename: \ / : * ? " , . The descriptive name usually consists of two parts: the name and the extension, separated by a full stop (.). The file extension is three or four letters that follow the full stop. When renaming a file, do not delete or change file extensions, as this may cause problems when opening the file.

For example, the file name RESUME.DOC has RESUME as the name and DOC as the extension. The extension tells you and the computer what type of file it is, in this case, a DOCument. When you click on the file to open it, the computer then knows which application is needed. The RESUME.DOC file is opened by Microsoft Word (or another word processing package you have installed) since DOC is a common file extension for Word documents. Table 6.1 gives some extensions and their associations.

Extension	Association
BAT	**BAT**ch files containing a series of DOS commands
COM	Executable **COM**mand files
EXE	**EXE**cutable command files
SYS	Various types of **SYS**tem files – usually drivers to control devices
DOC	**DOC**ument files created by, for example, Microsoft Word, the word processing program
XLS	A spreadsheet file created by, for example, Microsoft Excel, a spreadsheet program
WPD	**W**ord **P**erfect **D**ocuments (WordPerfect is another word processing program)
TXT	Te**XT** files – associated with the 'Notepad' program
JPG or JPEG	A graphics file commonly used for photos and illustrations
BMP	**B**it**M**a**P**ped graphics, such as photos and illustrations
PDF	**P**ortable **D**ocument **F**ormat – a file type that displays finished text and graphics in an application such as Acrobat® Reader®.

▲ Table 6.1 Some file extensions

Emerging technology

Interface developer Synaptics has announced a new partnership with Advanced Micro Devices, Inc. (AMD). AMD is an American multinational semiconductor company that develops computer processors and related technologies. The goal of the partnership is to help to secure many of the operating systems of the future with a new fingerprint sensor. If this happens, it will add a new layer of security to biometric login by storing the fingerprint signature on the sensor itself, making it self-contained and less susceptible (vulnerable) to hackers and data thieves. Synaptics and AMD are just two of many companies that want to move ICT towards a password-free future.

Chapter 6: Summary

- 'Software' is the general name given to all the programs (sets of instructions) that computers use to perform different tasks.
- Application software programs carry out specific tasks or solve particular problems.
- General-purpose software is not written for any specific business or organisation but can be used or adapted to suit anyone's specific needs.
- An integrated software package is a set of related, specialised programs combined in a unified package that allows data to be transferred easily between each program, for example, Microsoft Office.
- Specialised software is written for a specific task.
- Customised software is general-purpose software that has been modified to better meet the needs of an individual or organisation.
- Macros are short programs written to automate several steps in software, such as in a database.
- Custom-written (tailor-made) software is software that is written to meet the specific needs of a specific company or organisation; it is therefore expensive and highly specialised.
- System software is software that manages and supports the resources and operations of a computer system; it includes the operating system, the user interface and utility programs.
- An operating system is a set of programs that governs the operation of a computer. It manages computer resources, files, memory, tasks and maintains security.
- Multitasking is the ability of the computer to appear to run more than one program at the same time.
- Multiprogramming refers to the computer's ability to run two or more programs at the same time, using a single processor.
- Multiprocessing refers to a computer system's ability to support more than one process (program) at the same time using multiple processors. This generally increases processing times.
- A time-sharing processing system makes users in a multi-access environment believe they have the undivided attention of the CPU. It does this by giving each terminal, in turn, a small amount of processing time before going on to the others, then quickly returning to the first terminal again.
- A batch-processing system is one where data is collected in a sequenced batch queue before processing starts. The program is then run without interaction from the user.

- Real-time operating systems are designed to respond to an event within a predetermined time. The response may, in turn, create a response in the user, for example, in computer games.
- Online processing, also known as transaction processing or pseudo-real-time processing, processes data as soon as it is available.
- Utility programs are system software programs that provide useful services by performing common tasks and 'housekeeping' routines, such as backup and disk repair.
- Device drivers are programs that enable a computer to interact with hardware devices.
- Firmware is programming that is added to a computer's non-volatile memory at the time of manufacturing. It is used to run user programs on the device.
- A language translator is a program that translates a program written in a particular programming language into another programming language without losing the functional or logical structure of the original code.
- The user interface is the user-controllable part of the operating system that allows you to communicate, or interact, with it.
- The command-driven interface requires you to enter a command by typing in codes or words. An example is MS-DOS.
- Menu-driven interfaces allow you to use either a mouse or cursor movement (arrow keys) to make a selection from a menu.
- The graphical user interface (GUI), also called WIMP (windows, icons, menus and pointing devices), allows the use of graphics (icons), menus and simple keystrokes to choose commands, start programs, see lists of files and many other options.
- The touch user interface (TUI) allows the user to choose commands, start programs, see lists of files and many other options by touching icons on a screen.
- Directories or folders are used to hold documents, programs, files and even further sub-directories and folders.
- File names can be up to 255 characters long and must not contain symbols such as: \, /, :, *, ?, ", and ,.
- A file name consists of two parts: the name and the file extension (identifies the type of file).

Chapter 6: Questions

Fill in the blanks

1 _____ software is written for a specific task rather than for a broad application area.

2 Software written to meet the specific needs of a company is known as _____.

3 Software that manages and supports the resources and operations of a computer system is known as _____.

4 Programs developed to carry out specific tasks or solve particular problems are called _____.

5 _____ refers to a computer's ability to support more than one process at the same time.

6 The _____ is a set of programs that governs the operations of a computer.

7 Software can be classified into two major types: _____ and _____ .

8 The _____ is the user-controllable part of the operating system that allows a user to communicate or interact with it.

9 The processing of loading operating system software into a computer's main memory from disk is known as _____.

10 A set of related, specialised programs combined in a unified package that allows data to be transferred easily between the programs is known as _____ .

True or False?

1 Computer games are an example of application software.

2 A word processor is an example of general-purpose software.

3 Integrated software packages take up more storage space than individual applications.

4 A payroll program is an example of specialised software.

5 Customised software and custom-written software are the same.

6 Custom-written software has an increased probability of undetected error.

7 The operating system is one category of system software.

8 The operating systems of smartphones and tablets are embedded in a RAM chip.

9 Batch processing can be used in airline booking systems.

10 Assemblers, compilers and interpreters are all language translators.

Multiple-choice questions

1 Which of the following is not a utility program?
   a Disk repair program
   b Backup program
   c Spreadsheet program
   d File defragmentation program

2 Application software consists of:
   a entertainment software.
   b productivity software.
   c speciality software.
   d all of the above.

3 An integrated software package:
   a can transfer data from one component to another very easily.
   b costs less than individual applications.
   c takes up less disk space than individual applications.
   d contains all of the above.

4 Which of the following is not considered to be system software?
   a Graphics presentation software
   b Operating system
   c Utility program
   d Language translators

5 Which of the following is not a function of the operating system?
   a Managing files and memory
   b Managing tasks
   c Creating a document
   d Managing input and output devices

Short-answer questions

1 Draw a diagram to represent the relationship between the operating system, the application software and the hardware.

2 What are the advantages and disadvantages of integrated software?

3 a Define the term 'operating system'.
  b List THREE types of operating systems.
  c List FOUR functions of the operating system.

4 Explain the terms: 'time-sharing', 'batch processing' and 'real-time processing'.

5 Explain the difference between multiprogramming and multiprocessing.

6 a List THREE types of user interfaces.
  b Explain how each type of user interface operates.

7 a Define the term 'utility program'.
  b Give the functions of any THREE utility programs.

8 Explain the difference between batch processing and online processing.

9 Name a broader category of software that best describes the following software.
  a Microsoft Office 2016   b Windows 10
  c Medical Expert System

10 a Which interface requires the user to input commands by typing in the instructions to perform tasks?
  b Which interface requires the user to use a mouse to select icons to perform tasks?
  c Name an interface other than the answers for parts (a) and (b).

Research questions

1 You are the IT security analyst at a manufacturing company. Your company would like to purchase new computers and needs to decide which type of operating system would be best for the company. You are asked to prepare a comparative report on the latest versions of the Windows, Linux and macOS® operating systems.

2 Your school recently upgraded the operating system on all the computers in the school to Windows 10. The principal of the school asks that you explore the tools that are included in the Windows 10 operating system and determine if they are sufficient for the security needs of the school. You need to use the web to research firewalls, automatic updates and malware software included in the Windows 10 operating system. If your research suggests that any of the tools are inadequate, then you should recommend other software. You are required to present a detailed report to the principal.

3 Your friend would like to purchase a smartphone and has come to you for advice because you are studying ICT. Use the Web to conduct research on Android and iOS: examine the differences in the features, security options, speed and reliability of these two operating systems. Create a short report to assist your friend in making a decision.

Crossword

Across

5 The ability of the computer to appear to run more than one program at the same time (12)

7 The process of loading operating system software into a computer's main memory from disk (7)

8 A rectangular area that displays information on the screen of a computer (6)

Down

1 A pictorial representation of a file, folder or program (4)

2 A processing system where programs and data are collected in a queue before processing (5)

3 An area of memory that temporarily holds data being transferred to be processed or output (6)

4 Short programs are written to automate several steps in software, such as databases, spreadsheets and word processors (6)

6 System software programs that provide a useful service by performing common tasks and 'housekeeping' routines (7)

Data communications, networks and the internet

Objectives

At the end of this chapter, you will be able to:

→ define 'data communications'
→ explain the terms 'bandwidth', 'narrowband', 'voice-band' and 'broadband'
→ define 'simplex', 'duplex' and 'half-duplex'
→ understand the terms 'wireless communications', 'network', 'LAN', 'WAN', 'PAN' and 'MAN'
→ describe the three types of transmission cables used in a cabled LAN
→ explain the functions of NIC, access point, network adaptor, switch and router
→ explain the terms 'bluetooth' and 'Wi-Fi'
→ understand the terms 'internet', 'ISP', 'TCP/IP', 'hypertext' and 'hypermedia'
→ understand the different communications links used to connect to the internet
→ appreciate the hardware and software needed to connect to the internet
→ understand the terms 'email', 'mail server', 'mail client', 'VoIP' and 'podcasting'
→ create and send email
→ understand the WWW and URL
→ surf the Web to find information using the directory in a home page, keywords and known URLs
→ explain the structure of a URL
→ explain the terms 'html', 'webcasts', 'webinars', 'Web 2.0' and 'wiki'
→ explain the differences between an intranet and an extranet
→ give examples of different types of websites and their uses
→ explain the term 'mobile network'
→ describe the different types of mobile networks and their applications.

Data communications

Rapid advances in communications systems, computer use and multimedia technologies are changing the way people communicate and transmit data. Data communications can be broadly described as the transmission of data from one location to another for direct use or for further processing. A data communications system is made up of hardware, software and communications facilities. Communications systems may be set up to serve a small area; or they may be set up on a global scale. Data in any communications system is moved from one location to another via data communications channels or transmission links. These channels are classified according to bandwidth. Bandwidth determines the volume of data that can be transmitted in a given time. The wider the bandwidth, the more data it can transmit. Bandwidths can be grouped into three classes of channels.

A narrow-band channel, which is almost obsolete, for example, a telegraph system, can transmit data at slow speeds of between 10 and 30 bits per second (bps).

A voice-band channel can transmit data at the rate of up to 64 Kbps. A telephone line/landline is voice-band and is one of the most widely used methods of transferring data.

A broadband channel can transmit large volumes of data at speeds of over 45.48 Mbps (the global average). In some countries the speeds are much higher than in others. For example, in Trinidad the average fixed broadband download speed is 50 Mbps, whereas in Jamaica it is about 40 Mbps. Communications satellites, coaxial cables, fibre optic cables and microwave links are commonly used to provide these channels. Microwave signals are very high frequency radio signals that can be transmitted through space. A communications satellite accepts signals beamed to it from a point on Earth and then reflects the signals to another point as shown in Figure 7.1. Communications satellites can transmit data that includes text, voice, pictures and video.

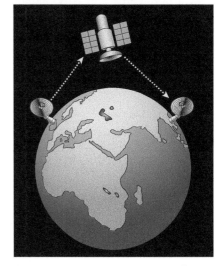

▲ Figure 7.1 A communications satellite linking two points on Earth

Data transmission direction

In data networking, the term 'transmit' means to issue signals to the network medium. Transmission refers to either the process of transmitting or the progress of signals after they have been transmitted. Data transmission, whether analogue or digital, may also be characterised by the direction in which the signals travel over the media.

■ A simplex line permits data to flow in only one direction. You can send data or receive data, but not both. An example of simplex communication is a principal speaking to students over the schools' public address system (PA). In this example, the principal's voice is the signal, and it travels in only one direction – away from the PA system and towards the classrooms or student assembly. Simplex is sometimes called one-way, or unidirectional, communication.

■ A half-duplex line can alternately send and receive data. This means that at any particular time you can either send data but not receive it, or receive data but not send it. An example of half-duplex communication is a two-way radio system, which allows the operator to talk or listen, but not at the same time.

■ A full-duplex line can simultaneously send and receive data. A telephone is an example of a full duplex system. When you call a friend on the telephone, your connection is an example of a full-duplex transmission because your voice signals can be transmitted to your friend at the same time your friend's voice signals are transmitted in the opposite direction to you. In other words, both of you can talk and hear each other simultaneously.

> **Did you know?**
>
> There are currently over 4,600 satellites orbiting the Earth of which the majority are used for communication and Earth observation.

Networks

Many businesses, organisations, universities and schools have networked computers. A network is a group of two or more computers linked together so that they can share resources (hardware, software and data) and communicate with one another. We tend to describe networks in terms of the area they cover and how they are arranged (topology).

Network types

One way we describe computer networks is by the geographical area they cover. These are:

■ local area networks (LANs)
■ wide area networks (WANs)
■ personal area networks (PANs)
■ metropolitan area networks (MANs).

Local area networks (LANs)

A local area network (LAN) consists of a collection of microcomputers, such as in an office building, department or school that can share peripherals, files and programs, and communicate on the network. Each microcomputer that forms part of the network is connected either by cables or by a wireless link. Each computer can function both as an independent personal computer running its own software, and as a workstation on the network accessing information from the network server. The server runs the networking software that allows resources to be shared with the other computers (called clients) on the network. The devices shared by a LAN may include printers, hard drives, optical drives (CD-ROM, CD-RW, DVD-ROM, DVD-RW), modems and fax machines. A LAN's ability to share information and communicate with the devices and computers on the network has many benefits for its users:

- Hardware such as printers can be shared.
- Storage facilities can be shared.
- Software and data files can be shared by many users.
- It is usually cheaper to buy one copy of a software application and pay the licence fee for several machines, than to buy individual packages for each computer.
- Users can work together on a single document.
- Users can communicate using email.

However, there are also some disadvantages:

- The initial set-up costs are high.
- Since many users use the system, there is a greater chance of corrupted data or data tampering.
- There is a greater risk from malware, because they are easily spread between the computers that are part of the LAN.
- If the file server fails, all the workstations are affected and work stored on shared hard disk drives will not be accessible; nor will it be possible to use network printers, and so on.
- Networks can be complicated to maintain and may require a network manager. Additional costs may therefore be incurred.

Wide area networks (WANs)

A wide area network (WAN) can connect mainframes, LANs and PCs across a large geographical area such as a city, a state or a country. LANs are often connected to WANs using a special interface device called a gateway. A gateway is an interface that enables communication between two different networks. Information can be transmitted using special high-speed telephone lines, microwave links, satellite links or a combination of all three. WANs are used mainly by universities and research centres so that information can be shared, and by large organisations, companies and banks with branches in different countries, to share information and process loads between the various branches. WANs can also be used to publish documents and distribute software. The internet is an example of a massive WAN. Figure 7.2 shows LANs in different countries, connected to form a WAN, using telecommunications links.

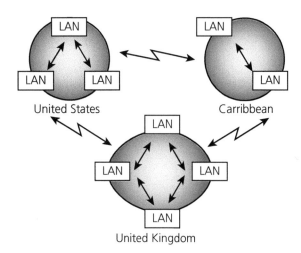

▲ Figure 7.2 LANs connected to form a WAN

Personal area network (PAN)

A personal area network (PAN) is a computer network organised around an individual person and is set up for personal use only. PANs typically involve a computer, smartphone, printer, and/or some other personal device such as a tablet. You can use these networks to transfer files including email, calendar appointments, photos and music. PANs can be wired, using USB or FireWire, or they can be wireless (WPAN: wireless personal area network), using infrared and Bluetooth. The range of a PAN is typically a few metres.

Metropolitan area network (MAN)

A metropolitan area network (MAN) is a network that interconnects users with computer resources in a geographic area or region larger than that covered by a large local area network (LAN), but smaller than the area covered by a wide area network (WAN). The term is applied to the interconnection of networks in a city into a single larger network. It is also used to mean the interconnection of several local area networks by bridging them with higher-capacity lines. The latter usage is also sometimes referred to as a campus network.

Network topologies

LANs can be described by the way in which the computers are connected and how they communicate with one another: client or server networks and peer-to-peer networks.

Client or server networks

A client or server network is one in which any computer on the network can be designated as the server, although most such networks will have a specially designed computer that operates as a dedicated server and has a faster processor, more RAM and a lot more storage space. This is the most common form of network and if your school has a network, it is likely to be set up in this way. Client or server networks are easier to manage when the networks are large, as changes can be made on the server and these are passed on to the clients when they log in.

A large LAN may have several servers to perform different tasks. For example, a file server may look after the organisation of the files on the network while a print server coordinates printing on the network and looks after the sending and receiving of faxes and email. The server or servers contain the software that manages:

- a shared hard disk
- requests from users
- the protection of data
- the security of the system.

Peer-to-peer networks

A peer-to-peer (P2P) network allows every computer to communicate with every other computer in the network. No computer is designated as a server. Instead, each computer can be considered as both a client and a server. This is because a user can access data from any computer on the network and vice versa. For this type of networking, P2P networks are limited to about ten machines, after which the performance drops and the system becomes cumbersome. They are used mainly in small businesses and departments, as they are easy to set up for small networks where you perhaps only need to share files and a printer.

Some uses for which P2P networks are very good, are for networks that are very large in size. Spotify, the music streaming site, is a good example that uses P2P techniques. Bitcoin is a cryptocurrency that uses P2P techniques to spread the information about how coins are spent around the internet to improve security and reliability, rather than relying on all that information being in one place such as a traditional bank.

Network technologies

Networks use a number of specialist technologies including transmission media, wireless technologies and network hardware.

Transmission media

In a cabled network, all the computers and other peripheral devices on the network are attached by cables. These cables fall into three categories.

- Twisted pair cable is a convenient and inexpensive method of connecting computers and peripherals in a network. It is the most common method for the cabling of a LAN in a building. It is quite flexible, and the plugs and sockets used are easy to install, so installers like to use these cables, as they are easy to lay around a building. There are several types, but the newest cabling is the so-called CAT6, which can carry data at 10 Gbit/sec over distances of up to 100 metres.
- Coaxial cable is more expensive than twisted pair cable because its transmission capabilities are higher; it is used to transmit voice, video and data. It is also stiffer and more difficult to fit connectors to, but it can carry signals over longer distances. It is most commonly found in cable television networks.
- **Fibre optic cable** is relatively expensive. It enables large volumes of digital data to be transmitted extremely fast and virtually error-free. A single strand of a fibre optic cable is a hair-thin piece of glass tubing. The inside of the tube acts as a mirror, allowing pulses of light, carrying data, to travel along it. A cable consists of thousands of these hair-thin strands. Adding connectors to these is a specialist job. Fibre optic cable is also well suited to sending signals over long distances and so are often used for the cabling under the streets that link phone and data networks.

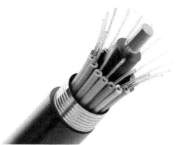

▲ Figure 7.3 Twisted pair cable (top), coaxial cable (middle) and fibre optic cable (bottom)

Wireless communications

Wireless communications offer organisations and users many benefits such as portability, flexibility, increased productivity and lower installation costs. Wireless technologies, in the simplest sense, enable one or more devices to communicate with each other without physical connections – without cabling. They use radio frequency, microwave or infrared transmissions as the means for transmitting data. Wireless communications range from complex systems, such as Wi-Fi networks and mobile phone networks, to simple devices such as wireless headphones, microphones and other devices that do not process or store information.

These simple devices include infrared (IR) devices such as remote controls, some cordless computer keyboards, mice and wireless hi-fi stereo headsets, all of which require a direct line of sight between the transmitter and the receiver to close the link.

Wi-Fi

Wi-Fi is the most popular means of communicating data wirelessly within a fixed location. It is a standard way of replacing the cables in a LAN. A LAN can mix cabled and wireless devices, and Wi-Fi is the way in which these devices connect into the rest of the LAN. A LAN that uses wireless technology is often called a wireless LAN or WLAN.

Most modern devices support Wi-Fi so that they can access a network to get internet access and share network resources. In a typical home, a router, connected to a LAN or directly to the internet, transmits a Wi-Fi signal and delivers that service to nearby devices that can reach the wireless signal.

The wireless part of the LAN, provided by Wi-Fi, can be used in places where it may be difficult or impractical to use a cabled LAN – for example, in homes, large offices, warehouses and lecture halls. In a building with many rooms or large halls, a few access points (a networking hardware device that allows a Wi-Fi device to connect to a wired network) may be needed. A user may take a laptop and walk from one room or from one end of a building to the next without losing network connectivity. This is because the laptop will lock onto the strongest signal from an access point and will transfer its link to another access point if the signal there is stronger.

The same features that are available in a wired LAN are also available in the WLAN. It provides more flexibility in acquiring information, as mentioned. Less wiring also means increased efficiency and reduced wiring costs. However, there are disadvantages. Besides the relatively slow speed at which a WLAN operates, there is also the problem of interference from other users or devices using the same 2.4 GHz band and the risk of illegal access to information. Interference can corrupt data and is, therefore, a major concern when installing a wireless LAN. Illegal access is also a major concern since anyone with a compatible network interface card (NIC – covered in the network hardware section later in the chapter) can access the network. The need for encryption is therefore of the utmost importance.

Hotspots
Another way to use Wi-Fi is a Wi-Fi hotspot whereby computers and mobile devices such as smartphones and tablets can share its wireless or wired internet connection to transfer files or carry voice messages.

Bluetooth

The other widely-used technology is Bluetooth technology. Bluetooth is a standard developed by a group of electronics manufacturers that allows any type of electronic equipment (computers, digital video cameras, cell phones, tablets, keyboards, cars, and so on) to automatically make their own connections to each other when they are close enough without wires, cables or any direct action from a user. The manufacturers program a Bluetooth radio transmitter into each unit with an address that falls into a range of standard addresses established for a particular type of device.

> **Did you know?**
>
> Vic Hayes has been called the 'father of Wi-Fi' because he chaired the IEEE committee that created the 802.11 standards in 1997. Before the public even heard of Wi-Fi, Hayes established the standards that would make Wi-Fi possible.

When a device is turned on, it sends out radio signals asking for a response from any unit with an address within a particular range. For example, if a computer and a printer are turned on and their addresses are within the established range, they will respond to each other and a tiny network (piconet or personal area network (PAN)) is formed. Once the networks are established, the systems begin communicating among themselves. Note that this is different from a standard LAN. Bluetooth networks are formed, broken up and reformed all the time, simply by switching on Bluetooth-enabled devices when they are in close proximity to each other.

These 'ad hoc' networks, as they are called, allow data synchronisation with network systems and the sharing of applications between devices. Bluetooth functionality also eliminates cables from scanners and other peripheral devices. Handheld devices such as tablets and smartphones allow remote users to update personal databases and provide them with access to network services such as wireless email and internet access. The Bluetooth method of wireless networking is already being used by many companies with great success. However, like any network, there are risks. Some of these risks are similar to those of wired networks, whereas others are the same as for other types of WLAN.

Microwave

Wi-Fi is suitable for short-range wireless connections, but it is not a good choice for applications that require longer wireless links. Microwave communication allows you to create wireless links over a wider range and with a higher data-carrying capacity. It is often used in places where it is not practical to lay a fibre optic cable. It needs to have a line of sight and uses a dish aerial, like a larger version of a television satellite dish. A typical application might be to link two campuses of a university, where the aerials can be mounted on top of tall buildings with a clear view of each other.

Infrared

Infrared uses infrared light, which is invisible to our eyes, to transmit small amounts of data over short distances. Devices such as keyboards and mice can use infrared to connect wirelessly to a computer.

Network hardware

Network interface cards

Before a PC can become part of a network it must be fitted with a network interface card (NIC). An NIC is a device that enables wireless or wired capabilities on a device that did not previously support it. This card fits into an expansion slot in the motherboard and enables the computers on the network to send and receive messages. In the case of a wired network, the card has an external outlet into which one end of the network cable is plugged. The other end of the cable plugs into a connection based on the configuration of the network.

Most modern devices come pre-equipped with an NIC that is installed on the device's motherboard. Laptops, tablets, cell phones, and other wireless devices have Wi-Fi NICs built into the devices.

> **Did you know?**
>
> The Bluetooth logo is a Viking inscription, known as a 'bind rune' that merges the two initials of the Danish king Harald Blatand (Bluetooth) who was famous for uniting the people of Denmark and Norway. In creating the Bluetooth standard, the inventors felt that they were, in effect, doing something similar in uniting the PC and cellular industries.

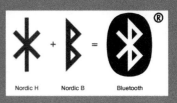

Nordic H + Nordic B = Bluetooth

> **Did you know?**
>
> Configuration refers to how a network is set up on hardware, software and other supporting devices.

Modems

A modem (short for 'modulator/demodulator') is a hardware device that allows a computer to send and receive data over a telephone line or a cable or satellite connection. In the case of transmission over an analogue telephone line, which was once the most popular way to access the internet, the modem converts data between analogue and digital formats in real time for two-way network communications. In the case of the high-speed digital modems that are popular today, the signal is much simpler and does not require the analogue-to-digital conversion.

▲ Figure 7.4 Transmission of data over a telephone line

The main purpose of a modem, when used in a home networking environment, is to establish a connection between your home internet connection and your internet service provider (ISP). The type of modem supplied to a home or business entity or organisation will depend on the type of transmission channel used. Each type of modem is capable of transferring data over a different type of physical connection using a set of communications standards, or protocols, which it was designed to support. It is important to know which modem you are using, as they provide different speeds and bandwidth.

Routers

A router acts as an interface between two networks. It helps to facilitate communications between your home's network and the internet service provider's (ISP's) network. It takes the information provided by the modem and routes it to the various devices that are connected. Devices (such as computers, TVs, gaming consoles, digital picture frames, and so on) can be connected to a router in one of two ways – wired directly to the router or wirelessly. A router can also select the best route for packets (data broken into small pieces for easier transmission) to take in large interconnected networks. Routers also provide advanced functionality such as a built-in firewall to help protect the network from unwanted attacks from hackers and some malware. Many routers aimed at home use have the modem to connect to the broadband network that is built into it.

Switches

A network switch is used to share network connections and boost the signal so that it can go over longer distances. In a typical home network, your router might have four connections for wired devices. If you wanted to add more than that you would connect a switch to one of these connections and the switch would have four, eight or more connections on it.

In the transmission media section, we said that the twisted pair cables should not be longer than 100 m. This might be a problem in a big office. Here we would have a switch at the server connected to other switches in each area of the building. This would allow us to connect the second switch up to 100 m from the first and then connect a workstation a further 100 m away.

> **Note**
>
> Here are some examples of types of modems and the different transmission channels they require.
>
> - A DSL modem is capable of transferring data over a standard copper telephone line.
> - A cable modem is capable of transferring data over a coaxial cable line.
> - A fibre modem is capable of transferring data over a fibre optic line.
> - A satellite modem is capable of transferring data over a satellite connection.

> **Did you know?**
>
> 'Mbps' is short for 'megabits per second', a megabit being just over a million bits.

Access points

An access point is a device that is attached to a LAN network, which contains a radio transmitter/receiver, encryption facility and communications software. It translates computer signals into wireless signals, which it broadcasts to wireless NICs on the network. NICs equipped for wireless communications receive these signals and can transmit back. They have a fixed or detachable radio antenna instead of the usual coaxial cable.

The access point and the NIC communicate with one another using a 2.4 gigahertz (GHz) radio band. The access point performs its role in reverse when transferring signals from a wireless NIC to the conventional network: it translates wireless signals received from NICs into wired signals.

Mobile networks

Mobile networks are something that we use on a daily basis to be in contact with the rest of the world. These networks have become the backbone of telecommunications in recent years, with the widespread adoption of cell phones, tablets and other mobile devices. Mobile networks have become a common carrier in the same way that the cabled phone network has been. Mobile networks, also known as cellular networks, are made up of 'cells' that connect to one another and to telephone switches or exchanges. These cells are areas of land that are typically hexagonal and overlap each other to form a large coverage area. Users on the network can cross into different cells without losing connection.

Each cell contains a base station or mobile phone tower that sends and receives the mobile transmissions. They connect to each other to hand off packets of data, voice and text signals – ultimately bringing these signals to mobile devices such as phones and tablets, which act as receivers. A mobile device will connect to the nearest or least congested base station. The base stations are connected to a digital exchange where the communication is sent to other telephone or data networks. Each base station is also connected to the main telephone network and can relay mobile calls to landline phones.

In Trinidad and Tobago, the main mobile network providers are Digicel and bMobile. Digicel and FLOW are also leading providers in many other Caribbean countries such as Jamaica and Grenada.

Types of mobile networks

Different types of mobile technologies are used to provide mobile network services to users. The large service providers vary as to which technologies they use, so mobile devices are typically built to use the technology of the intended carrier. The most commonly-used radio systems are GSM (Global System for Mobile Communication) and CDMA (Code Division Multiple Access). One of the newest technologies is Long Term Evolution (LTE), which is based on GSM and offers greater network capacity and speed. GSM phones do not work on CDMA networks, and vice versa. Although GSM and CDMA do not differ much in quality, there are significant differences in the way they work.

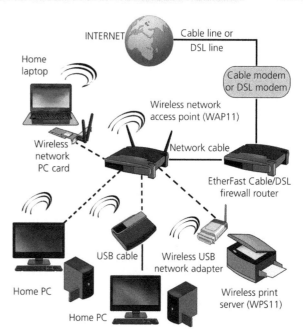

▲ Figure 7.5 The components of a WLAN

▲ Figure 7.6 Mobile network coverage area

1G: Analogue cellular networks

The first commercially automated cellular network (the 1G generation) was launched in Japan by NTT in 1979. 1G is an analogue technology, and the phones generally have poor battery life and voice quality, without much security, sometimes experiencing dropped calls. The maximum speed of 1G is 2.4 Kbps. Since 2018, only Russia has a limited service of 1G.

2G: Digital networks

In the 1990s, the 'second generation' (2G) mobile phone systems emerged, primarily using the GSM standard. The 2G phone systems used digital transmission instead of analogue transmission, and introduced advanced and fast phone-to-network signalling. 2G telephone technology is capable of speeds of between 40 Kbps to 50 Kbps. This allows call and text encryption, plus data services such as SMS (short message service), picture messages, and MMS (multimedia messaging service). Although 2G has replaced 1G and has been superseded by technologies such as 3G and 4G, described below, it is still used in a few countries.

3G: High-speed IP data networks

3G mobile networks were introduced in 1998, bringing with it faster data-transmission speeds. This allowed users to use their mobile phone in more data-demanding ways such as for video calling and mobile internet. The high connection speeds of 3G technology enabled media streaming of radio and even television content to 3G handsets. The maximum speed of 3G is estimated to be around 2 Mbps for non-moving devices and 384 Kbps in moving vehicles.

4G: Growth of mobile broadband

The fourth generation of mobile networks (called 4G) was released in 2008. In addition to mobile web access (such as 3G), 4G also supports gaming services, HD mobile TV, video conferencing, 3D TV and other applications that demand higher speeds. It is basically an extension of the 3G technology with more bandwidth and services offered than in 3G. The first two commercially available technologies characterised as 4G were the WiMAX standard and the LTE standard. Although these standards can theoretically reach mobile internet connection speeds in excess of 50 Mbps, most providers offer much less – between 6 and 45 Mbps, depending on the country.

Network privacy

The internet

The internet is a network, made up of other networks, which connects computers worldwide via a huge set of telecommunications links. The individual networks may be owned by universities, research facilities, governmental organisations, business corporations, non-profit organisations and private individuals. Being part of the network means you can access, share and exchange information. Much of the information on the internet is free, since many government and non-profit organisations use this avenue to educate and entertain the public. Some of these sites are open to anyone to access, but individual sites and servers may restrict access.

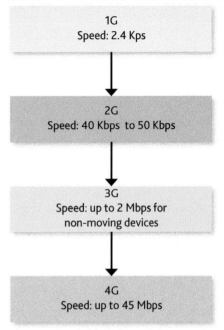

▲ Figure 7.7 Generations of mobile networks

Did you know?

5G is the fifth-generation cellular network technology that is currently being developed and will be in used in 2019.

5G delivers vastly increased capacity, lower latency, and faster speeds. 5G networks will operate in a high-frequency band of the wireless spectrum, between 28 GHz and 60 GHz. 5G network speeds should have a peak data rate of 20 Gb/s for the downlink and 10 Gb/s for the uplink. Not only will people be connected to one another but so will machines, automobiles, city infrastructure, public safety and more.

Intranets

An intranet can be thought of as a micro version of the internet within a company or organisation. It offers the same features as the global internet but in a localised environment, such as a factory site or an office. Many companies handle large volumes of information such as:

- training manuals
- company reports
- job openings and descriptions
- newsletters.

Authorised users within a company can use the company's intranet to find information stored on it easily and quickly. The documents in an intranet contain tags that provide links to other documents found in the company's network (or outside on the wider internet). This is handled using the same browsers, other software and TCP/IP, as used for the internet.

Extranets

If a company has an intranet and allows limited access to it by people outside the company, the intranet is referred to as an extranet. A company may set up an extranet, for example, to provide technical support information to its customers based on products it sells or services it provides.

Exercise 1

Fill in the blanks

1. The transmission of data from one location to another for direct use or further processing is known as _____.
2. The three classes of bandwidth channels are broadband, voice-band and _____.
3. A _____ line can simultaneously send and receive data.
4. Computers on a network can share software, data and _____.
5. The three types of LAN cables are twisted pair, fibre optic and _____.

True or False?

1. A broadband channel can transmit between 1,000 and 8,000 Mbps.
2. A half-duplex line can alternately send and receive data.
3. Wireless communications use cables to transmit data.
4. A LAN connects computers in a small geographical area such as an office building or school.
5. There is an increased risk of data corruption if computers are part of a LAN.

Multiple-choice questions

1. A simplex line permits data to flow:
   a in one direction only.
   b simultaneously in two directions.
   c in two directions but one at a time.
   d in none of the directions in (a) to (c).
2. The device that allows computers on a LAN to send and receive messages is known as a:
   a modem.
   b network receiver.
   c network interface card.
   d network adapter.
3. Which of the following networks has a range of a few metres?
   a LAN   b WAN   c MAN   d PAN
4. Which of the following devices is needed for setting up a WLAN?
   a Fibre optic cable   b Printer   c Access point   d Hard drive
5. Which network is the most suited for a school or office building?
   a LAN   b WAN   c MAN   d PAN

1 A reliable data communications system is an important asset to any business organisation.
   a What is 'data communications'?
   b What is meant by the term 'bandwidth' as it relates to data communications?
   c Identify and explain the different types of bandwidth.
2 List and explain the THREE types of data transmission channels.
3 Define the following terms:
   a Simplex   b Half-duplex   c Full-duplex.
4 Many university campuses have established LANs.
   a What is a LAN?
   b What are the main reasons for establishing a LAN?
   c State TWO methods used by computers to communicate using a LAN.
5 a Explain the term 'Wi-Fi hotspot'.
   b Define the term 'MAN' as used in networking.
   c Explain the difference between a MAN and a WAN.

The internet

We saw earlier in the chapter that the internet is a network, made up of other networks, which connects computers worldwide via a huge set of telecommunications links.

The internet does not have a central authority. There are organisations that develop technical aspects of the network and set standards for creating applications on it, but no single governing body or government is in control. The internet, therefore, has very few rules and answers to no single organisation. It consists of independently maintained and administered networks. Each network on the internet is responsible for formulating its own policies, procedures and rules. No one is in charge of the internet. The internet backbone, through which internet traffic flows, is owned by private companies.

One organisation that plays an important role in making sure that the network is stable and secure is ICANN (Internet Corporation for Assigned Names and Numbers). This is a private (non-government) non-profit corporation with responsibility for internet protocol (IP) address space allocation, protocol parameter assignment, domain name system management, and root server system management functions. Some of these will be discussed later in the chapter.

Advantages of the internet

- Vast volumes of information are available on virtually any topic.
- Information can be updated regularly.
- Much of the information is free.
- It allows people to 'telecommute', that is, to work from home using internet facilities such as email, and to keep in touch cheaply and quickly with friends and relatives.
- It is convenient for many common tasks, such as booking flights and checking bank balances online.
- It is easily accessible: all you need is an internet-ready device (PC, smartphone, tablet, and so on) and an internet service provider.

Disadvantages of the internet

- Large amounts of incorrect information are also available; there is no authority to check the accuracy of internet documents, and so on.
- It can be difficult to find exactly what you need because of the large volume of information available.
- Computer viruses can be downloaded easily without the user knowing.
- There are many undesirable websites on the internet (pornography, racist propaganda, and so on).
- The security of computers and WAN/LAN systems connected to the internet may be at risk from 'hackers'.

How the internet works

In this section, we will look at Transmission Control Protocol/Internet Protocol (TCP/IP) (the protocol used by devices to connect to and communicate over the internet) and how it uses IP addresses and domain names, the communications links that are used, and what an internet service provider is and what it does.

TCP/IP

All forms of communication, either electronic or other means, are based on some form of protocol. Computers connected to the internet use a TCP/IP, which is a set of protocols used to transfer data from one computer to another over the internet. A protocol is a set of rules that defines how computers interact or communicate with each other. TCP/IP is a non-proprietary protocol suite (it is not designed for any specific type of computer) that enables hardware and operating systems software from different computers to communicate. For example, a PC computer can communicate with an Apple® Macintosh® or another computer.

TCP/IP is actually two protocols: the TCP portion divides the data that is to be transmitted into smaller pieces called packets. This allows data to travel more easily, and therefore quickly, along communications lines. Each packet is numbered so that the data can be reassembled when it arrives at the destination computer. The IP sends each packet by specifying the address of both the sending and the receiving computers.

Each packet may take a different route depending on the amount of network traffic or on the location of the destination computer. The packets are sent by routers, which choose the best route to send data to its destination. Data arriving at the destination computer is reassembled. If a packet does not arrive or is corrupted, the entire file does not have to be resent – just the packet that was lost or corrupted.

Internet protocol (IP) addresses

Each computer on the internet has a unique address that identifies it as a node on the internet, so that information can be sent to it. This unique address, which is similar to your home address, is really a number called the internet protocol (IP) address. There are two standards for IP addresses: IP Version 4 (IPv4) and IP Version 6 (IPv6). Almost all computers at present have an IPv4 address, although many are starting to use the new IPv6 address system. IPv4 uses 32 binary bits to create a single unique address on the network.

An IPv4 address is expressed by four numbers separated by dots. Each number is the decimal (base 10) representation for an eight-digit binary (base 2) number, also called an octet.

An IP address has two parts. The first part is used as a network address and the last part is the host address. For example, the IP address 192.168.1.152 can be divided into two parts, as follows:

- 192.168.1. refers to the network
- 152 refers to the host.

The network part of the address is similar to a house address, number or postcode. The host part of the address is similar to a person's name on the mail who lives at that address. In essence, an IP address is a unique number used to identify a device or machine on the internet.

The IP address might be constant – that is, remain the same every time you connect to the internet (static) – or it could be a temporary address that changes each time you connect to the internet (dynamic). The IP address used by software is difficult for people to remember, as they prefer to use names.

Domain name system (DNS)

IP Addresses work really well, but they are not particularly easy for people to use. The domain name system (DNS) was developed as a simpler system to allow users to refer to hosts by names. This system divides the internet into a series of domains. It uses a hierarchical naming system or tree structure to represent a host. A domain is divided into second-level domains, which further subdivide into third-level domains and so on. A host is therefore named for the largest domain to which it belongs, then for any sub-domains within the largest domain, and then finally for the unique hostname. The DNS system allows an internet host to find another internet host by translating the hostname to the IP address of the computer.

At the top level, there are domains corresponding to educational institutions (edu), commercial entities (com), public organisations (org), governmental bodies (gov) and the military (mil). Individual organisations each get their name at the second level of the naming hierarchy. For example, Microsoft has 'Microsoft.com' and the Association of Curriculum Developers has 'ASCD.org'.

Departments within an organisation will be at the third level of the hierarchy, for example, 'shop.ASCD.org' (Figure 7.8). Sometimes a fourth level, which includes the unique hostname, is included. For example, if your domain is 'fun.com', which points to your website, you can create 'holiday.fun.com', which points to the holiday section of your website. You may also have a 'Caribbean.holiday.fun.com' which now gives the name of the computer in the holiday section of the website. The complete name of a host, therefore, includes the unique hostname, all sub-organisation units, the organisational name and the top-level domain. Table 7.1 shows a list of the current top-level domains in the United States.

Communications links

Connecting to the internet requires a physical link. As you learned earlier in the chapter, we use a modem to connect to the communications link. The four communications links that we will look at in this section are Satellite broadband, ADSL, cable broadband and fibre optic.

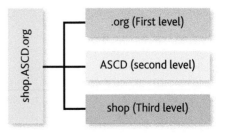

▲ Figure 7.8 DNS hierarchical naming structure

Domain name	Purpose
.com	Commercial
.edu	Educational institutions
.gov	Government bodies
.mil	US military institutions
.net	Computer networks
.org	Other types of organisations, for example, non-profit organisations
.rec	Recreational organisations
.store	Retailers on the internet
.info	Distributors of information
.int	International bodies

▲ Table 7.1 Current top-level domains in the United States

- **Satellite broadband** works by transmitting data thousands of kilometres up into the atmosphere to a satellite in orbit, and then back down to your internet service provider's hub back on Earth. Setting up a satellite broadband connection requires a satellite dish and a transmitter. The long distance that your data must travel in space results in a relatively slow download connection speed of up to 30 Mbps. The connection can also be unstable due to weather interferences such as thunderstorms. Satellite broadband is an option available for those who live in rural areas where traditional fixed-line broadband services are not available.
- **Asymmetric direct subscriber line (ADSL)** is the traditional type of broadband connection that works by transmitting data over copper telephone lines. This is the same line that is used to deliver your landline calls. It can provide speeds of up to 100 Mbps.
- **Cable broadband** uses coaxial cable to transmit information at speeds ranging from 36 Mbps to over 300 Mbps to homes or businesses. A cable broadband connection can provide cable TV, phone and internet-ready technology.
- **Fibre optic** broadband transmits information through pulses of light sent via dedicated fibre at speeds of over 1,000 Mbps. As with cable broadband, fibre optic provides cable TV, phone and internet-ready technology to homes or businesses using one cable. Many companies in the Caribbean such as Digicel, Flow and bMobile now provide both cable broadband and fibre optic services to homes and businesses.

Internet service provider (ISP)

An internet service provider (ISP) is a company that has a direct connection to the internet and gives users access to it, usually for a fee. The company generally has a small network that is connected via a high-speed communications link to a high-speed link that forms part of the internet's backbone (supercomputers and other large networks that make up the internet worldwide). Some of the companies providing internet services in the Caribbean are Digicel, Flow and bMobile.

Applications of the internet

The internet has a large number of applications. Some of the common applications are for communication; searching for information (job searches, finding books and study material, health and medicine, travel and so on); entertainment; shopping; stock market updates and research.

Services of the internet

There are four main types of services available on the internet:

- terminal emulation services (TES)
- file access and transfer services
- communications services
- the World Wide Web (WWW).

Terminal emulation services (TES)

These services enable you to connect your computer to a remote host and use the services available as if your computer were a terminal of that remote host. This can give you access to specialist offerings such as online databases, library catalogues and chat services.

An important TES is Telnet, a special program that allows you to access data and programs from a Telnet server. When connected to a Telnet site, your computer becomes a 'dumb' terminal that can be used only to send text-based messages to the Telnet site and to view the results. The Telnet program provides a window into which you can type commands and access information from the host computer. Some browsers, such as that of CompuServe, have built-in Telnet software, whereas others such as America Online (AOL) allow users to access the Telnet software, but do not run it themselves.

File access and transfer services

These services enable you to locate and use electronic files stored on computers across the internet.

File transfer protocol (FTP)

File transfer protocol (FTP) is a set of rules for communicating over the internet. It enables you, through an FTP program, to find an electronic file stored on a computer somewhere else and to download it (take a file from one computer on the internet and copy it to a storage device on your computer). It also enables you to upload files (send files to other computers on the internet). The electronic files are stored on what are called FTP sites, which may be maintained by universities, government agencies and large organisations. Some of the sites are private, and you may have to pay to retrieve or store information on those sites.

The files in an FTP site are stored in directories. Each file has a name and an extension, with the name labelling the contents of the file and the extension indicating the type of file – text, sound, program, image, video, and so on.

Communications services

Electronic mail (email) and email addresses

Email is the most popular and widely-used service on the internet today. It enables users locally and worldwide to send electronic messages (text, sound, video and graphics) to one individual or to a group of individuals, and to receive messages from others. A powerful feature of email is the option to send attachments. For example, a document created in Microsoft Word can be attached to an email message and received by the recipient with an email program.

Email is much faster than mail delivered by the traditional postal system. An email can be sent to an email subscriber in any part of the world in a matter of seconds or minutes (depending on the 'traffic' on the internet). Also, a subscriber can access his or her email from any part of the world as long as internet access is available. Apart from the fee that a subscriber has to pay to an ISP for internet access, sending email is free. You can send as many emails as you like at no additional charge and at your own convenience, any time of the day or night. This does not cause any problems for the person receiving it, who does not have to be present to receive the email. They collect the email (for example, from their ISP) at a time that is convenient to them.

To be able to send and/or receive email, each user must have an email address and an email program such as Mailbird or Microsoft Outlook. The address is unique to the user and consists of two parts separated by the @ ('at') symbol. The first part is the user name, which can be a real name, a shortened form of a real name or some made-up name. The second part is the domain name – the location of the email account on the internet, for example, with your ISP. The general form of an email address is as follows: Username@Domainname

For example, an individual who has a Gmail account may have an email like this: rolbirbal@gmail.com

Internet users can also use the other free email services offered by websites such as Yahoo!, Outlook.com, ZOHO mail and Fastmail. Examples of these addresses are: pettipoo@yahoo.com and madd@hotmail.com

For an email message to be sent and received, the following must be in place.

- **Mail server:** This is a computer on the internet that operates like the traditional post office. The mail server receives incoming messages and delivers outgoing messages. It allocates a certain amount of storage to hold mail for registered users. The area of storage allocated to you is your mailbox. You can retrieve your mail by supplying your username and password. This is necessary to protect your email from unauthorised access.
- **Mail client:** This is a program that enables you to read and compose email messages, send email and access email from the server. If you are using Microsoft Office software, you may use the popular Outlook Express program as your mail client. Figure 7.9 shows the Microsoft Outlook Express email screen for creating a new message; the format used by other email software is similar.

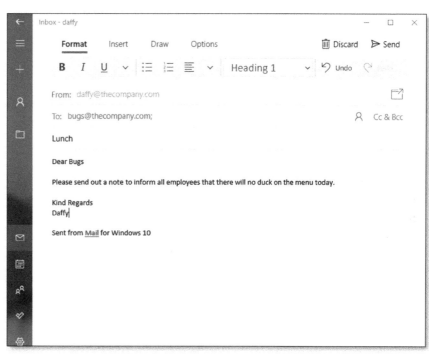

▲ Figure 7.9 The Microsoft Outlook Express email screen

Voice-over internet protocol (VoIP)

VoIP is the transmission of telephone calls over computer networks. It uses the internet rather than traditional communications lines to support voice communications. To place telephone calls using VoIP requires an internet telephone (or other appropriate input and output devices), an internet connection, sound card and special software.

The two most popular VoIP communications are as described below.

- **Computer-to-computer communications:** This is the least expensive and allows individuals to place long-distance calls between computers without incurring traditional long-distance telephone charges.
- **Computer-to-traditional telephone communications:** This allows a user to call almost any traditional telephone from their computer. Compared to computer-to-computer communications, however, this application requires an internet phone service provider.

Podcasting

Podcasting is online audio content that is delivered via an RSS feed over the internet. The term 'podcasting' derives its name from Apple's iPod®. However, to create a podcast or even to listen to one, does not require you to own an iPod or any portable music player.

Podcasting gives far more options in terms of content and programming than those provided by traditional radio. It lets you create your own syndicated online talk show or radio programme, with the content of your choosing. In addition, with podcasting, listeners can determine the time and the place of their interaction, which means that they decide what programme they want to receive and when they want to listen to it. Listeners can also retain audio archives to listen at their leisure.

World Wide Web (WWW)

The Web is a service offered on the internet. It was originally developed to help physicists in Geneva, Switzerland, to exchange data and research materials quickly with other scientists.

Many people believe the internet and the World Wide Web (also called the Web, WWW or sometimes W3) to be the same thing, but this is not so. In fact, the Web can be thought of as a large subset of the internet. The Web is a global collection of millions of hypertext and hypermedia documents and other resources, linked by hyperlinks and URLs. A hypertext document is a document that contains a hyperlink to another document located on the same computer or on another computer in any part of the world. Hypertext allows you to move easily from one document to the next.

For example, if you have used the Help files in any of Microsoft Office's application programs, you have already encountered hypertext. You may have asked for help with a certain topic and been shown a displayed explanation, in which you saw certain words highlighted in blue and underlined. If you clicked on such a word, you would get an additional help screen. The word is associated with a hyperlink to somewhere else in the computer (either in the same file or in a different file).

Hypermedia is a general name for documents that contain links to text, graphic, sound or video files. A computer that stores and makes available hypertext and hypermedia documents is called a server (or web server), and a computer that requests such a document is called a client.

HyperText Transfer Protocol (HTTP) is a set of rules that controls how data travels between server and client. In order to find, retrieve, display and send hypertext and hypermedia, you need a browser.

Podcasting can be used for:

- self-guided walking tours – informational content
- music – band promotional clips and interviews
- talk shows – industry or organisational news, investor news, sportscasts, news coverage and commentaries
- training – instructional informational materials
- stories – storytelling for children or the visually impaired.

Browsers

In order to navigate the World Wide Web (WWW), you need a web browser. A web browser is a program that is in your computer and enables you to find, retrieve, view and send hypertext and hypermedia documents that have been created using HyperText Markup Language (HTML) – (see below) over the Web. Popular browsers include Microsoft Internet Explorer, Google Chrome™ browser, Opera, Microsoft Edge and Mozilla Firefox.

All web browsers operate in a very similar way and have similar features. If you are using Google Chrome™ browser, the following points are some of the things you can do or can control with associated software accessible through its 'toolbar'.

- **View hundreds of millions of web pages:** The information on these web pages from all over the world is created in HTML and downloaded from a web server.
- **Send and receive email:** Outlook Express enables you to create and exchange email globally.
- **Participate in 'conferences':** For example, NetMeeting conferencing software in conjunction with a sound card, speakers and a microphone enables you to talk and listen to other users in real time.
- **Chat:** This program gives you the opportunity to join discussion groups and converse online.
- **Develop web pages:** Use the ActiveX controls software to build your own web pages.
- **View channels:** A channel is a website that automatically transmits information to your computer at the time you specify.
- **Shop online:** Buy books, CDs, clothes … almost anything is available to purchase online.
- **See and hear recorded broadcasts:** See and hear information as it is downloading; you do not have to wait until all of it has arrived.

HyperText Markup Language (HTML)

HTML is a programming language that you can use to create web pages. It contains standard codes that are used to specify how a web page is structured and formatted. These codes determine the appearance of the web page when it is displayed by your browser. HTML also contains tags that are used to create hyperlinks to access related information on the Web.

Finding information on the Web

You can retrieve information by clicking on a direct link using your browser, or by using one of the many search engines. A search engine, also sometimes called a web portal, is a website that allows users to find information quickly and easily. Each search engine has its own database of web documents. Items are continually added to the site by a program called a web crawler or spider, which searches the Web looking for new pages to add to the database. In addition to giving access to information in its database, a search-engine site may also provide features such as a free email service, chat rooms, news and facilities for online shopping. Some of the best-known search engines are Google™ search, Bing, Yahoo, Ask.com, AOL.com and Baidu.

Gain access to web pages by doing the following:

- Search through subject directories linked to organised collections of web pages.
- Enter an internet address or URL and retrieve a page directly.
- Enter a keyword or a search statement at a search engine to retrieve pages on the topic of your choice.
- Browse through pages and select links to move from one page to another.

Finding information using a uniform resource locator (URL)

You can find information by typing in a website's direct address or uniform resource locator (URL) into the 'Address' field, located at the top of the browser window, just below the menu bar. A URL is the address of an internet file, and is usually in this format, made up of four parts:

Protocol://Server/Path/Filename

- **Protocol:** The name of the internet protocol, usually 'http', giving access to the site
- **Server (hostname, for example, WWW):** The computer on which the document is located
- **Path (directory hierarchy):** The top-level directory and any lower-level sub-directories (separated by '/' characters) in which the required file is to be found
- **Filename:** The actual file name of the document.

An example is:

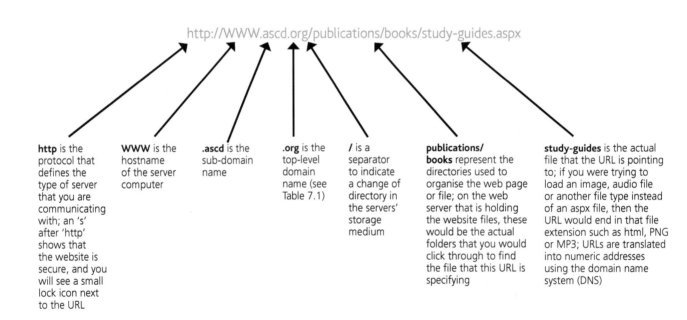

http://WWW.ascd.org/publications/books/study-guides.aspx

http is the protocol that defines the type of server that you are communicating with; an 's' after 'http' shows that the website is secure, and you will see a small lock icon next to the URL

WWW is the hostname of the server computer

.ascd is the sub-domain name

.org is the top-level domain name (see Table 7.1)

/ is a separator to indicate a change of directory in the servers' storage medium

publications/ books represent the directories used to organise the web page or file; on the web server that is holding the website files, these would be the actual folders that you would click through to find the file that this URL is specifying

study-guides is the actual file that the URL is pointing to; if you were trying to load an image, audio file or another file type instead of an aspx file, then the URL would end in that file extension such as html, PNG or MP3; URLs are translated into numeric addresses using the domain name system (DNS)

Other services offered using the World Wide Web (WWW)

- **Webcasts:** The delivery of live or delayed sound or video broadcasts over the World Wide Web is called webcasting. The sound or video is captured by conventional video or audio systems. It is then digitised and 'streamed' on a web server. Live webcasting is commonly used to transmit radio. For example, if you are a student from St Lucia studying a long way from home in the United States, it might still be possible for you to listen to your favourite radio station in Castries live, using your computer's speakers and an internet connection. With delayed webcasting, individual web users can usually connect to the server via a website to view/listen to the webcast at a time of their choosing. In both cases, the transmission is one-way, without any interaction between the presenter and the audience.

- **Webinars:** The term webinar is short for web-based seminar and refers to conducting a seminar or lecture via the World Wide Web, using graphics (often slides), text and even live voice. Unlike webcasting, the audience is able to interact with the presenter, for example, by 'asking' questions sent in an instant message. This interactive element allows the presenter and the audience to give, receive and discuss information.

- **Web 2.0:** Web 2.0 is the popular term for a group of internet technologies and applications that includes blogs, wikis, podcasts, RSS feeds and social bookmarking. These technologies enable enhanced creativity, communications and collaboration. They allow for a more socially connected Web where everyone is able to add to and edit the information space.

▲ Figure 7.10 Web page in Wikipedia

- **Wiki:** A wiki is a website where users can add, remove and edit every page using a web browser. A wiki allows a group of people to collaboratively develop a website with no knowledge of HTML or other markup languages. Anyone can add to or edit pages in a wiki. Anyone can create new wiki pages simply by creating a new link with the name of the page. Pages are not connected hierarchically, but rather by hyperlinks between pages. One of the best-known wikis is Wikipedia.

▲ Figure 7.11 Wikipedia edit screen

Types of websites

The first websites on the internet were used for informational purposes. However, with the development of the World Wide Web (WWW) several other types of websites were created.

- **Personal websites:** Individuals can create a personal website that can be used to display family photos, an online diary or information that they would like to share. These websites can be created from scratch using HTML or by using free website building sites such as Weebly, Wix.com, GoDaddy® and WordPress.

- **Photo-sharing websites:** Websites such as Flickr. com and Google Photos™ photo storage and organising platform offer free photo-sharing and hosting services. Also, many digital cameras, photo printers and smartphones come with software to create digital photo slide shows, which can be uploaded to the Web.

▲ Figure 7.12 Flickr photo-sharing website

- **Community building websites (social websites, forum websites, and sharing websites):** These websites build online communities of people who want to interact with other people socially or meet people who share their interests. Some of the best-known websites of this type are facebook.com, Linkedin.com and Twitter.com. For sharing and discussing mutual interests, there are online forums for practically any subject you can think of. These forum websites can be a great source of information.

▲ Figure 7.13 About LinkedIn page

- **Mobile device websites:** Mobile devices (smartphones, tablets, watches, and so on) are used extensively today. One problem is that standard websites are difficult to view and sometimes take a long time to download on some of these devices, with their small screens and wireless connections. Websites whose pages are narrower in width and take up less bandwidth work much better for mobile devices. A new domain designation .mobi, which has been available since the year 2006, has been created to identify websites that are 'mobile friendly'.

    Increasingly, designers are being encouraged to make their websites responsive so that they can adapt to different screen sizes. This reflects the changing way in which we are using the Web, with more of us using small screens such as smartphones and tablets rather than computers with larger screens. Google™ search now favours responsive designs in its searches.

▲ Figure 7.14 A mobile-friendly website

- **Informational websites:** Informational websites are websites that provide information on a wide range of topics. Newspaper companies, television companies, governments and business organisations all have websites that offer information to the public. One of the main informational sites available is wikipedia.org, the online encyclopaedia. This site allows members to contribute and edit articles. In addition, business owners often create websites to provide information about the products they sell. They can create a hybrid website by adding an e-commerce feature whereby the company can perform business transactions.

- **Directory websites:** Directory websites are the modern version of the printed Yellow Pages in phone books to find services and businesses. Directories can be dedicated to a certain topic or industry, or they can cover geographical areas. Some examples of general website directories are real estate, events, jobs, hotels, restaurants, and so on.

- **E-commerce websites:** There are millions of small businesses who use their e-commerce websites to sell their products over the internet. Just about anything that can be sold in a brick-and-mortar store can be sold online – with far fewer overheads! Some popular e-commerce sites are AMAZON, eBay, Tmall and Alibaba.

▲ Figure 7.15 An informational website

▲ Figure 7.16 Directory website

Mobile network applications

The use of mobile wireless data services continues to increase worldwide. The ever-increasing speeds of wireless networks have resulted in their use in diverse applications such as education, commerce, journalism, military, package delivery, disaster recovery and medical emergency care. Some of these applications are discussed below.

Mobile learning

Mobile learning represents a way to address a number of our educational problems and enhance learning. Devices such as smartphones and tablets enable innovation and they help students, teachers and parents to gain access to digital content and personalised assessment. Mobile learning makes it possible to extend education beyond the physical confines of the classroom and beyond the fixed time periods of the school day. The value of mobile devices is that they allow students to connect, communicate, collaborate and create digital resources that use text, sound, graphics, images and video (rich resources). The greater flexibility this gives students has resulted in more students finishing courses and continuing to study.

▲ Figure 7.17 Amazon e-commerce website

Mobile commerce

The continuous increase in the number of people owning and using mobile devices has provided a large and growing marketplace for various goods and services, as well as mobile commerce (m-commerce). M-commerce refers to conducting business activities via mobile devices – such as mobile phones or tablets – over a wireless internet connection. This method of conducting business provides many advantages for individuals, and for large and small businesses, for the following reasons:

- Businesses do not need expensive high street shops.
- Customers can shop from anywhere and get purchases delivered anywhere.

M-commerce can make services or applications available to consumers whenever and wherever a need arises. Users can get any information they need, whenever they want regardless of their location, via mobile devices that are able to connect to the internet. Through mobile devices, business entities can approach customers anywhere and anytime. As a result, customers are no longer restricted by time or place in accessing e-commerce activities. In addition, mobile devices are easy to carry and can connect easily and quickly to the internet, Intranet, other mobile devices and online databases, therefore making accessing services more convenient.

Mobile networks and journalism

Mobile devices such as smartphones enable journalists to quickly capture and create news content that can be broadcast live in a simpler and less expensive way than with traditional equipment. Live streaming through social platforms also enables journalists to engage with their audience while broadcasting.

Emerging trends

The Internet of Things (IoT) is the use of network sensors in physical devices to allow for remote monitoring and control via a network. This technology has gained wide acceptance in areas such as healthcare, banking, retail, manufacturing and consumer goods. Devices such as cell phones, automobiles, home appliances, headphones, manufacturing machines, wearable devices and almost anything else you can think of that can be fitted with web-enabled devices. These internet-ready devices allow for the collection and exchange of data, which create opportunities for more direct integration of the physical world into computer-based systems. The results are efficiency improvements, economic benefits and reduced human labour demands.

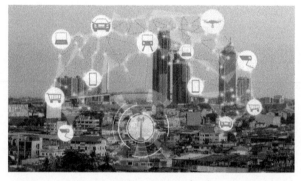

▲ Figure 7.18 In the Internet of Things (IoT), transportation examples such as automobiles, buses and trains are web-enabled.

Several applications of this technology are already in use. For example, web-enabled lights can help to reduce electricity use (automatically turning off the lights when no one is in a room) or helping to secure your home while you are away by turning your lights on and off. Similarly, smart outlets such as the WeMo allow you to instantly turn on and off any plugged-in device from across the world or from your living room. This allows users to save money and conserve energy over time by eliminating standby power, measure and record the power usage of any device, and increase its operating lifespan through more efficient use and scheduling. Individuals can also be part of the system by wearing web-enabled devices that can capture and upload personal adventures as they happen. Additionally, the system can assist in the care of the elderly by monitoring them through the use of wearable devices that can track their daily routine and provide alerts in the event of any serious disruptions in their normal schedule.

Chapter 7: Summary

- 'Data communications' refers to the transmission of data from one location to another for direct use or for further processing.
- The data communications channels used to carry data can be classified into narrow-band, voice-band and broadband, depending on the volume of data that can be transmitted.
- The transmission lines that carry the data are classified according to the direction of data flow: simplex, half-duplex or full-duplex.
- A local area network (LAN) is a collection of microcomputers connected within a small geographical area so that they can share information and peripherals, and also communicate with each other.
- The two types of LANs are client or server networks and peer-to-peer networks.
- The connection in a LAN can be through cables or wireless.
- A wide area network (WAN) can connect computers and peripherals across a large geographical area such as a city, a state or countries.
- The internet is a network, made up of other networks, which connects computers across the globe.
- A standard phone modem is a hardware device that converts analogue signals to digital signals and vice versa. Other types of modems that do not convert analogue to digital signals are ISDN modems and ADSL modems.
- An ISP is a company that has a direct connection to the internet and gives users access to it, usually for a fee.
- To transfer data from one computer to the next, computers must follow a set of rules called protocols. The protocol used over the internet is TCP/IP (Transmission Control Protocol/Internet Protocol).
- Each computer on the internet has a unique address called the IP address.
- The following four main types of services are available on the internet:
  - communications services, including email and electronic discussion forums
  - file transfer protocol (FTP)
  - terminal emulation services
  - the World Wide Web (WWW).
- VoIP is the transmission of telephone calls over computer networks via the internet.
- Web 2.0 is the popular term for a group of internet technologies and applications that includes blogs, wikis, podcasts, RSS feeds and social bookmarking.

- A podcast consists of audio files that are published via the internet and can be accessed via an RSS feed.
- A wiki is a website on which users can work collaboratively to add, remove and edit every page using a web browser.
- Webcasting is the delivery of live or delayed sound or video broadcasts conducted over the WWW.
- A webinar is the conducting of a seminar or lecture via the World Wide Web.
- The World Wide Web consists of hypertext and hypermedia documents. A hypertext document enables you to use hyperlinks to move from one document in a computer to another related document, either in the same computer or in another computer elsewhere.
- HyperText Transfer Protocol (HTTP) is a set of rules governing how data travels between server and client computers on the internet.
- A website consists of web pages built using specialised programming languages such as HyperText Markup Language (HTML). Each web page has a unique address called its uniform resource locator (URL).
- To find, retrieve, view and send hypertext and hypermedia documents over the Web, you need a browser. Browsers also give you access to search engines such as Yahoo!, Google™ search and MSN, enabling you to find information quickly by typing in keywords, a phrase or a website address.
- An intranet provides many of the features of the internet within a company or organisation.
- An extranet is similar to an intranet except that it allows limited access to individuals outside the company or organisation.
- Several types of websites exist on the internet. Some of these are personal websites, photo-sharing websites, community-building websites, mobile device websites, informational websites, directory websites and e-commerce websites.
- Mobile networks are made up of 'cells' that connect to one another and to telephone switches or exchanges.
- The most commonly used radio systems are GSM (Global System for Mobile Communication), CDMA (Code Division Multiple Access) and LTE (Long-Term Evolution).
- Mobile networks are used in diverse applications such as education, commerce, journalism, military, package delivery, disaster recovery, and medical emergency care.

Fill in the blanks

1 The internet is a _____ that connects computers worldwide via a huge set of telecommunications links.

2 A _____ converts analogue signals to digital signals for transmission over telephone lines.

3 A/(n) _____ modem is a digital device that allows voice, video and data to be sent as digital signals over ordinary copper wire telephone lines or fibre optic cables.

4 Computers connected to the internet use a protocol called _____.

5 The _____ address identifies a computer as a node on the internet.

6 The _____ system was developed to allow users to refer to hosts by names.

7 _____ enable users to send electronic messages (text, sound, video and graphics) to one individual or to a group of individuals on the WWW.

8 The _____ is a computer on the internet that operates like the traditional post office.

9 A/(n) _____ is a group of people using email to communicate their views.

True or False?

1 The internet is owned by the American government.

2 The internet is a worldwide network of networks.

3 All modems convert digital signals to analogue signals and vice versa.

4 Some internet connections allow users to have continuous internet service.

5 TCP/IP is a hardware device found on the motherboard of the computer.

6 A browser is used to navigate the WWW.

7 Each computer has a unique IP address that identifies it on the internet.

8 The internet and the WWW are the same.

Multiple-choice questions

1 The internet is owned by:
    a a world-wide governing body.
    b the United States government.
    c large organisations.
    d no single organisation.

2 TCP/IP is a protocol suite that was designed to be used with:
    a Apple® computers.
    b all computers.
    c IBM-compatible computers (that is, PCs).
    d none of the above.

3 Which of the following is not a browser?
    a Google™ search
    b Microsoft internet Explorer
    c Netscape Navigator
    d Mozilla Firefox

4 Which of the following can you do with browsers?
    a View hundreds of millions of web pages all over the world
    b Send and receive email
    c Participate in online conferences
    d All of the above

5 The IP address of a computer on the internet consists of:
    a 4 bits.   b 8 bits.
    c 16 bits.   d 32 bits.

6 Which of the following would you use to create web pages?
    a HTML   b FTP
    c HTTP   d TCP/IP

7 Each website on the internet has a unique address. What is the address referred to as?
    a HTML   b URL
    c HTTP   d TCP/IP

8 Which of the following network devices is best suited to connect two different networks?
    a Network interface card   b Switch
    c Gateway   d Modem

9 Which of the following network devices connects multiple devices on the same network to facilitate communication among the devices?
    a Network interface card   b Switch
    c Router   d Modem

10 Which of the following devices allows your home computer to connect to your internet service provider?
    a Network interface card   b Switch
    c Router   d Modem

Short-answer questions

1. a What is the internet?
   b List the hardware requirements needed to connect to the internet.
      i Explain the term 'internet service provider'.
      ii List and explain THREE types of communications links that may be used to get an internet connection.
      iii What is an IP address and why is it necessary?

2. List the different types of modems and explain how they differ.

3. Many people now use email for sending letters.
   a What is email?
   b List THREE advantages and TWO disadvantages of email over normal mail.
   c Why does a user need to have a password to access and send email?
   d Give TWO advantages of using email as opposed to using a phone.

4. How do you believe podcasting should be used in schools?

5. Give TWO examples of how a browser may be used for:
   a business purposes.   b personal use.

6. With the aid of examples, explain what URLs are.

7. What are some of the benefits that can be gained by a company that has set up an intranet?

8. Using an example, briefly explain how the domain name system (DNS) operates.

9. List THREE types of websites and explain their purpose.

10. The use of mobile wireless data services continues to increase worldwide. Mobile commerce is one application that has been continuously growing.
    a Explain THREE advantages of mobile commerce.
    b Explain how mobile data services can be used in education.

Research questions

1. A school has recently been granted an internet connection. The school principal intends to network all the computers on the school compound. As the president of the ICT club at the school, she has come to you for advice. She would like answers to the following questions:
   a What type of network (wireless or wired) is best suited for the school?
   b What are the advantages and disadvantages of this network?
   c What equipment would be required to set up this network?
   d What software would be required to ensure that both networks will function?
   e Will you please provide a sketch of all the devices in a wired and wireless solution?

2. The principal has also asked that you provide her with a report on how the availability of the internet and networked computers can improve student learning.

Crossword

Across
1 An area of storage allocated to you by a mail server (7)

3 A set of rules that defines how computers interact or communicate with each other (8)

6 This topology connects the computers on the network through a central hub (4)

7 It runs the networking software that allows resources to be shared with other computers on the network (6)

8 The term used to describe the copying of a file from one computer on the internet to a storage device on your computer (8)

Down
2 Used to navigate the WWW (7)

4 A device or computer designed specifically for sending packets of data to their correct destination (6)

5 An interface that enables communication between two different networks (7)

Problem-solving and program design

8

Objectives

At the end of this chapter, you will be able to:

→ define the term 'computer program'
→ outline the steps in problem-solving
→ explain the steps in algorithm development
→ develop an algorithm.

We are faced with problems every day, from the time we get out of bed in the morning until the time we fall asleep at night. A problem is any task that requires a solution.

Steps in problem-solving

A problem may be simple or complex. In order to come up with a solution we must follow these steps:

1 **Define the problem.**
In order to define a problem, we must have a clear understanding of the problem, determine what we need to help us to solve the problem and decide what results we want to achieve.

2 **Analyse the problem.**
Analysing a problem involves determining the possible options and identifying what information is needed to solve the problem. There are often several ways to solve a problem, so at this stage, we need to consider what these may be and what their strengths and weaknesses are.

3 **Select the most efficient solution.**
Choosing the most efficient solution involves deciding which solution provides the best answer to the problem. You need to decide which of the strengths and weaknesses you found in the last step are most important. Then you need to choose a solution that has more of those strengths and fewer of the weaknesses. This might be the quickest solution or it might be the cheapest.

4 **Develop a method or algorithm to solve the problem.**
For many everyday problems, you will often just go ahead and solve them. However, for some problems, you will be making a solution that you will use many times, for example, a company making boxes will need to set up their machines to make boxes in a particular way and repeat that process again and again.

5 **Test and validate the solution.**
Finally, we need to make sure a solution works as well as we planned. In the example of the company making boxes, they might realise that the glue they are using is taking too long to dry and so change it, or that if they change the shape they cut out, the machine can fold it into a box a little quicker. If they act on these problems to resolve them, they can improve the solution.

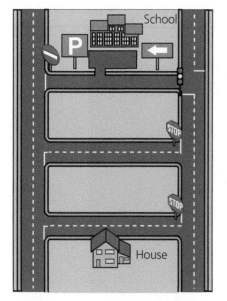

▲ Figure 8.1 A neighbourhood showing a house and a school

Let us look at a real example of problem-solving. Figure 8.1 shows a neighbourhood in which a house and a school are located.

We need to solve the problem of the best way to drive from the house to the school. We can then start looking at different routes (solutions). We will probably want to choose the quickest route and this is likely to be the shortest. Some routes will not work, for example, the road outside the school is a one-way road so you won't be able to go down it the wrong way. Eventually, you can come up with a step-by-step sequence of instructions to get from the house to the school. For example:

1   Enter the car.
2   Turn right into the road when safe to do so.
3   Drive forward to the stop sign.
4   Stop the car.
5   Turn left onto the main street when safe to do so.
6   Drive forward to the traffic light.
7   Turn left on the signal of the traffic light.
8   Drive forward to the school.
9   Turn right into the car park when safe to do so.
10 Park the car.
11 Exit the car.

Did you know?

A recipe is a good example of an algorithm because it tells you what you need to do, step by step.

You then go outside and use the directions. You might find that as you use them more and more, the amount of traffic on the road makes a bigger difference to the time taken than the distance, so you end up taking a longer route that has less traffic, as it takes less time.

This problem, and its solution, is from the real world; computers can also solve problems, using similar logic.

A computer program is a series of coded instructions for the computer to obey in order to solve a problem. The computer executes (obeys) these instructions when told to do so by the user. The number of these instructions varies, depending on the complexity of the problem.

An algorithm is a sequence of instructions that has a finite number of steps, which, if followed, produces a precise solution to the given problem, or part of the problem. At the end of each instruction, there is no question as to what needs to be done next, so there is a flow of control from one process to another. The instructions produce an unambiguous result (the result can only be one of a limited number of things) and eventually come to an end (terminate). An algorithm is written using special rules and statements. Simple computer programs are sometimes just made up of many different algorithms.

Algorithms can be written using pseudocode or flowcharts.

- Pseudocode is a language that models or resembles the real programming language of the computer. It cannot be executed by the computer.
- Flowcharts are diagrams that visually represent the sequence of instructions of algorithms.

Algorithms, pseudocode, flowcharts and computer programs are written using specific rules and statements, much like grammar rules in the English language. Computer programs are written in different computer languages and each of these has its own set of rules and statements. The specific rules for writing in a particular computer language are known as syntax.

Exercise 1

1   What is an algorithm?
2   Why do we need to try several solutions to a problem?
3   What do we mean by the most efficient solution?

Steps in algorithm development

As we saw at the start of the chapter, we can approach a problem by going through a set of steps. In this section, we are going to look at how we can take a problem and use flowcharts and pseudocode to design and test a solution. In the next chapter, we will look at how we turn that design into a computer program. As in the problem-solving steps earlier, there are a number of steps to create a design for an algorithm:

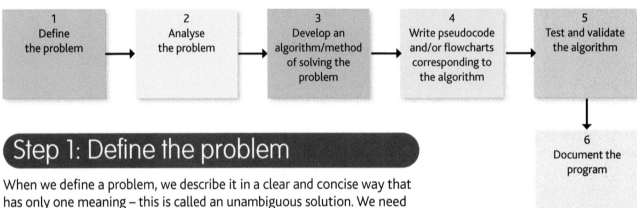

| 1 Define the problem | → | 2 Analyse the problem | → | 3 Develop an algorithm/method of solving the problem | → | 4 Write pseudocode and/or flowcharts corresponding to the algorithm | → | 5 Test and validate the algorithm |

6 Document the program

Step 1: Define the problem

When we define a problem, we describe it in a clear and concise way that has only one meaning – this is called an unambiguous solution. We need to do this because computers work in an unambiguous way. A computer would answer the question, 'Is this jacket grey?' with a yes or no, but we would answer in a slightly different way, perhaps saying 'dark grey' or 'light grey' or 'bluey-grey'.

Examples of unambiguous problems for which we could create an algorithm are:

■ calculating the price of an item after a 10% discount
■ converting a temperature from °C to °F
■ computing the average rainfall for the month of May in a certain place.

We call this clear description a problem definition.

Step 2: Analyse the problem

In order to write a program to accomplish a certain task, you must analyse the task as a sequence of instructions that can be performed by the computer. This process of breaking a problem definition into a set of steps that can be written as a computer program is called **decomposition**.

If our problem definition is clear and unambiguous, we should be able to identify three significant components: input, process and output. We will look at each of these components and the types of instructions that are associated with them.

Input

These instructions allow information or data to be accepted by the computer. The input is information that is needed by the computer to solve the problem. We often need to store this information somewhere, but we will look at that in detail later in this chapter. Words such as 'Enter', 'Input' and 'Read' within problem definitions usually indicate what data the computer requires. See Example 1.

Process

These instructions manipulate the input data. They involve calculations, that is, mathematical operations (for example, addition, subtraction, multiplication and division), repeating instructions, selecting instructions and comparison instructions. They also include commands and constructs. See Example 2.

A command is a word that instructs the computer what must be done to accomplish a specific task. Commands are specific to a particular programming language: for example, WRITE, PRINT, READ, INPUT, and so on.

A construct is a group of instructions that work together with commands to accomplish a specific task. An example is the 'IF–THEN' construct.

Problem statements that contain the words 'calculate', 'compute'. 'convert', 'add', 'sum', 'subtract', 'minus', 'multiply', 'divide', 'percentage' and 'average' indicate what needs to be done. Problem statements can also imply what needs to be processed by looking at the results that are required for output, for example: 'Print the **area** of the room.'

Repeat statements and comparison statements

Repeat statements and comparison statements are the repeating instructions and comparison instructions mentioned above.

- **Comparison/selection/decision statements:** These involve checking if a condition is true or false in order to perform a set of instructions. For example:
  Read the weekly hours worked by an employee. If the hours worked are greater than 40, then calculate overtime salary at 1.5 times the standard hourly rate of $8.50, for those hours over 40.
  The condition that is checked to see if it is true or false is the number of hours worked. The condition is true if it is more than 40 and false if it is less.

- **Repeat statements/loopings/iterations:** These are used when a problem has to be done a number of times.
  For example:
  Read the marks for three subjects, English, Maths and Spanish, for each student; find the average mark of each student in a class of 15, over the three subjects.
  The process of finding the average for the three subjects has to be repeated 15 times.

Example 1

In these problem definitions, what are the input instructions?

1. Read the price of an item and calculate the discount of 10%.

2. Enter the name and year of birth of a person and calculate the person's age.

3. Input the length of a side of a square tile and find the area.

Solution

Let us analyse these instructions to determine the inputs and what we need to store.

1. Read and store the price of an item.

2. Enter the name and year of birth of a person.

3. Input the length of the side of a square tile.

Example 2

What are the processing instructions here?

1. Read the price of an item and calculate the new price after a 10% discount.

2. Enter a temperature in degrees Celsius and convert it to degrees Fahrenheit.

3. Input the name and year of birth and compute and print the age of a person.

Solution

Let us analyse these instructions to determine what we need to process.

1. Calculate the new price after a 10% discount.

2. Convert it to degrees Fahrenheit.

3. Compute the age of a person.

Output

The instructions in Example 3 allow information to be displayed on the screen. Problem statements that include keywords such as 'print', 'output', 'display', 'return' and 'write' indicate what data should be output to the screen.

Input, process, output (IPO) charts

One tool we can use to help us to record and organise the instructions is an IPO chart. This allows us to organise the instructions we find in the problem definition so that we can clearly see the input, process and output components. Example 4 shows how an IPO chart is used.

> ### Example 3
>
> What are the output statements here?
>
> The IPO chart
>
> 1 Enter the name and year of birth of a person and compute and display the age of the person.
>
> 2 Write an algorithm to print a conversion table of degrees Celsius to degrees Fahrenheit, 10 °C to 20 °C inclusive.
>
> Let us analyse these instructions to determine what we need to output.
>
> 1 Display the age of the person.
>
> 2 Print a conversion table.

> ### Example 4
>
> Write a program to **enter** the **base** and **height** of a triangle and **find** and **print** the **area**.
>
> The IPO chart
>
>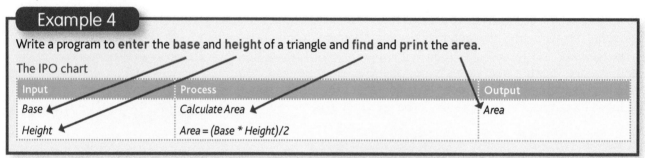
>
> | Input | Process | Output |
> |---|---|---|
> | Base | Calculate Area | Area |
> | Height | Area = (Base * Height)/2 | |

You will see that we have also added the formula to calculate the area into the processing instructions. Sometimes common calculations like this will not be written in the problem definition but are important in solving the problem, so if it is fine to use, then we will do so; it is a good idea to write them in.

Let us analyse a few more problems, as shown in examples 5 to 8.

> ### Example 5
>
> Write a program to read the temperature in degrees Celsius (°C) and convert it to degrees Fahrenheit (°F) where F = 32+(9C/5). Output the temperature in degrees Celsius and Fahrenheit.
>
> The IPO chart
>
> | Input | Process | Output |
> |---|---|---|
> | C | Calculate Fahrenheit F = 32+(9C/5) | C |
> | | | F |

> ### Example 6
>
> Write a program to read the answer to the sum 10 * 12. (The answer is 120.) Return the comment "Correct" if the answer is right and "Incorrect" if the answer is wrong.
>
> The IPO chart
>
> | Input | Process | Output |
> |---|---|---|
> | Answer | If Answer = 120 then print "Correct" otherwise print "Incorrect" | "Correct" or "Incorrect" |

Example 7

Write a program that reads the result of 10 games played by a team and find the percentage of games won by the team. Output the percentage of games won.

The IPO chart

Input	Process	Output
GameResult	• Repeat 10 times READ GameResult add 1 to TotalWins if Game Result is a "Win" • PercentageWins = (TotalWins/10)*100	PercentageWins

Exercise 2

Analyse these problems by finding the input, process and output and producing an IPO chart.

1 Write a program to enter an individual's year of birth and the current year, and calculate and return the individual's age.
2 Write a program to enter a number, double the number, and output the result.
3 A box can hold one-and-a-half-dozen cans of tomatoes. Read the number of boxes and the price of a can of tomatoes; then calculate and print the total cost of all the cans of tomatoes.
4 Write a program to accept four numbers and produce an output of their sum, average and product.
5 Write a program to read a month in the year and print 'This is the month of the rights of the child' if the month entered is 'October'.
6 Persons under 18 are not allowed in at 'Shutters Night Club'. Write a program to read a person's age. If it is under 18, output 'Underage'.
7 Students are awarded extra credit points depending on how they perform in their coursework; if they score more than 80 marks they are given a bonus credit point. Read the student course mark and add one bonus point to the total credit points if the student's mark is higher than 80. Print the students' total credit points.
8 Write a program to input a number N. If the number is greater than 50, subtract 10 from the number, otherwise multiply the number by 2 and add 5. Print the number and the result.
9 Three football teams are awarded points based on matches they played. Read the team, the team total and whether it won, drew or lost the match and print the team total. Award the points to the teams' total points as follows: 2 – win, 1 – drawn, 0 – lost.
10 Write a program to print the average age and height of students in a class of 35. Read the age and height of each student.
11 A computer technician works for $50 an hour at his regular paying job of 40 hours a week. If he takes on private jobs, he charges $150 an hour. Write a program to read the number of private jobs he has this week and the number of hours it takes him to perform the jobs. Calculate the total amount of money he earns.
12 To enter a theme park, children under 12 pay $3; children older than 12 and adults pay $7; babies 2 years and younger pay $0. Input the number of people entering the park. Read whether a person entering the park is an adult, child or baby, and calculate the total revenue earned by the park for that day.

Example 8

A school has implemented a house system. Points are awarded to a house based on the performance of its members.

- 1st place – 4 points
- 2nd place – 3 points
- 3rd place – 2 points
- 4th place – 1 point
- Last place – no points.

Read the names of 10 members of the Aripo house and the place they came in the events; calculate and print the total points awarded to the house.

The IPO chart

Input	Process	Output
Name	• Repeat 10 times • Check Place If Place = 1 then add 4 to Total If Place = 2 then add 3 to Total If Place = 3 then add 2 to Total If Place = 4 then add 1 to Total	Total

Step 3: Develop an algorithm

Once you have analysed the problem, the next step is to develop an algorithm. To do this, you need to take several factors into account.

- **Storage:** This involves understanding what constants and variables are and why you need them.
- **Flowcharts:** These involve learning how to show the flow of an algorithm in a diagram.
- **Pseudocode:** This involves learning a way to describe how a program will work. We will also look at the different operators of pseudocode: instructions; relational, arithmetic and logical operators; and conditional branching and loops.

Storage

As mentioned earlier, we often need to store the items we identified as input in our IPO chart. There may also be other items we need to store as we work through our algorithm. For example, in Example 8 on page 133, we need to keep track of how many house members there are, for which we have added scores, as well as the individual and total scores.

We are going to look at two types of storage used in programming – constants and variables.

Constants

Constants refers to the data that does not change but remains the same during the execution of the program. For example, pi is 3.14159 or 22/7 – this value does not change. Other examples of constants are 15% VAT, or the name of a person, 'Jack'.
There are two types of constants:

- Numeric constants are simply numbers – integers and whole numbers with fractions (called real or floating-point numbers), for example, 39, −6, 3.25. The value of a numeric constant is the actual number.
- String constants/**character strings** are a set of characters or text enclosed in single or double quotation marks, for example: 'James', "SUM =", 'Average', and so on. The value of a string constant is the characters without the quotation marks. Different programming languages use single or double quotation marks. Throughout this chapter, we will use double quotation marks.

Variables

The memory of a computer contains storage cells (or bytes), each of which has a unique address. Data occupies these storage locations rather like the way people occupy houses. A person living in a particular house can be located by their surname or house number; similarly, memory locations are given names that allow the computer to locate the relevant data easily. It is easier to refer to the data by name.

When we run or execute a program, instructions may cause the contents in these memory locations to change or vary, hence the term **variable**. Variable names should always be meaningful: they should convey (show) the meaning of what is being stored.

There are two types of variables: numeric and string variables. Numeric variables are used to store numbers only and can be integers and floating point numbers such as constants. String variables are used to store a set, or string, of characters. There is a third type, Boolean expression, and these can only take the values TRUE or FALSE. Look at this example:

Variable names

Firstname	Height	Age	Marks
Jack	160	13	78

Contents of storage locations

Note

Notice that you cannot store the name "Jack" in the storage location for age.

Flowcharts

Flowcharts are diagrams that are used to represent the sequences of algorithms visually. They use a set of symbols with a little text in each. Simple tasks have simple flowcharts and complex tasks can have flowcharts with thousands of components. Flowcharts are especially useful for novice programmers if it fits onto one page; however, if it takes up several pages , it becomes difficult to follow and may be ineffective. In that case, pseudocode becomes a more effective algorithmic tool.

Programmers use many different symbols to draw flowcharts but some basic symbols that we will be using are listed in Table 8.1.

Symbol	Representation
	Rectangle – process to be performed, for example, arithmetic
	Oval – the start and stop boxes
	Diamond – decision or question boxes
	Parallelogram – an input or output operation
	Arrow – denotes the flow or path of the algorithm, that is, where to go next after an operation has been carried out
	Connector – indicates an exit from or an entry to part of the program
	Off-page connector – denotes that the flowchart continues on another page

▲ Table 8.1 Basic symbols used by programmers

An example of a flowchart to find and display the sum of three numbers, is as shown in the flowchart on the right.

Pseudocode

Pseudocode is a way of writing a description of an algorithm or program that allows it to be read and converted easily into a computer language. In the next section, we will look at the operators.

Exercise 3

These questions will allow you to recognise constants and variables and their types. Answer each question by saying whether the data is a constant or variable and give its type: Integer, floating point (Float), String or Boolean.
1 Student's name
2 Cost of a bus ticket
3 Hours in a day
4 Whether or not a student is at school today
5 Length of a table
6 Number of centimetres in a metre

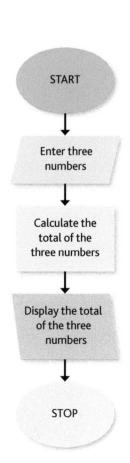

135

In this section, we will use a set of rules that will help you to recognise the parts of the pseudocode.

- The operators that are words, for example, instructions, logical operators, arithmetic operators, conditional branching and loops, all use capital letters. For example: PRINT, READ, WHILE, DIV, AND
- When we want to indicate the type of information that follows an operator, it will be in angle brackets. For example, if we want to explain that a variable follows a 'READ' operator, we write: READ<Variable name>
- Variable and constant names are mixed uppercase and lowercase, usually without spaces between words, for example: BoxHeight, ChildAge, DateOfBirth, Area

Instructions

Data input and storage instructions
These instructions accept data that is entered into the computer and store the value in the location with the given variable names.
Commands used to input data are READ or INPUT.
Syntax: READ<Variable name>, <Variable name>
Example: READName, Score

Prompting instructions
Prompting statements are used along with input statements to request or notify the user to enter data into the computer. These statements are usually displayed on the screen. Prompting instructions usually precede (come before) input instructions.
Commands used to prompt the user are PRINT or WRITE.
Syntax: PRINT<String>
Example: PRINT "Enter student name"
See Example 9.

Example 9

Note: In all of the examples, the purple boxes show the algorithms and the flowcharts show the sequence of the algorithms.

a Let us look at the question from Example 4:

Write a program to enter the base and height of a triangle and find and print the area. The inputs were base and height.

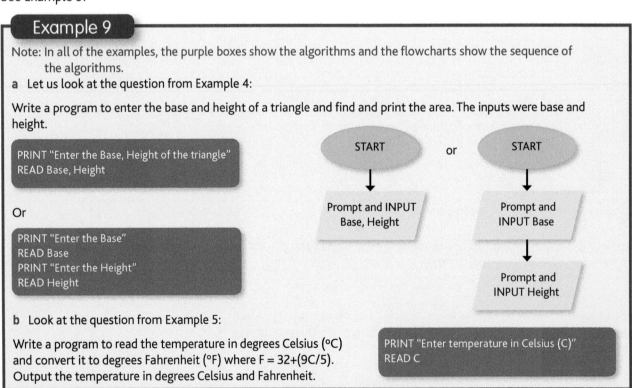

```
PRINT "Enter the Base, Height of the triangle"
READ Base, Height
```

Or

```
PRINT "Enter the Base"
READ Base
PRINT "Enter the Height"
READ Height
```

b Look at the question from Example 5:

Write a program to read the temperature in degrees Celsius (°C) and convert it to degrees Fahrenheit (°F) where F = 32+(9C/5). Output the temperature in degrees Celsius and Fahrenheit.

```
PRINT "Enter temperature in Celsius (C)"
READ C
```

c Look at the question from Example 6:

Write a program to read the answer to the sum 10 * 12. (The answer is 120.) Return the comment 'Correct' if the answer is right and 'Incorrect' if the answer is wrong.

```
PRINT "Enter answer for the problem 10 * 12 ="
READ Answer
```

d Look at the question from Example 7:

Write a program that reads the result of 10 games played by a team and find the percentage of games won by the team. Output the percentage of games won.

```
PRINT "Enter game resutls (Results)"
READ Results
```

Exercise 4

These questions will allow you to practise writing prompting, input and storage instructions.
The first question has been answered for you.

1 Write an instruction to read N.

```
Answer:
PRINT "Enter a value for N"
READ N
```

2 Write an instruction to enter the length and width of a pool.
3 Write an instruction to read the height and weight of an individual.
4 Write an instruction to read the names of students, their school houses and the places they came in a sporting event.
5 Write an instruction to read a time.
6 Write an instruction to enter values for a, b, c and d. $\dfrac{+b-c(c+d)}{a}$
7 Write an instruction to input the price of a textbook and the percentage discount given.
8 Write an instruction to enter the size (length and width) of a wall and the size of a tile (length and width) used to cover the wall.

Output instructions

These instructions display and output the data in the computer's memory.

Commands used to output data are PRINT or WRITE. You can output string variables and numeric variables as shown below.

Syntax: PRINT<Variable name>, <Variable name>
Example:

```
PRINT Name, ScoreJaneDoe, 78
PRINT Percentage 15
```

The values of the variables are printed, for example, 'Jane Doe' and '78' are printed.

Outputting a string constant

When a string constant is printed, the exact characters within the quotation marks are printed.

Syntax: PRINT"String"
Example:

```
PRINT "Carlosismyname."   Carlos is my name.
PRINT "Time"              Time
PRINT "Sum = 3+4"         Sum = 3 + 4
```

Outputting a string constant and a variable:
It may become necessary to output a label for a variable to identify what is being printed.

For example, if $4.35 is printed by itself, you may not know what it means unless a descriptor or label goes along with it, such as:
The total cost is: $4.35

Syntax: PRINT"String", <Variable>

Example:

> PRINT "Thetotalcostis:", Cost

Calculations

The arithmetic operators for addition (+), subtraction (−), multiplication (*), division (/), MOD and DIV are used when writing calculation statements. The equals sign in a calculation statement is known as the assignment symbol. Variables are assigned the results of the calculation.

For example:

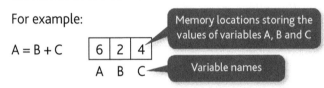

A = B + C | 6 | 2 | 4 |

Memory locations storing the values of variables A, B and C

Variable names

In this statement, the variable A is assigned the result of the calculation of B + C so that the memory location A will hold the result of the calculation performed on the variables B and C.

Syntax: <Variable> = <actual calculation>
Example algorithm:

> Area = (Base * Height)/2
> F = 32+(9C/5)
> PercentageWins = TotalWins/10

Calculation statements are always written with a variable being assigned the value of a calculation, rather than a calculation being assigned a variable.
Incorrect syntax: <actual calculation> = <Variable>
Incorrect example:
(Base * Height)/2 = Area

Brackets
In arithmetic calculations, the order in which calculations are carried out is controlled by brackets. The calculations inside the brackets are always worked out first. In the example of Area above, (Base * Height) is calculated first and the result is divided by 2.

Exercise 5

Write output instructions for these problems.
1   Write an algorithm to display 'My name is Carla'.
2   Write an algorithm to output the number of adults and children on a flight, appropriately labelled.
3   Write an algorithm to output the message: 'Warning: Read all labels before washing'.
4   Write an algorithm to output the message: 'At times like this, who needs enemies'?
5   Write an algorithm to read a time, and output the message: 'At a time like this', time, 'who needs enemies?'
6   Write an instruction to print the average score of 25 students and the name and mark of the person receiving the highest mark.
7   Print the name of an item, cost of the item, the price inclusive of the VAT, the discount, and the final price of the item.
8   Write an algorithm to read the name and amount on a cheque and display this information.
9   Input and output the following information: the name, age and sex of a person, appropriately labelled.
10 Print the principal, rate, time and interest for a loan.

Flowchart symbols for calculation instructions

> Area = (Base*Height)/2

> Let
> F = 32+(9C/5)

Did you know?

There are three operators that relate to division: /, MOD and DIV

/ — performs a division and gives a full answer, including the fractional part, for example: 7/3 = 2.3333

DIV — Integer division gives the whole number (integer) part of the answer to the division, for example: 7 DIV 3 = 2

MOD — Modulus gives the remainder of the division, for example, 7 MOD 3 = 2 (because 7/3 = 2 remainder 1)

Relational operators

Sometimes we have to compare the value of a variable to the value of another variable or we have to compare the value of a variable to that of a constant.

The relational operators shown in Table 8.2 are used to make these comparisons.

A **condition** is an expression that, when evaluated, gives either a TRUE or a FALSE. This expression is called a Boolean expression. These conditions use the relational operators between two variables, or between a variable and a constant.

Examples:
Boys in Class >= 35
Number of Boys <> Number of Girls

Relational operator	Meaning
=	Equal to
<>, #	Not equal to
>	Greater than
<	Less than
>=	Greater than or equal to
<=	Less than or equal to

▲ Table 8.2 Relational operators and their meanings

Conditional branching

The IF–THEN construct
The IF–THEN construct contains a condition that is tested before an action can be undertaken. If the condition holds true, then the action is taken. It is a good idea to add an ENDIF, as shown in the syntax below, as this makes it clear where the actions taken if the condition is true finish. Otherwise, the instruction statements between IF–THEN and ENDIF are ignored and not taken. See the flowchart on the right. Then see Example 10 and Example 11.

Syntax:
IF <condition> THEN
<Action to be taken if the condition is true>
(that is, instruction statements that would be performed if the conditions are met)
ENDIF

Exercise 6

Write calculation instructions for these problems.
1. Enter the length and width of a pool and calculate and print the length of rope needed to cordon (block) off the pool.
2. Input the price of a textbook. Calculate and print the total cost of the book after 15% VAT is added.
3. Pipes are laid by an oil company. If the company has to lay 3 km of pipes and each pipe is 25 m long, calculate and print the number of pipes needed to cover the distance.
4. Enter the size of a wall in square metres to be laid between two columns. If the area of one brick is 0.6 m², calculate and print the number of bricks required to build the wall.
5. Read the cost of a meal at a restaurant. If a 10% service charge were added to the bill, write an algorithm to calculate and return the total amount on the bill.
6. Write a program to read the temperature in degrees Celsius (°C) and convert it to degrees Fahrenheit (°F) where F = 32+(9C/5). Output the temperature in degrees Celsius and Fahrenheit.
7. $\dfrac{+b-c(c+d)}{a}$

   Write an instruction to enter values for *a*, *b*, *c* and *d* and compute and print the result of the equation.
8. Write an instruction to enter the size (length and width) of a wall and the size of the tile (length and width) used to cover the wall, in square metres. Estimate the number of tiles needed to cover the wall, adding 10% more tiles to cover for breakage. Print the size of the wall, the size of tiles used and the total number of tiles needed, inclusive of the number of tiles added to cover breakage.
9. Read the height in centimetres and mass in kilograms of an individual and compute and print their BMI (body mass index). BMI = ((mass/height)/height) * 703.
10. A carpenter is paid a contract fee of $2,000 for 3 days work. He hires 3 workers who work for the 3 days at $75 a day. Calculate and print the amount of money paid to each worker, the total paid to all the workers and the amount the carpenter is left with.

Flowchart syntax for the IF–THEN construct

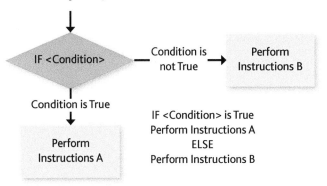

IF <Condition> is True
Perform Instructions A
ELSE
Perform Instructions B

Example 10

A company gives out bonuses based on the amount of income generated by its sales representatives per month. Once the income is greater than $5,000, a bonus of 10% of the generated income is given to the employees. Read the income generated and print the bonus.

Solution

The decision to give a bonus is based on the amount of income the sales representative generates.

Input/read the Income Generated.

The action to be taken is the calculation and printing of the bonus.

Only if the Income Generated is greater than $5,000 is the bonus calculated.

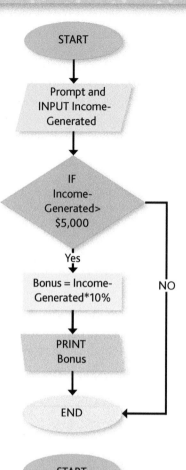

Case 1

We must be aware of where the PRINT statement is placed. If it is placed within the IF–THEN–ENDIF construct then *only* if the income generated is greater than $5,000 is the bonus printed.

```
READ IncomeGenerated
IF IncomeGenerated > 5000 THEN
        Bonus = IncomeGenerated/10
        PRINT "Bonus is", Bonus
ENDIF
```

Case 2

In this case, the PRINT statement is placed outside the IF–THEN–ENDIF construct. So, the word 'Bonus' is printed regardless of whether the bonus is actually calculated or not.

```
READ IncomeGenerated
IF IncomeGenerated > 5000 THEN
        Bonus = IncomeGenerated/10
ENDIF
PRINT "Bonus is ", Bonus
```

Initialising a variable

It may sometimes be necessary or wise to **initialise** a variable, that is, to give the variable a starting or initial value.

A variable is assigned to a position in memory that is not used. That position may nevertheless have data stored there (from some previous operation); this data, therefore, needs to be erased by setting an initial value for the variable.

In Case 2 in Example 10, since the bonus is printed regardless of whether the employee generates an income > $5,000, it is necessary to void the memory location where the variable is assigned and initialise it to $0.

In this way, a figure will be printed along with the word 'Bonus', and not the data that was stored from a previous operation.

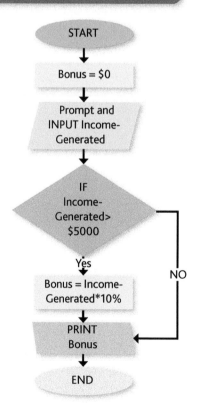

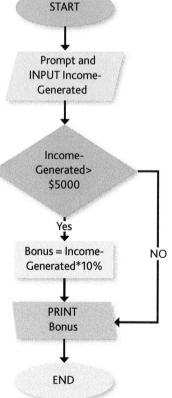

Case 3

In Case 3, if the income generated is less than or equal to $5,000 and no bonus is calculated, then the bonus printed will be $0. This is because the figure has previously been stored in memory, when we initialised the variable to $0.

```
Bonus = 0
READ IncomeGenerated
IF IncomeGenerated > 5000 THEN
        Bonus = IncomeGenerated/10
ENDIF
PRINT "Bonus is ", Bonus
```

Example 11

A car rental firm leases its cars for $250 per day. The manager gives a discount based on the number of days that the car is rented. If the rental period is greater than or equal to 7 days, then a 25% discount is given. Read the rental period and print the discount given.

Input the rental period.

The decision is based on the length of time the car is rented. The action is to calculate the discount to be given for the rental period. Only if the car is rented for 7 days or more is the discount calculated.

```
READ RentalPeriod
Discount = 0
IF RentalPeriod>=7 THEN
    Lease = 250*RentalPeriod
    Discount = Lease*0.25
ENDIF
PRINT "Discount is $", Discount
```

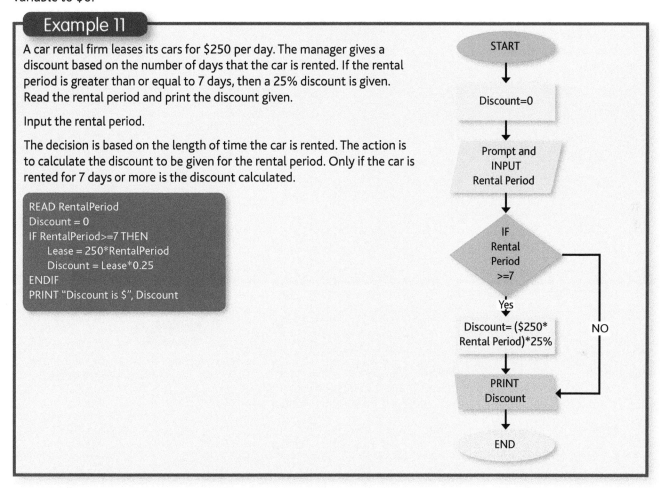

The IF–THEN–ELSE construct

The IF–THEN–ELSE construct contains two parts: the THEN part and an ELSE part. The condition is tested before an action can be undertaken. If the condition holds true, the THEN action is taken. If the condition is false, the ELSE action is taken. See Example 12.

As shown in the syntax below, indentation is used for readability, so that you can see at a glance the structure of the construct, and especially which statements belong to the THEN part, and which belong to the ELSE part.

Syntax:
```
IF <Condition> THEN
    <THEN part: Action to be taken if the condition is true>
ELSE
    <ELSE part: Action to be taken if the condition is false>
ENDIF
```

Example 12

A company gives out bonuses based on the amount of income generated by its sales representatives per month. Once the income is greater than $5,000, then a bonus of 10% of the generated income is payable; otherwise, the bonus is 3% of the generated income. Read the income generated and print the bonus.

```
READ Income
Bonus = 0
IF Income > 3000 THEN
    Bonus = Income * 0.1
ELSE
    Bonus = Income * 0.03
ENDIF
PRINT "Bonus", Bonus
```

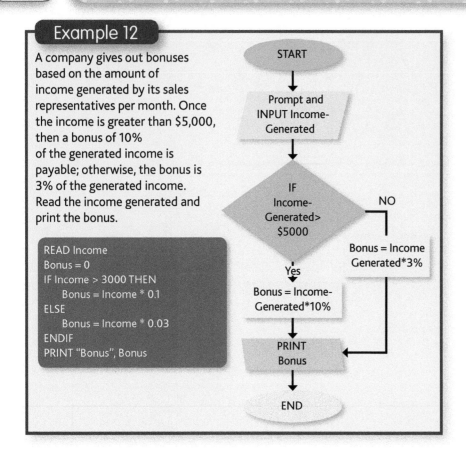

Boolean operators

When a selection is based on one or more expressions/decisions being true or false, it is possible to combine the expressions/decisions together using the Boolean operators AND or OR. See Example 13.

If the AND operator is used, *both* conditions must be met, in order for the *total* expression to be true or false. We can use a truth table, as follows, to show the results.

AND	TRUE	FALSE
TRUE	TRUE	FALSE
FALSE	FALSE	FALSE

If the OR operator is used, *either* condition must be met, in order for the *total* expression to be true or false. Again, we can use a truth table to show the results.

OR	TRUE	FALSE
TRUE	TRUE	TRUE
FALSE	TRUE	FALSE

There is also a NOT operator and this inverts the condition put into it. So, NOT TRUE = FALSE and NOT FALSE = TRUE

Note

A truth table is a logic table that is used to show if a statement is true or false.

The outcomes or results are shown in the last column.

Example 13

A club plays cricket only on Sundays, and only if it is not raining. Read the day and the weather and print 'Game on' if it is a suitable day for playing.

What happens with each of the two operators: AND and OR? Let us try some algorithms.

With the AND operator

Both conditions must be met for the expression to be true and 'Game on' is printed. If either condition is not met, such as the day is not 'Sunday' or the weather is 'Rain', then the action (printing 'Game on') is not taken.

```
READ Day
READ Weather
IF Day = "Sunday" AND Weather = "No Rain" THEN
        PRINT "Game ON"
ENDIF
```

With the OR operator

In this case, if either condition is true then the action is taken. So, if the day is 'Sunday', regardless of the weather, the game is on. If the weather is 'No Rain', regardless of the day, the game is on.

```
RREAD Day
READ Weather
IF Day = "Sunday" OR Weather = "No Rain" THEN
        PRINT "Game ON"
ENDIF
```

In this case, the game would always take place on a Sunday regardless of the weather; the game would also be played any other day of the week, as long as there is no rain. The only time the game is not played is if it is any of the days Monday to Saturday, and it is raining on that particular day. But, note that this is not exactly what the club wants. So, only the AND operator works to meet the conditions set out by the club.

The AND operator is also used to limit values within a particular range. See Example 14.

Example 14

A company gives out bonuses based on the amount of income generated by its sales representatives per month. Once the income is greater than $5,000 and less than or equal to $8,000, then a bonus of 10% of the generated income is given to the employee. Read the generated income and print the bonus.

```
READ Income
Bonus = 0
IF Income > 5000 AND Income <= 8000 THEN
        Bonus = Income * 0.1
ENDIF
PRINT "Bonus is $", Bonus
```

Nested conditions

IF statements that are embedded one within another are said to be nested. For every IF–THEN statement, there must be an ENDIF.

Syntax:

```
IF <Condition 1> THEN
    <Action to be taken if condition 1 is true>
ELSE
IF <Condition 2> THEN
    <Action to be taken if condition 2 is met>
ELSE
IF <Condition 3> THEN
    <Action to be taken if condition 3 is met>
ELSE
    <Action to be taken if conditions 1 to 3 are not met>
ENDIF
ENDIF
ENDIF
```

If the first condition is not met, the second condition is checked; if the first and second conditions are not met, then the third condition is checked; and so on. See Example 15.

Example 15

A company gives out bonuses based on the amount of income generated by its sales representatives per month. Once the income generated is greater than or equal to $10,000, a bonus of 20% is given. If the income generated is greater than or equal to $8,000 but less than $10,000, a bonus of 15% is given. If the income generated is greater than or equal to $5,000 but less than $8,000, a bonus of 10% is given. If the income generated is less than $5,000, then a 3% bonus is given. Read the income generated and print the bonus.

```
READ Income
Bonus = 0
IF Income >= 10000 THEN
        Bonus = Income * 0.2
ELSE
IF Income >= 8000 AND Income < 10000 THEN
        Bonus = Income * 0.15
ELSE
IF Income >= 5000 AND Income < 8000 THEN
        Bonus = Income * 0.1
ELSE
IF Income Income < 5000 THEN
        Bonus = Income * 0.03
ENDIF
ENDIF
ENDIF
ENDIF
PRINT "Bonus is $", Bonus
```

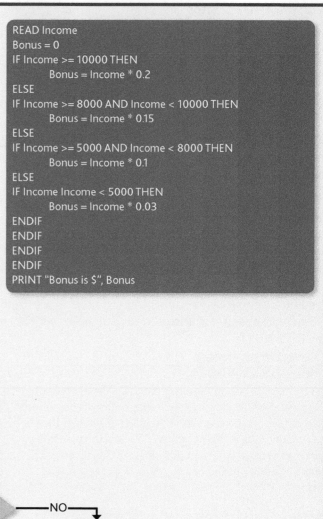

Exercise 7

Using the IF–THEN and IF–THEN–ELSE construct, write instructions for these problems.

1 Write an algorithm to read the number of days a person has been using a demo and display the message 'Time Up' if the number of days exceeds 12.

2 A video club rents videos for three days. Write an algorithm to read the date borrowed and the present date; calculate the number of days borrowed. If the number of days borrowed exceeds three days, compute the number of days overdue and the overdue charge. Use a rate of $1.50 for every day overdue or part thereof.

3 Read the weather; if the weather is sunny, output 'Good day for the beach'.

4 Read the present date, appointment date, time, place and contact name. If the appointment date is equal to the present date, display the appointment information appropriately labelled.

5 Read N; if N is greater than 100 then subtract 50 from N, otherwise multiply N by 3.

6 A club plays cricket only on Sundays and only if it is not raining. Read the day and the weather and output 'Game on' if the weather is good and the day is Sunday, or 'Play suspended' if it is Sunday and it is raining.

7 Write an algorithm to read the name of the student and the value of the student's mark. Print the name of the student and the appropriate grade based on the following grading scheme:

80 or more	A
Less than 80 but more than or equal to 65	B
Less than 65 but more than or equal to 50	C
Less than 50 but more than or equal to 35	D
Less than 35	F

8 Write an algorithm that reads three values, for a, b and c, and prints the roots of the quadratic equation $ax^2 + bx + c = 0$. The roots are given by:

$$\frac{-b+\sqrt{b^2 - 4ac}}{2a}$$

and

$$\frac{-b+\sqrt{b^2 - 4ac}}{2a}$$

provided that $b - 4ac < 0$ and $a <> 0$.

9 Write an algorithm to read the withdrawal amount from a savings account. Determine if there are sufficient funds in the account and whether the daily withdrawal limit has been exceeded. Output, appropriately labelled, 'Not enough funds' and 'daily withdrawal limit exceeded'.

10 Read the height in inches and weight in pounds of an individual, and compute and print their BMI (body mass index). BMI = ((weight/height)/height) * 703. If the BMI is less than 18.5, output 'You are underweight'; if the BMI is between 18.6 and 24.9, output 'Your weight is normal'; if the BMI is between 25 and 29.9, output 'You are overweight'; if the BMI is greater than 30, output 'Your health is at risk, you are in the obese category'.

Loops

It is often necessary to repeat certain parts of a program a number of times. One way of doing this is to write that part of the program as many times as needed. However, this is impractical as it would make the program lengthy. In addition, in some cases, the number of times that the section of code needs to be repeated is not known beforehand.

A group of statements/instructions that is repeated is called a loop. There are two types of loops.

- A finite loop is where the number of times the instructions are repeated is known.
- An indefinite loop is where the instructions are repeated an unspecified number of times until a result is achieved.

Two methods used to repeat sections of instructions or codes are the FOR construct and the WHILE construct.

You need to keep track of how many times the instructions are repeated. Counting or **iteration** involves increasing the value of a counter variable by a fixed number (this can be any value, such as 1, 2, 5, and so on) every time the instructions are repeated. When the counter reaches the number of iterations needed, the instructions are no longer repeated.

This counter can be part of a condition for stopping the instructions from repeating when the value of the counter becomes equal to a certain value. So if you wanted to keep track of a team's score in cricket and PRINT 'Winner' when they pass the other teams score, you could keep adding each batsman's score until it is bigger than the other team's total and use that to exit the loop.

The FOR construct

In the FOR construct, the loop is controlled by a counter that increases each time the set of instructions is executed. This construct is used when the number of times a set of instructions has to be repeated is known.

Syntax:
FOR <Variable> = <Beginning value> TO <Ending value> DO
    <Action to be repeated >
ENDFOR
or
FOR <Variable> = <Beginning value> TO <Ending value> STEP <incremental value> DO
    <Action to be repeated >
ENDFOR
Example:
For Counter = 1 TO 4 DO
    <Action to be repeated >
ENDFOR

When this statement is executed, the counter variable is initially set to the beginning value, in this case, 1. After the execution of the instructions between the FOR and the ENDFOR, the counter variable is increased by 1. The instructions are repeated and the counter variable increases until it becomes equal to the Ending value, in this case, 4. So the instructions are repeated four times.

See Example 16.

> **Note**
>
> The variable in the FOR construct is a counter variable that keeps track of the number of times the loop is executed.

Example 16

A car rental firm leases four cars in one day. Read the number of days for the lease of each car and calculate the total rent paid to the firm if a car is leased for $250. Print the total rent paid to the rental firm.

```
Total Rent = 0
FOR Counter = 1 TO 4 DO
        PRINT "Enter the number for days for lease"
        READ NoofDays
        Rent = NoofDays * $250
        Total Rent = Total Rent + Rent
ENDFOR
PRINT "Total rent paid to firm", Total Rent
```

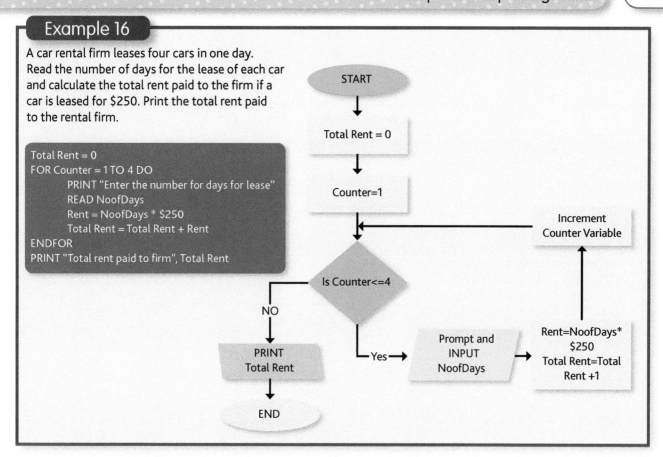

The Step clause allows you to increase the counter by the increment value every time the instructions are repeated, until it becomes equal to or exceeds the ending value. It is often used when we want to print tables.

Now look at the examples from Example 17 to Example 21.

Example 17

A Print a table to find the square and cube of numbers 1 to 10.

- In this case, Number becomes set to the initial value 1.

- The first time through the loop, Square becomes equal to Number * Number, which is 1 * 1 and Cube becomes equal to Number * Number * Number, which is 1 * 1 * 1.

- Then the Number, Square and Cube are printed.

- The second time through the loop, Number becomes set to 2 and the Square and Cube are calculated and printed.

- This continues until Number becomes equal to the ending value, which is 10.

```
PRINT "Number", "Square", "Cube"
FOR Number = 1 TO 10 DO
        Square = Number * Number
        Cube = Number * Number * Number
        PRINT Number, Square, Cube
ENDFOR
```

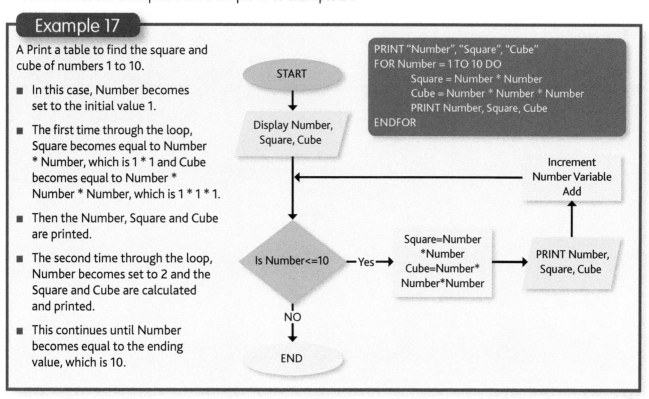

Example 18

Print a table to find the square and cube of all even numbers between 2 and 20 inclusive.

- In this case, Number becomes set to the initial value 2.

- The first time through the loop Square becomes equal to Number * Number, which is 2 * 2 and Cube becomes equal to Number * Number * Number which is 2 * 2 * 2.

- Then the Number, Square and Cube are printed.

- The second time through the loop Number becomes set to 4 as the STEP clause increases the value of the Number by 2 every time it goes through the loop. The Square and Cube are calculated and printed.

- This continues until Number becomes equal to the ending value, which is 20.

```
PRINT "Number", "Square", "Cube"
FOR Number = 2 TO 20 STEP 2 DO
        Square = Number * Number
        Cube = Number * Number * Number
        PRINT Number, Square, Cube
ENDFOR
```

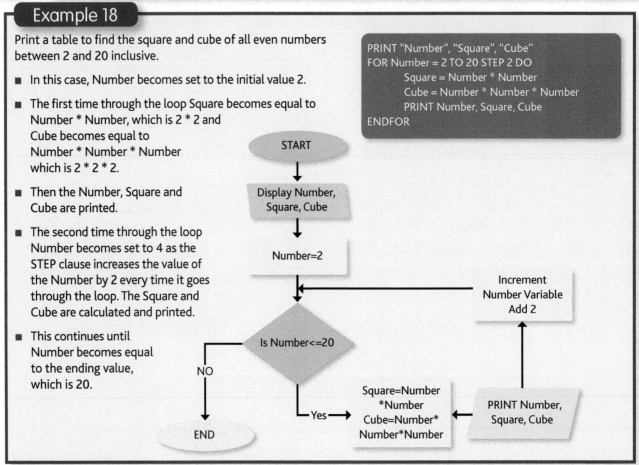

Example 19

Calculate the sum of all the odd numbers between 1 and 20. Print the total.

The statements that make up the body of the FOR loop can consist of other constructs such as the IF–THEN, and IF–THEN–ELSE constructs.

```
Sum = 0
FOR Oddnumber = 1 TO 20 STEP 2 DO
        Sum = Sum + Oddnumber
ENDFOR
PRINT Sum
```

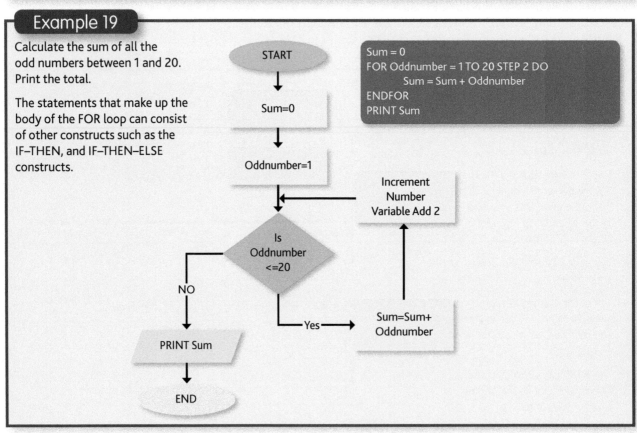

Example 20

A company gives out bonuses based on the amount of income generated by its sales representatives per month. Once the income generated is greater than or equal to $10,000, a bonus of 20% is given. If the income generated is greater than or equal to $8,000 but less than $10,000, a bonus of 15% is given. If the income generated is greater than or equal to $5,000 but less than $8,000, a bonus of 10% is given. If the income generated is less than $5,000, then a 3% bonus is given to the employee. Write an algorithm to read 10 employees' numbers, their income generated, and determine the bonuses of 10 employees. Print the employee number, income generated and the bonus earned by the employee.

The FOR loop can be used to find the maximum and minimum values in a set of numbers.

```
PRINT "EMPLOYEE NUMBER", "INCOME GENERATED", "BONUS"
FOR NumEmployees = 1 TO 10 DO
        PRINT "Enter Employee Number, Income-Generated"
        READ Employee Number, Income-Generated
        IF (Income-Generated >= $10000) THEN
                Bonus = Income-Generated * 20%
        ELSE
        IF (Income-Generated >= $8000) AND (Income-Generated < $10,000) THEN
                Bonus = Income-Generated * 15%
        ELSE
        IF (Income-Generated >= $5000) AND (Income-Generated < $8000) THEN
                Bonus = Income-Generated * 10%
        ELSE
                Bonus = Income-Generated * 3%
        ENDIF
        ENDIF
        ENDIF
        PRINT Employee Number, Income-Generated, Bonus
ENDFOR
```

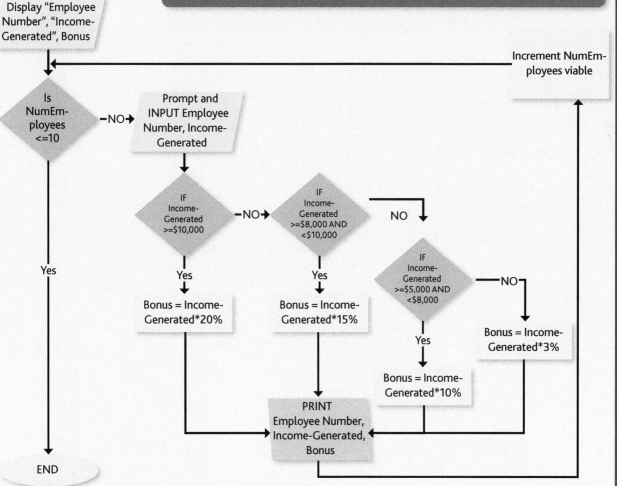

Example 21

Write an algorithm to read 25 numbers and print the lowest.

You need to choose an initial value for Lowest so that any number entered would be lower than that value. You cannot choose 0 (zero) as an initial value for Lowest, as, of the 25 numbers entered, it may not be the lowest value. The variable 'Count' is chosen as the variable counter to keep track of the number of times the instructions are executed.

```
Lowest = 999999
FOR Count = 1 TO 25 DO
        PRINT "Enter a number"
        READ Number
        IF Number < Lowest THEN
        Lowest = Number
        ENDIF
ENDFOR
PRINT "The lowest number entered is:", Lowest
```

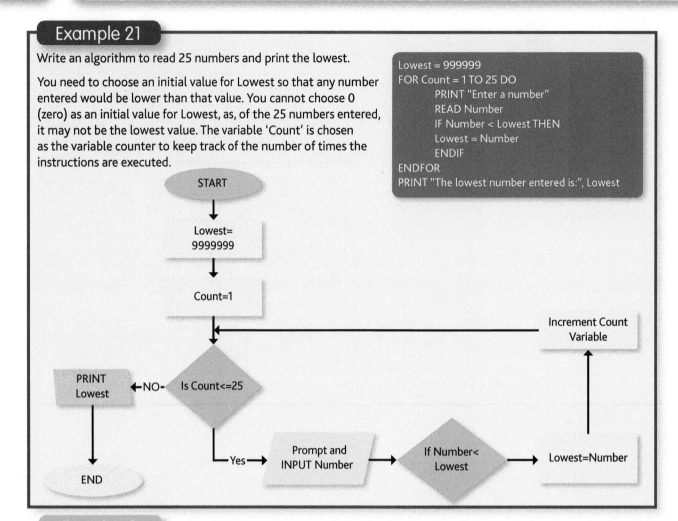

Exercise 8

Using the FOR construct, write instructions for each of these problems.

1 Write a program that reads the result of 10 games played by a team and finds the percentage of games won by the team. Output the percentage games won.
2 Write an algorithm to enter 10 numbers and output the highest and lowest numbers appropriately labelled.
3 Write an algorithm that finds the total of the numbers 10 to 25 and prints the total.
4 Write an algorithm to compute the following expression:
   Y1 = 2 (2–x2) and Y2 = 2–(2–x2) using values –4 to +4 for the value of x. Print x, Y1 and Y2.
5 An airline does not charge for babies 2 years and younger; it charges half price for children aged 2 to 12 years and the full price for persons older than 12 years. Read the airfare and the age of the person; calculate and print the total amount paid by a family of five.
6 A school has implemented a house system. Points are awarded to a house based on the performance of its members: 1st place – 4 points, 2nd place – 3 points, 3rd place – 2 points, 4th place – 1 point and last place – no points awarded. For 10 members of the Aripo house, read the place they came in the events; calculate and print the total awarded to the house.
7 Print a five-times multiplication table for numbers 1 through to 20.
8 Write an algorithm to input an integer N. Find and output the value generated when 2 is raised to the power N, where N is between 0 and 10.
9 Write an algorithm to input a country and exchange rate of that country's currency against the US dollar. Output a table showing the amount of US dollars and the equivalent amount of the country's currency, for 1 to 20 US dollars.
10 Write an algorithm to output the sum of all the even numbers in the range 2 to 40.
11 Write a program that accepts a positive integer and prints all numbers from the given number down to 1.

The WHILE construct

In the WHILE construct, the computer executes a set of statements or instructions repeatedly, for as long as a given condition is true. When you do not know beforehand how many times statements within a loop are to be repeated, use the WHILE construct.

- In the WHILE construct, the condition is tested; if it is true, the instructions within the WHILE and ENDWHILE are executed until the condition becomes false and the loop is then exited.
- Statements or instructions before the WHILE construct are carried out once. The WHILE loop is executed until the condition becomes false, which forces the loop to stop. Then the statements after the ENDWHILE are carried out once.
- If, after carrying out the instructions before the loop, the condition in the WHILE loop is tested and is false, the computer skips the instructions within the WHILE loop and continues with the statements after the ENDWHILE.

While <Condition> is True Perform Instructions

← Condition is not True — <Condition>

Perform Instructions

Condition is True

- The trigger that causes the loop to stop is a value that is entered for the input data. This value is read in within the loop and it is called a dummy value, a **terminating value** or sentinel value. It must not be one of the values in the list of data to be processed. For example, when calculating the average age of students in a class, a dummy value could be 999, since no one in the class will be 999 years old. This value signals the end of the data to be entered.

Syntax:
WHILE <Condition> DO
    <Action to be taken if condition is true>
ENDWHILE
See examples 22 to 24.

Example 22

Write an algorithm to enter the age and count the number of students in a class. Calculate the average age of the group of students if the data is terminated by the value 999. Print the number of students in the class and the average age of the students.

The statements that make up the body of the WHILE loop can consist of other constructs such as the IF–THEN, and IF–THEN–ELSE constructs.

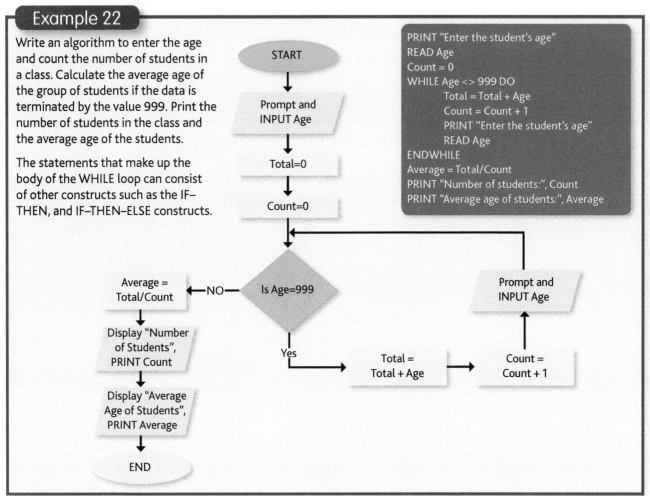

```
PRINT "Enter the student's age"
READ Age
Count = 0
WHILE Age <> 999 DO
        Total = Total + Age
        Count = Count + 1
        PRINT "Enter the student's age"
        READ Age
ENDWHILE
Average = Total/Count
PRINT "Number of students:", Count
PRINT "Average age of students:", Average
```

Example 23

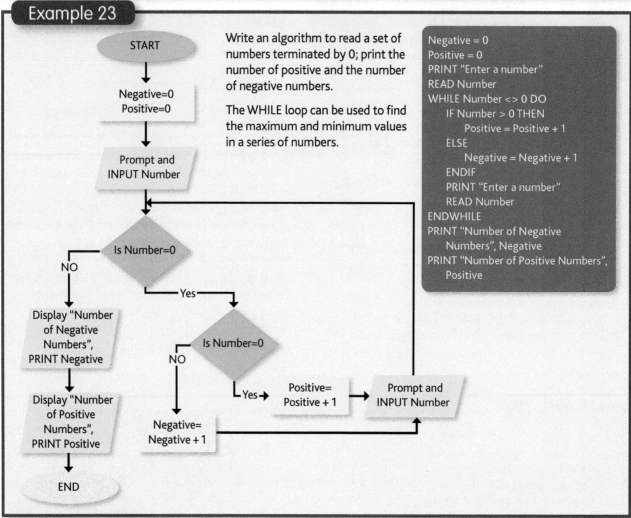

Write an algorithm to read a set of numbers terminated by 0; print the number of positive and the number of negative numbers.

The WHILE loop can be used to find the maximum and minimum values in a series of numbers.

```
Negative = 0
Positive = 0
PRINT "Enter a number"
READ Number
WHILE Number <> 0 DO
    IF Number > 0 THEN
        Positive = Positive + 1
    ELSE
        Negative = Negative + 1
    ENDIF
    PRINT "Enter a number"
    READ Number
ENDWHILE
PRINT "Number of Negative
    Numbers", Negative
PRINT "Number of Positive Numbers",
    Positive
```

Example 24

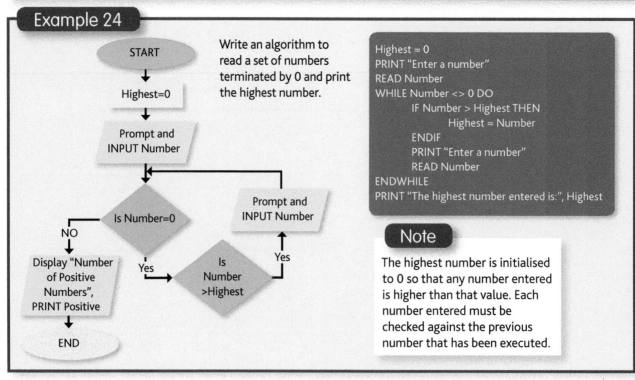

Write an algorithm to read a set of numbers terminated by 0 and print the highest number.

```
Highest = 0
PRINT "Enter a number"
READ Number
WHILE Number <> 0 DO
    IF Number > Highest THEN
        Highest = Number
    ENDIF
    PRINT "Enter a number"
    READ Number
ENDWHILE
PRINT "The highest number entered is:", Highest
```

Note

The highest number is initialised to 0 so that any number entered is higher than that value. Each number entered must be checked against the previous number that has been executed.

The REPEAT...UNTIL construct

In the REPEAT...UNTIL construct, the computer executes a set of statements or instructions repeatedly until the given condition becomes true. Similar to the WHILE construct, you do not know beforehand how many times the statements within the loop are to be repeated.

- In the REPEAT...UNTIL construct, the condition is tested; if it is true the instructions within the REPEAT and UNTIL are executed until the condition becomes false and the loop is then exited.
- Statements or instructions before the REPEAT construct are carried out once. The REPEAT loop is executed until the condition becomes false, which forces the loop to stop. Then the statements after the UNTIL are carried out once.
- If, after carrying out the instructions, the condition in the UNTIL part of the construct is tested and is false, the computer continues with the statements after the UNTIL.
- Similar to the WHILE construct, the trigger that causes the loop to stop is called a dummy value, a terminating value or sentinel value. It must not be one of the values in the list of data to be processed. For example, when calculating the average age of students in a class, a dummy value could be 999, since no one in the class will be 999 years old. This value signals the end of the data to be entered.

Syntax:
REPEAT
      <Action to be taken if the condition is true>
UNTIL <Condition>;
See Example 25.

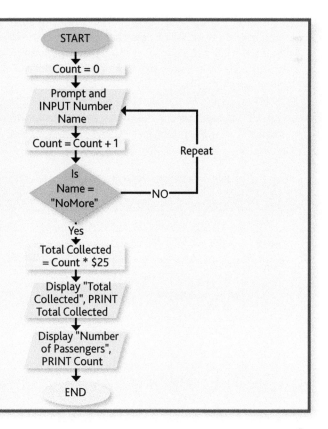

Example 25

Write an algorithm to enter the passenger name and count the number of passengers registering for the tour. Calculate the total paid to the tour guide if a fee of $25 per person is paid. Print the total collected and the number of passengers. The data is terminated by the passenger name "Nomore".

```
Count = 0
REPEAT
        PRINT "Enter Passenger Name"
        READ Name
        Count = Count + 1
UNTIL Name = "Nomore"
Total_Collected = Count * $25
PRINT "Total Collected = ", Total_Collected
PRINT "Number of Passengers =", Count
```

153

Exercise 9

Using the WHILE and also the REPEAT...UNTIL construct write instructions for each of the following problems.

1   Persons working for an income between $20,000 and $30,000 dollars per annum pay an income tax of $12,000 per annum. Persons working for an income of between $30,000 and $40,000 per annum pay an income tax of $15,000 per annum. Read the employee number and income, and calculate the total tax paid by employees. Data is terminated by employee number 000.

2   Enter the marks of students terminated by 999. Find and print the average and the highest mark.

3   A resident person leaving their country is required to pay a departure tax of $100. However, if the person is a visitor to the country, an additional $20 must be paid. Read in the passenger number, terminated by 0, and whether the passenger is a visitor or resident. Write an algorithm to calculate the total amount of tax collected for the day.

4   A company gives out bonuses based on the amount of income generated by its sales representatives per month. Once the income is greater than $5,000, a bonus of 10% of the generated income is added to the sales representative's salary of $4,000. Write an algorithm to input the sales representative's number and income generated; calculate the bonus, and salary plus bonus. Data is terminated by entering the value 000 for the sales representative number.

5   Write an algorithm to find and print the mean of a list of positive integers. The number of integers is not known in advance. The procedure is terminated by the value 0.

6   A car rental firm leases its cars for $250 per day. The manager gives a discount based on the number of days that the car is rented. If the rental period is greater than or equal to 7 days, then a 25% discount is given. Read a car number and the rental period, and calculate the total amount earned by the car rental firm after discounts, if the number of cars rented is not known in advance. The process is terminated by car number 0.

7   A supermarket is keeping track of the amount in stock of an item. Write an algorithm to keep track of how many of the items remain at the end of the day if the initial quantity was 210. Input the quantity bought at each purchase; calculate the total amount sold and the quantity remaining, if the number of sales and quantity purchased is not known in advance. Terminate the data by entering 0 for quantity.

8   Write an algorithm to accept a list of positive integers. Each sub-list of non-zero integers is terminated by a zero. Each time zero is read, output the sum of the non-zero integers. The data is terminated by –1. Indicate the number of non-zero integers and the number of sub-lists.

9   Write an algorithm to input integers until a sentinel value of 0 is entered; print the sum of all the positive numbers entered and the sum of all negative numbers entered. The number of positives and negatives must also be printed.

10 Write an algorithm to accept a number of integers until a sentinel value of 0 is reached. The algorithm must print each pair of consecutive numbers where the first number is larger than the second. For example: if the inputs are 1, 3, 2, 4, 5, 2, –1, 0 and 0, the output would be "3, 2" and "5, 2" and "2, –1".

Using a connector

A connector symbol is used to continue a flowchart from one page to another or from a decision symbol to a process or another page. Two symbols with corresponding letters included in them indicate where the chart continues, as shown with Connector A in Example 26.
(Also see the connector symbol in Table 8.1 on page 135.)

Example 26

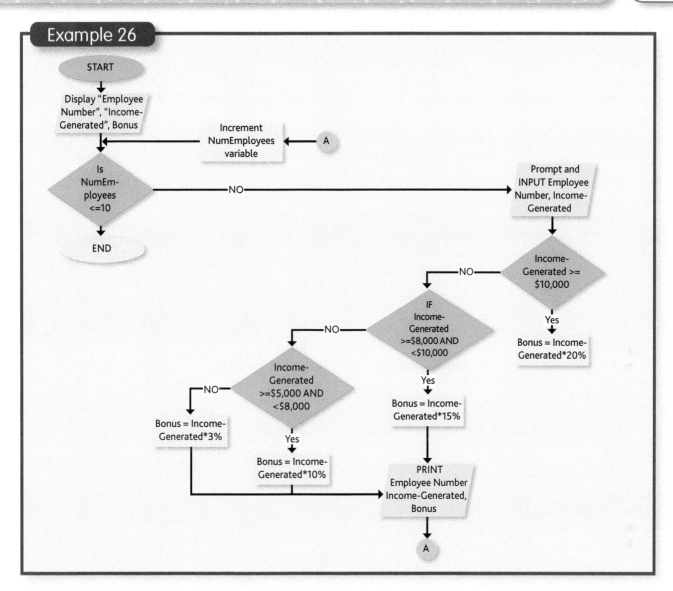

Arrays

An array is a special variable that is used to store a number of elements of the same type. So far, we have been using simple variables that store one value. If we wanted to store the names of 10 students, we would most likely have to give a variable name to each student, which can become awkward to manage. We declare an array:

StudentName : array [1..10] of string

Where:

StudentName[1] refers to the first student name

StudentName[2] refers to the second student name

⋮

StudentName[10] refers to the tenth student name

The value in the [ ] is called an index or subscript – this is the position in the array. Therefore, an array is referred to as an indexed or subscripted variable.

StudentName

Jonathan	StudentName[1]
Martha	StudentName[2]
Sue-Ann	StudentName[3]
Lewis	StudentName[4]
Jarvid	StudentName[5]
David	StudentName[6]
Trevin	StudentName[7]
Camille	StudentName[8]
Shaquille	StudentName[9]
Marsha	StudentName[10]

Components of the array are accessed by referring to the subscript.

Example:

StudentName[7] = Trevin

There are two types of arrays: one-dimensional arrays, which are also known as vector arrays, and multi-dimensional arrays, which are also known as matrix arrays, for example, (a two-dimensional array).
At this level, we will only be looking at one-dimensional arrays.

Initialising an array

On page 140, we learned the reason for initialising a variable. We also need to initialise an array variable. In order to give each element in the array a specific initial value, we can use the FOR or WHILE constructs. Every time the loop has executed, a location in the array is set to 0. That is when j = 1, StudentScore[1] is set to 0, when j = 2, StudentScore[2] is set to 0, and so on.

Using FOR construct
Syntax:
FOR <subscript variable> = <Beginning value> TO <Ending value> DO
    ArrayName[subscript variable] = <value>
ENDFOR
Example:
FOR j = 1 TO 10 DO
    StudentScore[j] = 0
ENDFOR

Using WHILE construct
Syntax:
Subcript variable = beginning value
WHILE <subscript variable <= Maximum subscript value> DO
    ArrayName[subscript variable] = <value>
    Subscript variable = subscript variable + 1
ENDWHILE
Example:
j = 1
WHILE j <= 10 DO
    StudentScore[j] = 0
    j = j + 1
ENDWHILE

Storing values in an array

Values can be read and stored in an array to be processed later. If we know the number of items to be read into the array, we can use the FOR construct. If we do not know the number of items to be read into the array, we can use the WHILE construct.

Using the FOR construct
Syntax:
FOR <subscript variable> = <Beginning value> TO <Ending value> DO
    READ ArrayName[subscript variable]
ENDFOR
Example:
FOR j = 1 TO 10 DO
    READ StudentScore[j]
ENDFOR

Using the WHILE construct
Syntax:
Subcript variable = beginning value
READ <variable>
WHILE <variable <> terminal value> DO
    ArrayName[subscript variable] = <variable>
    Subscript variable = subscript variable + 1
    READ <variable>
ENDWHILE
Example:
j = 1
READ Score
WHILE Score <> 999 DO
    StudentScore[j] = Score
    j = j + 1
    READ Score
ENDWHILE

Displaying the values stored in an array

This is similar to reading values into an array. We can either use the FOR construct or the WHILE construct.

Using the FOR construct
Syntax:
FOR <subscript variable> = <Beginning value> TO <Ending value> DO
    PRINT ArrayName[subscript variable]
ENDFOR
Example:
FOR j = 1 TO 10 DO
    PRINT StudentScore[j]
ENDFOR

Using the WHILE construct
Syntax:
Subcript variable = beginning value
WHILE <Subscript variable <= ending value> DO
    PRINT ArrayName[subscript variable]
    Subscript variable = subscript variable + 1
ENDWHILE

Example:

```
j = 1
WHILE j <= 10 DO
    PRINT StudentScore[j]
    j = j + 1
ENDWHILE
```

> **Note**
>
> Ending value is the total number of elements in the array list.

Navigating an array

If it becomes necessary to manipulate the components of an array, we will need to visit each element in the array. This is called navigating an array or traversing an array. To traverse an array means to visit each element in the array in turn.

Sequential search

One of the things we may want to do is to search for an element in the array. To do this we need to know the index or subscript at which the element is located. The simplest method is to look at each element in turn and compare it with what we want to find, by looking at ArrayName[1] up to ArrayName[Arraysize] for the element being sought. If we find the element, we are finished searching and Found becomes True; otherwise we have come to the end of the array and the element has not been found.

Example:

```
Arraysize = 10
Targetvalue = 55
Increment = 1
Found = False
WHILE (Found = False) AND (Increment <= Arraysize)
DO
IF (ArrayName[Increment] = Targetvalue) THEN
        Found = True
    ELSE
        Increment = Increment + 1
    ENDIF
ENDWHILE
IF Found = True THEN
PRINT "The target value", Targetvalue, "has been found
at location", Increment
ELSE
PRINT "The target value", Targetvalue, "has not been
found"
ENDIF
```

Modular programming

Modular programming, also called top-down analysis or top-down design methodology, allows us to write longer and more complex programs by breaking them into smaller tasks. Many problems or tasks can be broken into smaller sub-tasks or sub-problems. In programming, we call these sub-tasks 'modules', where each module performs a single task. This can make a major or complex problem much more understandable and manageable. Modular programming reduces the number of times that a set of statements may have to be repeated if it is not contained in a loop.

Top-down design moves a problem from being general to being more specific, that is, breaking down the sub-task into smaller tasks. Using top-down design to take the bus to get to school can be broken down into a set of related tasks:

1. Leave home to catch the bus.
2. Board the bus.
3. Ride to the destination.
4. Disembark from the bus.

Task 1 can be broken down even further:

1. Leave home to catch the bus.
   a. Leave home.
   b. Walk to bus stop.
   c. Wait on bus to arrive.

Task 2 can be broken down even further:

2. Board the bus.
   a. Board bus.
   b. Pay fare.
   c. Receive change.
   d. Take a seat.

However, a task must not be broken down into so small a sub-task that it becomes trivial.

A sub-task module in programming, called a subroutine, procedure or function, is a small program within the main program. For example, the main program of GetToSchool may have a number of procedures like CatchBus procedure, BoardBus procedure, RideBus procedure and DisembarkBus procedure.

Another example:

A program to tile the floor of a room may have the following procedures:

1   Get the size of tile and size of the floor.
2   Calculate the area of the floor.
3   Calculate the number of tiles.
4   Calculate the cost of the tiles.
5   Print the room size, number of tiles and cost of tiles.

Algorithm:

```
BEGINMAIN
    Procedure GetTileFloorSize
    Procedure CalculateFloorArea
    Procedure CalculateNumTiles
    Procedure CalculateCost
    Procedure DisplayResults
ENDMAIN
PROCEDURE GetTileFloorSize
    PRINT "Enter length and width of tile"
    READ TileLength, TileWidth
    PRINT "Enter length and width of floor"
    READ FloorLength, FloorWidth
PROCEDURE CalculateFloorArea
    FloorArea = FloorLength * FloorWidth
PROCEDURE CalculateNumTiles
    TileArea = TileLength * TileWidth
    NumTiles = FloorArea/TileArea
PROCEDURE CalculateCost
    PRINT "Enter price of tile"
    READ TilePrice
    Cost = TilePrice * NumTiles
    VAT = Cost * 15%
    TotalPrice = Cost + VAT
PROCEDURE DisplayResult
    PRINT "Floor size =", FloorArea, "Cost of tiles =", Total-
Price, "Number of Tiles =", NumTiles
```

Flowchart:

The flowchart symbol for a module or sub-task is:

Flowchart

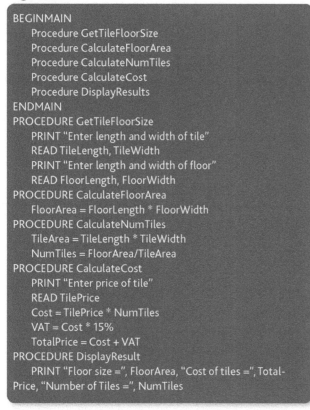

Communicating between modules or procedures

Procedures can be written as separate entities, which means that variables within the module are not shared with another module. However, there may be a need to pass information from one module to another. These variables need to be declared outside the modules so that they can be accessed by other modules. When variables are declared outside the modules, they are known as global variables. In a large program, the value of a global variable may be changed by more than one module, which may have unwanted effects in the program's execution.

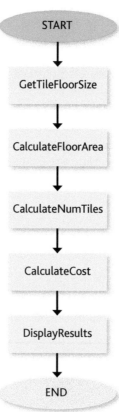

Chapter 8: Summary

- An algorithm is a sequence of instructions that, if followed, produces a solution to a given problem.
- A pseudocode is an algorithm that models or resembles real programming language syntax.
- A computer program is a series of coded instructions for the computer to obey in order to solve a problem.
- Computer programs are written using specific rules and statements of the particular computer language of the program, known as syntax.
- Flowcharts are diagrams that are used to represent the sequences of algorithms visually. They use a set of symbols with a little text in each.
- Programming instructions can be divided into three main types: Input and Storage instructions, Processing instructions and Output instructions.
- A command is a word that instructs the computer what must be done to accomplish a specific task.

- A construct is a group of instructions that works together with commands to accomplish a specific task.
- Data that does not change but remains the same during the execution of the program is called constant; if it changes during the execution of the program, it is called variable.
- When you know how many times statements within a loop are to be repeated, the FOR construct is used.
- In the WHILE construct, the computer executes a set of statements/instructions repeatedly for as long as a given condition is true. When you do not know beforehand how many times statements within a loop are to be repeated, the WHILE construct is used.

Chapter 8: Questions

True or False?

1 An array is a special variable that is used to store a number of elements of the same type.

2 Pseudocode is a programming language.

3 In the WHILE construct, the computer executes a set of statements or instructions repeatedly, for as long as a given condition is false.

4 Modular programming is also called 'top-down analysis' or 'top-down design methodology'.

5 In the REPEAT…UNTIL construct, the computer executes a set of statements or instructions once.

6 Programming instructions can be divided into three main types: Input and Storage instructions, Processing instructions and Output instructions.

7 When you know how many times statements within a loop are to be repeated, the WHILE construct is used.

8 A computer program is a series of coded instructions for the computer to obey in order to solve a problem.

9 Flowcharts are diagrams that are used to represent pseudocode visually.

10 A construct is a word that instructs the computer what must be done to accomplish a specific task.

9 Program implementation

Generations of computer languages

Computer languages can be classified according to whether they are low level or high level.

Low-level languages are machine dependent. Different brands of computers use different program codes. The program code written for one brand of CPU will not run on another brand of CPU, as the code is written for the internal operations and internal organisation (architecture) of a particular CPU.

High-level languages are independent of the machine. They are not specifically designed for any one brand of computer.

Many computer languages have been developed and have evolved over the years. They can be classified according to the different generations.

First generation (1GL) – low-level language

The first-generation of computer languages (1GLs) is machine language, which is written using 1s and 0s, that is, binary code. This is the internal language of computers as you have seen in Chapter 5. It is the only instruction that the CPU understands and can obey or execute directly without having to translate it. The physical workings of computers rely on this system. An example of machine code is:

1101 1101 1011 1011
1110 00011100 0111
0010 11101011 0011

Characteristics of 1GL

- It is the fastest to execute because the code is already in the language that the computer can understand.
- It is difficult to decipher (requires the aid of a reference manual to decipher the meaning of each code).
- Mistakes in the sequence of 1s and 0s are easy to make; replacing a 1 for a 0 can result in the wrong command or instruction being executed.
- It is time-consuming and tedious to write.
- It is machine dependent.
- Programming becomes more difficult as the complexity of the program increases.

Second generation (2GL) – low-level language

The second-generation of computer languages (2LGs) is an **assembly language**, which is written using mnemonic codes, or short codes that suggest their meaning and are therefore easier to remember. These codes represent the operations, addresses that relate to main memory and storage registers of the computer. Typical codes might be: LDA, STO, ADD, NOP, and so on.

An example of a program code to add and store two numbers would be:

LDA   A, 20   *load accumulator A with the value 20*
ADD   A, 10   *add the value 10 to accumulator A*
STO   B, A   *store contents of accumulator A into storage register B*
NOP   *no operation (stop here)*

Characteristics of 2GL

- It is easier to write than machine language.
- As with machine language, assembly language is machine dependent.

Third generation (3GL) – a high-level language

The third generation of languages (3GLs) has been designed to be even easier for humans to understand. Table 9.1 shows some examples of 3GLs.

Characteristics of 3GL

- It uses English words and symbols and is therefore even easier to write.
- It is machine independent.

Language	Example

Pascal – Designed to be used in teaching programming, and in business programs.
 	
Pascal was developed by Niklaus Wirth, a Swiss computer scientist in 1970, and is named after Blaise Pascal, the 17th-century mathematician who invented the mechanical calculator.
	Program Addition (Input, Output);
	
	Var
	
	    Num1, Num2, Sum: Integer;
	
	BEGIN
	
	    READLN (Num1, Num2);
	
	    Sum := Num1+Num2
	
	END.

BASIC (Beginner's All-purpose Symbolic Instruction Code) – Designed for beginners to use.	10 INPUT Num1 20 INPUT Num2 30 Sum 3 = Num1 + Num2 40 PRINT Sum

C – Developed by Bell Laboratories in the USA (now AT&T). Used for both high-level and low-level programming.	#INCLUDE <STDIO.H>
	
	MAIN ( )
	
	{
	
	    INT Num1, Num2, Sum;
	
	    Read (Num1, Num2);
	
	    Sum = Num1+Num2;
	
	    Printf (Sum);
	
	}

FORTRAN (FORmulator TRANslator) – Designed for use by engineers and scientists for complex mathematical calculations.	Program to find the sum of 2 numbers INTEGER Num1, Num2, Sum READ (10, 20) Num1, Num2 10 Format (14, 14) Sum = Num1+Num2 Print, Sum Stop End
COBOL (COmmon Business Oriented Language) – Designed for use in business, finance and administrative systems to manipulate large databases, files and business applications. Can be a tedious language to write.	IDENTIFICATION DIVISION. PROGRAM-ID. SUM OF TWO NUMBERS. ENVIRONMENT DIVISION. DATA DIVISION. WORKING-STORAGE SECTION. 01 Num1 PIC 99 VALUE ZEROS. 01 Num2 PIC 99 VALUE ZEROS. 01 Sum PIC 999 VALUE ZEROS. PROCEDURE DIVISION. DISPLAY "Enter First Number:" WITH NO ADVANCING ACCEPT Num1 DISPLAY "Enter Second Number:" WITH NO ADVANCING ACCEPT Num2 ADD Num1, Num2 GIVING Sum DISPLAY "Sum is =", Sum END-PERFORM. STOP RUN.

▲ Table 9.1 Some examples of third-generation languages (3GLs)

Fourth generation (4GL) – high-level language

The fourth generation of computer languages (4GLs) has been designed for the development of commercial business software. It uses English-like statements that are very user-friendly.

Characteristics of 4GL

- It is much easier to write because of the English-like statements.
- It takes less time to write because of the user-friendly aspects of the language.
- It reduces the cost of software development.
- Fourth-generation languages contain a built-in 'function wizard' to assist users in solving problems.

4GL languages fall into the following categories:

- Database query languages, for example, SQL (Structured Query Language)
- Report generators, for example, Oracle Report, RPG-II, RPG-III, RPG-IV (Report Program Generator)
- Data-manipulation, analysis and reporting languages, for example, Focus
- Data stream languages, for example, Iris Explorer
- Screen painters and generators, for example, Oracle Forms
- GUI (graphical user interface) creators, for example, Visual Basic (VB).

Here is an example of SQL programming code:

```
USE STOCKLIST
SELECT ALL Items WHERE Price > $10.00
```

Did you know?

The standard international unit of pressure in physics — Pa, or Pascal — was also named after Blaise Pascal.

Fifth generation (5GL) – high-level language

The fifth generation of computer languages (5GLs) is designed to build specific programs that help the computer to solve particular problems. These languages are essentially 4GLs with a knowledge base (a large store of information about a topic). The programmer only needs to be concerned with the problem and the conditions and their limits (called constraints) to be met for that particular problem. The main difference between 4GLs and 5GLs is that 4GLs are designed to build specific programs, whereas 5GLs are designed to make the computer solve the problem for you: all codes for the 5GLs are automatically generated.

A 5GL program is written by specifying certain parameters and constraints. It uses a visual or graphical development interface to create a program that is usually compiled with a 3GL or 4GL programming language compiler (a program used to convert the programming language to machine code). 5GLs are used mainly in artificial intelligence (AI).

Examples of 5GLs are OPS5 (Official Production System), Prolog (Logical Programming) and Mercury.

Here is an example of Prolog programming language:

dog(sparkie).	(The program code "Sparkie is a dog")
?- dog(sparkie).	(Question asked, "Is Sparkie a dog?")
yes.	(The program returns yes)
?- dog(spot).	(Question asked, "Is Spot a dog?")
no.	(The program returns no.)

You must remember that the computer does not understand Pascal or any of the high-level languages. Computers work in machine code or machine language, as we saw earlier. A compiler or interpreter converts the programs into the machine language of the computer you are using, which is the language that that computer understands. Only then can the program be executed.

Exercise 1

1. Explain the difference between fourth-generation languages and fifth-generation languages.
2. List THREE characteristics of first-generation languages.
3. What is the difference between assembly language and machine language?
4. A programmer wishes to write a program in a low-level language rather than a high-level language. Explain why she would want to do this. List TWO advantages and TWO disadvantages of using low-level languages.

Step 4: Write a computer program

After developing an algorithm or method of solving a problem, the next step is to write a computer program that corresponds to the algorithm, using programming language. Converting the algorithm to the programming language requires the use of the specific **syntax** of that programming language. Syntax is the term for the specific rules and statements of that particular computer language (similar to the grammar rules in languages such as English or Spanish).

The four main stages of writing a computer program are the following.

1 Create the source code (program in a specific programming language).
2 Translate and/or link the source code into machine code.
3 Execute or run the program.
4 Maintain the program.

Coding a program using the Pascal programming language

Three of the more common programming languages are Pascal, C and Java.

The computer does not understand C, Java, Pascal or any other high-level programming language. A compiler or interpreter is needed to convert athe programs written in these languages into the language that the computer understands, which is machine code 1s and 0s, and then the program is executed.

At this level, we will look at coding in the Pascal programming language. The International Organization for Standardization (ISO) approved a version of Pascal as the standard, based on the original language created by Niklaus Wirth, with only a few minor changes. However, there are many variations of Pascal that are based on the standard.

Pascal has the following structure, divided into three distinct parts:

- the program header
- the program block
- the program terminator.

The basic program structure looks like this example:

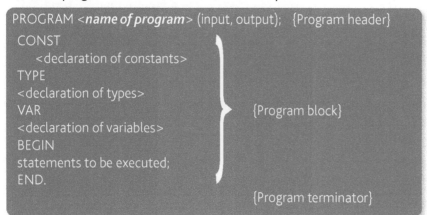

```
PROGRAM <name of program> (input, output);   {Program header}
    CONST
        <declaration of constants>
    TYPE
    <declaration of types>
    VAR
    <declaration of variables>         {Program block}
    BEGIN
    statements to be executed;
    END.

                                       {Program terminator}
```

Note

Even though Pascal is not case sensitive (text written in all caps or the first letter capital or all lowercase is considered to be the same: for example, NUM, Num and num are considered the same), we will use all capitals for keywords to make these clearer.

The first word in every Pascal program is the keyword PROGRAM. The name of the program is the name given by the programmer and should generally be an indicator of what the program does. The (input, output) part of the header statement indicates what the program does; for example, accept data (input) via the keyboard and display (output) via the monitor.

BEGIN signifies the start of the program and END. is the last statement of the program. The statements between the BEGIN and END. statements instruct the computer which task to perform.

All statements in Pascal end with a semi-colon (;) except for the BEGIN and END. keywords.
A semi-colon is placed:

- after the PROGRAM statement
- at the end of each CONST declaration
- at the end of each VAR declaration
- at the end of each TYPE declaration
- at the end of almost every statement.

It is not necessary to put a semi-colon (;) at the end of the statement directly before the END statement. However, it is not harmful to place one there, just in case you have to move the statement later on.

Although indentation is not required, it does make a program easier to read (see Example 1).

Example 1

Here is an example of some Pascal programming code. How can you make it easier to read?

Program Add_two_numbers (input, output); var Num1, Num2, Sum: integer; begin write ('Enter Num1 and Num2)'; read (Num1, Num2); Sum:= Num1 + Num2; write (Sum) end.

Solution
You can use indentation to make the code easier to read, as shown below.

```
PROGRAM Add_two_numbers (input, output);
VAR
   Num1, Num2, Sum: INTEGER;
BEGIN
   WRITE ('Enter num 1 and num 2');
   READ (Num1, Num2);
   Sum = Num1 + Num2;
   WRITE (Sum)  (* note the absence of a semi-colon in the statement before the END. *)
END.
```

Keywords

Keywords, also called reserved words, have a special meaning in a programming language: they are predefined; they can only be used in a specific way; and they cannot be used as variable names.
Some of these keywords are:
   PROGRAM, READ, READLN, WRITE, WRITELN, CONST, VAR, TYPE

Identifiers

Identifiers are names given to variables, constants and types. They are also the names given to the program. There are rules that govern how these names are written.

- They must begin with a letter.
- They can be followed by an alphanumeric character that is either a letter or a number.
- They can contain an underscore (_).
- They cannot contain any of the following characters ~ ! @ # $ % ^ & * ( ) + ' - = { } [ ] : " ; ' < > ? , . / | as these have special meaning in the Pascal language.

Declaring constants

Values declared in the CONST section cannot be changed during the course of the program. The syntax below and the code in Example 2 show how to declare constants.

Syntax:
CONST
    <identifier> = value;

> **Example 2**
>
> CONST
>   Name = 'Cobin';
>   Year = 2019;
>   Pi = 3.14;

Data types

A data type allows the computer to know what kind of data to process. The data needs to be of a specific type in order for the computer to manipulate the data and treat it in a specific way. Pascal uses the following data types, as shown in Table 9.2.

Data type	Keyword	Explanation
Integer	INTEGER	Can contain integers from −32768 to +32767
Real	REAL	Can contain real values from -3.4×10^{-38} to $+ 3.4 \times 1038$
Character	CHAR	Holds a single character but must be enclosed in single quotes, for example, 'a', 'H', '+'
Boolean/Logical	BOOLEAN	Can have either one of two values TRUE or FALSE
String	STRING	This is a string of characters enclosed in single quotes, for example, 'Smith'

▲ Table 9.2 Data types used in Pascal

A string is not a standard Pascal data type; however, modern compilers make use of this data type.

Declaring variables

Declaring a variable uses the ':' character and links the variable's name (identifier) to the data type (String, Real, and so on). The syntax below and the code in Example 3 show how to declare variables.

Syntax:
VAR
    <identifier> : data type;
    <identifier>, <identifier>, <identifier> : data type;

> **Example 3**
>
> VAR
>   Age, Sum, Total : integer;
>   Average : real;
>   Grade : char;
>   Fail : Boolean;

Assignment statements

A variable is assigned the results of a calculation. In Pascal, the assignment symbol has a colon preceding the equal sign (:=). The syntax below and the code in Example 4 show how to write assignment statements.

Syntax:

    <identifier> := <actual calculation>

> **Example 4**
>
> Area := (Base * Height)/2
> F := 32 + ((9*C)/5)

Mathematical operators

Some mathematical operators commonly used in Pascal are shown in Table 9.3. Example 5 shows a few examples of how to use them in code.

Operator	Operation	Operand value	Resulting value
+	Addition or positive	REAL or INTEGER	REAL or INTEGER
-	Subtraction or negative	REAL or INTEGER	REAL or INTEGER
*	Multiplication	REAL or INTEGER	REAL or INTEGER
/	Division	REAL or INTEGER	REAL
DIV	Division of integers	INTEGER	INTEGER
MOD	Modulus (remainder division), that is when the first number is divided by a second number it returns the remainder.	INTEGER	INTEGER

▲ Table 9.3 Mathematical operators used in Pascal

> **Example 5**
>
> Examples of using /, DIV and MOD:
>   9/4 = 2.25 (result is real)
>   9 DIV 4 = 2 (result is an integer)
>   9 mod 4 = 1 (the remainder and it is an integer)

Relational and equality operators

Table 9.4 shows a list of relational and equality operators used in Pascal.

Operator	Operation	Operand value	Resulting value
=	Checks if two values are equal	REAL, INTEGER	BOOLEAN
<>	Checks if the values of two things are not equal	REAL, INTEGER	BOOLEAN
>	Checks if the left value is greater than the right value	REAL, INTEGER	BOOLEAN
<	Checks if the left value is less than the right value	REAL, INTEGER	BOOLEAN
>=	Checks if the left value is greater than or equal to the right value	REAL, INTEGER	BOOLEAN
<=	Checks if the left value is less than or equal to the right value	REAL, INTEGER	BOOLEAN

▲ Table 9.4 Relational and equality operators used in Pascal

Logical operators

Table 9.5 shows a list of logical operators used in Pascal.

Operator	Operation	Operand value	Resulting value
AND	If both things are true, then the output is true.	BOOLEAN	BOOLEAN
OR	If either of the two things is true, the answer is true.	BOOLEAN	BOOLEAN
NOT	Reverse the Logical state, so True becomes False and False, True.	BOOLEAN	BOOLEAN

▲ Table 9.5 Logical operators used in Pascal

Comments

Comments are pieces of code that are not executed during the running of a program; they are statements that are ignored. Comments are used to explain what a variable name means or give an explanation as to what a program or part of a program does.

Standard Pascal uses:

- (* to start a comment
- *) to end a comment.

Modern Pascal compilers also recognise:

- { as the start of a comment
- } as the end of a comment.

The syntax below and the code in Example 6 show how to write comments.

Syntax:
```
(* Comment *)      or
{ Comment }
```

Example 6

(* This program adds two numbers and prints the result *)
{The variable name StuNam stores the name of the student}

Algorithms from Chapter 8

Let us look back at the algorithms we wrote in Chapter 8.

Prompting statements
Prompting statements send data to the standard output, which is usually the monitor. The syntax below and the code in Example 7 show how to write prompting statements.

Syntax:
```
WRITE ('String');
WRITELN ('String');
```

Example 7

WRITE ('Enter student name');
WRITELN ('Enter student name');

Difference between WRITE and WRITELN
WRITE places the cursor at the end of the output, whereas WRITELN places the cursor at the beginning of the next line. The syntax and algorithms showing the difference between WRITE and WRITELN are shown below.
WRITE

Syntax:
```
PROGRAM StudentInfo (input, output);
BEGIN
    WRITE ('Enter student name');
END.
```

Syntax:
```
PROGRAM StudentInfo (input, output);
BEGIN
    WRITELN ('Enter student name');
END.
```

Note

The underscore represents the position of the cursor.

The output will be:
Enter student name _
WRITELN

The output will be:
Enter student name
_

Data input and storage statements
Data input and storage statements read data from the standard input, which is usually the keyboard. The syntax below and the code in Example 8 show how to write data input and storage statements.

Syntax:
```
READ (identifier);
READ (identifier, identifier, identifier);
READLN (identifier);
```

Example 8

READ (Name);
READ (Name, Score);
READLN (Name);
READLN (Name, Score);

Difference between READ and READLN

READ accepts data on the same line, whereas READLN reads the first set of data values, discards the other values on the line and waits for the user to input a value. Table 9.6 shows examples of the differences in the code and result for READ and READLN. Example 9 shows the result for both READ and READLN.

Code	Result
READ (Name);	Jackie
READ (Name, Score);	Jackie 56
READLN (Name);	Jackie
READLN (Name); READLN (Score);	Jackie (waits for input)
READLN (Name, Score);	Jackie 56

▲ Table 9.6 Examples of the code and result for READ and READLN

Let us look at Example 9 from Chapter 8 – write a program to enter the base and height of a triangle.

The algorithms we wrote were:

```
PRINT "Enter the Base, Height of the triangle"
READ Base, Height
```

or

```
PRINT "Enter the Base"
READ Base
PRINT "Enter the Height"
READ Height
```

Here is the Pascal program for the Example 9 algorithm in Chapter 8.

```
PROGRAM Triangle_Problem (Input, Output);
VAR
    Base, Height: INTEGER;
{This program reads the base and height of a triangle}
BEGIN
    WRITELN ('Enter the Base, Height of the triangle');
    READLN (Base, Height)
END.
```

Output statements

Output statements will output data to the standard output, which is usually the monitor, although it can be a printer. The syntax below and the code in Example 10 show how to write output statements.

Syntax:
```
WRITE (identifier);
WRITE (identifier, identifier);
WRITE ('String', identifier);
WRITELN (identifier);
WRITELN (identifier, identifier);
WRITELN ('String', identifier);
```

Example 9

Data: Jackie 56

Example 10

```
WRITELN (Name);
WRITELN (Name, Score);
WRITELN ('Student name is ', Name);
```

Calculation statements

The syntax below and the code in Example 11 show how to write calculation statements.

Syntax:

    Identifier := calculation

Example 11

```
   Area := (Base * Height)/2;
PROGRAM Triangle_Problem (Input, Output);
VAR
   Base, Height: Integer;
{This program reads the base and height of a triangle
and calculates and prints the area}
BEGIN
   WRITELN ('Enter the Base, Height of the triangle');
   READLN (Base, Height);
   Area := (Base * Height)/2;
   WRITELN ('The area of the triangle is = ', Area)
END.
```

IF–THEN construct

Read Chapter 8 Example 10 Case 3 again. We can write the algorithm for Case 3 as shown below.

```
Bonus = $0.00
PRINT "Enter the Income Generated"
READ Income-Generated
IF Income-Generated > $5000.00 THEN
    Bonus = Income-Generated * 10%
ENDIF
PRINT "Bonus", Bonus
```

```
PROGRAM Employee_Bonus (Input, Output);
VAR
   Bonus, Income_Generated : Real;
{This program reads the income and calculates the bonus}
BEGIN
   Bonus := 0;
   WRITELN ('Enter the Income Generated');
   READ (Income_Generated);
   IF (Income_Generated > 5000) THEN
        Bonus := Income_Generated * 0.1;
WRITELN ('Bonus ', Bonus);
END.
```

If there is only one statement following the IF–THEN statement, then a semi-colon is placed after the statement. If, however, there is more than one statement to be executed once the IF–THEN statement is true, then the statements are placed between a BEGIN and END. A semi-colon may be placed after the END depending on what statement appears next. If the END is followed by END. or an ELSE then there is no semi-colon.

Here is the Pascal program for Chapter 8 Example 10 Case 3's algorithm.

```
PROGRAM Employee_Bonus (Input, Output);
VAR
   Bonus, Income_Generated, TotalPay : Real;
{This program reads the income and calculates the bonus}
BEGIN
   Bonus := 0;
   WRITELN ('Enter the Income Generated');
   READ (Income_Generated);
   IF (Income_Generated > 5000) THEN
   BEGIN
       Bonus := Income_Generated * 0.1;
       TotalPay := Income_Generated + TotalPay;
   END;   {Semi-colon is placed}
WRITELN ('Bonus ', Bonus);
WRITELN ('Total Pay = ', TotalPay)
END.
```

```
PROGRAM Employee_Bonus (Input, Output);
VAR
   Bonus, Income_Generated, TotalPay : Real;
{This program reads the income and calculates the bonus}
BEGIN
   Bonus := 0;
   WRITELN ('Enter the Income Generated');
   READ (Income_Generated);
   IF (Income_Generated > 5000) THEN
   BEGIN
       Bonus := Income_Generated * 0.1;
       TotalPay := Income_Generated + TotalPay;
       WRITELN ('Bonus ', Bonus);
       WRITELN ('Total Pay = ', TotalPay);
   END    {no semi-colon as statement precedes END.}
END.
```

Note

Comments can be placed anywhere within a program since they are not executed.

IF–THEN–ELSE construct

Look at the code in Example 12 and the corresponding algorithm below.

Example 12

```
{This program reads the income and calculates the bonus}
PROGRAM Employee_Bonus (Input, Output);
VAR
    Bonus, Income_Generated, Tax, TotalPay : Real;
BEGIN
    Bonus := 0;
    WRITELN ('Enter the Income Generated');
    READ (Income_Generated);
    IF (Income_Generated > 5000) THEN
    BEGIN
        Bonus := Income_Generated * 0.1;
        Tax := Income_Generated * 0.25;
    END    {No semi-colon as statement precedes ELSE}
    ELSE
    BEGIN
        Bonus := Income_Generated * 0.03;
        Tax := Income_Generated * 0.15;
    END;
    WRITELN ('Bonus ', Bonus)
END.
```

```
PRINT "Enter income generated"
READ Income-Generated
IF Income-Generated > $5000.00 THEN
    Bonus = Income-Generated * 10%
ELSE
    Bonus = Income-Generated * 3%
ENDIF
PRINT "Bonus", Bonus
No semi-colon is placed at the end of the statement that
precedes ELSE.
```

Here is the Pascal program for Example 12's algorithm.

```
PROGRAM Employee_Bonus (Input, Output);
VAR
    Bonus, Income_Generated : Real;
{This program reads the income and calculates the bonus}
BEGIN
    Bonus := 0;
    WRITELN ('Enter the Income Generated');
    READ (Income_Generated);
    IF (Income_Generated > 5000) THEN
        Bonus := Income_Generated * 0.1 {No semi-colon as
statement precedes ELSE}
    ELSE
        Bonus := Income_Generated * 0.03;
    WRITELN ('Bonus ', Bonus)
END.
```

Similarly, blocks of code can be grouped together between a BEGIN and END, if there is more than one statement to be executed once a condition is true or false.

Boolean operators

Here is the algorithm for Example 13 in Chapter 8.

```
PRINT "Enter the Day and the Weather"
READ Day, Weather
IF Day = "Sunday" AND Weather = "No Rain" THEN
    PRINT "Game on"
ENDIF
```

```
{Program using the Boolean operator AND}
PROGRAM Game_Condition (Input, Output);
VAR
    Day, Weather : String;
BEGIN
    WRITELN ('Enter the Day and the Weather');
    READLN (Day, Weather);
    IF (Day = 'Sunday') AND (Weather = 'No Rain') THEN
        WRITELN ('Game on')
END.
```

```
{Program using the Boolean operator OR}
PROGRAM Game_Condition (Input, Output);
VAR
    Day, Weather : String;
BEGIN
    WRITELN ('Enter the Day and the Weather');
    READLN (Day, Weather);
    IF (Day = 'Sunday') OR (Weather = 'No Rain') THEN
        WRITELN ('Game on')
END.
```

Nested IF–THEN–ELSE

Here is the algorithm for Example 15 in Chapter 8.

```
PRINT "Enter Income Generated"
READ Income-Generated
IF (Income-Generated >= $10,000.00) THEN
    Bonus = Income-Generated * 20%
ELSE
IF (Income-Generated >= $8000.00) AND (Income-Generated
< $10,000.00) THEN
    Bonus = Income-Generated * 15%
ELSE
IF (Income-Generated >= $5000.00) AND (Income-Generated
< $8000.00) THEN
    Bonus = Income-Generated * 10%
ELSE
    Bonus = Income-Generated * 3%
ENDIF
ENDIF
ENDIF
PRINT "Bonus", Bonus
```

Here is the Pascal program for Chapter 8 Example 15's algorithm.

```
PROGRAM Employee_Bonus (Input, Output);
VAR
    Bonus, Income_Generated : Real;
{This program reads the income and calculates the bonus}
BEGIN
    Bonus := 0;
    WRITELN ('Enter the Income Generated');
    READLN (Income_Generated);
    IF (Income_Generated >= 10000) THEN
        Bonus = Income_Generated * 0.2
    ELSE
        IF (Income_Generated >= 8000) AND (Income_Gener-
ated < 10000) THEN
            Bonus = Income_Generated * 0.15
        ELSE
            IF (Income_Generated >= 5000) AND (Income_
Generated < 8000) THEN
                Bonus = Income_Generated * 0.1
            ELSE
                Bonus = Income_Generated * 0.03;
    WRITELN ('Bonus ', Bonus)
END.
```

Note

The statements before the ELSE do not have semi-colons.

CASE–OF code

The CASE-OF code can replace lengthily nested IF statements. After the operator CASE, we define the variable being tested. Then, after the OF, list the different ranges of values that we are interested in.

Let us look at the previous program for nested IF statements (Chapter 8 Example 15's algorithm and Pascal program code). If Income_Generated is $4,000, then the first case is selected and the bonus is 3%, but if it is $8,500, then the third case is selected and the bonus is 15%.

```
CASE Income_Generated OF
    0..4999      : Bonus := Income_Generated * 0.03;
    5000..7999    : Bonus := Income_Generated * 0.1;
    8000..9999    :Bonus := Income_Generated * 0.15
    ELSE           Bonus := Income_Generated * 0.2
END;
```

Declaring constants

Look at the instruction in Example 13 and the corresponding algorithm below.

Example 13

Read the name and cost of an item and print the name, cost and final price if a discount of 5% is given and 15% VAT is added.

```
PRINT "Enter name and cost of item"
READ Name, Cost
Discount = Cost * 5%
AmountVAT = Cost * 15%
FinalPrice = Cost – Discount + AmountVAT
PRINT "Name", Name, "Cost", Cost, "Final Price",
FinalPrice
```

Here is the Pascal program for Example 13's algorithm.

```
PROGRAM DiscountedItem (Input, Output);
CONST
    VAT = 0.15;
    Percent_Discount = 0.05;
VAR
    Discount, AmountVAT, Cost, FinalPrice : Real;
    Name : String;
BEGIN
    WRITELN ('Enter name and cost of item');
    READLN (Name, Cost);
    Discount := Cost * Percent_Discount;
    AmountVAT := Cost * VAT;
    FinalPrice := Cost – Discount + AmountVAT;
    WRITELN ('Name: ', Name, 'Cost: ', Cost, 'Final Price: ',
FinalPrice)
END.
```

FOR construct

Here is how to write syntax for a FOR construct.

Syntax:

If a single statement is to be executed.
FOR identifier := Beginning_value TO Ending_value DO
    <Statement>;
If a block of statements is to be executed.
FOR identifier := Beginning_value TO Ending_value DO
BEGIN
    <Statement>;
    <Statement>;
    <Statement>;
END; {Semi-colon depending on the next statement}

Here is the algorithm for Example 19 in Chapter 8.

```
Total Rent = 0
FOR Counter = 1 TO 4 DO
    PRINT "Enter the number for days for lease"
    READ NoofDays
    Rent = NoofDays * $250.00
    Total Rent = Total Rent + Rent
ENDFOR
PRINT "Total rent paid to firm", Total Rent
```

Here is the Pascal program for Chapter 8 Example 19's algorithm.

```
PROGRAM Car_Rental (Input, Output);
CONST
    Rate = 250;
VAR
    Total_Rent, Rent : Real;
    NoofDays, Counter : Integer;
BEGIN
    Total_Rent := 0;
    FOR Counter := 1 TO 4 DO
    BEGIN
        WRITE ('Enter the number of days for lease');
        READLN (NoofDays);
        Rent := NoofDays * Rate;
        Total_Rent := Total_Rent + Rent;
    END;
    WRITELN ('Total rent paid to firm ', Total_Rent)
END
```

WHILE construct

Here is how to write syntax for a WHILE construct.

Syntax:

If a single statement is to be executed.
WHILE <Condition> DO
    <Statement>;
If a block of statements is to be executed.
WHILE <Condition> DO
BEGIN
    <Statement>;
    <Statement>;
    <Statement>;
END; {Semi-colon depending on the next statement}

Here is the algorithm for Example 25 in Chapter 8.

```
Print "Enter the student's age"
READ Age
Count = 0
While Age <> 999 do
    Total = Total + Age
    Count = Count + 1
    PRINT "Enter the student's age"
    Read Age
Endwhile
Average = Total/Count
PRINT "Number of students:", Count
PRINT "Average ages of students:", Average
```

Here is the Pascal program for Chapter 8 Example 25's algorithm.

```
PROGRAM Average_Age (Input, Output);
VAR
    Age, Total, Count : Integer;
    Average : Real;
BEGIN
    WRITELN ('Enter the student age');
    Read (Age);
    Count := 0;
        WHILE (Age <> 999) DO
        BEGIN
            Total: = Total + Age;
            Count: = Count + 1;
            WRITELN ('Enter the student's age ');
            READ (Age);
        END;
    Average := Total / Count;
    WRITELN ('Number of students: ', Count);
    WRITELN ('Average ages of students: ', Average)
END.
```

Exercise 2

1   Rewrite each of the following expressions using the correct Pascal code:
   Grade = A;
   Count = StartingValue := 1;
   Tax := 5%;
   Sum := 10 plus 8;
   Rate := .25;
2   Write the following instructions in Pascal code:
   a   Declare an integer called Number.
   b   Declare a character called LetterGrade.
   c   Declare a variable called Price.
   d   Declare an integer variable called Goals and initialise it to zero.
   e   Declare a String variable called StudentName.
3   This program code contains errors. Correct the errors by writing the corrected
   version of the program in your exercise book. There are 10 errors in the program.

```
PROGAM Addition (output)
    VAR   Num1, Num2, Sum ; integer;
    BEGIN;
        Num1 = 24;
        PRINT ('Enter a   number for Num 2');
        READ ('Num 2');
        Sum := Num1 +   Number2;
        WRITELN('Sum,Sum )
    END
```

Coding a program using the Visual Basic (VB) programming language

Here we will also look at coding in Visual Basic (VB) programming language.
The structure of Visual Basic (VB) is divided into four distinct parts:

- the Module header (or program header)
- the Subroutine block (or program block)
- the Subroutine terminator
- the Module terminator.

This is the syntax for a basic program structure:

```
Module <name of program>
Sub Main ( )
        <Block of instructions>
End Sub
End Module
```

Sub Main ( ) signifies the start of the program and **End Sub** signifies the end
of the program. There are no semi-colons at the end of a statement in VB.
   Similar to Pascal, indentation is not required in VB; however, it does
make a program easier to read.

Keywords in VB

Some keywords in VB are: MODULE, SUB, READLINE, WRITELINE, READ, WRITE, CONST, CONSOLE

Identifiers

Identifiers are names given to variables, constants and types. They are also the names given to the program. There are rules that govern how these names are written.

- They must begin with a letter.
- They can be followed by an alphanumeric character, which is either a letter or a number.
- They can contain an underscore (_).
- They cannot contain any of the following characters ~ ! @ # $ % ^ & * ( ) + ' - = { } [ ] : " ; ' < > ? , . / | as these have special meaning in the Pascal language.
- VB is not case-sensitive, which means that text written in all caps or with the first letter capital or in all lowercase is considered to be the same. For example, NUM, Num and num are considered the same. For clarity in this book, we will put keywords and identifiers in all capitals.

> **Note**
>
> Although an identifier can be any length, it is not advisable to use too long a name for an identifier. However, VB identifiers can be as long as 255 characters.

Data types in VB

A data type allows the computer to know what kind of data to process. The data needs to be of a specific type in order for the computer to manipulate the data and treat it in a specific way. VB uses the following data types, as shown in Table 9.7.

Data type	Keyword	Explanation
Integer	INTEGER	Whole numbers
Real/Floating Point	LONG	Contains numbers with decimals, for example, 3.4
Character	CHAR	Holds a single character but must be enclosed in single quotes, for example, 'a', 'H', '+'
Boolean	BOOLEAN	Can have either one of two values TRUE or FALSE
String	STRING	This is a string of characters enclosed in double quotes, for example, "Smith"
Double	DOUBLE	Floating point numbers but with greater accuracy

▲ Table 9.7 Data types in VB

Declaring constants

Values declared in the CONST section cannot be changed during the course of the program. If the constant declaration is placed within a module and prefixed with the keyword PUBLIC, it makes the constant available to other modules within the program. The syntax below and the code in Example 14 show how to declare constants in VB.

Syntax:
CONST <identifier> AS <datatype> = value
PUBLIC CONST <identifier> AS <datatype> = value

Example 14

```
CONST Name AS String = "Cobin"
CONST Year AS Integer = 2019
CONST Pi AS Long = 3.14
CONST Pi AS Double = 3.141592653589
```

Declaring variables

The syntax below and the code in Example 15 show how to declare variables in VB.

Syntax:

DIM <identifier> AS <datatype>
DIM <identifier> AS <datatype>, <identifier> AS <datatype>,
<identifier> AS <datatype>
DIM <identifier> AS String * n (where n is the number of characters)

Example 15

```
DIM Age AS Integer
DIM Sum AS Integer
DIM Average AS Long
DIM Grade AS Char
DIM Fail AS Boolean
DIM Num1, Num2, Sum AS Integer
DIM Name AS String
DIM Name As String *  10  (Note: in this example, the Variable Name can
only be 10 characters long)
DIM Name As String, Age As Integer, Fail As Boolean
```

Assignment statement

A variable is assigned the results of a calculation. In VB, the assignment symbol is the equal sign (=). The syntax below and the code in Example 16 show how to write assignment statements.

Syntax:

   <identifier> = <actual calculation>

Example 16

```
Area = (Base * Height)/2
F = 32 + ((9*C)/5)
```

Mathematical operators

Some mathematical operators commonly used in VB are shown in Table 9.8. Example 17 shows a few examples of how to use these operators in code.

Operator	Operation	Operand value	Resulting value
+	Addition or positive	Long or integer	Long or integer
-	Subtraction or negative	Long or integer	Long or integer
*	Multiplication	Long or integer	Long or integer
/	Division	Long or integer	Long or Integer
ROUND	Rounds up or down a value, for example, 8.7 will round up to 9.	Integer	Integer
SQRT	Square root	Long or integer	Long or integer
POW	Power, for example, 10 to the 2nd power is 10 squared or 10 * 10 = 100	Double	Double

▲ Table 9.8 Mathematical operators used in VB

Example 17

Examples of using /, SQRT, POW, ROUND
   9/4 = 2.25 (result is Long)
   SQRT(4) = 2 (result is integer)
   POW(10, 2) = 100 (result is integer)
   ROUND(3.4) = 3 (result is integer)

Relational and equality operators

Table 9.9 shows a list of relational and equality operators used in VB.

Operator	Operation	Resulting value
=	Is equal to	Num1 = Num2
<>	Not equal to	Num1 <> Num2
>	Greater than	Num1 > Num2
<	Less than	Num1 < Num2
<=	Less than or equal to	Num1 <= Num2
>=	Greater than or equal to	Num1 >= Num2

▲ Table 9.9 Relational and equality operators used in VB

Logical operators

Table 9.10 shows the logical operators used in VB.

Operator	Operation	Resulting value
NOT	NOT equal to	NOT x = y
AND	Both items being compared are true	Num1 AND Num2
OR	One or both of the items are true	Num1 OR Num2
XOR	Only one of the items is true	Num1 XOR Num2

▲ Table 9.10 Logical operators used in VB

Conditional operators

Table 9.11 shows the conditional operators used in VB.

Operator	Operation	Resulting value
&	Concatenation – joins two expressions together	FirstName LastName
	FirstName & LastName	

▲ Table 9.11 Conditional operators used in VB

Comments in VB

Comments are pieces of code that are not executed during the running of a program; they are statements that are ignored. They are used to explain what a variable name means or to give an explanation as to what a program or part of a program does. VB uses single line comments and begins each line of the comment with a single quote ('). The syntax below and the code in Example 18 show how to write comments.

Syntax:

```
'Comment
```

Example 18

```
'This program adds two
numbers and prints the result
'The variable name StuNam
stores the name of the student
```

Algorithms from the previous chapter

Let us look back at the algorithms we wrote earlier in this chapter.

Prompting statements

Remember, VB is not case sensitive. For readability, this book will place the keywords in uppercase. The keyword CONSOLE allows you to see the output on the standard output, usually your screen. The syntax below and the code in Example 19 show how to write prompting statements.

Syntax:

```
CONSOLE.WRITE ("String")
CONSOLE.WRITELINE ("String")
```

Example 19

```
CONSOLE.WRITE ("Enter student
name")
CONSOLE.WRITELINE ("Enter
student name")
```

Difference between WRITE and WRITELINE

WRITE places the cursor at the end of the output, whereas WRITELINE places the cursor at the beginning of the next line.

WRITE

```
MODULE StudentInfo
SUB Main ( )
    CONSOLE.WRITE ("Enter student name")

END SUB
END MODULE
```

The output will be:
Enter student name _

However, in order for you to see the output, you need to pause the output screen. You need to include CONSOLE.READKEY( ) or CONSOLE.READLINE ( )

WRITELINE

```
MODULE StudentInfo
SUB Main ( )
    CONSOLE.WRITELINE ("Enter student name")
    CONSOLE.READKEY ( )
END SUB
END MODULE
```

The output will be:
Enter student name

_

Data input and storage statements

Data input and storage statements take data from the standard input, which is usually your keyboard. The syntax below and the code in Example 20 show how to write data input and storage statements.

Syntax:
```
<identifier> = CONSOLE.READ ()
<identifier> = CONSOLE.READLINE ()
```

Example 20

```
Name = CONSOLE.READ ()
Name = CONSOLE.READLINE ()
```

Difference between READ and READLINE

READ accepts data on the same line, whereas READLN reads the first set of data values, discards the other values on the line and waits for the user to input a value. In VB, only one set of data should be read in one statement. Table 9.12 shows examples of the differences in the code and result for READ and READLN. Example 21 shows the result for both READ and READLN.

Example 21

Data: Jackie 56

Code	Result
Name = CONSOLE.READ ( )	Jackie
Age = CONSOLE.READ ( )	56
Name = CONSOLE.READLINE ( )	Jackie
Age = CONSOLE.READLINE ( )	

▲ Table 9.12 Examples of the code and result for READ and READLN

Let us look at Example 9 from Chapter 8 – write a program to enter the base and height of a triangle. The algorithms we wrote were as follows:

```
PRINT "Enter the Base, Height of the triangle"
READ Base, Height
or
PRINT "Enter the Base"
READ Base
PRINT "Enter the Height"
READ Height
```

Here is the VB program for Chapter 8 Example 9's algorithm.

```
MODULE Triangle_Problem
 'This program reads the base and height of a triangle
SUB Main ( )
    DIM Base AS Integer
    DIM Height AS Integer
    CONSOLE.WRITELINE ("Enter the Base of the triangle")
    Base = CONSOLE.READLINE ( )
    CONSOLE.WRITELINE ("Enter the Height of the triangle")
    Height = CONSOLE.READLINE ( )
    CONSOLE.READKEY( )
END SUB
END MODULE
```

Output statements

The syntax below and the code in Example 22 show how to write output statements.

Syntax:

```
CONSOLE.WRITE (identifier)
CONSOLE.WRITELINE (identifier)
CONSOLE.WRITE ("String" & identifier)
CONSOLE.WRITELINE ("String"& identifier)
CONSOLE.WRITELINE (identifier & identifier)
```

Example 22

```
CONSOLE.WRITE (Name)
CONSOLE.WRITELINE (Name)
Example of Concatenation
CONSOLE.WRITE ("My name is " & Name)
CONSOLE.WRITELINE ("My name is " & Name)
CONSOLE.WRITELINE (FirstName &" "& LastName)
```

Calculation statements

The syntax below and the code in Example 23 show how to write calculation statements.

Syntax:

```
Identifier = calculation
```

Example 23

```
Area = (Base * Height)/2;
MODULE Triangle_Problem
'This program reads the base and height of a triangle
and calculates and prints the area
SUB Main ( )
   DIM Base, Height, Area AS Integer
   CONSOLE.WRITELINE ("Enter the Base of the
triangle")
   Base = CONSOLE.READLINE ()
   CONSOLE.WRITELINE ("Enter the Height of the
triangle")
   Height = CONSOLE.READLINE ()
   Area = (Base * Height)/2
   CONSOLE.WRITELINE ("The area of the triangle is =
" & Area)
   CONSOLE.READKEY( )
END SUB
END MODULE
```

Note

Comments can be placed anywhere within a program since they are not executed.

IF–THEN construct

Here is the syntax example for an IF–THEN construct.

Syntax:

```
IF <condition> THEN
    Instructions
END IF
```

Let us look at Chapter 8 Example 10 Case 3's algorithm.

```
Bonus = $0.00
PRINT "Enter the Income Generated"
READ Income-Generated
IF Income-Generated > $5000.00 THEN
    Bonus = Income-Generated * 10%
ENDIF
PRINT "Bonus", Bonus
```

```
MODULE Employee_Bonus
SUB Main ( )
   'This program reads the income and calculates the bonus
   DIM Bonus AS Floating Point
   DIM Income_Generated AS Floating Point
   Bonus = 0
   CONSOLE.WRITELINE ("Enter the Income Generated")
   Income_Generated = CONSOLE.READLINE ()
   IF (Income_Generated > 5000) THEN
       Bonus = Income_Generated * 0.1
   END IF
   CONSOLE.WRITELINE ("Bonus " & Bonus)
END SUB
END MODULE
```

```
MODULE Employee_Bonus
'This program reads the income and calculates the bonus
SUB Main ( )
   Dim Bonus, Income_Generated, TotalPay As Double
   Bonus = 0
   CONSOLE.WRITELINE ("Enter the Income Generated")
   Income_Generated= CONSOLE.READ ()
   IF (Income_Generated > 5000) THEN
       Bonus = Income_Generated * 0.1
       TotalPay = Income_Generated + TotalPay
   END IF
   CONSOLE.WRITELLINE("Bonus", Bonus)
   CONSOLE.WRITELINE ("Total Pay = ", TotalPay)
END SUB
END MODULE
```

```
MODULE  Employee_Bonus
'This program reads the income and calculates the bonus
SUB Main ( )
   Dim Bonus, Income_Generated, TotalPay As Double
   Bonus = 0
   CONSOLE.WRITELINE ("Enter the Income Generated")
   Income_Generated = CONSOLE.READLINE ()
   IF (Income_Generated > 5000) THEN
       Bonus = Income_Generated * 0.1
       TotalPay = Income_Generated + TotalPay
       CONSOLE.WRITELLINE("Bonus" & Bonus)
       CONSOLE.WRITELINE ("Total Pay = " & TotalPay)
   END IF
END SUB
END MODULE
```

IF–THEN–ELSE construct

Look at the code in Example 24 and the corresponding algorithm below.

Example 24

```
MODULE  Employee_Bonus
'This program reads the income and calculates the bonus
SUB Main ( )
    Dim Bonus, Income_Generated As Double
    Bonus = 0
    CONSOLE.WRITELINE ("Enter the Income Generated")
    Income_Generated = CONSOLE.READ ()
    IF (Income_Generated > 5000) THEN
        Bonus = Income_Generated * 0.1
    ELSE
        Bonus = Income_Generated * 0.03
    END IF
    CONSOLE.WRITELINE("Bonus " &  Bonus)
    CONSOLE.READLINE( )
END SUB
END MODULE
```

```
PRINT "Enter income generated"
READ Income-Generated
IF Income-Generated > $5000.00 THEN
    Bonus = Income-Generated * 10%
ELSE
    Bonus = Income-Generated * 3%
ENDIF
PRINT "Bonus", Bonus
```

Boolean operators

Here is the algorithm for Example 13 in Chapter 8.

```
PRINT "Enter the Day and the Weather"
READ Day, Weather
IF Day = "Sunday" AND Weather = "No Rain" THEN
    PRINT "Game on"
ENDIF
```

Here is the VB program for Example 13's algorithm using the Boolean operator 'AND'.

```
MODULE Game_Condition
'Program using the Boolean operator AND
    SUB MAIN ( )
        DIM Day, Weather AS String
        CONSOLE.WRITELINE ("Enter the Day")
        Day = CONSOLE.READLINE ( )
        CONSOLE.WRITELINE ("Enter the Weather")
        Weather = CONSOLE.READLINE ( )
        IF (Day = "Sunday") AND (Weather = "No Rain") THEN
            CONSOLE.WRITELINE("Game on")
            CONSOLE.READKEY ( )
        END IF
    END SUB
END MODULE
```

Here is the VB program for Example 13's algorithm using the Boolean operator 'OR'.

```
MODULE Game_Condition
'Program using the Boolean operator OR
SUB MAIN ( )
    DIM Day, Weather AS String
    CONSOLE.WRITELINE ("Enter the Day")
    Day = CONSOLE.READLINE ( )
    CONSOLE.WRITELINE ("Enter the Weather")
    Weather = CONSOLE.READLINE ( )
    IF (Day = "Sunday") OR (Weather = "No Rain") THEN
        CONSOLE.WRITELINE ("Game on")
        CONSOLE.READKEY ( )
    END IF
END SUB
END MODULE
```

Nested IF-THEN-ELSE

Look at the code in Example 25 and the corresponding algorithm below.

Example 25

```
MODULE  Employee_Bonus
'This program reads the income and calculates the bonus
SUB Main ( )
    Dim Bonus, Income_Generated, Tax As Double
    Bonus = 0
    CONSOLE.WRITELINE ("Enter the Income Generated")
    Income_Generated = CONSOLE.READ ()
    IF (Income_Generated > 5000) THEN
        Bonus = Income_Generated * 0.1
        Tax = Income_Generated * 0.25
    ELSE
        Bonus = Income_Generated * 0.03
        Tax = Income_Generated * 0.15
    END IF
    CONSOLE.WRITELINE("Bonus  = "&  Bonus & " Tax
= " & Tax)
    CONSOLE READLINE ( )
END SUB
END MODULE
```

```
PRINT "Enter Income Generated"
READ Income-Generated
IF (Income-Generated >= $10,000.00) THEN
    Bonus = Income-Generated * 20%
ELSE
IF (Income-Generated >= $8000.00) AND (Income-Generated
< $10,000.00) THEN
    Bonus = Income-Generated * 15%
ELSE
IF (Income-Generated >= $5000.00) AND (Income-Generated
< $8000.00) THEN
    Bonus = Income-Generated * 10%
ELSE
    Bonus = Income-Generated * 3%
ENDIF
ENDIF
ENDIF
PRINT "Bonus", Bonus
```

Here is the VB program for Example 25's algorithm.

```
MODULE Employee_Bonus
'This program reads the income and calculates the bonus
SUB Main ()
DIM  Bonus, Income_Generated AS Double
    Bonus = 0
    CONSOLE.WRITELINE ("Enter the Income Generated")
    Income_Generated = CONSOLE.READLINE ()
    IF (Income_Generated >= 10000) THEN
        Bonus = Income_Generated * 0.2
    ELSE
        IF (Income_Generated >= 8000) AND (Income_Gener-
ated < 10000) THEN
            Bonus = Income_Generated * 0.15
        ELSE
            IF (Income_Generated >= 5000)  AND (Income_
Generated < 8000) THEN
                Bonus = Income_Generated * 0.1
            ELSE
                Bonus = Income_Generated * 0.03
            END IF
        ENDIF
    ENDIF
    CONSOLE.WRITELINE ("Bonus  = " & Bonus)
    CONSOLE.READLINE ()
END SUB
END MODULE
```

SELECT CASE code

The SELECT CASE code can replace lengthily nested IF statements. After the operator SELECT CASE, we define the variable being tested. The CASE IS statements then have the different ranges of values that we are interested in. Let us look at the previous program for nested IF statements. If Income_Generated is $4,000 then the first case is selected and the bonus is 3%, but if it is $8,500 then the third case is selected and the bonus is 15%.

```
SELECT CASE Income_Generated
    CASE IS < 4999
        Bonus = Income_Generated * 0.03
    CASE 5000 TO 7999
        Bonus = Income_Generated * 0.1
    CASE 8000 TO 9999
        Bonus = Income_Generated * 0.15
    CASE ELSE
        Bonus = Income_Generated * 0.2
END SELECT
```

Declaring constants

Example 26

Read the name and cost of an item and print the name, cost and final price if a discount of 5% is given and 15% VAT is added.

Here is the algorithm for Example 26 in Chapter 8.

```
PRINT "Enter name and cost of item"
READ Name, Cost
Discount = Cost * 5%
AmountVAT = Cost * 15%
FinalPrice = Cost – Discount + AmountVAT
PRINT "Name", Name, "Cost", Cost, "Final Price", FinalPrice
```

Here is the VB program for Example 26's algorithm.

```
MODULE DiscountedItem
SUB Main ()
    CONST Vat As Double = 0.15
    CONST Percent_Discount AS Double = 0.05
    DIM Discount, AmountVAT, Cost, FinalPrice AS Double
    DIM Name AS String
    CONSOLE.WRITELINE ("Enter name and cost of item")
    Name = CONSOLE.READ ()
    Cost = CONSOLE.READLINE ()
    Discount = Cost * Percent_Discount
    AmountVAT = Cost * VAT
    FinalPrice = Cost – Discount + AmountVAT
    CONSOLE.WRITELINE ("Name: " & Name & " Cost: " & Cost &
" Final Price: " & FinalPrice)
    CONSOLE.READLINE ()
END SUB
END MODULE
```

FOR construct

Here is how to write syntax for a FOR construct.

Syntax:
FOR <identifier> = <Beginning_value> TO <Ending_value>
    <Instructions>
NEXT

Here is the algorithm for Example 19 in Chapter 8.

```
Total Rent = 0
FOR Counter = 1 TO 4 DO
    PRINT "Enter the number for days for lease"
    READ NoofDays
    Rent = NoofDays * $250.00
    Total Rent = Total Rent + Rent
ENDFOR
Print "Total rent paid to firm", Total Rent
```

Here is the VB program for Chapter 8 Example 19's algorithm.

```
MODULE Car_Rental
SUB Main ()
    CONST Rate AS Integer = 250
    DIM     Total_Rent, Rent AS Double
    DIM NoofDays, Counter AS Integer
    Total_Rent = 0
    FOR Counter = 1 TO 4
        CONSOLE.WRITE ("Enter the number of days for lease ")
        NoofDays = CONSOLE.READLINE ()
        Rent = NoofDays * Rate
        Total_Rent = Total_Rent + Rent
    NEXT
    CONSOLE.WRITELINE ("Total rent paid to firm " & Total_Rent)
    CONSOLE.READKEY ()
END SUB
END MODULE
```

WHILE construct

Here is an example of how to write syntax for a WHILE construct.

Syntax:

```
WHILE <Condition>
    <Instructions>
END WHILE
```

Here is the algorithm for Example 25 in Chapter 8.

```
PRINT "Enter the student's age"
READ Age
Count = 0
WHILE Age <> 999 do
    Total = Total + Age
    Count = Count + 1
    Print "Enter the student's age"
    Read Age
ENDWHILE
Average = Total/Count
PRINT "Number of students:", Count
PRINT "Average ages of students:", Average
```

Here is the VB program for Chapter 8 Example 25's algorithm.

```
MODULE Average_Age
SUB Main ( )
    DIM  Age, Total, Count AS Integer
    DIM Average AS Long
    console.WRITEline ("Enter the student age ")
    Age = CONSOLE.ReadLINE ( )
    Count = 0
    WHILE Age <> 999
        Total = Total + Age
        Count = Count + 1
        CONSOLE.WRITELINE ("Enter the student's age ")
        Age = CONSOLE.READLINE ()
    END WHILE
    Average = Total/Count
    CONSOLE.writelINE ("Number of students: "& Count)
    CONSOLE.WRITELINE ("Average ages of students: " & Average)
    CONSOLE.READLINE ( )
END SUB
END MODULE
```

Exercise 3

1   Rewrite each of the following expressions using correct Visual Basic code:
Grade = A;
Count = StartingValue := 1;
Tax := 5%;
Sum := 10 plus 8;
Rate := .25;

2   Write the following instructions in Visual Basic code:
a   Declare an integer called Number.
b   Declare a character called LetterGrade.
c   Declare a variable called Price.
d   Declare an integer variable called Goals and initialise it to zero.
e   Declare a string variable called StudentName.

3   This program code contains errors. Correct the errors by writing the corrected version of the program in your exercise book. There are 10 errors in the program.

```
PROGAM Addition (output)
VAR   Num1, Num2, Sum ;   integer;
BEGIN;
    Num1 = 24;
    PRINT ('Enter a   number for Num 2');
    READ ('Num 2');
    Sum := Num1 +   Number2;
    WRITELN('Sum,Sum )
END
```

Step 5: Test and debug the program

Once an algorithm or a program is developed or written, the next stage is to check that the algorithm or program is doing what it was designed to do and is doing so correctly.

There are two types of testing:

- manual testing/dry running
- computer testing.

Manual testing/dry-running

The manual testing process involves using a technique called tracing, which allows the user to detect any logic errors in the program or algorithm. Also called dry-running or desk-checking, tracing involves executing the program manually by using input values for variables and recording what takes place after each instruction is executed.

A trace table is a table that is completed upon manual execution of an algorithm or program to determine what the program is doing. The first action when creating a trace table is to write down all the variables found in the algorithm as headings, as well as the heading 'output' to represent what is printed.

Example 27

What is printed by the following algorithms?

Solution

1
```
COUNT = 0
WHILE COUNT < = 10 DO
COUNT = COUNT + 2
PRINT COUNT
ENDWHILE
```

Count	OUTPUT	
0		Count is set as 0; Count < 10
2	2	2 is added to Count and 2 is printed; Count < 10
4	4	2 is added to Count and 4 is printed; Count < 10
6	6	2 is added to Count and 6 is printed; Count < 10
8	8	2 is added to Count and 8 is printed; Count < 10
10	10	2 is added to Count and 10 is printed; Count not less than 10 so the loop is exited.

2
```
FOR KG = 1 TO 5 DO
LB = KG * 2.2
PRINT KG, LB
ENDFOR
```

Kg	Lb	Output
1	2.2	1, 2.2
2	4.4	2, 4.4
3	6.6	3, 6.6
4	8.8	4, 8.8
5	11	5, 11

3
```
A = 3
B = 5
C = 6
D = B * A
E = C + B
IF E > D THEN
A = E
ELSE
A = D
ENDIF
PRINT A, B, C, D, E
```

A	B	C	D	E	OUTPUT
3	5	6	15	11	
15					15, 5, 6, 15, 11

At the end of the program, the values for B, C, D and E do not change.

Exercise 4

1 What is printed by the following algorithm?

```
R = 5
S = 6
IF S > 5 THEN
        T = S * R
ELSE
        T = S/R
ENDIF
PRINT T
```

2 What is printed by the following algorithm?

```
S = 25
N = 1
WHILE N < 12 DO
        = S - N
        PRINT S
        N = N + 2
ENDWHILE
```

3 Using numbers 5, 20, 25, 30, –1 for Num and 2, 4, 4, 3 for Rate respectively, what is printed by the following algorithm?

```
READ Num
WHILE Num >= 0 DO
        READ Rate
        Value = Num *
            Rate/100
        PRINT Rate,
            Num, Value
        READ Num
ENDWHILE
```

4 What is printed by the following algorithm if N = 4?

```
READ N
IF N < 3 THEN
        G = 1
        F = 2
ELSE
        F = 1
        G = 2
ENDIF
FOR J = 1 TO N DO
        H = F + G
        F = G
        G = H
        PRINT H
ENDFOR
```

5 What is printed by the algorithm?

```
For X = 1 to 6 DO
        R = X
        WHILE R >= 1 DO
            PRINT R
            R = R – 1
ENDWHILE
ENDFOR
```

6 What is printed by the following algorithm if Num is 10?

```
READ Num
FOR Count = Num to 1
        STEP –2 DO
        Sum = Count +
        Num
        PRINT Sum
ENDFOR
```

7 What is printed by the following algorithm if B = 5 and C = 4?

```
READ B, C
A = B
B = C
C = A
D = B + C
E = E * C
F = D – B
A = D
B = E
C = F
PRINT A, B, C, D, E, F
```

8 What is printed by the following algorithm?

```
X = 1
WHILE X <= 8 DO
        Y = 2X + (X *
            X) – 4
        PRINT Y
        X = X + 2
ENDWHILE
```

9 What is printed by the following algorithm?

```
Sum = 0
N = 25
WHILE N < 40 DO
        Sum = Sum + N
        PRINT N, Sum
        N = N + 4
ENDWHILE
```

Computer testing

Computer testing involves running the program using test data to discover any errors in the program. There are three types of errors: syntax, logic and runtime errors.

Syntax and logic errors

- A syntax error is an error in the grammar of the programming language.
- A logic error is an error in reasoning, such as the incorrect sequencing of instructions, and flawed comparisons and selection statements.

One of these errors within a program is known as a bug. The process of finding and correcting these errors is called debugging. Tracing is an invaluable tool that is used when debugging a program or algorithm.

In the process of debugging a program or algorithm, test data is used to make sure that the program is doing what it is supposed to. The program should be tested using suitable test data. If you test using only data from within a range of values that you think you will get (valid data), you would be assuming that only valid data will be used in the program. The data used must be chosen to deal with all the things that could happen and therefore, test data should include:

- data that is in the range you expect
- data that is much larger/above the range than expected
- data that is much smaller/below the range than expected
- the wrong type of data, for example, if you are expecting numbers, test the program by entering a word or an alphanumeric string that is a combination of letters and numbers such as 13no9.

For example:

```
Highest = 0
PRINT "Enter a number"
READ Number
WHILE Number <> 0 DO
        IF Number > Highest THEN
        Highest = Number
        ENDIF
        PRINT "Enter a number"
        READ Number
        ENDWHILE
PRINT "The highest number entered is:", Highest
```

Testing this program with data 2, 3, 0, 8, 1 would cause 3 to be printed as the highest number: once 0 is entered, the program would stop and you would not be able to enter any numbers after entering 0.

However, testing this program with –2, –8, –14, –1, 0 would cause –1 to be printed.

Runtime errors

Runtime errors are errors that occur after the program has been tested and debugged; they occur during the execution or running of the program. One of the reasons these errors can occur is if the program is stuck in an infinite loop. Since some computers set limits for how long your program is allowed to run, a runtime error may occur if the loop continues up to the time limit allowed.

During the computer testing process, the program is executed or run. This involves converting from the programming language to the language the computer understands, namely machine language or machine code.

The program written in the specific programming language is known as the source code. This source code is translated into object code by a compiler or an interpreter. Object code can be the same as or similar to machine or executable code.

The execution of a program can occur through an interpreter or compiler, as shown on page 186.

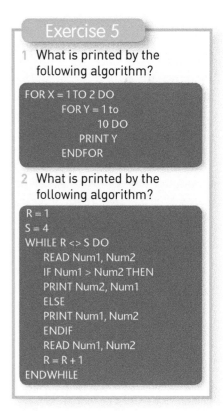

Exercise 5

1 What is printed by the following algorithm?

```
FOR X = 1 TO 2 DO
        FOR Y = 1 to
                10 DO
                PRINT Y
        ENDFOR
```

2 What is printed by the following algorithm?

```
R = 1
S = 4
WHILE R <> S DO
        READ Num1, Num2
        IF Num1 > Num2 THEN
        PRINT Num2, Num1
        ELSE
        PRINT Num1, Num2
        ENDIF
        READ Num1, Num2
        R = R + 1
ENDWHILE
```

In the case of an interpreter

The interpreter translates the source code to machine code and the machine code is executed (Figure 9.2). An interpreter translates and executes one instruction at a time as it is encountered. The machine codes are not saved after execution.

Advantages

- It translates one instruction at a time, therefore it uses a minimum amount of the computer's memory.
- It is also helpful in the debugging process, as the interpreter can relate error messages to the instruction being executed.

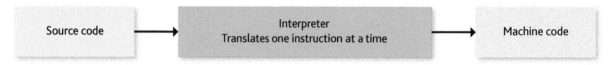

▲ Figure 9.2 An interpreter

Disadvantage

The interpreter takes longer to run a program, as time is spent interpreting the source code every time the program needs to be run.

In the case of a compiler

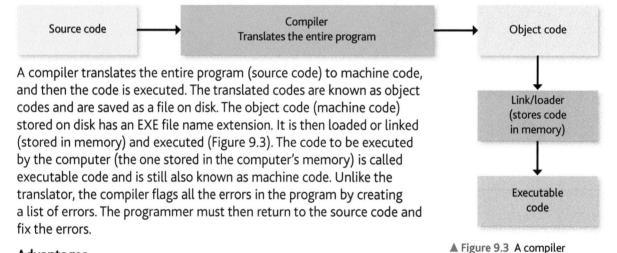

▲ Figure 9.3 A compiler

A compiler translates the entire program (source code) to machine code, and then the code is executed. The translated codes are known as object codes and are saved as a file on disk. The object code (machine code) stored on disk has an EXE file name extension. It is then loaded or linked (stored in memory) and executed (Figure 9.3). The code to be executed by the computer (the one stored in the computer's memory) is called executable code and is still also known as machine code. Unlike the translator, the compiler flags all the errors in the program by creating a list of errors. The programmer must then return to the source code and fix the errors.

Advantages

- It can be executed faster than when using an interpreter, as the object codes are saved and can be run at any time.
- Object codes are harder for a user to change than the source code. The object code is machine language and therefore a user will have difficulty reading and interpreting the code in order to make changes.

Disadvantage

- As the entire program is translated to object code, it uses much more of the computer's memory.

Step 6: Document the program

Documentation is a written explanation of how the program works and how to use it. It provides users with help in using the program and helps a programmer to understand the program so that changes can be made or bugs fixed more easily. There are two types of documentation: user documentation and technical documentation.

User documentation/user guides

User documentation is written to explain to users how to use the program. It is written in plain English and not in the specialist programming language found in technical documentation. It includes the following information:

- Hardware requirements
- How to install the program
- How to run the program
- How to enter data
- What the output looks like
- How to use any menus
- Special features of the program
- Error messages and advice on how to correct them (troubleshoot any errors).

Technical documentation

This documentation is for use by the programmer. It includes information on the program itself, that is, technical aspects of how it works. Some of the reasons for technical documentation include the following:

- When writing a long program, the programmer needs to understand what was written a few weeks or even months before.
- Extremely large programs are written in teams, where certain teams write particular sections of the program code. Each team needs to understand what the other teams have written so that the whole program code can fit together.
- A program may need modification in the future. It may need to be revised to fit a new situation, or corrected for a logic error that may show up after using extreme data. On many occasions, these modifications are not done by the original programmer; the new programmer will need to be able to read and understand the written program.

Technical documentation includes:
- the problem that the program is intended to solve (the purpose of the program)
- the algorithm
- the program code/listing with its internal documentation (see page 188)
- test data and results produced by the program
- data and file structures
- structure and flow diagrams, which show the relationships between the program modules.

Exercise 6

1 A programmer is asked to modify a program that has been in use by a company for a few years. However, there is no technical documentation for the program. List some of the problems that might result from this.
2 List FOUR requirements of a good user guide for a program.
3 Explain the difference between technical documentation and user documentation.
4 Explain the difference between an interpreter and a compiler. Discuss why a programmer might choose to use an interpreter rather than a compiler.
5 What does it mean to debug a program?
6 List the THREE types of programming errors and explain what they are.

Internal documentation within the program code/listing includes:

- using indentation and spacing (white space) to easily identify parts of the program helps with the readability of the program, so that the code can be easily read and the flow of the program control is easier to follow
- explanatory remarks (comments)
- suitable variable names, which can be associated with what is being stored so that further explanation is not needed.

Chapter 9: Summary

- The two levels of programming languages are low level and high level. High-level languages are machine independent; they are not specifically designed for any one brand of computer. Low-level languages are machine dependent and are designed for only one type of computer.
- Programs written in high-level languages must be compiled or translated before they are executed by the computer.
- There are five generations of computer programming languages.
- Program development is made up of six basic steps: defining the problem; analysing the problem; developing an algorithm/method of solving the problem; writing a computer program corresponding to the algorithm; testing and debugging the program; documenting the program.
- Tracing is a technique that allows the user to detect any logic errors in the program or algorithm.
- A syntax error is an error in the grammar of the programming language.

- A logic error is an error in reasoning, such as the incorrect sequencing of instructions and flawed comparisons and selection statements.
- Runtime errors occur during the execution or running of a program after testing or debugging.
- A program written in a specific programming language is known as source code. This source code is translated into machine language with the use of a compiler or an interpreter.
- Documentation written to explain to the user how to use a program is known as user documentation.
- Documentation for use by a programmer is known as technical documentation.
- Keywords, also called reserved words, have special meaning in a programming language. Identifiers are names given to variables, constants and types.
- A data type allows the computer to know what kind of data to process.
- Comments are pieces of code that are not executed during the running of a program and help to explain the action in the program.

Chapter 9: Questions

True or False?

1 Writeln or Write statement text is printed when enclosed with double quotations marks.

2 A Writeln statement causes the cursor to be positioned at the beginning of the next line.

3 The end of a Pascal program is terminated by the statement 'STOP'.

4 The Write statement causes the cursor to be positioned at the end of the statement being read.

5 A comment cannot be written anywhere in a program.

6 A comment in VB may be enclosed using { and }.

7 A comment cannot be enclosed using (* and *).

8 The '&' is an operator in Visual Basic.

9 Semi-colons are not placed at the end of statements in the Visual Basic programming language.

10 Every program statement in the Pascal program is terminated by a full stop.

Computer and cybersecurity and computer misuse

Technology has become an important part of everyday life for many people in the world. Governments, companies, organisations and individuals use technology to create, store and manage information. The increasing use of technology along with the expansion of the internet, and the many services available on it, have resulted in many risks to users and computer systems. System security is therefore essential to protect or safeguard computers, mobile devices, and data and software from loss, damage and misuse. The following text describes three important terms.

■ **Computer security** is about the security of a computer (or laptop, tablet or smartphone) and its software. Computer security covers things such as backups, so that data is secure if the computer breaks; password security to stop an individual who should not be using the computer from being able to login; and preventing viruses and other threats from damaging or stealing what is on the computer.
■ **Cybersecurity** is about making sure that the computer and its connections are secure. Cybersecurity covers how to prevent things such as viruses, malware, phishing and other threats from accessing information from a computer (or laptop, tablet or smartphone).
■ **Computer misuse** is about the way people use computers to access other people's computer systems and their information, or how they use computers to spread unfair, false or hurtful information. The first two points look more closely at preventing problems, whereas computer misuse looks at the ways in which people try to create the problems. These problems include cyberbullying, hacking, industrial espionage, trolling and fake news.

Risk assessment

To protect a system, you need to find out the parts of a system that could be affected by a system attack, and then identify the various risks that could affect those parts. The parts, often called the infrastructure, include computer hardware, network hardware (for example, routers and servers), communications systems, operating systems, application software and data files. This is called a system risk assessment, which would normally consider the following elements:

■ **Vulnerabilities** are flaws in a system that can be used to cause loss or harm. Vulnerabilities may be due to design, implementation or operational procedures and can exist at the network, host, or application levels. For instance, a system may be vulnerable to data manipulation by someone who should not have access to the system because the system does not check a user's identity before allowing computer and data access.

- **Threats** to a computing system are a set of circumstances that have the potential to cause loss or harm. They may or may not be damaging or malicious in nature. Threats to a computer system can be started (or exploited) by humans or by computers. Some of these threats include human errors, hardware design flaws and software failures. Natural disasters such as floods, earthquakes and hurricanes are also considered to be threats, as they can cause damage to a system.
- **Attacks** (or exploits) are actions taken that use one or more vulnerabilities in a system to realise a threat. For example, a human who exploits a flaw in the system causes an attack on the system. An attack can also be launched by another system, as in the case of 'denial of service' attacks, which work by causing a server or part of a network to be overloaded with data so that genuine users cannot use it.
- **Countermeasures** or controls are how we deal with and prevent these problems. A countermeasure is an action, device, procedure or technique that removes or reduces a vulnerability. It does not directly address threats; instead, it addresses the vulnerabilities to reduce the probability of an attack or the impact of a threat. Countermeasures can range from improving application design, programming code or operational practices.

Hardware and software security

Data integrity concerns the consistency, accuracy and reliability of data. Data is said to have integrity if it is accurate and complete when it enters a system and it does not become inaccurate after further processing. The goal of integrity is to protect against data becoming corrupted – being changed, deleted or substituted without authorisation. Data integrity can be compromised in a number of ways:

- human error (such as inaccurate data entry, accidental deletion and accidental changing of data)
- natural disasters such as fires, floods and earthquakes
- malware
- hardware failure
- fraud
- malicious deletion or changing of data.

Data security concerns protecting data from unauthorised access and is one of the methods used to ensure data integrity. Data can be secured using both physical and software safeguards.

Physical data security

Physical safeguards deal with the protection of hardware and software from accidental or malicious damage, destruction or theft. Whether a computer or computer system is used by an individual, an organisation or a government, the threats affect them all. However, some of these methods are not going to apply to an individual. Depending on the sensitivity of the data stored, a combination of the methods described in the text on the next page may be used.

Only allowing authorised personnel access

The goal is to stop unauthorised users from accessing the computer system. This is necessary to prevent equipment theft, media theft, console or network access and physical destruction of media or equipment. For an individual at home, making sure that you have good locks on your doors and a burglar alarm might be enough, but for an organisation or government you would look at a combination of all of these. One or a combination of the following methods may enforce this:

- locks
- security guards
- burglar alarms
- intrusion detection systems that use techniques such as monitoring video cameras, either watched by a security guard or using computer face recognition to identify anyone who should not be there
- authentication systems for checking identity, using some of the methods below, which only allow access to authorised people:
  - electronic doors that can only be opened using passwords or magnetic cards such as identification badges, magnetic stripe cards and smart cards with a PIN (personal identification number), as well as a numeric password assigned to each individual user of a system
  - biometric devices that confirm (authenticate) a person's identity by converting a personal characteristic, such as a fingerprint, into a digital code; this is compared with a digital code of that characteristic (stored previously on the system) for authentication. Examples of biometric devices and systems include:
    - a fingerprint reader, which reads the pattern of your fingerprints
    - facial recognition system, which recognises your face
    - hand geometry system, which identifies the shape of your hand
    - voice recognition system, which recognises your voice using a particular phrase
    - signature verification system, which recognises the shape and change of pressure when you sign
    - iris-recognition system, which recognises patterns in your iris
    - retinal scanners, which recognise patterns in the blood vessels in your retina at the back of your eye.

▲ Figure 10.1 Biometric scanning

Outer structural security

Outer structural security entails reinforcements to doors, windows, walls and roofs to make the building where hardware and data is stored more secure. It makes no sense installing expensive locks on fragile doors and windows; for this reason, structural security needs to look at many interlinked factors to ensure maximum physical protection.

Backup and recovery

Making a copy of your data and storing it safely so that you can recover the data is a simple and effective way to ensure data integrity. To do this, we use backup and recovery systems and software.

Modern operating systems such as Windows 10 have a built-in backup and recovery system. Windows 10 backs up your files to its OneDrive cloud storage on the internet, called remote or cloud backup. With an internet connection, you can retrieve the data on your computer if the data or computer are damaged or if there is a fire, earthquake or other disaster.

It is good practice to keep more than one backup, so in addition to using OneDrive, consider having an external hard disk drive for backup. You can secure this further by unplugging it at the end of the day and keeping it in a fireproof safe or cabinet, or in another building.

Organisations and governments invest heavily in backup because data is a very important part of their business. They will have more complex backup policies so that information is backed up in several places and will go back for different periods of time (for example, last week, last month, the last 5 years), and they will test that they can recover the information from the backup. Their backups will often be on several remote systems.

Organisations and governments will also use long-term data storage, known as archiving, a form of physical data backup involving the removal of inactive files from the computer. These files are no longer in use or have not been accessed for a long time, but may be needed at some future date, such as tax records where the law says you have to keep several years of accounts. They can be stored in The Cloud or in devices such as magnetic tape, microfiche or CD-R, and can then be retrieved if necessary.

Distributing work to a few employees, not just one

In this way, no one employee has access to all the data. This means that if someone is sick or on holiday, someone else can access the data.

Software-based data security

Software safeguards are another equally important method of protecting data from loss or damage. Data will never be fully secure unless both the physical safeguards and software safeguards are in place. Some of the most common onsite software safeguards are described below.

Passwords for the system

A password is a combination of characters used to control access to computers. In a password system, a user has to enter a password or PIN (personal identification number) to gain access to the computer system or unlock encrypted personal data on a device. This is basic security for any device, whether used by an individual or as part of an organisation or government. To create a secure password, you need to:

- make sure it contains a mix of uppercase and lowercase letters, numbers and keyboard symbols (?, £, $, !, %, and so on)
- avoid using information that could easily be found out about you, such as your name, part of your address or date of birth
- make it a reasonable length. A minimum of eight characters is a good starting point, but longer would be better.

Choosing a short phrase, perhaps from a movie you have seen, and substituting numbers or symbols for some of the letters is a good approach, for example, *The Jungle Book* becomes 'Th3Jung!e8**k'.

Passwords for individual files, folders, apps and websites

You have probably had to login to an app on your smartphone or a website. This is to protect your personal information that the app or website uses. You can often do the same with files and folders, for example, in Microsoft Excel you can password protect a spreadsheet file so that, for example, if you used it to keep track of your spending, you can prevent others from seeing that data. This authenticates you – confirms who you are and that you should have access to that app or data.

Multiple levels of passwords can provide entry to different levels of information in a database or other computer storage system. For example, in a company, everyone may have a password to gain access to the company's network. However, not everyone may be permitted to access all the different data stored on the network. This is because some files or folders may contain sensitive or highly confidential information and are not available to everyone. To gain access to some of these files or folders another password may be needed. Other levels of passwords may also be included, depending on the sensitivity of the data.

Increasingly, companies such as Google™ and Facebook are encouraging users to use two-factor authentication. This is when you have a second item that confirms it is you using your password. Examples of this are a one-off number texted to your phone or a USB key that you need to plug into the computer.

Audit trails or access logs

Many companies and governments use intrusion detection systems on their networks. These and other security software programs can audit computer use by providing a comprehensive record of all the network or system activity, including who is accessing what data, when, and how often. These can help to recognise unusual things happening, such as a computer that is supposed to be in the building appearing to be logging on from somewhere else, or an employee who has left the company logging in to the system. They can also help by providing logs of the individuals who may have used the network during a specific period of time or accessed a file. An audit trail can also be used to show when a file has been changed and by whom. This could be helpful in trying to work out what backed-up version of a file to recover if it has been damaged.

Encryption

Encryption is encoding (scrambling) data during storage or transmission so that it cannot be understood by someone who does not have the encryption key or software to convert it back to its original form. A key is a randomly generated set of characters that is used to encrypt/decrypt data. A mathematical algorithm determines the way an encryptor (the program that encrypts the text) alters the original communication, to produce enciphered (scrambled) text. This is a very effective method of preventing unauthorised persons from stealing, reading or changing data.

Using effective encryption techniques, sensitive valuable information can be protected against organised criminals, malicious hackers or spies from other companies or countries. Encryption is used to secure data such

▲ Figure 10.2 Comprehensive security software can track attempted logon activity.

Did you know?

Claude E Shannon is considered to be the father of mathematical cryptography. He wrote an article entitled 'A mathematical theory of cryptography', which was published in 1949 while he was working at Bell Labs.

as credit card numbers, bank account information, health information and even personal correspondence that is transmitted over the internet. Encryption is one of the most effective methods of securing data against electronic eavesdropping: the tapping of a data transmission line to access data being transmitted. Two of the most popular data encryption schemes are PGP (Pretty Good Privacy) and Triple DES (Data Encryption Standard).

Firewall

A firewall is a program, a hardware device or a combination of both that filters the information coming in through your computer system's or network's connection to the internet. It prevents unauthorised users from gaining access. A firewall can also perform audit and alarm functions that record all access attempts to and from a network. Three popular firewall software packages are Bitdefender Internet Security 2018, Kaspersky Internet Security 2018 and Norton Security Standard. Firewalls can protect systems from these dangers.

- **Remote login:** This is when someone is able to connect to your computer and control it in some form, ranging from being able to view or access your files to actually running programs on your computer.
- **Spam (electronic junk mail):** By gaining access to a list of email addresses, a person can send unwanted spam to thousands of users.
- **Denial of service:** This is an attack that floods a computer or website with data, causing it to overload and preventing it from functioning properly. This type of attack is more frequently targeted at businesses, rather than individuals.
- **Malware:** This is covered in its own section below.

Anti-virus software

Anti-virus software is a special type of software used to remove or inactivate known viruses from a computer's hard disk, or USB memory device. It scans the different storage media looking for known viruses; if viruses are found they are either removed or quarantined. These programs can also scan incoming and outgoing email messages to ensure they do not contain infected data. Anti-virus software should be updated via the internet regularly. Not doing this can make it easier for new viruses to infect your system, as they are created all the time and may pose serious risks to your computer system. Typical anti-virus software includes: Windows Defender, Symantec Norton AntiVirus, McAfee AntiVirus and Bitdefender Antivirus Plus.

Malware

Malware is a term used to describe different types of malicious software, which include viruses, worms, spyware, ransomware, trojans and bots. Criminals may use malware to monitor your online activity in the hope that they can steal some valuable personal information, such as your credit card details. This sometimes happens on a large scale, for example, British Airways had a lot of customer data stolen, including credit card details, by malware in a database. Malware may also try to cause damage to the computer or network if it is part of a government or organisation's network in order to stop them being able to do something, for example, to stop a big news organisation's website from being accessed during an election.

> **Did you know?**
> Encryption can be traced as far back as ancient Babylonian merchants who used an intaglio. This was a piece of flat stone carved into a collage of images and writing and was the equivalent of what today we call a 'digital signature'. Buyers knew that a particular intaglio belonged to a particular trader, since only he or she had the intaglio to produce that exact signature. Traders therefore used the intaglio to identify themselves when making transactions.

▲ Figure 10.3 A anti-virus software

▲ Figure 10.4 Many people are unaware that their computer systems contain malware.

Malware is often downloaded when someone opens an infected email attachment or clicks on a suspicious link in an email: a practice often used with 'phishing', which we look at below. Malware can also be used to steal your username, password or other information, which is then forwarded to a third party. These details can then be used to get access to other systems or to steal information such as credit card details.

Worms and viruses differ in the way they spread and how they function.

A worm is a program that uses computer networks and security holes (weaknesses in a security system) to repeatedly copy itself into a computer's memory or onto a magnetic disk, until no more space is left. A copy of the worm scans the network looking for another machine that has a specific security hole, and then starts to replicate itself again. For example, a worm known as 'Code Red' replicated itself over 250 000 times in about nine hours on 19 July 2001, causing traffic on the internet to slow down considerably.

A virus is a program purposefully written by someone to activate itself, unknown to the victim, to destroy or corrupt data. A virus must attach itself to some other program or document in order to be executed (executed here means 'started up'). Viruses are one of the main threats to a computer system and have caused many businesses to lose millions of dollars due to corrupted data, lost data and computer 'downtime' (times when computers are unusable).

Some common types of viruses are described in the following text.

- **File virus:** These are viruses that infect program files. The viruses attach themselves to executable program files, which are started each time the program is run. For example, a virus may attach itself to a word-processing program. Each time the word-processing program is run, the virus also runs.
- **Email virus:** This type of virus comes as either an attachment to an email or as the email itself. It usually spreads by automatically mailing itself to everyone in the address book of its victim. For example, in March 1999, the Melissa virus replicated itself so many times and so quickly that it forced Microsoft and a number of large companies to completely turn off their email systems until the virus could be contained. The ILOVEYOU virus in the year 2000 had the same effect.
- **Trojan horses:** A Trojan horse is a computer program that places destructive code in programs such as games. When the user runs the game, the hidden code runs in the background, usually unknown to the user, and it erases either their entire hard disk or some programs on the disk. Trojans are also known to create backdoors to give malicious users access to the system so they can steal personal or embarrassing information from individuals' computers, or perhaps sensitive information from an organisation or government's network. Unlike viruses and worms, Trojans do not reproduce by infecting other files, nor do they self-replicate. Trojans must spread through user interaction, such as opening an email attachment or downloading and running a file, from the internet.
- **Boot-sector virus:** The boot sector is part of the operating system; it tells the computer how to load the rest of the operating system when the computer is started up. A boot-sector virus corrupts or replaces the instructions in the boot sector, thereby preventing the operating system from loading properly and the computer from booting or powering up.

▲ Figure 10.5 A statue of a Trojan Horse in Turkey

- **Ransomware:** This is a type of malicious software that threatens to publish the victim's data or permanently block access to it unless a ransom is paid. Whereas some simple ransomware may lock the system in a way that is not difficult for a knowledgeable person to reverse, more advanced malware uses a technique called cryptoviral extortion, which encrypts the victim's files, making them inaccessible, and demands a ransom payment to decrypt them.
- **Bots:** 'Bot' is derived from the word 'robot' and is an automated process that interacts with other network services. Bots often automate tasks and provide information or services that would otherwise be conducted by a human being. A typical use of bots is to gather information, such as web crawlers (these find information for search engines), or interact automatically with Instant Messaging (IM), Internet Relay Chat (IRC), or other web interfaces. Bots can be used for either good (for example, web crawlers for search engines, IM and IRC, and so on) or malicious intent. A malicious bot is self-propagating malware designed to infect a host and connect back to a central server or servers that act as a command and control (C&C) centre for an entire network of compromised devices or 'botnet'. With a botnet, attackers can launch broad-based, 'remote-control', flood-type attacks against their target(s), such as the 'denial of service attacks' described above.

How viruses are spread

Viruses are usually spread by:

- unintended download of infected programs and files from the internet
- opening infected files received through emails
- unwanted attachments or embedded links in email
- using a storage medium such as a USB drive or CD that contains infected files
- self-propagation, which is where malware is able to move itself from computer to computer or network to network, thus spreading on its own.

Prevention of and protection against viruses

You need to be continually aware of the possibility of viruses entering your system. Some of the signs that may indicate that your system has a virus are:

- weird or obscene messages
- garbled information
- incorrect document contents
- missing files or folders
- your application crashes or hangs when opening documents.

To protect your system against viruses:

- Install an anti-virus software package on your computer system.
- Do not use storage media from other computers in your computer. If you have to use them, first run a virus scan to remove any viruses.
- Do not open any email attachments that contain an executable file: these have file extensions such as .exe, .com and .vbs.
- Use an operating system such as macOS®, Linux, UNIX or Windows 10, which has security features that protect computers from many types of malware.

> **Did you know?**
>
> In May 2017, the WannaCry ransomware, which was spread via a known problem with some versions of Windows, encrypted user's files so that they could not access them. The hackers then demanded a sum of money in return for a decryption key. It is believed that over 200,000 computers in 150 countries were infected. It affected the National Health Service in the UK, as well as companies such as Nissan, Renault and FedEx.

> **Did you know?**
>
> Windows 10 has the Windows Defender security centre, which provides protection for the system, files and online activities from malware and other threats.

Data privacy

Many businesses, government bodies and other organisations hold information on individuals. Information given to these bodies is given for a specific purpose. In many cases, the information is personal to the individual (for example, their name, address, age, gender and telephone number) and can be valuable to any number of organisations, not least, commercial organisations that want to approach you directly to offer a product or service. The ease with which data stored on databases can be accessed, cross-referenced and transmitted from one computer to the next in a LAN, WAN or over the internet, emphasises the need for data privacy laws, such as the General Data Protection Regulations that came into force in Europe in 2018. These are important because anyone trading with companies or individuals in Europe will need to comply with them. In many countries where there are no data protection laws, companies may be inclined to sell copies of their databases to other companies. The result is that personal or private information can now be used for purposes for which it was not intended, for example, Facebook has had a number of issues around how the data it collects has been used by other companies.

Computer surveillance

Computer surveillance can involve accessing the storage mechanism of an individual's computer, or monitoring an individual's use of a computer, in most cases without their knowledge. An individual in an organisation or government might also be targeted like this, as once you have access to one computer on a network you can often gain access to a lot of information on that network. Computer surveillance can be achieved by both hardware and software methods.

One hardware method of computer surveillance is keylogging or keystroke logging. A hardware keylogger is a device that plugs in between your keyboard and your computer. Once plugged in, all data entered via the keyboard is stored in the keylogger's memory.

The software method of computer surveillance involves the use of spyware. This type of software, which is usually secretly installed on a computer, covertly (secretly) monitors the user's actions without his or her knowledge. It can save its findings locally or transmit them to someone else. Spyware software can be categorised as surveillance spyware and advertising spyware. This is a type of malware, and all the suggestions to protect against malware, as that discussed in the last section, will help to stop spyware from being used illegally on a computer. Surveillance spyware includes software keyloggers, screen capture devices and Trojan horses. This type of software can be used by:

- law enforcement and intelligence agencies, to solve and/or prevent crimes
- corporations and companies, to monitor the use of their computer resources for many different reasons, including to help fix problems.
- criminals, to acquire passwords and credit card numbers
- private investigators, hired to spy on individuals or organisations
- government agencies, to spy on citizens
- parents, to monitor their children's use of the computer.

Exercise 1

1 List SIX ways in which data integrity can be compromised.
2 Distinguish between data integrity and data security.
3 Describe FOUR hardware methods used to protect data and FOUR software methods used to protect data.
4 a Define the term 'computer virus'.
   b Briefly describe FOUR types of computer viruses.
   c List FOUR methods to prevent and protect against viruses.

Advertising spyware, also known as adware, is used to gather personal information about computer users or to show advertisements. Some advertising spyware records information such as email addresses, web browsing history, online shopping habits, passwords and other personal information. Advertising spyware is usually bundled with freeware or shareware, when the unsuspecting user downloads it from the internet. Freebies such as screen savers, emoticons and Clipart will sometimes have spyware hiding in them.

Spyware can be legal or illegal. For example, law enforcement officials can use spyware legally after obtaining the relevant legal permission. However, it is illegal for a person to install software on another person's computer without that person's specific permission.

Cybercrimes

Cybercrime is an issue that impacts the lives of many people, businesses and organisations around the world. Cybercrimes are crimes that are directed at computers or other devices (for example, hacking), and where computers or other devices are integral to the offence. Cybercriminals are individuals or teams of people who use technology to commit malicious activities on digital systems or networks, with the intention of stealing sensitive company information or personal data, and generating profit. Common types of cybercrime include hacking, online scams and fraud, identity theft, attacks on computer systems and illegal or prohibited online content. For example, a cybercrime may occur if a person in an organisation (not a hacker) makes changes to information in a computer without authorisation, for personal benefit, perhaps so they can steal something of worth, or for malicious reasons, for example, if they had been fired they might delete some information in order to get even. Many computer crimes are committed by disgruntled employees who sometimes want to get even with their employer.

The effect of cybercrime can be extremely upsetting for victims, and not necessarily just for financial reasons. Victims may feel that their privacy has been violated, and that they are powerless. Unfortunately, as the reliance on technology grows worldwide, the cost and incidence of cybercrime is expected to increase.

Cyberbullying

Cyberbullying or stalking occurs when someone engages in offensive, menacing or harassing behaviour using electronic means. Although it has become increasingly common among teenagers, it can happen to people of any age, at any time, and often anonymously. It can affect the individual being bullied badly as, for example, you can walk away from a bully at school, but cyberbullies can reach you at home via your computer or phone. Examples of some of the ways cyberbullying can occur include:

- posting hurtful messages, images or videos online
- repeatedly sending unwanted messages online
- sending abusive texts and emails
- excluding or intimidating others online
- creating fake social networking profiles or websites that are hurtful
- nasty online gossip and chat
- any other form of digital communication that is discriminatory, intimidating, intended to cause hurt or make someone fear for their safety.

▲ Figure 10.6 With the increase in cybercrime, the police now need to establish specialised cybercrime units.

▲ Figure 10.7 Cyberbullying can be extremely upsetting to the individual and can lead to mental health issues.

Did you know?

Many companies use spyware to monitor their company resources. Employers use spyware to increase security, improve employee productivity and reduce information leaks. However, many employees and trade unions believe that the use of spyware to monitor individuals' computer use infringes on privacy rights. Employers counter by saying they have a right to protect their business from potential employee idleness, fraud and misbehaviour. Discuss this issue with classmates. In companies where spyware is being used, should the employees be informed?

Prohibited, obscene, offensive and illegal content

Illegal and prohibited content can be found almost anywhere online: newsgroups, forums, blogs, social media, peer-to-peer networks, live visual and audio. One of the major risks of illegal and prohibited content is that it may reach children, for whom such content can be especially damaging. In order to keep the internet safe for all users, you should report prohibited online content. The following types of content may be classified as prohibited, offensive and illegal content:

- child pornography or child abuse
- content that shows extreme sexual violence or materials that are overly violent
- content that provokes the viewer into committing crimes and carrying out violent acts
- content that promotes terrorism or encourages terrorist acts.

Software, music and video piracy

Piracy is the unauthorised copying, usage or selling of software, music or films that are copyrighted. Some of the main types of software, music and film piracy are listed in the following text.

- **Licensed-user duplication for unlicensed users:** If someone buys a new computer from a reputable (reliable) company, then within the overall price of the computer, the person may also be paying for copyrighted software that is on that machine. So, at the same time, a private purchaser of a computer is buying a single-user licence for the software on that machine. Licensed-user piracy occurs when the user makes copies of the machine's software and distributes or sells it to other individuals or companies. Another common example is if a company purchases a software package for use on, say 20 machines, but installs the software on more than 20 machines. All the computers in excess of the 20 to which the licence was granted are therefore using pirated software, since the licence was limited. Another example is if someone buys a DVD or CD and makes copies to sell or give to friends.

▲ Figure 10.8 All piracy is a crime.

- **Pre-installed software:** Software piracy can also occur when, for example, a computer store uses a copy of a software package that was licensed for use on one computer but installs it in many computers.
- **Internet piracy:** Some websites allow individuals to download unauthorised copies of software, music or films.
- **Counterfeiting:** This occurs when individuals or companies make illegal copies of software, music and films and package it to look like the original packaging from the manufacturer.

Piracy is an infringement of ownership rights. It is the theft of the work and effort of another individual or company. The owner may therefore lose money they could have earned as a result of piracy, just as if someone were to steal your hard-earned money by picking your pocket on the street. Pirated material is theft, and using it is morally wrong. Some of the other reasons why pirated material should not be used are:

- Pirated software may not contain all the elements and documentation of the program, causing problems for the user.

- Pirated software may not have the upgrade options often provided as an add-on (for example, with an encryption key) in legitimate software.
- Pirated software may have viruses that can be harmful to your hard drive or network.
- Pirated material is illegal – most countries have laws against it and individuals convicted of this crime can pay hefty fines or even be jailed.
- Income from pirated material is often used to support organised crime.

All software is copyright – the person or company who wrote it always retains the right to decide whether it can be copied or not. But it is not always illegal to copy and distribute such software.

For example, public domain software can be copied as many times as you like. Software is in the public domain when it is put on websites for free distribution, with the consent of the copyright owner. Popular freeware is Adobe®Reader®, available from www.adobe.com.

There is also 'freeware' software available at specialist websites, such as Ninite.WOT and softpedia.WOT; Free and Open Source (FOSS) and creative commons licensed software. Once again, this software may be copyrighted, but you may be allowed to copy it as many times as you like for personal use, though certain conditions on its use may be imposed (enforced).

▲ Figure 10.9 Adobe® Reader® is the free global standard reader for reliable viewing of PDF documents.

Phishing

Phishing refers to attempts by cybercriminals and hackers to trick you into giving away personal information to gain access to account numbers or to infect your machine with malware. Phishing attempts can happen through a variety of ways, including email, social media or text messages, and can compromise security and lead to theft of personal and financial data, for example, to get credit card details to use online. Phishing messages can come from hijacked accounts of people you know, making them hard to distinguish from real messages, or they can impersonate emails from real organisations such as banks. Additionally, cybercriminals commonly use infected documents or PDF attachments to aid in their phishing attempts.

How do you avoid phishing attempts?
Phishing attempts can often get through spam filters and security software that you may have in your computer. You therefore need to be vigilant. Keep an eye out for things such as poor spelling, unexpected urgency (for example, 'you must do this now') or a wrong salutation (for example, your bank saying 'hi Jones' rather than something more formal, such as 'Dear Mr Jones' or 'Hello Fred'. Think twice about clicking a link or opening a document that seems suspicious. Double-check that every URL or email address where you enter your password looks real, for example, it is spelled correctly. And if anything raises doubt, delete the communication.

Hacking

Hacking is the unauthorised accessing of a computer system; the individual who does this is referred to as a hacker. Hackers may gain access to your computer or device through security weaknesses, phishing or malware. Once they have compromised your email, banking or social media accounts, they can change passwords, preventing you from accessing your accounts. Scammers often send out messages impersonating you, directing people to fake websites, or asking them to send money.

Hackers are usually excellent computer programmers. Many hackers are young people who hack into systems just for the challenge or as a prank. Although this may seem harmless, it can cause considerable damage and is illegal in many countries. The more criminally-minded hackers access computer systems for one or more reasons:

- to steal important and highly confidential information
- to copy computer programs illegally
- to alter data
- to delete data or install a virus to destroy or corrupt it
- to transfer money from one bank account to another using electronic funds transfer (EFT).

These are some of the most common methods that hackers use.

- **Impersonation:** Pretending to be someone who is a legitimate user.
- **Brute force attacks:** Trying every possible combination of characters to find the password.
- **Remote login:** Using the flaws in operating systems to find a back door that allows a hacker to connect to a remote computer and control it.

Internet fraud

The term 'internet fraud' refers generally to any type of fraud scheme that uses one or more components of the internet – such as chat rooms, email, message boards or websites – to present fraudulent offers to prospective victims and conduct fraudulent transactions.

Some major types of internet fraud are listed in the following text.

- **Online trading schemes:** Online trading is the buying and selling of products over the internet. Companies or individuals set up virtual shops/malls on websites that users can access to view items on sale. These businesses appear to offer high-value items that are likely to attract many consumers, since the items are usually offered for sale at very reduced prices. Internet fraud occurs when the company or an individual bills the customer for the purchase, collects the money and then does not deliver the items purchased, or delivers a product that is substandard and far less valuable than what was promised. Another example includes impersonating charities and requesting donations for natural disasters.
- **Credit card fraud:** This is a slight variation on the above scheme. The fraud involves setting up temporary bogus businesses on the internet. These businesses lure individuals into giving their credit card numbers in order to steal their money. A common method is to send emails pretending to be from a major bank. These messages direct you to a fake website that asks you to type in your banking details, thereby allowing the fraudster to steal your money.
- **Business opportunity/'work-at-home' schemes online:** There are many fraudulent schemes that use the internet to advertise business opportunities, which supposedly allow individuals to get rich or earn large sums of money working at home. These schemes typically require individuals to pay for information and material to start a business or get a job, but then fail to deliver the materials, information or the job.

Are Our Personal Details Safe?

Teenager Arrested for Hacking

How the Hack did they do that?

Web Fraud Cases on the Rise

Government rushes Legislation for Internet Safety

▲ Figure 10.10 As technology advances, some criminals try to take advantage – in the most invasive way – by hacking.

INTERNET SCAM!
IF IT SOUNDS TOO GOOD TO BE TRUE THEN IT PROBABLY IS!

▲ Figure 10.11 Be vigilant about internet offers!

Other online scams or fraud

With the growth in online services and internet use, there are many opportunities for criminals to commit scams and fraud. These are dishonest schemes that seek to take advantage of unsuspecting people to gain a benefit (such as money, or access to personal details). These are often contained in spam and phishing messages. Here are some common types of online scams.

- **Unexpected prize scams:** These include lottery scams, 'scratchie' scams and travel scams. These scams can be delivered online, by telephone or by mail. They inform you that you have won a prize (for example, a large sum of money, shopping vouchers, a free holiday or travel-related products), and to claim it you are asked to send money or provide personal information.
- **Unexpected money scams:** These include inheritance scams, 'Nigerian' scams, money reclaim scams and other upfront payment or advance fee fraud. These scams ask you to send money upfront for a product or reward, to provide personal information, to pay lawyer fees, to claim your inheritance or large claim from a distant relative overseas, or to transfer money on someone's behalf with the promise of receiving money in return.
- **Threats and extortion scams:** These involve scammers sending random death threats via SMS or email from a supposed hired 'hit man'. The message will contain threats to kill you unless you send the 'hit man' cash.

Identity theft

Identity theft is a widespread crime that is continually evolving with the constant evolution of technology and trends. Cybercriminals have a variety of schemes to get a hold of your personal information and use it to steal your money, sell your identity and commit fraud or other crimes in your name. We have already looked at phishing and hacking as two ways criminals can access your personal information. The following are some other ways, criminals may steal your identity.

Types of identity theft attacks

- **Credit card theft:** One of the most common identity theft attacks occurs through the use of credit cards. Many people use credit cards everywhere; for shopping, entertainment and paying bills. This means that each time an individual purchases an item, several persons may have access to the individual's credit card. This provides many opportunities for a thief to steal the credit card number. If possible, individuals should use business establishments that allow them to swipe their own card, and they should not let their card out of sight.
- **Unsecure websites:** Whenever you shop or make a transaction online, there's a chance that an identity thief could intercept (get hold of) your personal information. Before making an online purchase, make sure the website is secure. Websites with a URL that starts with 'https' are usually safe (The 's' shows that it is a secure website.). Identity theft protection services can also help to protect your information when you are online.

- **Shoulder surfing:** Thieves will stand over the shoulder of unsuspecting individuals while they input their PIN and credit card numbers with the intent to steal the information. When typing your PIN at the ATM or your credit card numbers on your smartphone, make sure that there is no one looking over your shoulder. You should also cover your screen with your hand as you enter personal data in a public setting.
- **Skimming:** Skimming occurs when an identity thief installs an additional device onto an existing ATM or credit card reader. This device can read your credit card information, including your ATM or debit card PIN. If you notice an oddly shaped credit card reader, or there's a noticeable difference in your regular ATM reader, do not use the machine and notify the owner and police.
- **Dumpster diving:** Thieves will go through your trash looking for bills, receipts, credit card statements and other documents containing your personal information. Shred your statements or make your account numbers illegible when you throw them away.
- **Mail theft:** Thieves sometimes steal bank statements or new credit cards directly from the mailbox. If you notice someone has tampered with your mailbox or you think mail is missing, contact your local post office and report the incident to the police.

▲ Figure 10.12 Cover the keyboard with your hand when you put in your PIN at an ATM.

How to protect yourself from identity theft

- **Shred:** Shred any documents containing personal information before you toss them in the bin.
- **Use secure passwords:** Be sure to password protect all your devices, and use a different, unique, and complicated password for each of your online accounts.
- **Use secure connections:** Never log in to financial accounts or shop online while using free public Wi-Fi, and make sure you encrypt and password protect your Wi-Fi at home.
- **Monitor:** Review your credit reports and bank accounts periodically to look for suspicious activity and errors that could mean identity theft.
- **Detect:** Use an identity theft detection product that includes identity theft restoration. If you do become a victim of identity theft, you will be notified quickly and certified specialists will help to restore your identity.

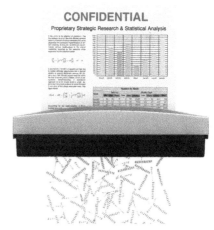

▲ Figure 10.13 Shred any documents that contain personal information to prevent dumpster divers from accessing your information.

Industrial espionage

Industrial espionage is when confidential information from within companies and other commercial organisations is obtained by spying, in an effort to gain some advantage. Spying is illegal in most countries. Such information may be anything from the design of a new gadget, to a list of unpublished prices of a new product or products, to a list of senior employees' names and addresses.

The spies 'on the ground' are usually employees (especially those who are still with the company but on the verge of leaving it) or on-site contractors. Companies that are victims of industrial espionage attacks may suffer financial losses as a result of the usefulness of the information to those spying – for example, if a competitor adjusts its prices in line with those of its victim, thereby gaining some of their customers. Companies may also have to deal with legal fees in the case of legal action, and reduced public trust if an attack is publicised.

Personal security practices

Many cybersecurity threats are largely avoidable. The following steps can assist in protecting you against cybercrimes:

- Beware of scams. If you receive an email or SMS that looks like a scam, delete it. Do not respond, attempt to unsubscribe, or call any telephone number listed in the message. Most importantly, do not send any money, credit card details or other personal details to scammers.
- Use good, cryptic passwords that cannot be easily guessed, and keep your passwords secret.
- Minimise storage of sensitive information.
- Do not send personal information such as bank account numbers and credit card numbers over open Wi-Fi networks, such as those available in airports and shopping centres. These do not use an encrypted connection so make it easier for hackers to gain access.
- Secure laptop computers and mobile devices; lock them up or carry them with you. Most smartphone and laptop operating systems allow you to encrypt data stored on them. If the device is stolen, no one can access the data on it unless they have the correct password.
- Do not install or download unknown or unsolicited programs or apps.
- Make sure antivirus and anti-spyware software are up to date.
- Shut down, lock, log off, or put your computer and other devices to sleep before leaving them unattended, and make sure they require a secure password to start up or wake-up.
- Make backup copies of files or data you are not willing to lose.

> **Did you know?**
>
> In June 2005, an industrial espionage ring was broken by Israeli police. The perpetrators of the crime hired a private programmer to custom-create a Trojan horse virus that was then planted on a rival company's PCs. The Trojan horse virus allowed the perpetrators to access PCs remotely and gather confidential commercial information, such as the amount of money bid by the company for lucrative commercial contracts. The investigation implicated car importers, cell phone providers and many other companies. The overall losses amounted to hundreds of millions of dollars. Victims said they lost competitive bids and thousands of customers because of the spying.

Emerging trends

An emerging approach to deal with the increasing number and sophistication of cyberthreats is to use blockchain principles to strengthen security. With blockchain technology, data is stored in many places around the internet (decentralised and distributed). Instead of residing in a single location, data is stored in an open source ledger – a record of when, how and who has changed it.
This makes mass data hacking or data tampering much more difficult because all participants in the blockchain network would immediately see that the ledger had been altered in some way. Blockchain has the potential to be a major leap forward for securing sensitive information, especially in industries such as finance, government, health and law.

▲ Figure 10.14 Blockchain means that data is stored in an open source ledger that has a record of when and how it was changed.

Chapter 10: Summary

- Computer security is the security of a computer (or laptop, tablet or smartphone) and its software.
- Cybersecurity is about making sure the computer and all the connections to it are secure.
- Computer misuse is the use of computers to gain access to other people's computer systems and their information or to use computers to spread unfair, false or hurtful information.
- A system security risk assessment identifies the various elements of a system's infrastructure (hardware, software and data) that could be affected by a system attack, and then identifies the various risks that could affect those elements.
- A vulnerability is a flaw in a system that can be exploited to cause loss or harm.
- A threat to a computing system is a set of circumstances that has the potential to cause loss or harm due to human errors or natural disasters.
- An attack is an action taken that uses one or more vulnerabilities in a system to realise a threat.
- A countermeasure is an action, device, procedure, or technique that removes or reduces a vulnerability.
- Data integrity concerns the consistency, accuracy and reliability of data. It can be compromised by human error (for example, inaccurate data entry, accidental deletion or changing of data), natural disasters (for example, fires, floods and earthquakes), viruses, hardware malfunctions, fraud and malicious deletion or changing of data.
- Data security concerns the safety of data and is one of the ways to ensure data integrity.
- Hardware protection methods include using locks, security guards, burglar alarms, monitoring systems, biometric scans; using doors that require passwords or magnetic cards; storing data in a fireproof safe; storing data in another building and distributing work to a number of employees.
- Software protection methods include using passwords for the system, and passwords for the files or folders; using audit trails; using encryption; adding anti-virus software and using firewalls.
- Malware is a term used to describe different types of malicious software, which includes viruses, worms, spyware, Trojans and bots.
- A virus is a deliberately written program that activates itself unknown to the user and destroys or corrupts data. A worm is similar to a virus; it copies itself repeatedly, using up memory or disk space to crash a computer.
- Viruses are usually spread by downloading infected programs and files from the internet, opening infected files received through email or using a storage medium that contains infected files. They are contained using anti-virus software. Avoid opening programs with certain extensions and avoid using unknown storage media in your computer.
- Computer surveillance can involve accessing or 'reading' the storage mechanism of an individual's computer, or monitoring an individual's operation of a computer, in most cases without their knowledge.
- Spyware is a type of software that is usually secretly installed on a computer and covertly monitors the user's actions without his or her knowledge.
- Data privacy refers to the right of individuals to determine what information is stored about them and how that information will be used.
- Cybercrimes are crimes that are directed at computers or other devices (for example, hacking) and where computers or other devices are integral to the offence.
- Computer fraud is using a computer in some way to commit a dishonest act by obtaining an advantage or causing the loss of something of value.
- Software piracy is the unauthorised copying, usage or selling of software that is copyrighted and is not public domain software or freeware.
- Hacking is the unauthorised accessing of a computer system to access, copy, steal, corrupt or destroy data. The individual who does this is referred to as a hacker.
- Internet fraud refers generally to any type of fraud scheme that uses one or more components of the internet – such as chat rooms, email, message boards or websites – to present fraudulent offers to prospective victims, to conduct fraudulent transactions or to transmit the proceeds of these.
- Industrial espionage is when secret commercial information about companies, organisations and even governments is obtained by spying in an effort to gain an advantage over a competitor.
- Phishing is an attempt by cybercriminals, hackers and some countries to lure individuals into giving away personal information to gain access to accounts or to infect an invidual's machine with malware.
- Identity theft refers to the theft of someone's personal information, such as credit cards numbers and banking information.

Chapter 10: Questions

Fill-in answers

1 One way of safeguarding a system is to perform a _____ assessment.

2 A _____ is a flaw in a system that can be exploited to cause loss or harm.

3 A set of circumstances that has the potential to cause loss or harm is known as a _____.

4 _____ concerns the consistency, accuracy and reliability of data.

5 _____ is one of the most effective methods of securing data from electronic eavesdropping.

6 _____ is used to scan your personal computer hard disk for known viruses and remove them once they are found.

7 A program, a hardware device or a combination of both, that filters the information coming in through the internet connection to your computer system or network is called a _____.

8 _____ is a term used to describe different types of malicious software, which include viruses, worms, spyware, ransomeware, Trojans and bots.

9 A _____ is a program that activates itself unknown to the user and destroys or corrupts data.

10 _____ refers to the rights of individuals to determine what information is stored about them and how that information will be used.

True or False?

1 Data integrity and security mean the same thing.

2 Distributing work to a number of employees instead of just one is a physical safeguard method of securing data.

3 Passwords for files and folders can be used to protect data.

4 Encryption is not a very effective method of protecting data during storage or transmission.

5 A firewall can consist of software, hardware or a combination of both of these.

6 Viruses can cause businesses to lose millions of dollars.

7 Viruses cannot be spread through emails.

8 Internet fraud occurs mainly through telemarketing.

9 In many countries, individuals are legally entitled to determine what information is stored about them and how that information will be used.

10 Hacking is the unauthorised accessing of a computer system.

Multiple-choice questions

1 Data integrity concerns:
   a consistency of data.
   b accuracy of data.
   c reliability of data.
   d all of the above.

2 Data integrity can be compromised by:
   a human error.
   b natural disaster.
   c viruses.
   d all of the above.

3 Which of the following is not a physical safeguard method used to secure data?
   a Biometric scans
   b Anti-virus programs
   c Security guards
   d Fireproof safe

4 Which of the following is not a software safeguard method used to secure data?
   a Passwords for the system
   b Audit trails
   c Encryption
   d The operating system

5 Which of the following is not a computer virus?
   a Worm
   b Trojan horse
   c Email virus
   d McAfee

6 You can protect your computer against viruses by:
   a installing an anti-virus package.
   b not using storage media from other computers.
   c not opening email attachments that contain any executable files with the extension .exe, .com or .vbs.
   d all of the above.

7 Which one of the following is not a type of software piracy?
   a Internet piracy
   b Copying freeware
   c Counterfeiting
   d Licensed-user duplication for unlicensed users

8 A criminally-minded hacker may access a computer system to:
   a install anti-virus software.
   b steal important and confidential information.
   c inform companies of security loopholes in their system.
   d play games.

Short-answer questions

1 Explain the term 'data privacy'.

2 a Define the term 'software piracy'.
  b Describe FOUR types of software piracy.
  c Do you feel someone should be jailed or fined if found guilty of software piracy?

3 a Define the term 'hacking'.
  b List FIVE reasons why people may hack.
  c List THREE methods used to gain illegal access to a computer.
  d State THREE methods that can be used to prevent unauthorised access to computer facilities.

4 a What is computer fraud?
  b Explain the term 'internet fraud'.
  c Briefly describe FOUR types of internet fraud.

5 List some steps that someone can take to protect his or her mobile devices.

6 a Explain the term 'identity theft'.
  b List some ways criminals use to steal someone's identity.
  c List some ways to protect oneself from identity theft.

7 a Define the term 'firewall'.
  b List THREE attacks to a computer system that can be prevented by a firewall.

8 a Define the term 'cybercrime'.
  b Give THREE examples of cybercrime.
  c Using an example stated in part (b) describe how the crime may occur.

9 a Explain the term 'phishing'.
  b State THREE tactics used in phishing attempts.
  c Describe TWO ways someone can avoid phishing attempts.

Research questions

1 You are an IT intern at a leading shoe manufacturing company. The IT manager said an employee came to him and said she found that since she downloaded an email attachment from a friend, her computer seems to be running very slow. The IT manager believes malware could be the reason for the employee's problem. The manager has asked you to prepare a set of guidelines for employees to follow when they perform the following:
  a Access email with suspicious attachments
  b Access email from unknown persons
  c Respond to emails that ask for personal information
  d Surf the Web

2 A shoe manufacturing company has lots of competitors who want to steal their designs and other company secrets. You have been asked to design security measures that include both hardware and software methods to protect the company secrets. These measures must be stated in a report to the IT manager.

3 At a local university, several students have been affected by cybercrimes. The student guild of the University has asked you to create a set of guidelines for students to follow, to protect themselves and their equipment.

Crossword

Across
1 A piece of software, hardware or both that is used to prevent unauthorised access to a computer network (8)

3 The unauthorised accessing of a computer system (7)

6 A type of software used to protect computer systems from viruses (9)

7 Another name for 'electronic junk mail' (4)

Down

2 A method used to encode data during storage or transmission (10)

4 It refers to the right of individuals to determine what information is stored about them and how that information will be used (7)

5 A small piece of software that uses computer networks and security holes to replicate itself (5)

Introduction to web page design

Many people interact with websites on a daily basis. A recent survey found that there are now over 1.8 billion websites on the internet. Websites are created by individuals, organisations, companies, governments and simply anyone who would like to display some type of information or conduct business.

Websites can provide a convenient way of purchasing items, paying bills, performing banking transactions, applying for jobs and much more. For example, suppose you want to make plans for a family vacation to Walt Disney World in Orlando Florida via the internet. You can book and pay for all your travel needs via the internet from home. You can book your tickets on the Caribbean Airline website, rent a vehicle via a website from a car rental company in Miami, pay for hotel accommodation in Orlando through the hotel's website and buy tickets for all the theme parks from Walt Disney's website.

However, even with the many uses of websites and a large number of people using the World Wide Web every day, few know how websites are actually built and how they can be used.

This chapter, therefore, looks at some basic ideas in website creation.

What is a website?

A website is a collection of related web pages linked together with hyperlinks that resides in a web server. Web pages are written in HTML (HyperText Markup Language). This is a language that web browsers use to understand how to display the contents of a web page. A web page can contain text, graphic images and multimedia effects such as sound files, video and/or animation files. Websites are accessible to users via the World Wide Web.

Web publishing

If you want to publish a website, you must first create the web pages that will be part of the website and link them together. Next, you upload these pages to a web server. There are six major steps in website publishing: planning; designing; creating; evaluating and testing; and hosting and maintaining. We will now look at each of these steps individually.

Planning a website

Planning is an important first step in ensuring the success of your website. During planning, the web designer must identify the purpose of the website and the intended audience. This will lead on to planning the layout – thinking about the number of pages needed, the content of those pages and the layout of the pages.

While planning the layout, the website designer should talk to the customer and the people they hope will use the website, in order to understand what the website needs to be able to do (user requirements) and how it will do it (technical requirements).

Purpose of a website

Before starting to build a website, the web designer must determine the purpose of the website. Is it to educate and inform? For example, is it for a school, training institution or community? Is it to gain publicity for a business? To sell or promote products? To promote or support a cause? To provide information about a club or institution?

Intended audience

It is important that the web designer has a good idea of their target audience for the intended website before it is created. Some examples of questions that the web designer may ask are:

- Who is the website for?
- What is the age range that the website is aimed at?
- Is it for everyone or is it aimed at a specific target group, for example, students, parents, teachers or members of an organisation, and so on?

Finding the user and technical requirements

Once a designer knows the audience and the purpose of the website, she or he can tailor almost every aspect of the website to satisfy the audience/ purpose – from the way the information is organised to the kinds of fonts and images used. In order to do this, the web designer should ask the customer and the audience specific questions, to determine the user and technical requirements that will meet the needs of the audience. These will give the web designer the information needed to create a design that allows the content to be organised in a layout that uses one or more pages to meet the purpose and requirements. Some of the questions that the web designer should ask to determine what format the website will take are:

- What information do the users want to be able to find – contact information, details of service, instructions, shopping, entertainment?
- How do the users want the information on the website presented to them – written words, pictures, sound, videos or a mixture of these?
- What other websites do they use often? (This question may give the designer some ideas about how the website should look and work.)
- Are there any legal or good practice requirements the website needs to follow, for example, content that does not break copyright laws or not using colours that make it difficult for someone with colour blindness to read?

Factoring the audience's preferences into the design will keep the target audience coming back to the site, and will encourage them to share it with their friends.

With the answers to these sorts of questions, you can design the website and think about what is going to go into the website, that is, how it will be organised over the pages of the website and on each page.

Designing a website

Design is a critical component of the success or failure of a website. The technical and user requirements help the web designer to make that design.

To start with, we are going to assume that our website is just one page. We need to make sure that all the things the audience wants to find are easy to find on that web page. The web page should also be well organised and look attractive. It's important to go through the web page to determine what design elements (for example, text menus, images, graphics and links) make the most sense for that page. All design elements should be designed in a way that fits together, such as the way the colours and badge of a school uniform go together, so you can recognise that several different students are at the same school.

The designer should work out the structure and layout of the website beforehand, in order to meet the purpose, user and technical requirements for the target audience and customer. One tool we can use for planning the layout of a web page is a wireframe.

Wireframe

A wireframe is a simplistic sketch and/or layout of a web page. Wireframes can provide a detailed view of the content that will appear on each page. Although they do not show any actual design elements, a wireframe provides a guide for the way the content is laid out on the page. Wireframes can be done using pencil and paper (see Figures 11.1a and 11.1b), software such as Microsoft Paint, Microsoft Word, or specialised tools such as Omnigraffle and Visual Paradigm, to create a sketch of the proposed website.

On a single web page, the designer will use the wireframe to plan where menus should go; where those menus link on the page, and where the headings, text, video and sound elements need to go. Using this, the designer can try out different designs and find the best way to organise the web page so that the users are able to find all the information they need by navigating the page.

This may show that there is a lot of information for a single page, making it hard to navigate the page. It might be more sensible to split the website into several pages, linked by hyperlinks. This is called a 'hierarchical structure'.

For example, a school website that tried to put information about all the classes on one page would be really hard to use. It would be better to have a home page, the first page you come to, with menus to link to other pages where most of the information is stored. The hyperlinks in the menus then take you from the home page to a separate web page for each class.

A designer can use a simple wireframe to design the structure of a website with several pages. The diagram looks a bit like the roots of a tree going into the ground. They would draw boxes to represent web pages and arrows for links to related pages of information. This process creates a basic visual outline or graphical map of the site. Figure 11.1a shows a typical example.

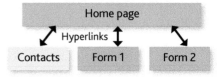

▲ Figure 11.1a First step in a hand-sketched wireframe

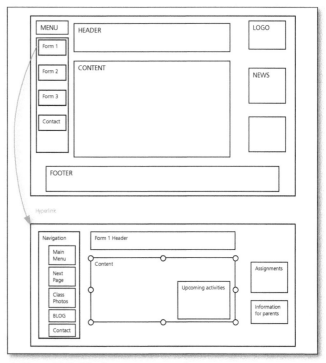

▲ Figure 11.1b Wireframe

The designer can elaborate on the design to show some of the elements on each page (Figure 11.1b). This is a critical step in any website, which has many different elements and/or content. Figure 11.2 shows an example of a website template.

Components of a web page

Let us go back to our single-page website. Figure 11.3 shows the layout of a typical web page.

Some of the basic components of a web page are listed in the following points.

- **Header:** A website header runs across the top of the page, appears on every page of the website and may contain a big heading and a logo. It may also contain common information about the website, such as site navigation and main contact information. Figure 11.4a shows the header for the Hodder Education website.

▲ **Figure 11.4a** Example of a header

- **Site navigation**: On the website, you will need navigation buttons. These can be part of the header, as in Figure 11.4a, or on the left or right as in Figure 11.3. These buttons allow you to click through to other pages if there is more than one page on the website. The buttons might also take you to other parts of a single web page.
- **Body/content area**: This is the big area in the centre that contains most of the unique content of a web page, for example, the photo gallery you want to display or a feature article you want visitors to read. This is the area that changes from page to page. Figure 11.4b shows part of the Hodder Education website. Have a look at the website at https://www.hoddereducation.co.uk/caribbean-curriculum.
- **Footer**: A page footer in a website operates in the same way as a footer in a Microsoft Word document.

    The footer may contain:
    - the web page author
    - the copyright statement
    - contact details
    - links to related sites.

▲ **Figure 11.2** Sample website template

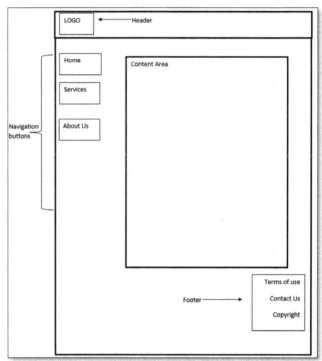

▲ **Figure 11.3** Layout of a typical web page

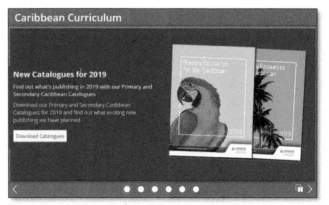

▲ **Figure 11.4b** Part of the content area of the Hodder Education Caribbean Curriculum website

Figure 11.5 shows the footer of the Hodder Education website.

Larger websites might also have the following features:

- a **Back to home page** button, which is a good design feature for the other pages to have a link back to the home page of the website
- a **site map** provides a list of hyperlinks to all the web pages on the site that can be accessed by search engines and users
- **Website Search** features that allow users to search the website for what they are interested in
- an **About us** page that could include:
  - a complete description of the individual/company/organisation
  - the objectives of the website
  - the name, address, phone numbers and email addresses of the individual/company/organisation
  - a **logo**, to be displayed in the left corner of each page of your website; often, clicking on the logo will take you back to the home page.

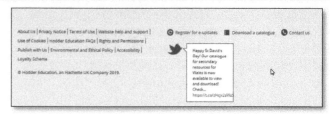

▲ Figure 11.5 Example of a footer from the Hodder Education website

Moving from wireframe to storyboard

Whereas a wireframe focuses on what the interface would resemble, a storyboard focuses on what the user would experience. Storyboarding your website is helpful in making your website accessible and convenient for users. A storyboard can show the direction of movement through the website by laying out the different buttons and links on each page. The storyboard should give a sense of the overall organisation, structure and mood of the website. It should show how all the pages work together, as well as what resources (videos, photos, graphics, colours, links) would be used to create the overall effect of the website. To storyboard your website, follow these simple steps.

- **Gather information:** Collect the information you want to incorporate on your website, such as tabs, buttons, images, videos and texts.
- **Create an outline:** Arrange and outline the information in your website based on the wireframe.
- **Link and connection:** Every button, tab, and active link on your website has a function and corresponding connection with other pages. Make sure you identify the pages to 'pop out', once a button or link is clicked.

Content

The content is the most important aspect of your website. Content includes text, graphics, animation, video, audio and links. Well-thought-out web content will make your website design engaging, effective and popular. By taking the time to create/acquire your content during the website design phase, you can make all the necessary changes before the site actually goes live. Here are some tips you need to take into consideration when working out the content for your website. The content should:

- be engaging, easy to understand and suitable for the intended audience (for example, if it is aimed at young children, the text should be suitable for their level of reading).
- contain keywords so that the site can be highly ranked on search engines, allowing it to draw more visitors.

- be written in such a way that naturally leads your reader through your website
- encourage readers to peruse the entire site.

The appearance and layout of the content also play an important part in the overall design of the website.

Appearance and layout of content
Scale
Scale is the sizing of individual elements to create emphasis, drama and add hierarchy. You can size your elements dramatically large or small to create effects, and to signal which parts of your design are more important and which are less important. The scaling of elements to signal importance is often referred to as 'hierarchy'.

Colour and format
Colour is an essential aspect of any website. Colour creates specific moods and atmospheres, and channels emotions. Each shade has specific meanings associated with it. You should use colours that look pleasant to the eyes and make the most sense for your website. You also need to consider what colours look good together and make the text easy to read. Using a single colour scheme throughout is a good way to achieve consistency. Some website builders have tools to help them to choose a colour scheme and use it consistently. You will usually need around five colours. When choosing a colour, ask yourself the following questions:

- What colours make the most sense for the website?
- What background colours and font colours will appeal to the target audience?
- What colours will support the theme of the site?

Font
The typeface of the text and size of the text on the web pages should be comfortable to read and make the matter easy to understand. The following are some suggestions that you should consider when using text in your website:

- Make sure your typeface is not too big or too small for the site you are building. Using two or three sizes will help to organise the text by making headings stand out.
- Try to avoid using too many typefaces at once. Two or three typefaces are probably enough.
- Left-alignment is easiest to read for large bodies of text.

Images
Images can add visual/aesthetic appeal to the information on a web page, and maintain viewer interest and attention. Images are also used to communicate or explain ideas visually. Here are some points to consider when using images on a website.

1 **Use high-quality images**: Start with high-quality images, either from a free website or use photographs taken personally.

▲ Figure 11.6 Interesting and high-quality images attract and maintain the viewer's attention.

2 **Use the right file type**: Photographs should be saved and uploaded as JPEGs. This file type can handle all the colours in a photograph in a relatively small, efficient file size. Graphics (for example, cartoons and diagrams) should be GIF or PNG files as these types of files mean the files can be kept small.

3 **Resize images to optimise page speed and appearance:** It is important for a web designer to find the right balance between size and resolution. The higher your resolution, the larger the file size will be, which also slows down the website's page speed. Resize images to optimise page speed and appearance. Some website building software recommends making your smaller images about 30 KB and your larger ones 60–100 KB.

4 **Make images the same size and style:** Images on a web page will look better if you use a consistent style and size/proportion. Consistency will also help when lining up your text, columns and the other information on your page.

5 **Name the image file correctly in order to help search engine optimisation (SEO)**: Rename your images before you upload them to your website to give your SEO a boost. When Google™ Chrome browser scans your website, it can read your text but it cannot see what is in your images. The file name provides information about what is in the image so that Google™ Chrome browser can interpret it correctly (think 'bluemountain.jpg' rather than 'DSC12345.jpg').

Creating a web page

Web pages can be created using:

- application software, for example, Microsoft Word, Excel and Access
- a text editor program such as Notepad to write an HTML program
- an HTML generator such as Aptana Studio 3
- website builders such as Sitebuilder, Site123, Wix.com and Jimdo
- specialist web creation programs such as Dreamweaver® and Webflow
- website writer software that allows you to write in HTML and create web pages as they appear on the screen, and provides tools to manage a website.

In this chapter, we will briefly discuss the creation of websites using Notepad, Microsoft Word and Wix.com.

Creating a web page using Notepad

Notepad is a basic Microsoft text editor program that you can use to create simple documents – a very basic word processor. The most common use for Notepad is to view or edit text (.txt) files, but Notepad can also be used for creating web pages (Figure 11.7).

Web pages can be created in Notepad by entering HTML code and saving the file as an .html or .htm file. The Notepad program can be accessed by clicking: **Start/Windows Accessories/Notepad.**

▲ Figure 11.7 Notepad window

HTML

An HTML file is a text file containing markup tags (commands). The markup tags instruct the web browser how to display the page. HTML has many tags that can be used to generate exciting web pages. To learn all the different tags in HTML would require an entire book. Therefore, in this section, we will only be looking at some basic HTML tags. Table 11.1 explains some examples of HTML tags.

All HTML tags are surrounded by the two characters (<, >) called angle brackets, which normally come in pairs , such as <P> and </P>. The first tag in a pair is the 'start tag', the second tag is the 'end tag'. The text between the start and end tags is the 'element content'. HTML tags are not case sensitive, for example: <b> means the same as <B>.

Tag	Explanation
<HTML>	This is the first tag in your HTML document. It tells your browser that this is the start of an HTML document.
</HTML>	This is the last tag in your document. This tag tells your browser that this is the end of the HTML document.
<HEAD> and </HEAD>	The text between the <HEAD> tag and the </HEAD> tag is header information. Header information is not displayed in the browser window.
<TITLE> and </TITLE>	The text between the <TITLE> tags is the title of your document. The title is displayed in your browser's caption.
<H1>and</H1>	Headings are defined with the <H1> to <H6> tags. <H1> defines the largest heading and <H6> defines the smallest heading. HTML automatically adds an extra blank line before and after a heading.
<BODY> and </BODY>	The text between the <BODY> tags is the text that will be displayed in your browser.
<P>and </P>	<P> and </P> defines the start and end of a paragraph. HTML automatically adds an extra blank line before and after a paragraph.

▲ Table 11.1 Some examples of HTML tags and their explanations

Activity 1

Writing a web page
Type in the following HTML code exactly as it appears on this page into Notepad. Save the file to your desktop, as an HTML file. View the page in your web browser.

```
<HTML>

<HEAD>

<TITLE>My First Web page</TITLE>

</HEAD>

<BODY>

<H1>Building Web sites</H1>

<P>THIS IS MY FIRST WEB PAGE.</P>

<P>I can start on a new paragraph by
enclosing my text within paragraph
tags.</P>

</BODY>

</HTML>
```

How it is done
1 Open Notepad.
2 Type in the HTML code exactly as shown above.
3 Click **File.**
4 Click **Save As.**

5 Change the Directory to your desktop.
6 Change the 'Save as' type to 'All Files'.
7 Type in the file name: 'My First Web page.html'.
8 Click **Save.**
9 Go to your desktop and open the file: 'My First Web page.html'.
10 The web page will be displayed as shown in Figure 11.8.

▲ Figure 11.8 Activity 1 HTML code displayed in a browser

Editing text

To edit text in an existing web page you must first open the web page in Notepad to view the page in HTML. You can then change the text as desired. If you are removing entire headings or paragraphs you need to also delete all the tags associated with the relevant section, so in Activity 1, you need to delete the <P> tag at the start and the </P> tag at the end, as well as the text if you delete one of the paragraphs.

Some more commonly used HTML formatting tags are shown in Table 11.2.

Tag	Explanation
<CENTER> and </CENTER>	Centres a heading, line or image. <H1> <CENTER> This is my first Web page.</CENTER> </H1> The sentence 'This is my first Web page.' will be centred.
<I> and </I>	Used to display text in italics
<B> and</B>	Used to bold text
<U> and </U>	Used to underline text

▲ Table 11.2 Commonly used HTML formatting tags

Activity 2

Formatting text

Retrieve the file 'My First Web page.html'. Type in the new lines of code exactly as they appear on this page. Save the file to your desktop, as an HTML file. View the page in your web browser.

```
<HTML>
<HEAD>
Building Websites
<TITLE>My First Web page</TITLE>
</HEAD>
<BODY>
<H1>Building Websites</H1>
<CENTER>
<P>Italics, Bold and Underline.</P>
</CENTER>
<P><CENTER>I can centre my text within a paragraph.</CENTER></P>
<P><CENTER><B>Making text bold is very easy.</B></CENTER></P>
<P><CENTER><I>Text can also be in italics.</I></CENTER></P>
<P><CENTER><B><I>Text can be bold and in italics.</I></B></CENTER></P>
<P><CENTER><U>You can also underline text.</U></CENTER></P>
</BODY>
</HTML>
```

How it is done

1 Open Notepad.
2 Retrieve the file 'My First Web page.html'.
3 Type in the new HTML code exactly as shown in Activity 2.
4 Click **File.**
5 Click **Save As.**
6 Change the Directory to your desktop.
7 Change the 'Save as' type to 'All Files'.
8 Type in the file name: 'Formatting.html'.
9 Click **Save.**
10 Go to your desktop and open the file: 'Formatting.html'.
11 The Web page will be displayed in your browser as shown in Figure 11.9.

▲ Figure 11.9 Activity 2 HTML code displayed in a browser

More HTML formatting tags to change the text and background colour, relative size and typeface are shown in Table 11.3.

Tag	Explanation
Attribute background-color	Attribute background-color changes the background colour to the selected colour. This code changes the background colour of the web page to yellow. <BODY BGCOLOR="YELLOW"> </BODY> To change to another colour, replace yellow with the desired colour.
<BIG> and </BIG>	Used to make text bigger than the current default
<SMALL> and </SMALL>	Used to make text smaller than the current default
<FONT> and </FONT>	Used to select a font typeface, size and colour <FONT SIZE=12 COLOR= "RED" FACE= "ARIAL"></FONT>

▲ Table 11.3 More HTML formatting tags with explanations

Activity 3

Type in the following HTML code exactly as it appears on this page into Notepad.
Save the file to your desktop, as an html file. View the page in your web browser.

```
<HTML>
<HEAD>
<TITLE>
Using tags to make text big or small
</TITLE>
</HEAD>
<Body style="background-color:yellow;">
<H1><CENTER><FONT SIZE =24>Building Websites</FONT></CENTER></H1>
<CENTER><FONT SIZE=14>Using tags to make text big or small</FONT>
<P><BIG>using the BIG tag</BIG></P>
<P><SMALL>Making text SMALL using the small tag</SMALL></P>
<P><FONT SIZE=1>This is font size 1.</FONT></P>
<P><FONT SIZE=2>This is font size 2.</FONT></P>
<P><FONT SIZE=12 COLOR= "RED" FACE = "ARIAL">This is font size 12, colour
red and font face arial.</FONT></P>
</CENTER>
</BODY>
</HTML>
```

How it is done
1 Open Notepad.
2 Type in the HTML code exactly as shown in Activity 3.
3 Click **File.**
4 Click **Save As.**
5 Change the Directory to your desktop.
6 Change the 'Save as' type to 'All Files'.
7 Click **Save.**
8 Type in the file name: 'Font.html'.
9 Go to your desktop and open the file: 'Font.html'.
10 The web page will be displayed in your browser as shown in Figure 11.10.

▲ Figure 11.10 Activity 3 HTML code displayed in a browser

Inserting a graphic

Graphics can be easily placed on a web page. Perhaps the most difficult part of inserting a graphic is acquiring the graphic. Sometimes, depending on the design of the web page, it may be necessary to place text at different positions in relation to the graphic. Text may be aligned vertically, meaning that it can be placed at the top, middle or bottom of the graphic. Text can also be aligned horizontally. This means you can place the image to the right or left of the text. If the image is aligned to the right, the text is on the left and seems to flow around the image. If the image is placed to the left, the text appears to the right.

▲ Figure 11.11 Use your own photographs or images. If you do not own the images, make sure that you have permission to use them.

The size of an image can also be adjusted to fit on your web page. You can make an image larger or smaller by changing the values in the "HEIGHT" and "WIDTH" attributes of the IMG tag. Adding these attributes can enhance the appearance of your web page and make it look more professional.

The format and size of an image determines the amount of storage space it requires. This directly impacts on the time it takes a web page to be loaded or displayed. To help reduce the time required to display a web page with graphics, thumbnail images may be used. A thumbnail is a smaller version of an actual image. When a user clicks on a thumbnail image, the actual full-size image, which is stored on another page, is displayed. Table 11.4 lists some of the tags that are used to insert images into a web page.

Tag	Explanation
<IMG SRC= "image.jpg">	This IMG tag inserts an image into a web page. To use this element, you supply the URL of the image you want to display in the SRC attribute. SRC stands for 'source'. <IMG SRC="School.jpg">
BORDER	Places a border around the picture, for example: BORDER=8. Changing the number changes the size of the border. <IMG SRC="School.jpg" BORDER=8>
ALT	ALT is used to define descriptive text that can be displayed in case the browser is not displaying the image. <IMG SRC="School.jpg" ALT= "Premier High School" BORDER=8>
WIDTH and HEIGHT	These <IMG> elements provide the width and height of the image in pixels. <IMG SRC="School.jpg" WIDTH="55" HEIGHT="75" ALT="Premier High School" BORDER=8>
ALIGN	ALIGN is used to align text and images. To align vertically, you can set the alignment to TOP, MIDDLE or BOTTOM. <IMG SRC="School. jpg" ALIGN=TOP> To align horizontally, you can set the alignment to RIGHT or LEFT.

▲ Table 11.4 Graphic tags and their explanations

Did you know?

Here are a few tips to use legal images for your website:

• Buy stock photographs from a photo agency.

• Use images with Creative Commons licenses.

• Go to sites that provide free stock images such as Pixabay.com or Picjumbo.com.

Always acknowledge the creator, such as the artist or photographer.

The following activity demonstrates how a graphic can be inserted in a web page.

Activity 4

Type in the following HTML code exactly as it appears on this page into Notepad.
Save the file to your desktop, as an html file. View the page in your web browser.<HTML>

```
<HEAD>
<TITLE> Aligning Text and Images </TITLE>
</HEAD>
<H1>
<CENTER> Aligning Text and Images</CENTER>
</H1>
<BODY>
<img src="cricket.png" style="width:100px;height:100px;"ALIGN=RIGHT
BORDER=0>
<P> Graphics can be easily placed in a web page. Perhaps the most difficult part of
inserting a graphic is acquiring the graphic. Sometimes, depending on the design the
web page, it may to necessary to place text at different positions in relation to the
graphic. Text may be aligned vertically - meaning that it can be placed at the top,
middle or bottom of the graphic.</P>
<img src="cricket.png" style="width:100px;height:100px;"ALIGN=LEFT BORDER=1>
Text can be aligned horizontally. This mean you can place the graphic to the right or
left of the text. If the image is aligned to the right, the text is on the left and
seems to flow around the image. If the image is placed to the left, the text appears
to the right.
<p> The size of the image can also be adjusted to fit on your web page. You can
make an image larger or smaller by changing the values on the "HEIGHT" and "WIDTH"
attributes of the IMG tag. Adding these attributes can enhance the appearance of your
web page and make it look very professional.</P>
<center>
<img src="cricket.png" style="width:100px;height:100px;"ALIGN=middle"
BORDER=3>
</P>
</BODY>
</HTML>
```

How it is done

1 Open Notepad.
2 Type in the HTML code exactly as shown in Activity 4.
3 Click **File**.
4 Click **Save As**.
5 Change the Directory to your desktop.
6 Change the 'Save as' type to 'All Files'.
7 Type in the file name: 'Graphics.html'.
8 Click **Save**.
9 Go to your desktop and open the file: 'Graphics.html'.
10 The web page will be displayed in your browser as shown in Figure 11.12.

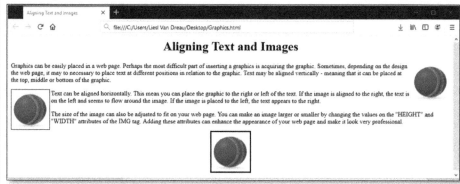

▲ Figure 11.12 Activity 4 HTML code displayed in a browser

Creating hyperlinks

A hyperlink is a reference (an address) to a resource on the Web. Hyperlinks can point to any resource on the Web: an HTML page, an image, a sound file, a movie, and so on. In HTML, the <A> tag is used to set up a hyperlink and the HREF attribute is used to set the target of the hyperlink. Hyperlinks can be either internal or external. An internal link allows you to jump from one section of your own website's page to another section in the same page or to another page in the same website, for example, from your home page to an 'About us' page. An external link allows you to open up a new browser window from another website, for example, from your home page to a Wikipedia article so that someone can read more about something on the site.

Internal and external links

To be able to jump from one section to another, you should first give a name to the section so that the tag can locate it when it is being called. The tag <A NAME="links"> has to be inserted in the lower section of the web page, just above the position where the 'link' value is located. For example, in Activity 5, the tag <A NAME="BOTTOM"> is inserted after the heading "End of Page".

The next step is to insert the link from which you want to jump. In the example, we want to jump from the top of the page to the bottom part of the page. We, therefore need to insert <A HREF="#BOTTOM">End of Page</A>. The hyperlinked text "Linking Tags" will appear, and when clicked, will jump from the current location to the indicated section.

To jump to another web page you need to create something the user can click on (some text or an image) and provide the address to link to. This can all be done using the <A> tags. The simplest thing to do is to use a piece of text to link to the other site. You put the <A> and </A> tags before and after the text you want to link from. You then use the HREF attribute to specify the website address to link to. For example, when: <A HREF="http://www.windiescricket.com /">West Indies Cricket Board WICB Official Website</A> is opened in the browser, the link will be displayed as 'West Indies Cricket Board WICB Official Website'. When you click on it, the web page will be displayed.

If you want to use an image, then instead of putting the text inside the <A> and </A> tags, you put <IMG> tags. For example: <A HREF= "https://www.windiescricket.com"><IMG SRC="cricket.png" style="width:100px;height:100px;"></A> displays the picture 'cricket.png' and this links to https://www.windiescricket.com when you click on it.

This can also be used to open a file, such as an audio file. Instead of the web page address, you would put the path to the file in the HREF attribute.

Link to email

You can add a hyperlink to an email address so that when you click on it, your email opens a new mail window, allowing you to send an email easily. Again, you use the <A> and </A> tags and put some text or an <IMG> inside them that you can click on. Like an external website, you use the HREF attribute to specify the email address, but you start the address with the word 'MAILTO'. For example: <A HREF=mailto:someone@somewhere. com>Click to send a message</A> will open a new email to someone@ somewhere.com when you click on the text 'Click to send a message'.

Exercise 1

1   List uses of websites.
2   List THREE types of content that can be included in a website.
3   How can users access websites?
4   What TWO factors inform the structure of a website?
5   Create a website that includes a photograph of your school or some building of interest in your community:
    a   Place a border around the photograph.
    b   Include a heading.
    c   Bold and centre the heading.
    d   Insert a body colour of your choice.
    e   Include a short description of the building.

Table 11.5 shows some examples of tags to use when you want to link to an email address.

Tag	Explanation
<A> and </A>	Used to set up a hyperlink
NAME	NAME specifies an anchor name. It is the name of the text, image, and so on, that you want to use as the target of a hyperlink.
<A HREF= "http://www. webaddress.com/">Web Address Link<A/>	This will display the "Web Address Link" as a hyperlink in your web page, and when you click on the text, it will load the page www.webaddress.com<html>. For example, when: <A HREF="http://www.windiescricket.com /">West Indies Cricket Board WICB Official Website</A> is opened in the browser, the link will be displayed as West Indies Cricket Board WICB Official Website. When you click on it, the web page will be displayed. The target web page will open in a new window if you use: <A HREF="http://www.windiescricket.com /" target= "-blank">West Indies Cricket Board WICB Official Website</A>.
 	Inserts a line break into your text or allows you to move to the next line of text

▲ Table 11.5 More HTML tags and their explanations

Activity 5

Type out the HTML code shown in Figure 11.13a below. Save the file as 'Links.html'. Display the file in a web browser.

```
<HTML>
<HEAD>
<BODY>
<h2 id="top">Top of page</h2>

<a href=#Bottom">Go to Bottom </a>

<H2>Local Links</H2>
<P><A HREF="https://windiescricket.com/">West Indies Cricket</A> is a link to the West Indies Cricket website on the World Wide Web.</P>
<P><A HREF="https://windiescricket.com/"><IMG SRC="Cricket Bal.jpg" STYLE="width:100px;height:100px;"></A>
<P> <A> The cricket ball is hyperlinked to the West Indies cricket website on the World Wide Web. Click on the cricket ball to move to the West Indies cricket website. </A></P>
</BODY>
</HTML>
<P>
<H2>West Indies Men's Cricket</H2>
</P>

<P><H4>The West Indies men's cricket team is a multi-national team representing several countries in the English-speaking Caribbean. As of 24 June 2018, the West Indian cricket team is ranked ninth in the world in Tests, ninth in ODIs and seventh in T20s in the official ICC rankings. From the mid-late 1970s to the early 1990s, the West Indies team was the strongest in the world in both Test and One Day International cricket. A number of cricketers who were considered among the best in the world have hailed from the West Indies: Sir Garfield Sobers, Lance Gibbs, Gordon Greenidge, George Headley, Brian Lara, Clive Lloyd, Malcolm Marshall, Sir Andy Roberts, Alvin Kallicharran, Rohan Kanhai, Sir Frank Worrell, Sir Clyde Walcott, Sir Everton Weekes, Sir Curtley Ambrose, Michael Holding, Courtney Walsh, Joel Garner and Sir Viv Richards have all been inducted into the ICC Hall of Fame. </H4> </P>
<P>
</P>
<P>
<H2>West Indies Women's Cricket</H2>
</p>
<P4><H4>The West Indies women's cricket team is a combined team of players from various English speaking countries in the Caribbean. The team competes in the International Cricket Council (ICC) Women's Championship, Women's Cricket World Cup and Women's One Day International Cricket.</H4></P>

<a href="stop">Go to top</a>

<h2 id="Bottom">Bottom of page</h2>
```

▲ Figure 11.13a HTML code

How it is done
1 Open Notepad.
2 Type in the HTML code exactly as shown above in Figure 11.13a.
3 Click **File.**
4 Click **Save As.**
5 Change the Directory to your desktop.
6 Change the 'Save as' type to 'All Files'.
7 Type in the file name: 'Links.html'.
8 Click **Save.**

9 Go to your desktop and open the file: 'Links.html'. The page will appear as shown in Figure 11.13b.
10 Clicking on the link 'West Indies Cricket' will take you to the West Indies Cricket website.
11 Clicking on the 'ball' will take you to the West Indies Cricket website.
12 Clicking on the internal link 'Go to Bottom' will take you to the bottom of the page.
13 Clicking on the internal link 'Go to top' will take you to the top of the page.

Top of page

Go to Bottom

Local Links

West Indies Cricket is a link to the West Indies Cricket website on the World Wide Web.

The cricket ball is hyperlinked to the West Indies cricket website on the World Wide Web. Click on the cricket ball to move to the West Indies cricket website.

West Indies Men's Cricket

The West Indies Men's Cricket team is a multi-national team representing several countries in the English-speaking Caribbean. As of 24 June 2018, the West Indian cricket team is ranked ninth in the world in Tests, ninth in ODIs and seventh in T20s in the official ICC rankings. From the mid-late 1970s to the early 1990s, the West Indies team was the strongest in the world in both Test and One Day International cricket. A number of cricketers who were considered among the best in the world have hailed from the West Indies: Sir Garfield Sobers, Lance Gibbs, Gordon Greenidge, George Headley, Brian Lara, Clive Lloyd, Malcolm Marshall, Sir Andy Roberts, Alvin Kallicharran, Rohan Kanhai, Sir Frank Worrell, Sir Clyde Walcott, Sir Everton Weekes, Sir Curtley Ambrose, Michael Holding, Courtney Walsh, Joel Garner and Sir Viv Richards have all been inducted into the ICC Hall of Fame.

West Indies Women's Cricket

The West Indies Women's Cricket team is a combined team of players from various English speaking countries in the Caribbean. The team competes in the International Cricket Council (ICC) Women's Championship, Women's Cricket World Cup and Women's One Day International Cricket.

Go to top

Bottom of page

▲ Figure 11.13b Activity 5 HTML code displayed in a browser

Creating a web page using Microsoft Word

Microsoft Word offers a variety of options for creating new web pages. Word's built-in HTML translator can automatically convert any text, graphics or hyperlinks that you insert into your Word document into a web-compatible format. Once you open a new blank document, you can start typing in text or add images, tables and hyperlinks, just as you would in a normal Word document. The document can be formatted and edited using all the formatting and editing features you will cover in Chapter 13 on word processing.

Hyperlinks

Hyperlinks can be inserted into a Word document. There are two different types of links: internal and external. An internal link is one that links to different points in the same web page. An external link is one that connects the page you are on to another page in the same website; to some other website on the internet; to an email address or to another file.

Creating a hyperlink

1 Open your Word document.
2 Place your cursor at the position at which you wish to insert your link, or select the word(s) or image you would like to click on to hyperlink.
3 Click the **Insert** tab, then select **Hyperlink** from the **Links** group. The Insert 'Hyperlink dialog' box appears, as shown in Figure 11.14.

If you did not select a word or image, type in whatever text you want to display as the link your web page visitor will click on in the 'Text to display' combo box.

Exercise 2

Create a web page for a club. The web page should contain the following:
1 A photograph of the club building
2 A brief history of the club
3 A link to a page listing and describing all the activities of the club
4 A suitable body colour should be added
5 Some text in bold, italics or both
6 Font of varying sizes
7 A link to an external website of interest to the club
8 A link to send an email to an official of the club.

Type in the full address or select from the list provided in the drop-down list in the 'Address' combo box of the website or file you want the user to access by clicking on the link. The words 'Application form' will hyperlink to the document 'Application form' on the 'Strikers Football Club' web page (Figure 11.15). Clicking the words **Soca Warriors** will take you to the 'Soca Warriors' website http://www. socawarriors.net/ on the internet.

If you wish to create a link to another web page in the same folder as the page you are creating or to an email or a file, follow the same instructions as above but instead of typing in a web address, type or select the filename of the '.htm' or other file, or add the email address with 'mailto:' in front (for example, mailto:someone@ somewhere.com) that you wish to access from this link.

To check to see if your links are working, you need to save your Word document as a web page and publish it to the web server.

Saving Word documents as web pages

1 Select **File/Save As** (the 'Save as' dialog box will appear).
2 Give the new web page a name that does not contain any spaces and is, preferably, eight characters or less in length.
3 Click the arrow next to 'Save as type' and change the type from Word document to Web page (*htm,*html).

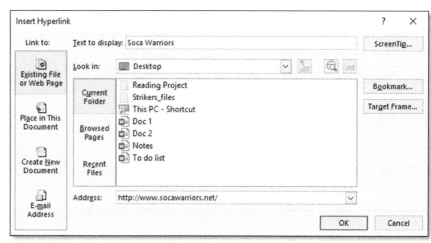

▲ Figure 11.14 Insert Hyperlink dialog box

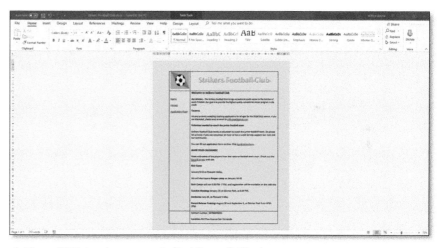

▲ Figure 11.15 A web page created in Microsoft Word

Word will automatically save the document in an HTML format and append the file extension '.htm' to the file name. It will also create a folder with the same name as the file 'plus _files' and will store an XML instruction file and all image files within this folder. In other words, if I created a Word document and saved it as a web page, giving it the name 'Strikers', Word would create a file called 'Strikers. htm' and a folder called 'Strikers_files'.

This folder contains a file with all the formatting instructions for the text and image layout on your new web page. It also contains all the image files for images you may have inserted within your web page.

Activity 6

Using the following content, create a web page for the Strikers Football Club, which looks like Figure 11.16.

How it is done

1 Create a folder in the desktop named 'Strikers Football Club'.
2 Open a blank Microsoft Word document.
3 Insert a table with three rows and two columns, as shown in Figure 11.16. Click the **Word Art icon** and type in the heading 'Strikers Football Club'. Change the colour of the font.
4 Find an image of a ball from the internet, or from your own images, and insert it in the appropriate location.
5 Type out the content shown on the right.
6 Format the document as shown in Figure 11.16.
7 Create a document named 'Application form' and save it in the folder you created.
8 Create another document named 'History' and save it in the folder you created. The 'History' document contains information about the history of the club.
9 Create a hyperlink to the application form:
   a Select the words **Application form**.
   b Click **Insert/Hyperlink** (a 'Hyperlink' dialog box will appear)
   c The words 'Application form' will be displayed in the 'Text to display' combo box.
   d Ensure that the 'Existing file or web page' option is selected in the 'Link to:' pane.
   e Click **Desktop** in the 'Look in' combo box.
   f Select the folder 'Strikers Football Club'.
   g Open the folder and select the document **Application form**.
   h The name of the document is displayed in the 'Address' box.

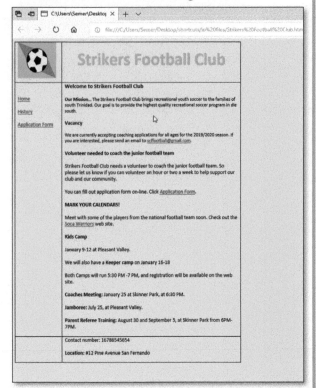

▲ Figure 11.16 Microsoft Word document saved as a web page

   i Click **OK** to confirm. The words 'Application form' will be displayed, as shown in Figure 11.16.
10 Create a hyperlink to the Soca Warriors website:
   a Select the words **Soca Warriors**.
   b Follow the steps as described in step 9.
   c In the Address box, type 'http://www.socawarriors.net/'.

Creating a website using the Wix.com website builder

Wix.com is an online website builder that uses templates that help to build a professional looking website, built on good practices.

1. Access the Wix.com site to sign up
To sign up as a first time user, you simply add your email address and set up your password to log in to your Wix account. The 'Let's get started' screen appears (Figure 11.17). Click on 'Create Your Website'.

▲ Figure 11.17 The 'Let's get started' screen on the Wix.com website

2. Answer the questions so Wix can recommend some designs

In this section, you can choose who you are building this for, what kind of website you want to create and your level of experience so that Wix can direct you to the right template. You can choose from the categories provided such as Business, Designer, Blog, Online store, Restaurants & food, Beauty & wellness, Photography, Accommodation, Portfolio & CV, Music, Events or Other. Figure 11.19 shows the options for the websites.

3. Choose how you want to create your website

The 'Choose how you want to create your website' dialog box appears (Figure 11.20).

Two options appear:
- a Let Wix ADI Create a Website for you. 'ADI' stands for 'Artificial Design Intelligence'.
- b Create your website with the Wix Editor.

4. Creating a website using option 1 'Let Wix ADI Create a Website for you'

This option allows the user to develop a website by answering a few questions. Try to answer all the questions given. This helps Wix to determine the best template for your website. These questions are:

1. **What type of site do you want to create?** The user is presented with several options from which to choose.
2. **Does your website need any of these features?** You can apply one or more of the following options: sell online, take bookings or get subscribers.
3. **What is the name of your business or website?** Add your business name or another name that is relevant to your business in a way that people can find it online.
4. **Where is your business located?** If the address is not relevant for you, you can skip to the next page.
5. **Review and edit your info.** In this step, you can modify your website name and additional information such as business email, address, phone number, fax number and a social network, if available. Once you complete all the information, Wix will process all the data given before continuing to the next step.
6. **Pick a theme you like.** You can choose a few designs provided in this step but you can also still change it later if desired. Next, Wix will direct you to the home page where you can actually manage your website.

▲ Figure 11.18 Welcome to Wix.com screen

▲ Figure 11.19 'What kind of website do you want to create?' category options

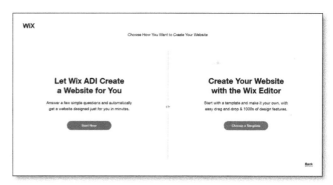

▲ Figure 11.20 'Choose how you want to create your website' dialog box

Manage your home page

Once you are on the home page, there will be a quick tutorial about each navigation tool. Now you can simply change the content or even modify the layout design based on your preference.

You can also always delete some sections if you find they are not relevant. Any work you do on Wix will be saved automatically. Avoid closing your work if you see the message 'Saving' instead of 'Saved'.

Publish your website

Once you are done managing your website, now it is time for you to publish your website online.

Creating a website using option 2 'Create Your Website with the Wix Editor'

Select 'Choose a Template'

You can choose from one of the preset templates. Alternatively, you can choose from a number of other templates, if the category you are looking for is not found in the preset templates by clicking on 'Other'.

Finding specific templates

Choose from a number of template category options.

Once you find the category you want, click on it to expand the menu.

You need to choose a category and a sub-category. The site will now be shown in Edit mode (see Figure 11.21). You will then be moved to the Wix.com Editor, from where you can edit your site.

You can select your domain name by choosing to save your site by clicking on **Save** in the Edit mode.

Once you click on **Save**, a pop up appears that lets you save the site to a particular domain. The first option lets you choose a name for your site under the Wix.com domain. The second option lets you connect to your own customised domain.

▲ Figure 11.21 The Wix.com website in Edit mode

Tools used to add content to your website

Wix provides the following options to create pages and add content to your chosen website.

- **Website menu:** Displays the website map. Pages can be renamed, duplicated, hidden or deleted. Transitions can also be chosen See Figure 11.22.
- **Page Background:** The Page Background enables you to add or change the background (colour, image or video) to one or more web pages of the website.
- **Add Web Elements:** Add web elements to your pages such as text, images, menus, shapes, boxes, buttons and many more.

▲ Figure 11.22 Site Menu

- **Wix App Market:** Wix enables you to add a number of apps and features to your site that are created by Wix or third-party developers. Apps enable you to add various types of functionality to your website, such as forms, calendars or stores.
- **My Uploads:** The 'My Upload' option allows users to upload their own media files to the Media Manager so that they are ready to use whenever they need to use them. Users can upload images, vector art, videos, fonts and documents.
- **Wix Bookings:** Wix Bookings is an easy-to-use scheduling system that lets customers book services online directly on the website.
- **Wix Blogs:** Wix blog allows you to easily create a blog and grow an online community with people who share your passion. Readers can join your blog, create member profiles, like and follow posts, comment with images and videos, and even become contributing writers.

Positioning and Editing Tools

The Positioning and Editing Tools Editor shown In Figure 11.23 provides several options to adjust elements on a web page.

▲ Figure 11.23 Wix.com Positioning and Editing Tools Editor

Publishing your Wix website

Once you preview your website by clicking on **Preview** and seeing that your site is exactly the way you want it, you can then publish it by clicking on **Publish**.

Evaluation and testing

Before you publish a website, you need to evaluate the website to make sure it meets the purpose, user and technical requirements. You also need to test the website to make sure that all the content works (for example, the videos all play); all the links and menus work; and all the content is up to date and formatted correctly.

Evaluation

Earlier in the chapter, we saw how the intended audience and purpose help us to generate user and technical requirements. When we are evaluating a website, we are checking that those requirements and the purpose have been met.

Our first step is to go through the website page by page and look for the features and content in the user and technical requirement. For example:

- If we have a requirement to use video, are there videos on the website?
- Are there clear contact, blog and 'About us' sections if the users want to be able to find addresses, read about what the writers have been up to and find out about the writers?
- The users want to be able to link to websites to buy the products that a site reviews – can they do that?
- You put reviews of local skate parks on your website and the users want to see where they are on a map. Does your website have a map or link to one?
- The users want your website to be 'easy to use'. Is it? How would you test that?

The last point on the previous page is very difficult to test, as your idea of 'easy to use' might be different from someone else's. One way around this would be to use a test audience. This is a group of people who match your intended audience whom you invite to try out the website before publishing it. By letting a number of people from your intended audience try it out, you will get a variety of opinions about how well it works, allowing you to improve it.

Testing

Testing involves making sure everything about the website works correctly. For large commercial websites, you would employ a company to do this and they would often use software to help with this. For most small websites, going through the website and carefully checking every aspect works well. Among the things to check are:

- **Do the hyperlinks and menus work?**
  - Check that the hyperlink or menu item takes you to the correct place when you click on it.
  - Check that you can get back to where you came from when you check a hyperlink or menu item.
- **Do different media play?**
  - Can you see all the images? Sometimes these are saved in the wrong place and then the image does not display.
  - Do videos and sound work? Sometimes this can depend on how your web browser is set up, so it is a good idea to check these on several different computers. See Figure 11.24.
- **Does all the content format correctly?**
  - Have all the formatting rules been applied correctly? If you want one heading to be in red text, is it actually red?
  - Does the text flow around the images properly?
  - Does the site look right on different screens? As more people use smartphones, this is becoming increasingly important. A website builder such as Wix will often create a website that will adapt to different sizes of screen. This is much harder to do using Microsoft Word or Notepad.

▲ Figure 11.24 Testing should be done on multiple devices such as laptops, tablets and smartphones.

Web hosting

Web hosting is a service that allows organisations and individuals to post a website or web page onto the internet. A web host, or web hosting service provider, is a business that provides the technologies and services needed for the website or web page to be viewed on the internet.

Websites are hosted or stored on special computers called servers. When internet users want to view your website, all they need to do is type your website address or domain into their browser. Their computer will then connect to the server in which your website is stored and your website will be made available to them through the browser.

Most hosting companies require that you own your domain in order to host with them. If you do not have a domain, the hosting companies will help you to purchase one. Two popular web hosting companies are Bluehost and HostGator.

Maintaining a website

To get the most from your website you need to maintain it. Websites quickly become outdated, old-fashioned and static. When information remains static, there is little reason for people to re-visit the site – and therefore the opportunity to promote new products, ideas and services is lost. Follow these steps to keep your website relevant and up to date.

1 **Keep the site secure:** Monitor for malware, viruses, hackers and errors.
2 **Keep a regular backup schedule:** This will ensure that you always have the latest content stored in the event there is an attack on your server or website and everything gets deleted.
3 **Keep monitoring for broken links:** These are hyperlinks that no longer work. This usually happens because a website has changed and the web page no longer exists. Website visitors and customers do not like broken links.
4 **Keep updated:** Update your website content regularly, with posts about recent events, promotions or news, to make it more appealing to clients.

Chapter 11: Summary

- A website is a collection of related web pages linked together with hyperlinks that resides in a web server.
- Web pages are written in HTML; this is a language that web browsers use to display the content of a web page. It can contain text, graphic images, and multimedia effects such as sound files, video and/ or animation files.
- The design of your website depends on the purpose and the intended users of the site, and these help you to produce user and technical requirements that explain to the designer how the site should look and what it should do.
- There are five major steps in website publishing. These are: planning; designing; creating; evaluation and testing; and hosting and maintaining.
- Web pages can be created using application software (Microsoft Word, Excel and Access), a text editor program (for example, Notepad), a HTML generator (for example, Aptana and Studio 3), website builders (for example, Sitebuilder, Site123, Wix.com and Jimdo), Specialist web creation programs (for example, Dreamweaver® and Webflow).
- Notepad is a basic text editor that you can use to create simple documents. A text editor is a very basic word processor. Web pages can be created in Notepad by entering HTML (HyperText Markup Language) code and saving the file as an '.html' or '.htm' file.

- An HTML file is a text file containing markup tags (commands). The markup tags instruct the web browser what the parts of the page are and how they should be displayed.
- Microsoft Word can automatically convert any text, graphics or hyperlinks that you insert into your Word document into a web-compatible format by the built-in Word HTML translator.
- A wireframe is a simplistic sketch and/or layout of a web page. Wireframes can provide a detailed view of the content that will appear on each page.
- A hyperlink is a reference (an address) to a resource on the Web. Hyperlinks can point to any resource on the Web: an HTML page, an image, and so on.
- Some of the basic components of a website are home page, site map, website search features (navigation buttons), 'About us' page, logo, header, footer and body/content area.
- Evaluation and testing are important steps to carry out before publishing. They ensure that the website meets the requirements decided on during planning and that everything works.
- A test audience is a good way of helping to evaluate a website.
- Web hosting is a service that allows organisations and individuals to post a website or web page onto the internet.
- Maintaining a website involves the following: keeping the site secure, updating content, fixing broken links and doing regular backups.

Chapter 11: Questions

Fill in the blanks

1 A _____ is a collection of related web pages linked with hyperlinks that reside in a web server.

2 Web pages are written in _____ code.

3 _____ is the language that web browsers use to understand how to display the contents of a web page.

4 Websites are accessible to users via the _____.

5 Notepad is a basic _____ program that you can use to create simple documents.

6 Web pages can be created in Notepad by entering HTML code and saving the file as an _____ file.

7 An HTML file is a text file containing markup _____.

8 _____ tells your browser that this is the start of an HTML document.

9 A _____ is a simplistic sketch and/or layout of a web page.

10 A service that allows organisations and individuals to post a website or web page onto the internet is known as _____.

11 Wix.com and Jimdo are examples of _____ software.

12 Websites are hosted or stored on special computers called _____.

13 Site _____ ensures that a website is secure, updated and working properly.

True or False?

1 Web pages are written in HTML.

2 HTML tags are case sensitive.

3 A server-based site is on the server and not on your computer.

4 Web pages can be created using application software such as Excel.

5 All HTML tags are surrounded by the two characters < and >.

6 The text between the <HEAD> tag and the </HEAD> tag is displayed in the browser window.

7 Word's built-in HTML translator can automatically convert any text, graphics or hyperlinks that you insert into your Word document into a web-compatible format.

8 Microsoft Expression Web is a website authoring application software.

9 The SRC tag in HTML inserts an image into a web page.

10 The attribution BGCOLOR is used with the BODY tag to change the background colour of a web page.

11 Website maintenance is not essential to keep visitors coming back to a site.

Multiple-choice questions

1 A website is a collection of:
   a sound files.   b animation files.
   c graphic images.   d web pages.

2 Which of the following is NOT a major step in website publishing?
   a Planning   b Designing
   c Executing   d Hosting

3 Web pages can be created using:
   a application software.
   b an editor program such as Notepad.
   c specialist web creation software.
   d all of the above.

4 Websites can provide a convenient way of:
   a advertising.
   b purchasing items.
   c paying bills.
   d all of the above.

5 The design of a website depends on:
   a the amount of memory space available on your computer.
   b purpose and intended users of the site.
   c the processing speed of your computer.
   d all of the above.

Short-answer questions

1 Define the terms 'website' and 'web page'.

2 List the FIVE major steps in website publishing.

3 Describe how you would go about building a web page.

4 Define the term 'wireframe' and explain its importance in building a website.

5 List FIVE basic components of a web page.

6 List FOUR different categories of software that can be used to create web pages.

7 What are the different types of links you can create in a web page?

8 Using the tags covered in this chapter, and those that you may have discovered on your own, create a web page about yourself.

9 Create a web page for your club using Microsoft Word.

10 Create a web page for the PTA of your school using HTML in Notepad or Microsoft Word.

11 Create a web page for your school using Wix.com.

12 Explain the term 'web hosting'.

13 Explain the purpose of maintaining a website.

Research questions

1 Make a list of FIVE of the most used website builder software. Place this information on a table under the following headings:
   a Name of software
   b Cost
   c Features offered
   d Support offered.

2 Make a list of FIVE of the top web hosting companies and their cost for their services.

3 Your friends have created a website using HTML. When they open it in the browser on the computer at school it seems to work fine. They would like to make the site available to everyone on the internet. Explain to your friends what they need to do to publish their website onto the internet.

4 Maintaining a website is very important to ensuring the success of a website. A few steps to maintain a website are listed in this chapter. Conduct research to find out about other ways to maintain a website. Use the information to prepare a list of instructions someone may follow to maintain a website.

Crossword

Across

3 The extension that must be used to save a Word document as a web page (4)

4 A collection of related web pages linked together with hyperlinks and residing in a web server (7)

5 A step in creating a website to make sure it meets the purpose, user, and technical requirements (10)

7 A simplistic sketch and/or layout of a web page (9)

Down

1 Allows you to move to another point within a document or a website by clicking on a word or image (9)

2 A basic text editor program that you can use to create web pages (7)

6 The types of brackets that surround HTML tags (5)

Presentations using PowerPoint

Microsoft PowerPoint is an application that allows you to create, print and show presentations. Presentations are often used to pass on information to an individual or a group of people in classrooms, lecture theatres or at work. When giving a PowerPoint presentation, your main aim is to get key points across to your audience in a way that allows them to understand the points quickly and completely. PowerPoint presentations help you to do this by showing information concisely (clearly), on a page-by-page basis. Each page of information is called a slide. PowerPoint's special features allow you to create imaginative and concise slides easily. A number of related slides can be viewed in sequence as a slide show. It is a dynamic way of presenting slides, as a simple click of the mouse allows you to move from one slide to the next, and back again, with ease. Once a presentation is created there are a number of ways to show it, as described below.

■ **On-screen presentation**: This is viewed on a PC screen by a small group of people at a time. Large (24 inch/61 cm) screens make this a convenient way of presenting. Sometimes several screens will be linked together for larger audiences.
■ **Digital projection**: For large groups of people, it is more convenient to project the presentation onto a large screen, as shown in Figure 12.1. The projector has an interface to the computer so that what you see on the PC screen is transmitted to the projector as a video signal, and is then converted by the projection engine into light. The three digital projection technologies are LCD (liquid crystal display), LED (light-emitting diode) and DLP (Digital Light Processing™).
■ **Printed handouts**: These are a duplicate of the slides that are printed on paper, with each sheet being able to hold between one and nine images of the slides, as shown in Figure 12.2. You can therefore hand these out to your audience so that they can review the information later, in their own time.

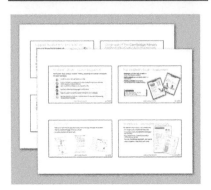

◄ Figure 12.2 Example of printed handouts of four PowerPoint slides

▲ Figure 12.1 Digital projection

Starting PowerPoint

1. Click on the **Start/Windows** button.
2. Select **PowerPoint 2013**, **2016** or **2019** (whichever version you are using) from the menu, as shown in Figure 12.3.
3. The New Presentation task pane appears, as shown in Figure 12.4. You can create a blank presentation by clicking on the **Blank Presentation** template.

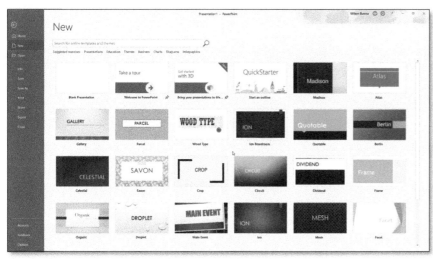

▲ Figure 12.4 The PowerPoint Getting Started task pane

▲ Figure 12.3 Selecting PowerPoint from the Windows drop-down menu

Microsoft PowerPoint 2016

Similar to Word and Excel, PowerPoint 2007, PowerPoint 2013, 2016, 2019 and Office PowerPoint 365 all use a single Ribbon with tabs at the top of the screen.

Commands are organised in logical groups, which are collected together under tabs. Each tab relates to a type of activity, such as **Home** (deals mostly with formatting of slides) or **Insert** (tables, graphics, movies, sounds, and so on). The Ribbon design makes it easier to quickly find the commands you need to be able to complete a task.

Starting PowerPoint 2016

PowerPoint allows you a number of options for creating a presentation, some of which are listed here.

- **Design template:** This allows you to choose from a number of backgrounds and colour schemes that are available before developing your new presentation.
- **Blank Presentation:** This gives you a blank page with no background or colour schemes.

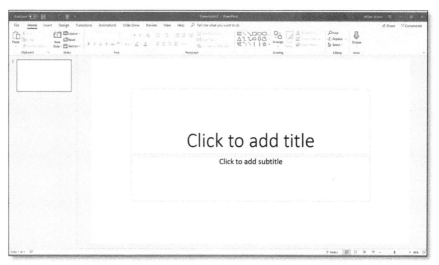

▲ Figure 12.5 Initial PowerPoint screen

233

■ **Open an existing presentation:** This displays a list of recently opened PowerPoint presentations from which you can choose to reopen one of the displayed files. You can also choose **More presentations...** If the file you want is not displayed, it allows you to select the location of the file by browsing other folders on your system.

In this chapter, we will look at creating a presentation using the Design template and Blank Presentation features.

Creating a new presentation

Having chosen a new presentation from either Design template or Blank Presentation, a Slide Layout task pane containing several layouts appears. This is called the Auto Layout. It consists of several predefined layouts, depending on what you want to illustrate. Once the mouse pointer is placed over a layout, the name of that particular layout appears.

When you click on a particular layout, PowerPoint opens this layout in its Normal view, which has a three-pane development area (Figure 12.6).

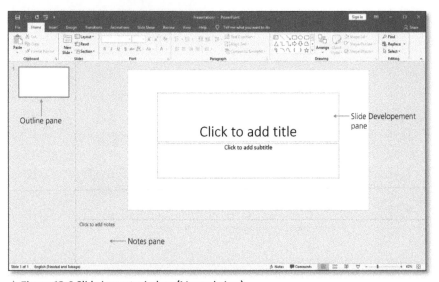

▲ Figure 12.6 Slide Layout window (Normal view)

■ **Outline pane** on the left: This contains the title of each slide, as well as the information typed into the placeholders.
■ **Slide Development pane**, top right. **Placeholders** are pre-selected boxes with dotted or hatched borders used to hold titles and other text or objects, such as charts, tables and pictures, within the slide.
■ **Notes pane**, bottom right.

Slide Layout

Click on the **Home** tab. Select **Layout** from the **Slides** group. See Figure 12.7.

Views

This toolbar is located at the bottom left-hand corner of the Outline pane (Figure 12.8). It allows you to move through the different views of your presentation.

Note: Different versions of Microsoft PowerPoint may have between three to five of these icons.

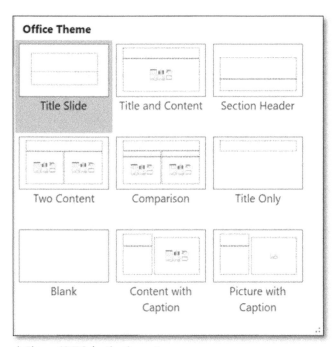

▲ Figure 12.7 Selecting Layout

Normal view: This is the default view and consists of the three panes (Outline, Slide Development and Notes panes).

Reading view: This view expands Slide Development to fill most of the screen and allows you to develop the slides of your presentation.

Slide Sorter view: This view shows a small picture of all your slides (a **thumbnail** – a miniature image of a graphic, document or slide), thus allowing you to move or rearrange the slides in the order that you would like them to appear. You can select a particular slide to view by double clicking on that slide.

Slide Show view: This view allows you to view an on-screen production of your presentation. Clicking the mouse button will change the slides.

▲ Figure 12.8 **The Views toolbar**

PowerPoint 2016

The Slide view and Outline view can be selected by choosing the **Outline** or **Slides** tabs on the left-hand side of the Normal view (the Outline pane).

Placeholders

The information within placeholders is used by PowerPoint so that you know where you are within your presentation document. The titles, as well as text in these placeholders appear in the Outline pane of the Normal view. This allows you to move to that particular slide in your presentation by clicking on these titles in the Outline pane.

Entering data in a placeholder

Click anywhere within the dotted borders and begin typing (Figure 12.9). If, however, you do not need to use a particular placeholder, you do not need to delete it – unused placeholders do not show up in a presentation.

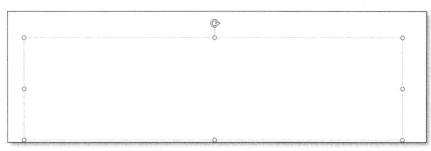

▲ Figure 12.9 A blank PowerPoint placeholder

Moving a placeholder

1 Click on the dotted border to select the placeholder.
2 Place the cursor on or near the border or box until a four-headed arrow appears.
3 Drag the placeholder to a new location.

Adding a new slide

Click on the **Home** tab. Select **New Slide** from the Slides group.

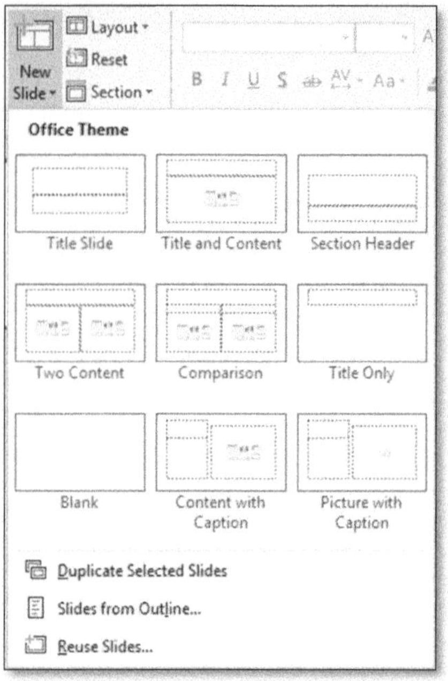

Office Theme

Title Slide   Title and Content   Section Header

Two Content   Comparison   Title Only

Blank   Content with Caption   Picture with Caption

Duplicate Selected Slides

Slides from Outline...

Reuse Slides...

▲ Figure 12.10 New Slides drop down

Activity 1

Creating a new PowerPoint presentation

1 Choose **Blank Presentation** from the 'PowerPoint' dialog box.
2 Select the **Title Slide** from the 'Auto Layout' dialog box.
3 Click in the **Title placeholder** box and enter the following title: 'Environmental Awareness'.
4 In the Sub-title placeholder, enter the name of your country, for example 'Trinidad'.
5 Insert a new slide by selecting **New Slide** from the Insert menu.
6 From the 'New Slide' dialog box that appears, select the **Auto Layout** with the bulleted list.
7 In the Title placeholder of this layout, type: 'Types of pollution'.
8 In the Bulleted List placeholder, enter FOUR types of pollution.
9 Insert a third slide from the Insert menu, choosing the same layout as the previous slide.
10 In the Title placeholder enter, the following text: 'What can we do?'
11 In the Bulleted List placeholder, enter the following information, which is relevant to ways we can reduce pollution.
   • Walk or cycle and reduce the use of vehicles for transportation.
   • Car pool to reduce the number of vehicles being used.
   • Recycle waste material.
   • Reduce the amount of energy used, turn off lights and machinery when not in use.
   • Conserve water.
   • Reduce noise by lowering the volume on your stereos.
12 Save your presentation as 'My Environment'.
13 Display your presentation as a slide show using the Slide Show view in the bottom left-hand corner of your screen, or by choosing Slide Show from the Slide Show menu.

Changing the slide layout

If you decide to change your slide layout afterwards, or to apply a different format to an existing slide, you can do so by clicking on the **Home** tab. Then select **Layout** from the **Slides** group.

Design templates

Changing or applying a new Design template

Each slide in your presentation can have a different design or the same Design template. The Slide Design template can be chosen from the **Design** tab. The Design tab appears as shown in Figure 12.11. This pane allows you to select from a variety of designs.

The background and other selections available in the Slide Design task pane have two options: **Apply to All** and **Apply**:

- **Apply to All** will apply your changes to each slide in the presentation, both the existing slides and the slides that will be created in the future for that particular presentation.
- **Apply** will cause the changes to occur only in the current slide.

▲ Figure 12.11 Design tab

▲ Figure 12.12 Slide designs available from the Design tab

Activity 2

Applying a design

1 Retrieve the presentation 'My Environment' that you created in the previous activity.
2 Choose a design from the **Themes** group of the **Design** tab.
3 Save your presentation.
4 Display your presentation as a **slide show** using the Slide Show view in the bottom right-hand corner of your screen, or by choosing **From Beginning** from the **Start Slide Show** group of the **Slide Show** tab.

Activity 3

Changing the background

1 Retrieve the presentation 'My Environment' that you created in Activity 1.
2 In the Outline pane of the Normal view, or in the Outline view, select your second slide.
3 Select **Format Background** from the **Customise** group of the **Design** tab (Figure 12.13). The Format Background pane appears to the right of your slide.

4 Select your background choices from the options listed.
5 Save your presentation.
6 Display your presentation as a slide show using the Slide Show view in the bottom right-hand corner of your screen, or by choosing **From Beginning** from the **Start Slide Show** group of the **Slide Show** tab. (Figure 12.14)

Click to add title

Click to add subtitle

◄ Figure 12.13 Format Background pane

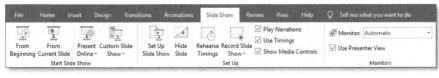

▲ Figure 12.14 Slide Show tab

Sound, video clips and photos

Sound, video clips and photos are inserted in your slide in the same way you would insert a Clipart image (a graphic). Once these images are inserted, they appear in the middle of your slide. They can then be moved or repositioned to any location by dragging. There are specially designed layouts that allow you to include video clips, sound, charts, tables and photos in the slide by clicking on the icons on the slide itself.

Look at the three figures on this page: 12.15, 12.16 and 12.17.

▲ Figure 12.15 Inserting a graphic, sound or video from the slide

Did you know?

The later version of Microsoft 2013, 2016, 2019 no longer has the Clipart organiser library as a built-in feature of the program. You have to search online for the Microsoft Clipart library through Bing Image Search.

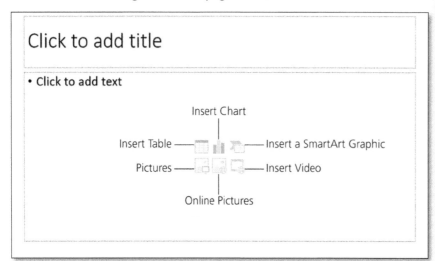

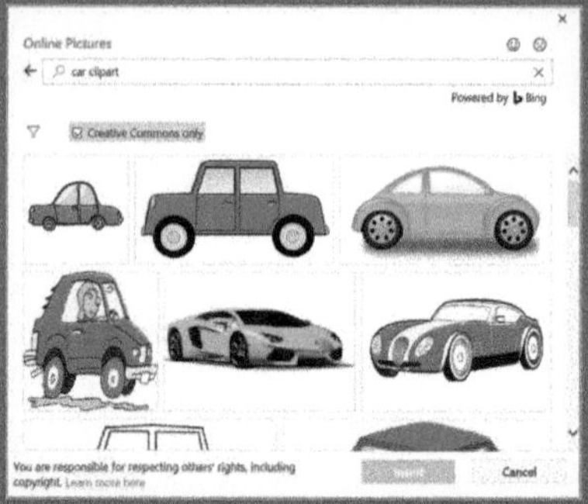

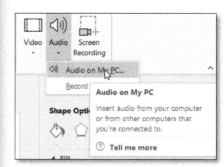

▲ Figure 12.16 Online search for Clipart through Bing Image Search

Activity 4

Adding graphics

1 Retrieve the presentation 'My Environment'.
2 Add a new slide to your presentation.
3 Choose the layout **Two Content** from the **New Slide** drop-down menu in the **Slide** group of the **Home** tab.
4 Click on the placeholder to add a Clipart.
5 Choose a map of the world for your presentation.
6 Enter the title 'Water Pollution'.
7 Enter some additional information about water pollution.
8 Save your presentation.
9 Display your presentation as a slide show using the **Slide Show** view in the bottom right-hand corner of your screen, or by choosing **From Beginning** from the **Start Slide Show** group of the **Slide Show** tab.

▲ Figure 12.17 Selecting sound clips

Changing the sequence of slides

Once you have produced a sequence of slides, you may want to change their order a little, in order to make the presentation more logical. Slides can easily be moved around within PowerPoint, in either the Outline view or Outline pane of the Normal view, or in the Slide Sorter view.

How it is done

1. Drag the slide to the position where you want it.
2. A grey vertical line indicates the slide's position as you are dragging when you are in the Slide Sorter view, and a horizontal line when you are in the Outline view.

Activity 5

Rearranging your slides

1. Retrieve the presentation 'My Environment'.
2. In the Slide Sorter view, move the third slide to the second position.
3. Save your presentation.
4. Display your presentation as a slide show using the **Slide Show** view in the bottom right-hand corner of your screen, or by choosing **From Beginning** from the **Start Slide Show** group of the **Slide Show** tab.

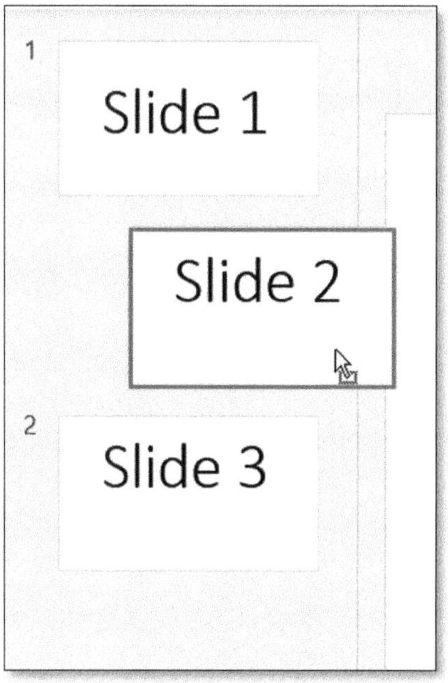

▲ Figure 12.18 In this sequence of slides, you may want to move the slides around for a better order of presentation.

Adding notes – speaker's notes

When using PowerPoint, speakers and presenters often like to make additional notes just for themselves, containing further details that remind them of what they plan to say about specific points during the presentation. These kinds of notes can be created in the Notes pane of the Normal view. You can also click on the **Notes** icon at the bottom right-hand corner of the screen, which allows you to expand the Notes section. As you would expect, the audience will not see the notes during the slide show, but the notes can be printed for the speaker's own benefit. On the printout, the speaker's notes normally appear below the printed slide. In this way, the speaker can look at his or her printout and see both the slide and the notes.

Activity 6

Adding speaker notes

1. Retrieve the presentation 'My Environment'.
2. Add an appropriate graphic to one of your slides.
3. Add one slide of your own to the presentation before the last slide.
4. Add speaker notes to each of your slides.
5. In the Slide Sorter view, move the third slide to the second position.
6. Save your presentation.
7. Display your presentation as a slide show using the **Slide Show** view in the bottom right-hand corner of your screen, or by choosing **From Beginning** from the **Start Slide Show** group of the **Slide Show** tab.

Slide Master/Master Slide

A Slide Master is a PowerPoint feature that allows you to create a presentation that contains objects, which appear on each slide of your presentation. It adds consistency to your presentation, so that once an object is added, it will automatically be added to each slide of your presentation.

The Slide Master has preset text boxes called 'Master Title' and 'Master Body'. Once these two aspects of your slides are formatted, they will appear the same way in each slide of your presentation. This feature is similar to the Header/Footer feature in Microsoft Word.

The Slide Master gives you a consistent starting point so that all your slides could contain a common feature, for example, a small piece of text, the same on each slide, indicating the overall title of the presentation. However, you are not limited to all the slides being the same: you can make individual slides that are different from other slides in your presentation. You can edit, delete, add, format or move various elements in the Master Slide so that all slides change accordingly, or you can make changes to individual slides.

▲ Figure 12.19 Master Views group on the View tab

Creating a Master Slide

How it is done

1. Click on the **View** tab. Select **Slide Master** from the **Master Views** group of the **View** tab (Figure 12.19). The Slide Master tab will appear (Figure 12.20).
2. Edit and modify the contents of the Slide Master by adding objects, background colour, specifying fonts and other similar features that you feel will enhance your presentation.
3. Add new slides and edit the contents.

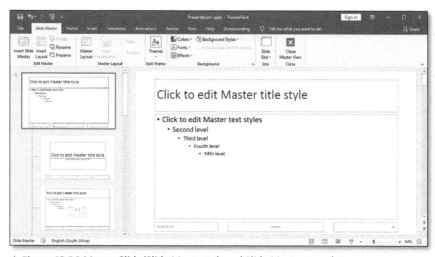

▲ Figure 12.20 Master Slide/Slide Master tab and Slide Master template

---

Activity 7

Using the Slide Master

Using the Slide Master template, create a five-slide presentation about your first day back at school.

Hint: Discussion points can be: Meeting up with friends you have not seen over the vacation period; Discussing your vacation; Changes at school; New classmates; New teachers; and Introduction to new subjects.

Adding a transition

You can choose to have a special effect to introduce a slide in your presentation. This special effect is known as a transition.

How it is done

1. Select the slide to which you want to apply the transition effect.
2. Select the effect/transition you want from the **Transition to this slide** group of the **Transition** tab. See Figure 12.21.
3. You can apply the effect/transition to that slide or click the **Apply to All** icon in the **Timing** group of the **Transition** tab.
4. You can add a sound by selecting the **Sound** drop-down arrow from the **Timing** group on the **Transitions** tab.
5. You can check your transition by going to the Slide Sorter view and clicking on the star icon at the bottom of the relevant slide. (Figure 12.22)

▲ Figure 12.21 Transitions tab

Timing your transition

There are times when you may want your presentation to run automatically; this is when the whole presentation is given at the click of a button and continues to the end without any further clicks, finishing after the amount of time that you decide it should take. For this to occur, you must add a timing to each slide. Timing specifies the length of time a slide remains on the screen – this is measured in seconds. You can practise your presentation timing (the length of time it would take you to discuss the points on each slide) and add the timing to the slide.

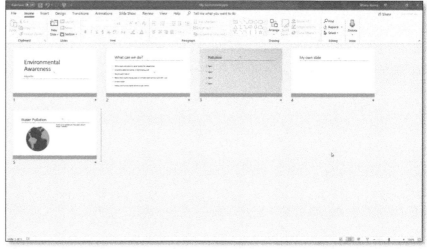

▲ Figure 12.22 Checking your transition in Slide Sorter view

How it is done

1. Select the slide to which you want to add timing.
2. You can select the **Duration** of your transition from the **Timing** group on the **Transitions** tab.
3. In the Advance slide section of the **Timing** group, select the **After** tick box and enter the number of seconds for the slide to remain on the screen.
4. Click on the slide to apply the timing. If you want to apply the same time to all the slides, then click on the **Apply to All** icon in the **Timing** group of the **Transitions** tab.

Activity 8

Transitions

1 Retrieve the presentation 'My Environment'.
2 Add two different transitions, one to slide 2 and another to slide 3.
3 Change the speed of each of the transitions.
4 Add a sound or audio to the transition.
5 Add a five-second timing to your transitions.
6 Save your presentation.
7 Display your presentation as a slide show using the Slide Show view in the bottom right-hand corner of your screen, or by choosing **From Beginning** from the **Start Slide Show** group of the **Slide Show** tab (see Figure 12.23).

▲ Figure 12.23 **Slide Show view**

Animating your presentation

Animations allow you to make your slide show more eye-catching or to include movement that will help to explain something. Presenters often use animations to bring the information up on the slide bit by bit as they explain something. For example, you could use this to create an opening slide that encourages the audience to guess what is being shown as an image or set of clues is built up on the slide. Animations can be useful, but they can also be distracting, so use them sparingly.

Animating a single object (a graphic or image)

1 Select the object you want to animate by clicking on it in the Slide Development pane.
2 Select an animation effect from the **Animation** group on the **Animations** tab (Figure 12.24).
3 View as a slide show.

You can choose whether you want your animation to start with either a mouse click or after a previous animation. You can also choose the speed of your animation.

▲ Figure 12.24 **Animation effects**

Animating more than one object on a slide

1. Choose the **Animation Pane** from the **Advanced Animation** group on the **Animation** tab.
2. The **Animation Pane** (Figure 12.25) will appear.
3. Click on the object you want to animate.
4. Click on the **Add Effect** button, a drop-down list will appear. Select the animation effect you want to apply.
5. The object you animated will appear in a list in the Animation Pane.
6. You can preview your animation by clicking the **Play** button in the Animation Pane.

▲ Figure 12.25 Advanced Animation group on the Animation tab

Activity 9

Animating an object

1. Retrieve the presentation 'My Environment'.
2. Select the first slide of your presentation.
3. Click on the **Title** placeholder.
4. Choose the **Animation Pane** from the **Advanced Animation** group on the **Animation** tab and choose an effect.
5. Save your presentation.
6. Display your presentation as a slide show.

Changing your animation order

1. Select the slide.
2. Choose the **Animation Pane** from the **Advanced Animation** group on the **Animation** tab.
3. The Animation Pane will appear.
4. A list of the animated objects in your slide will appear in the Animation Pane.
5. Clicking the up and down arrows (Reorder) allows you to change the order of the animation. Select the object and move it through the order list.

▲ Figure 12.27 Custom Animation Pane

Animating text

You can animate text either through Animation effects or by using the Animation Pane. Choosing Animation effect will automatically animate your text, one paragraph at a time. Using Custom Animation from the Animation Pane to animate your text allows you to animate your text as a whole, one paragraph at a time or various paragraph levels.

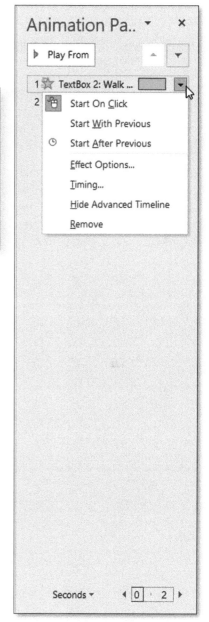

▲ Figure 12.26 Animation Pane

How it is done

1 Select the slide.
2 Choose the **Animation Pane** from the **Advanced Animation** group on the **Animation** tab.
3 The Animation Pane (Figure 12.26) will appear.
4 A listing of the animated objects in your slide will appear in the Animation Pane.
5 Click on the down arrow next to the listed objects and then click on **Effect Options**. The 'Effects Option' dialog box will appear (Figure 12.28).
6 Click on the **Text Animation** tab.
7 You can choose whether you want the text animation to start automatically, and in reverse order, by checking the appropriate check boxes (Figure 12.29).
8 Select an option from the **Group** text drop-down list.

You can also choose to have a special sound effect by clicking on the **Effect** tab of the same dialog box (Figure 12.28). Then click on the down arrow in the 'Sound:' window and a drop-down box with a list of sound effects will appear for you to choose from (see Figure 12.30).

▲ Figure 12.28 'Effect Option' dialog box

▲ Figure 12.29 'Text Animation' dialog box

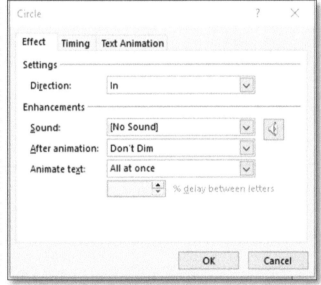

▲ Figure 12.30 'Sound Effect' dialog box

Animating charts

There are two ways to animate your charts.

1 You can animate the chart as a whole:
   a Choose the **Animation Pane** from the **Advanced Animation** group on the **Animation** tab.
   b Click on the object you want to animate.
   c Click on the **Add Effect** button, a drop-down list will appear. Select the animation effect you want to apply.

d The object you animated will appear in a list in the Animation Pane.

e You can preview your animation by clicking the **Play** button in the Animation Pane.

2 You can animate elements or parts of the chart:

a Choose the **Animation Pane** from the **Advanced Animation** group on the **Animation** tab.

b Click on the object you want to animate.

c Click on the **Add Effect** button, and select the animation effect you want to apply.

d The object you animated will appear in a list in the Animation Pane. Click on the down arrow next to the listed object and then click on **Effect Options**. A dialog box will appear.

e Click on the **Chart Animation** tab.

f In the **Group Chart** drop-down list, select an option (Figure 12.31).

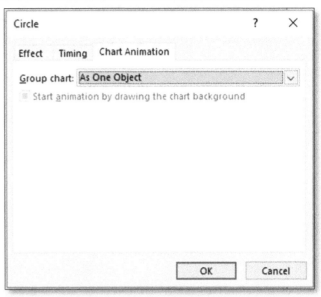

▲ Figure 12.31 'Chart Animation' dialog box

Tip: Do not include too many effects/animations in a single presentation or slide, since it can distract from the presentation rather than enhance it.

Click the **Preview** button to view your animation after making changes.

Activity 10

Animating more than one object

1 Retrieve the presentation 'My Environment'.
2 Select the fifth slide of your presentation.
3 Choose the **Animation Pane** from the **Advanced Animation** group on the **Animation** tab.
4 Open the document 'Env chart' (or any other chart you have available). Copy the chart and paste it into the sixth slide of your presentation.
5 Animate the chart.
6 Save your presentation.
7 Display your presentation as a slide show to check it.

Adding sound to an animation

Adding sound to an animation (briefly mentioned earlier in this chapter) can make your presentation more appealing, fun or even humorous for your audience.

How it is done

1 Choose the **Animation Pane** from the **Advanced Animation** group on the **Animation** tab.
2 Click on the object to which you want to add sound.
3 Click on the **Add Effect** button, and select the animation effect you want.
4 The object you animated will appear in a list in the Animation Pane. Click on the down arrow next to the listed object, and then click on **Effect Options**. A dialog box will appear.
5 Click on the **Effect** tab.
6 Click on the **Sound** drop-down arrow and select a sound.

Recording your own sound files

1 Plug your microphone into the microphone jack of your computer or you can use the built-in microphone on your laptop.
2 Select **Audio** from the **Media** group of the **Insert** tab.
3 Select **Record Audio** (Figure 12.32), and the 'Record Sound' dialog box will appear (Figure 12.33).
4 Enter the name of the recording (Figure 12.34).
5 Click the **Record** button and talk into the microphone.
6 Click the **Stop** button when you are finished with your recording.
7 You can play back your recording by pressing the **Play** button.

▲ Figure 12.32 Audio drop-down menu

If you want to add another segment to your recording, you can simply click the **Record** button and continue talking. Click the **Stop** button when you are finished. The new segment will be added to your previous recording.

If you are unsatisfied with your recording, you can simply click the **Cancel** button, and re-record your sound. If you are satisfied with it then click the **OK** button. The 'Record Sound' dialog box will close and a Speaker icon will appear in the middle of your slide. You can drag and position the icon anywhere on your slide.

▲ Figure 12.33 'Record Sound' dialog box

Playing sound files in your presentation

Double clicking the **Speaker** icon will play the sound that you recorded. Clicking anywhere on the slide will stop the sound before it finishes.

Adding music from CDs and other sources

You can add music to your presentation, such as your MP3s and other music formats from CDs or other sources. The music can be attached to your objects, transitions or animations within your presentation.

How it is done

1 Select **Audio** from the **Media** group of the **Insert** tab.
2 Select **Audio on My PC**.
3 Search for the sound on your computer.
4 After selecting the sound, a **Playback** tab appears (Figure 12.36). You can choose to select if you want the music or sound to automatically play in your presentation, or only when the icon is clicked. In the **Audio Options** group, **Start** drop-down list, choose either **On Click** or **Automatically**.
5 A Speaker icon will appear in your slide.
6 You can choose to hide the Sound icon (Figure 12.35) during the slide show by clicking the check box **Hide During Show** icon.

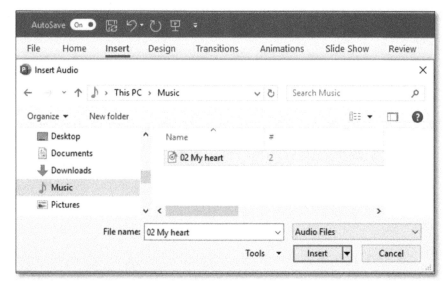

▲ Figure 12.34 Selecting sound from a file

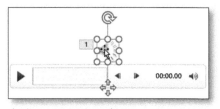

▲ Figure 12.35 Sound icon

▲ Figure 12.36 Playback tab

Activity 11

Adding sound

1 Retrieve the presentation 'My Environment'.
2 Add a voice recorded sound to one slide in the presentation.
3 Add a music file from an audio CD to the last slide in your presentation (if possible).
4 Save your presentation.
5 Display your presentation as a slide show to check the sounds.

Printing your presentation

As we saw earlier in this chapter, printing your presentation can be useful if you have added notes to it, so that you can refer to them as you give your speech. Printing your presentation can also be useful if you want to give a copy of it to your audience to take away with them to study in their own time. You can select whether you want to print each slide on a separate page or a number of slides on one page, for a more condensed handout. See Figure 12.37.

1 Select **Print** from the **File** tab; the Print window will appear.
2 Select **Slides** or **Handouts** from the **Full Page Slides** drop-down menu.
3 Selecting Slides will print a single slide on each page. Selecting Handouts allows you to choose how many slides will be printed on a page.
4 From the **Full Page Slides** drop-down menu, select the number of slides per page and whether you want it to be printed horizontally or vertically.
5 Click **OK** to print.

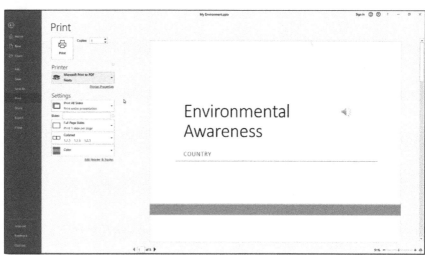

▲ Figure 12.37 'Print' dialog box

Printing your speaker notes or outline

1 Select **Print** from the **File** tab and the Print window will appear.
2 Select **Note Pages** or **Outline** from the **Full Page Slides** drop-down menu.
3 Click **OK** to print.

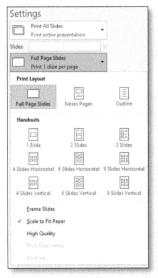

▲ Figure 12.38 'Full Page Slides' drop-down menu

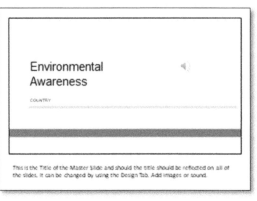

▲ Figure 12.39 'Note Pages' dialog box

Activity 12

Printing

1 Retrieve the presentation 'My Environment'.
2 Print the presentation so that six slides appear on one page.

Effective PowerPoint presentations

The purpose of creating a presentation is to get a message across to your audience. You may want to explain something or express an idea. A presentation can be exciting, fun and effective by holding the audiences' attention for the duration of the presentation, or it can be boring, unimpressive and ineffective, even leaving your audience at a loss as to what is being presented.

Here are some things to keep in mind when developing your presentation.

Guidelines for presenting

- Plan carefully and do your research.
- Practise and time your presentation.
- Speak clearly and enunciate your words; do not rush your presentation by speaking too quickly.

Guidelines for slides

- Use Design templates.
- Slides should have standardised colours and styles.
- Slides should include only necessary information, and the information on the slides should be limited to only the essentials.
- Slides should use colours that contrast.
- Limit the number of slides in your presentation – too many slides can lose you your audience.

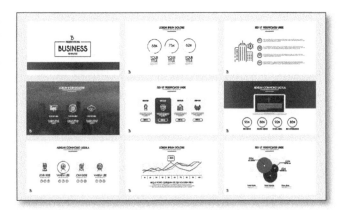

▲ Figure 12.40 Using a PowerPoint Design template can help to make presentations more interesting and appear more professional.

Guidelines for text

- Know your audience, that is, are you going to present this to adults or to children? This indicates that you may need to use simple or more complex language depending on the audience.
- There should generally be six to eight words on a line and six to eight lines on a slide, as the more words you place, the smaller the text is, and the audience may not be able to see the information.
- Try to avoid long sentences, as they may become difficult for your audience to read.
- The font size is important and should generally range from 25 to 48 points. Larger font sizes in a presentation usually indicate more important information.
- Fancy fonts can be hard to read – therefore, you should generally stay away from using them.
- Be sure that the text colour contrasts with the background, as text colours that are very similar to the background colours are difficult to see clearly.
- Words in all capital letters are difficult to read, so avoid this.
- Avoid abbreviations and acronyms unless they are explained somewhere in your presentation, as the audience may not understand what they mean.

Guidelines for graphics and Clipart

- Graphics and Clipart should enhance and complement the text, not overwhelm it.
- Graphics and Clipart should relate to the topic being presented and the information on the particular slide.
- There should generally be no more than two graphics per slide.

Transitions and animations

- Animations and transitions can enhance a presentation but can also distract from a presentation.
- Too many animations and transitions can confuse and distract the audience.
- Be consistent with your animations and transitions, many different types of animations on one slide can be distracting.

Sound and music

- Sounds can enhance a presentation but should only be added if they can boost the quality of the presentation.
- Be mindful of the fact that the sound you hear on your laptop or desktop may not be loud or clear enough to be heard by an audience in a large room.

Chapter 12: Summary

- PowerPoint is an application that allows you to create, print and show presentations.
- PowerPoint allows you to include sound, animation, videos, photos and graphics in your presentations.
- PowerPoint presentations are shown on a page-by-page basis, where each 'page' of information is called a 'slide'.
- These presentations are shown in the following ways: on-screen presentation, digital projection or printed handouts.
- PowerPoint allows you four options for creating a presentation: AutoContent Wizard, Design template, Blank Presentation and Open an existing presentation.
- PowerPoint opens this layout in its Normal view which has a three-pane development area (an Outline pane, which contains the title of each slide, as well as the information typed into the placeholders, a Slide Development pane and a Notes pane).
- Placeholders are boxes used to hold titles and other text or objects.
- The View toolbar allows you to move through the different views of your presentation. Normal view is the default view. Outline view allows you to develop the text of your presentation. Slide view allows you to develop the slides of your presentation. Slide Sorter view shows a small picture of all your slides and the Slide Show view allows an on-screen production of your presentation.
- Sound, video clips and photos are inserted in your slide in the same way as you would insert a Clipart graphic image.

- The sequence of slides in a presentation can be changed in the Outline pane of the Normal view or in the Slide Sorter view, by dragging the slide to the required new position.
- Speaker notes can be used by presenters to make additional notes containing further details to remind them about what to say about a specific point during a presentation.
- A Slide Master or Master Slide is a PowerPoint feature that allows you to create a presentation containing objects that appear on each slide of your presentation, giving a consistent appearance to all slides in the presentation.
- A transition is a special effect that introduces a new slide in a PowerPoint presentation, when moving from the previous slide.
- PowerPoint allows you to animate the objects on your slides.
- You can animate text either through Animation Schemes or Custom Animation.
- Custom Animation allows you to add sound and other effects to an animated object.
- You can add sound from a file, CD or your own recording to objects, transitions or animations within your presentation.
- Printing slides can be useful for looking at your presenter notes, or for handing out copies of your presentation to your audience.
- You can print each slide on a separate page or a number of slides on one page, using the Handouts option in the 'Print' dialog box.

Chapter 12: Questions

True or False?

1 PowerPoint does not allow you to include sound and videos in your presentation.

2 The Blank Presentation start-up option of PowerPoint gives you a blank page with no background or colour scheme.

3 AutoContent Wizard guides you through the development of your presentation.

4 The 'New Slide' dialog box consists of a number of different layouts.

5 There are four panes of development in the Normal view of PowerPoint.

6 You cannot change the colour and background once it is already selected.

7 You cannot change the sequence of your slides once you have developed your presentation.

8 Placeholders can only hold information that you have typed.

9 You can preview your animations after making changes.

10 You cannot control your PowerPoint presentation by setting the timing and order of animations.

11 An animated effect can be placed on an object by selecting either Animation Schemes or Custom Animation.

12 Both text and graphics can be animated.

13 You can only print six slides on a page.

14 Music from a CD cannot be added to a presentation.

15 It is appropriate to put as many animations on a slide as you can.

16 You cannot print speaker notes, you can only print slides.

17 A Master Title is a preset text box.

18 The audience will be able to see the speaker notes during a presentation.

Match the icons to their names

1 Slide Sorter view

2 Reading view

3 Normal view

4 Slide Show view

a   b   c   d

Multiple-choice questions

1 Which one of the following is not a means of delivering a presentation using PowerPoint?
   a A slide
   b Printed handout
   c Printed note pages
   d Notes

2 The following are start-up options. Which is not?
   a Open an existing presentation
   b Open a new presentation
   c Design template
   d Open Wizard

3 Which one of the following is not a pane in the Normal view of PowerPoint?
   a Outline pane   b Slide Development pane
   c Slide Show pane   d Notes pane

4 In which of these can moving slides take place?
   a Normal view   b Slide Sorter view
   c Outline view   d All of the above

5 Which of the following can be added to your presentation?
   a Sound   b Graphics
   c Video   d All of the above

6 To animate an object, which must you choose?
   a Slide Show from the File menu
   b Animation Effects from the Insert menu
   c Custom Animation from the Format menu
   d Custom Animation from the Slide Show menu

7 In which of these can moving slides take place?
   a Outline pane   b Slide Development pane
   c Slide Show pane   d Notes pane

8 The Notes pane allows us to:
   a   create our slide show.
   b   add an animation to our slide.
   c   add additional comments about the slide for the presenter.
   d   determine if an audience will like our presentation.

9 A Slide Master contains:
   a   preset text boxes.   b   consistent appearance.
   c   preformatted objects.   d   all of the above.

10 Which of the following are true about animating a presentation?
   i   Animation effects can be applied only to the first slide in your presentation
   ii   The order of an animation in a slide cannot be changed
   iii Animation Schemes can be used to add an animated effect to a slide
   a   i only   b   iii only
   c   i and ii   d   ii and iii

11 Which one of the following allows you to run your presentation automatically?
   a   Transitions   b   Timing
   c   Custom Animation   d   Preset text boxes

12 Which of the following is not a sound effect that can be added to your presentation?
   a   Music from a CD   b   Voice recorded sound
   c   MP3 and MP4 sound   d   Text

13 A presentation can include all of the following except which one?
   a   Video   b   Text
   c   Chat   d   Clipart

14 Which of the following is a special effect?
   a   Fly in   b   Notes
   c   Frame   d   Outline

15 Which of the following is not an effective guideline to follow when creating a presentation?
   a   Consistent animations
   b   Use as many graphics as possible
   c   Limit the number of colours
   d   Be mindful of the sound quality

Short-answer questions
1 What is a placeholder? Explain its use in PowerPoint.

2 List THREE situations in which PowerPoint presentation software can be used.

3 What is a thumbnail?

4 PowerPoint software can make presentations fun. Give THREE reasons for this.

5 List FIVE guidelines that should be followed to have an effective presentation.

6 Explain how sound can enhance your presentation.

7 List THREE guidelines that you should use when including sound, animation and transitions in your presentations.

8 Explain the purpose of using a Slide Master template.

9 What are speaker notes and how can they be used by a presenter?

10 Give ONE reason why you would want to automatically time your presentation.

Create a 10-slide presentation on one of the following topics
1 Safety during carnival time

2 Dangers of drinking and driving

3 Balanced diet and healthy lifestyles

4 Pollution in our community

5 Movies affect our perception of how things really are

6 Peer pressure: How does it affect us?

7 How piracy is affecting our local artists

8 Certain types of music influence our behaviour. Choose a position *for* or *against* and produce a PowerPoint presention to support your viewpoint.

9 How HIV and AIDS is affecting our lives

10 Safety on the internet

11 Our sedentary lifestyles are now blamed on computers and computer games

12 Choose a new or emerging technology and explain how you think it would affect our lives in the future.

13 Computers have changed how we do things

14 The pros and cons of wearing a school uniform

15 Literary devices (for example, simile, metaphor): their definitions and examples of how they are used

16 The benefits of playing sports

17 Projects that my peers and I can undertake to benefit my community

18 Hurricane preparedness

19 Poverty in my community

20 What my community is doing to help in the fight against cancer

21 Helping a needy family

22 Teenage driving is the cause of most major road accidents. Agree or disagree?

23 A friend of yours has been trying to influence you to smoke 'weed', marijuana. His argument is that it makes you mellow, not violent, and that it gives you a great high, helping you to forget all your problems. He says that many successful people think there are benefits to smoking marijuana. Present the facts to your class showing the ill effects of smoking marijuana.

Crossword 1

Across

1 Is used to assist the presenter when making a presentation (two words) (9)

5 Normal view has three of these (5)

6 The view that allows you to develop text (7)

7 Refers to the format of a slide (6)

Down
1 This is the default view (6)

2 The name of an application software package that allows you to create, print and show presentations (10)

3 An on-screen production of your presentation (two words) (9)

4 The menu that allows you to choose the Slide layout (6)

Crossword 2

Across

6 A special effect to introduce a slide (10)

7 Animating more than one object on a slide involves a _____ animation (6)

Down
1 What you do when you change the sequence of your animation (7)

2 This specifies how long a slide will remain on the screen (6)

3 You can attach this to your objects (5)

4 You can print a number of slides on one page by selecting this from the 'Print' dialog box (8)

5 You can add this to your presentation to make an impact (9)

13 Word processing

Word processing is the preparation of documents such as letters, reports, memos, books or any other type of correspondence. A word processor is an application package or program that allows you to edit, print and save these documents for use at a later date. A word processor also includes many other capabilities – such as the ability to copy and move text, find and replace specific words and phrases, delete, edit and format documents, and print documents.

Popular word processors include Microsoft Word, Lotus Word Pro, LibreOffice Writer, Corel WordPerfect, Adobe® InCopy® and Pages, a word processor for the Mac®. All these word processors contain similar functions. There is also an increase in the popularity and number of online word processors, for example, Google Docs™ and Microsoft Office Web Apps. For practical reasons, the particular operations described in this chapter feature Microsoft Word and its functions. 'Word' is part of the Microsoft Office package, which is currently the most popular integrated software package available.

Fundamentally, a word processor package on a computer allows you to enter text and make changes to that text without having to retype the entire document from scratch, as would be the case with a typewriter. You can save the document on disk and retrieve it at a later date, even if it is not yet complete. A word processor also allows you to perform complex formatting features that cannot be done on a typewriter.

Microsoft Office 2019, Microsoft's latest suite of office tools, was released in September 2018 as the successor to Office 2016. Office 2013, Office 2016 and Office 2019 are not significantly different from each other. There are minor upgrades from one Office version to the next. You may have also heard of Office 365, which is the cloud-based version of Office 2016. The cloud-based version requires you to pay an annual subscription to access the software, whereas the standalone versions only require a one-time purchase of the software.

Microsoft Word 2013 versus Microsoft Word 2016 versus Microsoft Word 2019

Most computers at your school would have either Microsoft Word 2013 or Microsoft Word 2016 installed. As already mentioned, there are not many significant differences between the three versions of Microsoft Word.

In all versions, commands are organised in logical groups, which are placed together under tabs. When you click on the tabs, they display these commands in a 'Ribbon'. Each tab relates to a type of activity, such as 'Home' (deals mostly with formatting) and 'Insert' (tables, graphics, date and time, and so on). To reduce clutter, some tabs are shown only when needed. The new Ribbon design makes it easier to quickly find the commands you need to complete a task.

In Microsoft Word 2016, all icons and tabs remain the same. The Page layout tab is now called Layout and the Review tab includes an additional feature called Start inking. Start inking allows you to include the features of Paint in your document. It allows you to draw directly onto your document if you are using a tablet or touchscreen. Figure 13.1 shows the Word 2016 Home tab.

In Microsoft Word 2019, all icons and tabs are the same as in 2016. This version contains a few additional features, of which two are located on the Insert tab. Two new icons have been added to this tab – the '3D model', where a three-dimensional diagram can be inserted, and one called, 'Icon', which allows you to insert an icon into your document. The other major additional feature is located in the File menu and allows you to link seamlessly to Office 365, which is the online version of Microsoft Office.

As all functions remain the same in all three versions of Microsoft Word, this chapter focuses on performing the various operations in Microsoft Word 2016.

▲ Figure 13.1 Word 2016 Home tab

Starting Microsoft Word

Starting Word using the Start button on the taskbar

1 Select the **Windows Button** menu.
2 When the **Programs** menu appears, select **Word 2013**, **Word 2016** or **Word 2019**, (whichever version your computer is using), and select **Word** from the **Microsoft Office** menu.

The Word window appears as shown in Figure 13.2.

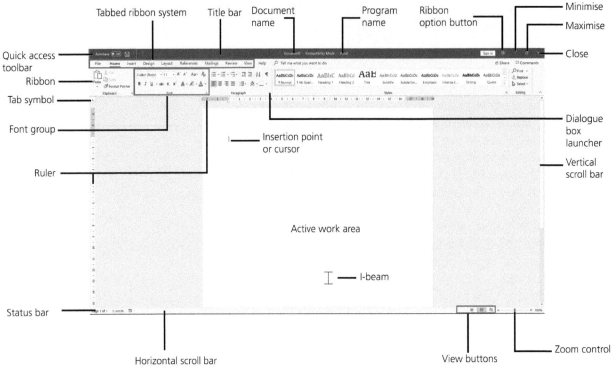

▲ Figure 13.2 Word 2013 or Word 2016 window elements

Word 2016 windows elements

In Word 2007 to Word 2019, the Ribbon system is used to make the commands more accessible. The Ribbon system contains various tabs, with each tab containing groups of related commands associated with that particular tab. Table 13.1 shows the key elements of the Word window.

Element	Function
Title bar	Displays the document name and the program name, as well as the Ribbon option button and the Minimise, Restore and Close buttons
Quick Access Toolbar	Can be customised with icons that you use most frequently
Ribbon	Allows you to access all features and commands of Word, such as formatting, editing and others
Formatting toolbar	Contains buttons that are shortcuts for formatting a document; usually one or two bars are shown; right-clicking on these allows you to add or remove further toolbars, such as the drawing toolbar
Ruler	Shows the margins, the tab setting and the indents
Insertion point or cursor	A flashing vertical line, which indicates the position where the next character will be inserted
I-beam or mouse pointer	Allows you to move to a specific position where the next character will be inserted: position the I-beam where you want the character to be inserted and click on the left mouse button; the beam converts to a pointed arrow when you move it into the margin
Vertical scroll bars	Allow you to scroll up or down a document
Horizontal scroll bars	Allow you to scroll from left to right or vice versa in a document
Status Bar	Displays a variety of information about the document, such as the number of pages and words, and the language used, and can be customised to display other information about the document
Zoom Control	Allows you to zoom in or zoom out of your page, in other words, the Zoom (+) magnifies your page, whereas the Zoom (–) shrinks your page
View buttons	Allow different views of the document on the screen

▲ Table 13.1 Key elements of the Word window

The keyboard

▲ Figure 13.3 A computer keyboard

Entering text

Once Word has been started, a new document is automatically opened. Before using your keyboard, familiarise yourself with the elements of the keyboard in Table 13.2. Match these to Figure 13.3, which shows a computer keyboard. Then you can begin typing immediately in the active work area of the window. This workspace will contain what you type or draw. The window displays a typing area similar to that of a clean sheet of paper. The document will be set up with default settings, which are features that have been preset such as page size, margin size, line spacing, and font style and size.

Word wrap

Word wrap is one such default setting; it is an important feature you should know about. Word wrap allows text to move automatically to the next line without you needing to press the 'Enter' key. When words approach the right margin, if the last word is too long to fit on the line, it automatically moves to the next line.
You should, therefore, use the 'Enter' key only when:

- you want to create blank lines
- you have reached the end of a line you want to keep short in appearance
- you have reached the end of a paragraph.

Different views of a document

Word allows you several different ways to view a document. These views include Web Layout, Print Layout and Read Mode. You can access them by selecting the desired view from the View tab, or by clicking the appropriate view button on the bottom left-hand corner of the document window. The icons are shown in Figure 13.4.

▲ Figure 13.4 View buttons

Key	Function
Enter	Moves the insertion point to the next line
Spacebar	Moves the insertion point one space to the right
Caps Lock	Toggles between uppercase and lowercase; pressing this key causes the 'Caps Lock' indicator light on the keyboard to light up and any letter that is typed will be displayed in uppercase.
Esc	Pressing this key immediately after an action takes you out of, or cancels, that action
Shift	This key is used along with other keys to allow second-function commands; for example, if the computer is not in 'Caps Lock' mode, you can get a capital letter by holding down the Shift key and pressing the desired letter
Backspace	Deletes the character to the left of the insertion point
Delete	Deletes the character to the right of the insertion point
Insert	Toggles between insert mode and overtype mode; the insert mode (the default mode) allows you to enter extra characters at the insertion point; in the overtype mode, new characters being typed erase the characters that were previously there
Num Lock	Toggles between a numeric keypad and directional keys that allow you to move text or the cursor around
Function keys	Function keys labelled F1 to F12 perform different functions depending on the program being used

▲ Table 13.2 Elements of the keyboard

257

These View options allow you to look at your documents in different ways.

- **Print Layout:** In this layout, you can create, edit and format your documents. It allows you to see how text and graphics are placed on the paper you may print the document on, as it shows the edges of the 'paper'. You can, therefore, adjust the position of text and graphics quite precisely on the page. This view displays the document fully formatted and shows how it would look if it were to be printed out on paper.
- **Web Layout:** This view enables you to look at a document as a web page to see what it would look like before it is published on the internet.
- **Read Mode:** This view enables you to view the document with minimum eye strain and with tools optimised for reading. It is designed to make reading documents on the screen more comfortable. In this mode, Word removes distracting screen elements, such as extraneous toolbars. Word also uses your computer's screen resolution settings to resize the document for optimum readability.

The Outline view and Draft view can only be accessed from the View tab, as they are not part of the View buttons on the Status bar.

- **Outline view:** This view shows the structure of a document. The extra symbols and indentation that appear in Outline View are not printed. This view enables you to make adjustments quickly to the structure of a document. For example, you can shift headings and text up or down by clicking on the up or down arrows.
- **Draft view:** In this view, the layout of each page of the document is simplified to enable you to enter text quickly, as certain page elements do not show up. In this layout, you can type, edit and format your documents.

Saving a document

Saving a document onto a backup storage device makes it available for editing and printing at a later date. A document temporarily resides in the computer's RAM memory as you work. If the computer is switched off, or there is a power failure, all the work you have done since the last time the document was saved would be lost. It is therefore important to save your document to backing storage regularly to avoid losing data.

Saving a document for the first time

1 Choose the **Save As** or **Save** command (we will look at the difference between these later in this section) from the **File** tab or click on the **Save** icon 🔲. When either of these commands is used to save a document for the first time, the 'Save As' dialog box appears (Figure 13.5).
2 Select the location where you want to save the document by selecting from the drop-down menu of the 'Save As' box.

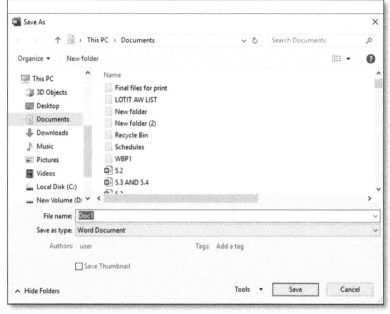

▲ Figure 13.5 'Save As' dialog box

3   Type a name for the new document in the 'File name' box. We look at file names in more detail below.

4   The 'Save as type' box lets you change the format of document you are saving. Most of the time you will leave the format unchanged and the document will be saved as a 'docx' file, which is Word's usual format. Occasionally you may need a different format, such as RTF, or an earlier version of Word, to use with a different word processor, or to make the text easier to use with a different program by producing an unformatted TXT file.

5   Click the **Save** button.

Saving a document that you have previously saved

Once you have saved a document, you can use the 'Save' function to save further changes to it.

1   Select **Save** from the **File** tab or click on the **Save** icon 🖫 to save the document in its current format with no change of where it is saved or what the file is named.

2   Select the **Save As** function as another option; the 'Save As' dialog box appears. You can either save changes to the previously saved document using its previously saved name or make another copy of the document by saving it under another name and/or storing it in another location.

File names

File names can have a length of up to 255 characters and contain letters, numbers and other characters. However, file names cannot contain the following symbols: ?, /, \, >, <, *, ", : or ;. It is a good rule to choose file names that are meaningful to you since they give an idea of what the contents of the file are.

Shortcut

Click on the Disk icon 🖫 on the 'Quick access' toolbar to save a document for the first time or to save changes to a document that has already been saved.

Closing a document

Closing a document removes it from your screen and stores it wherever you have placed it on your hard drive. You can close a document by either:

1   selecting the **Close** option from the **File** tab

2   clicking on the **Close** button ⊠ at the top right-hand corner of the document window.

If you try to close a changed document without saving it, a dialog box will appear, to give you an opportunity to save it (Figure 13.6).

Remember that if you do not save your work or changes that you made to a document, it will not be available for you to use again!

Opening a document

When you need to work with an existing document, you have to open it first. Opening a document places a copy of the original in your word processor window. The original is left intact in its location in backup storage.

▲ Figure 13.6 Opportunity to save

Retrieving a document

1 Select **Open** from the **File** tab.
2 Click on **Browse**.
3 The 'Open' dialog box appears (Figure 13.7). Using the 'Look in' box, select the location where the file is stored.
4 When the list of files or folders is displayed, you can do one of two options.
  a Type the name of the file you want to open in the 'File name' box and click **Open**.
  b Double-click on the name of the desired file.

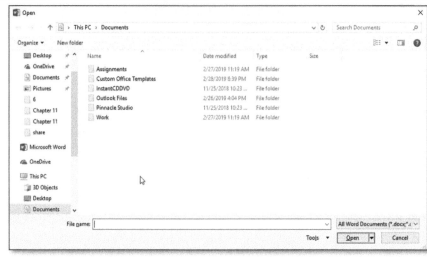

▲ Figure 13.7 'Open' dialog box

Printing a document

Printing a document allows you to produce a hardcopy of your work.

Shortcut

Click on the **Printer** icon on the 'Quick access' toolbar to print the entire document. Note also that the keystroke Ctrl + P opens the 'Print' dialog box.

Using the print option from the File tab

1 Select **Print** from the **File** tab. The 'Print' dialog box appears (Figure 13.8).
2 Make the appropriate selections (such as the number of copies or pages).
3 Click the **Print** icon to start printing.

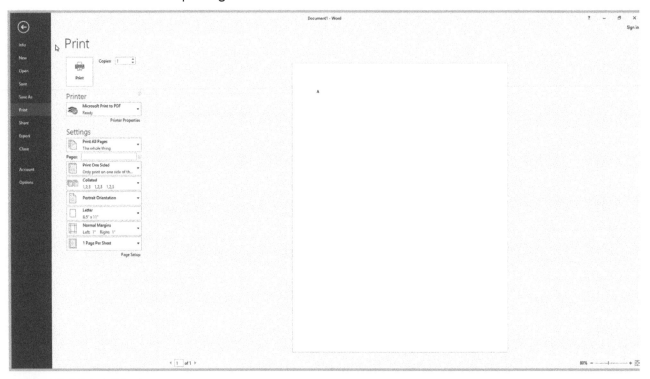

▲ Figure 13.8 'Print' dialog box

Exercise 1

1 What is the function of a word processor?
2 List the different ways of viewing a document in Microsoft Word.
3 What is the 'word wrap' feature and why is it useful?
4 Why do you need to save a previously-saved document after making changes to it?
5 Explain the difference between typeover mode and insert mode.

Activity 1

1 On your computer, double-click on the word-processing icon (Microsoft Word icon) to open the application.
2 Type the document below as accurately as possible.
   a Save the document as 'The argument' on the hard disk or on a USB memory stick.
   b Print the document.
   c Close the document.
   d Retrieve the document.
   e Resave the document as 'Cricket at the Oval' in the 'My Documents' folder.

The argument between the bat and the ball

It was a bright and sunny day at the Queen's Park Oval. The game started at eight o'clock. Brian Lara's family and supporters were there. It began, with Pakistan winning the toss. They made three hundred and sixty-five runs. They were really good.

Then it was West Indies time to bat. Our players were good too. We had three hundred runs when Brian Lara came to bat. 'Ah, there goes another six', said the commentator. 'Brian Lara is absolutely brilliant! Wow, look at that ball; it is high in the air. But a Pakistani player is right under it. Oh no! He caught it. Brian Lara is out and the West Indies team is down. What a sad day at the Oval.'

Meanwhile, the ball and the bat seemed to be having an argument. The bat asked the ball, 'Why did you have to fall in the man's hands?'

'Not me, it was your fault. It was you who sent me there.'

'If you did watch what going on we would never lose.'

'You old crooked bat, I'm not playing with you again.' And so they left the oval and so did I, very unhappy.

Jeremy Taylor
Std 5
Cunapo R.C., Sangre Grande, Trinidad

Editing and proofing text

There are many features in a word processor that permit quick changes to a document, which would be difficult and tedious to perform manually. Some of these features, such as deleting text using the 'Delete' and the 'Backspace' keys, and inserting and typing over text using the 'Insert' key, have already been discussed. Other editing features include:

- cutting, copying and pasting
- finding and replacing text.

Cutting, copying and pasting

The Cut function allows you to select and remove an item from a document – such as a character, a word, a line of text, or a picture – and place it in the Clipboard. This item can then be inserted anywhere, and as many times as you want, in any open document. This is the Paste function. You can do this within a Word document, between two different Word documents or between two programs. For example, you can cut and paste a table or graph created in the Excel application into a Word document.

The Copy function places a copy of an item selected onto the Clipboard; the original item remains exactly where it is. The copy on the Clipboard can then be inserted anywhere and as many times as you like in any open document.

The Clipboard is a temporary storage location in memory where cut or copied text and graphics are placed. The items remain on the Clipboard until you cut or copy a new item. The items can be copied from the Clipboard into different areas of the document or into another document or even another program, as many times as you like. The Clipboard can store up to 24 items. If you click on the dialog launcher button on the 'Clipboard' part of the 'Home' ribbon, you can see, and use, everything currently in your Clipboard.

To use the 'Cut' or 'Copy' feature; the item must first be selected. There are many ways to select items. For example, you can use:

- the menu bar to select an entire document
- the mouse by itself, or together with other keys.
- the arrow keys with the shift key to select characters and with both the ctrl and shift keys to select words.

Selecting an entire document

1 Choose **Select All** from the **Editing** group on the 'Home' tab. The entire document becomes highlighted. You can also use the keyboard stroke CTRL + A to select all.

Selecting text using the mouse

1 Position the mouse pointer in front of the first character of the block of text to be selected.
2 Hold down the left mouse button and drag the mouse over the text you want to select. The area becomes highlighted; release the mouse button at the end of the block of text.

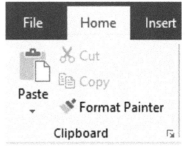

▲ Figure 13.9 Word 2016 'Copy', 'Cut' and 'Paste' icons

Other methods of selecting text

Table 13.3 shows other methods to select text.

Method	Result
Position the I-beam on a word and double-click.	Selects the word
Hold down the control key and click on a sentence.	Selects the sentence
Triple-click on a paragraph.	Selects the paragraph

▲ Table 13.3 Other methods to select text

Cutting and pasting (moving) text

1 Select the block of text to be cut.
2 Select the **Cut** icon from the **Clipboard** group on the 'Home' tab.
3 Click on the position where you want to place the removed (cut) text. This can be anywhere in the same document or in another opened document.
4 Click the **Paste** icon.

Copying and pasting text

1 Select the block of text you want to copy.
2 Select **Copy** icon from the **Clipboard** group on the **Home** tab.
3 Click on the position where you want to place the copied text. This can be anywhere in the same document or within another opened document.
4 Click the **Paste** icon.

Drag and drop editing

For some editing, it may be quicker to use drag and drop editing to move text and images around. This tends to work best when you are moving small bits of text around short distances, for example, rearranging sentences in a paragraph.

To do this, use the mouse and select the text you want to move. Keep the left mouse button pressed and a dotted rectangle will appear with the arrow as the mouse cursor. Then simply move the mouse cursor to where you want to move the text and release the left mouse button. The text is moved in exactly the same way as doing a 'Cut and Paste'.

Find and Replace

The Find function allows you to search a document for a particular word or string of characters that you may want to change or edit. Two options may occur:

Option one

1 Click **Find** from the 'Editing' group on the 'Home' tab.
2 Enter the word or phrase in the 'Find What' box.
3 Select **Find Next**.

Option two

1 Click **Find** from the 'Editing' group on the 'Home' tab. The 'Navigation' pane on the left of the window may appear.
2 Enter the word or phrase in the 'Search document' box.
3 All results appear highlighted in the document and a listing of the results appear in the 'Navigation' pane.

The Replace function allows you to search for a word or string of characters and replace it with another word or string of characters.

1 Select **Replace** from the 'Editing' group on the 'Home' tab (Figure 13.10).
2 Enter the word or phrase you wish to replace in the 'Find what' box.
3 Enter the word or phrase you wish to replace it with in the 'Replace with' box.
4 Click the **Find Next** button to find the first (and subsequent) occurrence of the word or phrase.
5 Click the **Replace** button to replace the word or phrase.

Did you know?

If you want to replace the word every time it appears in the document, you can simply click the 'Replace All' button.

Activity 2

1 Retrieve the document 'Honesty is the Best Policy' from the companion CD-ROM.
2 Find and replace all occurrences of the word 'girls' with 'boys'.
3 Save the document.

▲ Figure 13.10 'Find and Replace' dialog box

Spelling and grammar checks

Spelling and grammatical errors undermine the look of a document, whether it is a professional letter or your school assignment. To help you to create a more accurate and professional-looking document, use your word processor's spelling and grammar check facility. This checks the words in the document against a dictionary that can be selected to suit a particular language (See 'Language' section later in the chapter for how to select this).

Words that are misspelt or not recognisable by Word are highlighted by underlining the word with a jagged red line. If the spellchecker believes it has spotted an incorrectly-spelt word, it will display a list of possible suggestions in a suggestion box, from which you can choose an alternative.

When Word spots a phrase or sentence that contradicts grammatical rules, or when there is inaccurate spacing between characters, the text is identified using a green jagged underline. The grammar checker displays possible grammatical errors and correction suggestions. You could choose to 'Ignore' the suggestions or 'Change' and accept the suggestions.

Proofing a document

1. Position the I-beam at the point of the document where you would like to start the spelling and grammar check.
2. Select **Spelling and Grammar** from the 'Proofing' group in the **Review** tab. Or, press the function 7 (F7) key to activate the checker.
3. If there is a spelling error or a grammatical error, the 'Spelling and Grammar' dialog box or 'Navigation' pane is displayed (Figure 13.11). This box will show some possible suggestions in a 'Suggestions' box. You can choose any of the options displayed, or choose to ignore them (see Table 13.4).

Ignore	Choose this option if you do not want to change the word or this occurrence of the word.
Ignore All	Choose this option if you do not want to change any and all occurrences of the word throughout the document.
Change	Click on the appropriate word in the 'Suggestions' box and click the **Change** button.
Change All	Choose this option if you want to change all occurrences of the word in the document.
Add	If the computer has detected a word that it does not recognise and which is not in its dictionary, you can choose to add the word to the dictionary. Note that this word will be marked as 'incorrect' to start with.

▲ Table 13.4 The 'Spelling and Grammar' dialog box offers several correction options.

After making all the changes, the message 'The spelling and grammar check is complete' is displayed.

▲ Figure 13.11 'Spelling and Grammar' dialog box

Thesaurus

Sometimes we may want to replace a word in the document with another word of the same meaning. Word provides a 'Thesaurus', which gives us the list of synonyms (words with similar meaning).

1 Click on the word for which you would like to find a synonym.
2 Click on **Thesaurus** in the 'Proofing' group of the 'Review' tab. The 'Thesaurus' pane will appear (see Figure 13.12).
3 Select one of the words in the list of results to replace the selected word. You can choose one of these options:
   a Replace the word by clicking on the down arrow next to the selected work and then clicking **Insert**.
   b Select **Copy** and paste the word where you would like it to appear.

Language

There may be occasions where you need to set the language that the 'Spelling and Grammar' checker will use or the proofing language as Word refers to it. For example, in American English, we use 'color' and British English 'colour'. When you run a spelling check on a document, it is important to select the right language.

Word also allows us to translate our document into a number of different languages, as well as to set the language that we want to use to check our spelling and grammar.

Selecting the right proofing language

1 Select **Language**, set proofing language from the 'Language' group of the 'Review tab' and the 'Language Options' dialog box will appear.
2 Select the language you would like for proofing your documents.

Translating the language

1 Select **Translate** from the 'Language group' of the 'Review' tab and the 'Translation Language Options' dialog box will appear (see Figure 13.13)
2 Select the language you would like to translate to.

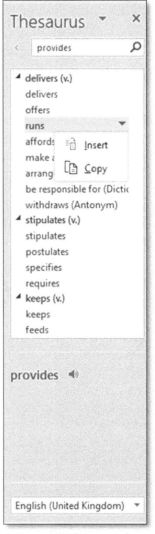

▲ Figure 13.12 'Thesaurus' pane

▲ Figure 13.13 'Translation Language Options' dialog

Undo and Redo

The 'Undo and Redo' function allows you to undo mistakes or changes made during editing, formatting or drawing. For example, if you intentionally or unintentionally change a document, the changes can be reversed using the 'Undo' button (or holding down 'Ctrl' and pressing 'z'). Actions are usually reversed right after you complete the action – that is the point at which you are most likely to change your mind. However, you can undo more than one previous action. A list of the most recent actions that can be undone is displayed when the arrow next to the 'Undo' button in the 'Quick access' toolbar is clicked. You can scroll down to undo as many of these recent actions as you wish.

The 'Redo' button (or holding down 'Ctrl' and pressing 'y') allows you to undo an undo (if you later decide that you actually did want to keep the original change).

Formatting

Changing the appearance of the text in a document is called formatting. The impact created on the reader of your document is greatly dependent on the appearance of your document. The final appearance of a document depends largely on the extent to which the user can effectively use the word processor's available formatting features.

Character formatting

The following are attributes that can be applied to characters, (that is, letters, numbers, symbols, punctuation marks and spaces):

- font type and size, for example, 12-point Times
- font style (Regular, **Bold**, <u>Underline</u>, *Italic*)
- font colour
- effects (strikethrough, superscript, subscript, shadow, outline, emboss, engrave, highlighting and caps).

Font

Font type refers to the typeface (shape of the character) that you wish to use for a particular piece of text. It is a collection of characters (letters, numbers, symbols, punctuation marks and spaces) with a consistent appearance. For example:

- **Font size** is measured in units called points; this refers to the height of a character, where one point is 1/72 of an inch (0.0352778 cm). Therefore, when you choose a font size of 72 points, your characters will be one inch (2.54 cm) in height, when printed. The larger the point size the larger the font.
- **Font style** changes the way the text appears. It includes Plain text, Bold (B), Italic (I), Underline (U), as well as many others or a combination of styles.

Activity 3

1 Retrieve the document 'Crime in Schools' from the companion CD-ROM.
2 Add the following text to the end of the document:

Many students have difficulty dealing with their problems and may exhibit poor behavioural responses to situations. Guidance counsellors are needed in the present system to help students deal with some of their problems.

3 Insert the heading 'Crime in Schools'.
4 Spell-check the document.
5 Save the document as 'A solution to crime'.

Activity 4

1 Retrieve the document 'Honesty is the Best Policy'.
2 Spell check the document.

Times New Roman	Times New Roman
Lucida Handwriting	*Lucida Handwriting*
Script MT Bold	*Script MT Bold*
Old English Text MT	*Old English Text MT*
Impact	**Impact**
Wingdings	✤✈■✌♓⚐✈■✌♓✦

▲ Figure 13.14 Examples of different font types

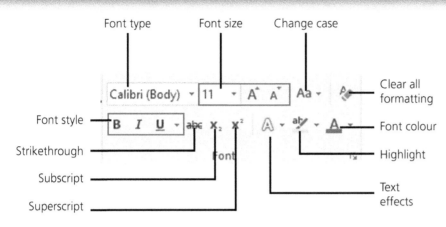

Font type Font size Change case

Clear all formatting

Font style

Strikethrough

Subscript

Superscript

Font

Font colour

Highlight

Text effects

▲ Figure 13.15 'Font ribbon' menu

Changing the font type

1 From the 'Font' group on the 'Home' tab, click on the arrow next to the displayed font type. A list of available font styles will appear (see Figure 13.15).
2 Select the desired style.

Changing the font size

1 From the 'Font' group on the 'Home' tab, click on the arrow next to the displayed font size. A list of available font sizes will appear (see Figure 13.16).
2 Select the desired size by clicking on the number.

▲ Figure 13.16 Font types and sizes

Changing the font style
From the 'Font' group on the 'Home' tab, click for bold (B), italic (I) or underline (U) as required.

Changing the font type, style and size using the 'Font' dialog box

1 The 'Font' dialog box will appear if the 'Dialog Box Launcher', which is located at the bottom right-hand corner of the 'Font' group is clicked.
2 The top part of the 'Font' dialog box window is divided into three sections: 'Font', 'Font style' and 'Size' (see Figure 13.17).
3 To select the required font type, use the scroll bar under the 'Font' heading and select the desired font.
4 To select the required font style (bold, italics, underline) select from the options available.
5 To select the required size click on the 'Size' box and select the desired size: 8, 9, 10, 11, 12, and so on.

You can see a preview of the options selected in the preview box at the bottom of the 'Font' window.

Many of the options, such as font type, style and font size, are available on the formatting toolbar.

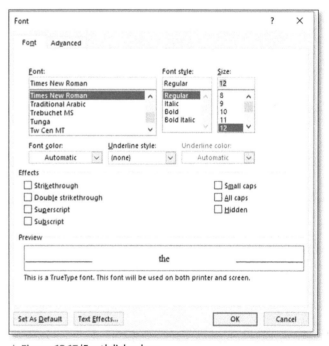

▲ Figure 13.17 'Font' dialog box

Did you know?
If the desired size is not displayed, you can type the number in the font size box and press the enter key.

Changing the font colour

1 Click on the down arrow next to the **Font Colour** button (a font colour box appears; see Figure 13.18).
2 Click on the colour you want.

Applying effects

Superscript and subscript

A superscript character is one that is raised above the normal line. For example, 3rd, 100 °C, $4x^2$ have the characters 'rd', '0' and '2' raised above the normal line and are superscript characters.

Subscript characters are placed below the normal line. For example, the chemical representation of water is H_2O or a number in base 2 can be written 1101_2. The number 2 in each of these cases is a subscript character.

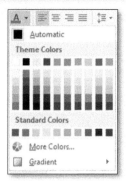

▲ Figure 13.18 Font colour box

Applying superscript and subscript

1 Select the text and then click the 'Superscript' or 'Subscript' icon from the Font Group. **Or**
2 Click the 'Superscript' or 'Subscript' icon, type the text and click the icon again to return to normal typing mode.

Applying superscript and subscript using the 'Font' Dialog Box

1 Select the text you would like to place as superscript or subscript.
2 Launch the 'Font' dialog box by clicking on the **Dialog Box Launcher**, which is located at the bottom right-hand corner of the 'Font' group.
3 Check the **Superscript** or **Subscript** box in the effects section of the 'Font' dialog box and click the **OK** button.

If you did not previously select the text you want to place as superscript or subscript before launching the 'Font' dialog box, you can simply check the 'Superscript' or 'Subscript' box, and type the character you want to format as superscript or subscript. However, you will need to change back to normal typing mode, by going back to the 'Font' dialog box and unchecking the 'Superscript' or 'Subscript' box.

The other effects can be applied by checking the appropriate box in the same way as for superscript and subscript. The results of applying some different format effects are shown in Table 13.5.

Effect	Outcome
Strikethrough	~~Strikethrough~~
Double strikethrough	~~Double Strikethrough~~
Shadow	**Shadow**
Outline	Outline
Reflection	Reflection
Glow	Glow
Small Caps	SMALL CAPS

▲ Table 13.5 Results of applying some font effects

Highlighting

Sometimes you will want to highlight a piece of text, for example, if you are editing a piece of work and want to pick out some text. This option lets you highlight the text in the same style as using a highlighter pen on paper.

1 Select the text to highlight.
2 Click on the highlight icon in the font group and the text is highlighted in the colour shown.
3 You can change the colour or remove the highlighting of the selected text by clicking the down arrow to the right of the icon and selecting the colour that you want.

Changing case (uppercase or lowercase)

On occasion, it may become necessary to change portions of typed text, for example, from lowercase (common letters) to uppercase (capital letters) and vice versa. This can be done easily using the 'Change Case' function.

▲ Figure 13.19 'Change Case' drop-down list

Changing case

1 Select the text.
2 Click on the drop-down arrow next to the **Change Case** icon from the 'Font' Group.
3 Select **Uppercase** or **lowercase** from the drop-down list (see Figure 13.19).

Activity 5

A car ride in Tobago

The first day of our vacation in Tobago began when we all piled into my mum's car. The car was a little blue 'bug', which we brought across from Trinidad to Tobago on board the Panorama. We drove around for a while until we came to Fort George, which was at the top of a very steep hill.

The engine stopped working and the car started to roll backwards. Foolishly, we kids were all excited, not realising what a dangerous predicament we were in. The car eventually came to a stop at the bottom of the hill. The car was easily restarted; apparently, the engine was not powerful enough to carry the load up the steep incline. We all came out of the vehicle and walked up to the Fort while my mum drove up the hill. It was an adventure I would never forget. Halfway up the hill, the car started to have engine trouble.

1 Type the document as shown above. The number of words per line may differ, but do not worry about this, just keep the paragraph structure.
2 Delete the heading.
3 Copy and paste the second-last sentence of the second paragraph as the new heading.
4 Bold and centre the heading.
5 Change the heading to uppercase.
6 Cut and paste the last sentence of the second paragraph to the beginning of the second paragraph.
7 Change the colour of the word 'Tobago' throughout the document, to blue.
8 Change the font of the words 'Fort George' in the first paragraph.
9 Underline and italicise the word 'Panorama'.

Paragraph formatting

A paragraph in Word can be any number of characters. It can include text, graphics, objects (for example, charts), blank lines and other items followed by the paragraph mark. The paragraph mark can only be seen by clicking on the **Show/Hide** button in the standard toolbar (see Figure 13.20). The paragraph mark appears each time the 'Enter' key is pressed and a new paragraph is created. A document can, therefore, have a number of paragraphs.

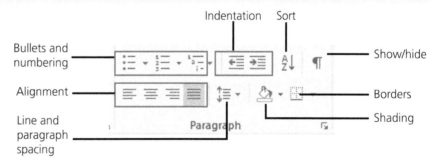

▲ Figure 13.20 Paragraph ribbon menu

The 'Show/Hide' button on the standard toolbar allows you to display all formatting marks such as white spaces and other markers not normally visible in the normal document.

Line spacing

Line spacing is the distance between lines of text. The spacing between the lines of text is also relative to the size of the font on a line. The larger the font size, the larger the line spacing. Appropriate line spacing improves the appearance and readability of a document. The line spacing available is 'single', 'double', '1.5', 'at least', 'exactly' and 'multiple'. The default line spacing for Word is single. It may be necessary to change the line spacing, depending on the nature of a document.

Shortcut

You can choose the desired spacing as shown in Figure 13.21 from the 'Paragraph' group. Place the insertion point in a paragraph or select multiple paragraphs.

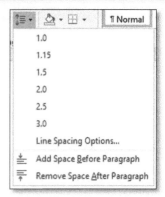
▲ Figure 13.21 Line spacing drop-down box

Changing line spacing

1 Place the insertion point in a paragraph or select multiple paragraphs.
2 Select the **Line and Paragraph Spacing** icon from the 'Paragraph' group.
3 Select the required spacing from the line spacing box.

Changing line spacing using the 'Paragraph' dialog box

1 Place the insertion point in a paragraph or select multiple paragraphs.
2 Select the **Dialog Box Launcher** from the 'Paragraph' group.
3 The 'Paragraph' dialog box appears (Figure 13.22).
4 Select the required spacing by selecting the option from the line spacing box.

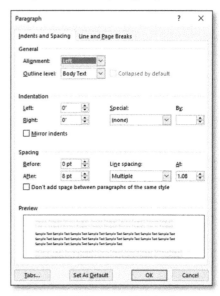
▲ Figure 13.22 'Paragraph' dialog box

Alignment/Justification

This is the process of aligning a block of text, paragraph or entire document within the text margins or frame borders. The default setting for Word is left justification. Text can also be right, centre or justify (fully justified).

- **Left justification (alignment)** means that the text is flush on the left margin (text at the right margin is uneven).
- **Right justification (alignment)** means that the text is flush with the right margin (text at the left margin is uneven).
- **Centre alignment** means that the text is centred in the middle of the document or frame.
- **Justify/Fully justified/Left and Right justification (alignment)** means that the text is flush with both left and right margins, and the spacing between the letters changes.

Changing the alignment using the dialog box

1 Select the text.
2 Select the desired alignment (**Left**, **Centered**, **Right** or **Justified**) icons from the 'Paragraph' group (see Figure 13.23).

▲ Figure 13.23 Toolbar buttons for justifying text

Changing the alignment using the dialog box

1 Select the text.
2 Select the **Dialog Box Launcher** from the 'Paragraph' group
3 The 'Paragraph' dialog box appears (see Figure 13.22).
4 Select the alignment from the 'Alignment' box by clicking on the down arrow and choosing the desired alignment (**Left**, **Centered**, **Right** or **Justified** – see Figure 13.23).

Indenting text

You can indent a line or a paragraph by pushing them away from the left or right margins. The size of an indent is the distance between the margins and the text. There are three indent settings: the left indent, the right indent and a special indent, (which includes 'First line/Hanging'). The default setting for all three indents is zero. This means that a paragraph would initially have no indentation.

- The 'Left' indent pushes the paragraph away from the left margin.
- The 'Right' indent pushes the paragraph away from the right margin.
- The 'First Line' indent is one in which the first line is shorter than the rest of the paragraph.
- The 'Hanging' indent occurs when the first line of a paragraph is left indented less than the rest of the lines in the paragraph. The first line will, therefore, be hanging to the left of the rest of the lines in the paragraph. It is used in bulleted lists, numbered lists, numbered paragraphs and bibliographies.

How to indent text
Click on the 'Home' tab. The 'Paragraph' group shows the commands available. (The 'Paragraph' dialog box appears, as shown in Figure 13.22, when the 'Paragraph Dialog Box Launcher' is clicked.)

You can set a left indent using the increase and decrease indent buttons in the toolbar. The 'Increase indent' button moves the left indent marker to the right, a distance of one tab stop at a time. The 'Decrease indent' button moves the left indent marker back (to the left) one tab stop at a time.

Indenting text using the 'Paragraph' dialog box
Place the insertion point in a paragraph or select the required paragraphs.

1 Select the **Dialog Box Launcher** from the 'Paragraph' group.
   The 'Paragraph' dialog box appears (Figure 13.22).
2 Specify the indentations in the 'Right', 'Left' and/or 'Special' indent boxes. The 'Preview' box at the bottom will show the effect of the changes on the text.
3 Click **OK** when you are finished.

The indent settings are maintained when each new paragraph is started by pressing the enter key.

Activity 6

1 Type out the document shown below. The number of words per line may differ, but keep the paragraph structure.

a Centre the first two lines of the document.

b Change the font size of the first two lines of the document to a size larger than the rest of the document.

c Change the first line of the document to uppercase.

d Change the font type of the second line of the document to Black Chancery.

e Place a blank line between the first two lines of the document and the date.

f Indent the first line of the first paragraph.

g Create a bulleted list for the type of forms to be used, that is the Cash-List Form and the Fund Raising Form.

h Use bold for the words 'Cash-List Form', 'Fund-raising Form', 'Approved Budget 2019/2020', 'Quantity', 'Items' and 'Cost'.

i Underline and italicise the words 'Items Approved'.

j Double space the approved items.

k Check for spelling errors.

l Save the document as 'New Record-keeping Practices'.

THE PANORAMA COMPANY

Wine and Cheese Club

26th January 2019

The Manager,

Wine and Cheese Club

As new members of the executive, we have decided that in order to promote transparency and proper accounting and record keeping, the following systems must be implemented:

Cash-List Form – This form will be used to record all petty cash transactions.

Fund-raising Form – This form will be used to inform the executive of all fundraising details.

Approved Budget 2019/2020

The items listed below have been approved for the 2019/2020 budget.

Items Approved:

Quantity	Items	Cost
2 dozen	Wine glasses	$84
4 dozen boxes	Chocolates	$400
6 cases	Wine	$6,000
2 dozen	T-shirts	$1,600
2 dozen	Cutlery items	$500

If there are any questions concerning the new forms, please contact the assistant treasurer. We look forward to your continued support.

The Treasurer

2 Type out the following and save to a single file called 'Practising Effects':

a $40\ °C$

b $3^3 \times 4^4 = y$

c $Fe^2 + $ ions

d $2P + 5Cl_2 \rightarrow 2PCl_5$

e $Ca(OH)_2 + 2HCl \rightarrow CaCl_2 + 2H_2O$

f $2Fe_2O_2 + 3C \rightarrow 4Fe + 3CO_2 \uparrow$

g $3X^3 - 4X^2 - 2X - 2 = Y$

Bullets and numbering

Bullets and numbers can be added to already-typed text or to text
that is being typed. Several different styles of bullets and numbering
are available.

Examples of numbering:

1. Monday	I. Monday	(a) Monday	A. Monday
2. Tuesday	II. Tuesday	(b) Tuesday	B. Tuesday
3. Wednesday	III. Wednesday	(c) Wednesday	C. Wednesday

Examples of bullets:

● Monday	❖ Monday	☜ Monday	❏ Monday
● Tuesday	❖ Tuesday	☜ Tuesday	❏ Tuesday
● Wednesday	❖ Wednesday	☜ Wednesday	❏ Wednesday

Adding bullets or numbers to a list

1. Select the list to which you want to add bullets or numbers.
2. Click on the drop-down arrow of **Bullets and Numbering** icons from
   the 'Paragraph' group.
3. Select the desired bullet or numbering style.

Note that the last bulleted or numbered style is displayed when the
numbers or bullets button is selected.

Removing bullets or numbers from a list

1. Select the numbered or bulleted list.
2. Click the **Bullet** or **Numbering** button to deselect or turn off the
   bullets or numbering.

Page layout/Layout

Figure 13.24 shows the 'Ribbon' menu under the 'Layout' tab. This allows
you to change the 'Page Setup', how the paragraphs are formatted and
how the elements are arranged.

▲ **Figure 13.24** Ribbon menu under Layout Tab

Paper size and page orientation

You may want to select the paper size and page orientation (portrait or
landscape) of your document before you begin to type in it.

Selecting the paper size and page orientation

1. Select **Page Layout/Layout** tab.
2. The 'Page Setup' group shows the commands available.
3. Click the **Orientation** drop-down arrow to select **Portrait** or **Landscape**.
4. Click the **Size** drop-down arrow to select the appropriate page size.

Selecting the paper size and page orientation using the Page Setup Dialog box

1   Select the **Dialog Box Launcher** from the 'Page Setup' group.
    The 'Page Setup' dialog box will appear. This box contains three tabs: 'Margins', 'Paper' and 'Layout'.

2   The **Margins** tab contains the options to select the page **Orientation** – **Portrait** (vertical) and **Landscape** (horizontal).

3   The **Paper** tab contains the option to select a paper size from the pull-down list provided or type in a width and height in the respective boxes for a custom size.

4   Click **OK**.

Margins

Margins are the blank areas around the work area of a sheet of paper, or the distance between the text and the edge of the paper. There are four margins: top, bottom, left and right. Then there is the gutter margin, which is the space allotted for binding. This is necessary so that work will not be hidden if the document is bound, that is, made into a booklet or book. A blank document in Word has a default setting of 1 inch (2.54 cm) for the top and bottom margins, 1.25 inches (3.175 cm) for the left and right margins, and 0 inches (0 cm) for the gutter. These default settings can be changed for the entire document or part of a document.

Changing margins using the Dialog box

1   Select the **Dialog Box Launcher** from the 'Page Setup' group.
    The 'Page Setup' dialog box appears (see Figure 13.25).

    This contains four options: 'Margins', 'Orientation', 'Pages' and 'Preview'.

    The 'Margins' tab dialog box displays the default values for the top, bottom, left, right and gutter margins.

2   These values can be changed by selecting the up arrow to increase the size or the down arrow to decrease the size of the respective margins, or by typing in the values.

3   As the values are changed a preview of how the document will change appears in the preview section.

4   You can change the margins for the whole document or from a particular point by selecting **Whole document** or **This point forward** in the 'Apply to:' section of the dialog box.

▲ Figure 13.25 'Page Setup' dialog box Margins Tab

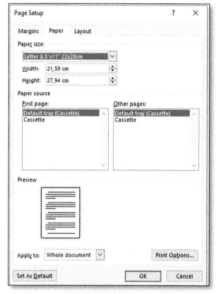

▲ Figure 13.26 'Page setup' dialog box Paper tab

Activity 7

1   Retrieve the document 'New Record-keeping Practices' you created earlier.

2   Change the left and right margins to 1.5 inches (3.81 centimetres).

3   Change the line spacing in the document to 1.5.

Headers and footers

A header or footer is text or graphics that appears in the top or bottom margins of every page in a document. The header appears in the top margin and the footer appears in the bottom margin. Headers and footers are usually used to print information such as the title of a document or chapter name and/or author name, page numbers, current date and time, letterheads and company logos. A different header and footer can be used for odd and even pages. The first page of a document can also have a different header and footer from the rest of the document.

▲ Figure 13.27 'Header & Footer' group on the 'Insert' tab

Creating a header and footer

1 Select **Header or Footer** from the 'Header & Footer' group of the 'Insert' tab. Or double click in the Header or Footer section of your document. The Header and Footer Design toolbar appears (see Figure 13.27).

You can type in the header in the 'Header 'textbox. Click on the **Switch between Header and Footer** button for the 'Footer' box to appear. Type in the footer. On screen, the text or graphics typed is displayed as dimmed, or lighter in colour.

Click the 'Insert' tab. The 'Header and Footer' drop-down arrow allows you to select from a variety of header and footer styles. It also allows you to edit the header or footer if 'Edit Header' or 'Edit Footer' is selected from the drop-down arrow. You can customise the header or footer from the 'Design' tab in the 'Header & Footer Tools' group.

▲ Figure 13.28 Word 2007 Header & Footer Tools Design

Deleting a header or footer

1 Double click in the header or footer section of your document. Or select the **Header** or **Footer** icon on the 'Insert' tab.
2 Select the 'Header' or 'Footer' text you want to delete.
3 Press **Backspace** or press **Delete**.
4 Click the **Close** button on the 'Header & Footer' toolbar to return to the document.

Footnotes and endnotes

You may want to insert a reference mark – such as a number, character or combination of characters – in the main body of your text, to indicate that additional information is provided elsewhere in the document to explain or expand on a word, a sentence or text. The reference is placed in a section of the document called a footnote or endnote (see Figure 13.29).

A footnote is placed at the end of the page containing the reference mark. It is usually positioned in the footer section of the page, below the text. Footnotes are usually used to expand the text and give detailed comments or explanations.

▲ Figure 13.29 A footnote

An endnote is placed at the end of the document or the end of a section (see Figure 13.30). Endnotes are often used for citing sources, for example, indicating another book that was used as a reference for the document that you are writing.

By default, Word places footnotes at the end of each page and endnotes at the end of the document.

Inserting a footnote or an endnote

1. Place the insertion point at the relevant section (that is, where the reference mark will be placed).
2. Choose the **References** tab (see Figure 13.31).
3. Select **Footnote**. The 'Footnote and Endnote' dialog box will appear (see Figure 13.32).
4. In the 'Location' section of the box, choose either **Footnotes** or **Endnotes** by clicking the radio buttons.
5. Select where you want to place the footnote or endnote.
6. Select the character (a number or custom mark/symbol) that will become your reference mark from the 'Format' section of the box.
7. If the reference mark is a number, select the starting number and whether you want to continue the numbering from the previous pages, or restart the numbering for each page or section.
8. Click the **Insert** button.

Click the 'References' tab. The 'Footnotes' group shows the commands available. (Display the 'Footnotes' dialog box by clicking the **Footnotes Dialog Box Launcher.**)

▲ Figure 13.30 Endnotes

▲ Figure 13.31 References tab

Deleting a footnote or an endnote

Delete the reference mark, not the text in the note. Word automatically renumbers the notes accordingly.

Page numbering

You will often want to number the pages of a document when it becomes longer than a few pages.

Inserting page numbers

Click the **Insert** tab. Click the **Page Number** icon in the 'Header & Footer' group; a drop-down menu will appear from which you can select where you would like to place the number (see Figure 13.33).

Page and section breaks

Word automatically determines the end of a page depending on the paper size selected. These automatic page breaks, which are called soft page breaks, can be seen as a single dotted line at the end of a page when you view the document in 'Normal' view. In 'Page Layout' view, you literally see the end of the page.

▲ Figure 13.32 'Footnote and Endnote' dialog box

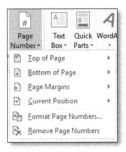

▲ Figure 13.33 Page number options

Despite this automatic function, you may still choose to insert a page break before the actual end of a page – for example, when you want to finish a section halfway down a page and start a new section immediately on the next page. This type of page break is called a hard page break and, once inserted, is seen as a solid horizontal line marked 'Page Break'.

Page breaks are used to control the lengths of a page, but we also have section breaks that control the formatting of a section. You might want to add a landscape formatted page in a portrait formatted document or have a section that uses a different header. To do this you would use a section break. These control the formatting of the text that comes before them, so a section break at the start of page 2 controls the formatting on page 1.

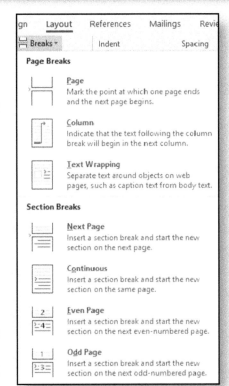

▲ Figure 13.34 Inserting a break

Inserting a hard page break

Position the insertion point where you would like to end the page.

You can click the **Page Break** icon in the 'Pages' group displayed on the 'Insert' tab or you can also select the **Breaks** icon from the 'Page Setup' group of the 'Page Layout' or 'Layout' tab.

Deleting a hard page break

1 Ensure the **Show/Hide** button in the 'Home' tab, 'Paragraph' group is in the 'on' position.
2 The page break will be displayed as a solid line, plus the words 'Page Break'.
3 Select the line and press the **Delete** key.

Inserting a section break

Position the insertion point where you would like to end the section.

You can click the **Breaks** icon from the 'Page Setup' group of the 'Page Layout' or 'Layout' tab. This gives you four options:

- **Next page**, which inserts a section break and starts the next section on a new page
- **Continuous**, inserts a section break and continues with the next section on the same pag
- **Even page**, which inserts a section break and start the new section on the next even-numbered page
- **Odd page**, which inserts a section break and start the new section on the next odd-numbered page

Activity 8

1 Retrieve the document 'Art' from your companion CD-ROM.
2 Move the article 'What is Art?' above the article 'Ancient Art'.
3 Centre and bold each article heading.
4 Insert a header 'The Artist Newsletter – Volume 1, Number 2'.
5 Right-align and italicise the header.
6 Insert automatic page numbering at the bottom centre of each page.
7 Double-space each article.
8 Change the left margin to 2" and all other margins to 1".
9 Insert the following footnote to refer to 'Paleolithic period' in the article 'Ancient Art'. Use this reference mark: 'The Paleolithic period refers to the second part of the Stone Age, beginning about 750,000 to 500,000 years BC, and lasting until the end of the last Ice Age, about 8,500 years BC.'
10 Spell-check the document.
11 Fully justify the paragraphs of the document.
12 Change the font size of each article to 16 points.
13 Save the document as 'Art Newsletter'.

Tabs

Tab stops are used to place text or numbers at predetermined positions in a document. This is a helpful feature that allows you to spread text or figures across a page evenly. The default tab position is 1.27 centimetres (or 0.5 inches). This means that every time the 'Tab' key is pressed, the cursor moves 1.27 centimetres (or 0.5 inches).

Tabs can be used for creating simple tabular-style documents or tables within a document. However, they are not an alternative to proper tables. You can also specify a particular character such as a full stop or a dash to precede a tab stop. Word offers five types of 'Tab' stops (see Table 13.6).

Tab	Function
Left	Text starts and is aligned at the tab stop
Right	Text ends at the tab stop
Centre	Text is centred under the tab stop
Decimal	Lines up the decimal point in numbers in a column at the tab stop
Bar	Creates a thin vertical line at the tab stop

▲ Table 13.6 Tabs and their functions

|
Tab stop button on ruler

▲ Figure 13.35 Setting tabs using the Ruler

Setting tabs

Click the **Home** tab or the **Page Layout** or **Layout** tab. Display the 'Paragraph' dialog box by clicking the **Paragraph Dialog Box Launcher**. Clicking the **Tabs...** button at the bottom of the dialog box will display the 'Tabs' dialog box (see Figure 13.36).

Setting tab stops using the ruler

1 Click on the **Tab Alignment** button at the extreme left of the ruler until the desired icon is displayed (see Figure 13.35). Click on the ruler where you want to place a tab stop for the paragraph.

Removing or moving a tab stop

1 Select the paragraph(s) that contains the tab stop markers you want to remove or change.
2 Drag the tab stop marker off the ruler to remove it. **OR**
3 Drag the tab stop to the left or right to change its position.

Clearing tab stops

1 In the 'Tabs' dialog box, select the tab and click on **Clear** to select one at a time or click on **Clear All** to remove all the tabs.

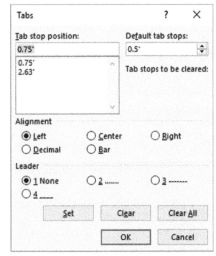

▲ Figure 13.36 'Tabs' dialog box

Activity 9

1 Type the following menu, setting a centre tab at 1.5" (3.81 cm) and a decimal tab with dots leader (...) at 4" (10.16 cm).
2 Centre the heading.
3 Change the font to 'Bookman Old Style'.
4 Change the font size to 14 points.
5 Below is a list of five students with their corresponding student number, name, mass (kg), height (cm) and age.

    111, Tricia Bridgemohan, 40.5, 110.5, 16
    112, Kizzy Joe-Johnson, 45.2, 180.3, 15
    113, Phillip McIsaac, 50.6, 141.0, 17
    114, Dwane Philips, 49.3, 150.2, 16
    115, Richard Williamson, 66.0, 195.3, 18

a Type out the data in a tabular format with the given headings, using appropriate tabs.
b Separate each column with a vertical line.
c Bold and underline each heading.

Breakfast Special	
Bake and Shark	$5.00
Bake and Saltfish	$3.50
Egg and Toast	$2.00
Cowheel Soup	$11.25
Tea	$1.50
Coffee	$2.00
Juice	$3.00

Drawing a line

In Word, you can also draw objects, the simplest of which is a line. A line is treated as an object and can, therefore, be moved. However, a point to note is that underlining is associated with text and cannot be moved by itself. It has to be moved with the accompanying text.

Drawing lines

Click the 'Insert' tab. Click **Shapes** from the Illustrations group; a drop-down listing will appear from which you can select the type of line object you desire (see Figure 13.37).

1 In your document, move the indicator to the desired starting position for your line.
2 Click, hold and drag the mouse button to make the line, in any direction you wish.
3 Click off the line to deselect.

You can also select **Drawing Canvas** from the 'Shapes' drop-down menu in which you are to perform your drawing. If you do not want to draw within this designated area, press the 'Esc' key to remove the 'Drawing Canvas'.

Mail merge

The mail merge feature can produce large volumes of personalised letters, mailing labels, memos and emails without having to type each one individually for each recipient. For example, many companies send standard letters to customers in which the body of the letter is the same but the name, address and a few pieces of additional information may be different. This type of multi-recipient correspondence can be produced easily using mail merge. Merging requires the use of two files: the main document (primary file) and a data source (secondary file). Data from the data source is inserted into the main document to produce personalised documents. Figure 13.38 on the next page shows a diagram of the mail merge process.

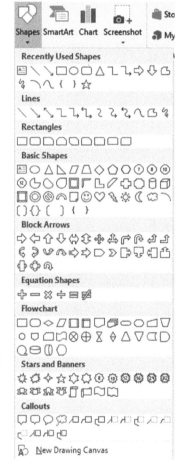

▲ Figure 13.37 'Shapes' drop-down menu

The mail merge process works as follows:

- The main document (or primary file) contains the letter or other document that is meant for each recipient. It also contains the merge fields, which are positioned at the points where the information from the data source is to be inserted. When the mail merge begins, the merge fields are replaced with the information from the data source.
- The data source (or secondary file) contains the personalised information that would vary in each document, such as the names and addresses of individuals. The data source can be an existing data source, or you can create a new data source by using the 'Mail Merge Helper'.

The information stored in the data source is organised in the form of a table. The first row, known as the header row, contains the merge fields. A merge field is the name of a data item that will be stored in the data source and later be merged into the main document. Some common field names are Title, Firstname, Address, Phoneno, and so on. When creating merge fields, you must ensure that each merge field:

- is unique
- begins with a letter
- contains no more than 40 characters
- does not contain any blank spaces.

Each row after the header row contains the information that is unique to each document and is known as a data record. The collection of data records is called a data file.

Creating the main document

You can create the main document before you access the Step-by-Step 'Mail Merge Wizard Task Pane'. The areas designated to hold the data that will be unique to each recipient could be indicated as blank spaces, or by typing dummy field names enclosed in double angle-brackets, for example, << Name >>. This is necessary so that the field codes will be inserted in the correct positions, even though the actual codes will not be available to be inserted into the main document until you have created the data source document.

The following are steps to create a mail merge document (see Figure 13.39):

1. Decide on the type of document you are going to create, for example, letter, email message, label, envelope, directory.
2. Decide on the starting document: either use the currently active document or open a document from storage.
3. Change the document layout if necessary (for envelopes and labels only).
4. Decide on the recipients: decide what data source to use, that is, whether to create it or to use an existing data source.

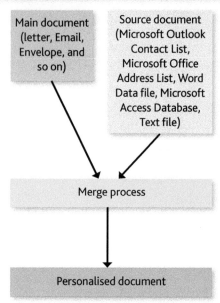

▲ Figure 13.38 Diagram of the mail merge process

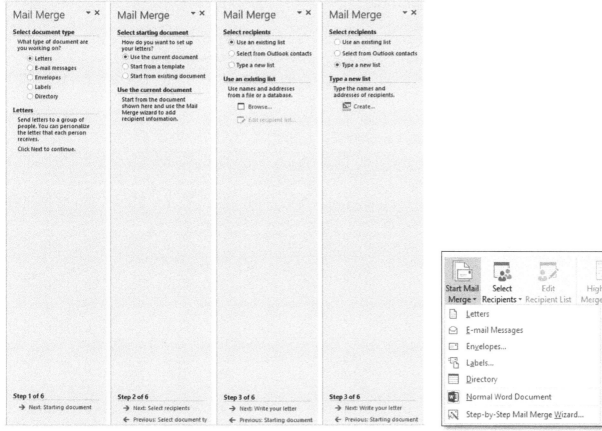

▲ Figure 13.39 Steps In the 'Mail Merge' menu

▲ Figure 13.40 'Start Mail Merge' options

Starting the mail merge

Step 1: Click the **Mailings** tab. In the Start Mail Merge group, select **Start Mail Merge** followed by **Letters** from the drop-down menu (see Figure 13.40).

Creating the data source

Step 2: In the Start Mail Merge group on the **Mailings** tab, choose **Select Recipients** followed by **Type a New List** from the drop-down menu (see Figure 13.41).

▲ Figure 13.41 'Select Recipients' options

Step 3: The 'New Address List' dialog box appears. You can customise the predefined fields by clicking the **Customize Columns** button (see Figure 13.42).

Step 4: Fill in the information for a record by clicking **New Entry**.

Step 5: Save the address list by clicking **OK**.

Step 6: Insert the merge fields. Click on the **Mailings** tab. Select **Insert Merge Field** from the 'Write & Insert Fields' group (see Figure 13.43).

Step 7: Place the fields in their respective locations.

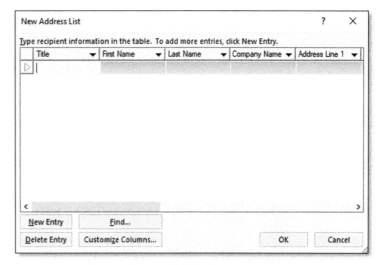

▲ Figure 13.42 'New Address List' dialog box

Step 8: Click the **Mailings** tab. Select **Finish & Merge** from the Finish group (see Figure 13.44). You can merge to a new document by selecting **Edit Individual Documents** from the drop-down list.

Renaming, deleting or adding fields

1 a Choose the **Customize** button. The 'Customize Address List' dialog box will appear.

  b Select the field you want to delete or rename and click the **Delete** or **Rename** button.

  c To add a field, click the **Add** button. The 'Add Field' dialog box will appear. Type the name of the field and click **OK**.

  d You can rearrange the order of the fields in your list by clicking on the field and then clicking the **Move Up** or **Move Down** button.

  e After you have finished customising your listing and entering all the field names, click **OK**. You will be returned to the 'New Address List' dialog box (see Figure 13.42).

2 Fill in the information for one record. To fill in another record, click **New Entry**. After filling in all the records, click **Close**.

3 A dialog box entitled 'Save Address List' will appear (see Figure 13.45). Type a name for the data file and click on **Save**.

4 The 'Mail Merge Recipients' box will appear, showing all records that are listed in the data source (see Figure 13.46).

5 You have now created the data source. Click **OK**.

6 The main document appears and the **Insert Merge Field** button in the Mailings tab is activated. The next step is to insert the merge fields into the main document.

The 'Write & Insert Fields' ribbon menu (Figure 13.47) becomes available at this point in the mail merge process.

▲ Figure 13.43 'Insert Merge Field'

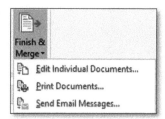

▲ Figure 13.44 'Finish & Merge'

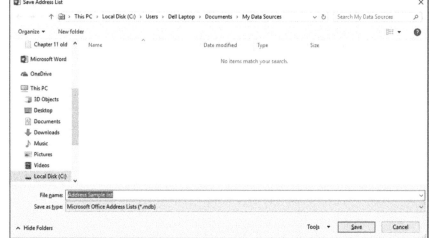

▲ Figure 13.45 'Save Address List' dialog box

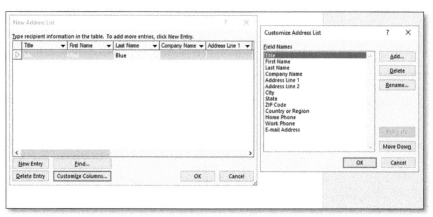

▲ Figure 13.46 'Mail Merge Recipients' box

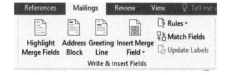

▲ Figure 13.47 'Write and Insert Fields'

Inserting the merge fields

1 Position your insertion point where the first merge field is to be inserted into the document.
2 Click on the **Insert Merge Field** button. The 'Insert Merge Field' dialog box appears (see Figure 13.48).
3 Select the desired field and click the **Insert** button. The field appears in the position you indicated (see Figure 13.49).
4 Place all the other fields in their respective positions.

Updating the data source

Once you have created a data source, you can make changes to it later.

1 Click on the **Mailings** tab and click **Edit Recipient List**; the 'Mail Merge Recipients' dialog box appears.
2 Under the 'Data Source' section, select the data file you would like to edit.
3 Select **Edit**.
4 The 'Address List' dialog box appears. Choose **Customize** and follow the instructions to rename, delete and add fields, as you wish.

Deleting a record

1 Click on the **Mailings** tab and click **Edit Recipient List**; the 'Mail Merge Recipients' dialog box appears.
2 a Uncheck the boxes to remove the records from the mail merge. **OR**
  b Click the **Edit** button, select the record to be deleted from the 'Address List' dialog box and click **Delete Entry**.

Editing a record

1 Click on the **Mailings** tab and click **Edit Recipient List**; the 'Mail Merge Recipients' dialog box appears (see Figure 13.50).
2 Click on the **Edit** button.
3 Select the record to be edited and select the data item; insert, change or replace the existing data as you wish.

▲ Figure 13.48 'Insert Merge Field' dialog box

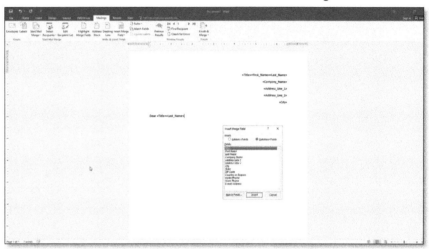

▲ Figure 13.49 Inserting the merge fields in their correct positions

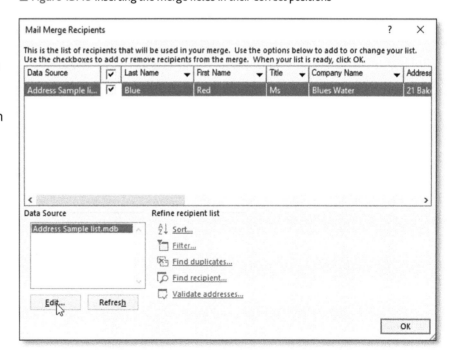

▲ Figure 13.50 'Mail Merge Recipients' dialog box

Activity 10

Patients of the Diamond Valley Clinic are sent letters to remind them of their appointment date and what they are required to bring with them.

1 Type in this document below to be used in a mail merge and save it to a file called 'Appointment Reminders'.
2 Indent the name and address of the clinic to 4 inches (10.16 centimetres).
3 Create a secondary document, called 'Patients', using the following data as a basis:

Title	Mr
Patient First Name	Martin
Patient Surname	Jades
Patient Address	65 Pine Drive, Mavewood Park
Time	9.30 a.m.
Appointment Date	1/6/19
Date of Last Visit	2/1/19
Doctor	James Mahabir
Sample	Urine
Title	Ms
Patient First Name	Leselle
Patient Surname	Kotes
Patient Address	Banana Bread Lane, Diamond Village
Time	2.00 p.m.
Appointment Date	10/6/19
Date of Last Visit	22/3/19
Doctor	James Mahabir
Sample	Stool

4 Add THREE records of your own to the data file.
5 Delete the 'Patient First Name' field from the data file.
6 Merge the two files to produce the personalised letters to be sent to patients.
7 Save the letters to a file called 'Appointment Letters'.

Diamond Valley Clinic   28 Diamond Boulevard   Cape Town

<Title> <First Name> <Last Name><Address Line 1><Address Line 2>

Dear <Title> <Last Name>,

This is to remind you of your appointment with us at <time> on <appointment date>. This is a follow-up of your last visit on <date of last visit>. Please bring this letter when you arrive at the Medical Out-Patient Consultant No. 3. You will be attended to by Dr. <Doctor>.

Please bring a sample of <sample>.

Yours respectfully,

_____

Clinic Administrator

Newspaper columns

Text columns are a very useful feature when you want to produce newsletters, newspaper-style documents, indexes or any text that needs to be in continuous columns. When the first column is filled at the bottom of the page, the text continues in the next column at the top of the page. Figure 13.51 shows a page divided into into three columns. When the first column is completed, the insertion point goes to the start of the second column.

Creating columns

1 Click the **Page Layout** or **Layout** tab, choose **Columns** from the 'Page Setup' group; a drop-down menu will appear allowing you to make a selection as to the number of columns. Clicking **More Columns** opens the 'Columns' options box (Figure 13.52), allowing you to select three or more columns or left and right columns.

2 Select the number of columns required by clicking on one of the presets; or move to the 'Number of columns' section and use the up-arrow to increase the number of columns or the down-arrow to decrease the number of columns.

3 The 'Width and spacing' section allows you to specify the width of each column and the spacing between them. A preview of the selections made can be seen in the 'Preview' section.

4 The 'Apply to' box lets you choose between formatting the entire document or formatting it just from a specified point.

You can also insert columns by using the 'Columns' button in the 'Page Setup' group of the 'Layout' tab. Clicking on this button produces a drop-down set of icons, from which you can select the number of columns required. These columns would all be of equal width. However, note that the width of a column and the spacing between columns cannot be changed when the 'Columns' button is used.

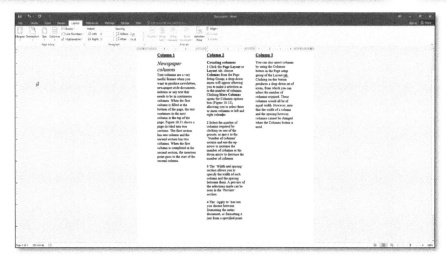

▲ Figure 13.51 Document with several columns

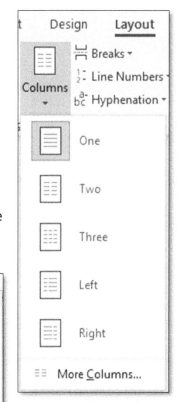

▲ Figure 13.52 'Columns' options

Column break

The position in a column where the text ends and the next column starts is called a column break. If a document has two columns and you reach a particular point in the first column where you would like to finish and start the next column, you can insert a column break.

Inserting a column break

1 Position the insertion point where you want to end the column.

2 Select **Breaks** from the 'Page Layout' or 'Layout' tab. A drop-down menu appears (Figure 13.53).

3 Select **Column** from the list.

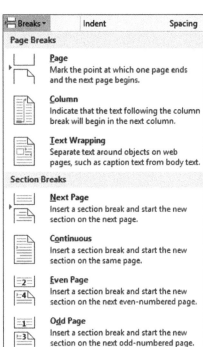

◀ Figure 13.53 'Page Breaks' and 'Section Breaks' menu

Activity 11

The Royal Bank of Grenada produces a newsletter called Bank News. The articles shown below are to be included in the next newsletter. You will create the document by doing the following:

1 Type out the articles for the document, as shown opposite.
2 Insert a title-heading, 'Bank News', in at least 24-point text.
3 Centre and bold the heading. Ensure that it uses a large font.
4 Use a bold font and capital letters for the title of each article – at least 18-point text.
5 Use at least 14-point text for the body of each article.
6 Double line-space each article.
7 Change the left and right margins to 1.5 inches (3.81 centimetres) and the top and bottom margins to 1.25 inches (3.175 centimetres).
8 Format the document using two newspaper-style columns. The title-heading should not be part of any column.
9 Insert the following header into every page of the document:
   ■ Bank News, Volume 3, Number 8
10 Insert the page number into the footer. Centre the page number.
11 Fully justify each article.
12 Correct all spelling and any grammatical errors in the document.
13 Save the document as 'Bank News'.

Here are the articles for the newsletter:
Staff Departures

The bank would like to express its sincere appreciation to the following for their services, which will be sadly missed:

■ Mr Frank Jackson, Accounts Development Officer, West Cape branch, has resigned his position with effect from 27 July 2019. Mr Jackson was employed at the bank continuously over the last seven years.

■ Miss Janet Jebodsingh, Regional Manager, Wester Isle, has resigned her position with effect from 11 June 2019. Miss Jebodsingh served the bank for eleven years.

New Staff
The bank would like to welcome the following new employees:

■ Mrs Laura Ellison has been employed as a computer programmer in the M.I.S. department at headquarters and will take up her position on 23 August 2019.
■ Mr Alton Royal has been employed as a teller in the South Wiscombe branch and will take up his position on 10 August 2019.

Staff Promotions
The bank would like to congratulate Sheena MacDonald, currently Junior Accounts Supervisor at headquarters, on being promoted to the position of Accounting Supervisor for West Cape branch. Miss MacDonald will move to the branch on 3 September 2019.

Training News: Seminar on Money Laundering
The Bank's Inspection Department will be conducting a seminar for supervisors between 10 and 14 October 2019, at the training centre at headquarters. The seminar is designed to empower all staff with the necessary skills to spot, report and explain possible cases of money laundering occurring in customers' accounts.

Supervisors attending the seminar will conduct knowledge-sharing presentations at their respective branches upon their return.

Sport News
The Bank's Annual Sports and Family Fun Day, 2019, will be held at the Centre of Excellence at headquarters, on 25 July 2019, from 10:00 a.m. All branches are asked to elect their team captains and start making preparations for this grand annual event. There will be events for the whole family, such as games, team sports, music, and of course, the barbecue. Branches of the bank will distribute tickets nearer the time of the event.

Tables

Tables are very useful for displaying numerical and statistical data within a document, and can also be useful for keeping text aligned. They are one way of enhancing the presentation of data within documents.
A table is made up of three components: rows, columns and cells.

1. A row runs horizontally
2. A column runs vertically
3. A cell is an individual 'box' in the table, in which you place data. It is at the intersection of a row and a column.
4. Information can be inserted in the table by placing the insertion point in the appropriate cell and typing.

Inserting a table

1. Click on **Insert** tab in the 'Table' group, a drop-down box will appear.
2. You can choose to insert the table using the grid or the 'Insert Table' dialog box
3. When using the grid, drag the mouse down to select the number of rows and then right to select the number of columns. A highlighted grid of the number of rows and columns is displayed as you are selecting (Figure 13.54). Release the mouse button; the table will be inserted into the document.
4. When using the 'Insert Table' icon, the 'Insert Table' dialog box appears (Figure 13.55). Make the appropriate selections and click **OK**.

Click anywhere in the table and 'Table Tools' appear at the end of the 'Word' ribbon.

Adding rows and columns in a table

1. Place the insertion point in the row or column next to where you would like to insert the new row or column.
2. Select **Insert** from the 'Table' menu. A drop-down list with the following options appears: Columns to the 'Left', Columns to the 'Right', 'Rows Above', 'Rows Below' and 'Cells' (see Figure 13.56).
3. Clicking on the desired option places the new row or column in the position relative to the selected row or column.

Deleting a row or column

1. Place the insertion point in the row or column you would like to delete.
2. Select **Delete** from the 'Table' menu. A drop-down list with the following options appears: 'Table', 'Column', 'Row', 'Cells'.
3. Select the desired option.

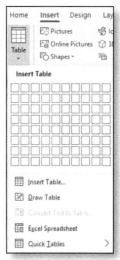

▲ Figure 13.54 'Table' drop-down menu

▲ Figure 13.55 'Insert Table' dialog box

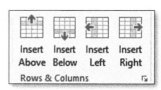

▲ Figure 13.56 'Rows & Columns' drop-down menu

Drawing a table using the Tables and Borders toolbar

You can draw tables using the 'Tables and Borders' toolbar.

Displaying the 'Tables and Borders' toolbar

1 Select **Toolbars** from the 'View' menu.
2 Click on **Tables and Borders** from the drop-down list.
3 The 'Tables and Borders' toolbar is displayed (Figure 13.57).

▲ Figure 13.57 'Tables and Borders' toolbar

Drawing the table

1 Click on the **Draw Table** button (the 'table-and-pencil' icon).
2 Change the line weight if necessary, that is, the line thickness. (Click on the 'line weight' drop-down arrow.)
3 The mouse pointer is displayed as a pencil. At the insertion point, press and hold the mouse button. Drag the pencil to draw tables and add lines.

Deleting lines

In the latest versions of Word, you can easily delete individual lines within tables.

1 Click on the **Eraser** button on the toolbar. The pointer becomes an eraser.
2 Click on the line to be erased.

▲ Figure 13.58 Table Tools showing the 'Design' and 'Layout' tabs

'Table Tools' allows you to select two options, 'Table Design' or 'Layout'. Click on the **Layout** tab option (see Figure 13.58).
In the 'Rows & Columns' group, to insert a row select **Insert Above** or **Insert Below**, and to insert a column, select **Insert Left** or **Insert Right** (see Figure 13.59).

▲ Figure 13.59 'Table Tools' showing the 'Layout' tab

To delete a row or column, click on **Delete** in the 'Rows & Columns' group and choose from the options shown (see Figure 13.60).

▲ Figure 13.60 Deleting rows and columns

Styling a table using the Design menu

Once you have created a table, clicking anywhere in it will cause two new tabs 'Design' and 'Layout 'to appear in the menu. Selecting 'Design' gives you options to change the style of the table, by adding shading, adding borders and styling them (see Figure 13.61).

▲ Figure 13.61 'Table Tools' showing the 'Design' menu

Adding table styles

The quickest way to style a table is to use one of the ready-made styles. These styles change the font, font colour and font styles in the table, as well as the borders and border styles, and the background shading. Many of these ready-made styles offer a quick way of creating an attractive and easy-to-read table.

To change the style, click inside the table and then click on the style you want. This modifies (changes) the whole table.

Adding shading

You can add a background colour to a cell or group of cells in a table by selecting the cell or cells and then clicking on the 'shading' icon and picking a colour, or picking no colour to remove the shading.

Adding or changing borders

If you select a cell, a group of cells or the whole table, you can use the 'Borders' group to change the border styles. The 'Borders' drop-down menu lets you choose which borders to display, and if you select the style, thickness and colour from the menus to the left, these options allow you to change just the parts of the border you choose. 'Border Painter' allows you to change the style of borders that you draw over with the mouse. When you select this option, the cursor changes to a paintbrush.

Changing the layout of a table

As we mentioned above, creating a table in the document will bring up two new tabs. Here we are looking at the second of these, 'Layout' menus. (see Figure 13.62).

▲ Figure 13.62 'Table Tools' showing the 'Layout' menu

Inserting and deleting rows and columns

In the menu, the 'Rows & Columns' group allows you to access 'Insert' and 'Delete' columns and rows.

- 'Insert' allows you to insert rows above and below the row selected. If you select one row, then one row is added, but if you select, say three rows, then three are inserted. 'Insert Left' and 'Insert Right' work in a similar way, but insert columns.
- 'Delete' has a drop-down menu that lets you delete the selected cell; the column the cell is in; the row the cell is in or the whole table.

Merge cells

The 'Merge' group lets you join and split cells. 'Merge Cells' lets you join the selected cells. You might use this in a table in which you want to use one heading above or beside several cells, as shown in Table 13.7.

Month	Sales			
	North	East	South	West
January	$40,000.00	$25,000.00	$18,000.00	$35,000.00

▲ Table 13.7 Merging cells to create a heading

The 'Split Cells' command lets you do the opposite – it lets you split a cell across one or more rows or columns. In our example above, if we wanted to add the year that the sales are in, we could split the 'Month' cell across two rows, move 'Month' to the lower cell and put the year in the top-left cell.

The 'Split Table' feature allows you to split the table along the row underneath the cell selected. This only works along a row.

Alignment

The 'Alignment' group lets you change how the text is placed inside a cell. The nine boxes of 'Cell Alignment' show how the text is aligned horizontally and vertically. Selecting one or more cells and clicking on one of these will change the alignment to match the icon.

'Text Direction' changes the direction of the text of the selected cell or cells. Clicking on the button cycles through horizontal, vertically down and vertically up.

'Cell Margin' changes the space above, below, to the left and to the right of the contents of the cell, putting more or less space around them. This can help to make what is in the cell easier to read, or to squeeze a big table onto a page.

Cell size

Autofit adjusts the size of the cells depending on which option you select:

- 'Autofit contents' changes the row height and column width to match the largest item in each.
- 'Autofit Window' keeps the proportion of the table, but stretches it to fit the width between the margins.
- 'Fixed Column Width' sets each cell to the height and width in the boxes to the right.
- 'Distribute Rows' and 'Distribute Columns' set the row height or column width equally across the width of the table. This is useful for making a table you have edited or added to look more even.

Activity 12

1 Here is a list of some foods we typically eat and the approximate amount of energy we get from them, measured in kilojoules.
- A portion of fish   363
- A portion of potatoes   129
- One boiled egg   380
- A slice of bread and butter   180
- One peanut   25
- One carrot   85

a Create a table with TWO rows and TWO columns.

b Put the information above into the table under the headings 'Food' and 'Energy'.

2 Information about the planets in the Solar System is listed below, in the following order: Planet; Diameter (km); Distance from the Sun (millions of km); and length of a year.
- Mercury; 4,840; 58; 88 Earth days
- Venus; 12,200; 108; 225 Earth days
- Earth; 12,800; 150; 365 Earth days
- Mars; 6,750; 228; 687 Earth days
- Jupiter; 143,000; 778; 12 Earth years
- Saturn; 121,000; 1,430; 29 Earth years
- Uranus; 47,200; 2,870; 84 Earth days
- Neptune; 44,600; 4,500; 154 Earth years

a Create a table with TWO rows and FOUR columns.

b Put the information above into the table under headings in the appropriate columns.

c Centre justify the data in the second and third columns.

Inserting graphics

Graphics are another way of enhancing the presentation of a document. Word allows you to search your computer or online for pictures. You can also scan drawings or photos using a scanner, or download graphics from a digital camera or the internet, saving these to a graphics file that can be inserted into documents.

Inserting a graphic into a document

1 Place the I-beam to the left of the point where you want the graphic displayed.

2 Click on the **Pictures** icon from the 'Illustrations' group of the 'Insert' tab.

3 Choose the graphic by searching for it on your computer.

4 Click the picture once and then click on **Insert** to insert the graphic in the document.

If you are not happy with the position and/or size of the graphic, you can change both quite easily.

Resizing a graphic

1 Click once on the graphic. The graphic is displayed with eight selection handles around it (Figure 13.63). Placing the mouse pointer on the selection handles changes the mouse pointer to a double-headed arrow (vertical, horizontal or diagonal).

2 Follow these steps to reduce or enlarge the graphic proportionately:

a Click on any of the corner handles (the mouse pointer becomes diagonal double-headed arrows).

b Drag away from the centre of the graphic to enlarge.

c Drag towards the centre of the graphic to reduce.

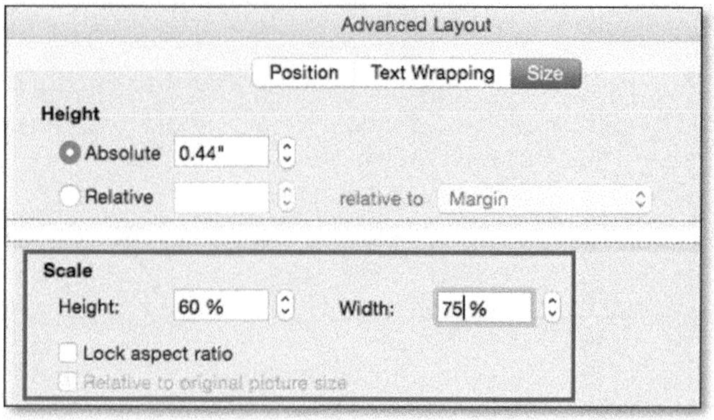

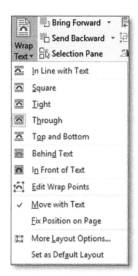

▲ Figure 13.63 Resizing a graphic

Changing the position of the graphic

1 Place the mouse pointer anywhere within the graphic except on any of the eight handles.

2 Click and hold down the left mouse button within the handles until a small square appears on the tail of the pointer.

3 The graphic can then be dragged to the desired position.

Wrapping text around a graphic

When a graphic is placed in a document, by default the text is placed at the top and bottom of the graphic. However, it may be necessary – especially in the case of newsletters, newspapers and magazines – to have the text flow or wrap around the graphic, to save space and enhance presentation (Figure 13.64).

▲ Figure 13.64 Text can be wrapped around a graphic

▲ Figure 13.65 'Wrap Text' drop-down menu options

Click on the graphic and the Format tab appears at the end of the Ribbon. In the 'Arrange' group click the **Wrap Text** icon; a drop-down menu will appear, allowing you to make your selection (see Figure 13.65).

Inserting a border or effects for a graphic

1 Click once on the picture to select the picture; the 'Format' tab will appear at the end of the ribbon.

2 In the 'Picture Styles' group, select **Picture Border** and choose the colour, weight, no outline or dashes (see Figure 13.66).

3 You can also select the **Picture Effects** from the 'Picture Styles' group (see Figure 13.66).

Inserting symbols and characters

In a number of cases, you may be required to prepare documents that need symbols that do not appear as keys on the keyboard. For example, p, 4, and a are all symbols that might be part of a document. These can be found in the 'Symbol' dialog box as shown in Figure 13.67. These symbols and characters are easily inserted in a document.

Inserting a symbol/special character

1 Click the **Insert** tab. In the 'Symbols' group, click on the 'Symbol' drop-down menu. If the symbol or character is not in the list shown, click 'More symbols', which will display the 'Symbol' dialog box.

2 Select the desired symbol.

3 Position the insertion point where you want the symbol/special character inserted. Click on **Insert**.

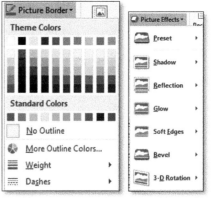

'Picture Border' options   'Picture Effect' options

▲ Figure 13.66 Picture border and effect options

▲ Figure 13.67 'Symbol' dialog box

Activity 13

1 Enter the following text and save it as 'Math Notes'.

  1 Acceleration is the rate of increase of velocity. If v is velocity, and a is the acceleration of an object at time t, then:

$$v = Ú\ a\ dt$$

  2 The angle between two lines where O is the origin and A and B are points, one on each line passing through O, each point being 1 unit of distance from O.

$$|AO| = 1$$

A has coordinates (p_1, m_1, n_1)

B has coordinates (p_2, m_2, n_2)

Therefore $(AB)^2 = (p_2 - p_1)^2 + (m_2 - m_1)^2 + (n_2 - n_1)^2$

$$= Âp_1{}^2 + Âp_2{}^2 - 2Âp_1p_2$$

   a Insert the heading 'Vectors'.

   b Italicise the coordinates p, m and n.

   c Change the numbering to bullets.

2 Create the following table.

Traditional	Arcade	Puzzles
Solitaire	Pacman	Big Money
Chess	Ping Pong	Mah-jong
Scrabble	AstroPop	Bejeweled
Hangman	Heavy Weapon	Mummy Maze

a Bold and centre the headings.

b Autofit to the contents of the table.

c Insert a column to the right of the Puzzles column and insert the heading 'Word'.

d Enter the following data for the Word column: Bookworm, Psychobabble, Text twist, Typer Shark

3 Retrieve the document 'Art Newsletter' that you saved earlier.

a Insert a title for the document 'Art is Life'.

b Centre and bold the title and increase the font size to a size larger than in the rest of the document, including the subheadings.

c Change the line spacing to 1.5.

d Centre the header in a smaller font that is used elsewhere in the document.

e Except for the title of the document, format the rest of the document in two fully justified newspaper columns.

f Remove the page numbering from the first page.

g Insert an appropriate graphic of your choice, within the article 'What is Art' with square text wrapping.

h Save your document.

Creating a fillable form in Word

Fillable forms allow you to enter data easily in a predesigned fillable document. Word now allows you to create a form in which you can fill in the contents. Content controls allow you to enter text in boxes, select options by clicking checkboxes, use date pickers, and select from the drop-down list. To create these fillable forms, we start by creating a template. A 'Template document' is a document saved with some predesigned features using a special format. Once opened, this document can be modified and/or the details filled in.

Before creating a 'Fillable form', the 'Developer' tab must be added to the ribbon if it is not visible.

Adding the Developer tab to the Word ribbon

- Click the **File** tab, click on **Options** and click on **Customize Ribbon**.
- Under 'Customize the Ribbon', under 'Main Tabs', select the **Developer** check box, and click **OK**.

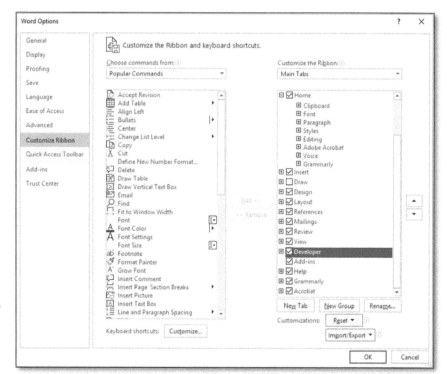

▲ Figure 13.68 'Customize Ribbon' dialog box

▲ Figure 13.69 The 'Developer' tab once added to the ribbon

Starting from blank document

1 Open a blank document by clicking on the **File** tab and then **New**.
2 Click on **Blank Document**.
3 Create your form by adding content to it.

If you already have a form created, you can open it or select an already-created form from the online templates.

1 Open an online template by clicking on the **File** tab and then **New**.
2 In the 'Search online template' box, type in the kind of form you would like to create and press the **Enter** key.
3 Select the template you want and then click **Create**.

On the 'Developer' tab, click the **Design Mode** icon, and then insert the controls that you want. To exit 'Design Mode', click the **Design Mode** icon again and view your fillable form.

Inserting a text control

A text control allows users to enter text into a form. There are two types of text controls:

- **Rich text content control** allows the user to format the text (for example, bold, italics, underline and allows for long paragraphs).
- **Plain text** content control limits what the users can add.

1 Click where you want to insert the control.
2 On the 'Developer' tab in the 'Controls' group, click the **Rich Text Content Control** icon or the **Plain Text Content Control** icon (see Figure 13.70).
3 Set the specific properties on the control (see setting or changing the properties for content control).

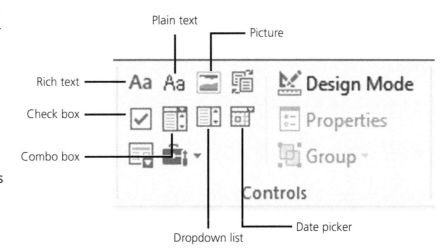

▲ Figure 13.70 'Text Content Control' dialog box

Inserting a Picture Control

You can also add a picture control to a form where you want the user to insert a picture.

1 Click where you want to insert the control.
2 On the 'Developer' tab in the 'Controls' group, click **Picture Content Control**.
3 Set the specific properties on the control (see setting or changing the properties for content control).

Inserting a combo box or drop-down list

A combo box allows users to select from a list of choices or type in their own information. A drop-down list allows users to only select from the list of choices provided.

1 On the 'Developer' tab in the 'Control' group, click the **Combo Box Content Control** icon or the **Drop-Down List Content Control** icon.

Setting or changing the properties of Content Controls

Each 'Content Control' has properties that you can set or change. For example, the properties of 'Date Picker Control' allows you to select options for how you would like to display the date that is the date format.

1 Select the **Content Control**, and then click on the **Developer** tab in the 'Control' group, and then click **Properties**.
2 To create a list of choices or options, click **Add** under the 'Drop-Down List Properties'.
3 Type your options in the 'Display Name' box.
4 Repeat this step until all of the choices or options are in the drop-down list.

If the 'Contents cannot be edited' check box is selected, users would not be able to make a selection. If you want users to replace the specified text with their own, do not check the 'Contents cannot be edited' check box.

Inserting a date picker

1 Click where you want to insert the 'Date Picker Content Control'.
2 On the 'Developer' tab in the 'Controls' group, click the **Date Picker Content Control**.
3 Set the specific properties on the control (see setting or changing the properties for content control).

Inserting a checkbox

1 Click where you want to insert the checkbox control.
2 On the 'Developer' tab in the 'Controls' group, click the **Check Box Content Control**.
3 Set the specific properties on the control (see setting or changing the properties for content control).

Inserting instructional text

Instructional text gives the user of the form instructions on how and what is needed to fill in the form. It enhances the form by making it more user-friendly.

1 On the 'Developer' tab in the 'Control' group, click the **Design Mode** icon.
2 Click the content control of the placeholder of the instructional text.
3 Edit the instructional text and format it any way you want.
4 Set the specific properties on the control (see setting or changing the properties for Content Control).

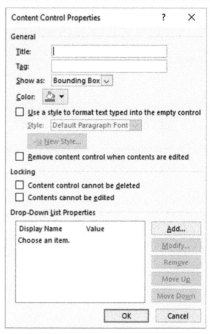

▲ Figure 13.71 Content Control Properties

Did you know?

Fillable forms can be printed; however, the boxes around the 'Content Controls' will not be printed.

Adding protection to a form

You may want to restrict what users and others can change in your document. The 'Restrict Editing' command prevents or limits users from editing or formatting a form.

1   Open the form that you want to lock or protect.
2   Click the **Home** tab; in the 'Editing' group, click **Select**, and choose **Select All** or **Select Objects**.
3   Click the **Developer** tab; in the 'Protect' group, click **Restrict Editing**.
4   Select the appropriate restrictions.
5   Click **Yes, Start Enforcing Protection**.

Creating a table of contents

Word can automatically create the table of contents for any document that you may be writing. You will need to set the headings and subheadings in your document using heading styles so that Word can recognise that these are the headings you want in your table of contents.

Setting heading styles

For each of the headings that you want as part of your table of contents, do the following:

- Select the text for the heading.
- On your 'Home' tab, from the 'Styles' group, select **Heading 1** for the main heading or **Heading 2** for the subheading (see Figure 13.72).

▲ Figure 13.72 Heading 'Styles' menu

Inserting a table of contents

Place the cursor in your document where you want the insert the table of contents.

Click on the **References** tab, in the 'Table of Contents' group, click on the **Table of Contents** icon and choose 'Automatic Table 1', 'Automatic Table 2' or 'Custom Table of Contents' to create your own style (see Figure 13.73).

Once changes are made to your document, you will need to update the table of contents as it does not automatically change if you have added or deleted information from your document. A 'Table of Contents' example is shown in Figure 13.74 on the next page.

Updating your table of contents

1   Place your mouse pointer over the table of contents, and the 'Update Table' icon will appear (see Figure 13.75 on the next page).
2   You can also select 'Update Table' from the 'Table of Contents' group of the 'References' tab.
3   You can choose to update the entire table or only the page numbers.

Exercise 2

1   Retrieve the document 'Doggie Day Care Registration Form'.
2   Save the document as a template.
3   Format the form by including an appropriate logo in the Header area.
4   Centre and bold the heading of the form.
5   Insert appropriate controls to make the document a fillable document: 'Text Content Control' ('Rich' or 'Plain'), 'Date Picker Content Control', 'Combo Box Content Control' and 'Drop-down List Control'.
6   Create a 'Picture Content Control' on the form for persons to attach a copy of their dog's vaccination document.

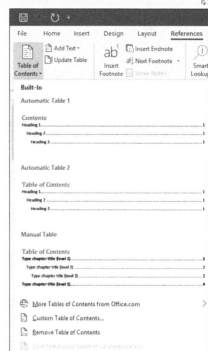

▲ Figure 13.73 'Table of Contents' menu

▲ Figure 13.74 A typical Table of Contents

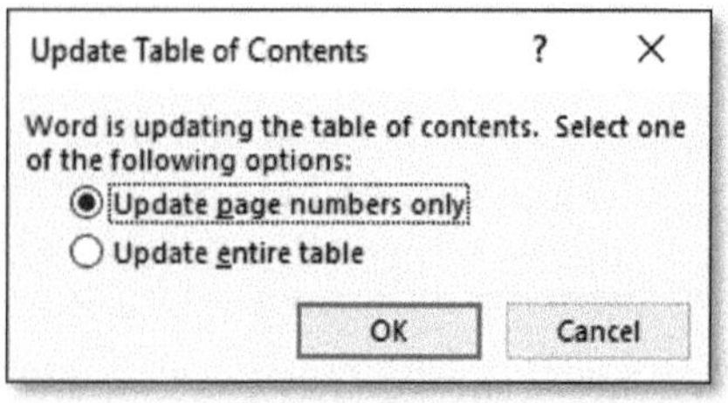

▲ Figure 13.75 Update 'Table of Contents' dialog box

Adding protection to your document

You may want to restrict what users and other people can change in your document, or you may want to restrict access to a particular document. The 'Restrict Editing' command prevents or limits other users from editing or formatting your document (see Figure 13.76).

1 Click the **Review** tab, in the 'Protect' group and click **Restrict Editing**; the 'Restrict Editing' pane will appear.

2 In the 'Editing restriction' section, check the **Allow only this type of editing in the document**.

3 In the drop-down list, select **No changes (Read only).**

4 Select the part of the document where you do not want any changes to be made. You can select a word, phrase, sentence, heading or paragraph.

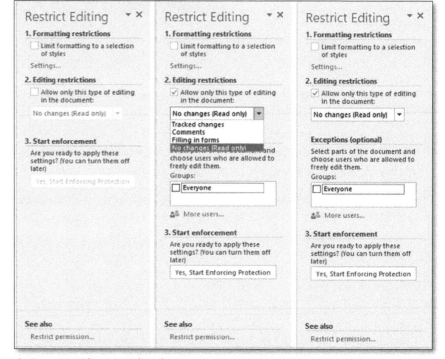

▲ Figure 13.76 'Restrict Editing' menus

5 In the 'Exceptions (optional)' section you have two choices:

a You can allow anyone who opens the document to make changes to the part that you selected, by selecting the **Everyone** check box in the 'Groups' list.

b You can allow only certain individuals to make changes to the part that you selected, by clicking **More users**, and then typing in their user names.

6 In the 'Start Enforcement' section, click **Start Enforcing Protection**.

a You can add a 'Password' so that users who know the password can make changes to the document (see Figure 13.77).

b You can add 'User Authentication', so that users must verify who they are by checking their email and clicking the link. Only authenticated users can remove the protection on the document.

▲ Figure 13.77 'Start Enforcing Protection' dialog box

Removing protection from a document

You can remove all protection from a document if:

- you need to know the password that was applied to the document
- you are listed as an authenticated owner for the document.

1 Click on the **Review** tab, in the 'Protect' group, and click the **Restrict Editing** icon.
2 In the 'Restrict Editing' task pane, click **Stop Protection**.
3 You will be prompted to enter a password; type the password.

Comments and track changes

Often, there may be times when you need to collaborate with your peers on an assignment or get feedback from your teacher or another person on a document. Word allows you to add comments and track changes made in your document.

Adding comments to a document

1 Select the text you want to comment on.
2 Click on the **Review** tab and click **New Comment** from the 'Comments' group. Make your comment (see Figure 13.78). You can make changes to any of your comments by simply going back and editing them.

▲Figure 13.78 Comment added to a document

Deleting a comment

1. Click on the comment.
2. Click on the **Review** tab and click **Delete** icon from the 'Comments' group. **OR**
3. You can delete a comment by right clicking on the comment and choosing 'Delete'.

Track Changes

Turning on 'Track Changes' (see Figure 13.79) allows you to see any additions and deletions made by individuals on your document. Additions are marked with a coloured underline and deletions are marked using strikethroughs. Once turned off, Word stops marking any changes made.

You can choose to show the changes by doing the following.

▲ Figure 13.79 'Track Changes' options

- **Simple markup:** This is indicated by a red vertical line in the margin of the document.
- **All Markup:** This gives a more detailed view of the changes within the document.
- **No Markup:** This gives a view of how the document would look if all the changes were accepted.
- **Original:** This gives a view of the original document before changes are made.

You can also choose to accept or reject the changes made on the document.

- **Accept:** This makes the change permanent.
- **Reject:** This removes the change.
- **Previous and Next:** This moves from one change to the next.

Exercise 3

1. Open the document 'Banking News'.
2. Set the following headings as Heading 1: 'Staff Departures', 'New Staff', 'Staff Promotion', 'Training and Staff Development News', and 'Upcoming Events'.
3. Set the following subheadings as Heading 2: 'Seminar on Money Laundering', 'Conference', 'Sports News' and 'Annual Charity 10K for Autism Awareness'.
4. Click at the top of the document and insert the table of contents.
5. Insert a page break at Staff Promotions.
6. Update the table of contents.
7. Save the Document as 'Banking News Updated'.

Chapter 13: Summary

- A word processor is an application package that allows you to prepare letters, reports, memos, books or any other type of correspondence. Once created, these documents can be saved to be worked on later or printed.
- The word-wrap feature means that, when entering text, you do not have to worry about where the end of each line stops. The word-wrap feature allows you to move automatically to a new line. You only need to press the Enter key if the line is a short line, or to move to a new paragraph.
- A word processor contains many editing and proofing features that enable users to make changes to a document quickly and easily. Some of the editing features are:
  - deleting (characters, words and blocks of text can easily be deleted)
  - inserting (characters, words and blocks of text can easily be inserted)
  - cutting, copying and pasting (characters, words and blocks of text can be removed or copied from one part of a document and placed in another part of the same document or in another document that is currently on the desktop)
  - finding and replacing text (you can search for a word or string of characters and replace it with another word or string of characters)
  - checking a document for correctness by using tools such as the spelling and grammar checks.
  - a thesaurus feature that allows you to replace a word in the document with another word of the same meaning
  - a language feature that allows you to translate text in your document into another language.
- Formatting determines the final appearance of a document. Formatting can be carried out at three levels – character, paragraph and page.
- Characters can be formatted using:
  - font type (Times New Roman, Old English, and so on)
  - size (height of a character)
  - font style (regular, bold, underline, italic)
  - font colour
  - special effects (superscript, subscript, strikethrough, shadow, outline, emboss, engrave, highlight and caps).
- Paragraph formatting includes:
  - line spacing (distance between lines)
  - justification (alignment of a block of text according to the margins, for example, left, centre, right and full justification)
  - indenting (pushing a line or paragraph in or out from the left or right margin).
- Pages can be formatted by adjusting the margins and by including headers and footers (text or graphical items that appear at the top or bottom of every page of a document) and page numbers.
- An endnote is placed at the end of the document or section and a footnote is placed at the end of a page. They give additional information to explain, expand on or make reference to a word, sentence or text within the document, using reference marks.
- A document can be displayed using any number of columns, for example, to produce newsletters and newspaper-style documents.
- Tables can be inserted into a document to display statistical and numerical data, and their contents can be styled in the same way as other text.
- The mail merge feature allows you to produce a large number of personalised letters, mailing labels and memos without having to type each one individually. Mail merging requires two files:
  - The main document or primary document contains the letter or other material meant for each recipient, and also contains the merge fields, which are positioned where information from the data source should be placed.
  - The data source or secondary document contains the personalised information needed to complete the main document.
  - A table of contents can be created automatically by specifying the heading styles.
  - Fillable forms allow you to enter data in a predesigned document with ease.

Chapter 13: Questions

Fill in the blanks

Text or graphics that appears on the top and bottom margins of every page of a document is called _____ and _____. The _____ appears in the bottom margin and the _____ appears in the top margin. A _____ is placed at the end of the document or the end of a section and a _____ is placed at the end of a page. They give additional information to explain, comment on or give reference to a word, sentence or text within the document with the use of _____ _____.

True or False?

1 You can reverse an undo action by clicking 'Redo'.

2 You cannot ignore a suggestion given by Word to say you should correct a spelling error.

3 When the OVR on the status bar is dimmed it indicates that you can type over the text.

4 You can only view a document in two views: 'Print Layout' view and 'Outline' view.

5 When you select text the area becomes highlighted.

6 The default setting for page margins can be changed.

7 To move text from one place to another, you need to copy and paste.

8 Endnotes are placed at the end of a page.

9 Page numbering can be placed in the header or footer area of a document.

10 There are a number of ways in which text can be wrapped around a graphic.

Multiple-choice questions

1 From which menu would you be able to find 'Columns'?
  a File   b Edit
  c Insert   d Format

2 Which of the following is not considered a formatting feature?
  a Font style   b Redo and Undo
  c Font size   d Underline

3 Which of the following is involved in creating a document?
  a Saving and storing   b Entering text
  c Formatting text   d All of these

4 Which of these sequences of actions allows you to double underline a piece of text in your document?
  a Edit, Insert, Underline, Double
  b Format, Paragraph, Underline, Double
  c Format, Font, Underline style, Double
  d Format, Font, Spacing, Underline style, Double

5 The difference between copy and paste and cut and paste is that:
  a cutting moves the text to where you want it to appear and also leaves a copy in the original position.
  b copying moves the text to where you want it to appear; cutting does not.
  c copying leaves a copy of the text in the original position; cutting deletes it from its original position.
  d cutting leaves a copy of the text in the original position; copying deletes it from its original position.

6 Footnotes refer to and expand on text within a document; they are placed:
  a at the end of the document.
  b in the top margin of the document.
  c at the bottom of the section.
  d at the end of a page.

7 Mail merge allows you to create multiple copies of a single document, such as a letter, so that it is partly personalised for a number of different recipients. You need to have the main document and a:
  a secondary data file.
  b primary document.
  c primary file source.
  d merged letter.

8 Which menu would most likely allow you to adjust your line spacing?
  a Edit   b File
  c Format   d Insert

9 Which key allows you to type over text?
  a Backspace   b Insert
  c Caps Lock   d Num Lock

10 Which of the following is not a type of tab?
  a Full Justify   b Decimal
  c Right   d Left

Short-answer questions

1 Explain what mail merge is and state ONE way in which a small T-shirt supply company can use mail merge.

2 Give TWO advantages of using a word processor over a traditional typewriter.

3 Name THREE important features that a word processor provides for a newspaper journalist.

4 Name THREE features of a word processor that allow you to present information that is difficult or impossible to do manually or using a traditional typewriter.

5 Give TWO ways in which word-processing software can be used by individuals in the following jobs:
   a Teachers
   b Musicians
   c Construction workers
   d Police officers
   e Caterers

Crossword

Across

1 A feature that will allow you to go automatically to the next line without pressing the 'Enter' key (two words) (8)

7 Used to place text or numbers in a predetermined position in a document (4)

8 A reference to text in a document, which is placed at the end of the document (7)

9 Remove text from its original position (3)

Down

2 The unit used to measure the size of a character (6)

3 The process of creating personalised mailing letters for a number of individuals (two words) (9)

4 Text that appears at the bottom of every page (6)

5 A type of page break that is inserted before the actual end of the page (4)

6 Another word for the typeface (4)

14 Spreadsheets

What is the purpose of a spreadsheet?

A spreadsheet package is a piece of software that stores and displays data as a table consisting of cells (columns, row locations). It can hold accounting or financial data, for example, and simulates the traditional paper-based spreadsheet that accountants used to use.

As well as capturing and displaying data it allows you to manipulate the data because you can also store formulae to carry out operations on the numerical data. These formulae are applied to the data in the sheet whenever you make a change to it. So, if you change any data values, the entire spreadsheet is automatically re-calculated, updating other numbers as necessary. Automatic re-calculation is one of the most important features of a spreadsheet. The ability to represent the numerical data quickly and easily in one of many graphical forms (such as pie charts, bar graphs, histograms, and so on) is another important advantage.

A spreadsheet package is a flexible modelling tool that can be used in any job that involves repetitive numerical calculations. This is because it allows you to obtain quick answers to what are called 'what-if scenarios'. Suppose your cricket club wants to predict the income it would earn from fundraisers based on last year's income. Using a spreadsheet program such as Excel you can set up the appropriate model and then test various assumptions. For example, 'What if the raffle sales increased by 10%?' or 'What if the Bar-B-Que sale made 15% less?' Some other examples of uses for spreadsheets are for:

- statistics, for example, finding averages or calculating the standard deviation
- loan calculations
- financial plans, for example, budgeting
- stock-keeping in a supermarket
- payrolls
- company accounts
- keeping accounts in a club
- schools to prepare end-of-term school reports.

Note

This entire chapter focuses on Microsoft Excel 2016. However, if the computers at your school have Excel 2010 or Excel 2013 installed, there is no need to worry as the differences between these versions would not affect your ability to complete the requirements of the CSEC syllabus.

Features of Excel equivalent or similar to Word

Excel is one of the applications in the Microsoft Office Suite. As such, many of the operations are the same for all the applications. In Excel, all the basic commands such as 'Open', 'New', 'Close', 'Save' and 'Save As', work in the same way as they do in Word. The only difference to note is that when you save an Excel file it is given the file extension **.xls**.

Other features that are similar are 'Spell Check', 'Find and Replace', 'Page Setup for margins', 'Page Orientation' and many of the formatting features.

Starting Excel

Excel is started in much the same way as any other program. Excel can also be started using the following steps:

1. If the Windows taskbar includes a Microsoft Office Excel 2016 shortcut icon, you can start Excel by double-clicking on the **Excel** icon.
2. Excel can also be accessed by performing a search using the 'Search' box. Simply type the name of the program 'Excel' and it will be displayed as shown in Figure 14.1. Click on the **Excel** icon to start the program.
3. Excel can also be started by clicking the **Start** button and searching the menu displayed. The programs are stored in alphabetical order. Scroll down until you see the 'Excel' program.

▲ Figure 14.1 Starting Excel 2016 in Windows 10

Workbooks and worksheets

Excel refers to its files as workbooks, so when you open Excel, the table you see is a workbook made up of three worksheets. You can add extra worksheets to the workbook and, if you open Excel with a new workbook, at the bottom of the table you will see tabs saying 'Sheet 1', 'Sheet 2' and 'Sheet 3'. You can add extra worksheets by clicking the next tab, which has an icon of a folder on it, or by pressing the shift key and F11 key together.

The Excel application window

The initial Excel application window includes the following elements.

- **Title bar:** This displays the name of the program, as well as the name of the current workbook if it has been saved. (If the workbook has not been saved, it is identified by a number; for example, 'Book1'.)
- **Ribbon tabs**: These are usually seen at the top of a worksheet with keywords that represent a group of closely related commands.
- **Vertical/horizontal scroll bars**: These are used to scroll the workbook window vertically/horizontally through a worksheet.
- **Worksheet tabs**: These identify the various worksheets in a workbook and allow you to move from one worksheet to another.

- **Status bar**: This displays helpful information as you use the program. The 'Ready' indicator that currently appears lets you know that the program is ready for data input.
- **Name box**: This identifies the active cell.
- **Formula bar**: This displays the contents of the active cell, if any.
- **Workbook window**: This window, which occupies the majority of the screen, displays an Excel workbook.

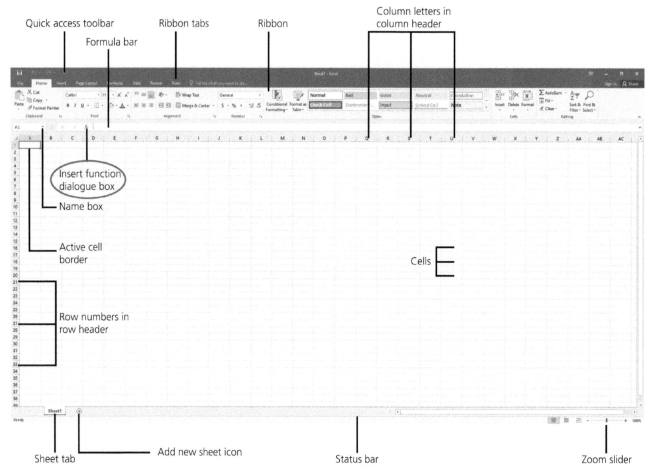

▲ Figure 14.2 Some elements of the Excel 2016 window

A workbook initially contains three worksheets, which are saved in a single file. A worksheet can be thought of as an electronic version of an accountant's pad (sometimes called analysis pads). It is a large grid divided into rows and columns. The rows run up and down and are numbered, whereas the columns run left to right and are lettered. Since an entire Excel worksheet can contain 1,048,576 rows and 16,384 columns of data, only a small part appears in this window at one time. A typical screen display may contain 39 rows and 29 columns. The intersection of a row and a column is called a cell. Each cell in the spreadsheet can be identified by its cell address or cell reference. The cell reference is simply the column position and the row position combined. For example, the address F6 means that the cell is in column F and row 6. Notice that cell A1 in Figure 14.2 is currently surrounded by a border. This border, or cell pointer, identifies the active cell; that is, the cell in which any information entered from the keyboard will be stored.

Basic concepts

A cell can contain one of three types of information: a label (text), a value (number) or a formula and is referred to by its column and row number, for example, A6. You can also address a range of cells. A range can be cells in a row, for example, A1:E1; cells in a column, for example, A1:A6; or a block of cells, for example, A1:E6.

- A label can be used as a title or heading to describe an aspect of the worksheet. It can contain any string of characters (letters or numbers) but must only start with a character that does not indicate a formula or number. A label cannot be used in a calculation.
- A value is a piece of data that can be used in a calculation.
- A formula is an instruction to perform operations on values. Depending on the package you are using, a formula must start with one of these special symbols: +, −, @, = to identify it as a formula. All formulae in Excel start with an equals sign (=).
- A function is a built-in formula. In Excel, there are many of these, including AVG, which finds the average of a range of cells and SQRT, which finds the square root of a number. The 'Insert Function' dialog box can be found by clicking on 'fx' in the 'Formulas' bar or the Formulas ribbon, see Figure 14.3.

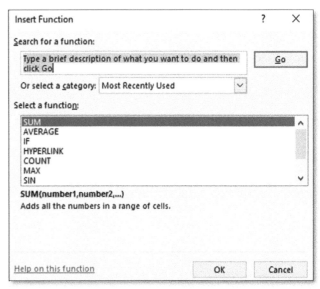

▲ Figure 14.3 'Insert Function' dialog box

Navigating around worksheets

Table 14.1 lists the navigation keys and their results.

Key	Result
Mouse click	Used to select a cell, by clicking any cell with it
Cursor keys on keyboard	Used to move in the direction of the arrow one cell at a time
Enter	Moves one cell down
Tab	Moves one cell to the right
CTRL+HOME	Moves back to cell A1
HOME	Moves to the first cell in a row
END	Moves to the last cell in the worksheet
PgDown	Move one screen down in a worksheet
PgUp	Move one screen up in a worksheet.
F5	Moves to a designated cell

▲ Table 14.1 Navigation keys

Entering data

Before data can be placed in a cell, the cell must be selected. You can do this by simply moving the cursor to it and clicking the left mouse button or by using the arrow keys. Notice that when you type data, it is displayed in the entry line of the formula bar, as well as in the cell itself as it is being entered. The data enters the cell when keys such as the 'Enter' key or arrow keys are pressed.

Once you start entering data, the formula bar buttons (Cancel and Enter) are activated (see Figure 14.4).

After you have typed all you require into a cell, you need to confirm the data entry (say that this data should stay in this cell). There are various ways of doing this. One way is to click on the **Enter** formula bar button. If you make a mistake while entering data, click the **Cancel** button on the formula bar to discard the entry and clear the cell. This will also switch off the formula bar buttons. Alternatively, press the **ESC** key on the keyboard.

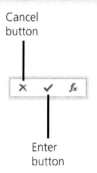

▲ Figure 14.4 Excel formula bar

Confirming data entry

We see from above that the **Enter** button on the formula bar will confirm entry, but there are alternative methods. The method used will depend on where you wish to type next. Table 14.2 summarises the different methods of confirming data entry and how the position of the active cell will change.

Default text formatting

Excel applies the following defaults to text:

- The text is automatically left aligned; 'text' includes a string of numerical characters that include hyphens or spaces, such as telephone numbers.
- Numbers are automatically right aligned.
- The text is 11-point Calibri by default. If you type text that is longer than the width of a column, it will appear to flow into the next cell if that cell is empty. If the next cell is not empty, the text that does not fit into the cell will be hidden.

Method of confirming entry	The position of active cells
Enter button on the formula bar	Active cells remain the same
Enter key on the keyboard	Cell below original becomes active
Tab key on the keyboard	Cell to the right of the original becomes active
One of four cursor keys on the keyboard	A cell in direction of cursor key becomes active
Click any other cell in the worksheet (do not use this method when entering formulae)	New cell clicked becomes the active cell

▲ Table 14.2 Methods of confirming data entry

Activity 1

Create the worksheet shown in Figure 14.5 as follows:

1. Select cell **B1** and enter the label 'Trinidad Wholesalers Ltd'.
2. Select cells **B2** to **D2** one at a time and enter the labels 'January', 'February' and 'March' respectively. Select cells **A3** and **A4** and enter the labels 'Sales' and 'Expenditure'.
3. Select the appropriate cells and enter the values as shown in the worksheet.
4. Save the worksheet as 'Sales'.

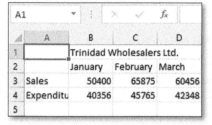

▲ Figure 14.5 Sample worksheet for Activity 1

To retrieve a worksheet from a USB device or hard disk

1. Pull down the **File** menu.
2. Select **Open**. The 'Open' dialog box appears. Choose the appropriate location where the document is stored, for example, Recent: shows a list of recent worksheets you may have worked on and appears in the far-right column. Other options include OneDrive or This computer where you can access your hard disk (C:), USB (E:) – from the window.
3. Double-click the icon of the selected worksheet or click the icon once and then click **Open**.

Exercise 1

1. What is the name and version of the spreadsheet package you are using?
2. Define the following terms:
   a. Cell
   b. Cell reference
   c. Label
   d. Value
   e. Formula.
3. a. What is the default alignment for text and numbers in Excel?
   b. What is the default font type and size in Excel?
   c. What happens to text that exceeds the width of a cell?
   d. List THREE features of Excel, which make it a very useful package.
4. Look at the worksheet in Figure 14.5.
   a. How many rows and columns are there?
   b. What is the content of cell C4?
   c. What is the address of the selected cell?
5. Besides the examples listed in the chapter, give TWO additional situations where you think a spreadsheet may be used. Give reasons for your answers.

Ranges

A range can be a cell or a group of adjoining cells, which are treated as a unit. A range can be represented by the address of the first cell and last cell in a group of continuous cells. For example, in Figure 14.6, the cells A1:D4 represent a range. To select a range of cells, click on the first cell and then drag down to the last cell.

A1				f_x
	A	B	C	D
1		Trinidad Wholesalers Ltd.		
2		January	February	March
3	Sales	50400	65875	60456
4	Expenditu	40356	45765	42348

▲ Figure 14.6 Selecting a range of cells

Selecting a non-adjoining cell range

1. Select the first range (for example, A2:A4).
2. To select the non-adjoining cell range, hold down the CTRL key and select the second range (for example, C2:C4).

This feature comes in very handy when selecting data to create graphs. Figure 14.7 shows the non-adjoining cell ranges selected.

After entering the data, notice that the numbers move to the right of the cells (they are right aligned) and the labels (text) move to the left (they are left aligned). These alignments occur automatically (by default). However, you can change the alignment of a cell or range of cells as follows.

C2				f_x	Fe
	A	B	C	D	
1		Trinidad Wholesalers Ltd.			
2		January	February	March	
3	Sales	50400	65875	60456	
4	Expenditure	40356	45765	42348	

▲ Figure 14.7 Selecting a non-adjoining cell range

Shortcut

You can justify the contents of a cell or range of cells by highlighting the cell or range of cells and clicking one of the Align buttons in the Home tab, such as left, centre or right.

Changing the alignment of a cell or range of cells

1 Select the cell or range of cells.
2 Click the **Home** tab.
3 Select the option you require from the 'Alignment' group. The 'Alignment' group has many options to change the way text is displayed in a cell (see Figure 14.8).
4 More options are available from the 'Alignment' launcher (bottom right-hand arrow in the 'Alignment' group) which will display the 'Format Cells' dialog box (see Figure 14.10).

▲ Figure 14.8 Excel 'Alignment' group

Wrapping text

The 'Wrap text' option allows a label that is more than one word and which exceeds the width of a cell to move to another line in the same cell. For example, the company name in cell B1 in Figure 14.11 is wrapped.

Wrapping text

1 Select the cell or range of cells.
2 Click the **Home** tab.
3 Select the **Wrap Text** icon from the Alignment group.

Basic editing

If you make a mistake when entering data into a cell, you can easily change the data or remove it entirely. The procedure is as follows.

Changing the contents of a cell by editing inside the formula bar or cell

1 Click once in the cell requiring the edit.
2 Click inside the text in the formula bar (a cursor or insertion point appears in the formula bar). Edit the contents.
3 Confirm the entry using any of the methods outlined earlier.

Or

Double-click on the cell to open it for editing and edit directly in the cell, then confirm the entry.

To delete the content of cells

1 Select the cell or range of cells.
2 Click **Delete** from the cells group in the **Home** tab, as shown in Figure 14.9.

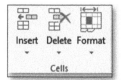

▲ Figure 14.9 'Cells' group

Activity 2

Create the spreadsheet shown in Figure 14.6 on page 309. You are required to:

1 Change the contents of cell B3 from 50400 to 54000. Perform the edit within the cell.
2 Centre align all the values.
3 Change the orientation of the labels in cells B2, C2 and D2 to 45 degrees.
4 Wrap the label in cell B1.

How it is done

1 Double-click on cell B3. The cursor appears in the cell. Edit the number.
2 Select the range B3 to D4. Select the centre to align the shortcut icon on the 'Alignment' group of the **Home** tab.
3 Select the range B2 to D2.
4 From the **Home tab**, click on the 'Alignment' launcher (bottom right-hand arrow in the 'Alignment' group), which will display the 'Format Cells' dialog box (as shown in Figure 14.10).
Click the up-arrow in the degrees box in the orientation pane until you reach 45 degrees. Click **OK**.
5 Select cell B1. Click the **Wrap text** box in the 'Text control' panel on the 'Alignment' group. Click **OK**.

Figure 14.11 shows the result of the activity.

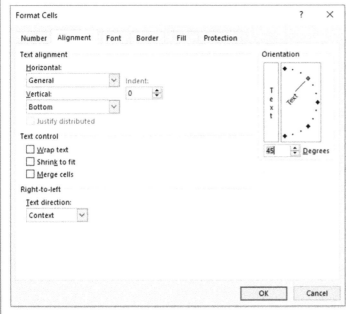

▲ Figure 14.10 'Format Cells' dialog box

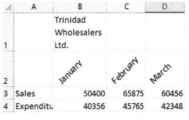

▲ Figure 14.11 Sample worksheet for Activity 2

Inserting and deleting rows and columns

A row or column can be inserted between existing rows or columns.
You can also delete rows and columns.

To insert a row

1 Click on a cell in the row below the row where you want the new row to go.
2 **Home** tab/Cells group/**Insert Sheet Rows.**

To insert a column

1 Click on a cell in a column to the right of the column where you want the new column to go (see Figure 14.12).
2 **Home** tab/Cells group/**Insert Sheet Columns.**
3 If you wish to insert more than one row or column, for step 1 select the exact number of rows or columns you require and then carry out step 2.

An alternative method (Click on column/Right click/click insert/choose an entire column from the dialog box)

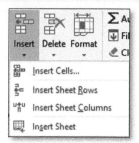

▲ Figure 14.12 'Insert' options

To delete a row or column

1 Click on a cell or cells in the row or column that you want to delete.
2 **Home** tab/Cells group/**Delete Sheet Rows** or **Delete Sheet Columns** (see Figure 14.13).

*An alternative method (Click on a row or column/Right click/click **Delete**)*

▲ Figure 14.13 'Delete' options

Right-click method for inserting rows and columns

1 Select the whole row(s) or column(s) to the right, or below, of where you want to enter the new one.
2 Right-click anywhere in the selected area.
3 The 'Insert' drop-down menu shown in Figure 14.14 appears. Select **Entire row** or **Entire column** as desired.

To delete a row or column, follow the same procedure as above and click **Entire row** or **Entire column** when the 'Delete' dialog box appears.

▲ Figure 14.14 'Insert' dialog box

Formatting

Using formatting, you can control the appearance of cells and of the worksheet in general. We have already looked at one aspect of formatting – the alignment of the contents of cells. We will now look at other aspects of formatting.

Resizing columns/rows

Columns and rows may be resized in various ways.

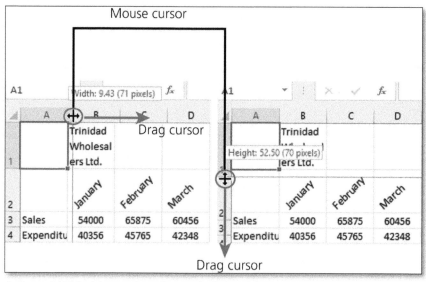

▲ Figure 14.15 Resizing a column/row with click and drag

Resizing with click and drag

The height of each row and width of each column in a worksheet can be adjusted using the mouse. When the mouse pointer is moved between the row and column headings, it changes shape to a two-way arrow as shown in Figure 14.15. When the two-way arrow appears, click and drag to the desired position. For example, to increase or decrease the width of the 'A' column, click between the A and B column heading and drag either to the right or left to the position you require.

Resizing with autofit

To **autofit** a column, double-click the right boundary of the column heading. To autofit a row, double-click on the lower boundary of the row heading. Excel then 'looks' at all the entries in the column or row and will resize the column or row to match the width or height of the longest or tallest entry.

Resizing using the cells group

From the Home tab, select 'Format' and then the 'Cell Size' group. Then select **Row Height** or **Column Width** from the drop-down menu (see Figure 14.16). When the 'Column Width' dialog box appears (see Figure 14.17), enter an exact measurement. *Only a value between 0 and 255 will be accepted.*

Formatting numbers

Another aspect of formatting is the way in which numbers are represented. For example, some of the standard formats (see Figure 14.18) are as follows.

- **General:** Use this if you want no specific number format.
- **Number:** Use this for general display of numbers (decimal places and negative). You have options to set the number of decimal places; to use a ',' as a thousands separator and how you show negative numbers.
- **Currency:** Use this if you want to represent monetary values (for example, $589.54). You have options to set the number of decimal places; choose a currency symbol and how you show negative numbers.
- **Accounting:** Use this format for lining up currency symbols and decimal points. You have options to set the number of decimal places and choose a currency symbol.

To format cells for currency data

1. Highlight the cell or range to be formatted.
2. If your chosen currency is not shown in the 'Number' group of the 'Home' tab, click the down arrow at the bottom right of the 'Number' group. The 'Format Cells' dialog box appears as shown in Figure 14.18.
3. Select the **Number** tab, then select **Currency** from the displayed list categories.
4. Choose the number of decimal places and the currency symbol you want to use.

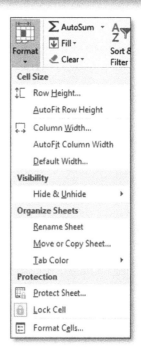

▲ Figure 14.16 'Format' options to change row height and column width

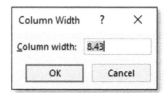

▲ Figure 14.17 'Column Width' dialog box

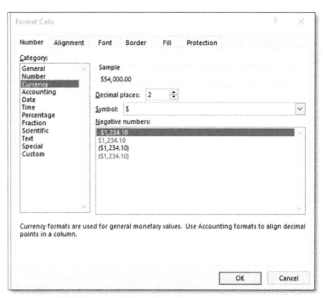

▲ Figure 14.18 'Format Cells' dialog box

Shortcut

Highlight the cell or cells that you want to format as currency data, and click the **Currency** icon ($) in the 'Number' group of the 'Home' tab shown in Figure 14.19.

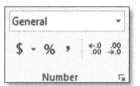

▲ Figure 14.19 'Number' group

Editing

Copying data

It is possible to copy data from cell(s) to cell(s) within a worksheet, across to a different worksheet or even to a different workbook. This can be achieved using one of several methods.

Fill down

1 Select the cell that has the data you wish to copy.
2 Click on the bottom right-hand corner of the cell (fill handle), as shown in Figure 14.20, and drag down or across as desired. The value in the first cell will be copied to all the cells selected.

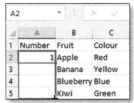

▲ Figure 14.20 Spreadsheet cells selected to be filled using the fill handle

Cut, copy and paste commands

1 Select the cell(s) or range of cells you want to cut or copy to other cells.
2 Select the **Cut** or **Copy** icon from the 'Clipboard' group of the 'Home' tab (see Figure 14. 21).
3 Select the cell or the first cell of the range where you wish to copy the data.
4 Select the **Paste** icon.

Working with worksheets

By default, each new workbook is provided with three worksheets (Sheet 1, Sheet 2 and Sheet 3) of which the active worksheet is always white. These sheets allow you to keep varied and large amounts of information together in one workbook. To move from worksheet to worksheet, click on the worksheet tab for the worksheet you require, at the bottom of the screen.

Inserting, deleting, renaming worksheets

Right-click one of the worksheet tabs and then select the command you require from the drop-down menu shown in Figure 14.22. Any inserted worksheet will be given a default name, for example, 'Sheet 4'. Selecting **Rename** allows you to change the name of the worksheet. Figure 14.23 shows 'Sheet 1' renamed as '1st Quarter Report'.

Note

■ When you **Copy**, and then use the **Paste** command, the data remains on the clipboard so you can repeat the paste many times. The cell containing the original data will have a broken line around it, indicating that the data is still on the clipboard. To get rid of the broken lines around the cell containing the original data and remove the data from the clipboard, press the **ESC** key.
■ When you use the **Cut** command when moving data, or if you use the **Enter** key to paste data you have copied, you will find that you can only paste once as the data does not remain on the clipboard. To paste again you will have to copy or cut again.

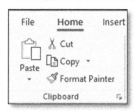

▲ Figure 14.21 Commands in the 'Clipboard' group

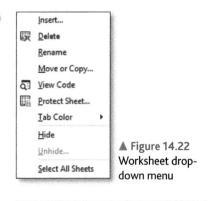

▲ Figure 14.22 Worksheet drop-down menu

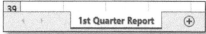

▲ Figure 14.23 Renamed worksheet

Activity 3

▲	A	B	C
1	Surname	Firstname	Position
2	Abbot	John	Supervisor
3	Alexis	Mark	Carpenter
4	Brown	Kerry	Carpenter
5	Berch	Tom	Mason
6	Cameron-E	Phillip	Labourer
7	Hugh-Baile	Shane	Mason
8	Dobson	Jonny	Labourer
9	Henry	Lelsie	Labourer

▲ Figure 14.24 Worksheet for Activity 3

Create the worksheet shown in Figure 14.24.

1 Insert the details of a new employee between rows 4 and 5: Surname – McLoclanding, First name – Johnathan, Position – Mason.
2 Insert a column to the left of column A.
3 Type the label 'Worker ID' in cell A1.
4 Input the following worker ID numbers for the nine workers. Starting from the first worker: 10, 11, 12, 13, 14, 15, 16, 17, 18.
5 Resize all columns to make all the data visible.
6 Insert the label 'Health Surcharge' in cell E1.
7 Input the value 20 for each worker in the 'Health Surcharge' column.
8 Format the 'Health Surcharge' values as currency.
9 Delete row 4.
10 Change the name of the worksheet to 'Salary'.
11 Save the worksheet as 'Payroll'.

How it is done
1 Place the cursor anywhere in row 5. Click the **Home** tab, then click **Insert** from the 'Cells' group. Click the **Insert Sheet Rows** option. Enter the data in the appropriate cells. (**Home** tab/**Cells** group/ **Insert** menu/**Insert Sheet Rows** option).
2 Select any cell in column A. Click the **Home** tab, then click **Insert** from the 'Cells' group. Click the **Insert Sheet Columns** option. Enter the data in the appropriate cells. (**Home** tab/**Cells** group/**Insert** menu/**Insert Sheet Columns** option).
3 Select cell A1 and input the label 'Worker ID'.
4 Select cell A2. Type 10 and press **Enter**. Continue entering the other Worker ID numbers.
5 Place the cursor between column B and column C. Double-click the mouse.
6 Select cell E1. Type in the label 'Health Surcharge'.
7 Select cell E2 and enter the number 20. Using the fill handle at the bottom right corner of the cell, drag to fill the cells for each worker.
8 Select the range E2 to E10. Click on the dollar sign ($) in the formatting toolbar or click the **Home** tab/ **Number** group/click the down arrow/**Currency**.
9 Place the cursor anywhere in row 4. Click the **Home** tab, then click **Delete** from the 'Cells' group. Click the **Delete Sheet Rows** option. (**Home** tab/**Cells** group/**Delete** menu/**Delete Sheet Rows** option).
10 Right-click **Sheet 1**. Select **Rename**. Type 'Salary'.

Figure 14.25 shows the completed worksheet.

▲	A	B	C	D	E
1	Worker ID	Surname	Firstname	Position	Health Surcharge
2	10	Abbot	John	Supervisor	$20,00
3	11	Alexis	Mark	Carpenter	$20,00
4	13	Mc Loclanding	Johnathan	Mason	$20,00
5	14	Berch	Tom	Mason	$20,00
6	15	Cameron-Brown	Phillip	Labourer	$20,00
7	16	Hugh-Bailey	Shane	Mason	$20,00
8	17	Dobson	Jonny	Labourer	$20,00
9	18	Henry	Lelsie	Labourer	$20,00

▲ Figure 14.25 Completed worksheet for Activity 3

1 Using the worksheet in Activity 3, complete the following.
  a Insert an empty row above row 1.
  b Type the label 'Ace Construction Company' in cell B1.
  c Change the contents of cell B5 to 'McLocland'.
  d Change the orientation of the labels in cells A2 to F2 to 45 degrees.
  e Insert a column between columns D and E.
  f Type the label 'NIS'.
  g Type the value 80 in cell E3.
  h Fill in the NIS value of 80 for each worker.
  i Format all monetary values to currency.
  j Rename the worksheet as 'Paysheet'.

Formulae

Formulae are used to perform calculations using data contained in the cells and to display the results. Some of the features of formulae are:

- A formula is entered in the cell in which the result is to be displayed.
- A formula begins with an equals sign (=).
- A formula includes arguments (such as cell references, text or numbers) and operators. Operators are mathematical symbols that are used in formulae. Examples of operators used in formulae include:

Addition	+
Division	/
Subtraction	–
Exponentiation	^ (raising to a power)
Multiplication	*

After a formula has been confirmed in a cell, only the calculation result will be displayed in that cell; the formula will be displayed in the formula bar. If you double-click on a cell containing a formula the full formula will be displayed and will be ready for you to edit.

BODMAS rule

An expression in a formula in a spreadsheet package follows the same order of precedence as for normal arithmetic. This means that whatever is within brackets is performed first, followed by exponentiation, then multiplication and/or division, and then addition and/or subtraction.

Figure 14.26(a) shows examples of various formulae on the values in the range A3 to B7. Figure 14.26(b) shows the results of applying the formulae.

Did you know?

Notice that to calculate the formula for the percent profit in cell G5 of Figure 14.27 we did not write the formula as: $F5/B5*100$ as you would do in mathematics. If you did this, the result would be expressed in the cell just as a number without a percentage symbol. If you format it to a percentage at this point, it would be multiplied by 100. Therefore, when you write your formula to calculate percentages, you must remember to leave the formula expressed just as a fraction and not multiply by 100.

	A	B	C
1	Various Formulae		
2			
3	25	2	=A3+B3
4	25	2	=A4-B4
5	25	2	=A5*B5
6	25	2	=A6/B6
7	25	2	=A7^B7

▲ Figure 14.26(a) Examples of various formulae

	A	B	C
1	Various Formulae		
2			
3	25	2	27
4	25	2	23
5	25	2	50
6	25	2	12.5
7	25	2	625

▲ Figure 14.26(b) Results of applying various formulae

Activity 4

The worksheet in Figure 14.27 shows the sales and expenditure for the first quarter of 2018 for a business named Optimum Trading Company. You are required to calculate:

1 The profit before tax for each month
2 The tax on the profit, which is set at 15%
3 The profit after tax
4 The percentage of profit (profit %) made each month
5 The total for sales, expenditure, profit before tax, tax, profit after tax and profit percentage
6 Format the range B5:F8 as currency and G5:G8 as percentage

How it is done

1 Select cell D5 and type the formula =B5–C5. Copy this formula to cells D6 and D7.

2 Select cell E5 and type the formula =.15*D5. Copy this formula to cells E6 and E7.
3 Select cell F5 and type the formula =D5–E5. Copy this formula to cells F6 and F7.
4 Select cell G5 and type the formula =F5/B5. Copy this formula to cells G6 and G7.
5 Select cell B8 and type the formula =B5+B6+B7. Copy the formula to cells C8, D8, E8, F8 and G8.
6 a Select the range B5:F8, Click on the dollar sign ($) in the Number group from the Home tab or click **Home** tab/**Number** group/click the down arrow/**Currency**.
   b Select the range G5:G8.
   c Select percentage (%) sign in the Number group from the Home tab or click **Home** tab/**Number** group/click the down arrow/**Percentage**. Figure 14.28 shows the completed worksheet.

Figure 14.27 shows the formulae used to create the worksheet.

	A	B	C	D	E	F	G
1				Optimum Trading Company			
2	Quarterly Sales Report						
3							
4		Sales	Expenditure	Profit before Tax	Tax (15%)	Profit after Tax	Profit %
5	January	456852	154275	=B5-C5	=0.15*D5	=D5-E5	=F5/B5
6	February	654587	256478				
7	March	554587	268975				
8	Corporate	=B5+B6+B7					

▲ Figure 14.27 Worksheet showing formulae for Activity 4

It is important to note that the formula includes the cell addresses and not the values that are currently in the cells. If you type the values themselves, the re-calculation feature of the spreadsheet package would not work. For example, typing the formula =456852 + 654587 + 554587 in cell B8 would give the correct answer for the 'Corporate' sales but the re-calculation feature would not work. If any of the values in the cells were changed, the total in cell B8 would remain the same. If the value in cell B5 were changed from 456852 to 556852, the formula =456852 + 654587 + 554587 in cell B8 would remain unchanged, which would result in the wrong total for the new value in cell B5. However, when we use cell addresses in a formula, any changes to the content of a cell that forms part of a formula, results in immediate adjustments to any cell that depends on the value that was changed.

	A	B	C	D	E	F	G
1				Optimum Trading Company			
2	Quarterly Sales Report						
3							
4		Sales	Expenditure	Profit before Tax	Tax (15%)	Profit after Tax	Profit %
5	January	456852	154275	$302 577,00	$45 386,55	$257 190,45	56%
6	February	654587	256478	$398 109,00	$59 716,35	$338 392,65	52%
7	March	554587	268975	$285 612,00	$42 841,80	$242 770,20	44%
8	Corporate	1666026	679728	$986 298,00	$144 944,70	$838 353,30	50%

▲ Figure 14.28 Completed worksheet for Activity 4

Exercise 3

1 a Create the spreadsheet shown in Figure 14.29.
  b Insert a row between row 1 and row 2 and insert the label 'First Quarter Sales' in cell D2.
  c Insert the label 'Total' in cell E3.
  d Find the total sales for each branch for each month.
  e Find the Corporate total for each month for all branches.
  f Centre align the labels January, February and March.
  g Format the range B4:E9 as currency.
  h Save the worksheet as 'Home Makers'.
2 a Create the worksheet shown in Figure 14.30.
  b Insert a blank column between column A and column B.
  c Insert the label 'Profit' in cell A5.
  d Insert the label 'Total' in cell F2.
  e Calculate the total sales and total expenditure.

  f Calculate the profit for each month and the total profit.
  g Format all values with currency.
  h Save the worksheet as 'Trinidad Wholesalers'.
3 Create the worksheet shown in Figure 14.31.
  a Insert the label 'Total' in cell E4.
  b Calculate the Total for each item.
  c Insert the label 'VAT' in cell F4.
  d Calculate VAT on each item at 15%.
  e Calculate the final cost of each item.
  f Insert a label 'Total cost' in an appropriate cell and calculate the total cost of all the items.
  g In an appropriate cell, calculate a discount of 20% of the 'Total cost'.
  h In an appropriate cell, calculate the amount the customer has to pay.
4 Create a spreadsheet to calculate the percentage change in sales for each month and the total for the period January to March 2016, and the same period in 2017 (see Figure 14.32).

	A	B	C	D
1		Home Makers Furniture Store		
2		January	February	March
3	North	26500	22442	23456
4	South	45600	23246	67543
5	Central	34568	29687	46578
6	East	78540	98755	65981
7	West	53546	94786	65847
8	Corporate			

▲ Figure 14.29 Worksheet for question 1

	A	B	C	D
1		Trinidad Wholesalers Ltd.		
2		January	February	March
3	Sales	50400	65875	60456
4	Expenditure	40356	45765	42348

▲ Figure 14.30 Worksheet for question 2

	A	B	C	D	E
1			Triple Point Stationary Supplies		
2	Purchase order		Order No:125		
3					
4	Item	Unit	Unit Price	Quantity	
5	Erasers	Box	8.99	5	
6	Pencils	Box	9.6	20	
7	Pens	Box	18	15	
8	Paper	Box	250	3	
9	Markers	Box	60	8	

▲ Figure 14.31 Worksheet for question 3

	A	B	C
1		2016	2017
2		Percentage Change (%)	
3	January	$254,781.00	$547,869.00
4	February	$652,457.00	$654,785.00
5	March	$547,896.00	$745,895.00
6	Total		

▲ Figure 14.32 Spreadsheet for question 4

Functions

There are easier and faster methods to find the total of a group of cells. The **SUM** function could accomplish the same task as the formula we used in Activity 4 to calculate the total sales for the first quarter. A function is a *predefined* formula in Excel that can automatically calculate results, perform worksheet actions or assist with decision making based on the information provided in your worksheet. Functions fall into several categories including:

- **Math and Trig:** This category includes functions for computing totals, square roots, tangents, and so on.
- **More Functions:** This category includes functions for Statistical analysis, Engineering, Cube, and so on.
- **Financial:** This category includes functions for computing loan repayments, rates of return, depreciation, and so on.
- **Date and Time:** This category includes functions for computing the number of days in a specific date interval, the number of hours in a specific time interval, and so on.

The SUM function

The SUM function starts with an equals (=) sign, followed by the word 'SUM', an open bracket, the arguments and a closing bracket. An argument is information passed to a function on which it operates. The general form of the SUM function is as follows:

The worksheet in Figure 14.29 shows the first-quarter sales figures for the five branches of Home Makers Furniture Store in North, South, Central, East and West branches. To find the total sales for the North branch for the period January to March, we need to find the total of cells B5, C5 and D5. The formula would be =B5+C5+D5 or, using the SUM function, the formula to put into cell E5 will be =SUM(B5:D5). Whenever we want to add up the values of a column or row of continuous cells, we can use the SUM function. Every time cell E5 is highlighted, the content box will show the formula.

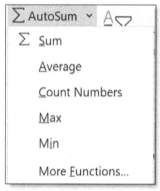

▲ Figure 14.33 'AutoSum' and options

If we wanted to find the total for the South branch for the period January to March, we would now have to go to cell E5 and type out another formula. The formula would be =B6+C6+D6 or =SUM(B6:D6). The formula to calculate the total for the Central branch would be =SUM(B7:D7) and for the East branch would be =SUM(B8:D8) and for the West branch it would be =SUM(B9:D9). Notice that the formula is almost the same for each branch except that the cell addresses are different. So instead of making us type out five different formulae, the package lets us copy the original formula to the other cells. The structure of the formula remains the same, but the addresses of the cells used in the formula will change, relative to the position of the formula. This feature is called relative cell addressing.

AutoSum button

Another method of easily summing a row or column of cells is to use the AutoSum button. To use AutoSum either:

1 Click in the cell where you want the result to appear: in this case, the first vacant cell under the five cells we are summing (B10).
2 Click the **AutoSum** button [∑].

AutoSum function

1 **Home** tab Editing group/Click on the **∑ AutoSum** icon.
2 Figure 14.33 shows the other functions available if the arrow in the icon is clicked.
3 Check the formula entered by Excel, to ensure that the correct range of cells has been chosen. If an incorrect range of cells has been selected by Excel, simply click and drag to select the correct range.
4 Confirm the entry.

Or

1 Select the range of cells to be added and also the cell where you wish to place the formula. In this case, it will be cells B5:B10 as shown in Figure 14.34.
2 Click the **AutoSum** button. In this case, the formula is entered and confirmed automatically.

◢	A	B	C	D	E
1				Home Makers Furniture Store	
2					
3				First Quarter Sales Report	
4		January	February	March	
5	North	26500	22442	23456	
6	South	45600	23246	67543	
7	Central	34568	29687	46578	
8	East	78540	98755	65981	
9	West	53546	94786	65847	
10	Corporate	238754			

▲ Figure 14.34 Worksheet showing the use of AutoSum

The Insert Function button

1 Click in the cell where you want the result to appear. Using the worksheet in Figure 14.34, this is the first vacant cell under the five cells we are summing (B10).
2 Click the **Formulas** tab.
3 Click the **Insert Function** button in the 'Function Library' group. The 'Insert Function' dialog box appears as shown in Figure 14.35.
4 Select the 'SUM' function from the 'Insert Function' dialog box and click **OK**. The 'Function Arguments' dialog box appears.
5 Check that the correct cell range is selected for summing. Here the range B5:B9 should be displayed.

If an incorrect range has been selected, move the 'Functions Arguments' dialog box out of the way if necessary, select the correct range with your mouse, and then click **OK** on the dialog box.

The resulting formula will appear identical to the formula constructed by the previous methods.

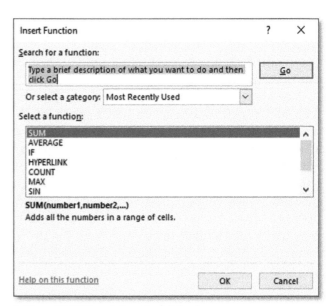

▲ Figure 14.35 'Insert Function' dialog box

AutoSumming many columns/rows at once

If you have a table of data, you can sum all the columns and rows at once. To do this:

1 Select all the rows and columns of data *and* one blank cell under each column and to the right of each row.
2 Click the **AutoSum** button.

Each column and row will now contain the correct formula to sum the cells above in the case of columns and to the left in the case of rows.

Other functions

AVERAGE function

The **AVERAGE** function is used to find the mean of a set of values. The general form of the function is =AVERAGE(first cell:last cell). For example, if you want to find the average of the range A2 to A9, the formula would be =AVERAGE(A2:A9). It can be entered into a worksheet either manually or by expanding the 'AutoSum' button and by selecting the AVERAGE option in the list that appears.

MAX function

The **MAX** (maximum) function is used to find the largest value in a set of values in a row or column. The general form of the maximum function is =MAX(first cell:last cell). For example, if you want to find the largest value in the range A2 to A9, the formula would be =MAX(A2:A9).

MIN function

The **MIN** (minimum) function is used to find the smallest value in a set of values in a row or column. The general form of the minimum function is =MIN(first cell:last cell). For example, if you want to find the lowest value in the range A2 to A9, the formula would be =MIN(A2:A9).

COUNT function

The **COUNT** function returns the number of entries in its argument list that represent numbers. For example, if you wanted to count the number of number values in the range A2 to A9 the formula would be =COUNT(A2:A9). The COUNT function does not count blank cells or labels.

Like the AVERAGE function, the MAX, MIN and COUNT functions can be entered into a worksheet either manually or by expanding the AutoSum button and selecting the appropriate option in the list that appears.

COUNTA function

This works by counting the number of cells that are not empty. You would use this to check how many cells have data in, whether that is a number or text.

COUNTIF function

This function counts the number of cells that meet a given criteria. In Figure 14.34, if you wanted to count how many of the regions had sales greater than 90000 in February you would use =COUNTIF(C5:C9, >90000). This gives the answer '2' as only East and West are bigger.

Rank function

The **RANK** function returns the rank of a number in a list of numbers that is not sorted or sorted in ascending or descending order. There are three arguments for the RANK function =RANK(Number, Ref, Order)

Number: is the number for which you want to find the rank (In Figure 14.36, we want to locate the rank of the number in A2)

Ref: is an array of, or a reference to, a list of numbers. Non-numeric values are ignored. (We want to compare the number in A2 to the list of numbers in range A2 to A31. Use an absolute reference ($A$2:$A$31), instead of a relative reference (A2:A31) so the referenced range will stay the same when you copy the formula down to the cells below

Order: (optional) This argument tells Excel whether to rank the list in ascending or descending order.

- If the third argument is omitted (or 0), Excel ranks the largest number first, second largest number second, and so on. In Figure 14.37, the order argument was left blank, to find the rank in descending order.
  =RANK(A2,$A$2:$A$31)
- For ascending order, type a 1, or any other number except zero.
  =RANK(A2,$A$2:$A$31,1)

PMT function

The **PMT** function (see Figure 14.38 on the next page) is a financial function that can be used to calculate the total payment (principal and interest) required to settle a loan if given the loan amount, number of periods and the interest rate. The general form of the PMT function is =PMT (rate, nper, pv, [fv], [type]).

COMPULSORY PARAMETER:

1 **Rate:** Rate represents the interest rate for the loan amount. If you are taking a monthly payment in this PMT Excel function then you should convert the rate in a monthly rate and should convert the nper to months.

2 **Nper:** Nper is the total number of instalments for the loan amount. For example, considering the 5-year terms in Figure 14.38 means 5*12=60.

3 **Pv:** Pv is the total loan amount or present value.

▲ Figure 14.36 Locating the RANK function

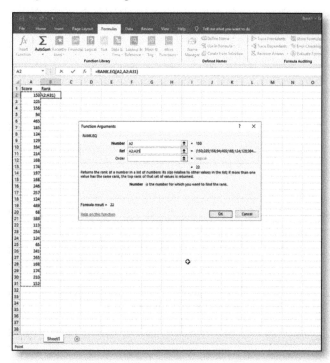

▲ Figure 14.37 Applying the RANK function

OPTIONAL PARAMETER:

1 **[Fv]:** It is also called the future value and it is optional in this PMT Excel and if not passed in the function, then it will be considered as zero.
2 **[Type]:** It can be omitted from the PMT function and used as 1 in case the payments are due at the beginning of the period and considered as 0 in case the payments are due at the end of the period.

Suppose the loan amount is $25,000 and interest rate is 10% annually and the period is 5 years.

Here the number of payments will be 60 payments (5*12=60) in total. In this PMT Excel function, we have considered C4/12 because 10% rate is annually and by dividing by 12 we get the monthly rate. Here the future value and type are considered as zero.
The output will be as follows:

■ This will return the value as a negative amount. This is the amount that will be credited from your bank.
■ To convert it in the positive value, simply use the negative sign before this PMT excel.
■ Then the output will be $531.18.

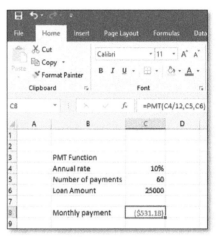

▲ Figure 14.38 PMT function

VLOOKUP function

The VLOOKUP function allows you to look up a value from a table.

Interpreting formula and function error messages

Error messages will appear when you use incorrect syntax or try to do something that prevents Excel from calculating the formula.
Some common examples are shown in Table 14.3.

#####	Means that the column is not wide enough to display the value. Use any of the methods described earlier to widen the column to allow the value to display.
#DIV/0!	The formula is attempting to divide by zero. Check the values of the cell in the formula.
#NAME?	Excel does not recognise text in a formula. Check the spelling of your function or check that a name exists.
#NUM!	Appears when Excel encounters a problem with the number in the formula, such as the wrong type of argument in an Excel function or a calculation that produces a number too large or too small to be represented in the worksheet.
#REF!	Appears when Excel encounters an invalid cell reference, such as when you delete a cell referred to in a formula or paste cells over the cells referred to in a formula.
CIRCULAR	The formula is referencing itself. The cell reference containing the formula is also part of the formula.
#VALUE!	Occurs when the wrong type of operand (item on either side of a formula) or argument is used.

▲ Table 14.3 Some common formula error messages

Whenever an error message appears, you will also see a green marker in the top left of the cell Figure 14.39). If you click on the cell to select it, an information symbol will appear. Click on this symbol to display a drop-down menu that offers you many choices, including a 'Help on this error' option, which will take you to a help file explaining the message error in detail.

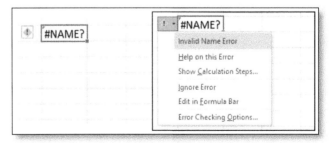

▲ Figure 14.39 'Help on this error' menu

Activity 5

Retrieve the worksheet 'Home Makers'.

1 Insert a row between row 1 and row 2 and insert the label 'First Quarter Sales' in cell D2.
2 Change the label 'First Quarter Sales' to 'First Quarter Sales Report'.
3 Insert the label 'Expenditure' in cell F4.
4 Enter the following expenditure for each branch.

Branch	Expenditure
North	25000
South	32056
Central	30123
East	54345
West	45632

5 Calculate the following:
   a The amount of tax paid if the profit is taxed at 15%
   b The after-tax profit
   c The corporate totals for every column
   d The greatest after-tax profit, that is, which store performed best?
   e The lowest after-tax profit, that is, which store performed worst?
   f The mean after-tax profit across all the stores
   g The amount of branches processed.
6 Format all monetary values as currency.

How it is done
1 Retrieve the worksheet 'Home Makers'.
2 Select cell B3. Change 'First Quarter Sales' to 'First Quarter Sales Report'.
3 Select F4. Enter the label 'Expenditure'.

4 Enter the expenditure data in the appropriate cells.
5 Select cell G4. Enter the label 'Profit before tax'.
6 Change the width of the cell to accommodate the label.
7 Select cell G5. Enter the formula = E5-F5. Copy the formula down to G9.
8 Select cell H4. Enter the label 'Tax on Profit' and change the column width.
9 Select cell H5. Enter the formula = G5*.15. Copy the formula down to H9.
10 Select cell I4. Enter the label 'Profit after Tax' and change the column width.
11 Select cell I5. Enter the formula =G5-H5. Copy the formula down to I9.
12 Select cell B10. Enter the formula =Sum(B5:B9). Copy the formula across to I10.
13 Highlight or mark off the range B5 to I10. Change the number format to currency.
14 Select cell A13. Enter the label 'Maximum Profit'.
15 Select cell B13. Enter the formula =Max(I5:I9).
16 Select cell A14. Enter the label 'Minimum Profit'.
17 Select cell B14. Enter the formula =Min(I5:I9).
18 Select cell A15. Enter the label 'Average Profit'.
19 Select cell B15. Enter the formula =Average(I5:I9).
20 Select cell A16. Enter the label 'Branches Processed'.
21 Select Cell B16. Enter the formula =Count(I5:I9).
22 Highlight B13 to B15. Change the number format to currency.
23 Save the worksheet.

After completing steps 1 to 23, the worksheet should look like Figure 14.40, shown here.

	B16	fx	=COUNT(I5:I9)						
	A	B	C	D	E	F	G	H	I
1				Home Makers Furniture Store					
2									
3		First Quarter Sales Report							
4		January	February	March	Total	Expenditure	Profit before Tax	Tax on Profit	Profit after Tax
5	North	$ 26,500.00	$ 22,442.00	$ 23,456.00	$ 72,398.00	$ 25,000.00	$ 47,398.00	$ 7,109.70	$ 40,288.30
6	South	$ 45,600.00	$ 23,246.00	$ 67,543.00	$ 136,389.00	$ 32,056.00	$ 104,333.00	$ 15,649.95	$ 88,683.05
7	Central	$ 34,568.00	$ 29,687.00	$ 46,578.00	$ 110,833.00	$ 30,123.00	$ 80,710.00	$ 12,106.50	$ 68,603.50
8	East	$ 78,540.00	$ 98,755.00	$ 65,981.00	$ 243,276.00	$ 54,345.00	$ 188,931.00	$ 28,339.65	$ 160,591.35
9	West	$ 53,546.00	$ 94,786.00	$ 65,847.00	$ 214,179.00	$ 45,632.00	$ 168,547.00	$ 25,282.05	$ 143,264.95
10	Corporate	$ 238,754.00	$ 268,916.00	$ 269,405.00	$ 777,075.00	$ 187,156.00	$ 589,919.00	$ 88,487.85	$ 501,431.15
11									
12									
13	Maximum Profit	$ 160,591.35							
14	Minimum Profit	$ 40,288.30							
15	Average Profit	$ 100,286.23							
16	Branches Processed	5							

▲ Figure 14.40 Worksheet after Activity 5 is complete

Exercise 4

1 a Define a function.
   b List FOUR categories of functions.
2 Give the general form and an example of the following functions: SUM, AVERAGE, MAXIMUM, MINIMUM and COUNT.
3 The following table shows the gross pay for some employees of R and R Enterprises Limited.

Employee	Anderson K	Henry P	Joseph A	Jack M
Salary	$15 000	$16 575	$14 356	$18 675

Each employee has to pay a Health Surcharge (HSCH) of $120.00, National Insurance (NIS) of $150.00 and income tax based on how much is earned.
Income tax is calculated on the gross salary as follows:
Create a spreadsheet to calculate the net pay for each employee using the information above and below. Format the worksheet appropriately.

Income tax table

Income	Rate
< $5000	5 %
>= $5000 and <$10 000	10%
>= $10 000 and < $15 000	15%
>= $15 000 and < $20 000	20%

4 *Table A*

	A	B	C	D	E	F
1	Premier Services					
2	Sales Team Salaries	January 2019				
3						
4	Surname	Firstname	Sales	Basic Salary	Commission	Net Salary
5	Ramesar	Randal	$35457	$3500		
6	Mohammed	Aneesa	$75654	$3500		
7	Dean	Melissa	$18000	$3500		
8	Brown	Kerry	$67594	$3500		

Table A shows the name, sales and basic salary for some employees of Premier Services.
Each employee is given a commission based on sales shown in Table B.
Calculate the Net salary for each employee.

Table B

Sales	Commission
< $20 000	2%
>= $20 000 and < $30 000	3%
>= $30 000 and < $ 50 000	4%
>=$50 000	6%

Absolute cell references

As we saw earlier, you can copy a formula to another cell(s) in a row or column and let Excel change the formula relative to the position of the cell(s) (relative cell reference). However, there are situations where you do *not* want Excel to adjust the cell references when a formula is copied from one location to another. To prevent the cell references in a formula from changing, place a dollar ($) sign before and after the column. These are called absolute cell references. In Figure 14.41, the values of $B$1 and $B$2 remain unchanged, no matter where they are copied or moved in the worksheet.

Activity 6

	A	B	C	D	E
1	MARK UP	20%			
2	VAT	15%			
3					
4	Item	Cost Price	Marked-up price	Vat	Final Selling Price
5	Hat	$ 20.00			
6	Shirt	$ 75.00			
7	Pants	$ 235.00			
8	Jersey	$ 145.00			
9	Shoes	$ 225.00			

▲ Figure 14.41 Data for calculating a final selling price

	A	B	C	D	E
1	MARK UP	20%			
2	VAT	15%			
3					
4	Item	Cost Price	Marked-up price	Vat	Final Selling Price
5	Hat	$ 20.00	$ 24.00	$ 3.60	$ 27.60
6	Shirt	$ 75.00	$ 90.00	$ 13.50	$ 103.50
7	Pants	$ 235.00	$ 282.00	$ 42.30	$ 324.30
8	Jersey	$ 145.00	$ 174.00	$ 26.10	$ 200.10
9	Shoes	$ 225.00	$ 270.00	$ 40.50	$ 310.50

▲ Figure 14.42 Calculation of the final selling price

A store-owner would like to build a worksheet to calculate the final selling price of each item in his store. He first adds a markup of 20% to the cost price, to produce something called the marked-up price. He then adds 15% VAT to the marked-up price to get the final selling price.

How it is done
The values for markup and VAT are placed at the top of the worksheet so that they can be easily changed.

1 Enter the data as shown in Figure 14.41.
2 Move to cell C5. Type the formula =B5+ (B5* $B$1).
3 Copy the formula to cells C6, C7, C8 and C9.
4 Move to cell D5. Type the formula =C5 * $B$2.
5 Copy the formula to cells D6, D7, D8 and D9.
6 Move to cell E5. Type the formula =C5 + D5.
7 Copy the formula to cells E6, E7, E8 and E9.

Figure 14.42 shows the completed worksheet.

Reference to cells in other worksheets

Sometimes you may wish to refer to a cell in another worksheet when writing a formula. The general formula is:

=worksheetname!cellreference

For example, if you want to use the value of cell D11 from the worksheet 'Shares' in Figure 14.43(a) in cell B5 in the worksheet 'Assets' as shown in Figure 14.43(b), the formula will be =Shares!D11.

	A	B	C	D
1	Company	Amt. Share	Current Price	Current Value
2				
3	BBX	290	$ 25.00	$ 7,250.00
4	SBD	235	$ 15.25	$ 3,583.75
5	NTL	1000	$ 11.47	$11,470.00
6	CSQ	700	$ 12.80	$ 8,960.00
7	RPO	100	$ 62.40	$ 6,240.00
8	DHX	1820	$ 27.00	$49,140.00
9	LKT	700	$ 19.00	$13,300.00
10				
11	Total			$99,943.75

▲ Figure 14.43(a) Shares Worksheet

	A	B
1	Assets	2005
2	Top Money Mar	$ 72,998.07
3	Zenit Bank	$130,607.03
4	Bonds	$ 64,000.00
5	Shares	$ 99,943.75
6	Total	$367,548.85

▲ Figure 14.43(b) Assets Worksheet

Sorting

To 'sort' means to arrange in order. A typical spreadsheet package enables you to sort data (text or numbers) into ascending or descending order. If you do not specify an order, the rows and columns are sorted in ascending order (lowest to highest). This means the lowest is at the top of the sheet and the highest is at the bottom. The opposite holds for descending order.

Data can be sorted in a number of ways. For example, a teacher who enters the names of students and end-of-term marks for five subjects can sort the column of names into alphabetical order, with the students' marks also being moved accordingly. The teacher could also create a worksheet to rank the students according to a particular subject, again with a corresponding movement of all the other rows.

When sorting a list of data, most spreadsheet packages use the following guidelines:

- Rows with blank cells are placed at the bottom of the sorted list.
- Hidden rows are not moved.
- Numbers used as text are sorted before text alone.

Sorting data

1 Select the cells you would like to sort.
2 Click on the **Data** tab.
3 Click on the desired **AZ** or **ZA Sort** icon (ascending or descending) in the **Sort & Filter** group (see Figure 14.44). The table is sorted.
4 For more complex sorting options, click the **Sort** icon. The 'Sort' dialog box appears, as shown in Figure 14.45.

▲ Figure 14.44 'Sort & Filter' group

Sorting using more than one field

You may need to sort the data in a worksheet by more than one field. For example, a book store may want to sort all their books by author name. The owner may then want to sort each author's books alphabetically by title. The sorting procedure for a multiple sort is exactly the same as that for a single criterion, except that after the first criterion is selected you then move down to a second sort field and add additional sort criteria.

To sort by more than one field

1 Select the cells you would like to sort (the primary field).
2 Click on the **Data** tab.
3 Click the **Sort** icon. The 'Sort' dialog box appears as in Figure 14.45.
4 In the 'Sort by' box, select the primary column (primary field) by which you want your data sorted.

▲ Figure 14.45 'Sort' dialog box

5 Click on the order box and select **AZ** or **ZA**.
6 If you wish to sort a second column (secondary field) click the 'Add Level' button at the top of the 'Sort' dialog box.
7 Click on the order box and select **AZ** or **ZA**.
8 If you wish to sort the third column, repeat steps 5 to 6.
9 Click **OK**.

Exercise 5

1 Use examples to explain the difference between relative and absolute addressing.
2 a Define the term 'sorting'.
   b What are the advantages of sorting a worksheet?
3 The worksheet in Figure 14.46 shows a listing of books from a supplier to the Small Book Store. Do the following:
   a Create the worksheet.
   b Sort it into ascending order of classification.
   c Re-sort the worksheet in descending order by author and then by title.
   d Add a column to calculate the total cost for each title. (Total cost = No. of copies * Unit cost).
   e Sort the worksheet in descending order of total cost.

	A	B	C	D	E	F
1			The Small Book Store			
2						
3	Author Surname	Author First Name	Title	Classification	No. of Copies	Unit Cost
4	Brown	James	Back to Godhead	Religious	12	$ 50.00
5	Jaira	Khadine	Eagle and the Falcon	Thriller	4	$ 65.00
6	Lucas	Gary	Dracula	Horror	15	$ 85.00
7	Jaira	Khadine	Apocalypse	Thriller	24	$ 51.00
8	Lucas	Gary	Lost Forever	Thriller	6	$ 45.00
9	Mars	Gary	Star Chase	Science Fiction	8	$ 59.00
10	Brown	James	Faith Healers	Religious	21	$ 85.00
11	Lucas	Gary	Bad Omens	Horror	16	$ 66.00
12	Richards	Jenifer	Outer Planet Experience	Science Fiction	25	$ 48.00
13	Mohammed	Afzal	In Touch with God	Religious	31	$ 54.00
14	Lucas	Gary	The Dark Side	Horror	8	$ 38.00

▲ Figure 14.46 Worksheet showing a booklist

Filtering records

Filtering a worksheet displays records that contain a certain value or that meet a set of criteria. The two methods used for filtering records in Excel are AutoFilter and Advanced Filter.

AutoFilter

AutoFilter allows the selection of records based on one criterion. For example, from the worksheet in Figure 14.46 you can select all the books classified as 'Horror'.

Using the AutoFilter command

1 Using the worksheet in Figure 14.46, select all the religious books.
2 Select the range to be filtered. Select A3:F14.
3 Next, click the **Filter** option in the 'Sort and Autofilter' group on the Data tab.
4 The first row in the table (the header row) should change, with a small drop-down arrow on each cell in the header row, as shown in Figure 14.47.
5 Click on the drop-down list arrow in the cell with column label 'Classification'. A list of the different values (Religious, Science Fiction, and so on) contained in that column is displayed.
6 Select the desired criterion, in this case, 'Religious'.
7 All the records containing the classification 'Religious' will be displayed as shown in Figure 14.48.

Note

Before a worksheet can be filtered, it must have column labels.

	A	B	C	D	E	F
1			The Small Book Store			
2						
3	Author Surnam ▼	Author First Nam ▼	Title ▼	Classification ▼	No. of Copi ▼	Unit Cc ▼
4	Brown	James	Back to Godhead	Religious	12	$ 50.00
5	Jaira	Khadine	Eagle and the Falcon	Thriller	4	$ 65.00
6	Lucas	Gary	Dracula	Horror	15	$ 85.00
7	Jaira	Khadine	Apocalypse	Thriller	24	$ 51.00
8	Lucas	Gary	Lost Forever	Thriller	6	$ 45.00
9	Mars	Gary	Star Chase	Science Fiction	8	$ 59.00
10	Brown	James	Faith Healers	Religious	21	$ 85.00
11	Lucas	Gary	Bad Omens	Horror	16	$ 66.00
12	Richards	Jenifer	Outer Planet Experience	Science Fiction	25	$ 48.00
13	Mohammed	Afzal	In Touch with God	Religious	31	$ 54.00
14	Lucas	Gary	The Dark Side	Horror	8	$ 38.00

▲ Figure 14.47 The Small Book Store's worksheet using AutoFilter

	A	B	C	D	E	F
1			The Small Book Store			
2						
3	Author Surnam ▼	Author First Nam ▼	Title ▼	Classification ▼	No. of Copi ▼	Unit Cc ▼
4	Brown	James	Back to Godhead	Religious	12	$ 50.00
10	Brown	James	Faith Healers	Religious	21	$ 85.00
13	Mohammed	Afzal	In Touch with God	Religious	31	$ 54.00

▲ Figure 14.48 List of all the religious books at The Small Book Store

Advanced filter – filtering using multiple criteria

Sometimes you may want to select records based on more than one criterion. For example, using the spreadsheet in Figure 14.46, if you would like to select all the books that are written by the author Lucas and are classified as horror, you would need to use an advanced filter.

Performing an advanced filter

1. Select **Advanced** from the 'Sort & Filter' group of the **Data** tab. The 'Advanced Filter' dialog box appears, as shown in Figure 14.49.
2. The first step is to specify the 'List range'. This is the range on which you would like to perform the advanced filter. Excel automatically selects this area and displays it in the 'List range' combo box. If you would like to change the range selected, click on the **Collapse** button on the right side within the combo box. The 'List range' combo box will be displayed alone; the other options become hidden. Type in or drag the mouse over the area desired. The range will be displayed in the combo box. Click on the **Collapse** button again to see the entire 'Advanced Filter' dialog box.
3. The second step involves the selection of the criteria range. This refers to the different criteria you are going to use to select the records. For example, using the worksheet in Figure 14.46 you can select records by using the criteria author surname (for example, Lucas), classification (for example, Horror), No. of copies (for example, >10). To select the criteria range you need to move to another part of the worksheet and type in or copy and paste the column labels and the criteria you wish to use to select the records. The cells A17 to C18 in Figure 14.50 (Activity 7 on the next page) shows the criteria range for selecting records in that worksheet.
4. Finally, you can:
   - filter the worksheet in place; the selected records will be displayed and the other records will be hidden, or
   - copy the selected records to another location within the worksheet.

To filter the worksheet in place, click **OK**. To place the selected records in another location check the radio button **Copy to** in the 'Advanced Filter' dialog box. A third combo box appears in the 'Advanced Filter' dialog box. Select a cell in the area of the worksheet where you would like to place the selected records and click **OK**. The selected records will be displayed.

▲ Figure 14.49 The 'Advanced Filter' dialog box

Activity 7

Using the worksheet named 'Book Store' shown in Figure 14.46, select the records of all the books by the author 'Lucas', classification 'Horror' and 'No. of copies' greater than ten (10).

How it is done

1 From the **Data** tab, select **Advanced** from the 'Sort and Filter group'. The 'Advanced Filter' dialog box appears as shown in Figure 14.49.
2 Excel selects the list range 'Sheet 1!$A$17:$C$18' and places it in the 'List range' combo box.

3 To enter the criteria range select the following cells and enter the corresponding values: A17 – 'Author Surname', B17 – 'Classification', C17 – 'No. of Copies', A18 – 'Lucas', B18 – 'Horror', C18 – '>10'.
4 To filter the list in place click **OK**. The results are shown in Figure 14.50.
5 To copy the records to another location within the spreadsheet, check the **Copy to another location** radio button in the 'Advanced Filter' dialog box. Excel selects a location to copy the records to. In this example, Excel selects the range A19 to F19. The selected records are shown in Figure 14.51.

	A	B	C	D	E	F
1			The Small Book Store			
2						
3	Author Surname	Author First Name	Title	Classification	No. of Copies	Unit Cost
6	Lucas	Gary	Dracula	Horror	15	$ 85.00
11	Lucas	Gary	Bad Omens	Horror	16	$ 66.00
15						
16						
17	Author Surname	Classification	No. of Copies			
18	Lucas	Horror	>10			
19						

▲ Figure 14.50 Records selected when the list is filtered in place

	Author Surname	Author First Name	Title	Classification	No. of Copies	Unit Cost
1			The Small Book Store			
2						
3	Author Surname	Author First Name	Title	Classification	No. of Copies	Unit Cost
4	Brown	James	Back to Godhead	Religious	12	$ 50.00
5	Jaira	Khadine	Eagle and the Falcon	Thriller	4	$ 65.00
6	Lucas	Gary	Dracula	Horror	15	$ 85.00
7	Jaira	Khadine	Apocalypse	Thriller	24	$ 51.00
8	Lucas	Gary	Lost Forever	Thriller	6	$ 45.00
9	Mars	Gary	Star Chase	Science Fiction	8	$ 59.00
10	Brown	James	Faith Healers	Religious	21	$ 85.00
11	Lucas	Gary	Bad Omens	Horror	16	$ 66.00
12	Richards	Jenifer	Outer Planet Experience	Science Fiction	25	$ 48.00
13	Mohammed	Afzal	In Touch with God	Religious	31	$ 54.00
14	Lucas	Gary	The Dark Side	Horror	8	$ 38.00
15						
16						
17	Author First Name	Classification	No. of Copies			
18	Gary	Horror	>10			
19	Author Surname	Author First Name	Title	Classification	No. of Copies	Unit Cost
20	Lucas	Gary	Dracula	Horror	15	$ 85.00
21	Lucas	Gary	Bad Omens	Horror	16	$ 66.00
22						

▲ Figure 14.51 Selected records copied to another location

Creating graphs and charts

The ability to convert worksheet data into one of many graphical forms is a very important feature of any spreadsheet package. Graphs and charts are very useful because they can simplify numerical data that may otherwise be confusing. They make the data easier to interpret. They grab your attention almost instantly and allow information to be absorbed quickly. Therefore, charts can be important tools for data analysis and the presentation of data.

The first step in creating a chart is to select the data values you want to place in it. A spreadsheet package enables you to plot any row or column of data against any other row or column of data. For example, if you want to represent the first-quarter sales for the months of January to March for the five branches of the Home Maker's Furniture Store for the values shown in Figure 14.29 (page 318), you need to select the range A3:D7.

After selecting the data values, you need to select a type of chart that is relevant to the situation. The type of chart you choose depends on the type of data you have and how you want to represent it. Some charts are best for representing certain types of data. For example, the data that represents sales of different branches of a company over a period may be displayed using a column graph. Data that represent portions of a whole might best be represented using a pie chart.

If any values in the data selected are changed after the chart has been created, the changes are immediately reflected in the chart. Also, more data can be inserted between the first and last rows or columns. These changes will also be included automatically in the chart. Before creating a chart, make yourself familiar with the elements of a chart. Figure 14.52 shows a completed chart for the first-quarter sales of the Home Maker's Furniture Store.

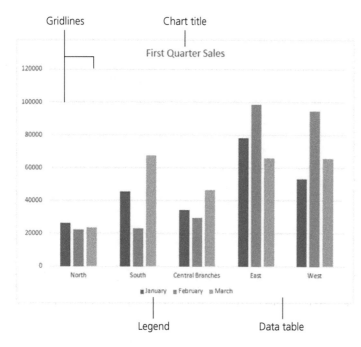

▲ Figure 14.52 Column chart for first-quarter sales with its elements named

Chart types

Excel offers many chart types, as well as the column chart shown in Figure 14.52. We will use a column chart as our example below, but different charts and graphs are used for different types of information. Table 14.4 summarises the main types and gives examples of what you might use them for.

Chart elements

A chart can include the following elements (see Figure 14.54), as listed.

- **Axes**: the vertical and horizontal lines against which data is plotted. The x-axis is referred to as the **category axis** and the y-axis is known as the **value axis**.
- **Data range**: The data selected to create the chart.
- **Series**: The row or column headings that make up the range of values from the worksheet that is used to create the graph.
- **Titles**: There are three titles: for the chart, category axis and value axis. They are lines of text used to describe the chart elements.
- **Gridlines**: Incremental lines that may appear along each axis; they help you to read values from the graph more easily.
- **Legend**: A cross-reference showing how each series is represented in the chart, that is a key.
- **Data labels**: The actual value, percentage or name of a bar or segment of a chart.
- **Data table**: The range of values, included at the bottom of the chart, that is used to chart the graph.

Creating a chart in Excel

Creating a chart using Excel's Chart options is a very simple process.

1 **Chart type:** Select the data in the worksheet to be used to create the chart. Select the **Insert** tab/ **Charts** group (see Figure 14.53) and choose the type of chart from what is displayed. Click the arrow button to launch the 'Insert Chart' dialog box (see Figure 14.54) for more options.

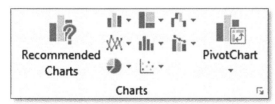

▲ Figure 14.53 Insert tab, showing the 'Charts' group options

Chart Type	Usage
Column chart	This is used to compare numerical values in a table across several categories. It is used when the order of the categories is not important. The sales chart in the example below is a column chart.
Bar chart	This is a different way to compare numerical values in a table across several categories. It is used when the category text is long or the category in the chart is duration. A chart to compare the time taken for different journeys would be a good example of this.
Line Graphs	Line graphs show trends – how one category changes compared to another. It plots the data as a series of points but then links those points with a line so you can estimate values between the ones recorded. You would use this for recording how a population changed over time, or how much liquid was in a bucket as it was poured in over time.
Pie Charts	These show categories as the proportions of a whole. You add up all the quantities in the category you are interested in and then turn each one into a percentage. Activity 10 below shows an example of different regions sales shown as a proportion of all the sales.

▲ Table 14.4 Excel chart types and their usage

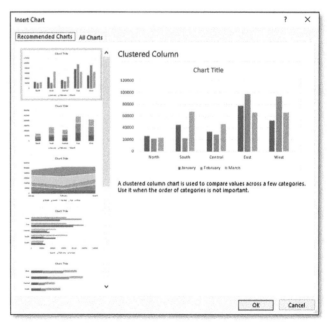

▲ Figure 14.54 'Recommended Charts' tab in the 'Insert Chart' dialog box

2 Select the type of chart you require from the options provided, for example, see Figure 14.55.

3 **Chart Design:** The Design tab shown in Figure 14.56 provides a number of options to change the features of the chart, such as titles, labels, legends, data tables, axes, gridlines and many more. The following groups are provided: Chart Layouts, Chart Styles, Data, Type and location.

4 **Chart Location:** You can choose where the chart is placed. The **Move Chart** icon (see Figure 14.57) is on the Location group at the end of the Chart Tools **Design** tab. Now look at Figure 14.58.

■ Axes – you can specify how the axes are labelled

■ Axis Titles – you can type a chart title, and titles for the category (*x*) axis and value (*y*) axis.

■ Chart Title.

■ Data Labels – you can include the values, percentage value and/or label for each data element.

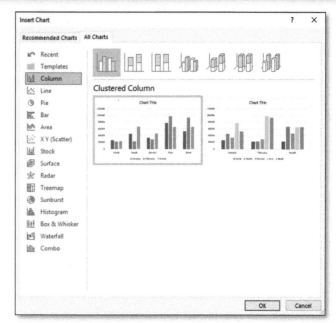

▲ Figure 14.55 'All Charts' tab in the 'Insert Chart' dialog box

▲ Figure 14.56 Chart Title options on the Labels group

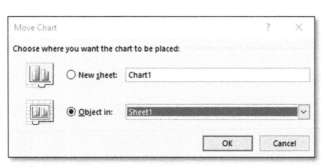

▲ Figure 14.57 'Move Chart' dialog box

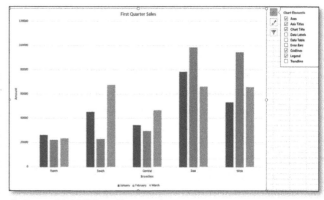

▲ Figure 14.58 'Chart Elements'

■ Data Table – you can choose whether or not to show in the chart the data range that was used to create it.

■ Gridlines – you can choose whether or not to include major and minor gridlines for the axes

■ Error bar – graphical representations of the variability of data Gridlines

■ Legend – you can include a legend and select a position to place it in the chart

■ Trendline – a best-fit straight line that is used with simple linear data sets.

Activity 8

Using the worksheet in Figure 14.59, create a column graph to show the first-quarter sales for five branches of the Home Makers Furniture Store.

How it is done

1 Select the ranges A3 to A7 and E3 to E7. (Select A3:A7 then hold down the CTRL key and select E3 to E7).
2 Click on the **Insert** tab.
3 From the 'Chart' group select the type of chart you require by clicking on the down arrow and selecting from the options.
4 Click the **Add chart elements** option from the Chart layout group.
Click the plus (+) sign. The 'Chart Elements' dialog box appears.
5 For each tab, do as follows.
  ▪ Titles: In the 'Chart title' field, type 'FIRST QUARTER SALES'.
  ▪ In the 'Category (X) axis' field, type 'Branches'.
  ▪ In the 'Value (Y) axis' field, type 'Amount'.
  ▪ Axes: Ensure the 'Category (X) axis' and the 'Value (Y) axis' boxes are checked, and check the Automatic radio button.

▪ Gridlines: Check Value (y) axis: Major gridlines.
▪ Legend: Check the Placement: Right radio button.
▪ Data Labels: Check the None radio button.
▪ Data Table: Check the Show data table box. (You may leave the box unchecked if you don't want to show the data table.) Click **Next**.
6 Leave the chart as an object in Sheet 1. Click **Finish**.

The chart created by this process is shown in Figure 14.60.

	A	B	C	D	E
1		Home Makers Furniture Store			
2		January	February	March	Total
3	North	$26,500.00	$22,442.00	$23,456.00	$72,398.00
4	South	$45,600.00	$23,246.00	$67,543.00	$136,389.00
5	Central	$34,568.00	$29,687.00	$46,578.00	$110,833.00
6	East	$78,540.00	$98,755.00	$65,981.00	$243,276.00
7	West	$53,546.00	$94,786.00	$65,847.00	$214,179.00
8	Corporate	$238,754.00	$268,916.00	$269,405.00	$777,075.00

▲ Figure 14.59 Worksheet to form the basis of a graph

Activity 9

Using the worksheet in Figure 14.59, create a graph to compare the total sales for the four branches.

▲ Figure 14.60 Graph of total sales

Activity 10

To create a pie chart

The data represented in Figure 14.59 can also be represented as a pie chart. The steps are as follows:

1 Select columns A3 to A7 and E3 to E7.
2 Click on the **Chart Wizard** icon.
3 With the Standard Types tab displayed, select **Pie** from the 'Chart type' box. Then select the first chart from the 'Chart sub-type' box. Click **Next**.
4 Select the **Series tab**. Type 'Total Sales' in the 'Name' field. Click **Next**.
5 On the Titles tab:
  In the 'Chart title' field, type 'First Quarter Total Sales'. (There are no other options available in this tab.)
  On the **Data Labels tab**, check the **Percentage** button.
  Click **Next**.
6 Click **Finish**.

The pie chart produced should look like Figure 14.61.

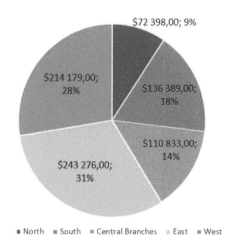

▲ Figure 14.61 Pie chart of total sales

Exercise 6

1 Table 14.4 shows the money spent by a student on different items over a four-week period.
  a Calculate the total amount of money spent on each item over the four weeks.
  b Create a pie chart showing the total amount spent on each item. The pie chart should display the percentage spent on each item.
2 Table 14.5 shows the cost of three types of juices, the quantity sold over a four-week period and the expenses of the Fresh Juice Stall. You are required to create a spreadsheet to calculate:
  a the income earned for each week
  b the profit or loss for each week
  c the total amount of each type of juice sold over the four-week period.

d Create an appropriately labelled column graph showing the total amount of each juice sold over the four weeks.

ITEMS	WEEK 1	WEEK 2	WEEK 3	WEEK 4	TOTAL
Food	200	245	180	80	
Stationery	50	25	20	40	
Travel	25	30	25	35	
Clothes	150				
Medical			125		
Books	50	75			
Other	120	45	94	65	

▲ Table 14.5 Money spent over four weeks

Fresh Juice Stall

Juices	Cost
Orange	$5
Melon	$7
Pineapple	$8

	Orange	Melon	Pineapple	Income	Expenses	Profit or Loss
WEEK 1	124	21	65		$120	
WEEK 2	135	80	45		$250	
WEEK 3	154	56	84		$165	
WEEK 4	110	85	94		$155	

▲ Table 14.6 The cost and number of juices sold over a four-week period, and the Fresh Juice Stall's expenses

The IF function

The IF function tests a condition that is either true or false. The general form of the function is as follows:

IF(logical_test, [value_if_true], [value_if_false])
   1   2   3

When the function is executed, the first instruction (the second argument) is executed if the condition tested is true, and the second instruction (the third argument) is executed if the condition tested is false. Either instruction can be text, a number, a formula, a function or a cell address. If the instruction is a formula, function or cell address, the result, and not the instruction itself, will be displayed.

For instance, consider the function =IF(F5>=50000,10,8). If the value in cell F5 is greater than or equal to 50000, the function will return the value 10. If the value is less than 50000, the function will return the value 8. The logical operators in Table 14.7 can be used in the IF function:

Operator	Meaning
>	Greater than
=	Equal to
>=	Greater than or equal to
<	Less than
<=	Less than or equal to
<>	Not equal to

▲ Table 14.7 Operators and their meanings

Activity 11

The First Trinidad National Bank pays a yearly interest of 8% on fixed-deposit balances that are less than or equal to $50 000, and 10% on fixed-deposit balances greater than $50 000. The interest earned is then added to the customer's balance at the beginning of the year to give the final balance.

The worksheet in Figure 14.62b shows some customers and their balances. The function =IF(C4<=50000,8%,10%) in cell D4 compares the value in cell C4 to see if it is less than or equal to 50 000. Since the value is 45 000, the condition is true, so the value 8% is returned. However, if the value in cell C4 had been greater than 50 000, the value 10% would have been returned, as is the case for D5, D6 and D8.

In Figure 14.62b, we have decided not to show the interest rate explicitly, but just the result of using it to calculate the interest earned. Look at the new formula for D4 at the top of the figure. The value in cell C4 is checked to see if it is less than or equal to 50 000. If the condition is true, the value in cell C4 is multiplied by .08 and if the condition is false it is multiplied by .10.

D4				fx	IF(C4<=50000, 0,08*C4, 0,1*C4)		

	A	B	C	D	E
1			Zenith Bank		
2					
3	First Name	Surname	Starting Balance	Interest Earned	Final Balance
4	Larry	Adams	$45 000,00	$3 600,00	$48 600,00
5	Marie	Balfour	$69 569,00	$6 956,90	$76 525,90
6	James	Chin-Fat	$84 254,00	$8 425,40	$92 679,40
7	Harry	Doodnath	$35 789,00	$2 863,12	$38 652,12
8	Krishna	Singh	$55 467,00	$5 546,70	$61 013,70

▲ Figure 14.62b Banking worksheet without an explicit interest rate

Nested IF statement

As you have seen, the IF statement can return one value if the condition is true or another value if the condition is false. The IF statement can also be used in situations where there are several conditions to be tested. For example, the worksheet in Figure 14.63 shows the identification number, first name, surname, marks for four subjects, total and average marks for a student in a class. Students are awarded grades based on the average mark.

The grades awarded for each range are:

Average mark	Grade
>=80	A
>=65 and <80	B
>=55 and <65	C
>=50 and <55	D
<50	F (fail)

To award grades we need to write a formula using several IF (called nested IF) statements, so we can test several conditions. In cell J2 we write the formula:

=IF(I2>=80,"A",IF(I2>=65,"B",IF(I2>=55,"C",IF(I2>=50,"D","F"))))

The formula is then copied to the other cells in the column.

L5				fx	=IF(K5>=80,"A",IF(K5>=65,"B",IF(K5>=55,"C",IF(K5>=50,"D","F"))))						
	A	B	C	D	E	F	G	H	I	J	K	L

	Student ID	Surname	First Name	Maths	Biology	Chemistry	Physics	English	History	Total	Average	Grade
1					Happy Valley High School							
2												
3					Form 4.1 Mark		Sheet					
4	Student ID	Surname	First Name	Maths	Biology	Chemistry	Physics	English	History	Total	Average	Grade
5	1354	Charles	Yvonne	84	78	78	85	75	85	485	80.8	A
6	1546	Dennis	Hall	45	40	60	65	65	76	351	58.5	C
7	1347	Estrada	Jean	85	89	69	72	75	88	478	79.7	B
8	1457	Eversley	Nadine	49	52	42	46	47	35	271	45.2	F
9	1436	Fung	Collin	68	65	72	65	84	81	435	72.5	B
10	1574	Grovia	Leslie	79	68	56	45	77	88	413	68.8	B
11	1642	Gower	John	85	79	67	65	69	67	432	72.0	B
12	1245	Brown	Jim	67	90	85	65	80	67	454	75.7	B
13	1342	Baker	Harry	85	82	76	68	68	40	419	69.8	B
14	1247	Cameron	Joanne	45	35	50	38	68	89	325	54.2	D

▲ Figure 14.63 Nested IF statements

Exercise 7

1 Create the worksheet shown in Figure 14.62b.
   a Insert five additional customers and their starting balances.
   b Sort the worksheet on customer name in descending order of surname.
   c A 15% tax is charged on interest earned IF the customer is under 55 years of age. Insert a column with the heading 'Age' and insert ages varying from 20 years to 70 years for each client on the spreadsheet. Calculate the tax, that are if any, on the interest.
   d Calculate the interest after tax.
   e Calculate the final balance (starting balance + interest after tax).

2 Create the worksheet shown in Figure 14.63.
   a Format the average mark as a percentage.
   b Insert a row above row 1.
   c Type the label 'Form Class 4s'.
   d Type in the label 'Comment' in cell K2.
   e Write an IF statement in column K to insert a comment based on the grades obtained using the following conditions:
      A – Very good
      B – Good
      C – Fair
      D – Try harder
      F – Much more effort needed

The date function

Dates are a special case in Excel. If you enter information that can be translated as a date then Excel treats it as a date. It converts your data into a serial number that is internally used to represent dates and times. To enter a date in Excel, use the ' / ' or '-' characters. For instance, any of the following entries will be translated to a date by Excel:

- 6/23
- 6-23/18
- 23 June
- June 23, 2018

To store dates in a particular format

1. Enter a date into an empty cell and confirm entry.
2. Select the cell with the date.
3. Click on the Home tab and click on the down arrow in the 'Number' group.
4. Select the format required (Short date or Long date) from the drop-down menu.

Excel has a number of functions that aid in computations involving dates. Some of the functions are as follows.

TODAY(): Gives today's date in date format (for example, 10/25/2018)

NOW(): Gives today's date and time (for example, 10/25/2018 11:45)

Because dates (and times) are stored as numbers, they can be used in calculations. For example, it is easy to work out the number of days between two dates. Consider the following example shown in Figure 14.64.

A video club rent videos to their customers for a down-payment of $3.00 and a daily rental of $2.00. The amount a customer pays is found by calculating the number of days from the day borrowed to the present day, multiplied by the daily rental.

	A	B	C	D	E	F	G	H	I	J
1	Member Number	First Name	Surname	Movie Borrowed	Date Borrowed	Cost per day	Down Payment	Date Returned	Number of Days	Cost
2	10	Brian	James	Venom	2/25/2019	$ 2.00	$ 3.00	3/4/2019	7	$ 11.00

▲ Figure 14.64 Date function

To get the present date, the function =TODAY() is entered in cell H2 (see Figure 14.64).

To get the number of days the video was rented, type the formula =(H2-E2) in cell I2 (see Figure 14.64).

To calculate the cost, enter the formula =I2*F2-G2 in cell J2.

PivotTables and PivotCharts

PivotTables are one of the most powerful and useful tools in Excel (see Figure 14.65). They will save you a lot of time by allowing you to quickly calculate, summarise, and analyse data that lets you see comparisons, patterns, and trends in your data.

How to insert and create a PivotTable

	A	B	C	D	E	F	G
1			The Small Book Store				
2							
3	Author Surname	Author First Name	Title	Genre	No. of copies	Unit cost	Total Cost
4	Young	William Paul	The Shack	Religious	12	$50,00	$600,00
5	Brown	Dan	Inferno	Thriller	4	$65,00	$260,00
6	Mary	Shelley	Dracula	Horror	15	$85,00	$1 275,00
7	Brown	Dan	Angels and Demons	Thriller	24	$51,00	$1 224,00
8	King	Stephen	The Shining	Thriller	6	$45,00	$270,00
9	George	Orwell	1984	Science Fiction	8	$59,00	$472,00
10	Lewis	C.S	The Screwtape Letters	Religious	21	$85,00	$1 785,00
11	Stephen	King	Pet Semetary	Horror	16	$66,00	$1 056,00
12	Atwood	Margaret	Oryx and Crake	Science Fiction	25	$48,00	$1 200,00
13	Lewis	Beverly	The Preacher's Daughter	Religious	31	$54,00	$1 674,00
14	King	Stephen	IT	Horror	8	$38,00	$304,00
15	Rowling	J.K.	The Philosopher's Stone	Fiction	15	$25,00	$375,00
16	Austen	Jane	Pride and Prejudice	Romance	20	$15,00	$300,00
17	Lee	Harper	To Kill a Mockingbird	Fiction	45	$37,00	$1 665,00
18	Orwell	George	Animal Farm	Fantasy	13	$34,00	$442,00
19	Meyer	Stephenie	Twilight	Fantasy	18	$43,00	$774,00
20	Huxley	Aldous	Brave New World	Science Fiction	7	$25,00	$175,00
21	Brown	Dan	The Da Vinci Code	Thriller	14	$18,00	$252,00
22	Hosseini	Khaled	Kite Runner	Fiction	13	$12,00	$156,00
23	Steinbeck	John	Of Mice and Men	Fiction	11	$13,00	$143,00
24	Shelley	Mary	Frankenstein	Science Fiction	6	$15,00	$90,00
25	Austen	Jane	Sense and Sensibility	Romance	7	$14,00	$98,00
26	Austen	Jane	Emma	Comedy	4	$14,00	$56,00
27	Dickens	Charles	Great Expectations	Aventure	34	$12,00	$408,00
28	Lowry	Lois	The Giver	Science Fiction	24	$13,00	$312,00
29	Atwood	Margaret	The Handmaid's Tale	Fiction	12	$14,00	$168,00
30	Coelho	Paulo	The Alchemist	Adventure	43	$19,00	$817,00

▲ Figure 14.65 Worksheet for PivotTable

To insert a PivotTable (see Figure 14.65), execute the following steps.

1   Click any single cell inside the data set.
2   On the Insert tab, in the Tables group, click PivotTable (Figure 14.66).

The 'Create PivotTable' dialog box appears (see Figure 14.67). Excel automatically selects the data for you. The default location for a new PivotTable is 'New Worksheet'.

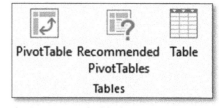

▲ Figure 14.66 'Tables' group

3 Click **OK**. The PivotTable Fields pane appears.
4 To get the total amount of each classification of books, drag the 'Genre' field to the 'Rows' area and the 'Sum of No. of copies' field to the 'Values' area.
5 Figure 14.68 shows the result.

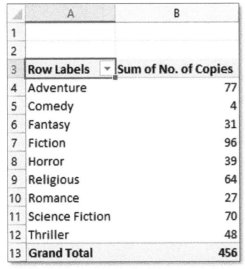

	A	B
1		
2		
3	Row Labels	Sum of No. of Copies
4	Adventure	77
5	Comedy	4
6	Fantasy	31
7	Fiction	96
8	Horror	39
9	Religious	64
10	Romance	27
11	Science Fiction	70
12	Thriller	48
13	**Grand Total**	**456**

▲ Figure 14.68 PivotTable

Sorting the PivotTable

To organise the results shown in Figure 14.68 in descending order, we need to sort the table.

1 Click any cell inside the 'Sum of No. of Copies' column.
2 Right click and click on Sort, click **Sort Largest to Smallest** (see Figure 14.69).

The result is shown in Figure 14.70.

	A	B
1		
2		
3	**Row Labels**	**Sum of No. of Copies**
4	Fiction	96
5	Adventure	77
6	Science Fiction	70
7	Religious	64
8	Thriller	48
9	Horror	39
10	Fantasy	31
11	Romance	27
12	Comedy	4
13	**Grand Total**	**456**

▲ Figure 14.70 PivotTable result

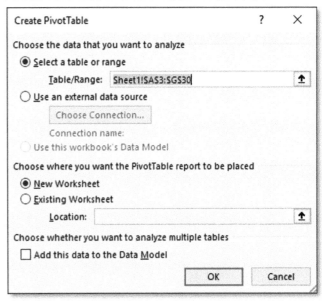

▲ Figure 14.67 'Create PivotTable' dialog box

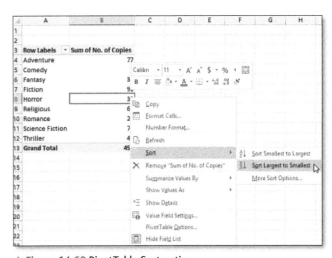

▲ Figure 14.69 PivotTable Sort option

Filter

If you wanted to find out the number of books by a particular author, you can add a filter. Check the Author Surname box and drag it to filter. Click the down arrow in the box to select the name of an author.

1   Click the filter drop-down and select Austen.

Result. The store has 31 books by Austen, 27 are Romance and 4 are Comedy (see Figure 14.71).

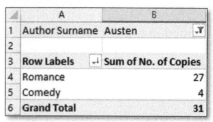

	A	B
1	Author Surname	Austen
2		
3	Row Labels	Sum of No. of Copies
4	Romance	27
5	Comedy	4
6	Grand Total	31

▲ Figure 14.71 PivotTable filtered

Two-dimensional PivotTables

If you drag a field to the 'Rows' area and 'Columns' area, you can create a two-dimensional PivotTable. For example, to get the total amount for each 'Genre' in stock, we need to check the 'Total Cost' field and drag the field to the 'Values' section of the PivotTable pane as shown in Figure 14.72.

Below you can find the two-dimensional PivotTable showing the number and total cost of books in each 'Genre'. The sum of the 'Total Cost' field has been formatted to currency. To do this you simply:

1   Select the range C4:C13.
2   Right click and select **Format Cells**.
3   Select currency from the 'Format Cells' dialog box.

Figure 14.73 shows the result.

	A	B	C
1			
2			
3	**Row Labels**	**Sum of No. of Copies**	**Sum of Total Cost**
4	Fiction	96	$ 2,507.00
5	Adventure	77	$ 1,225.00
6	Science Fiction	70	$ 2,249.00
7	Religious	64	$ 4,059.00
8	Thriller	48	$ 2,006.00
9	Horror	39	$ 2,635.00
10	Fantasy	31	$ 1,216.00
11	Romance	27	$ 398.00
12	Comedy	4	$ 56.00
13	**Grand Total**	**456**	**$ 16,351.00**

▲ Figure 14.73 Two-dimensional PivotTable

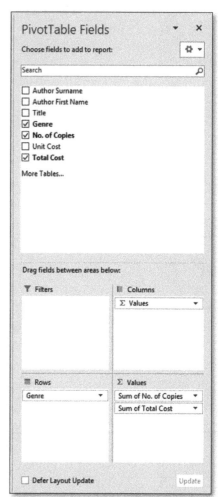

▲ Figure 14.72 PivotTable pane

Create a PivotChart

To easily compare these numbers, create a PivotChart. With the PivotTable displayed, click on the PivotChart option in the Charts group. A suggested chart will be displayed as shown in Figure 14.74. You can use this chart or make selections based on the chart options available.

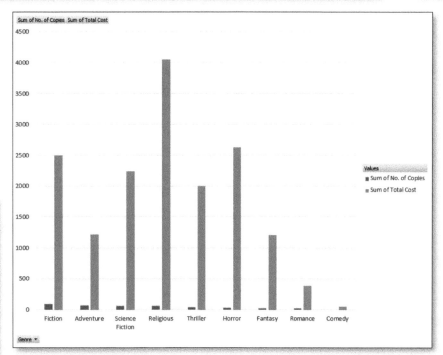

▲ Figure 14.74 PivotChart

	A	B	C	D
1	1 Surname	First Name	Student Scores
2	2 Bishop	Victoria	25
3	3 Eastman	Renee	25
4	4 Omar	Ravi	35
5	5 Cardinal	Melissa	38
6	6 Chen	Jason	46
7	7 Fredericks	Gary	47
8	8 Vaughn	Shimona	49
9	9 Brown	Jim	50
10	10 Baker	Harry	54
11	11 Cameron	Joanne	54
12	12 Carrington	Gloria	56
13	13 Diaz	Eric	57
14	14 George	Dominic	63
15	15 Homer	Bud	63
16	16 Jupiter	Neil	65
17	17 Charles	Yvonne	67
18	18 Hall	Dennis	67
19	19 Estrada	Jean	68
20	20 Eversley	Nadine	68
21	21 Fung	Collin	75
22	22 Govia	Leslie	75
23	23 Gower	John	75
24	24 Ferose	Ali	81
25	25 Jane	Mary	82
26	26 Bradshaw	Kimberly	84
27	27 Joseph	Ian	84
28	28 French	Jason	85
29	29 James	Sarah	87
30	30 Eden	Leo	98

▲ Figure 14.75 Students' marks for an activity

Activity 12

Create the worksheet shown in Figure 14.75. You are required to:

1 Create a PivotTable that group the marks from lowest to highest in an interval of 10.
2 Create a PivotChart to show the spread of the marks among the students.

How it is done

Refer to figures 14.76 and 14.77.

1 Select the cells you want to create a PivotTable from. (Note: Your data should not have any empty rows or columns. It must have only a single-row heading. Using the data in Figure 14.75, select A1 to C30.)

2 Select **Insert > PivotTable**.

3 Under 'Choose the data that you want to analyse', select **Select a table or range'**.

4 **Table/Range**, verify the cell range.

5 Under 'Choose where you want the PivotTable report to be placed', select **New worksheet** to place the PivotTable in a 'New Worksheet' or 'Existing Worksheet' and then select the location you want the PivotTable to appear.

6 Select **OK**.

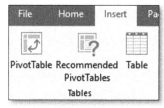

▲ Figure 14.76 Tables group from the Insert tab

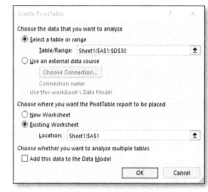

▲ Figure 14.77 PivotTable combo box

Activity 12 continued

The window in Figure 14.78 appears to check the student scores box in the PivotTable Fields and drag to Rows in the bottom left pane. The field Sum of Student Scores is added automatically.

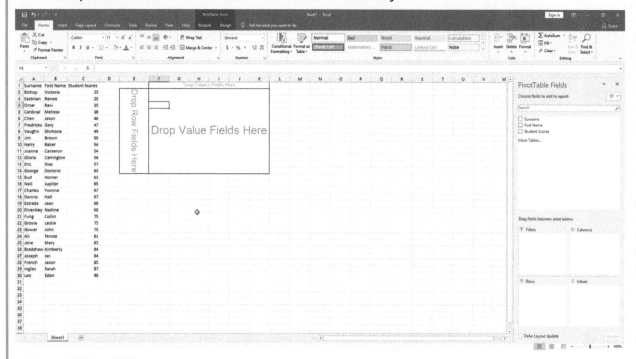

▲ Figure 14.78 PivotTable pane

Right-click on any number under the field sum of Student Scores. A drop-down menu appears. Select the **Group** option. The 'Group' dialog box appears. A set of predetermined groups appear. Make an adjustment or select **OK** to accept (see Figure 14.79). The student scores will be placed in groups as shown in Figure 14.80. Select any number under the 'Total' label. A drop-down menu appears. Select **Summarise Values by Count** (see Figure 14.81). The table is automatically updated with the number of values within each range (see Figure 14.82).

▲ Figure 14.79 'Grouping' dialog Dialog box

E	F
Sum of Student Scores	
Student Scores ▼	**Total**
25-34	50
35-44	73
45-54	300
55-64	239
65-74	335
75-84	556
85-94	172
95-104	98
Grand Total	**1823**

▲ Figure 14.80 Groups created

Activity 12 continued

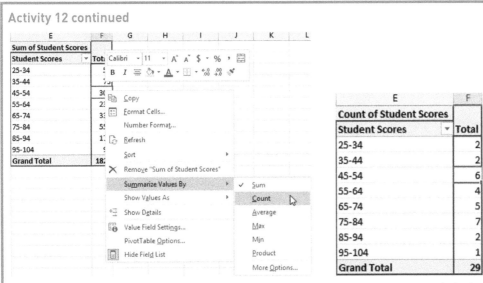

▲ Figure 14.81 Summarising by 'Count'

Count of Student Scores	
Student Scores	Total
25-34	2
35-44	2
45-54	6
55-64	4
65-74	5
75-84	7
85-94	2
95-104	1
Grand Total	29

▲ Figure 14.82 Spread of values

To plot a PivotChart (as in Figure 14.83), select the **Insert** tab and then choose 'PivotChart'. The chart will appear. You can make adjustments to the chart just as you did previously in the 'Charts' section.

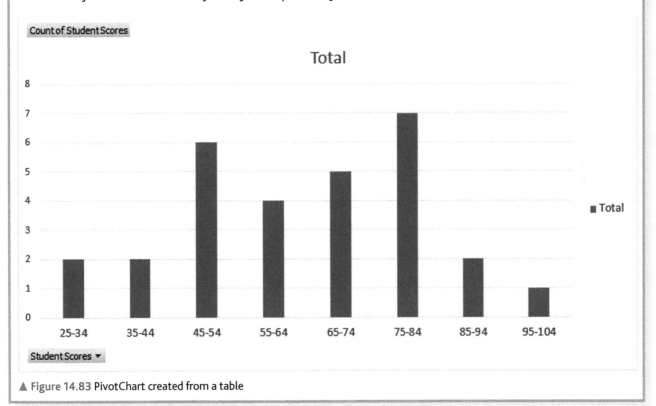

▲ Figure 14.83 PivotChart created from a table

Journey Car Rentals rent three types of cars at the rates shown in Table 14.7. A customer renting a car has to make a down payment of $200. If the car is returned in good condition, the customer is refunded the $200; if not, then the customer loses the down-payment.

Rental charge is calculated by multiplying the number of days rented by the daily charge. Using the present date on the computer as the date returned, create a spreadsheet to calculate the amount paid by the various customers in Table 14.8.

	A	B	C	D	E				
1	Journey Car Rentals								
2	Rate per day								
3	Class A	$400							
4	Class B	$300							
5	Class C	$200							
6									
7	Customer	DP#	Class	Date Rented	Down payment	Date Returned	Condition Returned	Amount Paid	
8	Jacob J	26548	A	11/08/19	$200		Good		
9	Hobson D	43577	A	13/08/19	$200		Bad		
10	Clarke G	24576	C	15/09/19	$200		Bad		
11	Jupiter V	34571	B	15/10/19	$200		Good		

▲ Table 14.8 Journey Car Rentals rates and rentals

Printing a worksheet

Printing allows you to get a hardcopy of your worksheet. However, before you print an Excel workbook, it is important to decide exactly what information you want to print. For example, if you have multiple worksheets in your workbook, you will need to decide if you want to print the **entire workbook** or only **active worksheets**. There may also be times when you want to print only a **selection** of content from your workbook.

To print an entire workbook or an active worksheet or a selection from a worksheet, you need to access the 'Print' pane from the 'File' menu.

To access the 'Print' pane:

1 Select the **File** tab (see Figure 14.84). The backstage view will appear.

▲ Figure 14.84 'File' Tab

2 Select **Print** (see Figure 14.85). The 'Print' pane will appear.

▲ Figure 14.85 'Print' pane

To print active sheets:

Worksheets are considered active when selected.

1 Select the worksheet you want to print. To print multiple worksheets, click the first worksheet, hold the Ctrl key on your keyboard, then click any other worksheets you want to select.
2 Navigate to the **Print** pane.
3 Select **Print Active Sheets** from the Print Range drop-down menu (see Figure 14.86).
4 Click the **Print** button (see Figure 14.87).

To print the entire workbook

1 Navigate to the Print pane.
2 Select **Print Entire Workbook** from the Print Range drop-down menu.
3 Click the **Print** button.

To print a selection

In our example, we will print a selection of content related to upcoming softball games in July.

1 Select the cells you want to print.
2 Navigate to the **Print** pane.
3 Select **Print Selection** from the Print Range drop-down menu.
4 A preview of your selection will appear in the 'Preview' pane.
5 Click the **Print** button to print the selection.
6 If you prefer, you can also set the print area in advance so you will be able to visualise which cells will be printed as you work in Excel. Simply select the cells you want to print, click the Page Layout tab, select the Print Area command, then choose Set Print Area.

▲ Figure 14.86 **Print Settings**

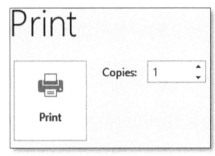

▲ Figure 14.87 **Print button**

Emerging trends

Coda the next-generation spreadsheet

Coda is a company co-founded by Mehrotra and Alex DeNeui. These innovators have created a beta version of a collaborative document editor that combines a word processor and a spreadsheet. It is a versatile tool that these developers hope will find a home in companies where diverse teams need regular access to shared sets of data but want to view and manipulate that data on their own terms.

Excel and other older documents also require formulae to be placed inside tables. In Coda, they can be placed anywhere; insert an '=' sign, and you can bring in data from anywhere else in your document. You can also include a summary section in your document that includes a written account of your progress, with embedded formulae that update key numbers automatically as you make progress.

The ability to link documents, infused with live data that updates automatically, has led Uber to use Coda. This new software has the potential to be used in ways that were not possible with Excel. The developers suggest that it can be used for everything from bug trackers to events planning to Salesforce-style customer relationship management software and much more.

The need to describe rows and columns in formulae using headings such as 'A1 to F7', does not exist in Coda. Instead in Coda documents, rows and columns are named objects, making formulae both easier to read and write. Formulae no longer have to refer to 'A1:F7'; instead you just type the name of the column.

Chapter 14: Summary

- A spreadsheet package is an application package that can be used for any job that involves repetitive numerical calculations. It is a large grid divided into rows and columns. The intersection of a row and a column is called a cell. Each cell is identified by its cell reference (column and row position). A cell can hold one of three kinds of information: label (text), value (number) or formula.

- Formulae are used to perform operations on numbers. A formula must start with an equal (=) sign, which is followed by numbers, different operators or cell references that are part of the calculation. Excel also contains built-in functions for performing calculations, including:
  - =SUM(First cell:Last cell). Finds the sum of a row or column of numbers.
  - =MAX(First cell:Last cell). Finds the maximum value in a row or column of numbers.
  - =MIN(First cell:Last cell). Finds the minimum value in a row or column of numbers.
  - =AVERAGE(First cell:Last cell). Finds the mean of a row or column of numbers.
  - =IF(logical_test, value_if_true, value_if_false). Tests a condition that is either true or false and returns a value.

- The **RANK** function returns the rank of a number in a list of numbers that are not sorted or sorted in ascending or descending order. There are 3 arguments for the RANK function =RANK(number, range, order)

- The **PMT** function is a financial function which can be used to calculate the total payment (principal and interest) required to settle a loan, given the loan amount, number of periods and the interest rate. The general form of the PMT function is =PMT (rate, nper, pv, [fv], [type]).

- The **COUNT** function counts the number of cells containing numbers in a range. It does not count empty cells.

- The **COUNTA** function counts the number of cells that are not empty. Compared to COUNT it would be able to count the number of cells in a range that had text in them.

- The **COUNTIF** function counts the cells in a range that meet a criteria, so if we had a range of cells with temperatures we could set it to count how many are greater than 10 degrees.

- **VLOOKUP** function allows you to look up a value from a table.

- Formulae usually contain cell addresses and not the values in the cell, so that if a value is changed in a cell, all the values in the dependent cells will automatically be updated. This is referred to as automatic re-calculation.

- A formula can be copied or moved from one cell to another cell or range of cells. When the formula is moved, all cell references in the formula change with respect to the formula's new cell location. This is called relative cell addressing. However, it may be necessary to move or copy a formula but keep the cell reference in the formula fixed. This is done using absolute cell referencing.

- Most of the editing features available in a word processor are also available in Excel – for example, 'Delete', 'Cut', 'Copy', 'Paste', 'Find' and 'Replace'.

- Formatting enables you to control the appearance of cells and the worksheet in general. Commands that control the formatting can be triggered from the toolbar or from the Format pull-down menu. Formatting includes:
  - Alignment of cells (left-, centre- or right-justified)
  - Representation of numbers (general, number, currency, accounting)
  - Changing the column width, row height, font size and style and including borders and patterns.

- A group of continuous cells that form a square or a rectangle is called a range of cells and is identified by the addresses of the first and last cells. You can use a single command to affect a range of cells. For example, a range of cells can be formatted for currency, or the contents of the cells can all be centre-justified, by selecting the range and using one command.

- A spreadsheet enables data to be sorted in ascending or descending order according to the content of one or more fields.

- Excel enables users to convert worksheet data easily into a wide range of charts and graphs. Simply select the data range that you want to use to create the graph and then follow the steps using the Chart Wizard.

- PivotTables allow you to quickly calculate, summarise, and analyse data that lets you see comparisons, patterns and trends in your data.

- Worksheets can be printed using the printer icon in the standard menu, or 'Print' in the 'File' menu.

Chapter 14: Questions

Fill in the blanks

1 A spreadsheet package is an _____ package that enables you to carry out numerical work easily and flexibly.

2 _____ re-calculation is one of the most important features of a spreadsheet.

3 A spreadsheet package is a flexible _____ tool that can be used in any job that involves repetitive numerical calculations.

4 When you save an Excel file it is given the file extension _____.

5 Excel is one of the applications in the _____ suite.

6 A workbook initially contains _____ worksheets, which are saved in a single file.

7 In Excel the rows run up and down and are _____, whereas the columns run left to right and are _____.

8 The intersection of a row and a column is called a _____.

9 Each cell in the spreadsheet can be identified by its _____.

10 A cell can contain one of three types of information: label, value or _____.

True or False?

1 In Excel, all the basic commands such as Open, New, Close, Save and Save As work in the same way as they do in Word.

2 The Status bar identifies the various worksheets in a workbook.

3 The Name box identifies the active cell.

4 A typical screen display of Excel may contain 39 rows and 29 columns.

5 The active cell is the cell in which any information entered from the keyboard will be stored.

Multiple-choice questions

1 Text entered into a spreadsheet is left aligned by default. Which of the following refers to textual data?
a Value b Label c Function d Formula

2 Which of the following is an example of a correct function in Excel?
a SUM(A1 to A5   b +SUM(A1:A5)
c =SUM(A1+A5   d =SUM(A1:A5)

3 Which of the following is the default font type in Excel?
a Times New Roman   b Arial
c Calibri   d Cambria

4 A group of adjoining cells treated as a unit is a:
a range.   b record.
c group.   d function.

5 How is a number formatted in Excel when the accounting option is selected?
a No specific number format is applied
b Decimal places and negative
c Represent monetary values (for example, $589.54)
d Lines up currency symbols and decimal points

Worksheet questions

1 A student receives an allowance of $100.00 a day. Table 14.9 shows how he spends the money from Monday to Friday.
Create a worksheet to:
a Calculate the total money spent each day
b Calculate the total money spent on each item for the five days
c Calculate his total expenses for the five days
d Calculate the amount left from his allowance.
e Format the worksheet with $ signs.
f Centre all headings.
g Save the worksheet as 'Allowance'.

	Monday	Tuesday	Wednesday	Thursday	Friday
Travelling	10	10	10	10	10
Lunch	15	25	20	15	25
Snacks	12	15	14	15	20
Games World	0	0	25	0	40

▲ Table 14.9 How a student spends his allowance

2 Currency conversion: the rates of exchange against the United States (US) dollar for some islands in the Caribbean in 2018 were as follows:
US $1 = TT $6.80 (Trinidad and Tobago dollars)
US $1 = BDS $2.00 (Barbados dollars)
US $1 = EC $2.70 (Eastern Caribbean currency)
US $1 = J$134.56 (Jamaica dollars)
a Create a spreadsheet to convert the following amounts of Trinidad and Tobago dollars – 1, 5, 10, 20, 30, 40, 50, 60, 70, 80, 90, 100 – to Barbados, Eastern Caribbean and Jamaican dollars. Save the worksheet as 'Currency'.

b Create a currency converter, to convert the United States (US) currency to the currency of the following countries Trinidad and Tobago, Barbados, Eastern Caribbean and Jamaican dollars. The user has to enter the amount of US dollars and the name of the currency he or she would like. The currency converter would convert the amount of US entered to the currency of the country requested.

3 Calculate the square, square root, cube, and the cube minus twice the number itself, for each of the following numbers – 1, 5, 7, 9, 12, 16, 20, 25, 36, 40, 64, 80.
   a Format the square root to TWO decimal places.
   b Centre all labels and numbers.
   c Add THREE numbers of your own to the table.
   d Save the worksheet as 'Numbers'.

4 The worksheet in Figure 14.88 shows the item code, name, quantity and unit price for seven different items bought from LowPrice Retailers. A discount of 12% is given on all purchases.
   a Calculate the total cost of each item.
   b Calculate the discount for each item.
   c Calculate the discounted price of each item.
   d Centre-justify all headings.
   e Modify the numbers in the Unit Price, Cost, Discount and Discounted Price columns to show dollar ($) values and TWO decimal places.
   f Save the worksheet as 'Purchases'.

	A	B	C	D	E	F
1			LowPrice Retailers			
2						
3	Item code	Name	Quantity	Unit cost	Discount	Discounted price
4	AA123	Underarm Deodorant	24	15		
5	AA128	Superior Cologne	15	65		
6	AB200	Dew Drop Perfume	20	95		
7	AC456	Gloss Powder	56	24		
8	CD231	Nail polish	65	10		
9	CF145	Mouthwash	50	35		
10	MN767	Dental Floss	96	8		

▲ Figure 14.88 Worksheet for items bought from LowPrice Retailers

	A	B	C	D	E	F	G	H	I	J
1				RB College Jamaica						
2										
3				Form 3.1 Mark		Sheet				
4	Surname	First Name	Mathematics	Biology	Chemistry	Physics	English	History	Total	Average
5	Bishop	Victoria	67	76	45	55	73	45		
6	Eastman	Renee	76	42	45	57	85	78		
7	Omar	Ravi	58	67	42	61	75	65		
8	Cardinal	Melissa	79	56	67	84	74	68		
9	Chen	Jason	87	43	64	83	85	84		
10	Fredericks	gary	65	67	38	76	78	67		
11	Vaughn	Shimona	61	65	56	65	82	71		
12										
13	Subject	Highest Mark	Lowest Mark							
14	Mathematics									
15	Biology									
16	Chemistry									
17	Physics									
18	English									

▲ Figure 14.89 Student marks in six subjects

5 Figure 14.89 shows the names of students and their marks in six subjects. Enter the data into a worksheet as shown.
   Complete the worksheet by carrying out the following tasks:
   a Enter a blank row between row 3 and row 4.
   b Calculate the total marks obtained by each student.
   c Calculate the average mark for each student.
   d Using a built-in function, extract the highest (maximum) mark and lowest (minimum) mark for each subject.
   e Calculate and display the mean mark for the class, correct to TWO decimal places.
   f Centre all headings.
   g Delete Melissa Cardinal and all her data from the worksheet.
   h Insert the name and marks for this student into the worksheet:
      Ishana Jyoti, Maths 75, Chemistry 85, English 71, Biology 80, Physics 60.
   i Move to an appropriate part of the worksheet and extract the highest total and lowest total.
   j Save the worksheet as 'School report'.

6 The Superior Car Company sells five different models of foreign used cars: the Vx5, Chameleon, Rhino, Speed Star and Pinnacle. The advertised car price is called the showroom price. The buyer also has to pay a 20% government tax on the showroom price and a fixed licence fee of $15 000. The final price is the price on the road. Table 14.10 shows how many of each model the company sold for the month of June.

The manager of the company wants to know the following information:

a The tax paid on each model of car
b The price including tax for each model
c The cost of each car on the road
d The total monthly sales value ($) for each model
e The average price of a car on the road
f The maximum sales total among the different models
g The minimum sales total among the different models
h On a graph, the comparative total monthly sales for each model.

Design and appropriately format a worksheet to show this information.

Model	Quantity	Showroom Price
Chameleon	5	$25 550
Pinnacle	7	$20 500
Rhino	4	$45 500
Speed Star	9	$17 850
Vx5	3	$50 450

▲ Table 14.10 Cars sold by the Superior Car Company

7 The Repeaters' College is a full-time school for students wishing to repeat their CSEC examination in various subject areas. The college has the following fee structure for each academic. which the student registers and the additional fee for each Lab subject. However, a student doing five or more subjects gets a 10% reduction in the total fee. A student is allowed three payments to complete the total payment of fees. The owners of the college need to know how much money each student listed in Table 14.11 has to pay, how much is received and how much is outstanding.

a Create a worksheet to satisfy the requests of the owners, using the data in the table.
b Format the worksheet as follows:
  - Centre all labels and values.
  - Set the discount given, total fees and balance to TWO decimal places.
  - Set total fees, payments and balance to currency.

c Edit the worksheet as follows:
  - Delete all information pertaining to Ian Sobers
  - Insert the names of two students of your choice along with the number of subjects and Lab subjects for which they wish to register
  - Sort the worksheet on the names in descending order.
d Save the worksheet as 'Payments'.
e Select all the students who are doing three or fewer subjects.
f Change the Lab fee from $100 to $150 and the Subject fee from $650 to $675.
g What is the maximum fee paid?
h What is the minimum fee paid?
i What is the average number of subjects being taken by students in the school?

Student's name	Total number of subjects	Number of Lab subjects
Carter, Daryl	4	1
Ali, Feroze	6	3
Brown, Michelle	3	1
Simmons, Pat	5	2
Simmons, Brandon	7	3
Foster, James	3	1
Maharaj, Rudy	4	2
Sobers, Ian	5	2
Roberts, Carl	6	3
Taylor, Petal	5	2

▲ Table 14.11 Subjects taken by Repeaters' College students

8 The owner of a small contracting firm has 12 employees, divided into two categories: skilled and unskilled. Each worker is contracted to work a 40-hour week at a set rate, and for any time worked above 40 hours is paid an overtime rate of 1.5 times the regular rate. The set rate for an unskilled worker is $20 per hour and a skilled worker gets $30 per hour. The rates of pay are subject to change over time. The names of the employees, category and the total number of hours worked for four weeks for the month of July 2019 are shown in Table 14.12.

Employee	Category	Hours worked			
		Week 1	Week 2	Week 3	Week 4
Jason Agard	Skilled	45	56	45	40
Ralf Brown	Skilled	56	45	50	68
Anslem Douglas	Skilled	40	45	40	55
Brian Despot	Skilled	40	40	45	56
Larry James	Unskilled	40	40	56	60
Rolston Granger	Unskilled	35	40	67	40
Rudy Maraj	Unskilled	40	55	43	55
Gerry Parker	Unskilled	56	45	76	45
Richard Bobart	Unskilled	65	45	45	57
Luke Thompson	Unskilled	70	45	34	45
Moses Fredricks	Unskilled	30	40	56	35
Vernon Johnson	Unskilled	40	40	64	62

▲ Table 14.12 Employees' categories and hours worked for four weeks

a Create a worksheet that will show the employee's name, category, a weekly number of hours worked and a weekly salary. It should also include the total number of hours worked and the total salary for all the employees for the month.

b Calculate and display:
- The average weekly salary
- The minimum salary for the week
- The maximum salary for the week.

c Format the salary with '$' and TWO decimal places.

d Format the worksheet so that all column labels are centre-justified.

e Sort the spreadsheet on name in ascending order.

f Select all the unskilled workers who work more than 200 hours for the four weeks.

g Save the spreadsheet as 'July wages'.

h Delete all information pertaining to Richard Bobart.

i Add the following data to the worksheet:
Employee – Wesley Taylor
Category – unskilled
Hours worked – week 1: 50; week 2: 60; week 3: 45; week 4: 40.

j Change the rate of pay for unskilled workers from $20 to $25 and for skilled workers from $30 to $40.

k Save the worksheet as 'July wages1'.

l Prepare an appropriately labelled bar graph to show the total weekly wages for the four weeks. Save the graph as 'Wage1'.

m Prepare an appropriately labelled pie chart to show the total number of hours worked for each week for the month of July. Save the chart as 'Hours'.

9 Figure 14.90 shows a Wholesaler's spreadsheet of the produce the company sold to countries around the world. Using a spreadsheet, you are required to do the following:
i Create a PivotTable to show the total amount of each product sold.
ii Sort the list from highest to lowest.
iii Display the total amount of each item exported.

	A	B	C	D	E	F
1	Order ID	Product	Category	Cost	Date	Country
2	1	Grapes	Fruit	$250 000,00	5/12/2020	Chile
3	2	Apples	Fruit	$300 000,00	6/14/2020	Barbados
4	3	Pears	Fruit	$150 000,00	6/17/2020	Jamaica
5	4	Peaches	Fruit	$120 000,00	6/23/2020	Trinidad and Tobago
6	5	Bananas	Fruit	$300 000,00	6/28/2020	St. Vincent
7	6	Sweet potatoes	Ground provision	$85 000,00	7/5/2020	St. Vincent
8	7	Carrots	Vegetable	$230 000,00	7/8/2020	China
9	8	Broccoli	Vegetable	$156 000,00	7/9/2020	Canada
10	9	Red beans	Grain	$450 000,00	7/10/2020	United States
11	10	Lentils	Grain	$230 000,00	7/10/2020	United States
12	11	Yams	Ground provision	$80 000,00	7/12/2020	St. Vincent
13	12	Dasheens	Ground provision	$12 000,00	7/14/2020	St. Vincent
14	13	Grapes	Fruit	$340 000,00	7/15/2020	Canada
15	14	Apples	Fruit	$340 000,00	7/18/2020	United
16	15	Grapes	Fruit	$230 000,00	7/19/2020	St. Lucia
17	16	Apples	Fruit	$120 000,00	8/12/2020	St. Vincent
18	17	Pears	Fruit	$300 000,00	8/14/2020	St. Vincent
19	18	Peaches	Fruit	$85 000,00	8/17/2020	China
20	19	Bananas	Fruit	$230 000,00	8/23/2020	Canada
21	20	Sweet potatoes	Ground provision	$156 000,00	8/28/2020	United States
22	21	Carrots	Vegetable	$450 000,00	9/5/2020	United States
23	22	Broccoli	Vegetable	$230 000,00	9/8/2020	St. Vincent
24	23	Red beans	Grain	$80 000,00	9/9/2020	St. Vincent
25	24	Lentils	Grain	$12 000,00	9/10/2020	Canada
26	25	Yams	Ground provision	$340 000,00	10/10/2020	United Kingdom
27	26	Dasheens	Ground provision	$340 000,00	10/12/2020	St. Lucia

▲ Figure 14.90 Worksheet for question 9

Research questions

1 Using the Web to conduct research suggest ways a spreadsheet package can be used in a bank.

2 Using the Web to conduct research, suggest ways a spreadsheet can be used in a school by the administrative staff in the office and by the classroom teachers.

15 Databases

Objectives

At the end of this chapter, you will be able to:

→ define the terms 'database' and 'database package'
→ list situations in which databases would be useful
→ list the similarities and differences between a manual and a computerised database
→ define the terms 'table', 'row' (record), 'column' (field), 'primary key', 'secondary key', 'candidate key', 'foreign key', 'query', 'form' and 'report'
→ define the data types 'numeric', 'text', 'logical', 'date/time' and 'currency'
→ create a database using Microsoft Access
→ create a table in Design view
→ enter, delete and edit records in a table
→ create a form using a wizard and edit the design
→ create and run queries to select, update, append and delete
→ create a report using the wizard and edit the design
→ establish relationships: show the joins between tables (one-to-one and one-to-many).

What is a database?

A database is an organised repository (collection) of related data. Data on any subject matter can be stored in a database as a collection of tables that are related to each other. It can be used to store information on students, patients in a doctor's or dentist's office, music or video collections, stock in a supermarket, employee records, information on various countries … almost anything.

Database management is the process by which information is organised and stored on a computer in such a way that there is efficient retrieval, updating and manipulation of the data.

A database package is a piece of software used to create and manage a computerised database. Using a computerised database is far more flexible than using a manual database. Information can be organised, retrieved, collated, displayed and printed much more easily this way.

Manual databases

Understanding how a manual database is set up will help you to understand how computerised databases are set up. A manual database is much like a filing cabinet in which you might keep all related information on a particular subject. Consider a filing cabinet at a doctor's office in which one drawer of the cabinet contains information on patients, another drawer contains information on employees and other information on stocks and suppliers. In the drawer that contains the patients' information, there is a folder containing patient records, such as information on medication prescribed to them. To find this information, the doctor opens the appropriate drawer, extracts the appropriate folder and reads through the documents one by one until she finds the one she wants. Things become difficult when the doctor tries to relate the medicines prescribed to each patient (in one drawer) to the supplies needed of that medicine (another drawer). These two concepts are related, and updating the records requires work on files in two different drawers. Manual databases, therefore, present many problems, including these points.

■ Finding records can be a time-consuming process.
■ Files and folders can easily be misplaced if they are not filed properly.
■ These databases require large amounts of physical storage space.
■ Cross-referencing information between files is difficult.
■ Accessing information from another location (for example, another office) is difficult.

Computerised databases

A computerised database allows you to create and manage your database much more efficiently and effectively than a manual database. It can summarise data, sort data, select data and answer ad hoc requests for specific information. In the manual example above, we could create a table in Excel to hold all the patient information. This would have some advantages over the manual system, but would still not let you relate the patients to the supplies of medicines.

In order to fix this, you need to use a database that links logically related data stored in several files or tables, known as a relational database. The name 'relational' explains one of the main advantages of databases: that you can set up relationships between tables and data within the database. In our example, when the doctor prescribes some medicine to a patient, she makes a link between the patient and the medicine in the database. Because the doctor is selecting the medicine from the Medicines Table, she cannot misspell the name, and the amount of the patient's prescription is added to the total needed for that medicine, so it is easier to make sure that there is enough medicine.

Database packages have many other built-in features that allow you to manipulate your data and extract information using a number of objects. An object is an option you can select and manipulate. These objects include tables, forms, queries, reports, macros and modules. We will look at some of these objects more fully in the course of this chapter.

Advantages of a computerised database

- Information can be accessed quickly and easily with little probability of it being lost.
- Related files can be linked – once one is updated, the related file(s) will also automatically be updated.
- Information need not be duplicated; it can be stored only once and accessed in several different ways.
- It is easy to update or change records and their structure in computerised databases.
- Data being entered can easily be validated, thereby preventing mistakes on entry (for example, the computer can tell you that you are entering an impossible date, such as '13' for the month).
- It is easy to store backup copies of the database 'offsite'.

Disadvantages of a computerised database

- Computer breakdown can cause files to become inaccessible or corrupted.
- It is easy to copy or steal files unless the files are stored and protected carefully.
- Database operators require training, which may take some time.

Basic concepts

- A database file is an entire database.
- A table is a basic unit of a database and contains data on a specific topic, for example, *all* the personal information about *all* the members of a video club.

- A table row (record) consists of a group of related fields containing information pertaining to *one* person, place or thing, for example, *all* the personal information about *one* member of a video club. Tables, therefore, have multiple records.
- A column (field) is an area within a record reserved for one very specific piece of data, for example, the *address* of *one* video club member. Tables, therefore, have multiple fields.
- Data is the information that is held in the table fields.
- A field definition is the attributes that describe a field. It consists of a field *name*, data *type*, and other attributes such as field *description*, field *size*/*width*, and so on (Table 15.1). A field definition determines the kind of work that can be performed with the field; for example, you can define a field to hold numbers or text. A field with numbers can allow you to perform calculations on those numbers.

Field Name	Field or Data Type	Field Size/ Field Width
Name (for example, Matthew Johnson)	Text	25
Sex (for example, M)	Text	1
Date of birth (for example, 22/03/19)	Date/Time	*
Address (for example, 23 Guiaco Street)	Text	50
Date of visit (for example, 11/03/19)	Date/Time	*

▲ Table 15.1 An example of a database record

Database keys

In a database, keys are used to uniquely identify a record in a table. In our patient example in Table 15.1, we might have a patient_no field, as well as perhaps driving license or health insurance numbers. Each of these could uniquely identify a patient, so are called 'candidate keys'.

A primary key is the most appropriate field in a table that uniquely identifies a record. In our patient example, we would probably use the patient_no field. An index is created when a primary key is set; this speeds up the operations of the database.

The fields that are candidate keys but are not used as the primary key are called 'secondary keys'.

A composite key is more than one field combined, which uniquely identifies a record.

A foreign key is a field in one table that uniquely identifies a record in another table, in other words, this field references the primary key in another table.

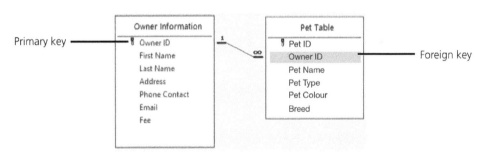

▲ Figure 15.1 Primary key and foreign key

For example, in Figure 15.1, Owner ID in the Owner Information table is the primary key of that table and Pet ID in the Pet Table is the primary key of that table. Owner ID in the Pet Table is the foreign key, as it links to a record in the Owner Information table, that is, it references the primary key in another table, so if one pet is selected, the owner's details are selected along with it.

However, the Owner ID, Pet Name and Pet Type can be used together to uniquely identify the pet, as it is unlikely that a pet owner would have two pets with the same name and pet type. The three fields used together to uniquely identify the pet is called a 'composite key', as shown in Figure 15.2.

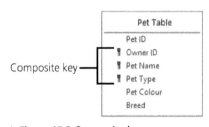

▲ Figure 15.2 Composite key

Creating a database using Access

Unlike spreadsheet or word processing documents, database documents have to be named before you start work on them.

1 Click on the Windows **Start** button.
2 Click on **Access 2013, 2016** or **2019**. The 'Microsoft Access' window appears, as shown in Figure 15.3, with the 'task pane' on the right side of the window.

The task pane gives you the option to:

- create a database from scratch
- use a template
- open an existing database.

Creating a new database from scratch

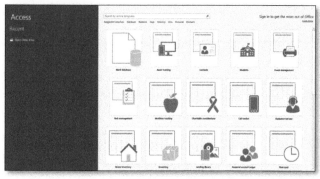

▲ Figure 15.3 The Microsoft Access window

1 Click **Blank Access Database**
2 Give your database a name by clicking in the 'File Name' box and typing a name.
3 Specify a location by selecting from the options available in the 'Save In' box.
4 Then click **Create** to create and save the database. Notice that the database window opens, as shown in Figure 15.4.

All the **objects** of the database are organised in the database window. The database window opens on the default setting from which tables can be created. This setting also displays all the tables in the database.

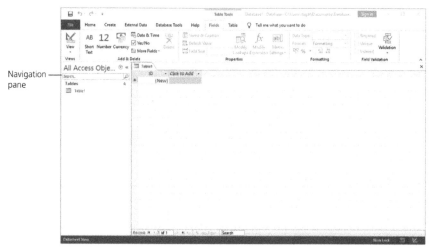

▲ Figure 15.4 The database window in Datasheet View

Creating tables

A table stores data about a specific topic. Creating separate tables for each topic allows you to store the data only once, hence limiting data entry errors and data duplication. It also increases the efficiency of the database. Tables can be created using any of the following three options.

1 **Datasheet View:** Data is entered into a datasheet grid, which consists of rows and columns labelled 'Field 1', 'Field 2', 'Field 3', and so on. The data type is determined by Access, based on the data that is entered. This is the view shown in Figure 15.4.

2 **Design View:** This option allows you to create a database from scratch. It allows you to define the fields in the database and set all the attributes of that field.
3 **Table Wizard:** The Table Wizard walks you through a four-step process that is easy to follow. However, the table produced may not meet your exact requirements. This method is the easiest and fastest way of creating a table.

Creating a table in Design View

1 Open the database.
2 If a blank table is already open, click on **View** and then **Design View** on the **Home** tab.
3 If a blank table is not already open, click on the **Create** tab in the **Tables** group and click on **Table Design** (Figure 15.5).

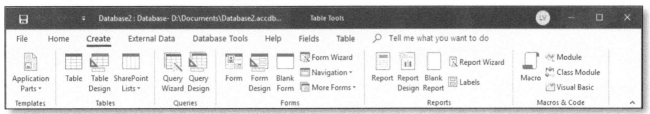

▲ Figure 15.5 Table Design under the Create group in the 'Table Tools' dialog box

4 Define each of the fields in your table (Figure 15.6). This is called 'table definition'.
   - Enter the field name in the 'Field Name' column. (*Note*: these field names become the headings for your table.)
   - Select the appropriate data type for that field in the 'Data Type' column.
   - Enter the text in the 'Description' column. This describes the data that will be entered in this field. (This field is optional.)

   The 'Data Type' column enables you to select an appropriate data type from a drop-down list. When you have selected a data type, the 'Field Properties' pane appears at the bottom of the window. Access provides default field properties that are suitable for many applications, but you can change these if necessary. Table 15.2 lists the various data types and an explanation of the data types.

▲ Figure 15.6 Design View with the Data Type drop-down menu

5 Select suitable properties for that field from 'Field Properties' in the bottom pane. A description of each of the field properties is given.
6 Choose **Save** or **Save As** to save the table within the current database.
7 Type the name of the table and click **OK** (Figure 15.7).

▲ Figure 15.7 'Save As' dialog box for a table

Field properties or definitions

Access uses the term 'field properties' rather than 'field definitions', so we will use that term in this section. Properties determine how a field is stored, works and is displayed. Access automatically assigns default field properties to each field, depending on the data type. You can see the 'Field Properties' under the table in Figure 15.6 on the previous page.

The default field properties are sufficient for many databases, but you can change them if necessary. Some field properties enable you to restrict data that is entered into a field, and this may increase the efficiency and accuracy of data entry. Different data types will have different field properties, and some of the key ones found in Access are explained below.

Field Size

This property specifies the number of characters you want the field to have. It is usually applied to text or number fields. This should cater to the longest data that would be entered into this field.

- **Text Field Size:** The default is usually 50 characters for text fields. However, up to 255 characters can be entered. Limiting the number of characters being entered can save disk space or even prevent data entry errors.
- **Numeric Field Size:** There are a few options available for the field size for numbers (Table 15.3).

Data type	Explanation
Number	Can store only a number, decimal point and a plus or minus sign. The number data type can be used in calculations, for example: 3, 4.7, 3.14125, -8
Text	Stores alphabetic, alphanumeric, numeric and special characters. A text field can store up to 255 characters. Calculations cannot be performed on numbers stored in text fields, for example: "M&N", "Fred", "14 Mill Lane"
Memo	Stores lengthy text such as notes and descriptions up to 65,536 characters in length
Date/Time	Stores several different formats of date and/or time
Currency	Used to store currency values. This data type prevents rounding off during calculations, for example: $12.25, $1,224.00
AutoNumber	Stores a unique sequential or random number, which is inserted when a record is added
Yes/No or Logical	Allows the storage of data that can have only two possible values: Yes/No, True/False or On/Off. Example: In an Employee database, to say whether an employee is a union member or not the field name, 'Union Member' could have a Yes/No data type in which the checkbox could be ticked if the employee is a union member and not checked if the employee is not a union member.
OLE Object	Used to store embedded objects such as word processing and spreadsheet documents, pictures and sound
Calculated	In Access, this is a field that is calculated from other fields in the table, for example: If you had one field as the date someone joined, you could calculate how long they had been a member.
Hyperlink	Can store a URL (website address) or a path to a file. Example: http://www.checkout.com C:\MyDocuments\mydatabase.mbd
Lookup Wizard	Selecting this data type starts a Wizard that allows you to choose a value from another table or select a value from a list of values in the 'Combo box'

▲ Table 15.2 Data types and their explanations

Numeric Field Size	Explanation
Byte	A positive integer between 0 and 255
Integer	Positive and negative integers between -32,768 and 32,768
Long Integer (default)	Larger positive and negative integers between approx. -2 billion (-2,147,483,648) and approx. 2 billion (2,147,483,647)
Single	A single-precision floating-point value with about 7 digits of accuracy
Double	A double-precision floating-point value with about 15 digits of accuracy
Replication ID	A special value known as a Globally Unique Identifier (GUID). It is used only with database replication
Decimal	A decimal number up to 28 digits in accuracy

▲ Table 15.3 Numeric Field Size options

Format

This (optional) property determines the way the field is displayed or printed.

- **Text and Memo Format:** This property conforms the data entered in the field to a specified format (Table 15.4).

Format	Data	Display	Symbol	Explanation
@@@-@@@@	8976543	897-6543	@	Indicates a required space or character
@@@-@@@&	897654	897-654	&	Indicates an optional character or space
< COMPUTER	computer	<		Converts the text to lowercase
> computer	COMPUTER	>		Converts the text to uppercase
@\EC	800	800EC	\	Adds characters to the end
@;"Not Yet Rated"	PG	PG		
@;"Not Yet Rated"	(blank)	Not Yet Rated		

▲ Table 15.4 Text and Memo Format

- **Number Format:** This property allows a selection from a drop-down menu, or values can be displayed according to different assigned formats (Table 15.5).

Format	Data	Display	Explanation
###,##0.00	476839.99	476,839.99	# is a placeholder that displays a digit or nothing if there is none. 0 is a placeholder that displays a digit or 0 if there is nothing (see this row and the one below)
$###,##0.00	0	$0.00	
###.00%	.055	5.5%	% multiplies the number by 100 and adds a percentage sign

▲ Table 15.5 Number format

- **Date Format:** This property displays the date and time in an appropriate format. The various formats can be selected from the drop-down menu or values can be displayed according to different assigned formats (Table 15.6).

Format	Display	Explanation
dddd"," mmmm d"," yyyy	Friday, March 3, 2019	dddd, mmmm, and yyyy prints the full names of the day, month and year. (*Note*: what is enclosed in quotation marks is printed as it is.)
ddd"," mmm"." d"," yy	Fri, Mar. 3, 19	ddd, mmm, and yy prints the first three letters of the day, month and the last two digits of the year.
dddd "is a sunny day"	Friday is a sunny day	
h:n:s: AM/PM	3:15:00 PM	'n' is used to represent minutes rather than 'm', so as not to confuse minutes with months.

▲ Table 15.6 Date Format

- **Currency Format:** The various formats can be selected from the drop-down menu.
- **Caption:** This is a label other than the field name that can be used in forms and reports.
- **Default Value:** This value is automatically entered in a field in each record of the table.
- **Allow Zero Length:** This allows a Text or Memo field to be filled with blanks or with a string of zero length.

- **Input Mask:** This only works with Text and Date fields. It enables you to define a character string to act as a template so that data entered is formatted in a specific way, for example, by only allowing a combination of numbers and letters in the right order for a number plate. It is similar to the Format property but displays the data on the datasheet before the data is entered (Table 15.7). The Input Mask Wizard takes you through the steps easily.
- **Validation Rule:** This specifies the condition that limits the values that can be entered into the field to either:
  - validate the field, so it meets a criterion, for example, '<> 0' the value must not be equal to 0, or,
  - validates a record, so that an entry in this field does not make the record nonsense. For example, in a library, you might record the start date and end date of each loan. An end date field cannot come before a start date field, so you could have a Validation Rule that checks this.
- **Validation Text:** A message you may want to be displayed if the Validation Rule is not met. This might be a message explaining what the rule is that the entry has failed to meet.
- **Required:** You may want to make sure that some fields in a record, for example, those that are part of a composite key, have some data in them. If 'required' is set to 'Yes' and no value is entered in this field, the record will be rejected and an error message is displayed.
- **Indexed:** Creating indexes on a field allows tables to be grouped, queried, sorted and searched faster.

Format	Explanation
0	A digit 0 through 9 without the + or – sign
9	A digit or space
#	A digit with +/- sign
A	A letter or digit
a	A letter
L	A Letter
C	Any character or space
&	Any character or space
<	Converts letters to lowercase
>	Converts letters to uppercase
!	Displays from left to right
\	Displays the next character

▲ Table 15.7 Input Mask Format

Adding a field between two rows

1 Open the table in **Design View**.
2 Select the row above which you want the new field to be inserted.
3 Choose **Rows** from the 'Insert' menu.
4 A blank row appears for you to type in the new field name, data type and description (optional).

Deleting a field

1 Open the table in **Design View**.
2 Select the row to be deleted.
3 Press the **Delete** key or select **Delete** from the 'Edit' menu.

Keys and relationships

A primary key is a selected field or fields in a table that uniquely identifies a record. When we link two tables, the primary key is used as a foreign key in the second table, to uniquely identify a record in the first table (see Figure 15.9).

In the example we used about owners and pets, Owner ID in the Owner Information table is the

◀ Figure 15.8 Primary key and foreign key

primary key of that table and Pet ID in the Pet Table is the primary key of that table. Owner ID in the Pet Table is the foreign key, as it links to a record in the Owner Information table, that is, it references the primary key in another table.

Characteristics of a primary key

A primary key:

■ is not allowed to be a null value (that is leaving a field blank indicates that there is no value for that field), it must always have a unique value
■ speeds up data storage and retrieval and the running of queries
■ sorts records according to the values in the field
■ enables a relationship between tables so that they can be joined.

Note

A primary key need not be defined, but it is usually a good idea.

Setting a primary key

If you do not select a primary key while building your database table structure, the message in Figure 15.9 will appear.

If **Yes** is selected, Access adds an 'AutoNumber' field to your table and sets it as the primary key (see Figure 15.10). If **No** is selected, the table is saved without a primary key being defined.

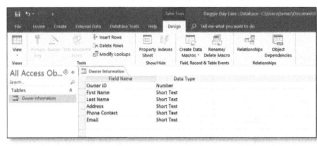

▲ Figure 15.9 No primary key

Defining a primary key

1　Open the table in **Design View**.
2　Select the field you want to define as the primary key.
3　Select the **Primary Key** icon in the 'Tools' group of the 'Design' tab.

▲ Figure 15.10 Defining a primary key

Deselecting a primary key

1　Open the table in **Design View**.
2　Click on the **Primary Key** icon in the 'Tools' group of the 'Design' tab.

Relationships

In the pet and owner example in the previous section, we saw how we used the primary key in the owner to create a link to the Pet Table. This sets up a relationship, relating a pet to an owner. There are three types of relationships.

1　**One-to-one relationship**: Here one record in one table relates to exactly one in another table. An example of this is the relationship between a country and a capital city. For each country, there is only one capital city and for each capital city, there is only one country.
2　**One-to-many relationship**: Here one record in one table can relate to several records in another table. Our 'pets and owners' is an example of this – one owner can have several pets.
3　**Many-to-many relationship**: Here many records in one table can relate to many records in a second table. Imagine a database for an online shop. There will be a table of many customers and a table of many products, and many customers will buy one product, but one customer will buy many products.

Exercise 1

1 The following are all objects in a database, except:
   a Text   b Form   c Report   d Table

2 An organised collection of related records is a:
   a Cell   b Table   c Field   d Report

3 All of the following are advantages of a computerised database except:
   a Once one file is updated all other files will automatically be updated if they are linked together.
   b Information can be stored just once and accessed in several different ways.
   c It requires training to use the system.
   d It is easy to update or change the record structure.

4 All of the following are problems associated with manual databases except:
   a Folders are easily misplaced.
   b Large amounts of storage space are required to store files.
   c Cross-referencing information from different files is difficult.
   d Retrieval of simple information is relatively fast and easy.

5 An area within a table reserved for a specific piece of data is called a:
   a Field   b Record   c Cell   d Query

6 Which of the following can be used as a primary key?
   a Make   b Order date
   c Serial Number   d Purchase date

7 Which of the following is not a characteristic of a primary key?
   a Enables you to establish relationships between tables
   b Can have duplicate values
   c Is automatically indexed
   d Speeds data retrieval

8 A field such as Item Price is considered _____ data type.
   a Currency   b Text
   c Autonumber   d Number

9 In a doctor's database the relationship between the Patients Table and Medicines Table is:
   a Many-to-many
   b One-to-one
   c One-to-many

1 Define the following terms.
   a Table   b Record   c Field   d File

2 Define the term 'database'.

3 What is a relational database?

4 What is a database package?

5 What are the functions of a primary key field?

6 What are the field properties?

7 List THREE field properties and explain their purpose.

8 Give an example of each of the THREE types of database relationships.

Activity 1

Tackle the following practical activities on your computer. There are some suggested solutions to start you off.

1 A wholesaler of appliances would like to change over from a manual method of stock keeping to a computerised method. Create a database called 'Tropical Appliances Wholesalers' to keep track of their stock using the structure in Table 15.8.

Field Name	Data Type	Description
Appliance	Text	Type of appliance
Manufacturer	Text	The manufacturer of the appliance
Model	Text	The model of appliance
Serial Number	Number	A 5-digit unique serial number for the appliance
Price	Currency	Appliance's selling price

▲ Table 15.8 Appliance Table

a Set the Serial Number as the primary key.
b Set appropriate field sizes for the Text Data Types.
c Save the table as 'Appliance Table'.

Activity 1 continued

How it is done

Creating the 'Tropical Appliances Wholesalers' database

1 Open the Access program.
2 Click **Blank Access Database** on the task pane.
3 Give your database a name by clicking in the 'File Name' box and typing a name.
4 Specify a location by selecting from the options available in the 'Save In' box.
   Then click **Create**, to create and save the database.
5 Click on **Tables**.
6 Click on **Design View**.
7 Place the cursor in the 'Field Name' column in the first row.
8 Type "Appliance" into the column.
9 Move to the 'Data Type' column. The default data type 'Text' will be displayed. To select a different field type, click on the down-arrow in the 'Data Type' box; a drop-down list will appear. Select the appropriate data type.
10 Click on the 'Description' column and type 'Type of Appliance'. This describes the data that will be entered in this field.
11 Move to the second row and enter the field name, data type and description for the second field.
12 Do the same for the remaining fields.

Setting the primary key

1 Click anywhere in the 'Serial No' row.
2 Click on the **Primary Key** icon in the Tools group on the Design tab

Saving the table structure

1 Once all the fields are complete, select the **Save** icon on the quick access toolbar or save from the File tab to save the table within the current database.
2 Type the name "Appliance Table" in the 'Save As' dialog box and click the **OK** button.

---

2 Retrieve the 'Tropical Appliances Wholesalers' database you created in the previous exercise.

a Change the field sizes for the following fields:

Field Name	Data Type
Appliance	25
Manufacturer	30
Model	15
Serial Number	Long Integer
Price	

▲ Table 15.9 Changing field sizes

b Format the Serial Number to accept a 5-digit number. Include a caption for each field.

Field Name	Caption
Appliance	Appliance Name
Manufacturer	Manufacturer Name
Model	Model Number
Serial Number	SN
Price	Item Price

▲ Table 15.10 Appliance Table

How it is done

Changing the field sizes for the fields

1 Display the 'Appliance Table' in Design View.
2 Click anywhere in the 'Appliance' row. The 'Field Properties' pane will be displayed.
3 Click on the 'Field Size' box; delete '50' and type '25'.
4 Do the same for the remaining fields.

Formating the Serial Number to accept a 5-digit number

1 Display the 'Appliance Table' in Design View.
2 Click anywhere in the 'Appliance' row. The 'Field Properties' pane will be displayed.
3 In the 'Format' box type '00000' where the 0 is a placeholder that displays the digit or 0.

Including a caption for each field

1 Display the 'Appliance Table' in Design View.
2 Click anywhere in the 'Appliance' row. The 'Field Properties' pane will be displayed.
3 In the 'Caption' box type "Appliance Name".
4 Do the same for the remaining fields.

Activity 1 continued

3 Retrieve the 'Tropical Appliances Wholesalers' database you created in the previous exercise.
  a Create another table to hold the client information with the structure as shown below.
  b Set Client ID as the primary key.
  c Save Table 15.11 as 'Client Records'

Field Name	Data Type	Description	Field Size	Caption
Client ID	AutoNumber	A unique number for the client		Client Identification Number
Client Name	Text	The name of the person	30	The client who makes the purchase
Business Name	Text	The name of the Client's business	30	Company
Address	Text	Address of the Client's business	50	Company Address
Phone	Number	A 7-digit phone number	Long Integer	Telephone Number
Date of Last Order	Date/Time	Date of last purchase from Tropical Appliances Wholesalers		Last Order Date

▲ Table 15.11 Client Records

4 A company that makes and sells quilts receives orders from various clients. The company wants to enter their orders into a database. Create a database called 'Quilts Incorp' using the structure given.
  a Set the order number as the primary key.
  b Format the order number to contain two digits followed by a dash followed by the remaining digits, for example, 26-3359.
  c Format the Date/Time field of the Order Date to Medium Date.
  d Format the Date/Time field of the Supply date to yyyy',' dddd d','F mmmm.
  e Save Table 15.12 as 'Order Table'.

Field Name	Data Type	Description	Field Size
Order Number	Number	A unique 6-digit number given to the customer for that particular order	Long Integer
Order Date	Date/Time	Date the order was placed	
Supply Date	Date/Time	The date for the order to be shipped to the customer	
Customer FName	Text	Customer's first name 15	
Customer LName	Text	Customer's last name 20	
Customer Phone	Number	A 7-digit phone number for customer Long Integer	
Delivery Address	Text	The address to which the order is to be delivered	50
Design Type	Text	A 6-character alphanumeric code that indicates the type of quilt design	6
King	Number	Number of king size quilts ordered	Integer
Queen	Number	Number of queen size quilts ordered	Integer
Full	Number	Number of full-size quilts ordered	Integer
Twin	Number	Number of twin size quilts ordered	Integer

▲ Table 15.12 Order Table

Entering records into a table

Now we have seen how to create the structure of the database we need to populate it with data so that it is useful.

Adding records

1 In the database window, click on **Tables** under 'All Access Objects' on the left side of the screen (which shows all the tables in the database).

2 Select the table into which you want to enter the records.

3 Click **Open** or double-click on the table. (*Note*: the Datasheet View Table contains the field names at the top of the individual columns.)

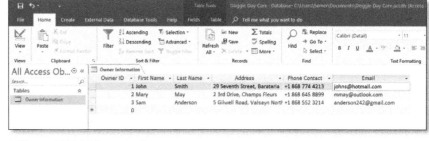

▲ Figure 15.11 Adding records

4 Type in the data in the respective columns. New records can be added to the table in the Datasheet View in the new record row denoted by the asterisk (*) (Figure 15.11). You can also select the **New** icon from the 'Records' group on the 'Home' tab.

Deleting a record

1 Open the table in Datasheet View.

2 Select the record to be deleted by placing the cursor in any field of the 'Record' row.

3 Select **Delete** icon from the 'Records' group of the 'Home' tab. You can also press the Delete key on your keyboard. (*Note*: A message appears to inform you that a record is about to be deleted.) See Figure 15.12.

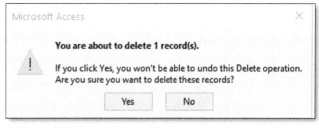

▲ Figure 15.12 Deleting a record

Editing a record

1 Open the table in Datasheet View.

2 Select the field of the record to be edited and make the necessary changes.

Copying data from one field to the next

If the same data has to be repeated in another record, you may need to use the Copy feature to copy data from one field to the next.

1 Open the table in Datasheet View.

2 Select the data in the field to be copied.

3 Click the **Copy** icon from the 'Clipboard' group on the 'Home' tab.

4 Click where you want the data copied, and click **Paste** from the 'Clipboard' group on the 'Home' tab.

Copying a table and its data

1 From the database window, select the table to be copied.
2 Click **Copy** from 'Clipboard' group on the 'Home' tab.
3 Click in the white space of the database window.
4 Click **Paste** from the 'Clipboard' group on the 'Home' tab.
   A 'Paste Table As' dialog box appears (Figure 15.13).
5 Select the **Structure and Data** option.
6 Type a name for the table in the 'Table Name' box and click **OK**.

Copying data from one table to another existing table

1 From the database window, select the table to be copied.
2 Click **Copy** from 'Clipboard' group on the 'Home' tab.
3 Click in the white space of the database window.
4 Click **Paste** from the 'Clipboard' group on the 'Home' tab. A 'Paste Table As' dialog box appears.
5 Select the **Append Data to Existing Table** option.
6 Type the name of the existing table that you want to add the data to in the 'Table Name' box and click **OK**.

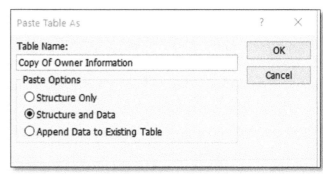

▲ Figure 15.13 The 'Paste Table As' dialog box

Activity 2

1 Retrieve the 'Tropical Appliances Wholesalers' database that you created in Activity 1.
  Add a new field in the 'Appliance Table' called Client ID with the following attributes:

Field name	Data type	Description
Client ID	Number	The ID number of the client who purchases the appliance

▲ Table 15.13 Appliance Table

2 Retrieve the 'Quilts Incorp' database that you created in Activity 1 and perform the following instructions.
  a Open the Order Table in Design View and change the field name of the Supply Date field to Shipping Date.
  b Insert a row after the Customer Phone field name.
  c Add a new field 'Client Address' to the Order Table.
  d Set the data type, description and the field size for this field as follows:
    Data Type – Text
    Description – The address of the client
    Field Size – 50
  e Delete the field 'Delivery Address' as deliveries are no longer made; clients collect their orders.
  f Save the table.

Designing a database

In designing a database some important questions must be asked, such as:

- What is the purpose of the database?
- What questions do you want the database to answer?
- What reports do you want to produce?
- How do you want the database sorted?

Example: A video club database

Platinum Members Video Club, owned and operated by Kaycee Kylock, has been in business for two years. Due to increased membership, Kaycee has decided to computerise her records to make the business more efficient (see Figure 15.14). Membership is free and at present Kaycee has 500 members. She maintains an inventory of 5,500 DVD movies and 2,500 Bluray movies.

Kaycee has assigned each member a unique 3-digit Member ID and has an index card for each member. The card contains information such as Member's ID, name, address and phone numbers for home and work. Kaycee keeps a note of what type of movies the member prefers under the category 'Preference'.

She also keeps a set of index cards of her Bluray and DVD movie inventory. The index cards contain a host of information: the Movie ID (a unique 5-digit alphanumeric), whether it is a Bluray or DVD, the movie title, the lead actors/actresses, the category (Family, Sci-fi, Adventure, Drama, Western, and so on.), the rating (G, PG, PG13, R), its condition (good, average, need to replace), date rented and duration rented.

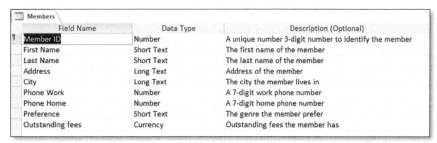

▲ Figure 15.14 Record table

Customers are allowed to rent up to five movies at a time. Movies can be rented for one day ($2.00), two days ($3.00) or a week ($6.00). A $1.00 late fee is charged if movies are not returned on time.

When a movie is rented, the movie card is placed together with the member card. When the movie is returned, the date on the movie card is checked and a late fee is calculated if the movie was returned late. In this case, the owner of the video club may want data on any number of things, such as:

- How many movies are out on loan?
- Which members have overdue movies or movies that are more than a certain number of days late?
- How many movies does the club have in each category?

In this section, we will be creating a database that can answer these kinds of questions.

Grouping related data and identifying fields

In creating the database, Kaycee needs to group all related data to form separate records, much like the card index files she currently uses. The most important factors in her database are the video club members, and then the movies they rent. It is therefore logical that the member information is grouped together and the movie information is grouped together. After grouping the data into these two different tables, individual fields need to be identified. Then, she will want to find a way of linking the two tables, so that she knows, for example, which member is renting which movie.

Within the Members table and the Movies table, the entries may be as shown in Figure 15.15.

Understanding relationships between groups of data

To retrieve data from both tables, there must be a relationship between them. The two tables must be linked by a field common to both tables. In this case, the Member ID can be placed in the Movie Table in order to pull up what movies that particular member has borrowed. The table entries may look like this (Table 15.14):

Movie ID	Movie Title	Category	Member ID
W0231	Unforgiven	Western	123
T0287	SAW	Thriller	123
D0026	The Graduate	Drama	123
S098	Avengers: Infinity War	Science Fiction	123

▲ Table 15.14 Movie Table

There are three types of relationships:

1 **One-to-many relationship:** One record or **entity** in a table or file is linked to many records/entities in another table/file. For example, one member can borrow many movies (Figure 15.15).

2 **Many-to-many relationship**: Many records/ entities in the primary file/table are linked to many records/entities in another file/table through a common entity. For example, a movie can have many actors and one actor can act in many movies (Figure 15.16).

Imagine that Kaycee expands her database later so that members can ask about all the movies the club owns in which a certain actor or actress has appeared. In this case, the database would now also contain many-to-many relationships.

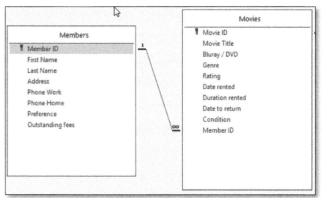

▲ Figure 15.15 A one-to-many relationship

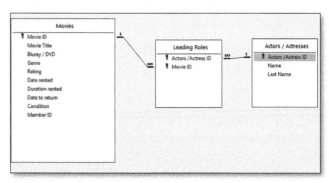

▲ Figure 15.16 A many-to-many relationship

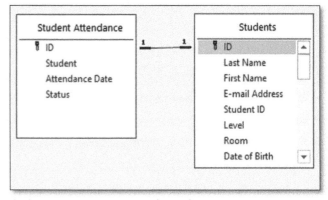

▲ Figure 15.17 A one-to-one relationship

3 **One-to-one relationship**: This is where one record or entity in a primary table or file is linked to exactly one record/entity in another file/table (Figure 15.17).
For example, a movie cannot be loaned to more than one person at the same time, so movie-to-person is a one-to-one relationship.

The steps required to design a database can be summarised in Table 15.15.

Step	Purpose
1	***Determine the goal of the database.*** This will help you to determine the needs of your database. Example: Your goal is to keep track of the books rented from your library. What do you need to know to accomplish this?
2	***Analyse your goal to determine your needs and wants exactly***. Make a list of statements to further define the problem. Example: I need to know who borrowed a particular book. I want to know which book is the most borrowed book. I want to know how many copies of a particular book we have.
3	***Determine the data items you need to store to meet your needs and wants.*** Make a list of relevant data items that will assist you in reaching your goal.
4	***Design your tables.*** Group related data items (books, library members). This will allow you to define your tables/files.
5	***Determine the field names and data types.*** Decide on a *field name* and *data type* for each data item and how the item is to be stored. For example: Storing the name of a person, the two field names 'First Name' and 'Last Name' will have a data type of 'Text'.
6	***Determine how the tables will be related.*** Create a relationship between the two tables that will allow them to link so that information can be cross-referenced. The two tables must, therefore, have a field in common.

▲ Table 15.15 Steps required to design a database

Creating relationships

The duplication of information caused by repeating fields in more than one table can be prevented by linking fields in the tables to establish a relationship.

Linking two tables

1 Click the **Relationships** icon in the 'Relationships' group on the 'Database Tools' tab. The 'Show Table' window will appear (Figure 15.18).
2 If the 'Show Table' window does not appear, click the **Show Table** icon on the 'Design' tab.
3 Select the tables you would like to include in the relationship from the 'Show Table' window by clicking on their names and clicking **Add** or double-clicking on the names of the tables.
4 Click **Close** after you have finished adding all the tables.
5 To link fields from two different tables, click and drag the field from one table to the corresponding field in the other table and release the mouse button. The 'Edit Relationships' window appears.
6 This window allows you to select different fields to link if necessary. You can also select the option to **Enforce Referential Integrity**. Enforcing referential integrity ensures that a value entered in one field of a linked table (related table) matches an existing value in the related field of the primary table.
7 If the **Cascade Update Related Fields** box is checked, changing a primary key value in the primary table automatically updates the matching value in all related records.

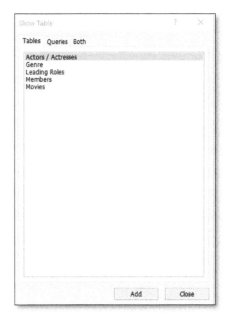

▲ Figure 15.18 'Show Table' window

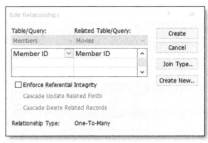

▲ Figure 15.19 'Edit Relationships' window

8 If the **Cascade Delete Related Records** box is checked, deleting a record in the primary table deletes any related records in the related table.

9 Click **Create** to create the link. A line connecting the two fields in the 'Relationship' window appears:
   - A one-to-one relationship is represented by a straight line.
   - A one-to-many relationship is represented by 1 and the infinity (∞) symbol on a line (Figure 15.20). The symbol indicates which table has what relationship to the other.

10 Expand and collapse indicators appear in the datasheet of a relational table, allowing you to view the sub-datasheets matching the information from the other table (Figure 15.21).

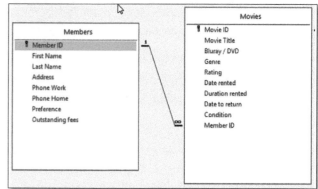

▲ Figure 15.20 One-to-many relationship between tables

Member ID ▾	First Name ▾	Last Name ▾	Address ▾	Phone Work ▾	Phone Home ▾	Preference ▾	Outstanding ▾	Click to Add ▾
002 Jason		Kanhai	Peter Trace, Pa	6879046	5674884	Western	$5.00	

Movie ID ▾	Movie Title ▾	Bluray / DVD ▾	Rating ▾	Date rented ▾	Duration ren ▾	Condition ▾	Return Date ▾	Click to Add ▾
W0231 Unforgiven		DVD	18	2019-03-03	3	Good	2019-03-06	
T0287 SAW		DVD	18	2019-03-02	2	Good	2019-03-04	
*					0			

▲ Figure 15.21 Table showing expand and collapse indicators

Activity 3

1 Retrieve the 'Tropical Appliances Wholesalers' database that you created in Activity 1. Set a relationship between the 'Client Record Table' and the 'Appliance Table'.

How it is done

1 Click the **Relationships** button on the toolbar. The 'Show Table' window will appear. If the 'Show Table' window does not appear click the 'Show Table' icon on the toolbar.

2 Select the 'Client Record Table' and the 'Appliance Table' from the 'Show Table' window by clicking on their names and clicking **Add**, or double-clicking on the names of the tables.

3 Click **Close** after you have finished adding all the tables.

4 Link the Client ID field from the 'Client Record Table' to the Client ID from the 'Appliance Table' by clicking and dragging the field from one table to the corresponding field in the other table and release the mouse button.

5 The 'Edit Relationships' window will appear.

6 Click **Create** to link the two tables.

Short-answer questions

1 Explain the purpose of field validation rules.
2 Explain, giving examples, how input masks are used to format data.
3 List THREE characteristics of primary keys.
4 Give TWO examples of how text and memos can be formatted.

5 What is the difference between the Integer Field Size and the Long Integer Field Size?
6 List FIVE field attributes or field properties and explain their purpose.

Exercise 2

This is an exercise in designing databases, by determining the fields needed, grouping the related fields and deciding on the relationships:

Example

Design a database to be used by your school's librarian to keep track of the library's collection and members/borrowers. See the example in Table 15.16.

Step	Purpose
1 Determine the goal of the database.	Your goal is to keep track of the books rented from your library.
2 Analyse your goal to determine your needs, and wants, exactly.	I need to know who borrowed a particular book. I want to know what is the most borrowed book. I want to know how many copies of a particular book we have. I need to know which books are overdue. I need to know how many days overdue a particular book is. I need to know when a particular book is due to be returned.
3 Determine the data items you need to store to meet your library's needs and wants.	Book number, Title, Author, ISBN number, Date Due, Date Borrowed, Number Borrower's Name, Borrower's Address, Number Borrower's Class, Subject (for example, Science), Category (for example, Fiction, Non-Fiction), Borrower's ID.
4 Design your tables.	Group related data items (books, library members). **Book Table** will contain Book Number, Title, Author, ISBN number, Subject, Category, Date Due, Date Borrowed. **Borrower's Table** will contain Borrower's ID, Borrower's Name, Borrower's Address, Phone Number, Borrower's Class.
5 Determine the field names and data types.	Decide on a *field name* and *data type* for each data item and the item is to be stored. **Book Table:** Book Number – Text, Title – Text, Author – Text, ISBN number – Number, Subject – Text, Category – Text, Date Due – Date/Time, Date Borrowed – Date/Time. **Borrower's Table:** Borrower ID – Number, Name – Text, Address – Text, Phone – Number, Class – Text.
6 Determine how the tables will be related.	**Borrower ID** can link the two tables, therefore it must be included in the Book Table to be able to determine who borrowed a particular book.

▲ Table 15.16 Steps in planning a school library database

1 Design a database to keep track of Dwayne Haze's music collection. As he frequently loans his friends his CDs, he needs to keep track of who has which CD.

2 A caterer has decided to computerise her business; she needs to keep track of her orders and the clients she services. Design a database to accomplish this.

3 Tiffs Flight Attendant Services owns a number of vehicles that are used to chauffeur its employees to and from work. Two flight attendants can share a vehicle, depending on the flight they are scheduled to work on and the area in which they live. Design a database that would keep track of the flight attendants, the vehicle pickups and the flight attendants' work schedule.
Hint: You may require three tables, one for the flight attendants information, one for the work schedule and one for the vehicles.

4 Joshua Bane owns a used car business in a small town. Joshua imports vehicles from Japan and sells them. Joshua has six salespersons working for him to whom he gives a commission based on the number of sales generated by the individual per month. He wants to keep track of his stock and his sales, as well as the employee who sold the vehicle. Design a database to help Joshua accomplish this.
Hint: You can use two or more tables, depending on whether you want to keep track of who bought the vehicles.

5 A Job Placement Company is looking to computerise its manual database. Clients usually approach the company for help in finding jobs, for which a small fee is charged. Information such as skill, personal information, available work hours, references and other relevant information on each client is kept. The organisation receives a list of available job openings from various firms, which they keep on file. These files are updated regularly as the post may become filled by means other than the Job Placement Company. A listing of clients and their skills is matched to the available jobs. Once the client is accepted for a job, an additional sum is paid to the organisation. You are required to design a database for the Job Placement Company.

Indexing and sorting data

Sorting a table

If you close and reopen a Datasheet, the records will appear to be sorted in ascending order according to the values in the 'Primary Key' field. If a primary key was not selected, the records would be displayed in the order that they were entered.

Sorting data on a single field

1 Click on the desired field (in any record or on the Field Name at the top).
2 Select **Sort Ascending (AZ)** or **Sort Descending (ZA)** from the 'Sort & Filter' group on the 'Home' tab.

Sorting on multiple fields

It may become necessary to sort the data in the table on more than one field; for example, sorting on surname and then on the first name or sorting by form and then by the student's surname in that form. You can use **Advanced Filter/Sort** to accomplish this.

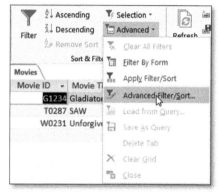

▲ Figure 15.22 Table 'Filter' window

1 Select **Advanced** from the 'Sort & Filter' group on the 'Home' tab.
2 Select **Advanced Filter/Sort** from the drop-down menu. The 'Filter' window opens, the top part of this window contains the table to be sorted, the bottom part contains a grid to select the fields you would like to sort (Figure 15.22).
3 Click on the first box in the 'Field' row and select the field you would like to sort on from the drop-down menu.
4 Click on the 'Sort' row and select the order of the sort, whether ascending or descending.
5 Similarly, select the other fields to sort.
6 Choose **Apply Filter/Sort** from the 'Filter' menu or click the **Apply Filter** icon on the toolbar (see Figure 15.23).

If you want to find out more about this topic you could look up the related animations and activities on your companion CD-ROM.

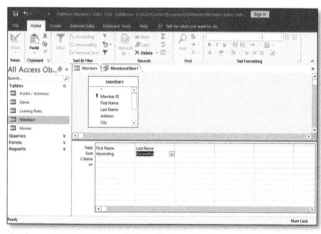

▲ Figure 15.23 Advanced Filter/Sort

Indexing

Records can be found and sorted faster using an index. Similar to the index in a book, Access uses indexes to find data by looking up the location of the data in the index.

An index can be created on a single field or in multiple fields. It is a table that has two columns:

- one stores a sorted list of values of the field or fields being indexed
- the other stores pointers to the data values that are stored in specific columns of the table. These pointers provide the location of each record in the table.

You should consider indexing fields that are searched and sorted frequently. The 'Primary Key' field is automatically indexed. A Multiple Field Index can be created if you search or sort on two or more fields at a time, for example, if you sort on both Last Name and First Name fields.

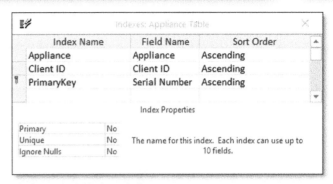

▲ Figure 15.24 Index window

Creating an index

1. Open the database in Design View.
2. Select the field on which you want to set an index, under 'Field Properties' of the table.
3. You can also click on the **Indexes** box in the 'Field Properties' for that specific field (see Figure 15.24).
4. Choose one of the following options:
   - **Yes (Duplicates OK)** – this creates an index on a selected field
   - **Yes (No Duplicates)** – creates a unique index for the selected field and prevents you from entering duplicate values in the field.
5. Save the changes to the table.

Creating a named index

1. Open the database in Design View.
2. Select the field on which you want to set an index.
3. Click on the **Indexes** icon from the 'Show/Hide' group of the 'Design' tab (Figure 15.25).
4. Type the name of the index in the 'Index Name' column.
5. Select the field on which you want to place the index from the drop-down menu in the 'Field Name' column.
6. Select the 'Order of sort' from the 'Sort Order' column.
7. Close the 'Indexes' dialog box.
8. Save the changes to the table design.

▲ Figure 15.25 Design tab

Deleting an index

1. Open the table in Design View.
2. Choose **Indexes** from the 'View' menu or click on the 'Indexes' icon on the toolbar.
3. Select the row selector for the index you want to delete.
4. Click the **Delete Row** icon on the toolbar or press the Delete key on the keyboard.
5. Save the table.
6. Click the **Table Tools Design** tab. Click on the field you want to define as the index and select the **Indexes** icon from the 'Show/Hide' group. The 'Indexes' dialog box will appear.

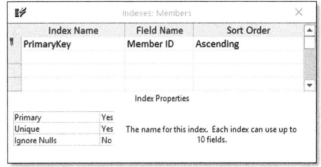

▲ Figure 15.26 Defining an index

Activity 4

1 Retrieve the 'Platinum Member Video Club' database from your companion CD-ROM.
   a Add the following data to the 'New Members Table'.
   b Index Table 15.17 on Member ID.

Member ID	First Name	Last Name	Address	City	Home Phone	Work Phone	Preference
007	Jason	Kanhai	Peter Trace, Palmiste Village	Chagg Town	687-9046	567-4884	Horror
008	Michelle	Lee	#4 Erin Road	Arima	644-6822	663-0987	Documentary
009	Devon	Amoraso	11 Mc Bean Main Road	Couva	772-0011	624-9908	Classics
010	Ethan	Nagra	Beckham Road, Smart Village	St. Helena	764-9034	622-0090	Science Fiction
011	Jack	Grant	#56 Extention Road,	Gulf City	722-8484		Comedy

▲ Table 15.17 New Members Table headings

How it is done

Entering the records

1 Open the Platinum Member Video Club database window.
2 Select the 'New Members Table'.
3 Click **Open**.
4 The 'Datasheet View' window appears with the field names as shown in Figure 15.26.
5 Type '007' under Member ID.
6 Press the Tab key to move to the next column.
7 Type the name 'Jason' in the 'First Name' column.
8 Continue to enter the data for the first record in the appropriate columns.
9 Press **Enter** or use the mouse to move to the next row.
10 Enter all records one by one.

Indexing the table on Member ID

1 Open the table in Design View.
2 Select the 'Member ID' field.
3 In the 'Field Properties' pane click on the **Indexes** box.
4 Choose **Yes (No Duplicates)**.

2 Retrieve the 'Tropical Appliances Wholesalers' database and perform the following instructions.
   a Enter the following records in the 'Appliance Table'.
   b Index Table 15.18 on Serial Number.

Appliance	Manufacturer	Model	Serial Number	Price	Client ID	Sold
Refrigerator	G.E.	R424	82736	$3,500	8	Yes
Stove	Consol	S789	45622	$1,999		No
Microwave	Sharp	M008	12312	$999	6	Yes
Refrigerator	Samsung	R324	22245	$10,500	6	Yes
Washing machine	Samsung	W212	56324	$3,000		No
Washing machine	Consol	W786	33233	$1,495		No
Stove	Atlas	S001	09876	$850		No
Convection oven	Mabe	O332	32109	$350	5	Yes

▲ Table 15.18 Appliance Table

   c Open the table in 'Design View' and add a new field name called 'Description' whose attributes are Text and Field Size 50.
   d Format this new field to display 'Description not available' if no data is entered.

Activity 4 continued

e Enter the following records in the 'Client Record Table' (Table 15.19).

Client ID	Client Name	Business Name	Address	Phone	Date of last order
1	John, Mark	S and M Appliances	James Smart Village, Tobago	663-9862	10/2/19
2	Ali, Devon	Ali's Furniture Store	Oren Road, Christ Church, Barbados	465-3820	20/12/19
3	Mohammed, Amy	Couva District Appliance Centre	Eastern Main Road, Couva	661-0048	2/1/19
4	Alexander, Ramond	Home Needs Wares	Maggie Road, Valley View, St. Lucia	398-0874	30/3/19
5	Blake, Karen	Blake Appliance Store	#44 Eastern Main Road, Sangre Grande, Trinidad	668-0025	7/8/19
6	Alexander, Leslie	LesAlex Home Centre	Baxtor Street, Grand Cayman Island, Grand Cayman	849-1829	3/11/19
7	Singh, Ryan	Drive Through Buyers	34 Fredrick Street, Port of Spain, Trinidad	622-1904	28/1/19
8	Singh, Rhyan	Market Centre	Mango Street, Caynan Bonacord, Tobago	639-6620	28/11/19
9	Gomez, Evon	Center City Appliance Centre	#67 Navet Road, St. Michael, Barbados	490-8383	5/1/19

▲ Table 15.19 Client Record Table

f Sort the Appliance Table according to Price in descending order.
g Index the Appliance Table on Manufacturer followed by Appliance in ascending order.
h Index the 'Client Record Table' on Client Name in ascending order.

3 Retrieve the 'Quilts Incorp' database and perform the following instructions.
a Enter the following records in the 'Order' Table (Table 15.20).

Order Number	Order Date	Shipping Date	Customer FName	Customer LName	Customer Phone	Address	Design Type	King	Queen	Full	Twin
100111	1/3/19	8/3/19	Liz	Massey	664-0938	Orange Grove, Belair, Trincity	MP3905	4	6	2	5
100112	1/3/19	15/3/19	Mary-Ann	Mohammed	668-5733	Breadfruit Lane, Santa Rosa	SUN289	1	8	1	1
100113	12/3/19	24/3/19	Jacque	Simmons	668-8390	Sangre Chiquito, Sangre Grande	MP3887	2	2	12	2
100114	13/3/19	14/3/19	David	Carter	691-9283	#43 Devon Lane, Mount Dor, Mount Hope	GR0290	3	1	7	0
100115	17/3/19	7/4/19	Ann-Marie	Waldross	660-3322	Eastern Main Road, Princes Town	FR0090	5	7	8	8
100116	2/3/19	12/3/19	Jennifer	Ramdass	622-7809	#11 St. Vincent Street, Port of Spain	SE5643	1	6	224	2
100117	31/3/19	31/4/19	Lee	Chan	621-4682	Amber Road, Valley View	SE5643	0	45	75	9
100118	1/4/19	3/4/19	Radha	Singh	720-5920	Peninton Ave. Guaico	FR0090	0	2	50	1
100119	3/4/19	3/4/19	Romaine	Singh	698-2201	Hights of Aripo Road, Wallafield	SE5643	2	5	25	25
100120	6/4/19	16/4/19	Darlia	Smith	758-2201	Common Main Road, Grand Rivera	DRY278	5	5	5	5
100121	8/3/19	20/3/19	Brian	Mohammed	654-2340	LP79 Toco Main Road, Toco	SUN289	11	12	0	0

▲ Table 15.20 Order Table

Activity 4 continued

b Create a table in the 'Quilts Incorp' database called 'Prospective Customers' with the structure, as shown in Table 15.21.

Field Name	Data Type	Description	Field Size
Customer FName	Text	Customer's first name	15
Customer LName	Text	Customer's last name	20
Customer Phone	Text	Telephone contact for customer	8
Address	Text	Customer's Address	50

▲ Table 15.21 Prospective Customers Table

c Enter the following data (Table 15.22) into the 'Prospective Customers Table' of the 'Quilts Incorp' database.

Customer Lname	Customer FName	Address	Customer Phone
John	Mark	James Smart Village, Sangre Chiquito	663-9862
Ali	Devon	Oren Road, Best Village, Point-a-Pierre	665-3820
Jessie	James	Novel Street, Little Dove Company, Diamond Vale	897-6654

▲ Table 15.22 The completed Prospective Customers Table

Manipulating data in a database

Queries

A query selects records from one or more tables, based on specific criteria, for example, to find all of the dog owners in a database of pets and their owners. This resulting set of records can be viewed and analysed and sorted. The resulting collection of records is called a dynaset (dynamic subset). As the original tables are updated, the dynaset is also updated when the query is run again.

There are several types of queries, as shown here.

- **Select query** – extracts data from tables based on a criterion or specified value.
- **Action queries**:
  - **Update query** – makes changes to a group of records, or all records in one or more tables.
  - **Append query** – adds a group of records from one table or more to the end of one or more other tables. The tables do not need to have the same number of fields for the tables to be merged. For example, if Table1 has seven fields and Table2 has four fields that are similar to those in Table1, and you want to append Table2 to Table1, the records will merge, minus the three additional fields from Table1.
  - **Delete query** – deletes a group of records from one or more tables.
  - **Make table query** – creates a new table from all or some of the fields of data in one or more tables. These queries are useful for creating tables to export to other databases or to other documents.
- **Crosstab query** – calculates and restructures data to make it easier to analyse.

Creating a select query in Design View

1. Click the **Create** tab. Select the 'Query Design' icon from the 'Queries' group (Figure 15.27). The 'Show Table' dialog box and the Query grid will be displayed.
2. Select tables and existing queries from the 'Show Table' dialog box (Figure 15.28).

▲ Figure 15.27 The Query Design icon in the Queries group on the Create tab

3. Click the **Tables** and/or **Queries** tab on the 'Show Table' dialog box (Figure 15.28) and click the **Add** button to add tables or existing queries to the new query. Click **Close**.
4. Add fields for the tables to the Query grid by double-clicking on the field name in the table boxes, or select the field from the 'Field' row drop-down menus (Figure 15.30).
5. Specify the sort order if necessary.

▲ Figure 15.28 The 'Show Table' dialog box

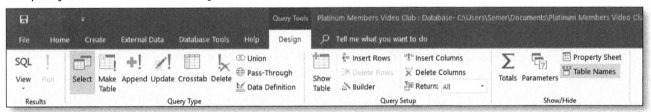

▲ Figure 15.29 Query Design tab

6. Enter the criteria for the query in the 'Criteria' row of the specified field. A criterion can contain values or expressions. Expressions can be equated to formulae much like those found in Excel. The Expression Builder can be used to write a formula/expression (see 'Writing expressions', later in this chapter).
7. After selecting all the fields and entering the criteria, click the **Run** icon [!] on the toolbar.
8. Save the query by clicking the **Save** button.

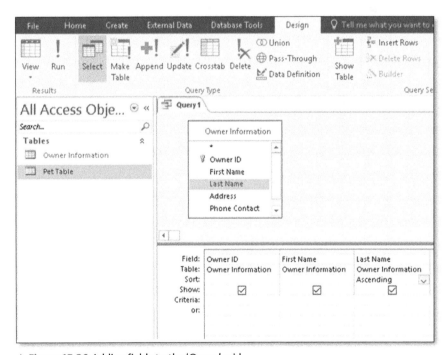

▲ Figure 15.30 Adding fields to the 'Query' grid

Activity 5

1 Retrieve the 'Tropical Appliances Wholesalers' database and perform the following instructions.
  a Create a query to show all the Manufacturers of the appliances where the price is greater than $3,000.
  b Create a query to select all clients who ordered refrigerators.
  c Create a query to select all clients whose last purchase was more than a year ago.
  d Create a query to select all the appliances sold and the names of the clients to whom they were sold.

How it is done

Showing all the serial numbers of the appliances where the price is greater than $3,000

1 Click on the **Query Design** from the 'Queries' group of the 'Create' tab in the 'Tropical Appliances Wholesalers' database window.
2 Select 'Appliance Table' from the 'Show Table' dialog box.
3 Click on **Add** (the table becomes visible in the upper pane of the 'Select Query' window).
4 Click on **Close** (the query grid will be displayed).
5 Click on the arrow in the first column of the 'Field' row and select Appliance or double-click on **Appliance** in the table box above the grid.
6 Move to the next column and select Serial Number or double-click on **Serial Number** in the table box above the grid.
7 Move to the next column and select Price or double-click on **Price** in the table box above the grid.
8 Enter the criterion '>3000' for the query in the 'Criteria' row of the 'Price' field.
9 Click the **Run** icon on the toolbar.
10 Save the query by clicking the **Save** button.

Creating a query to select all clients who ordered refrigerators

1 Click on the **Query Design** from the 'Queries group' of the 'Create' tab in the 'Tropical Appliances Wholesalers' database window.
2 Select 'Appliance Table' and 'Client Records' from the 'Show Table' dialog box.
3 Click on **Add** (the tables become visible in the upper pane of the 'Select Query' window).
4 Click on **Close** (the query grid will be displayed).
5 Link the two tables if they are not already linked, click and drag the Client ID from one table to the Client ID field in the other table and release the mouse button. A line connecting the two fields is displayed (Figure 15.31).
6 Fill out the query grid.
7 Enter the criterion 'Refrigerator' for the query in the 'Criteria' row of the 'Appliance' field.
8 Click the **Run** icon on the toolbar.

2 Retrieve the 'Quilts Incorp' database that you created earlier and perform the following instructions.
  a Create a query to select all customers who placed an order for quilts on 16/04/19.
  b Create a query to select all customers who ordered more than five king size quilts.
  c Create a query to select the design type of all full-size quilts.
  d Create a query to select all orders that are to be supplied between 1/5/19 and 15/5/19.

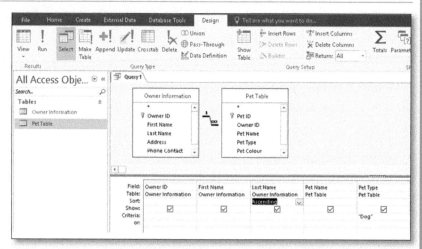

▲ Figure 15.31 Linked tables and query

Action queries

Creating an Update query

1. Click the **Create** tab. Select the 'Query Design' icon from the 'Queries' group. The 'Show Table' dialog box and the 'Query' grid will be displayed.
2. Select tables and existing queries from the 'Show Table' dialog box (Figure 15.32) and click the **Add** button to the new query. Click **Close**.
3. Click on the **Design** tab at the end of the ribbon.
4. Select **Update** from the 'Query Type' group on the 'Design' tab (Figure 15.33).
5. Select the field to update and enter the data you want to update in the 'Update To:' row. The Expression Builder can also be used to enter a formula or expression in the 'Update To': row.

▲ Figure 15.32 'Query Type' group

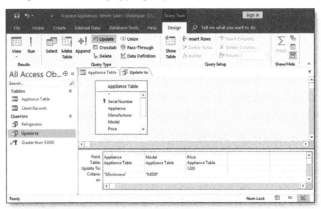

▲ Figure 15.33 'Update' query

Creating an Append query

1. Click the **Create** tab. Select the 'Query Design' icon from the 'Queries' group. The 'Show Table' dialog box and the Query grid will be displayed.
2. Select tables and existing queries from the 'Show Table' dialog box (Figure 15.33) and click the **Add** button to add tables or existing queries to the new query. Click **Close**.
3. Select **Append Query** from the 'Query Type' group on the 'Design' tab.
4. The 'Append' dialog box that appears (Figure 15.34). Select the name of the table to which you want to add the records.
5. Add fields to the query grid that would be added to the appended table.
6. Click the **Run** icon on the toolbar or select **Run** from the 'Query' menu.

> **Note**
>
> If you save an 'Update' query, every time you run the query by double-clicking on it, it will update the records to the table.

▲ Figure 15.34 'Append' dialog box

Creating a Delete query

1. Click the **Create** tab. Select the 'Query Design' icon from the 'Queries' group. The 'Show Table' dialog box and the Query grid will be displayed.
2. Select tables and existing queries from the 'Show Table' dialog box (Figure 15.35) and click the **Add** button to add tables or existing queries to the new query. Click **Close**.
3. Select **Delete Query** from the 'Query Type' group on the 'Design' tab.
4. Add fields to the 'Query' grid, and complete the criteria similar to the 'Select' query.
5. Select **Where** from the drop-down list in the 'Delete' row of the field.
6. Enter the criteria for the query in the 'Criteria' row of the field.
7. Run and save the query.

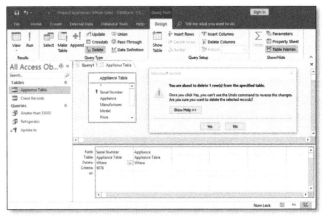

▲ Figure 15.35 'Delete' query

Writing expressions

You can use the Expression Builder to write an expression or formula for a criterion. Expressions can consist of identifiers (field names), operators (+, −, *, /, and so on.), functions, constants and values. An expression is used to perform a calculation, provide criteria for a query and also retrieve a value. Wildcards can also be used within expressions. They are symbols that can be used to specify characters that you do not know the value of or only know part of the value. For example, when a wildcard is used to search a particular field for names that end with 'son' many combinations of the word such as Davidson, Jamison, Johnson may be retrieved. Table 15.23 shows examples of expressions using both operators and wildcards.

To use the Expression Builder select the **Build** icon from the toolbar.

The 'Expression Builder' dialog box appears. The box consists of a top pane and three bottom panes (Figure 15.36).

> **Note**
>
> If you save an append query, every time you run the query by double-clicking on it, it will append the records to the table.

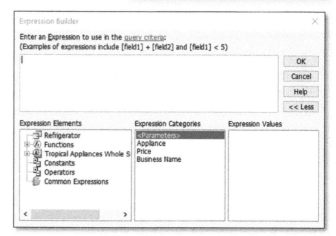

▲ Figure 15.36 'Expression Builder' dialog box

Example of wildcard/operator	Symbol	Explanation
?aren	Wildcard ? or _ (underscore)	Takes the place of a single character, therefore in this example, it finds any word where the first letter can be anything but the remaining letters are 'aren'.
Arima ( ) J B*n	Wildcard * or %	A wildcard that represents any number of characters. Words ending in 'Arima'. Words beginning with 'J'. Words beginning with 'B' and ending with 'n'.
<500	Relational operators >, <, >=, <=, =, <>	Values less than 500.
>=$5,000.00 AND <$8,000.00 "Smith" OR "Singh" BETWEEN #04/05/19# AND #18/05/19#	Boolean operators – AND, OR, NOT, BETWEEN	
=[DateReturned] – [DateBorrowed] =[UnitPrice]*[Quantity] *[Discount]		Calculates the difference between the two values. Calculates the discount on a number of items.

▲ Table 15.23 Wildcards and expression operators

Writing expressions

1 Click the **Create** tab. Select the 'Query Design' icon from the 'Queries' group. The 'Show Table' dialog box and the 'Query' grid will be displayed.
2 Select tables and existing queries from the 'Show Table' dialog box and click the **Add** button to add tables or existing queries to the new query. Click **Close**.
3 Select the type of query from the 'Query Type' group on the 'Design' tab.
4 Add the selected fields to the 'Query' grid. Click in the criteria row of the field you would like to add the expression to.
5 Click on the **Builder** icon from the 'Query Setup' group of the 'Design' tab. The 'Expression Builder' dialog box appears. See Figure 15.37.

▲ Figure 15.37 'Expression Builder' icon

Using the Expression Builder

1 Double-click on the **Tables** folder and select the table that contains the field or fields that will be part of your formula.
2 Double-click on the field(s) that would be part of your expression or formula.
3 Select any relational or Boolean operator and use them to build your expression.
4 Click **OK** when you are finished building your expression or formula.
5 Run and save your query.

Creating a calculated field

A calculated field is a new field where the result of an expression or formula that is created is displayed. The Expression Builder can be used to build the expression/formula.

1 Display the query in 'Design View'.
2 Select an empty field in the 'Query' grid.
3 Type a new field name followed by a colon (:), followed by the expression, which can be built using the Expression Builder or written using the field names that form part of the expression, each in square brackets along with the relevant operators.
   For example: Overdue:[Daysoverdue] * [Overduerate]
4 Click on the **Show** box of the field to display the new calculated field.

Activity 6

1 Retrieve the 'Tropical Appliances Wholesalers' database and perform the following instructions.
   a Create a query to change all Consol manufacturers in the 'Appliance Table' to G.E.
   b Create a query to increase all the prices in the 'Appliance Table' by $100.00.
   c Create a query to calculate the VAT of 15% of all appliances.
   d All Serial Numbers of the appliances are off by one due to a data entry error. Update the Serial Numbers in the 'Appliance Table' by adding one to the Serial Number.

How it is done

Creating a query to change all Consol manufacturers in the 'Appliance Table' to G.E.
1 Use an update query to change all Consol manufactures in the 'Appliance Table' to G.E.
2 Add the 'Appliance Table' to the Query grid.
3 Pull down the **Query** menu and select **Update Query**.
4 Add the 'Manufacturer' field to the Query grid.
5 In the 'Update To:' row of the 'Manufacturer' field type '**G.E.**': include the double quotes.
6 Save and run the query.

Creating a query to increase all the prices in the 'Appliance Table' by $100.00.
1 Add the 'Appliance Table' to the Query grid.
2 Click on Query Design from the 'Queries' group on the 'Create' tab and select the **Update** icon from the 'Query Type' group of the 'Design' tab.
3 Add the 'Price' field to the 'Query' grid.
4 In the 'Update To:' row of the 'Price' field, type "[Price]+100".
5 Save the query.

Creating a query to calculate the VAT of 15% of all appliances
1 Add the 'Appliance Table' to the 'Query' grid.
2 Select the fields to be displayed.
3 Click on the next empty column in the 'Field' row.
4 Type 'VAT:[Price]*[0.15]'.
5 Save the query.

2 Retrieve the 'Quilts Incorp' database and perform the following instructions.
   a Append the 'Prospective Customers Table' to the 'Orders Table'.
   b Delete all orders where the order amount is >=50 for all full sizes of quilts.

Including totals in a query

You can modify a query to include a summary or statistical information. Table 15.24 shows some examples.

How to include totals in a query

1 Display the query in Design View.
2 Click on the **Totals** icon ($\sum$) from the 'Hide/Show' group on the 'Design' tab (Figure 15.39).
3 Select the file(s) on which you want to find the totals (Figure 15.38).
4 A Total row appears in the 'Query' grid. Click on the drop-down arrow and select the function you want to perform.
5 Run and save your query.

Function	Explanation
Sum	Calculates the total of all the values in a field
Avg	Finds the average of all the values in a field
Min	Finds the lowest value in a field
Max	Finds the highest value in a field
Count	Finds the number of values in a field, ignoring the null values
StDev	Calculates the standard deviation of all the values in a field
Var	Calculates the variance of all the values in a field
First	Finds the first value in a field
Last	Finds the last value in a field

▲ Table 15.24 Functions

Finding duplicate queries

This displays the records with duplicate values for one or more specified fields. It filters out the records with duplicates in a specified field.

How to find duplicates

1 Click **Query Wizard** in the 'Queries' group of the 'Create' tab. The 'New Query' dialog box will appear.
2 Select **Find Duplicates Query Wizard** from the 'New Query' window and click **OK** (Figure 15.40).
3 Choose the table or query on which you want to find the duplicates and click the **Next** button.
4 Select the field(s) that may contain the duplicates by clicking on the **>** or **>>** buttons to move the fields from the 'Available Fields' pane to the 'Duplicate-value Fields' list and click **Next** (Figure 15.41).
5 Select additional fields if necessary to be displayed and click **Next**.
6 Give your query a name and click the **Finish** button.
7 Your query should be displayed (Figure 15.42).

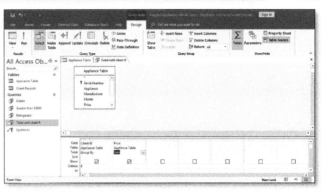

▲ Figure 15.38 Totals in a Query

▲ Figure 15.39 Access 2016 Totals icon

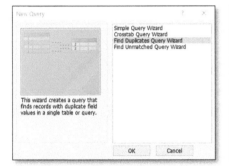

▲ Figure 15.40 New Query window with Find Duplicates Query Wizard highlighted

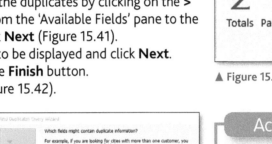

▲ Figure 15.41 Find Duplicates Query Wizard window

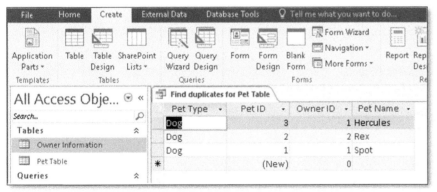

▲ Figure 15.42 The 'Find duplicates' query

Activity 7

1 Retrieve the 'Quilts Incorp' database that you created earlier and perform the following instructions.
 a Quilts are sold for $199.00 – King, $150.00 – Queen, $99.00 – Full, $56.00 – Twin. Create a calculated field that calculates the total cost of the order.
 b Create a query to find the total number of each size of quilt ordered.
 c Create a query to find the average number of each size of quilt ordered.
2 Retrieve the 'Tropical Appliances Wholesalers' database that you created earlier and perform the following instructions.
 a Create a query to find the total number of appliances sold.
 b Create a query to find the number of each type of appliance in the Tropical Appliances Wholesalers inventory.

Forms

A form is a graphical representation of a table. It allows you to create a more aesthetically pleasing display for data entry. You can add, update and delete records in the table from the form. A form can have a different name from the table but they both manipulate the same data in the same way. If a record is changed in the form it is also changed in the table.

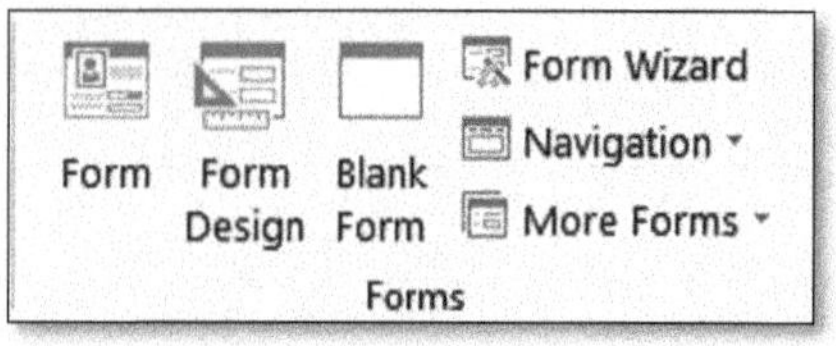

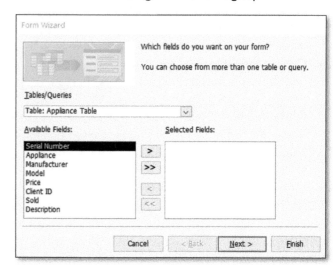

▲ Figure 15.43 Forms group

Creating a form using the Wizard

This is the quickest and easiest method for creating a form for data entry.

1 In the database window, click on the **Form Wizard** icon from the 'Forms' group on the 'Create' tab. The 'Form Wizard' window appears (Figure 15.43).
2 Select the table or query you want to use to create the form. Select the fields you want to view on your form:
    ▪ Click on the **>>** button (this will select all the fields from the specified table or query)
    ▪ Select the field and click on the **>** button or double-click on the field name (this option will select only certain fields)
    ▪ To deselect a field, click on either the **<<** or **<** button.
3 Click **Next**, and select the layout you would like for your form.
4 Click **Next**, and select the style for your form.
5 Clicking **Next** on the style options brings you to the final option screen where you give your form a title or accept the default title for the form.
6 Click the **Finish** button.
    The new form appears in the database window and will be ready for data entry (Figure 15.45). If the form is not open, double-click on the name of the form in the database window.
    One record at a time is displayed. You can scroll through the records by using the record selection buttons at the bottom of the form.

▲ Figure 15.44 The 'Form Wizard' dialog box

▲ Figure 15.45 Pet Table form

Modifying the design of the form

To modify aspects of the form, open the form in Design View.

1 If the form is already open, select **Design View** from the 'View' drop-down menu on the 'Home' tab (Figure 15.46).
2 If the form is not open, right click on the form and select **Design View**.
3 This layout allows you to adjust the width of the data entry fields. Access sets the width of the field to a default size, which may not be wide enough to display the data and hence needs to be adjusted. Place the mouse at the edge of the field box so that the cursor changes to a double-headed arrow. Hold and drag the mouse to adjust the width.

▲ Figure 15.46 View drop-down menu

4 To return to the Data Entry view, select **Form View** from the 'View' drop-down menu on the 'Home' tab. The design changes that were made can be seen in the 'Form' view (Figure 15.47).

Creating a form with a sub-form

A form with a sub-form (or a form within a form) occurs when two tables linked on a specific field are used to create one form. The tables must have a one-to-many relationship in order for a sub-form to be created. That is, a single record in one table must be linked to multiple records in another table. The quickest and easiest method to do this is using the Form Wizard.

1 In the database window, click on the **Form Wizard** icon from the 'Forms' group on the 'Create' tab. The 'Form Wizard' window appears (Figure 15.48).

2 Select the first table or query you want to use to create the form. Select the fields you want to view on your form:
- Click on the >> button (this will select all the fields from the specified table or query)
- Select the field and click on the > button or double-click on the field name (this option will select only certain fields)
- To deselect a field, click on either the << or < button.

3 Select the second table or query you want to use to create the sub-form and select the fields you want on that form.

4 Click **Next**, and select how you would like to view your data.

5 Click **Next**, and select the layout you would like for your form.

6 Clicking **Next** brings you to the final option screen where you give your form a title or accept the default title for the form.

7 Click the **Finish** button.

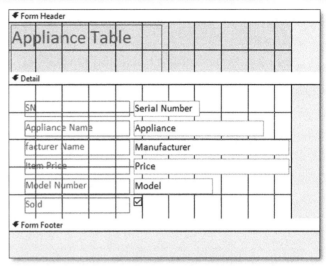

▲ Figure 15.47 The Form view, showing changes

Activity 8

1 Retrieve the 'Quilts Incorp' database that you created earlier and perform the following instructions.
  a Create a form to enter the Orders for Quilts Incorp.
  b Create a form to enter the Prospective Customers for Quilts Incorp.

2 Retrieve the 'Tropical Appliances Wholesalers' database that you created earlier and perform the following instructions.
  a Create a form to enter the records for the 'Appliance Table'.
  b Create a form to enter the 'Client Records'.

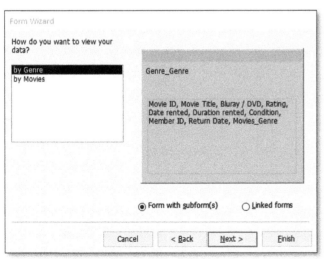

▲ Figure 15.48 Sub-form view

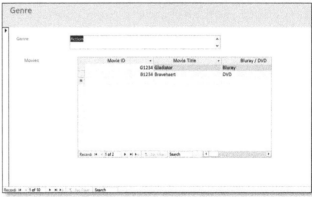

▲ Figure 15.49 Form with sub-form

Reports

Reports organise and group information from tables or queries and format the data in a way suitable for online viewing or for printing from the database.

Creating a report using the Wizard

This is the quickest and easiest method for creating a report.

1 In the database window, click on **Reports Wizard** in the 'Reports' group of the 'Create' tab.

2 The 'Report Wizard' window appears and takes you through a series of options (Figure 15.50).

3 Select the tables or queries that contain the fields you want to be displayed in the report by transferring them from the 'Available Fields' window to the 'Selected Fields' window. This can be done by double-clicking on the field name or clicking on the single right arrow button > to move the fields across one at a time or the double arrow >> to move all the fields at once. Once all the fields are selected, click **Next** to move to the next screen.

4 This screen (Figure 15.51) allows you the option to group your records.
For example, in the 'Pets Table', you can group the records according to the Owner ID.
You can have more than one grouping level. For example, in the 'Movie Table' you can group according to Category and then according to Rating. Use the Priority buttons to change the order of the grouping when there is more than one grouping level. Click the **Next** button to move to the next screen.

5 The 'Sort Order' dialog box appears (Figure 15.52). If the records are to be sorted, you can set the sort order here. You can sort up to four fields in either ascending or descending order. Select the fields to sort and click the **AZ** sort button to choose from ascending or descending order. Click the **Next** button to move to the next screen.

6 Select a layout and page orientation for the report (Figure 15.53) and click **Next** to move to the next screen.

7 This screen (Figure 15.54) allows you to give your report a name and select whether to open it in 'Print Preview' or 'Design View'. The default is the 'Print Preview'. Click the **Finish** button to create the report (Figure 15.55).

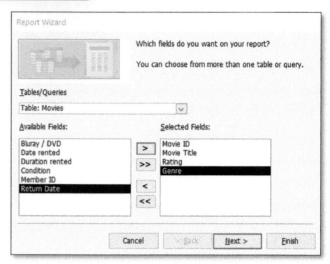

▲ Figure 15.50 The 'Report Wizard' dialog box

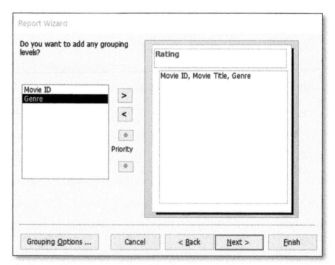

▲ Figure 15.51 Report Wizard Preference window

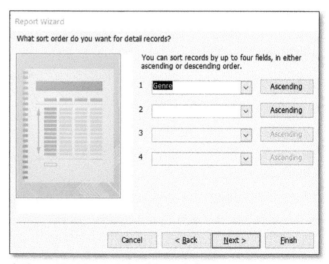

▲ Figure 15.52 Report Wizard Sort window

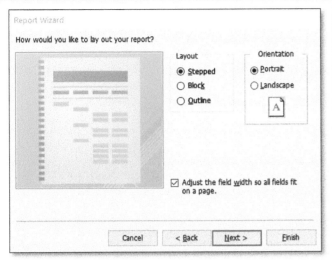

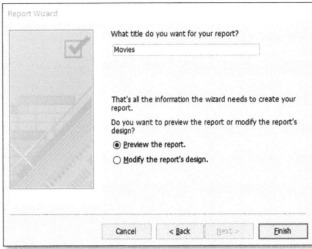

▲ Figure 15.53 Report Wizard Layout window

▲ Figure 15.54 Report Wizard Title window

▲ Figure 15.55 The report

Modifying the layout of the report

A Report layout is divided into sections (Figure 15.56 and Table 15.25).

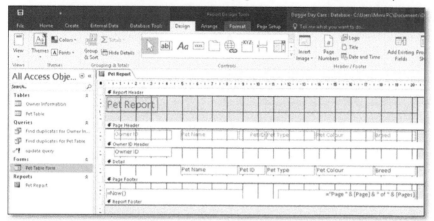

▲ Figure 15.56 A Report layout

Section	Description
Report Header	This section is at the beginning of the report. It usually contains the name of the report and describes the information listed in it.
Page Header	This appears just after the Report Header. It displays the column headings (field names) and page numbers.
Group Header and Group Footer	If records are sorted into groups based on a common value, a Group Header is placed at the start of each group and a Group Footer after the last record in the group.
Details Section	This section contains the primary information of the report. It contains data for each record.
Report Footer	This appears at the bottom of the last page of the report, before the Page Footer on that page. It holds summary information, such as the number of records, grand totals, and so on.
Page Footer	This is the last item on each page of the report. It could contain a page number or other descriptive information.

▲ Table 15.25 Report sections

Chapter 15: Summary

- A database is an organised collection of related data.
- Database management is the process by which information is organised and stored on the computer in such a manner that there is efficient retrieval, updating and manipulation of the data so that persons requiring the information will receive it in a timely manner.
- A database package is a piece of software that enables the user to organise and store related data together so that specific pieces of information can be retrieved quickly and easily.
- Manual databases have many problems associated with them, such as misplacing of files, difficulty cross-referencing data, requires large storage space and the length of time spent finding records.
- A database file is an entire database.
- A table is a basic unit of a database and contains data on a specific topic. Tables may contain multiple fields.
- A field is an area within a table reserved for a specific piece of data.
- A record consists of a group of related fields containing information pertaining to one person, place or thing.
- Data is the information that is held in the field.
- A field definition is the attributes that describe a field.
- Tables/Files can have one of three kinds of relationships to one another:
  - the one-to-many relationship, where one record/entity in one table is linked to many records/entities in another file/table
  - the many-to-many relationship, where many records/entities in one table are linked to many records/entities in another file/table through a common entity
  - the one-to-one relationship, where one record/entity is linked to exactly one record/entity in another file/table.

- A primary key is a selected field or fields in a table that uniquely identifies a record.
- Records can be found and sorted faster using an index. It is similar to the index in a book. Access uses indexes to find data by looking up the location of the data in the index.
- A query selects records from one or more tables based on specific criteria. This resulting set of records can be viewed, analysed and sorted. The resulting collection of records is called a dynaset (dynamic subset). As the original tables are updated the dynaset is also updated when the query is run again.
- A 'Select' query extracts data from tables based on a criterion or specified value.
- An 'Update' query makes changes to a group of records or all records in one or more tables.
- An 'Append' query adds a group of records from one or more tables to the end of one or more other tables. The tables do not need to have the same number of fields for the tables to be merged. For example, if Table1 has seven fields and Table2 has four that are similar to those in Table1, and you want to append Table2 to Table1, the records will merge minus the three additional extra fields from Table1.
- A 'Delete' query deletes a group of records from one or more tables.
- A 'Make Table' query creates a new table from all or some of the fields of data in one or more tables. These queries are useful for creating tables to export to other databases or to other documents.
- A calculated field is a new field where the result of an expression or formula that is created is displayed.
- A 'Form' is a graphical representation of a table. It allows you to create a more aesthetically pleasing display for data entry.
- Reports organise and group information from tables or queries. They format the data in a way suitable for online viewing or for printing.

Short-answer questions

1 List THREE capabilities of computerised databases.

2 What is a relational database?

3 What is a database package?

4 What is a database object? List FOUR of these objects.

5 Give TWO reasons for limiting the size of a field.

Crossword

Across

3 Extracts data from tables based on a criterion or specific value (6)

5 Adds groups of records from one or more tables to the end of one or more tables (6)

6 A database _____ is an entire database (4)

7 A group of related data belonging to one person, place or thing (6)

Down

1 An area in a table reserved for a specific piece of data (5)

2 A graphically pleasing display for information for online viewing or to print data from the database (6)

4 The basic unit of a database (5)

6 A graphical representation of a table (4)

Project

You are asked to design and create a database with at least TWO tables to organise the items in your family's bakery catering business. Your family's bakery sells in bulk to a number of businesses in the area, therefore you need to keep track of what your bakery sells and the businesses you sell to.

16 Integrating data

Objectives

At the end of this chapter, you will be able to:

→ create mail-merged documents using an Access or Excel table as the data source
→ integrate data and graphs from an Excel spreadsheet into a Word document
→ integrate reports and tables from an Access database into a Word document
→ export an Access database object to an Excel spreadsheet
→ import a spreadsheet to a database
→ tackle a sample SBA project involving data integration across all three applications.

Chapters 13, 14 and 15 dealt with Microsoft Word, Excel and Access, respectively, a word processing program, a spreadsheet program and a database program. These applications form part of the Microsoft Office 2016 integrated package. As such, data can be copied or moved from one application to another quite easily. For example, we have looked at mail merge in Word in Chapter 13 and used the address fields to create the data table required to perform the mail merge. With an integrated package such as Microsoft Office 2016, we can also use a table created in Microsoft Excel or Microsoft Access to perform a mail merge. Other examples of integration include moving an Access table to Excel to analyse or produce charts,or publishing an Access report in Word to enhance a report.

Mail merge

In Chapter 13, mail merge was explained using a data source that was created in Word. In this chapter, the data source will be a table created in Access or Excel. The steps to perform a mail merge are the same as outlined in Chapter 13, with the exception of selecting the data file.

Mail merge in Word (using an Access or Excel table as the data source)

1   Select the **Mailings** tab.
2   Click on **Start Mail Merge**.
3   Select **Step By Step Mail Merge Wizard**.
4   The 'Mail Merge Wizard' dialog box shown in Figure 16.1 appears on the right side of the Word document you are working on.
5   Follow the steps as shown in the Wizard.
    (As shown in the Mail Merge section in Chapter 13.)

Step 1 – Selecting the document type

The first step in performing a mail merge is to select the document type. You can perform a mail merge using any of the document types shown in Figure 16.1.

1   For our purposes, check the 'Letters' radio button.
2   Click on **Next: Starting document** at the bottom of the dialog box to move to the next step.

Mail Merge ▾   ✕

Select document type

What type of document are you working on?

◉ Letters
○ E-mail messages
○ Envelopes
○ Labels
○ Directory

Letters

Send letters to a group of people. You can personalize the letter that each person receives.

Click Next to continue.

Step 1 of 6

→ Next: Starting document

▲ Figure 16.1 'Select document type' pane of the 'Mail Merge' dialog box

Step 2 – Selecting the starting document

The 'Select starting document' pane gives you three options to choose from to select the main document. You can:

- use the current document
- start from a template
- start from an existing document.

1   Select the starting document by checking the appropriate radio button. Figure 16.2 shows the **Use the current document** option selected.
2   Click on **Next: Select recipients** at the bottom of the dialog box to move to the next step.

Step 3 – Selecting recipients

In the 'Select recipients' pane, you have to indicate the location of the recipients (the data source).

1   Since our data file will be coming from Access or Excel, you need to check the radio button for the option **Use an existing list** and then select **Browse** as shown in Figure 16.3.
2   The 'Select Data Source' dialog box appears as shown in Figure 16.4. Select the location of the data source from the '**Organise**' pane. Select the data source and click **Open**.

If the data source is from Access, follow the instructions in part a of 3. If it is from Excel, follow the instructions in part b.

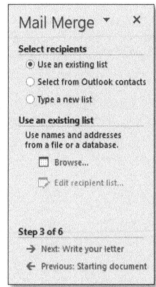

▲ Figure 16.2 'Select starting document' pane of the 'Mail Merge' dialog box

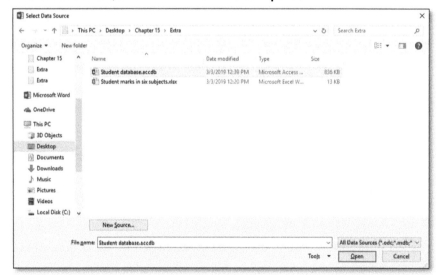

▲ Figure 16.4 'Select Data Source' dialog box

▲ Figure 16.3 'Select recipients' pane of the 'Mail Merge' dialog box

3   a   *Using an Access table as the data source*: When the data source file is opened, the 'Select Table' dialog box is displayed as shown in Figure 16.5.

- Select the table that will be used as the data source and click **OK**. The 'Mail Merge Recipients' dialog box displaying all the records in the table will be displayed, as shown in Figure 16.6 on the next page.

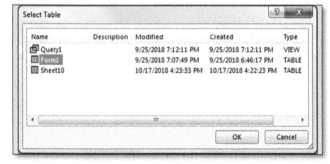

▲ Figure 16.5 'Select Table' dialog box

- Click **OK** to accept the records.
  The 'Mail Merge Select recipients' dialog box, as shown in Figure 16.8, appears again, displaying the name of the table and the name of the database from which it is being taken.
- To continue the mail merge process, click on **Next: Write your letter** to *go to step 4*.

b *Using an Excel table as the data source*: When the data source file is opened, the 'Select Table' dialog box, as shown in Figure 16.7, is displayed.

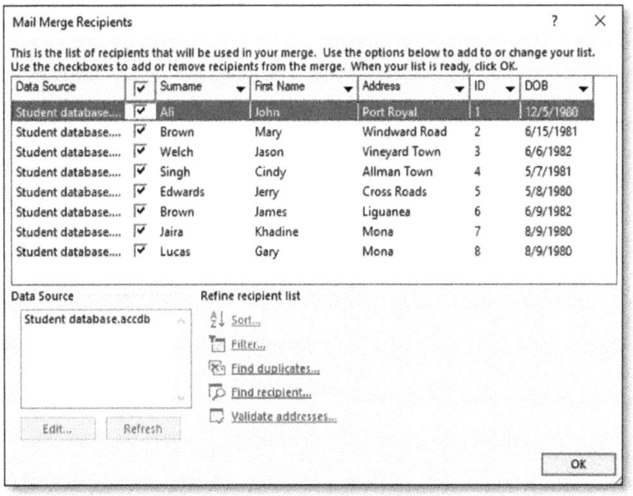

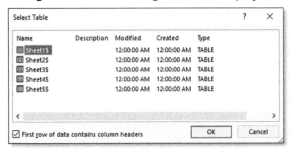

▲ Figure 16.7 'Select Table' dialog box

The dialog box in Figure 16.7 displays all the sheets from the workbook selected.

- Select the sheet containing the data source and click **OK**.
  As in step 3a, the 'Mail Merge Recipients' dialog box displaying all the records in the table is displayed, as shown in Figure 16.9.
- Click **OK** to accept the data.

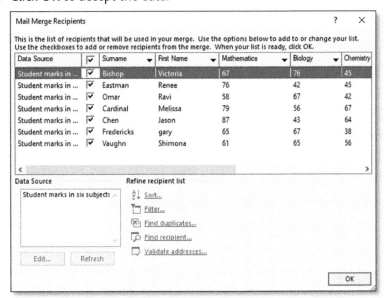

▲ Figure 16.9 'Mail Merge Recipients' dialog box

▲ Figure 16.6 'Mail Merge Recipients' dialog box

▲ Figure 16.8 'Select recipients' pane of the 'Mail Merge' dialog box showing the named Access file

- The 'Select recipients' mail merge dialog box displaying the name of the worksheet and workbook is displayed again.
- To continue the mail merge process, click on **Next: Write your letter** to *go to step 4*.

Step 4 – Writing your letter

The 'Mail Merge Write your letter' pane, as shown in Figure 16.10, is displayed. This option allows you to view the fields for the document.

1   Open your Word document and click a location in the document where you would like to place a particular field. Then click **More items** (Figure 16.10).
    The 'Insert Merge Field' dialog box as shown in Figure 16.11 appears.

2   Select the field from the 'Fields' Combo box and click **Insert**. The field will be inserted in the position selected. Repeat the process for each field.

3   When all the fields you require have been inserted, click **Next: Preview your letters**.

▲ Figure 16.10 'Write your letter' pane of the 'Mail Merge' dialog box

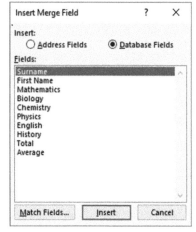

▲ Figure 16.11 'Insert Merge Field' dialog box

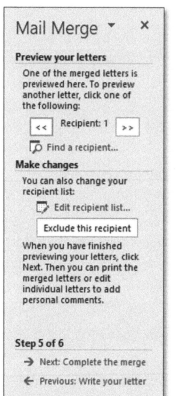

▲ Figure 16.12 'Preview your letters' pane of the 'Mail Merge' dialog box

Step 5 – Previewing your letters

1   The 'Preview your letters' pane appears as shown in Figure 16.12.

2   The 'Preview your letters' dialog box allows you to preview the merged letters. At this point, you can still make changes to the recipient list if you wish.

3   If you agree with the contents of the merged letters then click **Next: Complete the merge** to move to the next step.

Step 6 – Completing the merge

The 'Complete the merge' pane as shown in Figure 16.13 appears.

1   To display all the merged letters click on **Edit individual letters**. The 'Merge to New Document' dialog box appears as shown in Figure 16.14.

2   If you want to select all the records check the **All** radio button, otherwise, input the appropriate range and click **OK**.

▲ Figure 16.13 'Complete the merge' pane of the Mail 'Mail Merge' box

▲ Figure 16.14 'Merge to New Document' dialog box

Activity 1

1 a Type the following document and save it as 'Customers'.
  b Using data from the table 'Client Records' from the database 'Tropical Appliances Wholesalers', which you created in Chapter 15, perform a mail merge.

St. James

12/05/18

<<Business Name>>

<<Address>>

Dear <<Client Name>>

We would like to inform you that our offices will be closed for stocktaking during the period 20/05/18 to 25/05/18. We would be very happy if you could make arrangements to remove all items purchased on <<Date of Last Order>>.

Yours truly,

Jonathan King

Sales Supervisor

2 a Create the following document.
  b Using data from the spreadsheet 'School report' created in Chapter 14, perform the following mail merge.

Happy Hill High School

Report for Term 2 (January to March 2018)

Student : <<First name>> <<Surname>>

Subject	Mark
Mathematics	<<Maths>>
Biology	<<Biology>>
Chemistry	<<Chemistry>>
Physics	<<Physics>>
English	<<English>>
History	<<History>>
Total	<<Total>>
Average	<<Average>>

Ann Margot

Class Teacher

Integrating data and graphs

Many people have to write reports. For example, a teacher may have to write a report to the principal to show students' performance in her class. The principal may then have to write a report to show overall students' performances in the CSEC examinations. To make such a report more meaningful, it may be necessary to include data and charts from a spreadsheet. Moving data and graphs from an Excel spreadsheet to a Word document involves copying, cutting and pasting.

Copying data and charts/graphs from an Excel spreadsheet to a Word document

1 Open the Word document.
2 Open the Excel workbook.
3 Click the appropriate worksheet and select the data/chart required.
4 Select **Copy**.
5 Click the Word document on the taskbar to make it active.
6 Position the cursor in the Word document where you would like to begin to insert the data or chart.
7 Click on the **Paste** icon.

Activity 2

1 Copy and paste the data from the spreadsheet file 'School report' from Figure 14.63 in Chapter 14 (page 338) to the location specified in the letter.
2 Using the spreadsheet 'School report', create a column graph showing the average mark of each student.
3 Import the chart to the location specified in the letter to the principal.
4 Save all changes made to the document.

The Principal

Happy Hill High School

26 March 2019

Dear Mr John Bobb,

The following table shows the performance of students in my class for the different subject areas.

<<Paste spreadsheet table here>>

The average mark obtained by each student is represented as a chart for your convenience.

<<Paste chart here>>

Yours truly,

Darren Phillip

Class Teacher

Integrating objects from a database

You can export a table, query, form or report to Microsoft Word. When you export an object by using the Export – RTF File Wizard, Access creates a copy of the object's data in a Microsoft Word Rich Text Format file (*.rtf). For tables, queries, and forms, the visible fields and records appear as a table in the Word document. When you export a report, the Wizard exports the report data and layout — it tries to make the Word document resemble the report as closely as possible.

Exporting an Access object to a Word document

1 Open the source Access database.
2 In the Navigation Pane, select the object that contains the data you want to export. You can export a table, query, form or report.
3 Select the **External data** tab.
4 Go to the Export group and select **More**.
5 Select **Word** from the drop-down menu (Figure 16.15).
6 The **Export – RTF File** Wizard opens (Figure 16.16).
   a In the Export – RTF File Wizard, specify the name of the destination file.
   b The Wizard always exports formatted data. If you want to view the Word document after the export operation is complete, select the 'Open the destination file after the export operation is complete' checkbox.

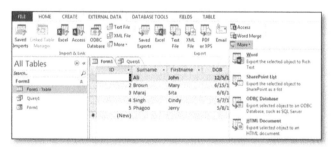

▲ Figure 16.15 Inserting a database table into a Word document

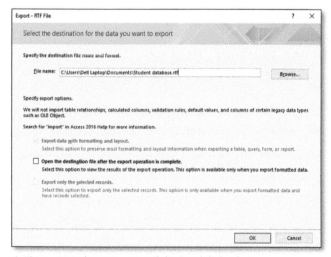

▲ Figure 16.16 'Export – RTF File' Wizard dialog box

7 If you selected the records that you want to export before you started the export operation, you can select the 'Export only the selected records' checkbox. However, if you want to export all the records in the view, leave the checkbox cleared. (*Note*: This checkbox appears unavailable (dimmed) if no records are selected.)

8 Click **OK**.

9 If the destination document exists, you are prompted to click **Yes** to overwrite the file. Click **No** to change the name of the destination file, and then click **OK** again.

The object will be published in a new Word document. To move the object to the document you are working on, you can copy or cut it, and paste it. Figure 16.15 shows the selections involved in publishing the Form1 table from the Student database.

Exporting a database

Data stored in tables in Access can easily be queried to extract information or produce reports. Sometimes, however, you may need to perform calculations on the data or represent the data graphically. Calculations can be carried out in Access but the process is much more difficult than in Excel. Therefore, tables from an Access database can be copied to Excel to be worked on.

Exporting an Access object to an Excel spreadsheet

1 Open the database file.
2 Click on the object.
3 Select the table, query, report, and so on.
4 Select the **External data** tab.
5 Go to the Export group and select **Excel**.
6 The **Export – Excel Spreadsheet** Wizard opens (Figure 16.17).

   a In the **Excel Spreadsheet** Wizard, specify the name of the destination file.

   b You can change the file format of the Excel worksheet by clicking the down arrow in the File format Combo box and selecting from the displayed options. If you want to view the Excel document after the export operation is complete, select the 'Open the destination file after the export operation is complete' checkbox.

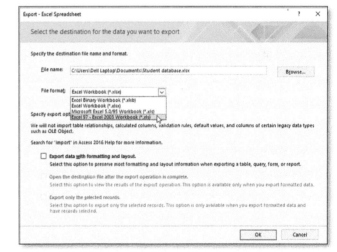

▲ Figure 16.17 Export – Excel Spreadsheet options to copy an Access table to Excel

7 If you selected the records that you want to export before you started the export operation, you can select the 'Export only the selected records' checkbox. However, if you want to export all the records in the view, leave the checkbox cleared. (*Note*: This checkbox appears unavailable (dimmed) if no records are selected.)

8 Click **OK**.

The object will be published in a new Excel worksheet. To move the object to the worksheet you are working on, you can copy or cut it, and paste it.

If you only want part of the table moved to the worksheet, select the content and follow the steps outlined on the previous page.

Importing data from Excel to Access

Importing an Excel spreadsheet into Access can go a lot more smoothly if you take some time to prepare and clean your data.

How to clean your Excel data before you import it into Access

- Convert cells that contain multiple values in one cell to multiple columns. For example, a cell in Excel may contain an individual's first name, middle name and surname. This should be separated into individual columns that each contain only one name (First name, Middle name and Surname).
- Remove non-printing characters.
- Find and fix spelling and punctuation errors.
- Remove duplicate rows or duplicate fields.
- Ensure that columns of data do not contain mixed formats, especially numbers formatted as text or dates formatted as numbers.

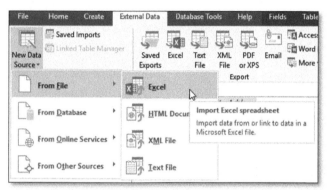

▲ Figure 16.18 Excel option from the Import & Link group

Using the Access Wizard to import a spreadsheet into Access

1 Open the Access program on your computer.
2 Open a new blank Access database to import the Excel sheet into it.
3 Choose 'Blank desktop database' to create a new database within the Access program. (Give it a new name if you wish).
4 Click **Create**.
5 Select the **Excel** option from the **Import & Link** group in the '**External Data**' tab (Figure 16.18). The 'Get External Data – Excel Spreadsheet' dialog box appears, as shown in Figure 16.19.
6 Click **Browse** to find your Excel sheet on your computer. Leave the box checked that says: 'Import the source data into a new table in the current database.' It will be checked by default.
7 When you find the Excel spreadsheet you want to import onto your computer, click on it. Click **OK**. This will take you into the 'Import Spreadsheet Wizard' (Figure 16.20).
8 Choose the worksheet within the Excel spreadsheet that you want to import (Figure 16.21). If there are multiple pages within a single Excel spreadsheet, you need to tell the Access wizard which spreadsheet you are choosing. Click **Next**.

▲ Figure 16.19 'Get External Data – Excel Spreadsheet' dialog box

▲ Figure 16.20 'Import Spreadsheet Wizard'

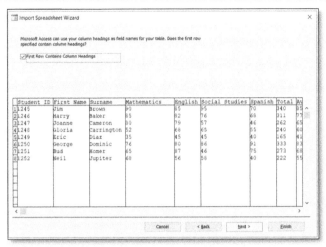

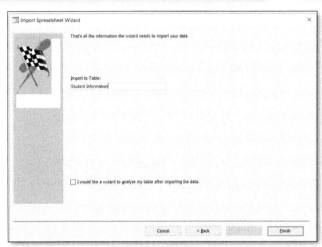

▲ Figure 16.21 Identifying the column headings in the 'Import Spreadsheet Wizard'

▲ Figure 16.22 'Import Spreadsheet Wizard' final step

9 The next page has a box asking if the first row in the Excel sheet has column headings (such as First name, Surname, and so on). Check 'Yes' that the first row contains column headings. Click **Next**.

10 The next page in the Wizard will ask if you want to identify a primary key. (You do not have to do this, but you can if you wish.)

11 The final screen in the Wizard has a space providing a default name. You can change the name of the Excel sheet you are importing (it will become a 'table' in Access on the left side of the page when you finish importing it).

12 Click **Finish** (Figure 16.22).

13 Click **Close**. You will see your table on the left side of the screen. It is now imported within Access (Figure 16.23).

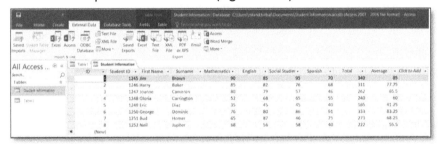

▲ Figure 16.23 Spreadsheet imported into Access

Chapter 16: Summary

- 'A mail merge can be performed using an Access table or Excel table as the data source.
- The steps involved in performing a mail merge using an Access or Excel table as the data source are:
  - selecting the document type
  - selecting the starting document
  - selecting the recipients
  - writing your letter
  - previewing your letters
  - completing the merge.

- Data and graphs from an Excel spreadsheet can be moved to a Word document by selecting the required data or graph and cutting or copying, and pasting into the Word document.
- Access objects such as tables, queries and reports can be published in a Word document.
- Tables from an Access database can be copied to Excel to be worked on.
- A spreadsheet table can be imported into an Access table. This may be necessary if you wish to perform more in-depth queries on your data.

Chapter 16: Questions

Fill in the blanks

1. If the data source of a mail merge is an Access table, the 'Select Table' dialog box displays the _____.

2. If the data source of a mail merge is an Excel table, the 'Select Table' dialog box displays the _____.

3. The 'Mail Merge Recipients' dialog box displays all the _____ in the table.

4. The Mail Merge 'Write your letter' dialog box allows you to view the _____ for the document.

5. Moving data and graphs from an Excel spreadsheet to a Word document involves copying or cutting and _____.

6. To convert an Excel table into an Access table, the first row of the spreadsheet should contain the _____ or _____.

True or False?

1. A mail merge can be performed with a table created in Access as the data source.

2. The first step in performing a mail merge is selecting the document type.

3. Labels cannot be used as a document type in a mail merge.

4. The starting document in a mail merge must be an existing document only.

5. The 'Select Recipients' dialog box allows you to indicate the location of the recipients.

6. The Mail Merge 'Write your letter' dialog box allows you to view the fields for the document.

7. The 'Preview your letters' dialog box allows you to preview the merged letters.

8. Moving data and graphs from an Excel spreadsheet to a Word document involves copying, cutting and pasting.

9. An Access object such as a table cannot be imported into a Word document.

10. To move an Excel table into an Access table you must ensure that the first row of the spreadsheet contains the field names or row headings.

Short-answer questions

1. Describe the steps to perform a mail merge if the data file is an Access table.

2. Describe the steps to perform a mail merge if the data file is an Excel table.

3. Explain ONE reason for moving data and charts from an Excel spreadsheet to a Word document.

4. Explain the steps involved in importing a spreadsheet table or chart into a word processing document.

5. Describe the steps involved in publishing an Access object to a Word document.

6. State ONE reason why you might want to export an Access table into Excel.

7. Describe the steps involved in importing an Access table into Excel.

8. Describe the process of importing an Excel table into an Access database.

9. State ONE advantage of importing an Excel table into a database.

Now that you have seen how data can be copied or moved from one application to another, we will walk you through the solution for a sample SBA (School-based Assessment) project. In this project, many of the features you have learned about in Word Processing, Spreadsheet, Database, Website creation and Programming, as well as in this chapter, will be used.

Description of your project

Tech Info Corporation, established in 2014, has decided, in January 2019, to implement employee salary increases based on seniority, performance and qualifications. The CEO of the company has asked the IT Department to computerise this process. In order to do so, employees' records need to be updated. So, you were asked to do the following:

- Create a fillable form for employees to update their records.
- Establish the present salaries of all employees.
- Establish the increment each employee will receive based on his or her performance, seniority and qualifications.
- Perform all the calculations necessary to work out the salary increases.
- Send out letters to all employees, informing them of their salary increase.
- Update all employee records with all the changes that were made.
- Record on a printout any assumptions that were made.
- Create a program to calculate the employees' new salaries.

Spreadsheet section

At present, increments are given to employees of rank 3 and above. Increments are fixed at 2% of their current salary. This increment is given every year after the first year of employment. The current salary plus increments become their new salary.

A completed SBA project can be found on your companion CD-ROM.

Table 16.1 shows the current starting monthly salaries of employees:

Position held	Rank	Starting monthly salary
Data Processing Manager	6	15000
Database Administrator	5	10000
Network Administrator	5	10000
Systems Development Manager	5	10000
Business Analyst	5	10000
Operations Manager	5	10000
Systems Analyst	4	8700
Programmers	3	8000
Computer Operators	2	5000
Technical Support	2	5000
Data Control Clerks	2	5000
File Librarian	1	3500
Data Entry Operators	1	3500

▲ Table 16.1 Current starting monthly salaries for various positions

After a series of meetings, the Board of Directors has decided to change the way the salary increment each employee receives is calculated each year. Instead of receiving fixed increments every year, increments will now be based on seniority and rank.

A new agreement between the workers' union and the company states that employees will get their increments as of January 2019, according to the criteria listed in Table 16.2.

Years of service	% increase
5	7
4	5
3	3
2	2

▲ Table 16.2

Sample project continued

You are required to:

A Use the data from Table 16.1, along with data you will make up, to create a spreadsheet of no less than 25 employees showing their Employee ID, Name, Position, Rank, Starting Monthly Salary, Year of Entry and Years of Service. Each employee has a 3-digit employee ID number. Ensure that your data includes all the positions in the company, along with a range of starting dates from the inception of the company.

Your spreadsheet should use labels appropriately, for example, bear in mind that you may be asked to sort the spreadsheet on Employee Surname. The information should be easily interpretable.

B Create a spreadsheet to determine the annual salaries of employees over the years from their date of entry into the company to December 2018. Use currency format to display the salaries.

C Modify the spreadsheet to reflect the new agreement for 2019 salaries.

D Use appropriate formulae to determine the highest and lowest salary increases in 2019.

E Add the following two employees to the spreadsheet:

Employee ID	Name	Position Held	Entry Year
339	Davanand Singh	Programmer	2015
340	Jessie Romero	Data Entry Operator	2018

F Sort the data worksheet containing the 2019 yearly salaries on employee Surname, followed by First Name, in ascending order.

G Extract the records of ALL employees whose monthly salary is >= $8,000.00 and who started working at the company in the year 2016 or after.

H Create a summary table to show the percentage of employees in each rank.

I Create a pie chart to show the percentage of employees in each rank. Label your chart appropriately.

J Create a graph to show the differences in the salaries between the old agreement in 2014 and the new agreement in 2019. Label your graph appropriately.

Database section

Records are kept by the company of all existing employees and the state of their due salaries over the years. There are six ranks of employee. The salaries payable to each employee is dependent on his or her rank.

The company's database has two tables, one holding personal information on each employee, the other holding the history of the annual salary paid to each employee.

The 'Employee Information' table maintains the following information on each employee: employee ID, name, address, phone number, date of birth and gender. Each employee is also assigned a unique identification number for database recording purposes.

The 'Salary History' table holds information on employee ID, employee position, rank, year of entry, years of service, starting monthly salary and also maintains a history of the yearly payments. For example, Jane Doe was employed in 2014, so the company will maintain records for 2014, 2015, 2016, 2017, 2018 and 2019. These records will indicate what salaries were paid under the old agreement and what is due under the new agreement.

You are required to:

A Design and create a set of database tables that will meet with all the criteria above.

B Populate your database with the names and data used in your spreadsheet section. Include payment information from the year of entry for each employee.

C Delete the Surname and First Name field from the 'Salary History' table.

D Create your database files so that you can respond to the following queries. Test your database by running samples of the following queries.

a What are the names, addresses and phone numbers of all the Data Entry Operators?

b List all the employees who occupy positions above rank 4.

c List all employees and their salaries for 2019.

d What is the total sum of money that has been paid out in increments during the year 2016 by Tech Info Corporation?

e Create a query to determine the salaries for 2018 of all employees who entered the organisation before the year 2017.

Further, test your database by performing the following operations on the database:

E   Delete all the records related to Davanand Singh, Employee ID 339, who has now left the company.

F   Prepare a report, which must display the unique employee number, starting salary, rank and position held. For each employee, the report should give information on the payment of salary (that is, 2014 to 2019) from the year they started with the company. The salary information should be grouped by rank and sorted by employee number in ascending sequence.

G   Create a control form to display information about the candidates.

Word processing section

At the end of the year 2018, Tech Info Corporation has finished its salary adjustments for all its employees and is now ready to publish all the changes made to every employee's salary.

You are required to:

A   Send out letters to every employee notifying them of the change in salary increment structure for 2019 as compared to 2018, and what their new annual salary will be. Letters must be prepared on the company's letterhead, including the company's logo, address, phone/fax number, email address and website address. Every letter must contain the following information:
   - The year the employee began to work at the company
   - The rank that the employee holds
   - The employee's starting monthly salary
   - The percentage increase that was received up to the year 2018
   - The percentage increase and new salary that the employee will receive at the beginning of 2019.
   - Populate each letter with the correct values, as obtained from either the spreadsheet or database that you have already produced.
   - The guidelines for writing the letter the employees will receive are as follows:

   - The letter must begin with:
     Maria Brown
     The Chief Financial Officer
     Finance Department
     Dear , _____
   - Every letter should have the following footer in a smaller font than the rest of the document and in italics.

     _____

     © Tech Info Corporation
     Finance Department, 2018
   - Include a space for the Chief Financial Officer's (CFO 's) signature.

a   Using the Mail Merge facility, create letters to send out to all the employees.

b   Make sure that you have spell-checked the letters have have used appropriate grammar, that is, a professional register.

c   Adjust the margin for each letter so that the top margin is 2 inches, in order to accommodate the letterhead, and the left margin is 1.5 inches, and the bottom and right margins are 1 inch each.

B   Each employee must update their records by completing and submitting an Employee Information Update Form. You are required to:
   - Design a fillable form to capture information about the employee, for example, employee name, address, phone contact, date of birth, email, gender, marital status, emergency contact information (that is, information on who to contact in case of an emergency), National Insurance number and tax number, and Employment start date.
   - The form must include the company's logo in the letterhead.

C   You are required to produce a financial report on the salary adjustments made, comparing 2018 and 2019 salaries.

a   The report must be addressed to the Board of Directors of Tech Info Corporation.

b   The report must inform the Board of Directors of the changes in increments and how the new increments will be adjusted.

c   The report must give a brief reason for the change.

d   The graph from your spreadsheet showing the percentage of employees in each rank of the organisation, and the graph comparing the 2018 salaries to the 2019 salaries, should also be included.

Web page design section

The Tech Info Corporation has requested that you design a web page to sensitise the employees of their rank and incremental percentage (%) increase, and to inform them about the need to update their records. The web page should include the following:

1 Tech Info Corporation's logo
2 Display information about the incremental increase based on job position and rank.
3 Link the form 'Employee Information Update Form' created in the Word Processing section to the web page.

Problem-solving section

A Develop an algorithm to accept and print the names, positions held and years of service of each employee, as well as their 2018 salary.

The algorithm should calculate the salary of each employee for the year 2019, based on the percentage incremental increase. Test the algorithm with 10 employees. Source data to test the algorithm from the Spreadsheet section of the project.

B Design and execute a trace table to test the algorithm development in Part A of this section. The table should have a maximum of 10 iterations.

Program implementation section

1 Develop a problem statement for the algorithm developed in the Problem-solving section part A.
2 Using the programming language Pascal, or Visual Basic, write the code to implement the algorithm.

A solution to the project

Spreadsheet section

Part A: Entering the data

1 Open the spreadsheet program Microsoft Excel.
2 Enter the headings in row 5, starting from column A: Employee ID, Surname, First Name, Position Held, Rank, Starting Monthly Salary, Year of Entry and Years of Service in sheet 1.
3 Enter data for 25 employees for each of the fields, except Years of Service field.
4 Enter in a cell above the table the label 'Current Year' and in a cell next to the label the year '2018'.
5 Enter the formula to calculate Years of Service where Years of Service = Current Year – Year of Entry. Use absolute referencing to refer to the cell holding the 'Current Year' value. Example: =$H$2–G6
6 Place the formula in the remaining cells below by filling down.
   a Rename the sheet by right-clicking on the sheet tab and choosing **Rename** from the pop-up menu.
   b Rename the sheet, **Current year**.

Part B: Determining the annual salaries from 2014 to 2019

1 For each employee, enter a formula to calculate the first-year salary for that employee by multiplying the starting monthly salary by 12. Place the formula in the cell that indicates the year of entry for that employee. Example: = F6*12 where F6 contains the starting monthly salary of that employee.
2 Enter the formula (a) to determine the yearly increments, (b) to determine the final yearly salary by adding the yearly salary to the yearly increment.
   a To determine the increment:
      i Enter in a cell above the table the label '% Increment' and in a cell next to the label '2%'.
      ii To do this, you have to determine if the employee's rank is greater than or equal to 3. If it is, you multiply the previous year's monthly salary by 2%, otherwise you multiply it by 0%. This requires you to use the IF function. Remember, the IF function is written in three parts: IF(Logical_Test,Value_If_True,Value_If_False)

- The Logical_Test part determines if the employee's rank is greater than or equal to 3.
- The Value_If_True part multiplies the employee's previous year's monthly salary by 2%.
- The Value_If_False part multiplies the employee's previous year's monthly salary by 0%. Multiplying the employee's previous year's monthly salary by 0% will give US$0.00 dollars as the increment.

Example: IF(Rank>=3,%increment*Yearly salary,0%*Yearly salary)
=IF(E6>=3,$E$3*J6,0%*J6) This calculates the increment.

b To determine the final yearly salary, add the yearly salary to the yearly increment: =I6+J6

c Fill down to put the formula in the cells for all employees.

d Select all monetary values and place them in currency format by clicking the **Currency** button in the **Number** group on the **Home** tab.

Note

Absolute referencing is used for the 'Rank' and the '% Increment', as these values do not change as you fill down.

Part C: Modifying the spreadsheet to reflect the new agreement for 2019

1 Copy the Current Year sheet by:
  a Right clicking on the **Sheet** tab – a pop-up menu will appear. Select **Move or Copy**. The 'Move or Copy Sheet' dialog box will appear.
  b Select the sheet to copy.
  c Check the **Create a Copy** box.
  d Rename the sheet by right-clicking on the **Sheet** tab and choosing **Rename** from the pop-up menu. Rename the sheet, **2019**.

2 Add the heading 2019 in cell B3.

3 Change the heading for the columns in the 2019 sheet from Current Monthly Salary to 2018 Monthly Salary, from Yearly Salary to 2018 Yearly Salary, from Yearly Increments to 2018 Yearly Increments, and from Final Yearly Salary to 2018 Final Yearly Salary.

4 Enter the formula to calculate the 2019 Increment using the information provided.

This requires the use of the nested IF function:

=IF(celladdress>=2,K6*2%,IF(celladdress>=3,K6*3%,IF (celladdress>=4,K6*5%,K6*7%)))

In the example, the second IF statement is also the Value_if_False argument/part to the first IF statement.

Similarly, the third IF statement is the Value_if_False argument to the second IF statement.

For example, if the first Logical_Test (Years of Service>=2) is TRUE, the increment I8*2% is calculated.

If the first Logical_Test is FALSE, the second IF statement is evaluated, and so on.

A function can contain up to seven levels of nested functions.

=IF(Years of service>=2;K6*2%;IF(Years of service>=3;K6*3%;IF(Years of service>=4;K6*5%;IF(Years of service>=5;K6*7%;0))))

for example,

=IF(E6>=2;K6*2%;IF(E6>=3;K6*3%;IF(E6>=4;K6*5%;IF(E6>=5;K6*7%;0))))

Enter the formula to determine the 2019 salary by adding the 2018 salary to the increment

= K6+L6

Part D: Determining the highest and lowest salary increases in 2019

1 Insert the heading 'Salary Increase' next to the 2019 Yearly salary.

2 Enter the formula to determine the salary increase by subtracting the 2018 salary from the 2019 salary. Example: =M6–K6

3 Place the formula in the remaining cells by filling down.

4 Four cells below the table, enter the labels 'Highest Increase' and 'Lowest Increase'.

5 Enter the formula for Highest Increase. Example: =MAX(O6:O30)

6 Enter the formula for Lowest Increase. Example: =MIN(O6:O30)

Part E: Adding two new employee records

1. After the last employee record, insert the given data for the two new employees, Davanand Singh and Jessie Romero.
2. Insert the Rank and Entering Salary corresponding to their position.
3. Enter the formula to calculate their salary for the year of entry of these employees.
4. Enter the formula of these 2019 salary by filling down.
5. Recalculate the Highest Increase and Lowest Increase by changing the range to include the two new employees.

Part F: Sorting the worksheet on employee name

1. Select all the employee records including the headings, that is, from Employee ID to Salary Increase and from the first employee record to the last.
2. Select **Sort** from the 'Editing' group of the 'Home' tab.
3. In the 'Sort by' box, select **Surname**. Ascending is the default sort order.
4. Click on **Add a Level**, in the 'Then by' box and select **First Name**.
5. In the 'My data range has' section of the dialog box, make sure that a 'Header row' is selected. This indicates that your table has headings.
6. Click **OK**.

Remember:
If you only select the column with the surname, the surnames will sort and the rest of the table will remain the same.

Part G: Extracting records based on particular criteria

1. Two rows above the '2018 Monthly Salary' heading, copy the '2018 Monthly Salary' heading.
2. Enter the criterion '>8000' below the heading you just copied.
3. Two rows above the 'Year of Entry' heading copy the 'Year of Entry' heading.
4. Enter the criterion '>=2016' below the heading you just copied.

5. Select all the employee records including the headings, that is, from Employee ID to Salary Increase and from the first employee record to the last.
6. Select **Advanced Filter** from the 'Sort & Filter' group on the 'Data' tab. The 'Advanced Filter' dialog box will appear.
7. Click the radio button **Copy** to another location.
8. The 'Data Range' has already been selected when you selected all the employee records.
9. Click in the **Criteria Range** box and select the criteria that you placed above the table. Select the headings 'Entering Salary' to 'Year of Entry', as well as the values placed below these headings '>=8000' and '>=2015'. The following range will appear in the Criteria Range box: $F$3:$G$4
10. Click on the **Copy to box** and a few rows below the table, click in cell A45.
11. Click **OK**.

Part H: Summary table to show percentage of employees in each rank

1. Click on a new worksheet. If there are only two worksheets showing, select **Insert sheet** from the 'Cells' group on the 'Home' tab.
2. Create a table with the headings 'Rank', 'Number of Employees' and 'Percentage'.
3. Enter the ranks 1 to 6.
4. Enter the formula to calculate the number of employees using the COUNTIF function.
5. The COUNTIF function is divided into two parts: =COUNTIF(Range,Criteria)
   - The range is the list of employee ranks in Sheet 2. Since this range does not change, you need to use absolute referencing.
   - The criterion is the rank that it is being checked against in the summary table. Example: =COUNTIF('2019'!$E$6:$E$32,A2)
6. Enter the formula to find the total number of employees. Example: =SUM(B2:B7)
7. Enter the formula to calculate the percentage of employees in each rank; that is, the number of employees in a rank divided by the total number of employees. Then click on the percentage button on your toolbar. Example: =B5/$B$8. Remember, you need to use absolute referencing so that the total number of employees does not change when you fill down.

Part I: Creating a pie chart to show the percentage of employees per rank

1. Since the ranks are numbers, you need to format these numbers as text by placing an apostrophe before the number. Example: '5 (Figure 16.33).
2. Select the ranks and percentages by holding the **Ctrl** key.
3. Click the **Recommended Charts** button from the 'Charts' group on the 'Insert' tab. The 'Insert Chart' dialog box will appear.
4. Select the type of chart **Pie** and Click **OK**.
5. The **Data Range** has already been selected.
6. Click on the title placeholder and enter a title for your chart.
7. Click the **Add Chart Element** in the 'Chart Layout' group on the 'Design' tab. You can adjust the placement of the legend by selecting **Legend**. You can also select the format of your **Data Labels**. Select **Percentage data** label from the 'Data Label' drop-down menu.
8. Click **Move Chart** from the 'Location' group and select **New Sheet** from the 'Move Chart' dialog box, to allow the chart to appear in a new sheet.

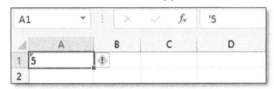

▲ Figure 16.24 Numbers formatted as text

Part J: Creating a graph to show the differences in the 2018 and 2019 salaries

1. Since the Employee IDs are numbers, you need to format these numbers as text by placing an apostrophe before the number, Example: '301. Or you can select the Employee ID's by right-clicking on them. Select **Format Cells** from the pop-up menu, and choose **Text** from the 'Category' list.
2. Select the Employee IDs and the 2018 and 2019 Yearly Salaries of all the employees from the 2019 sheet by holding the **Ctrl** key, you need to include the headings in your selection.
3. Click the **Recommended Charts** button from the 'Charts' group on the 'Insert' tab. The 'Insert Chart' dialog box will appear.

4. Select the type of chart, **Bar** or **Column**, and click **OK**
5. The **Data Range** has already been selected. Click **Next** to continue to the next window.
6. Click the **Titles** placeholder on the chart and enter a title for your chart.
7. Click the **Add Chart Element** in the 'Chart Layout' group on the 'Design' tab. You can adjust the placement of the legend by selecting **Legend**. You can also select the format of your **Data Labels**, as well as your **Axis Titles**.
8. Enter a title for the x-axis.
9. Enter a title for the y-axis.
10. Click **Move Chart** from the 'Location' group and select **New Sheet** from the 'Move Chart' dialog box, to allow the chart to appear in a new sheet.

Database section

Part A: Importing the spreadsheet data into the database

1. From the spreadsheet, create a new worksheet by right-clicking one of the worksheet tabs and then selecting the command **Insert** from the pop-up menu.
   Optional: You can rename the sheet by right-clicking on the sheet tab, choosing **Rename** from the pop-up menu and naming it 'For DB'.
2. Select the employee data from the '2019' sheet. including all the headings from A5 to N32.
   a Click on the worksheet you created, that is, 'For DB'.
   b Right-click on the first cell in the sheet A1 and select **Paste special** from the pop-up menu. The 'Paste Special' dialog box will appear.
   c Click **Values** icon from the 'Paste' section of the dialog box.
3. Save and close the spreadsheet.
4. Open a blank database.
5. Select **Excel** from the 'Import & Link' group of the 'External Data' tab.
6. Browse and select the file to import.
7. Select the worksheet that contains the data for the database table – 'For DB'. Click the **Next** button.
8. Indicate by checking the box **First Row Contains Column Headings**. Click the **Next** button.
9. *Optional*: You can further specify or modify information about each field. However, just click the **Next** button to move on to the next screen.

10 Click the radio button **Choose my own primary key** and select Employee ID as the primary key. Click the **Next** button.

11 In the 'Import to Table' box, type the name 'Salary History' and click the **Finish** button.

12 Open the 'Salary History' table in Design View and modify the data types, field sizes of all the fields, and format of salary to currency format.

Part B: Creating the 'Employee Information Table'

1 Open the database.

2 Click on the **Table Design** in the 'Tables' group of the 'Create' tab.

3 Define each of the fields in your table (table definition) – employee ID, Surname, Firstname, address, phone number, date of birth and gender.

- Enter the field names in the 'Field Name' column. (*Note:* these field names become the headings for your table.)
- Select the appropriate data type for that field in the 'Data Type' column.
- Enter text in the 'Description' column. This describes the data that will be entered in this field. (This field is optional.)

Part C: Deleting the Surname and First Name fields from the 'Salary History' table

1 Open the 'Salary History' table in Design View.

2 Select the row(s) to be deleted.

3 Press the **Delete** key.

Part D: Queries

Append Query:
Query 1: Append the ID, Surname and First Name from the Salary Table to the Employee Information Table.

1 Click on the **Queries** tab under 'Objects' on the left side of the screen.

2 Double-click **Create query** in 'Design View' or click on the **New** button (the 'New Query' dialog box appears) and select **Design View** then click **OK**.

3 Add the table 'Salary History' from the 'Show Table' dialog box and click the **Close** button.

4 Click the **Append** icon from the 'Query Type' group of the 'Design' tab. The 'Append' dialog box will appear.

5 Enter/Select the name of the table you want to append to 'Employee Information'.

6 Double click on the names of the fields you want to append. This will add the information to the 'Query' grid. Then **Run** the query.

Note

You do not need to save this query since once the data is added and if the query is run again, you will add the records again to the table.

Query 2: What are the names, addresses and phone numbers of all the Data Entry Operators?

1 Click on the **Queries** tab under **Objects** on the left side of the screen.

2 Double-click **Create query** in 'Design View' or click on the **New** button (the 'New Query' dialog box appears) and select **Design View**, then click **OK**.

3 Select the 'Employee Information' and the 'Salary History' tables from the 'Show Table' dialog box.

4 Click the **Tables** tabs and click the **Add** button to add the 'Employee Information' table and the 'Salary History' table. Click the **Close** button.

5 If the two tables are not linked on Employee ID, then link the two tables by dragging the Employee ID of the 'Employee Information' table to the Employee ID of the 'Salary History' table.

6 Add fields (Surname, First Name, Address and Phone Number) from the 'Employee Information' table and the field (Position Held) from the 'Salary History' table to the Query grid by double-clicking on the field name in the table boxes or by selecting the field from the 'Field' row drop-down menus.

7 Enter the criterion 'Data Entry Operator' for the query in the 'Criteria' row of the 'Position Held' field.

8 Click the **Run** icon on the toolbar.

9 Save the query by clicking the **Save** button and give the query the name 'Data Entry Operators qry'.

Query 3: List all the employees who occupy a position above rank 4.

1 Repeat steps 1 to 5 from Query 1.

2 Add fields (Employee ID, Surname and First Name) from the 'Employee Information' table and the field (Rank) from the 'Salary History' table to the query grid by double-clicking on the field name in the table boxes or by selecting the field from the 'Field' row drop-down menus.

3   Enter the criterion '>4' for the query in the 'Criteria' row of the 'Employee Rank' field.

4   After selecting all the fields and entering the criteria, click the **Run** icon on the toolbar.

5   Save the query by clicking the **Save** button and give the query the title 'Above Rank 4 qry'.

Query 4: List all employees and their salaries for 2019.

1   Repeat steps 1 to 5 from Query 1.

2   Add fields (Employee ID, Surname and First Name) from the 'Employee Information' table and the field (2019 Yearly Salary) from the 'Salary History' table to the query grid by double-clicking on the field name in the table boxes, or by selecting the field from the 'Field' row drop-down menus.

3   After selecting all the fields and entering the criteria, click the **Run** icon on the toolbar.

4   Save the query by clicking the **Save** button and give the query the title '2019 Salary qry'.

Query 4: What is the total sum of money that has been paid out in increments during the year 2018 by Tech Info Corporation?

You need to find the grand total of all the employees' increments for the year 2018.

To perform the first step, you need to perform a calculated query.

1   Repeat steps 1 and 2 from Query 1.

2   Add the 'Salary History' table. Click the **Close** button.

3   Select the next empty field in the Query grid.

4   Add the field (Increment) from the 'Salary History' table to the Query grid by double-clicking on the field name in the table boxes or by selecting the field from the 'Field' row drop-down menus.

5   Click on the **Totals** icon ($\sum$) on the **Design** tab in the **Show/Hide** group.

6   Click on the drop-down arrow of the 'Totals' row of the 'Increment' field and select the **SUM** function.

7   Run and save your query as 'Total Increments qry'.

Part E: Deleting all the records related to Davanand Singh, Employee ID 26

1   Repeat steps 1 and 2 from Query 1.

2   Select **Delete Query** from the 'Query' drop-down menu on the toolbar.

3   Add all the fields from the 'Employee Information' table to the Query grid by a double-clicking the asterisk (*) above the field names. Do the same step as above for the 'Salary History' table. Add the 'Employee ID' from the 'Employee Information' table to the Query grid.

4   Select **Where** from the drop-down list in the 'Delete' row of the field under the 'Employee ID' field.

5   Enter the criterion '26' for the query in the 'Criteria' row of the 'Employee ID' field.

6   Click the **Run** icon on the toolbar.

7   You do not need to save this query since, once the data is deleted, if the query is run again there will be no records to delete, as the record has already been deleted. You can also open the table, search for the record and click on the **Record selector** tab of the record. To delete it, click on the **Delete Record** button on the toolbar.

Part F: Creating the report

1   Select **Report Wizard** from the 'Reports' group of the 'Create' tab. The 'Report Wizard' dialog box will appear.

2   Select the 'Salary History' table: it contains all the fields you want displayed in the report. Transfer the fields (Employee ID, 2018 Final Yearly Salary, Employee Rank, Position Held, Year of Entry and 2019 Yearly Salary) from the 'Available Fields' window to the 'Selected Fields' window. This can be done by double-clicking on the field name or clicking on the single right arrow button > to move the fields across one at a time. Once all the fields are selected, click **Next** to move to the next screen.

3   This screen allows you the option to group your records. Group the records according to the Employee Rank.

4   Click the **Next** button to move to the next screen. The 'Sort Order' dialog box appears. If the records are to be sorted, you can set the sort order here. Select the field 'Employee ID' to sort, and click the **AZ** sort button to choose from ascending order. Click **Next** to move to the next screen.

5   Select a layout and page orientation for the report and click **Next** to move to the next screen.

6   This screen allows you to give your report a name 'Salary History rpt' and to select whether to open it in **Print Preview** or **Design View**. The default is Print Preview. Click the **Finish** button to create the report.

Part G: Creating a control form to display information

1. Select **Form Wizard** from the 'Forms' group of the 'Create' tab. The Form Wizard dialog box will appear.
2. Select the 'Employee Information' table: it contains all the fields you want displayed in the form. Transfer all the fields from the 'Available Fields' window to the 'Selected Fields' window. This can be done by double-clicking on the field name or clicking on the single right arrow button > to move the fields across one at a time. Once all the fields are selected, click **Next** to move to the next screen.
3. Select the layout you would like from the list and click **Next** to move to the next screen.
4. This screen allows you to give your form a name 'Employee Information frm' and select whether to open it in **Form View** or **Design View**. The default is Form View. Click the **Finish** button to create the form.

Word processing section

Part A: (i) Creating a letterhead with the company's logo

1. Adjust the margin for each letter so that the top margin is 2 inches (3.08 cm), in order to accommodate the letterhead. The left margin is 1.5 inches (2.31 cm) and the bottom and right margins are 1 inch (1.54 cm). To do this:
   a. Select **Page Setup** from the **File** menu.
   b. Click on the **Margins** tab and change the top margin to 2 inches (3.08 cm), left margin to 1.5 inches (3.08 cm) and bottom and right margins to 1 inch (1.54 cm) each.
2. Select **Header and Footer** from the 'View' menu.
3. Move to the Header section and create your letterhead. Make the letterhead attractive, include the following:
   - the name of the company in a larger font
   - the address, phone/fax number, email address and website address
   - the logo, which can be letters, a picture, a graphic or a symbol
   - borders and other formatting features.

Part A: (ii) Creating the primary document and merging to a new document

Before you start, you may need to check your database to ensure that all the fields required for the merge are in one table. If the data is in more than one table, then you may need to create a query to hold all the information you need to use in the letter.

1. Create your main document by typing a suitable letter, using areas designated to hold the data by typing dummy field names enclosed in double angle-brackets, for example, << Name >>. This is necessary so that the field codes will be inserted in the correct positions. Include all necessary information. Save your document.
2. Click the **Mailings** tab. In the 'Start Mail Merge' group, select **Start Mail Merge** followed by **Letters** from the drop-down menu.
3. Check the **Use the current document** option and click the **Next** button.
4. In the 'Select recipients' dialog box, you have to indicate the location of the recipients (data source). Since your data file will be coming from Access or Excel, you need to check the radio button for the option **Use an existing list** and then select **Browse**.
5. Select the data source and click **Open**.
6. Select the table/query that will be used as the data source and click **OK**.
7. The 'Mail Merge Recipient' dialog box appears, showing all records that are listed in the data source.
8. Insert the merge fields. Click on the **Mailings** tab. Select **Insert Merge Field** from the 'Write & Insert' fields group. The next step is to insert the merge fields into the main document. Position your insertion point where the first merge field is to be inserted into the document.
9. Place the fields in their respective location.
10. Once all the fields have been entered, Click the **Mailings** tab. Select **Finish & Merge** from the Finish group. You can merge to a new document by selecting **Edit Individual Documents** from the drop-down list.
11. Save both documents.

Part B: Creating a fillable form

1 Move to the Header section and create your letterhead. Use the letterhead you created in Part (i).
2 Design a form to capture information pertaining to the employee, such as: employee name, address, phone contact, date of birth, email, gender, marital status, emergency contact information (that is, information on who to contact in case of an emergency), National Insurance number and tax number, and Employment start date.
You can use all or some the following features to layout your form:
- tables, columns and/or tabs
- Format your document using any four of the following formatting features.
  - any TWO: bold, underline, italics
  - justification (centre, right, full)
  - changes in line spacing
  - superscript and/or subscript
  - changes in font or font size
  - page numbering.
3 Insert 'Text Control' to allow users to enter text into the form.
- Click where you want to insert the control.
- On the 'Developer' tab in the 'Controls' group, click the **Rich Text Content Control** icon or the **Plain Text Content Control** icon.
- Set the specific properties on the control (see 'Setting' or 'Changing the properties for content control').
4 Insert a combo box or drop-down list to allow users to select from a list of choices.
- On the 'Developer' tab in the 'Control' group, click the **Combo Box Content Control** icon or the **Drop-Down List Content Control** icon.
5 You can also choose to insert a date picker. checkbox or instructional text on the form you created.
- Click where you want to insert **the Date Picker Content Control/Check Box Content' Control**, or click the **Content Control** of the placeholder of the instructional text.
- On the 'Developer' tab in the 'Controls' group, click the **Date Picker Content Control/ Check Box Content Control** or **Edit the instructional text** and format it any way you would like to.

- Set the specific properties on the control (see 'Setting' or 'Changing the properties for content control').

Part C: Producing a financial report on the salary adjustments

- You can be creative in the design of your by using the letterhead you created earlier.
- Write the report, making sure that it is addressed to the Board of Directors of the company.
- Ensure that your report has a heading.
- Indicate who the report is coming from.
- The report must also be dated.

Insert the charts from the Spreadsheet section in the appropriate positions to do this:

1 Open the Word document (that is your report).
2 Open the Excel workbook containing your charts.
3 Click the appropriate worksheet and select the data/chart required.
4 Select **Copy**.
5 Click the Word document on the taskbar to make it active.
6 Position the cursor in the Word document where you would like to begin to insert the data or chart.
7 Click on the **Paste** icon or select **Paste** from the 'Edit' menu.

Website section

Web page design section

Create the website using Wix.com website builder. This is the easiest method and would allow you to produce an attractive website.

1 **Access the Wix.com website to Sign Up:** To sign up as a first time user, you simply add your email address and set up your password to log in to your Wix account. *If you already have an account, simply log in.*
2 **Choose a category from the 'What kind of website do you want to create?'**: You can choose what kind of website you want to create so that Wix.com can direct you to the right template. Select the most appropriate template.
3 Give your website a name.

4   Modify the template by adding and editing content.
    a   The information must sensitise the employees of their rank and incremental percentage (%) increase and inform them about the need to update their records.
    b   Include Tech Info Corporation's logo that you created in the Word processing section.
    c   Display information about the incremental increase based on job position and rank.
5   Attach the fillable form you created in the Word processing section.
6   Save and publish your website.

Problem-solving section

Part A: Develop an algorithm

1   You can either use pseudocode or a flowchart to develop your algorithm.
2   Start your algorithm by using the word **start** or the start symbol for a flowchart.
3   Initialise the variables for: 2019 increment, 2019 salary, years of service and percent and counter for your loop.
4   Prompt the user to enter the data for one employee: Employee name, position held, employee years of service 2018 final salary.
5   Calculate the 2019 increment based on rank.
    a   You can choose to use a nested 'if' statement or a case statement to determine the percentage to apply. For example, if employee years of service are equal to 3, then years of service percentage = <value> else if, and so on.
    b   Calculate 2019 increment: 2019 increment = 2018 salary * Rank percentage.

6   Calculate 2019 salary: 2019 salary = 2018 + 2019 increment.
7   Print employee name, position held, employee years of service, 2018 salary and 2019 salary.
8   Using a 'For loop', repeat the instructions from steps 4 to 7, 10 times. That is repeated for 10 employees.

Part B: Design and create a trace table

1   Select 10 records from your spreadsheet to use as data in your trace table.
2   The first step is to write all the variables found in the algorithm from part A as headings, as well as the heading 'output' to represent what is printed. In other words, create a table with the variables names as headings.
3   Manually execute the algorithm by writing the value for each variable under the heading. As the value changes, record the changes in the next row.

Program implementation section

1   Write a problem statement for the algorithm developed in the Problem-solving section part A. Remember, if you are coding in Pascal or Visual Basic, you will need to use the proper syntax for the particular language.
2   Code your algorithm using the appropriate syntax for the language you are coding.

Mark scheme

Word processing

Key skills The effectiveness with which the candidate(s) has/have confidently used and/or manipulated:	Mark Allocation	Maximum marks per sub-section
The following are compulsory		
Document formatting features		(4)
No more than FOUR features to be tested:		
■ Any TWO: bold, underline, italics		
■ Justification (centre, right, full)		
■ Changes in line spacing		
■ Superscript and/or subscript		
■ Changes in font or font size		
■ Page numbering		
Page layout		(2)
■ *Any* change in margins, page orientation, paper sizes or text orientation	1	
■ Correct use of header OR footer OR footnotes OR endnotes	1	
Select any TWO of the following.		
Inserting/importing files		
■ Graphic/chart in document	2	(3)
■ Graphic/Chart/Table sized appropriately to fit in desired location/margins	1	
Columns		(2)
■ Correct use in entire document or selected text	1	
■ Mostly correct in document or selected text	1	
Tables		(2)
■ Correct number of rows and columns	1	
■ Correct formatting of table (for example, border, shading of cells, colour)	1	
Select any TWO of the following.		
Table of Contents		(5)
■ Auto-generation of Table of Contents	1	
■ In suitable location	1	
■ At least TWO levels of headings	1	
■ Suitable headings chosen (1 mark EACH)	2	

Mail Merge Facility		(5)
Selection or creation of required merge fields in:		
▪ Data source	1	
▪ Primary document (final document consistent with merged document)	1	
Insertion of correct merge field in:		
▪ Appropriate section	1	
▪ Correct merge	2	
Fillable Forms		(6)
Appropriate use of at least THREE of:		
Option boxes, check boxes, text boxes, date picker, drop-down lists, and command buttons		
Layout of form for ease of use:	3	
▪ Layout clear and easy to follow	2	
▪ Some aspects of layout not clear or easy to follow	1	

Web-based design

Key skills The effectiveness with which the candidate(s) has/have confidently used and/or manipulated:	Mark Allocation	Maximum marks per sub-section
Appropriate design features to create a simple web page		(3)
▪ Inclusion of graphics and text	1	
▪ Appropriate use of text	1	
▪ Appropriate use of graphics	1	
Web page for intended audience		(2)
▪ Layout suitable for intended audience	1	
▪ Mostly suitable for intended audience	1	
Consistent information on the page, specific with requirements		(6)
▪ Majority of information consistent with requirements	3	
▪ Somewhat consistent with requirements	2	
▪ A few aspects are consistent with requirements	1	
Hyperlinks		(2)
The presence of a link for any TWO of the following:	2	
▪ Link to another web page		
▪ Link to a location within the web page		
▪ Link to an email address		
▪ Link to user created files		

Spreadsheet

Key skills The effectiveness with which the candidate(s) has/have confidently used and/or manipulated:	Mark Allocation	Maximum marks per sub-section
Pre-defined systems functions – 1 mark each for correct use of any THREE functions		(3)
■ Correct use of any THREE different functions	3	
Arithmetic formulae – 1 mark each for any THREE formulae		(3)
■ Correct use of any THREE different formulae	3	
Replicate formulae into other cells		(2)
■ Use of absolute addressing or range names (two different examples)	2	
Spreadsheet formatting		(4)
■ Any TWO: Decimal place, currency, comma, percentage features	2	
■ Justified, left, right, centre, font or font size	1	
■ Advanced use such as merging cells, wrap text	1	
Sorting data in the spreadsheet		(1)
■ Data sorted in ascending/descending order as required	1	
Extracting data		(2)
■ Simple filter in place	1	
■ Evidence of criteria (for example, B3<20)	1	
PivotTables		(1)
■ Use of PivotTables to summarise a large group of data	1	
Charting operations		(3)
■ Ability to select required range of adjacent/non-adjacent cells for use in a chart	1	
■ Appropriate chart such as bar/column chart, line graph, pie chart	1	
■ Appropriate labelling of chart title, chart axes and/or data labels	1	
Use of two or more sheets		(1)
■ Linking of cells in different sheets	1	

Database management

Key skills The effectiveness with which the candidate(s) has/have confidently used and/or manipulated:	Mark Allocation	Maximum marks per sub-section
Create a database		(5)
■ Appropriate field names	1	
■ Appropriate data types	1	
■ Populating table	1	
■ Create minimum of TWO database tables/files	1	
■ Selecting a suitable primary key	1	
Simultaneous use of two or more tables/files		(2)
■ Joining between pairs of database tables/files	1	
■ Evidence of relationship (1:1 or 1:M)	1	

415

Creating queries		(5)
■ Simple query (1 criteria)	1	
■ Complex query:>1 criteria (1) using more than one table (1)	2	
■ Correct use of and result from calculated field in query	2	
Creating forms		(2)
■ Form with sub-form created	1	
■ Appropriate fields for sub-form	1	
Sort a database table/file/report		(1)
■ Evidence of sort	1	
Generate reports		(6)
■ Selection of appropriate fields for report	1	
■ Statistical and/or summary features (for example, count, sum average)	1	
■ Grouping required fields	1	
■ Correct specific report title	2	
• Generic report title only	1	

Problem-solving and programming

Key skills The effectiveness with which the candidate(s) has/have confidently used and/or manipulated:	Mark Allocation	Maximum marks per sub-section
Flowchart or pseudocode		(6)
■ Start of Algorithm	1	
■ Identifying user-friendly variable names	1	
■ Initialising variables	1	
Processing		
■ Request for data (prompt)	1	
■ Storing data (reading data)	1	
■ Appropriate and logical use of structures	1	
Selection		
Looping		
Trace table		(5)
■ Variables identified in trace table	1	
■ Appropriate test data	1	
■ Changes in values correctly demonstrated	2	
• Some errors in manipulating the trace table	1	
Program execution		(1)
Working program	1	

Program language features/working solution		(3)
▪ Variable initialisation	1	
▪ Control structures:		
• Appropriate use of selection statements (if-then-else, or case statement)	1	
• Looping (while, repeat or for)	1	
Documentation		(1)
Program documentation (such as author, date created, statement of a problem and suitable inline comments)	1	

Project

There have recently been a number of natural disasters that have occurred and the Government has disbursed funds totalling US$2,000,000 (two million US dollars) to the Regional Corporation in various districts to assist in this regard.

The IT department of the Regional Corporation of the St. Ann's District has decided to implement a financial assistance scheme based on the amount of damage to property and the number of household members. You have been assigned the task as an employee of the IT department to create a solution for the Regional Corporation. You are required to utilise the following applications: word processing, web page design, spreadsheet, database management and a programming application to design and implement a program solution.

You are required to:

▪ Create a website where affected families can find information about the financial assistance provided by the Corporation, and be able to download the form where they can apply for assistance.
▪ Calculate the necessary financial assistance required and keep a budget of the expenditure of the Corporation in the financial assistance scheme.
▪ Produce a financial report to send to the Board of the Executive of the corporation and send individual letters to applicants to indicate whether they have been approved for assistance, and how much they qualify for. Create a form for persons to apply for assistance.
▪ Create a database of applicants and approved persons.
▪ Write a program to determine the amount for which affected persons qualify.

Web page design

St. Ann's Regional Corporation has requested that you design a web page to provide the community with relevant information about the services provided to affected individuals and families. You must include:

▪ the Corporation's logo
▪ displayed information on the financial assistance services provided.

Description	Maximum amount for which you can qualify
Household Items destroyed	$20,000.00
Clothing	$1,000.00 per household member
School supplies	$1,000.00 per school-age child
Electrical and plumbing repairs	$15,000.00
Home repairs	$20,000.00

▪ Link to the Assistance Application Form that you created in Word processing.
▪ Information explaining that representatives from the Regional Corporation will be visiting to verify their claims, if they qualify, and the exact amount for which they qualify.
▪ Affected individuals and families need to fill out and submit an application for financial aid. Certain information must be captured in order to determine the amount of financial aid needed.

Word processing

1 Design a fillable financial grant application form allowing for the entry of relevant data from the applicant to be captured. The form must include and capture:

a The Corporation's logo, the Corporation's address, phone/fax, email and website address

b The name of the applicant, number of adults besides the applicant, number of children and number of school-age children in the household

c The address of the applicant

d The estimated value of the items lost based on the categories: household items, clothing, school supplies, electrical and plumbing and house repairs.

2 You are required to produce a financial report for the Executive Board of the Corporation. Your report should contain the following:

a The number of applicants applying for assistance

b The total number of approved applicants

c Include a graph displaying the total amount paid for each category of loss: household items, clothing, school supplies, electrical and plumbing and house repairs.

d The grand total paid out by the Corporation to the applicant and the funds that remains if any.

3 Send out letters to every applicant notifying them of whether they have been approved or not for the financial assistance they seek.

a The report must begin with:
   Maria Brown
   The Chief Financial Officer
   Finance Department
   St. Ann's Regional Corporation

b Every letter should have a footer in italics, in a smaller font than the rest of the document.

c Indicate to the applicant that the visit and valuation to their home was completed on the specified date, and indicate the sum for each category of assistance if the applicant was approved.

d Include a space for the signature.

e Using the Mail Merge Facility, create letters to send out to all applicants.

f Make sure that the letters have been spell-checked and grammar-checked.

g Adjust the margins for each letter so that the top margin is 2 inches, in order to accommodate the letterhead, and the left margin is 1.5 inches and the bottom and right margins are 1 inch each.

Spreadsheet

1 Using the data from the application forms, enter the data into a spreadsheet.

2 After assessment and verification by the Corporation, the actual value was determined by the verifiers of the Corporation and recorded. Some of the applicants were approved, whereas a few were denied, and some were given a percentage of what they requested. Clothing of $1,000.00 per household member was given and $1,000.00 per school age child was also given. Funds for household items, electrical and plumbing and house repairs are awarded to a maximum value of $15,000.00, $15,000.00 and $20,000.00 respectfully. The Corporation has a budget of $2,000,000.00.

3 Enter the applicants request, as well as the Corporation's approved value.

4 Your spreadsheet should be labelled appropriately.

5 Determine what percentage of the amount requested by the applicant was approved.

6 Find the total paid out by the Corporation for each service and the grand total paid out.

7 Determine the balance, if any, from the Corporation's budget.

8 Sort the spreadsheet on the approved/denied applicants.

9 Create a graph to compare the Corporation's budget and expenditure.

Database

Records are kept by the Regional Corporation of all applicants who applied. Create a database that contains TWO tables:

1 One holding the personal information of each applicant. Use the information collected from the application form.

2 The financial assistance table holding the payment per category, as well as the verifier's amount and whether the applicant was approved or denied.

3 Create a query to determine the approved applicants and their qualified amount.

4 The Corporation was informed to reduce the approved applicants' qualified amounts by 10%. Create an update query.

5 Create a form to display the applicant's personal information.

6 Create a report of approved applicants and their new qualified amounts.

Careers in computing

Objectives

At the end of this chapter, you will be able to:

→ list major careers available in the field of ICT
→ describe the roles of various personnel in computer-related professions.

Information and communication technology (ICT) has a significant impact on almost all facets of our daily lives. ICT is now used in our homes, our schools, health centres, banks and many other organisations in society. With changes in technology and the expansion of the ICT industry, new skills are now required in many of our institutions and workplaces, to design and develop new hardware and software systems, and to incorporate new technologies. Every day, the local newspapers in many Caribbean countries contain numerous advertisements aimed at finding people to fill the many jobs available in the computer field.

This chapter looks at the job descriptions of people in the data processing (ICT) departments of large organisations such as banks, insurance companies, government agencies and educational establishments. For smaller companies or organisations, the range of personnel will be much smaller, and the overlap in duties more extensive. We also look at some job descriptions for people who work in the ICT industry but who may not be part of an ICT department within a company, as well as new and emerging IT fields.

Jobs in an ICT department

Look at Figure 17.1, which shows the jobs in an ICT department and how they are linked.

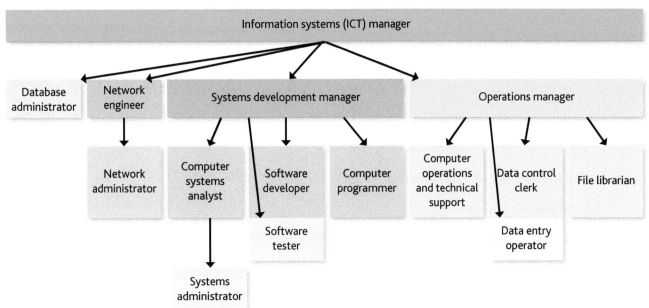

▲ Figure 17.1 Jobs in an ICT department

Information systems (ICT or data processing) manager

The ICT manager is responsible for planning, coordinating, managing and staffing the information systems department of a large organisation. The ICT manager plays an important role in defining the technological direction of the organisation, as such, he or she must clearly understand the organisation's purpose and goals, and its unique data processing needs.

An ICT manager must be aware of the latest developments in the ICT field and be able to chart the long-term vision, plans and policies of the way in which ICT can be used within the organisation.

Much of an ICT manager's time is spent reading reports on the system's performance and on developing strategies to improve it. A fair amount of time is also spent meeting users and members of other departments to discuss problems encountered with the system or new projects for computerisation. He or she is also responsible for preparing budget projections for the department, including the cost of new hardware and software for upgrades, and the training of employees.

An ICT manager is usually someone who has been in the ICT field for a number of years, and who has considerable technical and managerial skills. Many ICT managers started off either as programmers or systems or business analysts and worked their way up. They must possess strong interpersonal skills, since a major part of their job is people-oriented. They should be good leaders and must be capable of motivating their staff to perform at their best, as well as commanding the respect of other company executives.

People planning to seek a career in information systems management should pursue degree courses in Computer Studies, along with extra studies such as business administration and human resource management. Many information systems managers are now also required to obtain a Master of Business Administration (MBA) degree, with a strong emphasis on information technology, along with other business courses.

Summary of duties

- Plan, coordinate, manage and staff the data processing department
- Communicate with, motivate and lead a number of highly-skilled employees
- Be aware of the latest developments in the ICT field
- Read reports on the system's performance and develop strategies to improve it
- Meet users and members of other departments to discuss problems encountered with the system or new projects for computerisation
- Prepare budget projections for the department, including the cost of new hardware and software, and the training of employees.

Database administrator

Many organisations have computer databases that store information on employees, customers and inventory. A database administrator (DBA) is responsible for the administration and management of a company's database. This involves the effective and efficient storage, retrieval, customisation and archiving of data.

A database administrator is usually someone who can think logically and is experienced in the ICT field. She or he must also be able to pay close attention to detail. A DBA usually has a degree in Computer Studies or Information Systems and would have attended many other courses. In large organisations, the qualifications may also include a master's degree in Computer Science with an emphasis on database design, or an MBA degree.

Summary of duties

- Interact with managers and users to ensure that the database is accomplishing what they need
- Meet with users to make modifications to the database whenever there are changes in the company's operation
- Ensure that the database is performing at its optimum at all times to meet the needs of its users
- Develop policies and procedures to ensure the security and integrity of the system
- Select and maintain database management software
- Coordinate database design
- Establish a back-up and recovery procedure in case of failure or loss of data
- Establish a data dictionary that records company-wide data definitions and standards
- Coordinate the data collection and storage needs of users.

▲ Figure 17.2 Database administrator

Systems development manager

A systems development manager is responsible for the development, implementation and maintenance of a company's computerised system. In companies with smaller information systems departments, the systems development manager's job may be part of the information systems manager's job.

Summary of duties of a systems development manager

- Manage teams of information systems personnel (systems analysts, engineers, programmers, technicians, and others) to design, develop, implement, operate and administer computer software
- Oversee the professional development and training of personnel under his or her supervision.

Computer systems analyst

A systems analyst looks at the operations of a manual or computerised system in an organisation or company, and tries to find solutions to specific end-user problems by implementing a new computerised system or upgrading an existing one. He or she is directly in charge of the development of the system from start to finish.

Before embarking on a project, the systems analyst must have a thorough understanding of the existing system. This is done by planning and conducting studies to determine if the existing system needs to be upgraded, or if a new system has to be put in place.

The systems analyst then conducts a feasibility study and prepares a report giving:

- an analysis of the present system
- a proposal for a new or upgraded system (if required), including the hardware, software and personnel costs.

This study is presented to management, who will make the decision whether or not to continue with the project. If they approve, the analyst moves on to the next phase – designing the new system.

To accomplish this task, the analyst has to hold discussions with managers and users of the system to determine their exact needs. The input, output and processing specifications are worked out.

This leads to the implementation phase. The analyst can decide to purchase appropriate software, if it is available, or to direct a programming team to develop new software. If the programs are to be developed in-house, the systems analyst will work with a software engineer or software developer to develop the software. This software is then coded and tested to ensure that it meets the needs of the users and management. If hardware has to be bought, the analyst is the person who makes recommendations and helps in the procurement.

After the programs have been fully tested and debugged, the system is then installed. The analyst has to ensure a smooth transition from the old system to the new system. After the installation is complete, the systems analyst has to evaluate the performance of the system over a period of time to see if it is performing as expected.

The job of a systems analyst can be very demanding and challenging. To be able to perform the job of systems analyst competently, requires skills in the following areas.

- **Analysis/Problem-solving:** A major part of the job depends on the ability of the individual to define problems and then to use a methodical and structured approach to solving them. The systems analyst must also be able to find and evaluate alternative solutions so that the best method is used to solve a particular problem.
- **Communication:** Good systems analysts must be able to express their thoughts clearly in speech and in writing. A significant part of the systems analysis process requires that they meet with users and managers to obtain information and to make presentations.
- **Business:** Many systems analysts work in business organisations. Having a strong business background allows them to develop better systems because they can see the wider uses and implications of their systems for the overall success and profitability of the company.

The educational backgrounds of systems analysts vary, but a degree in Computer Studies or equivalent is generally required.

Summary of duties

- Plan and conduct studies to determine if the existing system needs to be upgraded or if a new system should be put in place
- Hold discussions with managers and users of the system to determine their exact needs
- Gather facts about, and analyse the basic methods and procedures of, current information systems
- Design new systems, integrate existing procedures into new system specifications as required, and assist in the implementation of new designs
- Make recommendations for the procurement of hardware and software, if necessary
- Test and debug the new system
- Create documentation for the system
- Assist in training employees to use the system
- Evaluate the performance of the system over a period of time to see if it is performing as expected.

Software developer or engineer

A software developer or engineer applies the principles of software engineering to the design, development, maintenance, testing and evaluation of the software that runs devices, or even controls networks.

Similar to a systems analysts, they start by establishing a client or company's needs. Then they design, develop, implement and test software systems to address those needs. They also oversee the entire software development process. In addition, they instruct and guide computer programmers who write the code for software.

▲ Figure 17.3 A software developer assists a computer programmer in debugging a new system

Summary of duties

- Analyse users' needs and then design, test and develop software to meet those needs
- Research software upgrades and make recommendations for customers' existing programs and systems, and design new software systems when applicable
- Design the larger system and then break it down into executable and testable pieces, and plan how the pieces will work together
- Show programmers the software code needed for an application, using a variety of diagrams and flowcharts
- Performing maintenance on the software and ensuring that the software remains relevant and up to date
- Manage the quality of work and ensure that software projects remain on track and within budget
- Hire, manage and mentor computer programmers and software testers.

Computer programmer

Computer programmers are individuals whose main job function is programming. Programmers write programs according to specifications determined mainly by computer engineers, software developers or systems analysts. Besides writing new programs, programmers also update, repair, modify and expand existing programs.

Summary of duties

- Discuss program specifications with the systems analyst
- Write programs
- Test programs for correct operation and intended results
- Debug programs
- Document programs, that is, produce system/program flowcharts and program listings (a list of variables used and an explanation of their purpose), details of data structures used (files, arrays, and so on), test data and expected output
- Update, repair, modify and expand existing programs.

Computer programmers can be classified into two categories, relating to the types of programs they develop:

1. Application programmers write software to meet end-user requirements and may produce applications such as payroll programs, science programs, and word processing programs.
2. Systems programmers write systems software, such as programs to monitor and control peripheral devices. Regardless of the category of the programmer, the job specifications are the same.

A programmer's job is usually very demanding. In order to meet deadlines, programmers may regularly have to work long hours and on weekends. The qualifications for this job vary between a diploma from a technical college and a degree from a university.

▲ Figure 17.4 Program code on a monitor

Network engineer

Network engineers are responsible for planning, designing, installing and maintaining the equipment that makes up a network. Their work covers all types and sizes of a network – LAN, MAN, WAN – as well as different types of data, including video and audio, as many computer networks now also handle broadcasting and telephony.

Network engineers work closely with network administrators, particularly once the network has been built, to make sure that it is reliable and can grow to meet the customers' needs. In smaller companies, the network engineer and network administrator jobs may be carried out by the same people. Many larger companies bring in an outside company (called subcontracting) to do this job.

▲ Figure 17.5 A network engineer carefully monitoring a company's network

The network engineer will be heavily involved in planning and designing a network, turning the customers' requirements into something that can be built. They will also be involved with either installing all of the equipment and cabling or managing someone else who is able to do this.

Once the equipment and cabling are installed, the network engineer will be configuring the network equipment and working with the network administrator to connect users to the network. Part of their role is testing the network to make sure that it is performing as required. This job will often continue once the network is up and running, and the results of those tests will help the network engineer to see if it continues to function properly.

When everything is running, the network engineer will continue to be involved in maintaining and, if necessary, repairing the network. This is where they are often alerted to problems by the systems administrators and can then perform their own tests to find where the problem occurs.

A network engineer would normally have a Computer Science or Electronic Engineering degree, as well as professional qualifications, such as those from the CISCO Networking Academy.

Summary of duties

- Plan and design the network
- Oversee the installation of the network's hardware and software
- Test the network to ensure that it is functioning properly
- Monitor the network's performance to ensure that it is working at its optimum
- Troubleshoot and solve problems on the network.

Network administrator

Network administrators are responsible for the creation, administration and security of computer networks. The creation of a network starts with planning and designing, after which the hardware and software are installed. This is followed by a short period of testing to ensure that the network is functioning properly.

Once the installation problems have been solved, the network administrator starts to set up user accounts and arrangements for access, also ensuring that staff is trained to use the hardware and software that forms part of the network.

The network engineer focuses on hardware, whereas the network administrator is more focused on software and the running the network.

Summary of duties

- Plan and design the network
- Oversee the installation of the network's hardware and software
- Test the network to ensure it is functioning properly
- Set up user accounts and arrangements for access
- Ensure that staff are trained to use the hardware and software that form part of the network
- Monitor the network's performance to ensure that it is working at its optimum
- Troubleshoot and solve problems on the network
- Create security policies for the network
- Set up systems to ensure compliance by users of the network.

The network administrator also monitors the network's performance to ensure that it is working at its optimum. In the event of users encountering these, the network administrator is responsible for troubleshooting and solving these. She or he is further responsible for creating security policies for the network and ensuring compliance by its users. This includes regulating access to various computer files and enforcing rules on the changing of passwords.

Network administrators usually have a degree in Computer Studies along with some professional qualification in networking, for example, the Microsoft Certified Systems Engineer (MCSE) certification.

▲ Figure 17.6 Network administrator

Systems administrator

The systems administrator is responsible for running a computer system. Typically, this will be a key server or servers on a network. The systems administrator will work closely with the network administrator, network engineer, help desk staff and data security staff. They are often specialists in the system software that runs on servers, such as Linux.

Summary of duties

- Responsible for the day-to-day running of the servers, including to:
  - maintain and updat the server software
  - manage and run backups and recovery
  - monitor and manage traffic on the server so that it does not get overloaded
  - maintain and repair the hardware.

▲ Figure 17.7 A systems administrator working in a data centre

The systems administrator also helps to ensure that the system is secure. They will have access to logs and other information, which is often the first clue that there is a security issue or a fault developing.

Operations manager

The operations manager is responsible for the overall operations of a computer department on a daily basis. In companies with small information systems departments, the operations manager's job is sometimes performed by the information systems manager.

Summary of duties

- Supervise the use and maintenance of equipment
- Supervise data reception and preparation
- Schedule processing activities
- Allocate duties to members under his or her charge
- Consult with the data processing manager on staff issues (problems, training, and recruitment).

Computer operator

A computer operator is responsible for monitoring and controlling computer hardware systems – especially mainframes – to ensure the efficient use of these devices. He or she is stationed in the computer room, where they monitor and control a computer system by operating the central console (the main terminal in a mainframe or mini-computer system, used by operators to give instructions to the operating system).

A computer operator usually acquires the skills needed for the work by on-the-job training. Additionally, ordinary level examination passes and a diploma from a technical institute may be required.

Summary of duties

- Start up and shut down the system
- Respond to messages from system software and carry out the actions required
- Continuously observe the operations of the equipment, and report any faults to the supervisor
- Perform routine equipment maintenance, such as cleaning drive-heads
- Process jobs according to established procedures
- Load input and output units with materials such as tapes for tape drives and paper for printers
- Keep a log of matters such as machine performance, operating records and data processing supplies; maintain inventories and disk- and tape-library records.

Data control clerk

The data control clerk screens, edits and validates the input and output for a data processing unit. She or he also runs scheduled or requested jobs to provide clients with the necessary data.

Summary of duties

- Regulate workflow in accordance with operating schedules
- Responsible for receipt, safekeeping and retrieval of data, software, hardware, and security items
- Distribute materials on request and follow up on overdue items
- Help with the destruction of information-system materials.

Data-entry operator

A data-entry operator enters data into a system in a form that is suitable for processing. The individual must have a general knowledge of data-entry machines and their operations, and an ability to enter data at a rapid rate, making very few errors.

Summary of duties

- Transcribe data from a variety of source documents into the computer
- Keep records on the data transcribed
- Verify the data entered.

File librarian

A file librarian is responsible for keeping a company's data files and software organised and up to date.

Summary of duties

- Maintain and protect the company's programs and data
- Catalogue and store magnetic tapes and disks
- Supply magnetic tapes and disks to authorised users
- Clean and inspect storage media
- Keep records of the disks and magnetic tapes stored.

Other jobs within the computer industry

Data security analyst/Data security specialist

Security problems have become more prevalent with the spread of networks, since skilled hackers from outside an organisation may find it easy to gain access to a company's network. A data security analyst looks after the protection of a company's computer-based information banks and is responsible for keeping information safe from floods, fire, power outages, fraud, theft, invasion of privacy and viruses. A security analyst has to constantly analyse and assess the potential threats to a computer system.

The job entails working with different types of security software, including tools such as Nmap, which constantly scans the ports into the network from outside, and monitoring tools such as SpyNet. A security analyst has to keep up to date with cryptographic tools and techniques, and with the different types of security hardware and software available. In-depth knowledge of operating systems such as Unix and Windows NT networking, especially in TCP/IP communications and firewall technologies, is also required.

The educational background needed by someone in this field depends on the sensitivity of the data and the complexity of the network. Having a degree in Computer Studies, along with extra certificates in networking such as Microsoft Certified Systems Engineer (MCSE) and CISCO courses, is a distinct advantage.

Summary of duties

- Keep information safe from floods, fire, power outages, fraud, theft, invasion of privacy and viruses
- Analyse and assess the potential threats to a computer system
- Set up procedures to protect vulnerable information
- Develop, document and implement data security policies, standards and guidelines
- Identify and fix security vulnerabilities
- Work with different types of security software
- Ensure there are no security loopholes
- Conduct 'raids' on the system to try to expose security loopholes
- Keep up to date with cryptographic tools and techniques, and with all the different types of security hardware and software
- Have in-depth knowledge of operating systems and networking technology.

Computer consultant

A computer consultant is required to give an independent and objective opinion on how ICT can be used to meet the needs of an organisation. He or she is usually contracted for a short period of time, to provide technical assistance to an organisation in areas such as systems analysis, design and programming, in the formation or upgrading of a data processing department. A computer consultant is required to upgrade his or her skills constantly and keep in touch with the latest technology in the field. He or she is usually someone with much working experience in the field and usually has a first degree in Information Systems and Management, along with a master's degree in Computer Science or Business Administration.

Summary of duties

- Hold discussions with users to identify and clarify their information needs
- Identify and evaluate potential hardware and software
- Assist in the design, development and implementation of a company's computer system
- Assist in the development of programs, applications and documentation
- Develop training programmes for users.

Electronic data processing (EDP) auditor

Electronic data processing (EDP) auditors ensure that all aspects of a company's information systems perform in the manner stated in the system design. EDP auditors provide information systems managers with expert opinions about the reliability of results and operations of computer systems. An individual interested in this job must have a logical and analytical approach to investigation, and the ability to pay close attention to detail. The individual usually has much experience in the computer field and possesses a degree in Computing or Information Systems and Management.

Summary of duties

- Inspect programs, systems, control techniques, operational procedures, documentation, disaster plans, insurance protection and fire protection
- Use sample data to test the accuracy of computer programs and the control procedures that are built into them
- Check and report on the use of computing facilities
- Examine the input and output of programs for accuracy (an auditor will report any discrepancies to upper management)
- Make recommendations for changes to ensure system integrity and accuracy (recommendations are often implemented by a data security analyst).

Web-page designer/Web developer

The World Wide Web (www) is growing at a tremendous rate, and so too are the business activities that are transacted over it. To conduct business over the Web, a company must advertise, which requires the building and maintenance of a website. A website consists of web pages. A web page designer creates web pages containing information such as text and graphics. Website development is not as difficult a task as it once was, as there are now many packages available, such as Microsoft FrontPage, ColdFusion or Macromedia Dreamweaver, which make the task easier.

There are no formal qualifications for designing websites. However, a background in programming will help, since some developers choose to create their sites using HTML or Java languages directly. Any form of experience in graphic art would also be an asset, as many people consider web page design to be more an artistic field than an exercise in programming. Web page designers frequently consult with graphic artists when developing websites. A webmaster may be responsible for all of the above duties, with an added emphasis on maintenance, expansion and improvement of the existing websites.

Summary of duties of a web-page designer/web developer

- Ensure that all the links on the site work and that the site is easy to navigate
- Ensure that the site contains the required information
- Develop a visually stimulating website
- Run the web server software
- Find and install tools to create web content
- Maintain and improve existing web pages.

Computer support specialists

Computer engineer

Computer engineers are found at all levels of the computer industry. They design, develop, test and supervise the manufacture of components (such as new computer chips or circuit boards) and peripheral devices. If the company employing them is a large one, a different set of engineers will take care of the assembly and testing of new designs for overall effectiveness, cost, reliability and safety.

Some computer engineers working for hardware dealers or manufacturers are also responsible for maintaining and repairing computer hardware that is sold to clients.

Summary of duties

- Design, develop, test and supervise the manufacture of components (such as new computer chips or circuit boards) and peripheral devices
- Assemble and test new designs for overall effectiveness, cost, reliability and safety
- Maintain and repair computer hardware sold to clients.

Software engineer

Software engineers are specialists who design or create software. They may or may not write actual programming code, however, they must be competent in programming. They work together with both the business functions and the programmers, explaining the business functions to the programmers and the technology to the non-technical personnel. The usual qualification for a software engineer is a Bachelor of Science degree in Computer Science. In addition, the software engineer must have relevant qualifications or knowledge in the related programming languages, such as Java, C++, C#.Net, and so on. Software engineers must have good communication and teamwork skills, as well as certification in business functions. Masters and Doctorate of Philosophy degrees in Computer Science are required for promotion to the higher levels in an organisation.

Summary of duties

- Develop and implement software services
- Evaluate software and software designs
- Perform design trade-off, depending on budget.

Computer technician

Computer technicians, sometimes called computer repair technicians, are called in when a computer system is not working as it should. They maintain, repair and install hardware and software. Computer technicians may be employed as part of an organisation or they can be outsourced, that is, they may have their own business and be called to perform a service (independent service providers). Qualifications for a computer technician can vary depending on the skill level attained. This can range from a simple computer repair course to courses with various levels of certification, for example, A+ certification, NET+, MCSE (Microsoft Certified Systems Engineer) and MCP (Microsoft Certified Professional) to Computer Technician Degree programmes and higher-level degree programmes.

Summary of duties

- Troubleshoot and diagnose computer problems
- Repair, replace and test computer parts
- Receive and set up hardware
- Communicate and return failed hardware to the vendor
- Maintain and set up servers and networks
- Set up and back up desktop computers and servers.

Software testers

Software testers, also known as software test engineers, are hired by companies to perform quality control tests on the software that they produce. Their remit (brief) is to find any bugs in the program. It is not necessary to have a computer degree to become a software tester, however, you need to be knowledgeable about how computers operate.

Summary of duties

- Set up and run simple to complex tests.
- Document the results of the tests.

Software trainer/IT trainer

Software trainers, also called IT trainers, design, develop and deliver training courses to individuals and organisations on a variety of software applications. A software trainer may require some form of recognised IT qualification. However, it is not a necessity to have formal IT certification to become a software trainer. It may become necessary to have technical qualifications for more complex technical trainer jobs. There are certified technical trainer courses available for those wanting to perfect their skills and become skilled trainers. Software trainers are required to have excellent presentation and communication skills.

> ### Did you know?
>
> There are new or emerging careers being established in IT where the focus is geared towards green technology. 'Green' careers or jobs are those that benefit both the economy and the environment. In IT, examples of such jobs include geographic information systems technicians and geospatial information scientists and technologists.

Summary of duties

- Assess client's needs
- Prepare learning materials and aids
- Set up the learning environment and resources
- Deliver the course
- Evaluate the course.

Multimedia artist and animator

Multimedia artists and animators develop moving pictures with the use of computers, for use in game development, use on the internet, in movies and television. They may work with a web developer/designer or a programmer to develop their design. A multimedia artist or animator can obtain their qualification from a number of courses offered at the level of associate, bachelor's or master's degrees. A multimedia artist or animator requires formal training in art, drawing, illustration or related areas.

▲ Figure 17.8 A computer game designer (a multimedia artist)

Summary of duties

- Create animated images and special effects
- Create storyboards (a series of images, similar to a comic strip, showing the sequence of a movie) for movies and video games
- Create drawing or illustrations by hand or computer to develop a series of images for animation.

Computer sales representative

Sales representatives are important to any organisation since they are the people responsible for bringing in the company's profits. Computer sales representatives must have an understanding of the products they are selling, whether hardware, software or services. This is especially necessary in the case of hardware and software, since the representative may often have to do demonstrations for customers. She or he should stay abreast of the changing needs of clients and the new products that are available to satisfy their needs.

Depending on the company and product being sold, a computer sales representative may work in a display room, or visit the business premises of clients, or both. The qualifications for this job may be ordinary level passes and a good knowledge of computers, or specialised training in computer repairs and computer applications, or a degree in computers. Computer sales representatives also need to have a shrewd business sense, since part of their earnings would usually come from the commission on sales.

▲ Figure 17.9 A sales representative should have good communication skills, a pleasant personality, and patience.

Summary of duties

- Explain the specifications, functions and capabilities of hardware and/or software products to their company's customers
- Help customers to install new equipment
- Attend trade shows and seminars to keep abreast of the latest trends or products in the field
- Demonstrate equipment to clients.

Mobile app developer

The increasing use of smartphones and tablets by people for communication and entertainment, as well as its increasing use for work the Mobile app developer, has become one of the fastest growing information technology careers worldwide. The advancement of mobile technology has caused an explosion in the development of software, specifically designed for these devices to meet the needs of the users.

Summary of duties

- Discuss program specifications with the systems analyst/client
- Write programs
- Test programs for correct operation and intended results
- Debug programs
- Document programs, that is, produce system/program flowcharts and program listings (a list of variables used and an explanation of their purpose), details of data structures used (files, arrays, and so on), test data and expected output
- Update, repair, modify and expand existing programs.

Social media specialist

Social media specialists work on a company's social media marketing. They are responsible for creating material that is published on different social media platforms (for example, Facebook, Twitter and Instagram). This role is important because it manages how the company is perceived by its prospective customers.

The social media specialists will research what people are searching for and discussing on social media, and try and find things that match the functions of the company. They then produce material to upload on various social media platforms to encourage people to look further into what the company offers and perhaps turn them from a Facebook or Instagram friend into a customer.

One of the things social media specialists will be involved with is search engine optimisation (SEO). By using this technique, they are trying to make sure that the company's material appears near the top of search engine lists and in searches on social media platforms. Social media specialist will also be involved in running advertising campaigns and managing the budgets.

Summary of duties

- Plan and set goals for social media campaigns
- Create the company's online image and reputation
- Create content to attract interest in the company
- Identify what a company's SEO needs to focus on.

Other ICT jobs

The computer games industry is rapidly expanding and has created a whole new range of jobs, including games programmer, games artist, games designer and games tester.

Others jobs available in the IT field include technical writer, ICT journalist, lecturer, e-commerce specialist, robotics engineer, 3D animator, and virtual reality specialist.

As the ICT industry expands and computers become more ingrained in our society, ICT skills will continue to change but will be in greater demand.

▲ Figure 17.10 Robotics engineers use both computer-aided design and drafting (CADD) and computer-aided manufacturing (CAM) systems.

Chapter 17: Summary

- The ICT manager is responsible for planning, coordinating, managing and staffing the information systems department of a large organisation.
- A database administrator (DBA) is responsible for the administration and management of a company's database.
- A systems analyst looks at the operations of a manual or computerised system in an organisation or company, and tries to find solutions to specific end-user problems by implementing a new computerised system or upgrading an existing one.
- A software developer or engineer applies the principles of software engineering to the design, development, maintenance, testing and evaluation of the software that runs devices, or even controls networks.
- Programmers write programs according to specifications determined mainly by computer engineers or systems analysts. Besides writing new programs, programmers also update, repair, modify and expand existing programs.
- Network engineers are responsible for planning, designing, installing and maintaining the equipment that makes up a network.
- Network administrators are responsible for the creation, administration and security of computer networks.
- The systems administrator is responsible for running a computer system. Typically, this will be a key server or servers on a network.
- The operations manager is responsible for the overall operations of a computer department on a daily basis. In organisations with smaller information systems departments, this function may be performed by the information systems manager.
- A computer operator is responsible for monitoring and controlling computer hardware systems, especially mainframes, ensuring the efficient use of these devices. This is done through the central console (the main terminal in a mainframe or mini-computer system).
- The data control clerk screens, edits and validates the input and output for a data-processing unit.
- A data-entry operator enters data into a system in a form that is suitable for processing. The individual must have a general knowledge of data entry machines and their operations, and an ability to enter data at a rapid rate, with very few errors.
- A file librarian is responsible for keeping a company's data files and software organised and up to date.
- A data security analyst looks after the protection of a company's computer-based information banks and is responsible for keeping information safe from floods, fire, power outages, fraud, theft, invasion of privacy and viruses.
- A computer consultant provides technical assistance to an organisation in areas such as systems analysis, design and programming, and/or in the formation or upgrading of a data processing department.
- Electronic data processing (EDP) auditors ensure that all aspects of a company's information systems perform in the manner stated in the design.
- A web page designer creates web pages containing information such as text and graphics.
- A webmaster may also create web pages, however, focuses on maintenance, expansion and improvement of the existing websites.
- Computer engineers develop, test and supervise the manufacture of components (such as new computer chips or circuit boards) and peripheral devices.
- Software engineers design or create software.
- Computer technicians, sometimes called computer repair technicians, maintain, repair and install hardware and software.
- Software testers, also known as software test engineers, are hired by companies to perform quality control tests on the software to find any bugs in the program.
- Software trainers, also called IT trainers, design, develop and deliver training courses to individuals and organisations on a variety of software applications.
- Multimedia artists and animators develop moving pictures with the use of computers for use in game development, use on the internet, in movies and television.
- Computer sales representatives market computer products and services.
- Mobile app developers create application software for mobile device, in order to meet the needs of its users.
- Social media specialists work on a company's social media marketing and are responsible for creating material that is published on different social media platforms.

Fill in the blanks

1 A _____ looks at the operations of a manual or computerised system in an organisation or company and tries to find solutions to specific end-user problems.

2 The _____ monitors and controls a computer system by operating the central console.

3 A _____ creates web pages that contain information such as text and graphics.

4 The _____ is responsible for planning, coordinating, managing and staffing of the information systems department of a large organisation.

5 A _____ is responsible for the administration and management of a company's database.

6 A _____ designs, develops, tests and supervises the manufacture of components (such as new computer chips or circuit boards) and peripheral devices.

7 A _____ explains the specifications of the different hardware and software products sold by their company to customers.

8 The _____ screens, edits and validates the input and output for a data processing unit.

9 A _____ enters data into a system in a form that is suitable for processing.

10 A _____ is responsible for keeping a company's data files and software organised and up to date.

11 A _____ writes software to meet end-user requirements.

12 A _____ writes programs to monitor and control peripheral devices.

13 _____ are responsible for the creation, administration and security of computer networks.

14 A _____ looks after the protection of a company's computer-based information banks, and is responsible for keeping information safe from floods, fire, power outages, fraud, theft, invasion of privacy and viruses.

15 A _____ is contracted to provide technical assistance to an organisation in the formation or upgrading of a data processing department.

16 _____ ensure that all aspects of a company's information systems perform in the manner stated in the design.

True or False?

1 The ICT manager plays an important role in the technological direction of the organisation.

2 A database administrator is responsible for the effective and efficient storage, retrieval, customisation and archiving of data.

3 A systems analyst selects and maintains database management software.

4 A programmer plans and conducts studies to determine if the existing system needs to be upgraded or if a new system has to be put in place.

5 Programmers update, repair, modify and expand existing programs.

6 The network administrator oversees the installation of the network's hardware and software.

7 The network administrator is responsible for creating security policies for the network and for ensuring compliance by its users.

8 The operations manager supervises the use and maintenance of equipment.

9 The computer operator can work from home.

10 Performing routine equipment maintenance, such as cleaning drive-heads, is not one of the functions of a computer operator.

11 A computer operator is responsible for transcribing data from a variety of source documents into the computer.

12 A file librarian is responsible for transcribing data from a variety of source documents into the computer.

13 A file librarian keeps records of the disks and magnetic tapes stored.

14 A data security analyst conducts 'raids' on the system to try to expose security loopholes.

15 A computer consultant holds discussions with users to identify and clarify their information needs.

16 Electronic data processing auditors make recommendations for changes to ensure system integrity and accuracy.

17 Experience in graphic art is never needed to become a good web page designer.

18 A webmaster may be responsible for the maintenance, expansion and improvement of existing websites.

19 Computer engineers are not responsible for maintaining and repairing computer hardware sold to clients.

20 Computer sales representatives are only responsible for selling computer products and services.

Multiple-choice questions

1 The ICT manager is responsible for:
  a preparing budget projections for the department.
  b reading reports on the system's performance and developing strategies to improve it.
  c planning, coordinating, managing, and staffing of the data processing department.
  d all of the above.

2 A database administrator:
  a interacts with managers and users to ensure that the database is accomplishing what they need.
  b conducts a feasibility study.
  c helps install new equipment.
  d has in-depth knowledge of operating systems and networking technology.

3 A systems analyst:
  a tests and debugs the new system.
  b develops a visually stimulating website.
  c maintains and protects the company's programs and data.
  d performs routine equipment maintenance, such as cleaning drive-heads.

4 Computer programmers:
  a discuss program specifications with the systems analyst.
  b write programs.
  c test programs for correct operation and intended results.
  d all of the above.

5 Network administrators are responsible for:
  a inspecting programs, systems, operational procedures, documentation, control techniques, disaster plans, insurance protection and fire protection.
  b monitoring the network's performance to ensure it is working at its optimum.
  c identifying and evaluating potential hardware and software.
  d all of the above.

Short-answer questions

1 List THREE duties of a data processing (or ICT) manager.

2 Describe TWO job functions of each of the following:
  a Operations manager
  b Network administrator
  c Database administrator

3 Distinguish between a systems programmer and an application programmer.

4 List FOUR duties of a systems analyst. What skills do you need to become a good systems analyst?

5 Why do companies that have confidential data stored in databases and accessed through a network need to have a data security analyst?

6 What skills must someone possess to become a web page designer?

7 Use the World Wide Web or any method available to you to find the job specifications of an e-commerce specialist.

8 List THREE duties of a computer technician.

Any job you apply for in today's society requires some form of IT or IT-related skill. This project is divided into TWO parts.

Part A: Creating a booth display

You are required to work in groups of four to create a career booth display. As part of a public relations team for your company, you are required to select an IT or IT-related company listed on the right to create a display for a career fair. You are to create brochures, newsletters, fliers, posters, call cards, applications form, PowerPoint presentation, websites and any other artifacts that can promote the IT careers available in your company. You are to give your company a name, give an overview of the company and what it does, specify the qualifications required for each of the IT jobs at the company and any specialised training that is required for the job(s). Some of the jobs listed on the right are new and emerging jobs in the IT field, therefore, research is required.

Part B: Applying for an IT Job

Each person will select and apply for ONE of the jobs. Each student will attend a mock interview for a specific job. All interview protocols will be observed, be guided accordingly. You must present your résumé and application.

Please note that you will be marked on your word processing skills (in your résumé and application letter).

You must know something about the company to which you are applying for the job.

You must also know the duties and responsibilities of the job to which you are applying.

Company	Jobs available at the company
A gaming company	Software engineer Game designer Graphic artist Game tester Animator Mobile game developer
A web development company	Graphic artist Web page designer e-Commerce developer iPad®/Android app developer Web content manager Internet security engineer/specialist
A computer school	IT lecturer/teacher/trainer Online course developer Computer technician Software trainer Technical writer ICT journalist
A computer sales company	IT sales manager Marketing manager Public relations officer (PRO) Computer sales representative IT technician IT consultant
Research company	Data entry operator Data warehouse manager Information systems manager File librarian Data control clerk Computer operator
Large company with IT department	Systems analyst Information technology manager Computer engineer Network administrator Database administrator Technical support staff
Forensics company	Ethical hacker Vulnerability security research engineer Computer forensics analyst Computer consultant Information security crime Investigator/Forensics expert Security analyst

18 Applications and implications of IT

Collecting, storing and sharing information

Regardless of who we are and where we work, we collect, store and share information. Computers have made it easier for us to do this, both individually and within organisations, large and small, public and private. We collect information because it is useful to us in some way. Information can be something as simple as a map from the internet of a place we are going to visit. We store this information in order to be able to retrieve it or update it later – we create a personalised copy of the map on the internet. Similarly, many situations require us to share information: a police department in one district may share information about suspected criminals with a police department in another district. At a personal level, you may want your friends to have a copy of your map, so you share it with them by sending it to them as a link. Look at Figure 18.1.

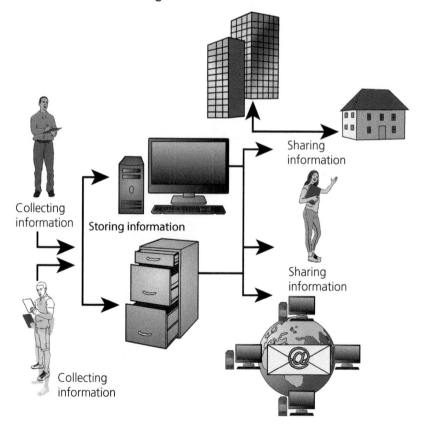

▲ Figure 18.1 Information collection, storage and sharing

436

Why we collect information

Information keeps us informed and is useful to us in a variety of circumstances. For example, a fisherman needs to be kept informed about the weather. This will help with deciding whether to take out the boat, or not. You may want to be kept informed about events in an election campaign in your country, so you listen to the radio and watch television to gather information: this information will help you to decide how to vote. Based on the information we receive, we can make suitable decisions. Information helps us to monitor, control and supervise systems, people and processes. If we do not have the information we need, we cannot take suitable action or make suitable decisions. Information may also have value and is therefore considered to be a commodity that can be sold and purchased.

In summary, information is collected for four main purposes:

1   to monitor, control and supervise systems, people and processes
2   to be used as a commodity
3   to be used in making tactical and strategic decisions
4   to keep us informed.

Let us look at each of these in turn.

Monitoring, controlling and supervising systems, people and processes

We need information in order to monitor, control and supervise systems, people and processes. For example, receiving information such as heart rate, blood pressure, sugar and cholesterol levels, allows a doctor to monitor her patient to determine whether he is improving or getting worse, and control the drugs that are then administered, accordingly. If the patient needs to go to the operating theatre, information received from equipment in the theatre allows supervision of the operating procedure.

Information as a commodity

Information can have commercial value; in business, it constitutes a percentage of the cost of any product. For example, if you had to estimate the cost of building a bridge, the materials and the labour will take up a percentage of the cost. On top of this, the information about how to build the bridge, the technical information provided by the chief engineer, and the information contained in the design plans also constitute a percentage of the cost of building the bridge. Information, once it is considered useful, can, therefore, be bought and sold. A simple example would be a police officer paying for information from an informant.

Information for tactical and strategic decision-making

All kinds of problems, challenges and circumstances arise in organisations or in individuals' lives. These necessitate decisions on how to deal with them. Organisations use the information to come up with strategies that will place them in a more favourable position than before. At any time, a company or individual may need to come up with a plan on how to proceed (a tactical plan) given certain circumstances.

Note

Here is an example of a tactical plan.

If you are about to build a house, you will need information about the design of the house, potential contractors and their past records in building, how to pass the safety inspection, and legal and financial matters. If problems arise during the construction of the house, you must develop a plan of action that is based on the information you receive or collect.

Information to keep us informed

Information is needed to keep us informed about a huge variety of things. In general, the more information we are able to store and have access to – whether it is about weather patterns, ancient civilisations, design and engineering techniques, or famous people's lives – the more informed we are about our world, and the more likely we are to learn from what we know. The fact that we have these details stored somewhere, may be of value to us at some future point in our lives.

Why we store information

It serves little purpose if the information we collect cannot be stored. Imagine that we simply collect information, use it and discard it. If we need that same information again, we will need to collect it again, thereby wasting time and money. Thousands of years ago information was stored on the walls of caves and on stone tablets. Today, we store information manually in files; in computerised databases; on diskettes, CDs, magnetic tape and other storage devices; and in cloud services such as OneDrive or DropBox on the internet. We do this in order to:

- refer to it when a decision has to be made or for confirmation of a fact
- keep a backup in case the original data is lost or corrupted
- analyse the information to come up with some interpretation, explanation or resolution of it
- distribute the information to persons or systems that can make further use of it.

Stored information should be organised. Organising information makes it easy to retrieve when we want it quickly, as we know exactly where it is. Computers – especially when used with specialist electronic databases – are highly efficient at organising information.

Why we share information

Information that we have stored is often valuable to, and needed by, someone else. Over the years, people have found many different ways of sending information to others, such as the traditional mail service, word-of-mouth, the telephone, and so on.

Information can be shared using manual files but there are numerous disadvantages to this. Manual files must first be organised (alphabetically, numerically or chronologically) and this is time-consuming work.

Exercise 1

Short-answer questions

1. Describe TWO reasons for collecting information.
2. Give TWO types of information that would be collected by a:
   a school teacher.   b police officer.
   c musician.   d doctor.
   e meteorologist.

   Why would each of these professionals decide to collect this particular information?
3. Give THREE reasons why we need to store information.
4. Describe TWO methods by which information can be shared.

Fill in the blanks

1. Files that are not frequently used are _____.
2. One of the fastest and cheapest ways of sharing information worldwide is _____ .
3. _____ decisions and plans that are made depend on the information received.
4. Information is a _____ when it something that can be bought or sold.
5. An efficient way of organising information is _____ it.
6. The weather forecaster uses information to _____ the weather.

Manual files can easily be misplaced; it is also difficult to distribute information manually when more than one group of persons require the same information at the same time.

Computer networks can offer a more efficient means of sharing this information. They allow several persons to use the same information from different places at the same time. Information can be easily updated from different sources since it can be stored in a central database and access to it can be made available to all computers on the network.

All modern computer networks contain tools for distributing information. Most obvious and popular of these is email: a fast, efficient and cheap way of sharing information. It allows you to send the same information to a number of people at the same time and you can receive feedback or acknowledgement very soon after delivery of the message, by the same method.

Computers and their related technology have become such an integral part of our daily lives that sometimes we barely notice their effect. They have had a major impact on the way we live, work and play. Even the most technophobe person is affected by computer technology and would live a drastically different life if this technology were removed from their lives. Computers impact both negatively and positively on our daily lives. We will now look at some of these applications and implications of information technology in greater detail.

Forms of information processing

Information processing is the method by which information is acquired, stored, organised, presented, retrieved, shared and used as an activity. In today's society, computers are used to perform many of these tasks. Information required for different purposes is processed differently. Data processing systems, or transaction processing systems as they are sometimes called, are designed to deal with such information. These may include automation, process control, commercial (such as payroll, stock inventory, and so on), industrial and scientific data processing. Data processing systems are also used for information retrieval and management. They are used to carry out tasks that are scheduled and repetitive with accuracy and speed. Automation of some procedures reduces the amount of time humans spend performing necessary but repetitive tasks.

An information processing system should ensure that:

- a transaction is processed quickly, as speed is an important factor in many organisations and can give a company a competitive advantage
- the system is reliable and limits failure
- transactions are processed in the same way every time to maximise efficiency – the processing of a transaction is standardised
- that a transaction, once started, can run its course
- that employees should have access to only parts of the system that requires them to perform their job.

Let us look at an example.

A computer rental company receives requests for computers over the phone, via fax, via the company's website or when a customer walks into the company. A request is entered into the computer by a data-entry clerk using a special form. The transaction processing system validates the data entered and creates a request order file by pulling information from the customer file and the stock file. Look at Figure 18.2.

There are three file organisation methods allowing files to be stored and retrieved. **Sequential access** files are stored one after the other in sequence, in either ascending or descending order based on a primary key; therefore, they can only be retrieved in sequence. **Indexed sequential access** files contain an index, which indicates to the computer where the file is located, much like the index at the back of a book, which tells a user where information is located. Indexed-sequential files have to be reorganised from time to time to free up disk space and discard deleted files. **Direct access (random access)** files are stored in random order on the disk. A relationship between the primary key and the location on the disk is established. With the use of a special algorithm, the computer can calculate the location of a file and go directly to the file.

There are two major ways in which transaction files can be updated: **batch processing** and **interactive processing**, sometimes referred to as **on-line processing**.

The basic principle of batch processing is that transactions are collected over a specific time period and processed all at once. The principle behind interactive processing is that it takes place as a transaction occurs.

The way in which a transaction is processed is based on the type of company and the company's needs. The computer company example shows a transaction that uses interactive processing as a request is handled once it is made. Batch processing is not appropriate for this type of transaction because computer rentals are not handled at the end of a specific time period but rather when a request is made. Direct access files or indexed sequential access files may be most suitable for this company, as files can be stored and retrieved faster using this method without having to read through a number of records to locate a record, as in sequential access.

> **Note**
>
> Further information on file access methods was described in Chapter 6.

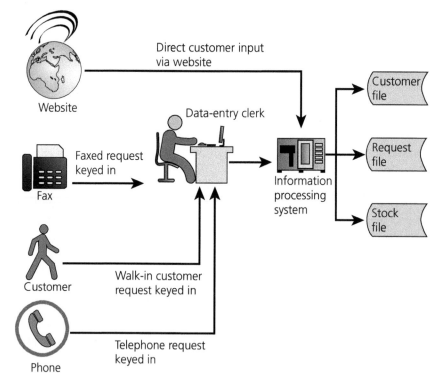

▲ Figure 18.2 Example of a transaction processing system

Batch processing	Interactive/Online processing
Data collected over a time period and processed all at once	Data processed as the transaction occurs
Sequential/Indexed sequential file organisation	Direct file organisation

Computers in banking

Even when we undertake a seemingly simple transaction, such as buying a few items from the grocery or supermarket, we interact with computers. The cashier may pass the barcode of the item over a barcode reader; you may then decide to pay using a debit card, credit card or contactless card. This scenario and many others in business and banking present many opportunities to use computer technology. Some of the hardware and software involved is listed in Table 18.1.

In banking, computers are used to:

- process customer transactions (withdrawals, deposits, loans, bill payments, card and contactless card payments in shops)
- online and phone banking
- process cheques
- transfer funds (electronic fund transfer) from one account to another.

Let us look in detail at some of these computer functions in banking.

Hardware requirement	Software requirement
Mainframe computer with networked terminals	Accounting and financial software
Printers (character, line and page) ■ Character: for printing transactions on passbooks ■ Line: for printing duplicate copies and statements ■ Laser: for printing reports	Word processing software for preparing documents
Contactless card and debit card readers	Security software (for example, intrusion and forensics for detecting and tracing unauthorised access)
Cheque encoders and writers (MICR)	Networking software for WAN
ATM machines	Video conferencing software
Magnetic/Chip and PIN readers	Internet access software
Currency counters	Email software

▲ Table 18.1 Banking hardware and software

Automated Teller Machines (ATM)

This machine, together with an ATM card (also known as a 'debit card'), allows you to perform a number of banking transactions, 24 hours a day. You can access your bank account to deposit and withdraw money, obtain balances, transfer funds and pay bills. The card contains a magnetic stripe, which holds a code to identify the cardholder's bank account so that the holder can perform banking transactions. The cardholder enters a PIN (personal identification number) to gain access to their account. ATMs can be found at a number of locations other than banks, such as supermarkets, airports, bus stations and shopping malls.

Using an ATM

A customer must have an ATM card or debit card issued by a bank. This card has a magnetic stripe at the back, which stores the customer's account number and name.

1 The customer inserts the card; the ATM reads the information from the stripe, and communicates with a central computer to access the customer's account.
2 A message appears on the ATM screen requesting the customer to enter his or her personal identification number (PIN).
3 The customer enters the PIN using the ATM's keypad.

▲ Figure 18.3 Using an ATM

4   If the PIN does not match the one stored in the computer's memory, the customer is given two chances to enter the information again. If the correct PIN is still not entered, the ATM keeps the card and the customer cannot carry out any further transactions.

5   If the PIN is correct, the computer asks the customer to select a transaction from a list displayed on the screen. In the case of a withdrawal or transfer of funds, the computer checks the customer's account to determine if sufficient funds are available for the transaction.

6   If sufficient funds are available, the transaction is processed and the account will be updated immediately to reflect it. The customer is issued a receipt showing the date, time, amount and type of transaction. The transaction will also be reflected on the customer's monthly statement.

Cheque processing

Millions of cheques are written every day all over the world. This method of payment, though decreasing in use, is still an important way of paying for goods and services. Banks are increasingly using card payments and electronic payments, as these are cheaper to process and do not need cheques to be printed, and people and special equipment to process them. The electronic transfer is often significantly quicker too.

- The amount of money to be paid to an individual or organisation is printed at the bottom of the cheque using a magnetic ink recognition (MICR) font. This money is normally deposited into the bank.
- If the cheque is presented at the bank where the cheque originated, payment can be received immediately. If both parties have accounts at the same branch at which the cheque is cashed, the accounts of both parties are updated.
- However, a cheque originating from a different bank is sent to a central clearing house. In the Caribbean, the Central Banks are responsible for this task. An MICR reader reads the information at the bottom of the cheque and the cheque is sorted according to its bank of origin. Payments between the different banks are made according to the value of cheques received. The cheques are then sent to the original banks, where the information is read into the main computer so that customers' accounts can be updated. See Figure 18.4.

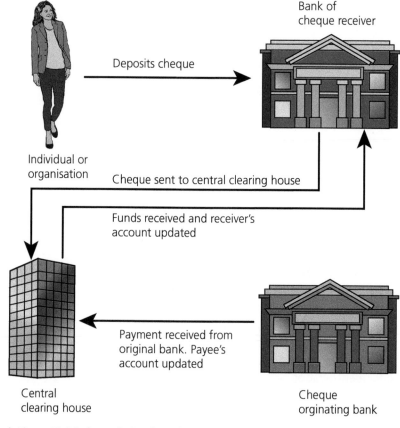

Bank of cheque receiver

Deposits cheque

Individual or organisation

Cheque sent to central clearing house

Funds received and receiver's account updated

Central clearing house

Payment received from original bank. Payee's account updated

Cheque orginating bank

▲ Figure 18.4 A cheque being cleared

Debit and credit cards

Most banks now issue a debit card or credit card that uses 'smart card' technology, a wafer-thin chip embedded in the card, usually called chip and PIN cards. These chips can store and encrypt information, and the information can be updated. The old style of card with magnetic stripes on the back can be altered or forged, but this is far more difficult with a smart card chip. The chip holds information that identifies the user, in combination with a personal identification number (PIN). This technology is also used for cell phone SIM cards, travel cards and passports.

Eventually, smart card technology may combine many functions, storing information about a person's driving history and their birth certificate or paper, for example, and could even be imprinted with the holder's voice, fingerprints and retinal scans, for identification purposes.

Both debit and credit cards work in a similar way. They give you access to funds in your account. Credit cards give you access to funds in your credit account, whereas debit cards access your main bank account. When the card is 'swiped' in the store where you are purchasing goods, the card's magnetic stripe or smart chip is read and the information is transmitted to the bank or credit card company. A check is performed to determine if sufficient funds are available for the purchase before payment can be transferred to the merchant's account. If there is not enough money available, the transaction is denied or declined. The transaction is verified by the cardholder signing a receipt or entering their PIN. Paying for an item in this way uses electronic funds transfer (EFT). The balances in both the merchant's account and your account are updated.

Contactless payment, also called tap-and-go, is becoming increasingly popular. Many credit cards contain not only the smart chip and magnetic stripe but also RFID embedded in the card. Other devices such as smartphones (for example, Apple Pay®, Samsung pay, Google Pay™ payment service), keyfobs, smartwatch and fitness tracker (for example, Fitbit pay) have near-field communication (NFC), which requires the device to be within about 7.5 cm (3 inches) of the payment terminal. This type of payment is usually for small purchases, as it does not require the user's PIN nor signature, thus making the transaction faster. However, as this type of payment does not require authentication, there is a possibility of fraud occurring, hence the limit on the type of purchases that can be made.

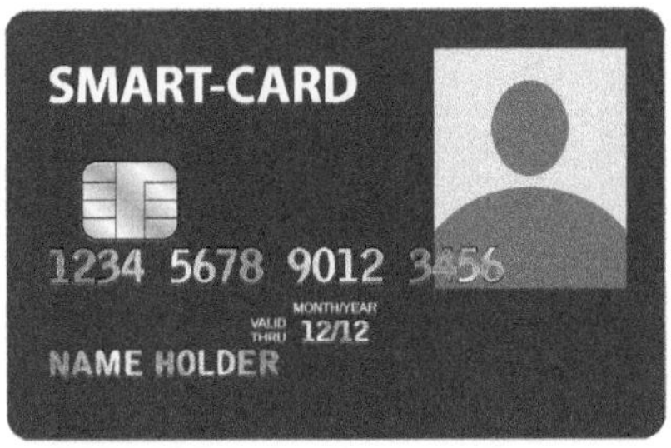

▲ Figure 18.5 A smart card

> **Did you know?**
>
> Magnetic stripe-only credit cards will no longer be accepted after December 31, 2018, in other words, magnetic stripe-only credit cards will become obsolete. The magnetic stripe on credit cards that also contain the smart chip is used to hold backup information. Eventually all bank card 'debit cards' will be smart cards.

Stored-value cards

Stored-value cards are cards that are reloadable or disposable and store a certain amount of money for a specific transaction. They include prepaid phone cards, prepaid debit cards, travelcards for public transport and merchant gift cards. Stored-value cards are one of the most commonly available and fastest growing retail products. When they are passed through an appropriate reading system linked to a computer, they can be updated, for example, to reflect the fact that you have purchased something using the card. Many of the reloadable cards now use smart card technology. Although the cards are more expensive, companies benefit because people pay for, for example, bus or train trips before they use them and they can use self-service terminals to top them up, saving on staff costs.

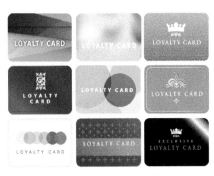

▲ Figure 18.6 Store loyalty cards

Home or internet banking

Home or internet banking gives you the convenience of doing transactions from home or anywhere there is internet access. You can check your accounts, order cheque books, pay bills, transfer funds and even apply for loans via the internet. The convenience associated with doing banking at home is appreciated by many customers. This is also cheaper for the banks, as often, it means they can reduce the number of bank branches.

Computers in business

It is hard to imagine a modern business functioning without computers – they permeate (spread throughout) every aspect of 21st-century business life. Computers are used to create bills (invoices), monitor inventory (stock control), in point-of-sale (POS) systems (store checkouts), in accounting (profit and loss accounts), in marketing (promotion of merchandise), in logistics (organising and planning deliveries), as well as in new developments such as e-commerce and telecommuting.

In this section, we will look at some of the areas just mentioned. Meanwhile, some of the hardware and software commonly used by modern businesses are listed in Table 18.2.

Stock control

Most companies use the computer and its related technology to keep track of their stock inventory. For example, when an item is purchased in a store it is often swiped over a barcode reader. The reader sends a message to the stock computer to update the record of that particular item – decreasing the quantity in stock by one (POS system).

The reverse occurs when items are added to the stock and scanned by a reader in the warehouse. This system allows companies to set up their system to automatically re-order a quantity of an item. When the number of items sold diminishes to a point where the stock is low – at the designated re-order level – the system can warn the stock manager to re-order.

This allows many companies to use a system called 'just in time'. Because the computer records exactly what customers buy, and what is in the company's (and perhaps their supplier's) warehouse, the company can ensure that they get products just in time to sell them. This means that they don't have to hold as many of a product. That saves money because the company doesn't need as big a warehouse to store stock, and can often deliver a product to a customer so fast, that the customer pays for it before the company has to pay the supplier.

Hardware requirement	Software requirement
POS terminals	Inventory software
Barcode readers	Payroll software
Mainframe or mini-computers	Accounting and financial software networked terminals and cash registers
Printers (character, line, laser, thermal for printing statements, reports, bills)	Word processing software
Magnetic card readers (for the reading of credit cards, debit cards)	Web, audio and video conferencing software
Video/Teleconferencing devices	Web browsers
Robots	Email software
	Scheduling and routing software

▲ Table 18.2 Hardware and software used in business

In a supermarket, another benefit is that a lot of fresh food is managed 'just in time' so that there is less wastage. Supermarkets have very sophisticated stock control systems so that they don't run out of things or are left with too much of something that then goes to waste or needs to be discounted. For example, they will make sure they know when big sporting events are scheduled, as this often means that people will buy more drinks and snacks.

E-commerce

E-commerce or **electronic commerce** consists of the buying, selling, marketing and servicing of products and services over computer networks. It also includes the transfer of funds in the buying process. There are two types of e-commerce:

1 B2C or Business to Consumer (where businesses retail their supply goods and services over the internet to individual private consumers)
2 B2B or Business to Business (where businesses supply other businesses with products and services the operations of that business requires).

In 2017, e-commerce sales worldwide were 2.3 trillion US dollars. Many people will know and use Amazon, which is now one of the world's wealthiest companies. They do not use a shop, traditional store, but allow you to choose products from their website, which are delivered by couriers from warehouses that use a lot of automation. This cuts the cost of selling the goods for Amazon, allowing them to sell goods cheaper than in many shops. It does mean that more shops are closing, which often means that towns and cities end up with many empty shops and cannot benefit from the rent and tax income from those shops, which could help to pay for things such as roads and schools.

Traditional companies have also adopted e-commerce as an important part of their business. For example, supermarkets in the USA are offering a home shopping and delivery service; other companies have started up in the last few years purely as online businesses. In some cases, even the products have gone digital, so while CD and DVD sales have fallen, streaming services such as Spotify and Netflix have grown.

This growth in e-commerce has also benefitted small companies, particularly those doing something that may be quite specialised. These companies can now advertise and sell their products worldwide much more easily by setting up an e-commerce website.

The advantages of e-commerce include:

- It allows companies to reach a wider market of potential customers globally, via the company's website. Similarly, potential buyers, whether individuals or companies, have the ability to source products and services from a wider range of potential suppliers, globally.
- The intermediary, usually a physical store, is cut out of the buying process, so, in theory, at least, prices should be cheaper.
- Shopping is easy and convenient this way: it can be done from the comfort of your own home or office. It is usually just a matter of browsing items for sale on the website, putting them in a 'virtual shopping basket' and going to the 'checkout' where you punch in your credit card details to pay for the item(s). The transaction is now complete: just sit back and wait for the items to be delivered.

Did you know?

Supermarkets even link their stock control systems to the weather forecast as a heatwave, for example, increases the demand for things such as cold drinks, ice cream, salads and barbeque foods, and cold weather can increase demand for things such as soup.

- Automated computerised invoices, tied directly to the purchase made via the website, mean fewer processing errors. This automation also helps with stock control and accounting. An e-commerce company can tie-in all its software to work in an integrated way, thus smoothing its operation.
- Data about what a customer is buying or looking at, using a website, allows a company to know what customers are buying, but also to know what things they have looked at on the website. This means that the company can make suggestions or target advertisements at the customer based on what they have bought and looked at, hopefully encouraging them to buy more.
- Companies have the ability to respond to customer demands, queries and comments: this can be done quickly, cheaply and easily, for example, via email.

The disadvantages of e-commerce include:

- The lack of a 'customer facing' operation, that is, a normal physical store, can reduce buyer confidence, especially when the customer would like to see the product they are considering buying, and have it explained to them in person.
- There is a perceived risk of fraud, and/or of data privacy being compromised: there have been documented cases of fake online stores being set up, which are simply a vehicle for stealing people's money. Consumers are therefore often wary of doing business over the internet. Reputable e-commerce sites, though, use web servers that encrypt customer data (such as name, address, credit card number) when it is in transit between the customer's computer and their own.
- Although e-commerce websites have the ability to reach a wide market, the number of business sites on the web increases daily, and the probability of your site being visited may be reduced; traditional advertising may still be necessary, and costly.
- E-commerce has the potential to make small companies seem larger than they actually are, and in some cases, these companies are unable to handle the volume of orders received.
- There are significant cost and training issues associated with setting up e-commerce companies, such as the outlay on hardware and software, and the expense of training and/or recruiting computer-literate staff.
- The change from a shop to e-commerce often means jobs are lost or become less skilled. A good shop assistant can help a customer to make a choice, which takes skill and knowledge of the shop's products. Many e-commerce sites have automated this part of the job and need staff to select products from the shelves in warehouses or to act as delivery drivers.

Telecommuting

Technology has made it possible for individuals to stay at home and work yet communicate with their offices using a combination of computer, modem or broadband connection, telephone, email, teleconferencing, online applications and faxing. Telecommuting, also called teleworking, is just this type of employment: working from home and communicating with colleagues and customers using computer facilities.

> **Note**
>
> Telecommuting can be part-time (1–2 days per week) where employees can avoid the commute to and from the main office every day, and full-time (4–5 days per week) where the employees are part of 'virtual teams' who work from various, often changing, locations to perform the requirements of their business. This can enable companies to use smaller offices and perhaps to be based in less costly parts of the country.

This is becoming easier with the growth of applications that are built to allow people to collaborate. For example, Google Docs™ and Microsoft Word 365 both allow several people to work on a word processor document together. New forms of communication and messaging software such as Slack and Microsoft Teams help teams to manage and run projects. These types of software allow you to quickly set up teams, share messages, have meetings, share documents, and share and track task lists.

There are advantages and disadvantages to telecommuting, both for the employee and the employer.

Advantages of telecommuting to the employee:

■ It reduces the time and cost of commuting to and from the employee's main office.
■ It reduces stress, as there is no need to beat the early morning rush hour to get to work or to be exposed to regular office politics.
■ It allows better organisation of personal time. If the employee is to work eight hours per day, there is a certain amount of flexibility as to when he or she can decide to do so.
■ There is less distraction from co-workers on the job.
■ The full-time teleworker does not need to relocate to take on a new job – he or she can live virtually anywhere.
■ It means that staff, such as sales staff, who need to go and meet customers can be based near to those customers, so saving on the amount of travel they need to do.

Advantages of telecommuting to the employer:

■ In general, there seems to be less absenteeism due to sick days: employees who may have been too sick to travel to work can sometimes do some work at home.
■ Productivity may increase – employees may be more relaxed and concentrated in a home office, without the distractions of colleagues' chatter, and may, therefore, work harder.
■ There is less expense in overheads, such as the need to rent large office space.
■ When recruiting, there is naturally an increased number of potential employees, since potential teleworkers are available all over the country.
■ Work does not necessarily have to stop in extreme weather, for example, when hurricanes cause transport disruptions.

Disadvantages of telecommuting to the employee:

■ There are potential distractions from family, neighbours and household chores; home life and work life may merge, benefiting neither.
■ A teleworker may feel overly isolated from their employer, as there is less interaction with other workers.
■ There is a possibility that either the employee may work excessive hours, since there isn't a clear 'going home' time, or the opposite, that motivation may reduce due to lack of supervision.
■ The employee may be less aware of global changes that take place within the company and therefore may feel less connected and loyal to the organisation.

▲ Figure 18.7 With the help of modern technology you can work from the comfort of your home.

- There may also be a fear that the employee can be overlooked for promotion or other benefits, as they are not a regular face who is seen at the office.
- Many of the services that a company would pay for if the employee was in the office may now partly be paid for by the employee, for example, heat and power.

Disadvantages of telecommuting to the employer:

- Employee supervision is potentially the biggest disadvantage. For example, there may be difficulties contacting the employee, he or she could simply choose when to be available and may become something of a 'law unto themselves'.
- Only certain kinds of work can be done well via telecommuting; many jobs still benefit from face-to-face contact between colleagues and customers in meetings.
- It may be more costly to set up an employee with all the equipment they would require at home, rather than the shared equipment that is used by several employees in a normal office.

Exercise 2

1 Banks issue their customers with debit cards, containing a smart card chip, which can be used to draw money from an ATM machine.
 a Describe how the information stored on the card is secured.
 b How can a bank customer use the card to draw money from the ATM?
 c How does the bank prevent its customers from withdrawing more money than they have in their account?
2 a What is meant by the term 'e-commerce'?
 b Describe TWO advantages and TWO disadvantages of e-commerce.
3 a What is telecommuting?
 b Name THREE pieces of hardware that you would need if you were to telecommute.
 c Give THREE reasons why someone might want to telecommute.
 d Give TWO reasons why their employer might agree to this.
 e Describe TWO disadvantages of telecommuting.

Computers in education

Computers are a major part of the global community because they can perform certain tasks more efficiently and effectively than humans. We now even use computers to assist with teaching and learning, since computers sometimes have the capacity to communicate information more effectively than humans – especially with the arrival of multimedia.

Recently, companies such as Microsoft and universities such as Harvard, have started to produce massively open online courses (MOOCs). These are courses delivered over the internet, combining multimedia, text, images and interactive materials. These allow the organisations to teach courses to much bigger groups than they could on campus or in a school, so making them cheaper to teach. MOOCs such as those on edX and HarvardX use many of the techniques described in the section that follows.

Some of the hardware and software used in education are listed in Table 18.3.

CAA, CBA, CAL and CAI

The four acronyms, CAA, CBA, CAL and CAI, represent computerised innovations that are helping to extend the educational options available to teachers and students alike. Let us look at them in turn.

Hardware requirement	Software requirement
Computers (stand-alone and networked)	Word processing for creating documents
Printers (laser, inkjet and sometimes character printers)	Web and video conferencing software
Devices for the learning disabled such as concept keyboards, voice synthesisers	CAI/CAL software for a variety of subjects and levels (simulations, drills and tutorials)
	Database software for managing student records
	Spreadsheet for grading students' marks
	CML (Computer Managed Learning) software which is used as an administrative tool for creating timetables, and so on

▲ Table 18.3 Hardware and software used in education

Computer-assisted assessment (CAA)/Computer-based assessment (CBA)

CAA is the use of computers and computer technology to assist in the marking of examination scripts, such as multiple-choice papers, where you mark a box in pencil to indicate your preferred answer. An electronic reader that is sensitive to shading can assess which boxes have been marked, and give a score accordingly. As CAA can mark this type of script much faster than a person can, it saves money and allows marks to be produced more quickly. Also, it means the teacher can focus on how to improve a student's learning rather than spending a lot of time marking.

CBA is the use of computers to deliver and mark computerised assessments. This type of assessment can be reused, reordered (randomised) and automatically graded with students getting results of their assessment as soon as the assessment is completed. Automatic feedback can also be a feature of computer-based assessment. This again, can free up teacher's time to really help students with the things they are having difficulty with. Being able to randomise and reuse the material will also save money because the tests don't have to keep being rewritten.

Computer-assisted learning (CAL)/Computer-aided instruction (CAI)

CAL and CAI involve the use of computers and appropriate computer software to allow students to learn at their own pace, and/or to create a more interesting learning environment in which teaching material is presented. As with the other techniques above, these tools can help to save money by making better use of the teacher's time, for example, being able to use the same material to teach many more people than in a classroom, or by not needing a classroom at all.

There are three basic forms of CAL/CAI.

- **Drills and practices:** This is where students are repeatedly given a range of questions from a data bank, to especially practise skills and concepts that require repeated practice in order to become ingrained (such as vocabulary work, or mastering rules in mathematics). These questions will usually have an exact right or wrong answer and are therefore very easy for the computer to mark.
- **Tutorials:** These are self-paced, self-instructional programs that guide student through new material, acting as their tutor. Students can repeat a lesson as often as they like if they do not understand the material. The lessons can also be adjusted depending on the level of the student's competence – the tutorial may even test the student's competence at the outset and adjust the tutorial scheme accordingly.
- **Simulations:** These use sound, text, video and graphics (multimedia) to demonstrate a realistic-looking and sounding outcome, based on a specific scenario. For example, a simulation may show you what happens when you mix two chemicals together in a test tube (for example, bubbles, changes in colour, production of gas, and so on). Simulations, therefore, provide the opportunity for individuals to learn in a safe environment, without material wastage or high-risk situations. Note, though, that simulations can only produce sound and sight, not touch and smell.

▲ Figure 18.8 Hodder Education's Dynamic Learning offers CAL/CAI

CML/CMI

Computer managed learning (CML) and Computer managed instruction (CMI) are other tools used in education. However, unlike CAI and CAL, CML and CMI software is used as an administrative resource rather than an instructional source – to organise students' data and timetables, and in libraries to manage indexes.

Referencing information

Computers are a popular means of sourcing information. Since information is knowledge, and knowledge is part of education, computers are inherently educational, especially when connected to the internet.

For example, online libraries are becoming popular, as individuals can stay at home and access most of the information they need relatively quickly and easily. Through these libraries, you can find information from books, magazines, journals, articles and newspapers around the world from both academic and commercial publishers. They range from subject-specific libraries, such as medical libraries or law libraries, to general libraries that cover a wide range of subject areas. Many require you to register and subscribe to their service by paying either a monthly or an annual fee, for example, Questia (www.questia.com). Once you are a member, you are given a password and a user name that allows you access. Others do not charge a fee. However, for key books and articles, your access may be limited to the abstracts and summaries, for example, Google Books™ service. Traditional encyclopaedias are now also available on CD-ROMs or online. The advantages of these are clear:

- They can be updated regularly; new information can be added.
- The electronic versions need less storage space and cost less than the printed encyclopaedias.

Wikipedia is an online alternative to many traditional encyclopaedias. It is written collaboratively by anyone who wants to contribute. The contributors are required to show that what they are publishing is true, by being able to reference a reliable source for that information. Over time, articles are reviewed and amended by a number of contributors, so should become more accurate over time. Despite this, you need to take care of what you use from Wikipedia and understand when an article might be unreliable.

Distance teaching and learning

Distance learning involves classes being conducted via the internet, an extranet or intranet, satellite broadcasting, interactive television and CD-ROM. It includes:

- Web-based learning (WBL)
- Tele-collaboration, which means using global computer networks in a teaching/learning environment to connect students all over the world. Learners can collaborate or work together on projects through the use of email, synchronised chat, threaded conversations and other forms of electronically mediated conversation such as video conferencing
- Virtual classrooms, which is an online learning environment designed to carry out some of the roles of a physical school/classroom.

Many institutions are now conducting classes through distance learning. In the Caribbean, The University of the West Indies has its own distance learning programme conducted through the University of the West Indies Distance Education Centre (UWIDEC). Similarly, 'virtual schools' and 'virtual classrooms' (VCs) are used as a means of homeschooling. You can apply and enrol in classes for your age group. The teaching environment provides training materials, newsgroups, annotation facilities, teleconferencing and video conferencing, all integrated into a single learning environment.

In some virtual classrooms, students can follow the lecture from their computer. These schools offer support materials and information for both students and parents. There are several projects to launch virtual classrooms in the Caribbean that are in various stages of development, such as VCOIN (Virtual Classroom Over the internet) developed at Florida Atlantic University.

> **Did you know?**
> Google Classroom and Edmodo are popular virtual classrooms used by many Caribbean schools today.

Advantages of IT in education

The advantages of IT in education include the following:

- CAI and CAL use multimedia that make learning more interesting and interactive.
- Students can learn on their own and at their own pace, even in the absence of a teacher.
- Feedback is immediate after answering the question or at the end of a simulation.
- An abundance of educational resources is available on CD-ROMs and on the internet.
- Abstract concepts can often be explained more clearly with the use of multimedia.
- Dangerous experiments, experiments requiring expensive equipment and materials, and experiments that are difficult to perform, can be done through simulations.
- IT can assist the teacher in giving instructions to students where she or he may otherwise lack time, competence or resources. Freeing up the teacher's time by using IT to mark multiple-choice papers or using CAL to assess allows teachers to focus on where students are having difficulty.
- IT can also allow schools, universities and companies to train many more people than they could fit into a building, so saving money.

Disadvantages of IT in education

The disadvantages of IT in education include the following:

- It reduces face-to-face interaction with others.
- Computer-aided instructions are set up in a pre-defined order; hence students can only follow in that order. This may sometimes be restrictive, not allowing for creative flow in lessons.

Computers in engineering and manufacturing

In engineering and manufacturing, computers are used to:

- direct assembly line operations
- perform simulations
- design, draw and manipulate engineering, architectural, product, graphic and textile designs.

Some of the main hardware and software requirements are listed in Table 18.4.

Hardware requirement	Software requirement
Robots	CAD and CADD software for design and draughting
Sensors	
Mainframes, mini- and microcomputers	Specialised software to control machines
Printers and plotters (for printing drawings)	CAE or simulation software
3D printers (for printing solid objects)	Modelling software
Digitised tablets and stylus	
Monitors (high-resolution)	

▲ Table 18.4 Hardware and software used in engineering and manufacturing

Computer-aided design (CAD) and Computer-aided design and drafting (CADD)

This includes hardware and software to draw, manipulate and design for example, engineering and architectural designs, electronic products and even clothing designs. There are many types of CAD software; the one used depends on the specific kind of design that is taking place. Adjustments, updates and duplications of designs can be done easily on the computer. CAD systems can allow designers to create three-dimensional (3D) objects that can be easily manipulated, rotated and viewed from many angles. The CAD package contains basic elements such as points, lines, circles, shapes and solids, from which all CAD drawings are constructed. In addition, the computer keeps track of design dependencies, so that when a value is changed, all other dependent values are automatically changed.

Because CAD systems are often used to build a 3D model of whatever is being built, information about the materials used is often added at this stage. This allows the CAD system to create something that can be fed into the CAE or modelling software to test. For example, Solidworks is a well-known 3D CAD package, which has simulation tools that can work with its models to simulate how heat will flow through a design, how a structure like a building will behave in different conditions, or how best to design plastic parts to cut the number of rejects when you make them.

A high-resolution graphics monitor is needed to show the details of drawings done with a CAD package. The input devices needed for a CAD system include a mouse and a digitising tablet or 3D mouse for drawing. Output devices such as a special printer or a plotter are needed for printing design specifications.

Some advantages of using CAD are:

- Drawing a design takes less time, allowing the designer to do more.
- It is easier to make changes or update the original design.

- The design is an important piece of data for CAM, CAE and modelling systems. The design is often a computer model in 3D rather than a simple set of drawings.
- Duplicates of the design are easy to produce and to distribute to various interested parties or other parts of the company.

Computer-aided manufacturing (CAM)

Computer-aided manufacturing (CAM) systems are used to control manufacturing plant equipment and production equipment, for example, in a car manufacturing plant or a factory that makes microprocessors for computers. CAM translates the design into the actual product, such as moulding a bottle or spoon. Many CAM systems use robots and sensors along with computers in the manufacturing process.
The advantages of CAM include:

- faster production of parts and products to meet customer demand
- the ability to control and maintain the quality of the product better, so that it is produced more consistently
- the robots work faster than humans and need less supervision, reducing the number of people needed, so saving costs, or allowing the same number of people to make more items.

▲ Figure 18.9 Computer-aided manufacture

Computer-aided engineering (CAE) and modelling

Computer-aided engineering (CAE) and modelling systems analyse engineering designs, by simulating varying conditions to determine in advance whether the design is likely to work. For example, an aeroplane manufacturer might be able to simulate the forces of a hurricane wind on a plane wing using a CAE computer, or an engineer might be able to simulate the stresses applied to a bridge.

These allow a company to experiment with their designs at less cost. In the past, a company would either have built actual models or made something stronger than the design calculations suggest. Both of these solutions are expensive. With modelling you can often trial thousands of designs quickly, often allowing new and exciting designs to be built.
For example, look at the design of new skyscrapers and bridges around the world. They are often bigger, longer or look very different from what has been built in the past. This is usually because computer modelling has allowed the designers to experiment at a lot less cost, but still ensure that their design can be made and will be safe.

Computers in artificial intelligence (AI)

Artificial intelligence (AI) has become one of the most innovative ways of using computers today. In artificial intelligence, computers are used to:

- control robots
- control systems and processes (through the use of sensors, temperature, air and water flow, pressure, light and other physical elements can be monitored)

- produce voice recognition and synthesis systems
- produce virtual reality and sensory capability systems
- produce expert systems.

Some of the main hardware and software used in AI are listed in Table 18.5.

Hardware requirement	Software requirement
Robots	Software to control machinery such as robots, process, sensors
Sensors	Virtual reality software
Voice recognition and voice synthesis systems that include microphones and speakers	Voice recognition and voice synthesis software
Virtual Reality (VR) systems that include special clothing, headgear, data gloves, joysticks and handheld wands	Expert systems

▲ Table 18.5 The main hardware and software used in AI

Robotics

Robotics is the use of computer-controlled machines instead of humans to perform repetitive and dangerous tasks. They are normally found in the industry on assembly lines. For example, in the automotive industry, robots are used for welding, paint spraying, assembling and loading. They are used to perform high-precision tasks, which they can perform faster and with fewer errors than humans. They do not get sick, complain or take strike action. Robots are also able to operate in extreme environments where it might be difficult or impossible for human beings to operate. Robots have been developed to perform specialised tasks.
For example:

- Canadarm2 is a robot that plays a critical role in building and maintaining the International Space Station, currently under construction.
- Dante is a robot that enters active volcanoes to gather information about the potential volcanic activity.
- Remotely operated vehicles (ROVs) are able to perform tasks such as searching for and recovering ship and plane wreckage, specialist scientific studies and the burial and repair of underground telecommunications cables.
- Other robots clean up hazardous waste sites or handle wastes that are too dangerous for humans to handle (such as bomb disposals).

▲ Figure 18.10 An astronaut anchored to a foot restraint on the International Space Station's Canadarm2 robot

Control systems

Control systems use sensors to detect physical changes in the environment. Having gathered information, the sensors interface with software on the computer. The computer then tells an output device what to do, depending on the information given to it by the sensor. Sensors can detect changes in temperature, pressure, light, sound, pH, humidity, position and proximity of an object … the list goes on. For example, in some modern cars, light sensors turn headlights on automatically when the light intensity drops below a certain level; as with some street lamps.

Process control

Process control is the automatic monitoring and control of a process by an instrument and computer that has been programmed to respond appropriately by taking corrective measures, if necessary, in industrial settings such as chemical plants, steel mills and oil refineries.

> **Did you know?**
>
> NASA's new rover 'Insight' landed on Mars on November 26, 2018. Its purpose is to deploy scientific instruments and capture seismic and other scientific data about the planet. Because it takes time for data to travel from Mars to Earth, the rover has to be able to move around with very little intervention from Earth, so uses a number of AI technologies to help it navigate its way around and avoid hazards.

The advantages of process control include the following:

- Data from the process can be stored and displayed so that changes over time can be seen.
- Safety can be ensured by sounding an alarm, if necessary, and shutting off the process.
- Product quality can be maintained.
- Employees can have better working conditions.
- Operating costs are lower because the system is efficient.

Natural language processing (NLP)

The goal of natural language processing (NLP) is to create computer systems that recognise, understand and process written and spoken language. Many of us are familiar with voice assistants such as Siri or OK Google™ on smartphones, where instead of typing, we tell our phone what we want to do. These, along with smart home assistants such as Alexa, are starting to demonstrate that accurate recognition of natural speech is a reality. NLP is a growing technology that may become as important a way to work with our devices as keyboards and touchscreens are now.

The following points describe some other applications that use NLP.

- **Voice recognition systems** process the spoken word and match it to a word stored in the computer's memory. If they match, the command or data being entered is accepted by the computer and processed. Simple commands can be used to control machines or even 'type' letters in a word processor. Voice recognition has made life easier for people with movement difficulties, such as the paralysed, who with suitable equipment can now operate a wheelchair, adjust lighting and even open doors using voice commands.
- **Voice synthesis systems** produce sounds resembling human speech. They convert written text to computer-generated speech (Text to Speech). They are used for computer-aided conversation by hearing- and speech-impaired persons, or for converting conversations or text written in one language into another.

Other applications of NLP include:

- Translation of one human language text into another. An online example that does this is the Babel Fish translator, found at https://www.babelfish.com, or Google Translate™ translation service
- Information retrieval and database queries. For example, the Grolier and Encarta encyclopaedias use NLP to find answers to users' questions.
- Grammar checking, for example, as found in Microsoft Word.

Many companies use speech recognition as part of their phone systems. It can be a cheaper way to direct calls to the right team to handle a query. With increasingly sophisticated AI, it is also possible to use a computer to handle some phone queries without the need of a person. While this saves money, it also means fewer jobs. However, by using this intelligently it means that the people working there need to be more skilled, as they will end up dealing with more complicated enquiries, so this should retain better-paid jobs.

Simulation of human sensory capabilities

Simulation of human sensory capabilities technology is available to varying degrees. Computer simulation of human sensory capabilities includes computers with the ability to see, hear, speak, feel (touch) and smell (detect odour). For example, some cars are fitted with sensors that detect how far you are from the edge of the road, or how close you are to another vehicle. The onboard computer can warn you about possible dangers.

Virtual reality (VR) systems include hardware and interactive graphics software that can replicate sensations which imitate the real world. You need special clothing, headgear and equipment to use VR systems, such as data gloves and joysticks. In these systems, you can almost believe that you are in the actual situation because ultra-modern technologies are used to create a more physical sensation.

Virtual reality systems are used in gaming, to train military personnel, in medicine and in the space programme.

▲ Figure 18.11 A data glove

Expert systems

Expert systems provide a vast knowledge database of information in specific fields such as medicine, mathematics, engineering, geology, computer science, business, law, defence and education. Expert systems or knowledge-based systems make decisions based on the results of questions put to the user; the program analyses input data and provides answers at the level of an expert in that particular field. By looking at various possibilities, the computer makes the best-informed decision. These systems perform the function of a human expert consultant in a particular field, providing support for decision-making. They can also 'suggest' alternatives or other issues to be considered.

Expert systems consist of two parts: the knowledge base and the inference engine. The knowledge base contains a large volume of information in a particular field, for example, a medical expert system knowledge base contains a vast array of information about different types of diseases, symptoms and possible treatments. The inference engine complements the knowledge base: it analyses the input data using 'reasoning' methods, along with the knowledge base, to arrive at a conclusion. It also provides the user with an explanation of how it arrived at its conclusion, by showing the concepts that were used.

> **Did you know?**
>
> The fingertips of a data glove contain sensors that detect when the tip of a finger touches the sensor. The glove is tracked using a transmitter and a receiver; the information is fed into the computer, which then renders a perfect replica of the position of the hand. The computer can then send 'tangible force feedback' to the glove — such as pressure, vibration and sound, creating a physical sensation.

Computers in law enforcement

Computers are now an integral part of law enforcement in all its aspects. National databases have been set up to hold information such as criminal records, profiles of wanted persons, data on stolen cars, fingerprints of convicted individuals and drivers who have had their licences suspended or revoked. These databases, such as the National Crime Information Center (NCIC) in the United States and the Police National Computer (PNC) in the United Kingdom, can be accessed by officers in law enforcement departments throughout the country.

In law enforcement, computers are used to:

- maintain criminal databases
- examine forensic evidence
- communicate with other departments and agencies
- provide electronic surveillance
- control traffic systems
- provide assistance to officers through easy access to information
- computerise many of the traditional office tasks.

Crime often has a financial cost, for example, repairing the damage done after a break in, the cost of someone's stay in hospital or the extra costs of insurance after a burglary. If crimes can be prevented, then these costs do not happen. Technology helps the police to prevent crimes, as well as to solve them, and it helps them to do that as efficiently as possible.

Some of the key hardware and software involved in law enforcement is listed in Table 18.6.

Hardware requirement	Software requirement
Robots (bomb detection and disarming)	Database management software
Security cameras and electronic surveillance equipment	Biometric identification software such as DNA, voice analysis, facial image identification and fingerprinting identification software
Biometric identification systems	
Scanners	Composite profiling software
Networked PCs, Mainframes and microcomputers	Video processing software
Printers	Statistical analysis software

▲ Table 18.6 Hardware and software used in law enforcement

Security cameras

Security cameras can act as a visible deterrent to a criminal. Sometimes they are hidden in order to catch criminals in action. They can capture video footage of a crime in progress and the images can be used to identify the criminals. Most cameras today are linked to computer systems that can store and process the raw data. These often link to tools such as facial recognition and number plate recognition, helping the police to quickly track down persons of interest.

Security cameras allow the police to check on a far broader area than traditional patrolling, as one camera operator can monitor several cameras at once. This means that fewer people are needed and officers can be directed to a possible incident as it is happening, hopefully preventing it from getting worse. This has a number of economic benefits:

- Police officers can be used more efficiently.
- Crimes can often be stopped so the amount of damage or injury occurring is reduced.
- Crimes may not happen, because there is a higher risk of being caught.

Biometric identification systems

'Biometrics' refers to the science of identifying an individual through their body characteristics, such as face geometry, hand geometry (for example, fingerprints), iris or retinal scans and veins and voice patterns. All these forms of identification can be input into a computer system set up for security purposes. Two of the most commonly used methods are:

- **Fingerprints** obtained from a crime scene can be matched against a database of known criminals' fingerprints to identify a suspect. The complex patterns of the prints are stored and analysed by computer.

- **Computer-assisted facial image identification systems** use computers to identify a person from an image captured by a surveillance camera or photograph. There are three ways to do facial image identification:
  1 **Morphological comparison of facial features** – 2D and 3D images are obtained and directly superimposed on a second image to see if they match.
  2 **Anthropometrical analysis** – points are plotted on two images and distances and angles are measured to compare the images.
  3 **Face-to-face superimposition** – anthropometrical points of one image are superimposed on the points of the second image to see if they match.

▲ Figure 18.12 Image built up by a facial image identification system

All three methods are used together to identify a person. They can also be used to create an on-screen 'three-dimensional' facial reconstruction, based on the dimensions of the skull of a dead person, to show what an unidentified person might look like if they were alive.

Did you know?

The way we move when we walk and run, called our gait, can be as distinctive as our fingerprints. Research is being carried out to see whether this could be used to identify a person on security cameras.

Profiling (computer composites)

Appropriate software can be used by the police to compose a picture of an alleged criminal based on the description of a witness. The picture can then be compared to those stored in the national databases. This method reduces the cost of police stations having a traditional composite artist, and the sketch can easily be transmitted over the internet to other police departments.

Another form of profiling has been used in the US, called predictive policing. Predictive policing uses computers to analyse data about crimes, to predict where they are most likely to occur, or who might be the most likely suspects. It helps the police to concentrate on those areas or to watch those people in order to make the crimes less likely or to catch the criminals quickly after a crime has taken place. It also helps to reduce crime (and the cost of crime), for example, in Santa Cruz, California there was a 19% drop in burglaries after it was introduced. However, there is also a lot of criticism of predictive policing because many people think the data used to train the system is biased and so, for example, it might reinforce that an area is 'where the criminals live'. Another common criticism is that there is a tendency for predictive policing to introduce racial bias.

Traffic control

Computerised traffic light systems control traffic flow using a specific sequence of lighting managed by the computer. These sequences are adjusted throughout the day, depending on the flow of traffic. The systems use a sensor in the road to detect traffic flow. The data from the sensors is sent via wire-based or fibre-optic cables to the processing computer.

The traffic computers then process this raw data, adjusting traffic lights as necessary to promote the maximum flow of traffic at different times of the day by building a model of how the traffic changes during the day. That model is then used to try out different patterns of lights in the computer to see which helps the traffic to flow best. The settings from this are then used to run the lights. It allows the traffic light system to react to changes in the amount of traffic, so that if there is extra traffic from a concert or sports event, the lights can adapt to the extra traffic flow. Keeping the traffic flowing smoothly helps to cut the cost of driving; it cuts pollution; and it helps to ensure that people arrive at their destination on time.

Electronic surveillance

Wiretaps, email and online communications interception, location information (for example, determining where you are from calls going to your cell phone) and communications analysis (for example, monitoring when and where credit cards are used) are all forms of electronic surveillance. Such surveillance can help the police to track criminals' movements and activities. One of the benefits of this is that it can help to prevent crimes from happening, or that criminals can be caught more quickly after a crime has taken place.

In-car computers

Many police patrol vehicles are now retrofitted with computers, allowing police officers to have an abundance of information at their fingertips. These computers are linked to the police local and national databases and allow police officers to make enquiries about vehicle registration, drivers' licences and wanted criminals. They facilitate quick access to information. In the Caribbean, a number of police vehicles are now retrofitted with these onboard computers.

Computers have a number of other functions in law enforcement, including:

- preparing reports
- equipment inventory
- tracking the history of calls from a particular address
- managing cases
- identifying trends and patterns
- carrying out statistical analysis
- tracking parolees (criminals who have been released before the end of their jail term because of good conduct)
- posting surveillance photographs of wanted criminals and missing persons on the internet
- transmitting, exchanging and obtaining information from other police officers in other departments or other countries via the internet
- developing contacts with other police organisations.

These computers help police officers to be more efficient by providing the information they need to do their job where they are doing it.

Computers in medicine

Computers are now virtually indispensable in the field of medicine. They can be used to:

- monitor patients' vital signs
- maintain databases of patients, diseases and drugs
- aid in detecting and diagnosing diseases
- help patients through online access to health services, information and tools to self-diagnose
- help doctors to collaborate with colleagues and administer treatment over the internet
- perform research.

Some of the key hardware and software requirements in medicine are listed in Table 18.7.

Patients' records

Electronic patients' records help doctors to provide medical care. Records of patients' health history, as well as their personal information, can be easily accessed if this information is computerised. This would be especially helpful where information about one patient exists in several different institutions. An extranet or central database could allow the patient's main doctor to access more complete information about the patient's treatment in several different institutions, thereby helping their analysis.

Hardware requirement	Software requirement
Mainframes, micro and supercomputers (for performing research and diagnoses)	Database management software
Sensors (heart rate, temperature, pressure)	Patient monitoring system software
Printers/Plotters	Expert systems
Magnetic Resonance Imaging (MRI) systems	Imaging software
Computerised Axial Tomography (CAT) scanning (X-ray tubes)	
Monitors (high-resolution)	

▲ Table 18.7 Hardware and software used in medicine

Most doctors' offices in the Caribbean still use manual databases to store information about their patients' diagnosis, symptoms and treatment. Computerised records can reduce the time spent looking for patient records in the case of an emergency. The computer records are also easier to share with other health care professionals, so if a doctor refers someone to a consultant, they can have access to all the notes and results that the doctor had, saving them time as they do not have to repeat things. Modern computer systems are also very good at looking for patterns in data and can help to look for trends in diseases across medical records.

However, potential challenges exist, such as maintaining the privacy of these records, how much access should be granted to health insurers and researchers, and what level of control should be given to patients regarding the content of their records.

Patient monitoring systems

Patient monitoring systems help doctors to monitor and treat patients – either at home or in hospital intensive care – by providing a 24-hour service that can reduce false alarms. These are computerised systems that monitor a person's vital signs, such as blood pressure, temperature and heart rate, using sensors attached to the patient. The system records the information at specific intervals and may sound an alert in the event of a dangerous abnormality in the readings.

These systems are becoming increasingly miniaturised, allowing them to be wearable so the patient can go about their normal day while something is monitored. One example of this is the latest version of the Apple Watch®, which contains a heart rate sensor and software to capture electrocardiogram (ECG) data and so, recognise irregular heartbeats. This could act as an early warning of a heart problem or inform a doctor of the best course of treatment. Another example of miniaturisation is a pill camera that you swallow, which allows the doctor to see the inside of your gut, replacing things such as a colonoscopy, which can be unpleasant and a relatively expensive procedure in comparison.

These new forms of patient monitoring can potentially help to reduce the cost of health care by detecting problems early on, or by better understanding how a patient's condition is changing. Knowing more about a patient's condition allows the doctors to adjust medication or other treatments so they can make efficient use of these.

Computer-aided detection and computer-aided diagnosis

Both of the following systems assist doctors in detecting or diagnosing abnormalities in the tissues of their patients.

- **Magnetic Resonance Imaging (MRI)** uses magnets to create two- and three-dimensional images of tissues such as the brain (Figure 18.13). The images are processed by computers for analysis by doctors. This helps to detect strokes, tumours, infections and even haemorrhages.
- **Computerised Axial Tomography (CAT) scanning:** A CAT scanner is an X-ray tube that takes as many as 30 pictures per second as it rotates around the patient. The computer system reconstructs a three-dimensional view of parts of the patient's body from the pictures taken. This aids in the diagnosis of brain diseases, tumours, and so on.

These imaging technologies are developing all the time and increasingly including real-time imaging, where you can see changes as they happen, so you can see how the patterns of electrical activity in a patient' brain changes as they do something, allowing doctors to understand how the brain works.

All of these help doctors to diagnose problems earlier, which can make curing an illness more likely. This often means that treatments are cheaper and the patient needs less care.

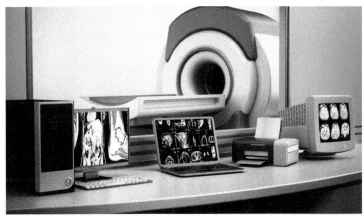

▲ Figure 18.13 A Magnetic Resonance Imaging (MRI) scanner

Expert medical systems and AI in health care

This type of system analyses data and provides answers to questions in the field of medicine. It can imitate the behaviour of a human advisor, or analyse information about a patient or patients to help find patterns. Active knowledge systems use two or more items of patient data to generate case-specific advice.

The Quick Medical Reference (QMR) system (available from the Camdat Corporation) is a medical expert system that performs differential diagnosis in many areas of internal medicine. Other examples of expert systems are Mycin and Dentral. These could be used, for example, for people to enter their symptoms so the system can advise whether they need to see the pharmacist, the doctor or go to casualty.

Recent advances in AI have used deep learning techniques to help look for patterns in data. One example has been a recent system that was better at accurately detecting skin cancer from images than a team of dermatologists. This kind of system could help to free up a doctor's time to deal with more serious cases, by sifting through lots of data and highlighting the ones that need attention. Other systems look at patterns of data in an area to predict the spread of disease, so doctors might try to encourage more people to have immunisations in an area because there is a nearby outbreak of a disease.

The advantages of expert medical systems and AI are:

- It can support a doctor who is doubtful of his or her decision because of a lack of knowledge or experience.
- Experts can use this system to arrive at a faster, more accurate conclusion.
- The systems can often work through data faster than humans can.
- The theory behind the conclusion can be given.

The disadvantages of expert medical systems and AI are:

- Instinct and common sense, which this system does not have, are often a good part of decision-making.
- The system cannot learn from its mistakes, unlike a real doctor, although modern deep learning AI can adjust their algorithms.
- AI systems make decisions in a different way from humans, so it is not always clear how they have reached a decision. This means it is not always clear how good and bad decisions are arrived at.
- It could have disastrous effects if used by unqualified individuals.

Practising medicine via the internet (telemedicine)

Doctors can use the internet in any number of ways. They can send information to patients or other physicians. They can send X-rays, MRIs and CAT scans to other medical institutions or doctors. The process of sending X-rays, CAT scans and MRIs from one location to another to be shared with other radiologists or doctors is called teleradiology. Doctors can even use the internet to collaborate with colleagues on surgery 'live' in different parts of the world. Video and broadband connections may allow a specialist far away from the location of a surgical operation to give advice to the surgeon actually present, and even remotely carry out the surgery, based on what the distant specialist is seeing on the computer screen.

▲ Figure 18.14 A doctor does a patient consultation and looks up her health information from a medical record system.

Some doctors are now diagnosing patients' illnesses and prescribing medication online. However, potential legal problems may occur with this innovation, since it is not always clear who would be responsible if a patient were to worsen as a result of a poor web-based diagnosis. Many medical websites contain disclaimers warning patients that they should seek appropriate medical follow-up by meeting one-on-one with a real doctor.

The explosion of information on the internet has seen an increase in self-diagnosis by individuals. Self-diagnosis is the process of identifying a medical condition oneself by researching in books and on the internet. This can be extremely useful, as it can provide patients with reassurance and practical advice on how to deal with illness, sometimes meaning they don't need a doctor's visit. However, this also has the potential to be extremely disastrous to the individual, as the information on the internet can be misinterpreted or be unreliable, or both.

The internet has also made it possible for persons to have online access to health care services. In the Caribbean, however, many institutions offer various degrees of online health care services. These services may include access to your medical/patient records, requesting repeat prescriptions, booking appointments or contacting your physician. Challenges with online access, are ensuring that the information remains private.

Computers in entertainment

Computers also feature heavily in the production, distribution and consumption of all forms of modern entertainment, from games to movies and music. In recent years, the way we access media has changed enormously and this has had a big influence on entertainment.

In entertainment computers are used to:

- record, synthesise, edit and distribute music
- create and play computer games
- create animations and special effects in movies
- stream music, video and games.

Table 18.8 lists some of the hardware and software requirements in entertainment.

Hardware requirement	Software requirement
Microcomputers, tablets, smartphones with high-speed internet connections	Music recording and editing software
Speakers/Headphones	Animation software
Gaming consoles	Special effects software
Gaming wheel, joystick, game-pad	Actual games
Monitors (low- and high-resolution for graphics and animation)	Game editors used to create new levels in games
VR glasses	VR software
	Streaming software

▲ Table 18.8 Hardware and software used in entertainment

Music and sound

The natural sounds of most musical instruments have been digitised into electronic versions and can now be played from a single instrument such as a keyboard. When the keyboard is connected to your computer, you can record, playback and enhance the music. The use of software to edit sound and music clips, and insert these clips into other pieces of music, is used extensively today. More and more music is being produced electronically in this way.

Another application of computers in music is at the distribution and consumption end. It is now very common to download popular music to smartphones and MP3 players from the internet. This can be done legally for a relatively small transaction fee via various websites, where you can buy tracks or albums like at traditional record shops. The convenience and choice available online – where you only buy the songs you actually want – contrasts with the traditional method of having to visit a real store and buy a complete ready-packaged CD. Increasingly, people are turning to subscription services such as Spotify and Deezer, where, for free with advertisements, or for a monthly fee, the users get access to a vast range of music.

Streaming services have been incredibly popular, yet many artists do not like them, as they pay very small royalties (the money paid to an artist when their song is played) compared to what they can earn from CD sales. Artists are adapting to this by focusing on playing more live music, however, many artists are struggling to make a living from music. The streaming services also mean you borrow the music, like taking a book out of a library, rather than owning the CD. For many people, being able to listen to a wider range of music is much better than not owning it. Recently, vinyl records have started to become popular again because people like owning something, and because it is a bit of a luxury item, which also helps to make some money for the artists.

Movies and animation

Computers play a big part in the making of movie CGIs (computer generated images) as featured in popular films such as *Transformers*, *The Matrix*, *Finding Nemo* and *The Lord of the Rings* trilogy. Animations are now part of many popular movies; the old method of sketching on paper to create an animation is rapidly becoming defunct. Anime, a new method of animation, has also become popular in recent times. The Anime software allows persons without much computer skill to develop an animation from the beginning to the final product. Popular anime software, such as Moho and Adobe® Animate, allows you to develop an animation from an idea to the finished colour video product. This product can be observed and recorded in real time.

Another commonly used technique is a green screen. This allows a real actor to be placed in an animation. The actor performs against a bright green background pretending to react to things going on in the animation. The computer is then used to remove the green screen and insert the animation in its place.

▲ Figure 18.15 A CGI laden still shot from the movie *Transformers*

Many movies also use a technique called 'motion capture with animation'. Here an actor is filmed performing the movements of the character, often wearing a suit with markers attached at important points on their body, such as their hip joint or knees. This image allows the animators to create a 'stick man' character that moves like the actor. They can then use this to build their animated character using the movements of the actor. One example of this is the character Gollum in the *Lord of the Rings* movies, who was created by using motion capture of the actor Andy Serkis.

All of these techniques allow movies to be made, which would be impossible, or too costly to make using real actors or models.

Movie streaming

As in the music industry, streaming has grown enormously in the movie industry with companies like Netflix and Amazon offering streaming services of TV series and movies. Increasingly, these companies are making their own movies and TV series, and are competing with broadcasters and film studios.

Some of the same problems as with music streaming exist, but perhaps the biggest casualty has been cinemas. Cinema audiences have dropped dramatically as streaming services and the cost of high definition TVs have dropped. Cinemas have also had to change, and streaming is helping them to do that. Many cinemas now have the movies they are showing sent to them digitally, rather than having a series of cans of the movie delivered. This has allowed cinemas to do new things, for example, in the UK many leading theatres, particularly in London, now stream performances of a popular play, ballet or opera to cinemas around the country. With the cinema's big screen and sound system, customers get to see the performance in a very realistic way.

Games

The gaming industry is another hugely successful entertainment arm of computing. Games for pure entertainment, or educational games, known as 'edutainment', have become big business. The Nintendo Wii U, 2DS and Nintendo Switch, PlayStation 4 Pro and Slim, Microsoft X-Box One S and 360, and Game Boy (special computer game playing consoles), as well as computer games for the PC and the Mac®, have become very popular, grossing millions of dollars every year.

▲ Figure 18.16 A motion sensor on a game console

Computers in weather forecasting

Weather forecasting is the practice of trying to predict what the weather conditions will be like by measuring and observing the current weather conditions around the world. As we saw earlier, accurate weather forecasting helps supermarkets to plan what they have in their shops. This information is also important for farmers, to plan when to harvest crops; transport planners, to ensure transport runs smoothly in bad weather; emergency services, to respond to really serious weather such as hurricanes and hospitals, where a sudden heatwave may cause an increase in people with heat-related illnesses. All of these applications help organisations to respond efficiently to weather-related events, so keeping down the cost of those events.

In weather forecasting computers are used to:

- gather and store data
- analyse the data
- display the data in an animated, easily digestible way.

See Table 18.9 for the hardware and software required for weather forecasting.

Hardware requirement	Software requirement
Supercomputers	Database software
Satellites	Statistical software
Doppler radar and other advanced radars	Weather model forecasting software
Weather balloons	
Sensors (pressure, humidity, temperature)	
Plotters and printers (to print weather maps and charts)	

▲ Table 18.9 Hardware and software used in weather forecasting

Data obtained from a variety of sensors and instruments are sent to a supercomputer to be logged and analysed. Supercomputers, along with a number of complex instruments, are used to predict weather conditions.

- Doppler radar gives the locations of storms. It also gives an indication of wind speeds, wind direction and precipitation.
- Weather balloons with radiosondes measure pressure, temperature and humidity in the air at many locations around the world. Radiosondes are packages of light-weight measuring instruments that produce electrical signals, which can be sent back to Earth by radio.
- Satellites such as the GOES-8, orbiting high above the Earth, take pictures to help create surface weather maps showing types of clouds and precipitation. These allow meteorologists to observe clouds across the entire globe.

The information gathered using these instruments, together with mathematical models, is used by the supercomputer to make predictions about the weather. The mathematical models are programs that contain complex mathematical equations. These models try to predict weather conditions based on historical data. Even with the fastest computers, though, meteorologists cannot forecast day-to-day weather for more than a week ahead because elements of the weather may change quite radically.

▲ Figure 18.17 Supercomputer showing a predicted weather pattern

Many new models are currently being developed. Some of these will help to forecast tropical features, such as hurricanes. Other models of the future will help to forecast smaller scale features, such as thunderstorms and severe weather outbreaks in fairly specific locations. Forecasters will be able to issue better and more timely warnings and advice. In the United States, the National Weather Service's National Centers for Environmental Predictions (NCEP) runs the computer models. All weather forecasters in the US rely on these models.

Computers in mass media

Mass media is the use of media that is specifically designed to reach large sections of the public or very wide audiences. They include media such as print (newspapers, books, magazines, and so on), television, radio, cinema, recordings (pre-recorded DVDs, videotapes, CDs, and so on), internet and, most recently, cell phones.

Some of the main hardware and software used in mass media are shown in Table 18.10:

Hardware requirement	Software requirements
Computers (stand-alone or networked)	Word processing for creating documents
Printers and plotters (for print media)	Internet browser and web development software
Devices for video production such as digital cameras, video camcorders, voice synthesis systems, microphones, webcams, televisions, DVDs, CDs, Blu-ray disc players and headphones	Video editing software
Devices for audio production such as audio consoles, microphones, headphones, CD players, microwave receivers and relays and satellite dishes (broadcasting equipment)	Audio editing software

▲ Table 18.10 Hardware and software used in mass media

Print media

Computers are used to produce books, newspapers and magazines with the use of word processing software and other desktop applications. Popular novels are written and sold, and posters, banners and billboards are produced using wide-format printers and plotters, allowing their messages to be viewed by thousands, even millions of people.

Cinema and television

We connect with large audiences via cinema and television, through the viewing of advertisements, documentaries and movies. In today's society, cinemas have become popular in many countries and a television exists in almost every home. The production of these media utilises both computer and computer-related devices, as well as audio and video editing software.

Television has increasingly become digital over recent years. This has meant that it is cheaper to produce programs. Anyone with a PC and a video recorder can produce and edit video that could be good enough to broadcast. It has also meant that more channels can be transmitted, providing more choice. Computers are also increasingly built into TVs and satellite boxes, and along with increasing use of streaming, allowing us to choose when we watch something and to interact with a program.

Recordings

Video and audio programmes also reach large audiences via the use of pre-recorded video tapes, DVDs, CDs, Blu-ray discs and others. Many homes have computers, CD, DVD and Blu-ray disc players, which can be used to view or listen to these recordings.

Radio

There are numerous radio stations that broadcast audio programmes. Many of the programmes that are broadcast are live, though some are pre-programmed. When personnel are unable to be present to run a programme, sophisticated software can be used and programmed to run on autopilot. Many, if not all radio stations, have switched their entire operations over to digital production. Many radio stations use digital turntables. The use of vinyl record turntables by radio disk jockeys is highly unlikely. A fairly recent development is the introduction of satellite radio. This radio covers a much wider geographical area than the traditional radio stations. A listener can listen to the same radio programme/radio station wherever they are in the country. Radio stations such as XM Satellite Radio and SIRIUS Satellite Radio are two of the leading satellite radio stations in America.

▲ Figure 18.18 Inside a radio station

The internet and social media

With the advent of the internet and digital technology, there has been a move to convert many of the printed texts to digital format. This has led to the production of the electronic book or ebook. Innovations such as the Kindle and Kindle 2 allow the user to pay for and download books off the internet to read at their convenience. Podcasts are now used quite extensively. This is an audio or video programme that is uploaded to the internet and can be listened to live or downloaded to computers, MP3 and MP4 players, CDs and DVDs, for later viewing or listening. Websites, blog sites and emails are used to broadcast information to a wide geographical area. Twitter is a free online social network that allows a user to send and read other users' updates, also called microblogging. In 2019, Barack Obama and Katy Perry both have about 108.7 million followers.

Cell phones

Smartphones are now one of the most popular devices of the twenty-first century. People have their cell phones virtually 'joined to their hips' or 'permanently attached to their ears'. They are carried by everyone almost everywhere, from restrooms to bedrooms. Some people even take their cells to bed with them. Therefore, to say that this device is one of the most revolutionary mediums to reach large audiences would not be an exaggeration. With the advent of the mobile internet, mobile radio and mobile TV, programmes can now reach the person 'on the go'. This form of media has the characteristics of being personal, always carried and always on. Many companies make use of these characteristics to communicate by broadcasting information to individuals via text messaging, mobile internet, mobile radio and mobile TV.

▲ Figure 18.19 The latest versions of e-readers have the ability to wirelessly download books, blogs, magazines and newspapers.

Social effects of computers

Computers are useful tools and we have seen that, in many ways, they are indispensable to our modern lives. Computers have both good and bad effects on our society; we will examine some of these in this section.

Effects of computers on employment

Perhaps the area where computers have most greatly affected our lives is in the world of work. These effects are both good and bad.

Loss of jobs

Some jobs have become extinct with the advent of automation, and more are under threat. Many jobs previously done by humans are now being done by computers or computer technology. Automated assembly lines (for example, in car production plants) can perform many assembly jobs more efficiently and effectively than humans, allowing cars to be produced more cheaply. As a result, companies have increased productivity, but there have been significant job losses in production lines over the last two or three decades around the world.

In the banking industry, the increasing popularity of internet banking has resulted in less need for bank branches and less need for cash, so bank branches are closing and ATMs are being removed. This means that there are many job losses in the banking sector.

Automation can also sometimes be used to replace humans where the jobs are boring, monotonous or dangerous. Dangerous or potentially hazardous jobs, such as the handling of chemicals, are now often done by robots instead of humans. In other cases, job losses have occurred because jobs previously requiring two or more people to do them are now being done by just one person with a computer. Employees are being made redundant.

Job creation

Although there have been many job losses due to computerisation, there has also been millions of jobs created. Some jobs that have been created as a direct result of computerisation are in areas such as research, design, manufacturing, programming, maintenance, communication, education, consultation, marketing and security. Computerisation has resulted in the creation of high-tech companies and jobs that require highly-skilled workers. There is still a general shortage of workers for these types of high-tech jobs.

Computerisation has also made jobs more accessible to the disabled person.

Computerisation can do some things really well, but jobs such as a therapist or personal shopper, which involve spending time with people and talking to and understanding them, are still best done by people.

Change in job skills

With the introduction of computers into the workplace, many workers now need new skills or the upgrading of old ones. Most countries are making computer training more important in schools as they recognise this. Many jobs now require basic computer knowledge, for example, draughtsmen and architects are now required to produce their drawings and designs on computers using computer-aided design (CAD) packages.

Changes in work patterns

Computers have also been changing the way people do their jobs. People can sit on a bus or in a café and work on their laptops. Teachers can send homework to absent students via email, after normal school hours. A police officer can access and retrieve information from the computer in his or her police car, rather than go back to headquarters. Computers, therefore, allow us to work outside 'normal' working hours, and away from our 'normal' workplaces, that is, telework or telecommute.

There may be consequences for family and social life as a result of this, both good and bad. It is now possible to choose when to work. If you are a teleworker you can juggle your work responsibilities with your family commitments, such as picking up your children from school. But it may not always be possible to have a full weekend off, dedicated to spending time with family and friends.

Effects of computers on society

Computers have affected how we save or access information. It has allowed us to save a lot more information than we could traditionally, and we can also retrieve the information quickly. Computers have also affected the way we conduct warfare. Cyber warfare is now used as a means of attacking one's opponent information systems. Online shopping has the ability to promote the economic growth of a company and encourages ease of shopping, however, it has affected the physical stores, as they have lost customers who have chosen to stay at home to shop online.

Effects of computers on communication

Computers have allowed us to communicate almost instantaneously. We no longer use just telephones and mail, but also texting and email, which are both very cheap and very fast. Texting has developed its own style of writing, a language with shortened words and symbols called 'emoticons'. This texting language, a kind of jargon, aids quick communication but may have consequences in that traditional standards of grammar, spelling and punctuation are being eroded.

Email is also impersonal. By using it, we express ourselves in ways that we may not normally do in a face-to-face meeting.

Effects of computers on the environment

Technology has been blamed for polluting the environment. The use of solvents in the manufacturing of computers, and the disposal of old and used computer parts (commonly called technotrash or electronic waste/e-waste) can harm the environment unless care is taken over this process. Production of computers consumes valuable non-renewable resources and renewable resources that are used faster than they can be renewed. However, computers can have a positive impact on the environment. Telecommuting means that less people travel to and from work, which means less traffic and less air pollution. Computers can also help to reduce the use of paper by the use of paperless communication, e-paper and e-ink. Computers can also be used for helping to monitor pollution in our environment.

The potential for overdependence on computers

The potential for overdependence on computers is a big issue. Computers can be used to manage critical systems in a power plant or an aircraft, to support the operations of large and small companies, transfer millions of dollars around the world and even assist a doctor performing a life-threatening operation. Despite all this, computers still fail – complete trustworthiness is so far elusive (out of reach). For example, viruses can infect software and destroy data, with disastrous effects on individuals and organisations. Without a backup plan, companies, governments and other organisations that are affected by a computer failure for an extended length of time can cease to function properly.

Computers' effect on employee health

Computer work is labour-intensive, requiring hours of repetitive work by the individual using the computer. Employees in this type of environment can suffer from a range of health problems known as computer work-related disorders.

Repetitive strain injury (RSI)

There are two key types of repetitive strain injury (RSI). Tendonitis is where a tendon is inflamed, as a result of some repetitive motion or stress on that tendon. Carpal tunnel syndrome (CTS) is an inflammation of the nerve that connects your forearm to the palm of your hand. Repeated or forceful bending of the wrist can cause CTS or tendonitis of the wrist. Symptoms of tendonitis of the wrist include extreme pain that extends from the forearm to the hand, along with tingling in the fingers. Symptoms of CTS include burning pains when the nerve is compressed, along with numbness and tingling in the thumb and first two fingers.

Excessive keying or mousing, bad posture and lack of rest are three key factors that may result in RSI.

Methods of preventing or reducing RSI

- Take frequent breaks during any long computer session. Roll your shoulders and exercise your hands and arms by shaking them and letting them hang loose.
- Type on the computer keyboard lightly, lifting your fingers up and down rather than moving your wrists.
- Position the mouse at the same height as your keyboard. When you slide the mouse around, move your entire arm and not just your wrist.

Computer Vision Syndrome (CVS)

Computer vision syndrome (CVS) may cause these conditions:

- sore, tired, burning, itching or dry eyes
- blurred or double vision
- headache or sore neck
- long-distance vision becoming blurred after prolonged staring at the monitor
- difficulty shifting focus between the monitor and documents

▲ Figure 18.20 Exercises to help prevent RSI

- 'colour fringes' or 'after images' when you look away from the monitor
- difficulty focusing on the screen image
- increased sensitivity to light.

CVS is not thought to have any serious or long-term consequences, but it is nevertheless disruptive and unpleasant.

Methods of preventing or reducing CVS

- Take a break of 5 to 10 minutes away from the computer every hour.
- Reduce glare and reflections from the computer screen – clean your screen and block out excessive sunlight and reflections from lamps.
- Adjust the contrast and brightness of the computer screen so that there is a high contrast between text on the screen and the screen background.
- Prevent eyestrain – the top of your screen needs to be at, or slightly below, eye level; find a comfortable distance between your eyes and the screen (usually 18 to 28 inches, or 46 to 61 centimetres).
- Gently massage your eyes, cheeks, forehead, neck and upper back from time to time to keep blood flowing and muscles loose.

Lower back pain

Lower back pain can be caused by bad posture or poorly designed or incorrectly assembled furniture or equipment.

Methods of preventing or reducing lower back pain

- Use a firm, adjustable and comfortable chair. Adjust the chair height so that your thighs are horizontal, your feet are flat on the floor, and the backs of your knees are slightly higher than the seat of your chair. The back of the chair should support your lower back.
- Stretch your lower back now and then by standing up and pulling each knee to your chest, holding that position for a few seconds.
- Relax your shoulders. When you are keyboarding, your upper arms and forearm should form a right angle, with your wrist and hand in roughly a straight line.
- Take short breaks (5 to 10 minutes per hour) – get up from your desk and walk around.
- Consider using a standing desk for part of your working time.

Ergonomics

Ergonomics is a science that determines the best working conditions for humans who work with machines. Using these principles, manufacturers can incorporate features for comfort, efficiency and safety into computer furniture and equipment. For example:

- The curvature of a computer mouse may be designed to fit the average shape of the cup of a human hand.
- Desktop lamps can be designed to be flexible, with a bright and focused light that aids reading of printed computer documents.
- Computer keyboards are sometimes designed to arch in the middle. This is said to allow the human hand and arms to adopt a more natural, slightly angled, position when keying. See Figure 18.21.

▲ Figure 18.21 An ergonomic keyboard

Chapter 18: Summary

- Information is collected for four main purposes: to monitor, control and supervise systems, people and processes; to be used as a commodity; to be used in making tactical and strategic decisions; to keep us generally informed.

- We store information to make it easy to retrieve when we want to make a decision that is dependent on it; to manipulate it or analyse it or distribute it, at a time of our convenience; as a backup.

- In banking, we use computers when we withdraw cash from ATMs, use our debit cards and smart cards in stores, write and process cheques using MICR, use home or internet banking, transfer funds by electronic funds transfer (EFT) and use stored-value cards.

- In business, we use computers in areas such as stock control and inventory, to set up or buy from e-commerce websites, and in telecommuting or teleworking. There are advantages and disadvantages to buying from websites. There are advantages and disadvantages to teleworking, both for the employer and the employee.

- In education, we use CAI and CAL tools to assist in teaching and learning, CAA and CBA tools to assist in assessment, and CML/CMI tools to administer resources. Computers are also used to find reference information (for example, online libraries) and in distance learning. Using computers to assist teaching and learning has a major disadvantage in that it reduces face-to-face interaction between individuals.

- We use computers in engineering and manufacturing for designing (CAD), drafting (CADD), manufacturing (CAM) and engineering (CAE).

- Artificial intelligence (AI) has become one of the most innovative ways in which computers are used today, in such fields as robotics, process control, natural language processing (NLP), expert systems (for example, in medicine) and virtual reality simulators.

- Computers are used in law enforcement in areas such as biometric identification systems; police car computers; national criminal intelligence databases; security cameras; profiling (computer facial composites); traffic control and electronic surveillance.

- Computers are also used in medicine in areas such as patients' records, patient monitoring, Magnetic Resonance Imaging (MRI scans), Computerised Axial Tomography (CAT scans), expert medical systems and medicine via the internet.

- In the entertainment industry, computers are used to record, edit and distribute music, to write and play sophisticated games, and to produce special effects in the movies.

- The social effects of computers are both positive and negative, and include: loss of jobs due to automation; the creation of many new jobs associated with computers; changes in job skills (necessitating retraining); changes in work patterns (times and places of work, telecommuting); changes in methods of communication (email shorthand replacing face-to-face meetings); pollution of the environment unless hardware is properly disposed of; the potential for overdependence on computers.

- Information processing is the method by which information is acquired, stored, organised, presented, retrieved, shared and used.

- There are three file organisation methods: sequential access files, indexed sequential access files and direct access files.
  - Sequential access files are stored one after the other in sequence.
  - Indexed sequential access files contain an index that indicates to the computer where the file is located.
  - Direct access or random access files are stored in random order on the disk.

- Transactions files can be updated using batch processing or interactive processing. In batch processing, transactions are collected over a specific time period and processed all at once, whereas in interactive processing, transactions are processed as they occur.

- Mass media is the use of media specifically designed to reach large sections of the public or very wide audiences. They include print, television, radio, cinema, recordings, internet and cell phones.

- Computers can have a negative impact on our health, the most common problems being repetitive strain injuries (RSI), such as tendonitis, where a tendon is inflamed, and carpal tunnel syndrome (CTS), an inflammation of the nerve connecting your forearm to the palm of your hand.

- Computer vision syndrome (CVS) and lower back pain are other problems that can occur when using computers for extended periods of time. These can be tempered by using ergonomic equipment, such as appropriately designed keyboards and mice, modern high-resolution screens, and chairs and desks designed specifically for computer work.

Chapter 18: Questions

True or False?

1 Virtual reality is a form of artificial intelligence.

2 A smart card stores information about your bank account on a magnetic stripe. Your bank card is called a debit card.

3 Educational gaming software is known as edutainment software.

4 An individual cannot use CAI and CAL software at his or her own pace.

5 Simulations allow you to perform dangerous experiments without risk to life or wastage of materials.

Multiple-choice questions

1 Which of the following is not a health problem associated with extended use of the computer?
   a Back pain
   b CVS
   c RSI
   d High blood pressure

2 A factor that does not result in RSI is:
   a sitting too close to the screen.
   b repetitive keystrokes.
   c lack of rest and breaks between computer work.
   d bad posture.

3 Information is collected for the purpose of:
   a making tactical and strategic decisions.
   b monitoring, controlling and supervising systems, people and processes.
   c using it as a commodity.
   d all of the above.

4 In the police service, computers are used to do each of the following except:
   a examine forensic evidence.
   b communicate with other departments and agencies.
   c design menus.
   d provide electronic surveillance.

Short-answer questions

1 What do the following stand for?
   a CAE   b CAL   c CAI   d AI
   e CML   f ATM   g NLP   h CBA

2 a Explain the term 'expert system'.
   b List THREE fields in which expert systems are used.
   c State ONE advantage and ONE disadvantage of using expert systems.

3 Describe TWO applications of CAD and CADD.

4 Name TWO devices that can be used in CAM systems.

5 State FOUR ways in which computers and their related technology are used in medicine.

6 The Head of the English and Mathematics departments of a school is attempting to convince their staff to use CAI and CAL software. Explain the benefits and limitations of introducing such software.

7 Describe TWO applications of AI in our homes.

8 Your friend is ill but feels that waiting at the doctor's office is too time-consuming. She has found a website where the doctor can diagnose illnesses online and prescribe medication. Discuss the benefits and implications (effects) of practising medicine via the internet, with her.

Crossword

Across

4 Allows you to perform banking transactions 24 hours a day (3)

6 An _____ system acts as a human advisor or consultant (6)

7 A feature used in making movies (3)

Down

1 A form of electronic surveillance (two words) (8)

2 Voice _____ systems produce sounds resembling human speech (9)

3 This card contains a memory chip that holds your banking transaction information (5)

5 Detects strokes and tumours (3)

Glossary

absolute cell reference A reference to a cell in a spreadsheet that remains unchanged if the formula that contains the reference is moved or copied to another cell.

access point A device attached to a LAN that contains a radio receiver, encryption and communications software. It translates computer signals into wireless signals, which it broadcasts to network interface cards (NICs) on the network.

active cell The cell that is available for data entry.

algorithm A sequence of instructions which, if followed, produces a solution to the given problem.

anti-virus software A special type of software used to remove or inactivate known viruses from a computer's hard disk, floppy disk or memory stick.

archiving A form of backup. Inactive files are removed from the computer and stored in case they need to be referenced at a later date.

argument Refers to cell references, text or numbers that are used in a formula.

artificial intelligence (AI) The science of attempting to develop machines that mimic human behaviours such as reasoning, learning, hearing, seeing and communicating.

assembly language A programming language written using mnemonic codes (short codes that suggest their meaning and are therefore easier to remember).

assignment symbol The equals sign in a calculation statement.

backup A duplicate copy of a program, disk or data file.

bandwidth A measure of the volume of data that can be transmitted in a given time.

barcode A series of thick and thin bars representing data, and usually encoding an item number.

base The number of single digits denoting different values in a positional numeral system, including zero.

binary number system Consists of two digits, 0 and 1.

biometric systems Refers to the science of identifying an individual through their body characteristics such as face geometry and hand geometry (for example, fingerprints), iris or retinal scans, vein and voice patterns.

bistable device A device that can function in one of only two positions.

bit The smallest unit of storage in a computer. It can be either a 0 or a 1.

Bluetooth A standard developed by a group of electronics manufacturers that allows any sort of electronic equipment (computers, digital video cameras, mobile phones, PDAs, keyboards, and so on) to automatically make their own connections without wires, cables or any direct action from a user.

Boolean expression An expression or statement whose value can either be TRUE or FALSE when evaluated.

Boolean operator Words such as AND, OR and NOT used in expressions of logic.

booting Loading the operating system into memory.

broadband channel A transmission channel capable of transmitting large volumes of data at speeds of over 100,000 cps.

browser A program that enables you to find, retrieve, view and send hypertext and hypermedia documents over the World Wide Web.

buffer A temporary area holding data that is in transit from one device to another, so that neither device is delayed by the other.

bug An error within a program.

byte A combination of eight bits that has the storage power to represent one character.

cache memory Very fast memory that the processor can access much more quickly than main memory or RAM.

calculated field A new field where the result of an expression/formula that is created is displayed.

cell The intersection of a row and a column in a spreadsheet, used to hold a label, value or formula.

cell address See *cell reference*

cell pointer Identifies the active cell.

cell reference The cell's (column, row) position. See *cell address*

central processing unit (CPU) See *processor*

character A letter, number, symbol, punctuation mark or blank space.

character set All the characters that a computer can store and process.

client or server network A network in which any computer can be designated as the server.

clipboard A temporary storage area used to hold information cut or copied from a document.

cloud storage Also referred to as 'The Cloud'; is a service where data is remotely maintained, managed, and operated by a cloud storage service provider. The service allows the users to store data online so that they can access them from any location via the internet.

coaxial cable A type of communications channel used to transmit voice, video and data.

command A word that instructs the computer what must be done to accomplish a specific task.

compiler Converts high-level programs into lower-level programs (machine code) that a computer understands.

computer A programmable electronic device that processes data following a set of instructions to produce information, which it can output or store for future use.

computer-aided design (CAD) The use of hardware and software for the drawing of engineering or architectural designs.

computer-aided engineering (CAE) and modelling The analysis and engineering of designs in advance (by simulating varying conditions) to see if the design is likely to work.

computer-aided manufacturing (CAM) The use of a computer to control manufacturing plants and equipment in a production system.

computer languages Each has its own set of rules and statements. *See also* syntax.

computer program A series of coded instructions for the computer to obey in order to solve a problem.

computer system The complete computer, which includes all the hardware and software required for the computer to work.

computer vision syndrome (CVS) Eye and vision problems that occur due to prolonged use of the computer, characterised by eyestrain, headaches, blurred vision and eye irritation.

condition An expression that when evaluated either gives a TRUE or a FALSE.

configuration How computers on a network are connected together.

constant A value that never changes throughout the course of a running program.

construct A group of instructions that work together with commands to accomplish a specific task.

continuous data Data that can be measured and recorded at many different points.

control system A device or devices that controls and manages the behaviour of other devices through the use of sensors.

copy This function places a copy of an item selected onto the clipboard; the original item remains exactly where it is. See also *paste*

cryptocurrency A digital currency in which encryption techniques are used to regulate the generation of units of currency, and verify the transfer of funds; it operates independently of traditional banks.

cut Remove selected material from a document and copy it to the clipboard. See *paste*

data All the raw facts and figures that a computer processes by following a set of instructions; called a program.

database An organised collection of structured data about a particular subject (person, place or thing).

database file See *data source*

database management The process by which information is organised and stored on a computer in such a way that there is efficient retrieval, updating and manipulation of the data.

database package A set of software that enables users to organise and store data so that specific items of information can be easily and quickly retrieved.

data capture The first stage of getting data into the computer using various input devices.

data capture forms On-screen forms designed to clearly submit data by data-entry personnel into the computer.

data communication The transmission of data from one location to another for direct use or for further processing.

data crunching The analysis of large amounts of data so that it becomes useful in making decisions.

data file Same as *data source*.

data integrity Ensuring the accuracy and completeness of data when it enters a system and throughout its subsequent processing.

data item An individual piece of information stored in a field.

data security The physical, hardware and software methods used to protect data.

data source A file that contains the information or records that are required to be merged into a main document. See *data file*

debugging The process of finding and correcting errors in a computer program.

dedicated server A server dedicated to a single function on a network.

default settings A preset number of features.

delete query Deletes a group of records from one or more tables.

desk-checking Involves executing the program manually by using input values for variables and recording what takes place after each instruction is executed. See *dry-running*

desktop The main screen in Windows where you can put files, folders and/or icons that act as shortcuts to various programs.

digitising tablet An input board that allows you to enter drawings and sketches into the computer by detecting the position of a pointing device on its surface.

direct access Means that you can go directly to a specific piece of data without having to access any other data either before or after the data you want.

directory A collection of files or other (named) subdirectories, as part of a tree structure.

discrete data Data that can be counted.

domain name system (DNS) A distributed database system for translating a host computer name (such as 'a.b.com') to an IP address (such as '192.54.122.5') or vice versa.

download Retrieve a file stored on another computer on the internet.

dry-running See *desk-checking*.

dummy value An input value that causes a loop to stop.

dynaset The resulting collection of records from a specific query.

e-commerce (electronic commerce) The buying, selling, marketing and servicing of products and services over computer networks.

electrically erasable PROM (EEPROM) A special type of ROM chip that can be erased and reprogrammed repeatedly by a user. It can be erased by exposing it to an electrical charge, which erases the entire chip.

electronic data processing (EDP) auditor The person responsible for ensuring that all aspects of a company's information systems perform in the manner stated in the system design.

electronic eavesdropping The tapping of a data transmission line to access data being transmitted.

electronic funds transfer (EFT) The movement of funds from one account to another electronically.

email The sending and receiving of electronic messages (text, sound, video and graphics) using electronic devices.

email address A unique address used to identify persons sending and receiving email.

encryption Encoding (scrambling) data during storage or transmission so that it cannot be understood by someone who does not have the encryption key.

encryption key Software to convert encrypted data back to its original form.

endnote Text at the end of the document or section that cites the source or additional information pertaining to text within the document.

erasable programmable ROM (EPROM) A type of ROM that can be erased and reprogrammed using special equipment.

ergonomics Determining the best working conditions for people who work with machines.

expert system A program that analyses input data and provides answers at the level of an expert in a particular field.

exponentiation The power to which the base of a number is raised.

extranet Limited access to an organisation's intranet by people outside the organisation.

fibre optic A communications channel consisting of hundreds of thousands of thin hair-like strands of glass that transmit pulsating beams of light.

field An area in a record reserved for a particular data item.

field definition The attributes that describe a field and determine how a field is stored, works and is displayed.

field size The maximum storage size allocated for a field.

file defragmentation Finding fragmented files and organising them back in a contiguous manner.

file librarian The person responsible for keeping all the data files and software organised and up to date in an enterprise.

file transfer protocol (FTP) A set of rules for transmitting stored files over the internet, either by downloading or uploading.

find function Search action that allows you to locate words, phrases or pieces of text within a document.

finite loop A loop where the instructions are repeated a specified number of times.

firewall A program or hardware device, or a combination of both, that filters the information coming through the internet connection into a computer system or network, to prevent unauthorised users from gaining access.

folder A directory.

font type A particular typeface (shape of the character); a collection of characters (letters, numbers, symbols, punctuation marks and spaces) with a consistent appearance.

font size Refers to the height of a character measured in a unit called points (1 point is 1/72 of an inch).

font style Refers to whether the font is standard, bold or italic.

foreign key A field in one table that uniquely identifies a record in another table, in other words, this field references the primary key in another table. See *HyperText Markup Language*

formula Used to perform operations on numbers. It must start with an equals (=) sign, which is followed by numbers, different operators or cell references that are part of the calculation.

full-duplex line A transmission line that can simultaneously send and receive data.

function A predefined method of performing a specific task.

gateway An interface that enables communication between two different networks.

global variables Variables declared outside a module so they can be accessed by other modules.

graphics/video card or **adaptor** An electronic link between the computer's processor and the monitor; a circuit board that connects the processor to the monitor.

gutter margin A margin setting that allows additional space for binding.

hacker A person who gains unauthorised access to a computer system.

hacking Unauthorised access to a computer system.

half-duplex line A transmission line that can send and receive data but not simultaneously.

hardcopy Printed output from a computer.

hard page break A page break deliberately inserted before the end of a page.

hardware All the parts of the computer system you can see and touch.

high-level language A machine-independent programming language that is not specifically designed for any one brand of computer.

home or **internet banking** A form of banking that gives you the convenience of doing transactions from home or anywhere there is internet access.

HTML see *HyperText Markup Language*

hub A common connection point for devices in a network.

human readable Output that can be read by human beings.

hyperlink An element in an electronic document that links to another place in the same document or to an entirely different document.

hypermedia Documents containing links to text, graphic, sound or video files.

HyperText Markup Language (HTML) A programming language used to create web pages. See *HTML; foreign key*

HyperText Transfer Protocol (HTTP) A set of rules that controls how data travels between server and client.

icon A pictorial object on your screen that represents files and activities with which you can work.

impact printer A printer that uses a number of metal hammers to strike an inked ribbon.

indefinite loop A loop where the instructions are repeated an unspecified number of times.

index A table containing two columns, one storing a sorted list of values in the field or fields being indexed, and the second storing pointers that give the location of each record in the table.

inference engine Part of an expert system that analyses input data using 'reasoning' methods, along with a knowledge base, to arrive at a conclusion.

input devices Pieces of equipment that are used to put data into the computer.

Input Processing Output Storage (IPOS) cycle The cycle for when a computer needs input, output and storage devices so that it can accept data, process that data and produce useful output.

instruction register Holds the instruction that is being processed.

integrated circuit (IC) A memory chip made up of millions of transistors and capacitors.

interactive A real-time 'conversation' between two entities, usually the user and the computer.

internet service provider (ISP) A company that has a direct connection to the internet and who gives users access to it, usually for a fee.

interpreter Interprets high-level programming language into lower-level programming language that a computer understands.

intranet A micro-version of the internet within a company or organisation.

internet protocol (IP) The unique address that identifies a computer on the internet.

iteration One execution of a set of statements.

joystick An input device that uses a lever to control movement of a cursor or graphic image.

keylogging A method used to record all the data entered via the keyboard.

knowledge base A database part of an expert system containing a large volume of information in a particular field.

label A title or heading to describe an aspect of a worksheet. It can contain any string of characters (letters or numbers) but must only start with a character that does not indicate a formula or number.

language translator Translates a program written by a programmer into machine language.

latency time The time it takes for the data to rotate under the read/write head of a disk.

LCD (liquid crystal display) A monitor that uses liquid crystals as part of the display.

local area network (LAN) A collection of computers in a building, department or school that can share peripherals, share information and communicate with each other on the internet.

logic error An error in reasoning, such as the incorrect sequencing of instructions, and flawed comparisons and selection statements.

low-level language Machine-dependent programming language, where different brands of computers use different codes.

machine code The type of instruction that the computer's CPU can directly execute. Different types of computer have different machine-code languages.

machine cycle The sequence of instructions performed to execute one program instruction.

machine language Normally written using binary code of 1s and 0s.

machine readable Computer output that cannot be understood by humans.

macro A short program written to automate several steps in software, such as in database, spreadsheet and word-processing programs.

magnetic ink character recognition (MICR) reader The use of magnetic ink, especially on cheques, to print and to detect special characters.

mailbox The area of storage allocated to a registered user by a server to hold incoming messages.

mail client A program that enables you to read and compose email messages, send email and access email from the server.

mail merge The ability to produce a large number of personalised form letters, mailing labels and memos without having to type each one individually.

mail server A computer on the internet that receives incoming messages and delivers outgoing messages.

main memory Holds data and instructions that the computer is processing at the time.

make table query Creates a new table from all or some of the fields of data in one or more tables.

many-to-many relationship Where many records or entities in one table are linked to many records or entities in another table through a common entity.

master file A controlling file that is updated as soon as a transaction takes place.

menu A list of commands for program action from which you can choose.

menu bar An area, usually horizontal and near the top of a program's window, containing the names of menus relevant to the program's operation.

merge field The name of the data that will be stored in the data source and later be merged into the main document as part of a mail merge.

mice Hand-controlled devices that roll across a flat surface and whose movement controls the action of a screen cursor.

microfiche An output medium consisting of rectangular sheets of film. Highly compressed storage can be achieved using this method.

microfilm An output medium consisting of a roll of film.

modem Modulator/Demodulator: a device to convert digital data from a computer into analogue form that can be passed along a telephone wire, and vice versa.

monitor The display unit (screen and controls) attached to your computer; also called the visual display unit (VDU).

multi-access system A system that allows a number of users with online terminals to interact with the same computer at the same time.

multiprocessing A computer system's ability to support more than one process (program) at the same time using multiple processors. This generally increases processing times.

multiprogramming The ability of the computer to appear to run more than one program at the same time, although at a specific instant in time, the CPU is dealing with only one instruction for one of the active programs.

multitasking A hardware device on a computer that enables it to communicate over a network.

narrow-band channel A communications channel, which can transmit data at slow speeds of between 10 to 30 characters per second (cps).

natural language processing (NLP) Computer systems that recognise, understand and process written and spoken language; includes voice recognition systems and voice synthesis systems.

netbook A small, low-power notebook computer that weighs less than 1.5 kg and has a battery that can provide between 6 to 12 hours of service before being recharged. It has a smaller screen size (less than 30 cm), smaller keyboard size and less processing power than a full-sized laptop.

network A group of two or more computers linked together so that they can share resources (hardware, software and peripherals) and communicate with each other.

network interface card (NIC) A hardware device on a computer that enables it to communicate over a network.

non-impact printer A printer in which the print head does not strike the paper.

non-volatile Cannot be changed easily.

numeric constant A constant that represents an integer, real, complex or byte number.

numeric variable A variable that stores only numeric data.

object An option you can select and manipulate; it includes tables, forms, queries, reports, macros and modules.

object code Machine code produced by a compiler.

one-to-many relationship Where one record or entity in one file or table is linked to many records or entities in another file or table.

one-to-one relationship Where one record or entity is linked to exactly one record or entity in another file or table.

online shopping Buying goods and services over the internet.

online system All the terminals or PCs and the computer are linked interactively.

online terminal/PC A device for entering or displaying data, which is connected to a computer system.

operations manager The person responsible for the overall operations of a computer department on a daily basis.

optical mark reader (OMR) A reader that detects the position of marks on a sheet of paper.

packet A group of bits transmitted as part of a data stream across the internet, numbered so that the data stream can be reassembled when it arrives at the destination computer.

parity bit An extra binary digit used to check for transmission errors, and appended to a binary word to make the total number of 1s odd (odd parity) or even (even parity).

paste Copy material from the clipboard into a document. See *cut*

peer-to-peer (P2P) network A network in which computers can communicate directly with each other, so that each can be considered as both a client and a server.

peripheral A device that is controlled or monitored by the CPU, usually for providing input or output facilities. They include keyboards, printers, speakers, mice and hard drives.

pixel One of the many tiny illuminated dots that make up the picture on the monitor screen; also known as picture element.

plotter A device that draws by moving a pen, and is especially suited for line drawings and charts in conjunction with CAD packages.

plugins Blocks of code that add features to the overall package.

pointing device Used by graphical operating systems (for example, Windows) to show the motion of a pointer or cursor, and enables the control and selection of objects on the display.

primary key A selected field or fields in a table that uniquely identifies a record.

printer A device especially designed to produce a hardcopy of computer output.

process control The use of digital computers to monitor external processes closely and take corrective action if necessary, in industries such as chemical plants, steel mills and oil refineries.

processor The 'brain' of the computer. It takes raw data and, following a set of instructions, converts it into information. See *central processing unit (CPU)*

program A set of instructions to the computer to complete a task.

programmable ROM (PROM) A type of ROM that can be programmed using special equipment; it can be written to, but only once.

program counter A register that holds the address of the current instruction (the instruction being processed).

programming language A series of coded instructions for the computer to obey, written using the specific rules and statements.

protocol A set of rules and procedures controlling the transmission and reception of data so that different devices or computers can communicate with each other.

pseudocode An algorithm that models or resembles the real programming language syntax.

public domain software Free software available for public use on the internet.

puck A mouse-like device moved over the surface of a digitising tablet for drawing and sketching.

query A method used for storing and answering questions about information in a database.

radio frequency identification (RFID) A chip connected to a small antenna, which makes up the RFID transponder or RFID tag and uses radio waves as a means of identifying animals, persons and objects.

Random Access Memory (RAM) A type of chip that holds data and instructions (programs) temporarily while processing is taking place using that data and program.

range of cells A group of continuous cells that forms a rectangle and is treated as a unit.

Read Only Memory (ROM) A type of chip that holds data and instructions necessary for starting up the computer when it is switched on.

record A collection of related data about a specific subject.

refresh rate The number of times a second the image is repainted or refreshed on the screen.

register A temporary storage location that holds a single instruction or data item.

relational database A database that links together logically related data stored in several files or tables.

relative cell addressing A reference to a cell in a spreadsheet that changes with respect to its current position when the formula is moved or copied.

repetitive strain injury (RSI) An injury that affects the tendons and nerves due to repeating the same movement continuously for extended lengths of time.

replace function Replaces all occurrences of a word or formatting within a document.

report To organise and group information from tables or queries to format the data for online viewing or to print the data from the database.

resolution The number of dots horizontally (w) and vertically (d) on a monitor screen, always specified in the form 'w × d'. It determines the clarity and sharpness of an image.

robot Computer-controlled machinery that includes functions such as locomotion, mobility, grasping and recognition.

root drive The base position of a disk.

router A specialised computer or a piece of electronic hardware designed to direct data efficiently towards its intended destination across a network.

runtime errors Errors occurring after the program has been tested and debugged during the execution or running of the program.

save Store a document on a secondary storage device so that it can be made available for editing and printing at a later date.

scanners Designed to scan pictures and text and translate them into a form that the computer can use.

search engine Software or a website that enables you to find information quickly by typing in keywords or phrases.

sector The amount of data that can be read from or written to a disk by the computer in one read/write operation.

sensor A device that measures physical quantities such as temperature, fluid flow, pressure, and so on.

sequentially Data is retrieved in the order in which it was stored.

server On a network, a computer running software that allows resources to be shared with the other computers (called clients).

simplex line A transmission line that can send or receive data but not do both.

slide A page of information displayed by a presentation application (for example, PowerPoint).

slide show A dynamic way of presenting PowerPoint slides, where a simple click of the mouse takes the user through a series of slides.

smart card A card similar in shape and size to a credit card, but with an embedded microprocessor (a thin gold-coloured memory chip) having processing and storage capacity.

smartphone A cell phone that performs many of the functions of a computer. It usually has a touchscreen interface, internet access, and an operating system capable of running downloaded apps.

softcopy A type of output, also called temporary output, this refers to information displayed on a screen or in audio or voice form through speakers.

soft page break Moving from a completed to a new page automatically.

software A set of instructions (a program) that a computer needs to carry out its tasks.

source code A program written in the specific programming language.

source document A document on which data is first recorded before it is entered into the computer. Data entered from these documents is transferred directly from the document into the computer's memory.

speech synthesis The ability of a computer to produce sounds resembling human speech.

spider A program that searches the Web looking for new pages to add to a search engine's database.

spyware Software that covertly monitors a user's actions without his or her knowledge and is capable of locally saving or transmitting those findings to someone else.

string constants A set of characters or text enclosed in single or double quotation marks, for example: 'James'.

stylus A pointing device in the shape of a pen, which allows you to make selections on the surface of a graphics/digitising tablet.

syntax The specific rules and statements of a particular computer language.

syntax error A programming error caused by incorrect use, violating the rules governing the structure of the language.

table A basic unit of a database that contains data on a specific topic.

tags Markup tags (in HTML) instruct the web browser on how to display the page.

telecommuting Working at home instead of the office, and transmitting work over a communication network to the computer at the office.

Telnet A terminal emulation program that enables you to access data and programs from a host computer.

text editor program A very basic word processor that can be used to create simple documents.

thumbnail A miniature image of a graphic, document or slide.

topology The way in which computers in a particular network are logically connected together.

touchscreen A device that enables you to input data by touching a screen with your finger or another object.

trace table A table of values that follows the effect of each line of program code on the variables being used within the program.

tracing A technique that allows the user to detect any logic errors in the program or algorithm.

track A set of numbered concentric rings on the surface of a disk.

Transmission Control Protocol/ Internet Protocol (TCP/IP) A set of protocols used to transfer data from one computer to another computer over the internet.

transmission time The time taken to read the data from a disk and transmit it to the CPU.

turnaround document A document produced at the output stage of the data-processing cycle that has more information added to it and is then input for further processing.

twisted pair cable A communication channel consisting of two strands of twisted insulated copper wire.

uniform resource locator (URL) The address of an internet file, usually in the format 'Protocol://Server/Path/Filename'.

upload Send files to other computers on the internet.

user interface The user-controllable part of the operating system that allows you to communicate, or interact, with it.

validation Checking performed by the computer to ensure that data entered obeys the rules which apply to it.

value A piece of data that can be used in a calculation.

variable A name that is given to represent a piece of data that can be changed/varied while the program is running.

virtual reality (VR) system Includes hardware and interactive graphics softwares that can replicate sensations which imitate the real world.

virus A program that activates itself, unknown to the user, and is capable of causing damage to your computer system.

visual display unit (VDU) A monitor.

voice-band channel A channel that can transmit data at a rate of 1,000–8,000 cps, for example, a telephone line.

voice recognition The ability of a computer system to accept spoken words as input for processing.

voice response systems A set of digitised pre-recorded words, phrases, music, alarms or other sounds selected and played back based on selections made by the user.

volatile Temporary and changeable.

Web 2.0 This is a popular term for a group of internet technologies and applications that facilitate enhanced communication and creative collaboration, including blogs, wikis, podcasts, RSS feeds and social networking.

webinar The conducting of a seminar or lecture via the World Wide Web.

web portal A website that allows users to find information quickly and easily.

web server A computer that stores and makes available hypertext and hypermedia documents.

website A collection of related web pages linked together with hyperlinks and which resides in a web server.

Wi-Fi The most popular means of communicating data wirelessly within a fixed location.

wide area network (WAN) A communications network that covers a wide geographical area such as a country.

wiki A wiki is a website where users can add, remove and edit every page – without any knowledge of HTML or other markup languages – using a web browser. One of the most well-known wikis is Wikipedia.

window A framed rectangular area on your display controlled by an executing program.

word The number of bits the computer can process in one operation.

workbook Contains a number of worksheets.

worksheet The grid of rows and columns used by a spreadsheet program.

worm A program that uses computer networks and security holes (weaknesses in a security system) to repeatedly copy itself into a computer's memory or onto a magnetic disk, until no more space is left.

Index

A

access point(s) 101, 106, 109
active cell(s) 306, 308
action queries *see under* queries
Alexa 455
algorithmic tool 135 *see also* pseudocode
application program interface (API) 85
application programmer(s) 423
archiving 192, 420
argument(s) 316, 319–23, 337, 348
arithmetic logic unit (ALU) 1, 4–5, 14
arrays 60, 155–57, 423, 431
artificial intelligence (AI) 2, 11, 13, 163, 436, 453–55, 461–62, 472
assessment 401, 418, 448–49, 472
    personalised 123
    risk 189, 205
assignment symbol 138, 167, 176
ATM (automated teller machine) 22–3, 63, 92, 203, 441–42, 468, 472
audio and video input devices 21, 30–2
audit trails 193, 205
automation 2, 439, 445–46, 468
autofit 290, 313

B

back pain *see* lower back pain
backup and recovery 191
backup storage 41, 46, 258–59
bandwidth 101, 108, 110, 122
banking 2, 26, 124, 200–1, 205, 436
    electronic 89
    internet 444, 468, 472
    phone 61, 441
banking transactions 29, 208, 441
barcode reader(s) 21, 27, 91, 441, 444
barcode(s) 18, 20, 27–8, 34
base-2 69–70, 72–3, 114, 268
base-10 12, 70, 72, 81, 114
binary code(s) 12, 70, 79–81, 160
binary number, converting a 70–1
binary number system 40, 69–70
biometric identification systems 457, 472
biometrics 32, 34, 457 *see also* data
    security
bistable device 40, 69
blog(s) 121, 125, 199, 225, 227, 467
Bluetooth 32, 64, 94, 101, 104, 106–7
BODMAS rule 316
Boolean expression 135, 139 *see also*
    Boolean *under* operators
booting 83, 86, 94, 195
broadband 101, 108, 110, 114–15, 125, 446, 462
broadcasting 124, 424, 450, 466–67

buffer 43, 86–7
bug 184, 347 *see also* debugging
byte(s) 21, 37, 40, 47, 54, 134, 358

C

cache memory 38
calculated field 381, 383, 389, 416
card(s) 83, 367
    credit 53, 194–95, 197, 200–5, 441, 443–46, 459
    debit 29, 203, 441, 443–44, 472
    flash RAM 31
    flash storage 43
    graphics/video 59–60, 66
    magnetic stripe 29, 37, 52–4, 191
    memory 31, 37, 39, 41, 47–9
    smart 21, 37, 52–54, 191, 443, 472
    sound 31, 61, 117, 119
    stored-value 443, 472
carpal tunnel syndrome (CTS) 470, 472
cell addressing 304, 319, 348
cell reference(s) 306, 316, 323, 326, 348
central processing unit (CPU) 1, 3–5, 14, 86
channel(s) 101, 108, 119
character set 69, 79–81
chat rooms 119, 201, 205
cheque processing 442
cinema and television 466
circuitry 9, 43, 77
client(s) 50, 101, 103–4, 117–18, 125
Clipart 198, 238, 249–50
clipboard 261–63, 314, 365–66
closing a document 259
cloud storage 37, 47, 50–1, 54, 90, 192
coaxial cable(s) 101, 105, 108–9, 115
coding 78, 164, 174
communication, effects of computers on 469
communications
    data 21, 34, 101, 125
    wireless 101, 105–7, 109
communications links 101, 113–14
complement 69, 75–8, 81
computer-aided design (CAD) 65–6, 452, 468, 472
computer-aided design and drafting (CADD) 431, 452, 472
computer-aided engineering (CAE) 452–53, 472
computer-aided instruction (CAI) 448–51, 472
computer-aided manufacturing (CAM) 431, 453, 472
computer-assisted assessment (CAA) 448–49, 472

computer-assisted learning (CAL) 448–51, 472
computer-based assessment (CBA) 448–49, 472
computer crime(s) 189, 198
computerised database(s) 353–54, 438
computer-managed instruction (CMI) 450, 472
computer-managed learning (CML) 448, 450, 472
computer program(s) 18, 128–130, 159, 164, 188, 195, 201, 428
computers(s)
    desktop 6–7, 14, 429
    embedded 1, 9, 14
    ENIAC 12
    in-car 459
    laptop 7, 22–3, 47, 58, 204
    mainframe 1, 10–11, 14, 42, 44, 62, 76, 86, 88, 432, 441
    micro 6, 14, 38, 61, 102, 125, 452, 457, 463
    mini 1, 10–1, 14, 426, 430, 432, 444
    netbook 8, 14
    notebook 7–8, 14
    personal 1, 3–4, 6–7, 14, 38, 48, 50, 103
    quantum 1, 13–14
    social effects of 436, 468–69, 472
    subnotebook 7–8, 14
    tablet PC 8, 14
    wearable 1, 9, 14
computer vision syndrome (CVS) 470–72
conditional branching 134, 136, 139
continuous data 69, 74, 81
control system(s) 57, 65, 445, 453–54
control unit (CU) 1, 4–5, 14
cryptocurrency 105
cybercrimes 189, 198, 204–5, 207

D

data, copying 314, 365–66, 395
database keys 355
database management 353, 389, 415, 417, 421, 457, 460
database package(s) 3, 87, 353–54, 389–390
data capture 17–8, 25, 34–5
data crunching 2
data integrity 47, 79, 189–91, 197, 205
data item 4, 14, 280, 283, 369
data preparation and data input 19–21
data security 51, 54, 189–90, 192, 205, 425, 427–28, 432
    physical 190–92
    software-based 192–94

Acknowledgements

The Publishers would like to thank the following for permission to reproduce copyright material. Every effort has been made to trace or contact all copyright holders, but if any have been inadvertently overlooked, the Publishers will be pleased to make the necessary arrangements at the first opportunity.

Photo acknowledgements

p. 1 *br* © Fizkes/Adobe Stock; **p. 2** *tr* © Korn V/Adobe Stock; **p. 2** *br* © Akarat Phasura/Adobe Stock; **p. 3** *tr* © Hachette; **p. 3** *b* © Hachette; **p. 4** *br* © Rost 9/Adobe Stock; **p. 6** *br* © Tim Urock/Adobe Stock; **p. 7** *tr* © Texelart/Adobe Stock; **p. 7** *br* © Scan Rail/Adobe Stock; **p. 8** *cr* © Patryk Kosmider/Adobe Stock; **p. 8** *br* © Scan Rail/Adobe Stock; **p. 9** *tl* © Tran/Adobe Stock; **p. 9** *tr* © Rawf 8/Adobe Stock; **p. 9** *cl* © Ralwel/Shutterstock; **p. 9** *cr* © Akarat Phasura/Adobe Stock; **p. 9** *cl* © Scan Rail/Adobe Stock; **p. 9** *cr* © Perfect Vectors/Adobe Stock; **p. 9** *br* © Matthew Benoit/Adobe Stock; **p. 10** *br* © Arnaud 25; **p. 11** *tr* © Courtesy of International Business Machines Corporation, © International Business Machines Corporation; **p. 11** *br* © Timofeev Vladimir/Shutterstock; **p. 12** *tr* © Everett Historical/Shutterstock; **p. 12** *br* © ZZ Midnight ZZ/Shutterstock; **p. 13** *cr* © Alexey Kotelnikov/Alamy Stock Photo; **p. 13** *br* © D-Wave Systems; **p. 18** *br* © Hachette; **p. 21** *tr* © Kritchanut/Adobe Stock; **p. 21** *br* © DGM Photo/Adobe Stock; **p. 23** *tr* © Nick/Adobe Stock; **p. 23** *cr* © Santy Pan/Adobe Stock; **p. 23** *cr* © Alice Foxart Box/Adobe Stock; **p. 23** *bc* © Lightfield Studios/Adobe Stock; **p. 24** *tl* © Hachette; **p. 24** *tr* © Hachette; **p. 24** *bl* © Hachette; **p. 25** *tr* © Hachette; **p. 25** *br* © Destina/Adobe Stock; **p. 26** *tr* © Sean Locke Photography/Adobe Stock; **p. 26** *cr* © Adam Gregor/Shutterstock; **p. 27** *tr* © Andrey Popov/Adobe Stock; **p. 27** *br* © Zapp 2 Photo/Adobe Stock; **p. 28** *cr* © Ideeah Studio/Adobe Stock; **p. 29** *tr* © Seksan 94/Adobe Stock; **p. 30** *tr* © Andrey Popov/Adobe Stock; **p. 31** *tr* © Hachette; **p. 31** *cr* © Hachette; **p. 31** *br* © Mr Garry/Adobe Stock; **p. 32** *tr* © Matthew Benoit/Adobe Stock; **p. 32** *br* © Oleksandr/Adobe Stock; **p. 32** *bl* © Michael D Brown/Shutterstock; **p. 33** *cr* © A Ralia/Shutterstock; **p. 37** *bl* © Joel Calheiros/Adobe Stock; **p. 38** *tr* © Timothy H/Adobe Stock; **p. 39** *tr* © Devy Atkin/Adobe Stock; **p. 39** *br* © Cake78 (3D & photo)/Adobe Stock; **p. 42** *br* © Bacho Foto/Adobe Stock; **p. 43** *tr* © Claudio Divizia/Adobe Stock; **p. 43** *br* © Science Photo/Adobe Stock; **p. 44** *br* © Eivaisla/Adobe Stock; **p. 45** *tr* © Jacky Kids/Adobe Stock; **p. 46** *tr* © Hachette; **p. 46** *cr* © Stock Photos Art/Adobe Stock; **p. 47** *br* © Ludo Design/Adobe Stock; **p. 48** *tr* © Vastram/Adobe Stock; **p. 48** *br* © Eye Matrix/Adobe Stock; **p. 52** *br* © Paul Velgos/Adobe Stock; **p. 53** *tr* © Real Stock Vector/Adobe Stock; **p. 53** *cr* © Miniloc/Adobe Stock; **p. 53** *br* © Billion Photos.com/Adobe Stock; **p. 58** *tr* © Lucian 3D/Adobe Stock; **p. 59** *tr* © Patryk Kosmider/Adobe Stock; **p. 60** *tr* © Andrey Popov/Adobe Stock; **p. 60** *cr* © Sand Sun/Adobe Stock; **p. 60** *br* © Zern Liew/Shutterstock; **p. 61** *tr* © Africa Studio/Adobe Stock; **p. 61** *cr* © Terry Lee White/Adobe Stock; **p. 63** *br* © Jack F/Adobe Stock; **p. 64** *tr* © Destina/Adobe Stock; **p. 64** *cr* © Stlee000/Adobe Stock; **p. 65** *tr* © James Steidl/Adobe Stock; **p. 65** *cr* © Kirill 4 Mula/Adobe Stock; **p. 65** *cr* © Gramper/Adobe Stock; **p. 65** *br* © Creativa Images/Adobe Stock; **p. 66** *tr* © Rio Patuca/Alamy Stock Photo; **p. 66** *cl* © Real Stock Vector/Adobe Stock; **p. 66** *cr* © DPA Picture Alliance/Alamy Stock Photo; **p. 69** *bl* © KTS Design/Adobe Stock; **p. 84** *tl, tr* © Acronis® is a registered trademark of Acronis International GmbH and or its affiliates in the United States and other countries; **p. 84** *cl* © Adobe product box shot(s) reprinted with permission from Adobe; **p.** *cr* © Box shot(s) reprinted with permission from Corel Corporation; **p. 84** *br* © Used with permission from Microsoft; **p. 90** *tr* © Yong Hian Lim/Adobe Stock; **p. 92** *tr* © Pedro Luz Cunha/Alamy Stock Photo; **p. 93** *br* © Hachette; **p. 105** *tr* © Yura Zaga/Adobe Stock; **p. 105** *cr* © Salita 2010/Adobe Stock; **p. 105** *br* © Destina/Adobe Stock; **p. 107** *tr* © The Bluetooth word mark and logos are registered trademarks owned by the Bluetooth SIG, Inc.; **p. 122** *br* © Hachette; **p. 124** *br* © Montri/Adobe Stock; **p. 191** *cr* © Usanee/Shutterstock; **p. 193** *br* © 123 Tin/Adobe Stock; **p. 194** *cr* © Philipp Schilli/Adobe Stock; **p. 194** *br* © 123 Tin/Adobe Stock; **p. 195** *br* © Nicky/Adobe Stock; **p. 198** *cr* © Zimmy TWS/Adobe Stock; **p. 198** *br* © Highway Starz/Adobe Stock; **p. 199** *cr* © Eldeiv/Adobe Stock; **p. 200** *cr* © Template Creator/Adobe Stock; **p. 201** *br* © Creative Soul/Adobe Stock; **p. 203** *tr* © Sylvia/Adobe Stock; **p. 203** *cr* © James Steidl/Adobe Stock; **p. 204** *br* © Thodonal/Adobe Stock; **p. 211** *tr* © Silver Tiger/123rf; **p. 211** © Hachette; **p. 211** © Hachette; **p. 212** © Hachette; **p. 213** *br* © Tom Sarraipo/Adobe Stock, © Andrea Willmore; **p. 218** *tr* © N Media/Adobe Stock; **p. 226** *cr* © Scan Rail/Adobe Stock; **p. 228** *cr* © Thodonal/Adobe Stock; **p. 232** © Thodonal/Alamy Stock Photo; **p. 248** *br* © Darko Vujic/Adobe Stock; **p. 257** *t* © Ojovago/Adobe Stock; **p. 421** *tr* © Biker 3/Adobe Stock; **p. 423** *tr* © RH 2010/Adobe Stock; **p. 423** *br* © RH 2010/Adobe Stock; **p. 424** *tr* © Frame Stock/Adobe Stock; **p. 425** *tr* © Rob/Adobe Stock; **p. 425** *cr* © Audy Indy/Adobe Stock; **p. 430** *tr* © Gorod Enkoff/Adobe Stock; **p. 430** *cr* © IMTM Photo/Adobe Stock; **p. 431** *tr* © Nestor/Adobe Stock; **p. 441** *tr* © Nenetus/Adobe Stock; **p. 443** *cr* © Sergey Yakovlev/123rf; **p. 443** © Barney Boogles/Adobe Stock; **p. 447** *tr* © Blue Sky Images/Adobe Stock; **p. 449** © Hachette; **p. 453** *tr* © Phonlamai Photo/Shutterstock; **p. 454** *cr* © NASA Photo/Alamy Stock Photo; **p. 456** *tr* © Manuel/Adobe Stock; **p. 458** *tr* © Юрий Красильников/ Adobe Stock Photo; **p. 461** *cr* © Destina/Adobe Stock; **p. 462** *cr* © P and P Stock 001/Adobe Stock; **p. 464** *tr* © NASA Photo/Alamy Stock Photo; **p. 464** *br* © Dmitri Maruta/Adobe Stock; **p. 465** *br* © Janice Barchat/Adobe Stock; **p. 467** *tr* © Engage Stock/Adobe Stock; **p. 467** *br* © Only 4 Denn/Adobe Stock; **p. 470** *br* © Juriah Mosin/Adobe Stock; **p. 471** *br* © P Rees/Adobe Stock.

Screenshot acknowledgements

pp. 90–96, 117, 214–224, 232–251, 255–300, 305–352, 355–388, 391–407 © Used with permission from Microsoft. **p. 121** © Wikipedia® is a registered trademark of the Wikimedia Foundation, Inc., a non-profit. **p. 122** © LinkedIn® professional networking services. **p. 122** © Flickr. **p. 123** © 1996-2019, Amazon.com, Inc. or its affiliate. **pp. 211, 212, 449** © Hachette. **pp. 229–227** © 2006-2019 Wix.com, Inc.

Text acknowledgements

pp. iii, 122, 214, 224–231, 411 © 2006-2019 Wix.com, Inc. **pp. iii–iv, 20, 22, 43, 50, 54, 83–84, 86–87, 90–100, 116–118, 192–194, 196, 208, 210–211, 214–252, 254–411, 427, 435, 438, 447, 455, 478–479, 482–483** © Used with permission from Microsoft. **p. 9** © iPhone® is a trademark of Apple Inc. **pp. 9, 122, 193, 197, 431** © Facebook © 2019. **pp. 9, 10, 460** © Apple Watch® is a trademark of Apple Inc. **pp. 11, 12, 13, 42, 50, 80** © Courtesy of International Business Machines Corporation, © International Business Machines Corporation **pp. 30, 33, 50, 66, 61, 85, 90, 119, 122, 125, 126, 193, 214, 254, 450, 443, 455, 477** © 2018 Google LLC All rights reserved. Google and the Google logo are registered trademarks of Google LLC. **pp. 51, 254, 464** © Mac® is a trademark of Apple Inc. **p. 83** © iWork® is a trademark of Apple Inc. **pp. 83, 113** © Apple® Macintosh® is a trademark of Apple Inc. **pp. 83, 97, 200, 214, 229, 254, 464** © Copyright © 2019 Adobe. All rights reserved. **p. 86** © OS X® is a trademark of Apple Inc. **pp. 86, 126** © Apple® is a trademark of Apple Inc. **pp. 86, 92, 100, 196** © macOS® is a trademark of Apple Inc. **pp. 114, 120** © located on ASCD's website: http://www.ascd.org/publications/books/study-guides.aspx. **p. 118** © iPod® is a trademark of Apple Inc. **pp. 121, 123, 220, 450, 480, 483** © Wikipedia and MediaWiki are trademarks of the Wikimedia Foundation and are used with permission of the Wikimedia Foundation. We are not endorsed by or affiliated with the Wikimedia Foundation. **p. 122** © LinkedIn Corporation 2019. **p. 122** © Weebly, Inc. **p. 122** © WordPress. **p. 122** © GoDaddy® is a registered trademark of GoDaddy Operating Company, LLC. All rights reserved. **p. 122** © Flickr. **pp. 122, 431, 467** © 2019 Twitter, Inc. **p. 200** ©2019 Secure by Design Inc. **p. 200** © 2001-2019 Softpedia. All rights reserved. Softpedia® and the Softpedia® logo are registered trademarks of SoftNews NET SRL. **p. 210** © 1994–2019 The Omni Group; Apple, MacBook, the Apple logo, iPad, and iPhone are trademarks of © Apple Inc., registered in the U.S. and other countries. App Store is a service mark of Apple Inc. **p. 210** © 1999-2019 by Visual Paradigm. All rights reserved. **p. 211** © Hachette. **pp. 214, 229** © 2019 Webflow, Inc. All rights reserved. **pp. 214, 229** © 2005 – 2018 Axway, Inc. **pp. 214, 229** © Sitebuilder. **p. 228** © 2002-2019 bluehost inc. All rights reserved. **p. 228** © 2019 HostGator.com LLC. All Rights Reserved. **p.435** © iPad® is a trademark of Apple Inc. **p. 443** © Apple Pay® is a trademark of Apple Inc.

Illustrations by
Val Myburgh

t = top, *b* = bottom, *l* = left, *r* = right, *c* = centre